RAVE REVIEWS FOR VOLUME 1

THE ULTIMATE BOOK ON STOCK MARKET TIMING: CYCLES AND PATTERNS IN THE INDEXES

"The Ultimate Book on Stock Market Timing Volume I: Cycles and Patterns in the Indexes" by Raymond Merriman is literally the ultimate book on the analysis of the stock market. We are especially impressed with various waves of long-term cycles for more than 200 years, which we have never seen before... a marvelous job."

- T. Kaburagi, Toshi Nippou Ltd. (Japan's major commodities' newspaper).

"As the first volume in what is designated to be a five-volume series, Ray Merriman has not only provided a unique and in-depth analysis of various cycles in the stock market indices, but he has done so with a clarity and enthusiasm that makes reading this "technical" book an exciting and illuminating journey into the cyclical ups and downs of the stock market. Guiding the reader through the complexities of cyclical analysis, Merriman explains step by step what defines a market cycle; the orb of time a cycle can take to unfold; reasons why a cycle might contract or expand; and most importantly, how to read the characteristics of a cycle to determine whether it is bullish or bearish.

"That Merriman has so generously shared this knowledge with us in this first volume, gives the reader/investor one of the most valuable market timing tools available. It is a book based not on subjectivity but on data that has revealed a complexity of market cycles to Merriman's unrelenting search to know "the soul of the stock market." For those who are fascinated with (market) cycles, this book is a classic. And for those who invest, this book is a must."

- Geraldine Hannon; Reviewer for The Mountain Astrologer

"Do stock markets rise and fall in accordance with some readily identifiable cycle? Most are familiar with the so-called "Presidential Election" or four year cycle, some are familiar with the 54-year Kondratieff Cycle. Author Raymond Merriman searches through centuries of stock market history with charts and data going back as far as 1695 to prove the existence of these as well as both short and longer stock market cycles.

"Analyzed in depth is the entire history of the New York Stock Exchange from 1789-1997 and the Japanese Nikkei Index from 1949-1997. The charts of these markets alone are fascinating!

"From all this data, we are provided with details on 15 separate long and short term recurring cycles, and a description of the patterns occurring in each one. Not only are we taught when to expect a cycle to unfold, but also how to recognize it when it does.

"Merriman also provides us with...(studies) on technical analysis, and helps us integrate the two together whether our time frame is next year - or 300 years.

"I recommend this book for all those interested in markets. I can't wait for Volume 2!"

- Ted Kunzog; Reviewer for Technically Speaking, newsletter for the Market Technicians Association (MTA), and editor of The Asset Allocator market letter.

"If you are done with Fourier transform cycle printouts, and cycles sent down from Sanai, this is your book. Raymond Merriman teaches you how to isolate and prove historical cycles: in an eighteen year cycle prices will do "this" at a certain point, but they will NOT do "that." In setting long (and short) term positions, what you want to know is what ARE the cycles and how do they perform? Merriman puts you in control and doesn't mandate a computing environment more complex than you and your pencil."

- Dr. Thomas Drake, Tenorio Research; Editor of the Gold Fax Market Letter.

RAVE REVIEWS FOR VOLUME 2

THE ULTIMATE BOOK ON STOCK MARKET TIMING: GEOCOSMIC CORRELATION TO INVESTMENT CYCLES

"Once in a great while a truly revolutionary trading book is published that creates and redefines a method of analysis."

-David Wierzba, Willow Financial, Atlanta, GA

"I just finished Volume 2 of The Ultimate Book on Stock Market Timing: Geocosmic Correlation to Investment Cycles, by Raymond A. Merriman. It is everything I was expecting and looking for, and is a landmark in research."

-Lukman Clark, Signal Hill, CA - The Future Works, and member of ISAR, Inc.

"Raymond Merriman has written an exceptional book on the correlation of stock market cycles with planetary alignments that is of tremendous value to market analysts and investors. It is a well researched and easy to read correlation of stock market tops and bottoms with planetary movements... If you often consider the possibilities of what the stock market is likely to do over the next 10 - 15 years, read this book. It will help you anticipate longer-term tops and bottoms of the stock market, and point out some time periods when you should be out of the market. With so much gloom and doom published today about the world economy it was very refreshing to read Merriman's longer term outlook for 2000-2015, based on well researched historical precedents. This book is a MUST for the serious investor."

-Walter J. Bressert, Chicago, IL - World-renowned cycles analyst

"Words can't even begin to express how extraordinary I think this volume is. (Merriman) has indeed handed over to us investors and market timers a blue-chip portfolio of substantive and ground-breaking research and information. This book is phenomenal!"

-Geraldine Hannon, Reviewer for The Mountain Astrologer

"When it comes to applying the principles of financial astrology to active analysis of the markets, few people have more credibility than Raymond Merriman. Merriman's latest contribution is Geocosmic Correlations To Investment Cycles, a great financial astrology tool that will save you incredible amounts of research time. Merriman's work is meticulously researched, carefully documented, and extremely helpful if you're trying to make meaningful and well-reasoned forecasts for the U.S. stock market. Since overall market direction has a huge impact on the fortunes of most individual equities, this is also important information if you hope to make wise investment decisions. Understanding cycles and developing market forecasts is a fairly complex task, but Ray Merriman does an excellent job of making the work accessible.

"An especially useful section of Geocosmic Correlations To Investment Cycles is the closing chapter on "The Art of Integration: Combining Long-Term Cycles in Stocks with Long-Term Geocosmic Cycles." In it, Ray Merriman guides you step-by-step in the process of developing a long-range market forecast, then illustrates his methodology with a couple of extremely detailed examples. This chapter alone is worth the price of the book. If you really want to sink your teeth into financial astrology as a vital, rigorous discipline, Geocosmic Correlations To Investment Cycles comes highly recommended, along with Ray Merriman's companion volumes. When you get your hands on these books, get ready for a lot of intensive study-- and a lot of profitable understanding too!"

- Tim Bost, editor of Financial, Sarasota, FL

THE ULTIMATE BOOK ON

STOCK MARKET TIMING

VOLUME 5

TECHNICAL ANALYSIS
AND
PRICE OBJECTIVES

THE ULTIMATE BOOK ON

STOCK MARKET TIMING

VOLUME 5

TECHNICAL ANALYSIS AND PRICE OBJECTIVES

BY
RAYMOND A. MERRIMAN

SEEK-IT PUBLICATIONS, P.O. BOX 250012, WEST BLOOMFIELD, MI 48325
Internet: http://www.mmacycles.com

DEDICATION

This book is dedicated Charles Drummond, who has served as my mentor in study of technical analysis. I am extremely grateful for his work and how it has enhanced my own skills as a market analyst and market timer.

DISCLAIMER

All information provided herein is based upon original research and observations of Raymond A. Merriman, except where cited elsewhere. It is written with sincere and reliable intent.

Although these methods and techniques have proved reliable over the years, there is no guarantee that these same methods will continue to work in the future. Therefore, neither the publisher nor the author assume any responsibility whatsoever for any reader's activities or decisions regarding trading or investing in any stocks or financial vehicles. The reader alone is responsible.

1st printing: September 2011
2nd printing: October 2012

ISBN: 0-930706-46-3

THE ULTIMATE BOOK ON STOCK MARKET TIMING, VOLUME 5: TECHNICAL ANALYSIS AND PRICE OBJECTIVES

Copyright © 2011 by MMA/Seek-It Publications

All rights reserved under international and Pan American Copyright Conventions. No part of this book may be reproduced or converted to computer usage without written permission from the publisher.

Published in the United States by:

    MMA/Seek-It Publications
    P.O. Box 250012
    West Bloomfield, MI 48325
    Phone: 1-248-626-3034
    Fax: 1-248-538-5296
    E-Mail: ordersmma@msn.com
    Internet: http://www.mmacycles.com

TABLE OF CONTENTS

Glossary of Terms Used in This Book i
Geocosmic Abbreviations and Symbols vii
Acknowledgements viii
Tools That You Will Need x

Introduction 1

Chapter 1:   Trend Analysis and Multiple Time Frames 3
Chapter 2:   Investors, Traders, and Their Charts 13
Chapter 3:   Support and Resistance 19
Chapter 4:   Price Targets for Long-Term Investors 25

Technical Analysis and Price Objective Calculations

Chapter 5:   Price Objectives: Basic Methods of Calculations 41
            Corrective Retracements
            MCP Price Targets
Chapter 6:   Price Objectives: More Advanced Methods 52
Chapter 7:   Price Objectives for Last Phase of a Three-Phase Cycle   57
Chapter 8:   Price Targets for Breakouts of Head and Shoulders 73
Chapter 9:   Gaps, Measuring Gaps, and Island Reversals 81
Chapter 10: Trendline Analysis (and Gaps That Follow) 91
Chapter 11: Stochastic Patterns: Identifying Cycle Troughs and Crests   101
Chapter 12: Intermarket Bullish and Bearish Divergence............... 112
Chapter 13: Moving Averages as a Trend Indicator & Confirmation Signal   119

Short-Term Trading Tools for the Professional Trader

Chapter 14: The Formulas for Short-Term Trading 144
Chapter 15: The Pivot Point (PP) 147
Chapter 16: The Trend Indicator Point (TIP) 151
Chapter 17: Support and Resistance for Short-Term Trading 185
Chapter 18: As Good As It Gets: Position Trading 200
Chapter 19: As Good As Gets: Short-Term and Aggressive Trading   231
Chapter 20: Creating Trading Plans 259
Chapter 21: Finis 291

TABLES:

Table 1:   4-Year Cycle Occurrences 6
Table 2:   18-Year Cycles: High, Lows, and Percent of Change ... 30
Table 3:   4-Year Cycles: High, Lows, Percent of Change 33

GLOSSARY OF TERMS USED IN THIS BOOK

The following represent terms that the reader will find throughout this book.

Bearish Intermarket Divergence: Occurs when a market makes a new cycle high, but is not confirmed by a new cycle high in another closely related market. If one makes a new high and the other does not during a cyclic time band for a high, it is considered a "sell" signal.

Bear Market: Consecutively lower troughs and lower crests of the same cycle type; "left translation" patterns of primary cycles. "Left Translation" means the crest occurs in the first half of the cycle.

Bullish Intermarket Divergence: Occurs when a market makes a new cycle low, but is not confirmed by a new cycle low in another closely related market. Examples would be Dow Jones Industrials and S&P futures, or Gold and Silver, or Corn and Soybeans, or Swiss Franc and Euro. If one makes a new low and the other does not during a cyclic time band for a low, it is considered a "buy" signal.

Bull Market: Consecutively higher crests and higher troughs of the same cycle type; "right translation" patterns of primary cycles. "Right Translation" means the crest occurs in the second half of the cycle, past the midway point of the two troughs that define the cycle.

Candlestick Patterns: A Japanese charting system that analyzes chart patterns based on the open high, low, and close of a financial market or security each day or week (or even hour) over a certain period of time.

Coincident Indicators: Technical studies that are designed to coincide with a low or high as it happens, or very nearby, such as oversold and overbought indicators.

CCI: Commodity Channel Index. A technical study tool that measures overbought and oversold readings based on the high, low, and close of a market over a period of time.

Congestion: The price area between support and resistance. When a market trades below a resistance zone but above a support zone for several days, weeks, or months, it is said to be in "congestion." At these times, traders will look to buy as prices fall nearby to support, and then to sell when they rally nearby to resistance.

Corrections: A counter-trend move following a cycle high or low that has culminated in the direction of the greater underlying trend. A correction is also known as a "retracement." It represents a percentage (less than 100%) of the prior move up or down.

For instance, if a market moves up from 50 to 100, that is a gain of 50 points. If it pulls back less than 50 points, it is known as a "correction" or "retracement" of the prior move.

Crest: A high in price; the peak of a cycle. It is the highest price between the troughs that define the cycle.

Crossover Zone, Bearish: A very powerful area of resistance. It occurs when the resistance range of a current time period is completely below the support range of the previous time period. The price range from the low end of the current period's resistance area to the higher end of the prior period's support area defines the bearish crossover zone. Oftentimes this occurs when there is a "gap down" between the two time periods.

Crossover Zone, Bullish: A very powerful area of support. It occurs when the support range of a current time period is completely above the resistance range of the previous time period. The price range from the low end of the prior period's resistance area to the higher end of the current period's support area defines the bullish crossover zone. Oftentimes this will occur when there is a "gap up" between the two time periods.

Cycle: A measurable phenomenon that occurs consistently at regular intervals of time. In markets, cycles are measured from trough (low) to trough, unless specified otherwise.

Cycle Pattern: There are three common cycle patterns: 1) The classical "three-phase" pattern, in which there are three sub-cycles (or phases) of approximately ⅓ the greater cycle length; 2) the classical "two-phase" pattern consisting of two sub-cycles (or phases) of approximately ½ the greater cycle length; and 3) a "combination" pattern, which has sub-cycles at the ½ and ⅓ intervals of the greater cycle, thus making it appear that there are 4 sub-cycles within the greater cycle. In longer-term cycles, we may skip one cycle and use 4-5 cycle phases to the greater cycle that is two levels above or below, i.e. 18- to 4-year cycle, and 4-year to 50-week cycles.

Double bottom: A chart pattern where the market makes a trough (low in price), then rallies, and then a few days (or weeks or months) later, it returns to that same price area to form a second trough, known as a "double bottom." It is usually a bullish sign, and the market will rise for awhile.

Double top: A chart pattern where the market makes a crest (high in price), then declines, and then a few days (or weeks or months) later, it returns to that same price area to form a second peak, it is known as a "double top." It is usually a bearish sign, and the market will fall for awhile.

Fibonacci: A series of sequential numbers, starting from the number 1, that are added to one another successively. For instance, 1, 2, 3, 5, 8, 13, 21, 34, 55 are all Fibonacci numbers that are derived by adding the last number to the number the preceded it. After a while, each number is 61.8% higher than the last. This percentage, and 38.2% (the difference of 100% - 61.8%) are considered the basic percentages of most market corrections. That is, if the market rallies 50 points in a bull market, the following correction is anticipated to be 38.2 – 61.8% of that move up, or 19.2 – 30.9 points, a Fibonacci correction to the primary swing. Other Fibonacci numbers include 23.6% and 76.4%. In addition to price ratios, these factors can also apply to time factors, such as days or weeks. If a market takes 100 weeks from a bottom to a top, it might then decline a Fibonacci 38-62 weeks

Geocosmics: The study of the mathematical relationships of planets to one another, as seen from either the Sun (heliocentric) or Earth (geocentric). It may also apply to the study of planets in relationship to signs of the zodiac. Geocosmic studies are used to determine critical reversal dates in financial markets. It is a tool used in market timing – the timing of highs or lows in financial markets.

Solar-Lunar Reversals: Refer to the sun-moon combinations that change every 2.5 days. Certain sun-moon combinations have a higher correlation to reversals in financial markets than others, such as certain new moons or full moons. These are different than geocosmic correlations to market reversals because they involve only sun-moon combinations, where as geocosmic correlations involved planetary relationships. Geocosmics have a much stronger correlation to stronger reversals than do solar-lunar reversal signatures.

Gap up: This occurs when the low of one time frame is above the high of the previous time frame. If, for instance, the high in a market on one day is 50.00, and the next day the low is 51.00, it is a "gap up" day. The entire price range of one day is completely above the entire price range of the previous day.

Gap down: This occurs when the high of one time frame is below the low of the previous time frame. If, for instance, the low in a market on one day is 51.00, and the next day the high is 50.00, it is a "gap down" day. The entire price range of one day is completely below the entire price range of the previous day.

Head and Shoulders Patterns: A bearish chart pattern that is formed when a market makes a high, pulls back, then makes a higher high, followed by another pullback in the vicinity of the earlier pullback, and then makes a lower high, in the vicinity of the first high. The first high is known as a left shoulder. The higher high is known as the head. The last high is known as the right shoulder. The line connecting the two lows is known as the neckline. When prices fall below the neckline, it is considered a valid head and shoulders, and the market is likely to fall harder.

An **Inverse Head and Shoulders Pattern** is a bullish chart pattern that occurs when a market makes a low, rallies a bit, then makes a lower low, followed by another rally in the vicinity of the earlier rally, and then makes another higher low in the vicinity of the first low. The first low is known as a left shoulder. The lower low is known as the head. The last low is known as the right shoulder. The line connecting the two highs is known as the neckline. When prices rally above the neckline, it is considered a valid inverse head and shoulders, and the market is likely to rally further.

Island Reversals: There are two types here; a bullish and bearish island reversal. A bullish island reversal occurs when there is a first a gap down in the market, followed by lower prices. After the low forms, there is then a gap up above the highest price that followed the gap down, making it appear as if all the price activity between the two gap days was in an "island" below the rest of the market. A bearish island reversal occurs when there is a first a gap up in the market, followed by higher prices. After the high forms, there is then a gap down below the lowest price that followed the gap up, making it appear as if all the price activity between the two gap days was in an "island" above the rest of market. If prices fill the first gap before the second gap occurs, the island pattern is negated.

Lagging Indicators: Technical studies that indicate a bottom or top is in after it happens, such as a when a market crosses above or below a particular moving average. It is a lagging indicator because the buy or sell signal is not generated until well after the high or low have formed.

Long: Buying the market. When you take a position that appreciates as that market goes higher. This is the opposite of a **short position,** where one sells the market at today's price and makes a profit if the that market declines in value.

Mid-Cycle Pause or MCP: A mathematical formula for determining a price target that is above the market in a bullish trend, or below the market is a bearish trend.

Moving Average: In this book, the simple moving average is used. The length of a moving average used in this book is usually one-half (and sometimes one-quarter) of the cycle length when longer-term cycles are employed. For shorter-term cycles, we will often use 25-day and 25-week moving averages simply because our experience demonstrates that they work well for the methodology outlined in this book. According to www.investopedia.com, "This is the most common method used to calculate the (simple) moving average of prices. It simply takes the sum of all of the past closing prices over the time period and divides the result by the number of prices used in the calculation. For example, in a 10-day moving average, the last 10 closing prices are added together and divided by 10. Increasing the number of time periods in the calculation is one of the best ways to gauge the strength of the long-term trend and the likelihood that it will reverse."

Oscillators: According to www.investopedia.com, "A technical analysis tool that is banded between two extreme values and built with the results from a trend indicator for discovering short-term overbought or oversold conditions. As the value of the oscillator approaches the upper extreme value the asset is deemed to be overbought, and as it approaches the lower extreme it is deemed to be oversold."

Overbought: A term used to describe a technical study, like an oscillator, that shows the market has advanced very rapidly and/or sharply to a certain high level as measured by that oscillator.

Oversold: A term used to describe a technical study, like an oscillator, that shows the market has declined very rapidly and/or sharply to a certain high level as measured by that oscillator, like a stochastic.

Phase: These are the sub-cycles within each cycle. Each cycle is comprised of two or three sub-cycles, or phases, which are approximately ½ or ⅓ of the greater cycle's length.

Pivot Points: The average of the high, low, and close for a specific time period, like a day or a week.

Position Trading: Entering a market with the idea of carrying it for several days, weeks, or even months.

Pyramiding: This is a trading strategy that adds on to positions in the direction of trend whenever a new high (buying) or new low (selling) occur within a cycle.

Resistance: An area above the current market price where we expect prices to hold on rallies; a "ceiling" for prices.

RSI: relative strength indicators.

Short Selling: Selling a market today with the idea that it will fall and can then be bought back at a lower price. A short seller is one who makes a profit when that market falls in price.

Short Term Trading: Entering a market with the idea of carrying it only for a few days, perhaps only 3 days to three weeks. **Aggressive short-term trading** would be even less, perhaps 1-4 trading days, and even day trading.

Stochastics: A technical momentum indicator that compares the closing price of a financial market to its price range over a given time period. According to www.investopedia.com, "The oscillator's sensitivity to market movements can be reduced by adjusting the time period or by taking a moving average of the result." In this book, we use a 15- and 3-bar study for calculations, as follows:

$$\%K = 100[(C - L15)/(H15 - L15)]$$

C = the most recent closing price
L15 = the low of the 14 previous trading sessions
H15 = the highest price traded during the same 15-day period.

$$\%D = \text{3-period moving average of } \%K$$

Stop-loss: A market order that may be placed below the current price after a long position, or above the current price in a short position, in order to protect one in the event the trade starts to move against the position. It can be used to lock in profits or to prevent further losses. For example, if one bought a stock at 25, but didn't want to risk more than 10% on the trade, he could entered an "stop-loss" order to sell if prices drop to 22.50. This is known as a "sell stop," but it is effectively a stop-loss position. If the market hits 22.50, his position is sold for a 10% loss, assuming it is in fact sold at 22.50..

Support: An area below the current market price where we expect prices to hold on declines; a "floor" for prices.

Trailing Stop: This is where one continually adjusts his stop-loss order based on the market's moves. If he is log, he may raise his stop loss higher and higher as the market goes higher and higher. If he is short, he may lower his stop-loss as the market continues to decline. This is known as a "trailing stop," and some traders use this type of protective ordering to guard against a sudden turn against their position, while still locking in a profit. Of course, once a position hits the trailing stop, the trader is taken out of that market.

Trend: Bull or bear (as above). Trend depends upon the cycle you are studying. The trend is usually determined by the *next* longest time frame or cycle than the one you are studying. For example, the trend of the primary cycle may depend upon the phasing of the 50-week cycle; the trend of the 50-week cycle may depend upon the phasing of the 4-year cycle. The first phase of cycle is usually bullish and the last phase usually bearish.

(TIP): Trend indicator point. The average of the last three-days (or weeks) high, low, and closes.

Trough: A low in price; the bottom of a cycle, from whence the cycle ends and begins.

Trendlines: A line that connects two or more lows (upward trendline) or highs (downward trendline) to one another. It is then extended. There are no lows below this trendline up, or above this trendline down. When the price breaks the trendline, it is said to be a signal that the trend of that cycle is over, but that is not always the case.

Trend Run Down: There are two types used in this book. One is based on two moving averages, where the shorter moving average is below the longer moving average, and the price is below each. The second is based on the market closing three consecutive days (or weeks, or whatever time frame is used) below the TIP (trend indicator point), especially when the third day is a down day on the close.

Trend Run Up: There are two types used in this book. One is based on two moving averages, where the shorter moving average is above the longer moving average, and the price is above each. The second is based on the market closing three consecutive days (or weeks, or whatever time frame is used) above the TIP (trend indicator point), especially when the third day is an up day on the close.

GEOCOSMIC SYMBOLS AND ABBREVIATIONS USED IN THIS BOOK

Throughout this book, abbreviations and symbols may be used to identify the various planets in the solar system, and signs of the zodiac. Those abbreviations and symbols are listed below. The name of the planet or sign is given first, followed by its abbreviation, and then followed by its astrological symbol. The abbreviations and symbols are consistent with those used in the study of astrology.

PLANETS			SIGNS		
SUN	SU	☉	ARIES	AR	♈
MOON	MO	☽	TAURUS	TA	♉
MERCURY	ME	☿	GEMINI	GE	♊
VENUS	VE	♀	CANCER	CA	♋
MARS	MA	♂	LEO	LE	♌
JUPITER	JU	♃	VIRGO	VI	♍
SATURN	SA	♄	LIBRA	LI	♎
URANUS	UR	♅	SCORPIO	SC	♏
NEPTUNE	NE	♆	SAGITTARIUS	SA	♐
PLUTO	PL	♇	CAPRICORN	CP	♑
			AQUARIUS	AQ	♒
			PISCES	PI	♓

ACKNOWLEDGEMENTS

The writing of Volume 5 took place over several months and in several different locations. As a writer, I do my best work with extreme quiet and visual inspiration from nature, such as oceans, lakes, rivers, mountains, and forests. Thus I travel in intervals of 2-6 weeks to go away to places that offer these inspiration vistas and write.

This book started in Tucson, Arizona, in the rugged mountains near Gates Pass, in a lovely large rental home founded by my daughter Alexandra, who was a student at the University of Arizona at the time. This was followed by a three-week writing retreat on the beautiful white beaches of the Emerald Coast in Destin, Florida, in a stunning high rise condominium with panoramic view of those lovely white sand beaches, courtesy of client, friend, and fellow trader Leonard Farina from Detroit, Michigan.

The next retreats would take place in Amsterdam, Netherlands and Cari Campello in Switzerland - again with the aid of two associates. In Amsterdam, I was able to rent a wonderful, cozy apartment in central city, not far from the Dam Square, with the aid of my Dutch associate Irma Schogt, president of Schogt Market Timing (www.schogtmarkettiming.nl). In Cari Campello I was given use of a home on a mountain side in southern Switzerland by client and trader Maurizio Monti of Italy.

This was followed by a three-week visit to Miami, Fl, where I wrote in the home of Bill and Lynn Hyde, right on the stunning Biscayne Bay. And finally the book was completed on a two-month visit to Europe, and the homes of well-known astrologer Antonia Langsdorf, and clients/friends Franco and Beatrice Bianchi of Lake Constance, Switzerland.

To all of these wonderful people who supported my desire to write in great places, I am eternally grateful.

I would also like to express my thanks to all the great minds in technical and cyclical market analysis who have contributed to my understanding of this fine art of technical analysis and market timing throughout my career, including (but not limited to): Walter Bressert (www.walterbressert.com), Charles Drummond of Nova Scotia (www.drummondgeometry.com, formerly lived in Toronto when we met), Robert Krausz (now deceased), Larry Brundage of Novi, Michigan, Patrick Shaughnessy (now deceased), and Rick Lorusso, Citi Bank technical analyst in New York City. I would particularly like to thank both Ted Hearne (Birmingham Michigan) and Charles Drummond, both of "Drummond Market Geometry," for their permission and assistance on the short-term trading material presented in this book related to the technical market analysis concepts of Charles Drummond. Ted has co-authored a learning course on the Drummond methodology and can be contacted at ted@DrummondGeometry.com.

Furthermore I would like to thank my editors for the time and care they have demonstrated in reading over this book and making corrections so that it is clear and understandable (not an easy job!). This was probably the hardest book I have ever written, and it is not a subject that can be easily incorporated with a cursory glance. It will take some effort to master, but the rewards in doing so are well worth it. Yet with the expertise of these editors, I think we managed to make the book both exciting and intriguing so that the reader will be anticipating each new chapter after completing the former one. The chief editor of this book has been Ursula Godwin Niesmann of Munich, Germany (ursula@jewellstreet.com). Additional editing was conducted by MMA's exceptional Operations Manager, Amber Lundsten of Farmington Hills, Michigan, my friend and astro twin Carol McAndrews of Birmingham, Michigan (cmcandrews25@gmail.com), and my long-term editor of the annual Forecast books, Roxana Muise of Kingsland, Texas (roxanamuise@wecred.net).

Additional thanks also go to graphic artists Tad Mann of Hudson, NY (atmann@atmann.net) and Mark Demaagd (demaagddesigns@yahoo.com) of Demaagd Designs in Farmington Hills, MI for their combined efforts in the design of the book cover.

And last but not least, I would like to give a very special thanks to Laurel Humphries, Frank Bozzelli, and Diane Western. Laurel and Frank traveled with me to many of these places to make sure I was healthy - Laurel with massage and Frank with cooking. Diane Western, who is a beautiful geek from The Web Emporium and has been involved in various international humanitarian efforts via the United Nations, is one of the coolest and kindest people on the planet. She did many of the graphic illustrations that appear in this book and made sure the technology matters functioned properly in each place we worked. She can be reached at diane@thewebemporium.com.

TOOLS THAT YOU WILL NEED
TO UNDERSTAND THIS BOOK
AND APPLY ITS METHODS

A calculator, data vendor, and a market charting program. Also, a good mind for numbers and to know your temperament as a trader is invaluable. That's it.

Any calculator that will add, subtract, divide and multiply will do.

Any data vendor who provides daily, weekly, and monthly high, low, and closing prices will be sufficient. If your data vendor also provides intraday prices, such as hourly, 30-minute, 5- and even 1-minute numbers, that is even better. For daily, weekly and monthly prices, this book uses MetaStock data, (www.equis.com, owned by Reuters) and also data from Commodity Services Incorporated (www.csidata.com) of Boca Raton, Florida. For intraday figures, we have used the Street Smart Program offered to clients of Charles Schwab brokerage house (www.schwab.com).

Any charting program that will perform various technical studies as outlined in this book will be useful. The charts used in the book came from either MetaStock charting services, FAR for the Galactic Trader (www.galacticinvestor.com, or www.mmacycles.com), or Street Smart by Charles Schwab.

INTRODUCTION

It's time. It's all about time. And "timing is everything" in trading. Well, almost everything.

It's been seven years since I wrote Volume 4 of "The Ultimate Book on Stock Market Timing" series. When I started the series in 1996, I promised five volumes. I wrote the first four approximately every two years and then I got busy. My business grew faster than I anticipated. Demands for public appearances increased markedly. The application of all my studies conducted in Volumes 1-4 led me to spend more and more time each year writing the annual Forecast Book, a yearly analysis of world and national political and economic trends, collective psychological dynamics, and financial markets. The size of the annual Forecast Book doubled, and the sales quadrupled during these years. The same was true with my daily and weekly subscription services. I ran out of time to write the final volume of this Stock Market Timing series.

I was busy being a Capricorn. Totally immersed in my career as a market analyst, I was independent and doing what I enjoyed, which was researching and writing about the correlation of geocosmic and cyclical studies to financial markets and world affairs.

Yet there was something missing, something still undone. In the back of my mind were two nagging thoughts. The first was that I needed to complete my promise of writing the fifth volume of the Stock Market Timing series. After all, if a Capricorn makes a promise, he has to fulfill it or he experiences guilt. It's just the way the instructions come when you are born a Capricorn. Commitment for a Capricorn is an "all or none" endeavor. It is why Capricorns seldom make a commitment. But I did. I promised to write five volumes, and I had stopped at four. And I knew it, which meant I had a sense of being incomplete. I wasn't whole.

The second nagging thought was that I needed to start training apprentices to my life's work, students who could carry on the basic principles of these studies - these methods of market analysis - that I had developed over the past 30 years. I needed to start teaching. Otherwise, what was the real purpose of this life? Almost as disturbing as not fulfilling a commitment, was the idea of living a life that, in the end, didn't achieve a purpose - the potential - it had defined for itself. But this later issue was very much related to the first. I couldn't in good conscience start the teaching phase of my life until I finished writing the complete set of books needed for instruction. It would be like trying to build a house or an automobile (or anything) without a complete set of tools. I needed to write Volume 5 before I could confidently transition into the role of mentor. I needed all my tools to be available before I set out on the next – and perhaps last – leg of my life purpose (well, one of my purposes in life). And I wasn't even sure if it was my plan not, but it was something I started, something I promised to do, something that had a purpose to it, and it wasn't complete. That made me uncomfortable because I am not quitter or someone who doesn't finish the job. I am a Capricorn, a builder. It is time to finish the project and get on with the next stage of this life.

For the past 30 years, and especially the last 15, I have been immersed in understanding the "soul of the stock market," if such a thing is possible. Perhaps it would be more precise to say I was driven by the desire to experience the "pulse" of the stock market and by an awareness of its interconnectedness to all of the people on the planet that invest and trade in financial markets. But beyond that I also experienced something even more fascinating: the connection of both the stock market and the people who make up this sector of human activity with the forces of nature and the cosmos.

The study of this correlation has never ceased to amaze me. It provided the basis for the material presented in the first four volumes. Through these studies, I believe I have achieved the status of an efficient and credible market timer. There is a rhythm to the rise and fall of stock prices, and it correlates to the rise and fall of man's hopes for a better and more secure future. This rhythm in the market correlates with rhythmic cycles in human activity, which in turn correlates with cycles in the cosmos. These are not only valuable principles to understand, but they are essential in one's quest to become a competent market timer. And as every successful trader knows, "timing is (almost) everything" in trading. You have to buy AND sell at the right time to make a profit.

You will notice that I stated "timing is (almost) everything." The word "almost" is important. One may have a knowledge, or sense, of "when" to buy or sell, but at "what price" do you buy and sell? Prices change constantly during a market day. What is "too much" to pay, or "too little" to sell, for a stock or commodity? Where is the "support" that defines the price at which buyers will enter the market and purchase, or sellers will decide to no longer sell? Where is the "resistance" that defines the price at which buyers will not purchase any more, and sellers will come out to sell? This is the subject of this final volume of the Stock Market Timing series.

The first four volumes addressed the issue of "when" to buy and sell. This fifth volume addresses the issue of "at what price" to buy or sell in order to maximize profit (or reduce loss). The first four volumes dealt with the subject of market timing. This volume will focus more upon the subject of technical analysis, chart patterns, and price objectives for optimal buy and sell points. Another way to view this is that these first four volumes on market timing are akin to understanding "leading indicators." Technical analysis, on the other hand, is more akin to understanding "coincident" and "lagging," or "confirming," indicators.

This book is the last volume of this series of instructional manuals on Stock Market Timing. For me, it will represent the end of a phase of life, and the start of a new one. One cycle in life is now complete, and another begins with the publication of this book. This book reveals the missing part of a successful trading plan that combines "market timing" with "right price for entry and exit," the very edge that all traders seek in trading financial markets. It is an invaluable way to integrate market timing studies (like cyclical and geocosmic analysis) with pattern recognition, trend analysis, and technical studies. It is, after all, the final volume in "The Ultimate Book on Stock Market Timing."

CHAPTER ONE

TREND ANALYSIS AND MULTIPLE TIME FRAMES

You have a choice when trading. You can either go with the flow, or go against it. In market terminology, this means you can choose to either trade in the direction of the trend, or against it. Most market people will tell you that "the trend is your friend," and you should only trade in the direction of the trend. But there are exceptions to this rule.

First of all, what defines a trend? Ask any ten market analysts for a definition of the trend, and you will get ten different answers. Secondly, there is the matter that the sharpest price moves in the shortest amount of time tend to occur in counter-trend moves. If you think it is a bull market, you will soon realize that it takes a lot of time for the market to move up in price, but a very short time to move down. Markets move up in steps, but they come down in elevators. It might take 15-20 weeks to advance 100 points, but only two or three weeks to lose 50 of those points. In terms of maximizing trading time efficiently, which is the better trade? Tying up your money for 20 weeks to make $10,000 on the long side of a trade, or two-three weeks to make $5000 by selling short?

The answer depends greatly on your psychological temperament, and how you approach markets. If you are a long-term investor, then a 15-20-week time horizon probably doesn't matter. So what if the market takes 15-20 weeks to move up 100 points, and then falls 50 points in the next two-three weeks? If it is a bull market, it will go up again after that decline, so why bother trading it? Trading takes time, attention, and study. Not everyone has the time or discipline required to engage in successful trading practices. On the other hand, these types of price swings are very important to those who have the temperament of a trader. A professional trader's creed is to find *maximum profit potential with minimal market exposure.* To a trader, sitting tight while the market makes sharp price swings at regular time intervals is akin to a lost opportunity.

UNDERSTANDING MULTIPLE TIME FRAMES

Knowing the trend at any point in time is important to successful trading. However, to a cycles' analyst, the "trend" depends upon which cycle you are analyzing. The four-year cycle, for instance, may be in a bull market (bullish trend). The trend may be up. But within that four-year cycle may be two half-cycles of 23 months each. After the crest of the first half-cycle is achieved, the trend of the 23-month cycle will be down for several weeks, even months. So this is a case where the longer-term cycle is still in an up - or bullish - trend, whereas the smaller cycle within it may be down, or in a bearish trend. So what is the correct trend? They are both correct given certain qualifications.

The opposite can happen too. Perhaps the four-year cycle has topped out, and is in its bearish phase down. But that bearish decline may take several months to complete. During that time, there may be two or three 50-week subcycles. After each 50-week subcycle is completed, the market can rally for several weeks. During that rally period, the market may be said to be bullish, or in an upward trend. So what is the trend then?

For this reason, it is important to understand the concept of multiple time frames, or cycles within cycles, and to correctly identify which phase of a cycle the market is in at any given time. Not only does this provide the investor and trader with a useful road map for making an intelligent trading or investment plan, but it also provides insight as to what the shorter-term, intermediate-term, and longer-term trend is likely to be. When all three time frames are in the same trend, one can trade or invest with greater confidence.

Using multiple time frames as well as multiple cycles is an essential task to successful trading and investing. The first is important in the art of mastering technical studies, and the second is important for mastering the art of accurate cycles' analysis. Together, these serve as powerful tools in building a successful trading or investing plan.

The multiple time frames for a technical analyst are usually daily, weekly, and monthly charts. But a more active trader will also want to apply these studies to intraday charts too, such as a 60-, 30-, 15-, 5-, and even 1-minute, or tick charts. The idea is to choose the time frame that is most suitable to your trading or investing style. And then to make sure it is in alignment with the next higher-up time frame, as well as supported by the next lower time frame. Let's give a couple of examples.

Let's assume an investor is most comfortable holding a position for about one year. His major time frame for analysis may be a weekly chart. The next higher-up time frame would be a monthly chart. The next lower time frame would be a daily chart.

The first step is to analyze the monthly chart. Let's assume the monthly chart is bullish. The various technical studies or chart patterns he examines point to higher and higher prices. The majority of his studies on a monthly chart are bullish, so he wants to be a buyer of this particular stock or commodity. He wants to buy when the weekly chart is also indicating the market will go higher.

The next step is to examine the weekly chart. Again, he examines his technical studies and chart patterns in a quest to determine a favorable price to buy. When his weekly studies have determined a level of support being built, he is ready to buy. But to maximize his "best entry" point, he would also be wise to wait for the daily chart to indicate that the market is bottoming, and ready to turn up. If the daily chart's technical signals are still pointing to lower prices, then it is best to wait a little longer in order to get a potentially better price for this long-term position.

The same principle works for short-term and aggressive traders. Let's assume a more aggressive trader likes to be in a position for perhaps 1-4 days, which seems common amongst many successful traders. In this case, the three time frames to study might be a daily, 30-minute, and 5-minute chart. Let's say this trader is looking to sell short a particular market. He wants to wait for the 30-minute chart to top out. For this set up to proceed smoothly, he should determine that the daily chart is already in a bearish mode. The daily chart indicators are pointing down. Since he wants to sell short, he wants to make sure the next highest time frame (the daily) supports this position. Once it points to lower prices, he then waits for the 30-minute studies to enter "overbought" conditions. He is now ready to sell short. But to maximize the potential profitability of this position, he is advised to also wait for the 5-minute technical studies to reach an overbought level, and then to start turning down. Once the 5- and 30-minute studies have topped out and are also pointing down (in the same direction as a daily), he should be on board - or short - for a high probability profitable trade of 1-4 days and maybe even up to three weeks.

UNDERSTANDING MULTIPLE CYCLES AND THEIR PHASES

Just as multiple time frames are important to successful forecasting or trading by means of technical analysis studies, so too is the ability to combine different cycle periodicities important to the cycles' analyst. This is known as "cycles within cycles."

The first rule to understand is that in the study of financial markets, cycles are measured from trough to trough. A trough is a clearly identifiable low in price on a given chart. The mean length of time between these two troughs is known as the cycle length, or periodicity.

In our use of these studies, a cycle is not static. Cycles are dynamic. Each cycle has an orb of time away from its "mean" length that is allowable. Generally speaking, that "orb" is about 1/6 of the mean cycle length. Thus if it is a six-week cycle, that does not mean it occurs exactly every six weeks. It means it has an allowable orb of about one week. When you apply that orb to the mean cycle length, you get the "range" of that cycle. Thus a 6-week cycle with an allowable orb of one week has a range of 5-7 weeks in which the cycle is likely to unfold.

In actual practice, a cycle may have an allowable orb of slightly more or less than 1/6 its mean length. We have "theory," and we have historical data studies that may support or refute the theory, or cause it to be slightly modified. When we have a historical study to refer to, we will use that body of knowledge over the theory. In this book, we will try to identify the differences between theory and historical studies as we outline our points regarding price objectives.

When determining a mean cycle length, one should use actual historical data whenever possible. For instance, before I began my own historical studies for this series on "The Ultimate Books on Stock Market Timing," the accepted "theory" was that the U.S. stock market had a 4-year cycle. That is, every four years, the U.S. stock market would make a pronounced trough, and it was usually in the middle of a U.S.A. President's 4-year term of office. The accepted belief was that stock markets rose into a presidential election, and then fell to the 4-year cycle trough in the middle of the president's term. The interval of time between the troughs was thought to be about 4 years, or actually a wide range of 3-5 years. But was that conventional wisdom really the case?

TABLE OF 4-YEAR CYCLES IN THE U.S. STOCK MARKET

Cycle Number	Date of Trough	Number of Months
1.	July 1893	
2.	Aug 1896	37
3.	Sep 1900	49
4.	Nov 1903	38
5.	Nov 1907	48
6.	Sep 1911	46
7.	Dec 1914	39
8.	Dec 1917	36
9.	Aug 1921	46
10.	Mar 1926	55
11.	Nov 1929	44
12.	July 1932	32*
13.	Mar 1938	68*
14.	Apr 1942	49
15.	Oct 1946	54
16.	Jun 1949	32*
17.	Sep 1953	51
18.	Oct 1957	49
19.	Jun 1962	56
20.	Oct 1966	52
21.	May 1970	43
22.	Dec 1974	55
23.	Mar 1978	39
24.	Aug 1982	53
25.	Oct 1987	62*
26.	Oct 1990	36
27.	Nov 1994	49
28.	Sep 1998	46
29.	Oct 2002	49
30.	Jul 2006	45
31.	Mar 2009	32*

Table 1: List of 4-year cycles (trough to trough) in the USA stock market, 1893-2009. Column to the right indicates how many months this cycle lasted (low to low). * means it was less than 36 months or greater than 56 months in length of time. These four-year cycles are given in groups of the greater 18-year cycle. It is possible that the low of March 2009 begins the current 18-year cycle group, instead of October 2002, as shown here.

In Volume 1 of this series, sub-titled "Cycles and Patterns in the Indexes," this theory was tested. A list of all 4-year cycle troughs since 1893 was given, along with the number of months between each successive cycle low.[1] From 1893 through 2002 there were 28 instances of 4-year cycles with a range of 32-68 months. In the updated table shown on the previous page, we now see 31 instances with the same range. This demonstrates that the "mean" length of this cycle is 50 months, with an orb of 18 months. However, when determining a mean cycle length using historical data, it is useful to eliminate the 20% of instances that are extremely long or extremely short. In other words, the correct mean cycle length will be determined best by using only the instances that comprise the middle 80% of the occurrences. If the two longest cycles (62 and 68 months) in this list were eliminated, as well as the three shortest cycles (each 32 months), then the shortest and longest of the remaining instances were 36 and 56 months. Using this revised list produced a mean cycle length of 46 months, with a 10-month orb, based on historical data. This is slightly different than the "theory," which would postulate a 4-year cycle with an orb of 8 months.

But what about those cases that fall outside the normal range for a mean cycle? How does one explain that? And doesn't that invalidate the cycle? The study of cycles allows for these "distortions." In fact, historical studies validate that the vast majority of distortions happen when a greater cycle is simultaneously occurring. Readers may have noticed that the most recent instance of a 4-year cycle (as of this writing) occurred in March 2009. It did not occur within the normal 36-56 month range when the 4-year cycle was due. That strongly suggested an even greater cycle was occurring than the 4-year cycle. It was at least a 6-year cycle, and quite possibly an 18-, 36-, and 72-year cycle as well. It will take some time to confirm those longer-term cycles, though. A market cycle is seldom confirmed until well into its first phase, or even its second.

Generally speaking, there is a 15-20% probability of a market's cycle distorting. However, when a greater cycle is also bottoming, the probability that the lesser cycles (i.e. the phases of the greater cycle) will distort increases to about 50%, according to the studies presented in Volume 1. That is why another rule applies: *the longer the cycle, the more difficult it will be to pinpoint the exact time of its top or bottom* (crest or trough). When long-term cycles come due, the shorter-term cycles will often distort and the market behavior will appear to be most bizarre. This is useful information. When you see this happening, it is wise to consider that perhaps a longer-term cycle is about to bottom. It also supports the theory that the greatest opportunities for profit occur when the market is most risky. At long-term cycle bottoms, markets are more risky, patterns are more bizarre, cycles are more distorted, and the opportunities for profit are greatest. It is the time when most investors and traders are selling, because the climate is fearful. But the smart money is buying. However, that too is just a theory, because I am not sure how one would define "smart money." Any position that is making money is obviously "smart money." As you will see, the conventional wisdom is made up of a number of sayings espoused by market players. The idea of "smart money" is one. "The trend is your friend," is another. And so is, "Bull markets climb walls of worry." Has there even been a time when there was not a "wall of worry" to climb? Conventional wisdom is nice, but ultimately it comes down to correct analysis of the present and forecasting of the future.

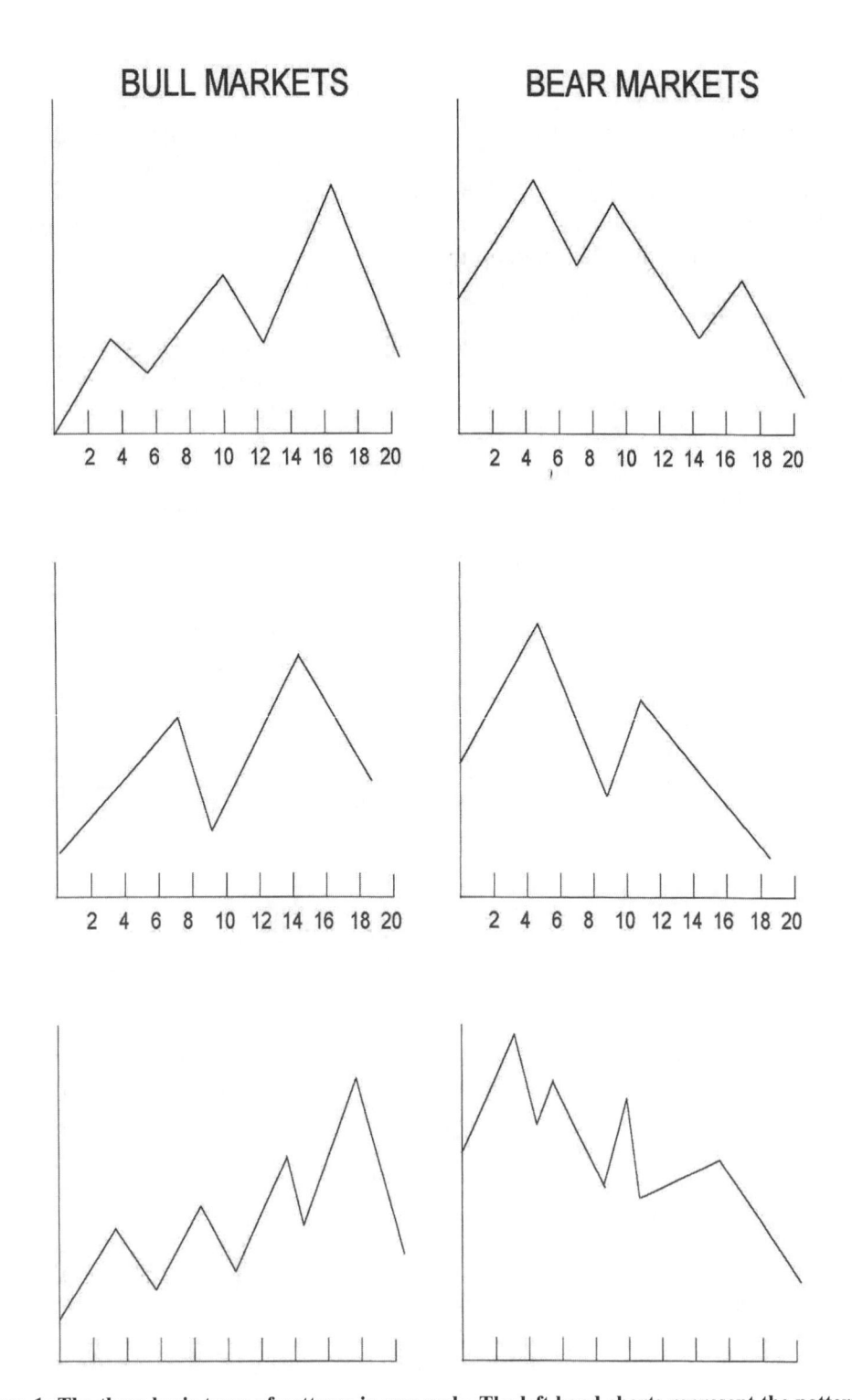

Figure 1: The three basic types of patterns in any cycle. The left hand charts represent the patterns of bull markets and right side the patterns of bear markets. The top two are classical "three-phase" patterns. The middle graphs depict the classical "two phase" pattern. The bottom charts depict typical "combination" patterns. From "Merriman on Market Cycles: The Basics."

Let us now return to the importance of using multiple time frames, or cycles, in the pursuit of understanding the trend of a market, which is so very important in successful trading and investing. Let us start with the concept that every cycle is comprised of smaller cycles, known as subcycles, or phases. In general, every cycle length, or periodicity, can be divided by the number two or three to determine the subcycles, or phases of that greater cycle. Thus any cycle is usually comprised of two or three phases of approximately equal length. These are referred to respectively as the "classical two-phase" or "three-phase" cycles. But sometimes both types unfold within a given cycle. That is, a cycle may be comprised of three subcycles, with each equal to about one-third of the greater cycle length. And it may also be comprised of two cycles, each equal to one half of the greater cycle length. Thus it may appear to have four phases within the greater cycle. This is known as a "combination" cycle. You can see these three patterns in the diagram on the preceding page.

The trend of a market depends upon which phase of the cycle it is in. The first phase of every cycle, for instance, is always bullish. There are some exceptions to this rule, but in the vast majority of cases, this rule will be true. That is, the first phase of a cycle will tend to exhibit the three characteristics of a bullish cycle, which are:

1. Each crest will be higher than the previous crest within that phase of the cycle.
2. Each trough will be higher than the previous trough within that phase of the cycle.
3. The structure of this phase of the cycle will be a "right translation," which means it will spend more time going up in price than coming down (see figure below).

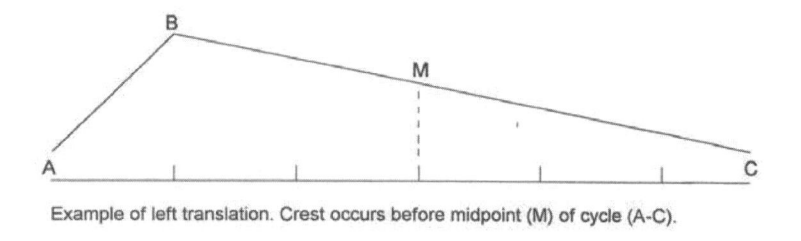

Example of left translation. Crest occurs before midpoint (M) of cycle (A-C).

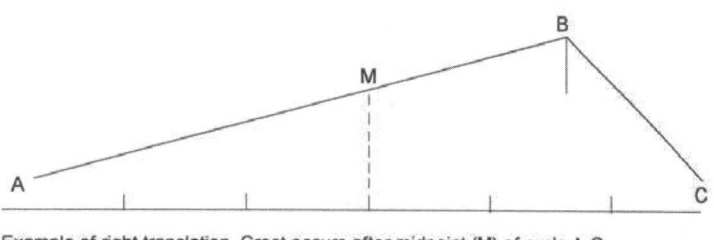

Example of right translation. Crest occurs after midpoint (M) of cycle A-C.

Figure 2: Left (bearish) and right (bullish) translation.

Likewise, the last phase of every cycle is either bearish, or contains the steepest decline within the whole cycle, assuming it has been a bullish cycle up until this phase. The three characteristics of a bearish cycle are:

1. Each crest will be lower than the previous crest within this phase of the cycle.
2. Each trough will be lower than the previous trough within that phase of the cycle.
3. The structure of this phase of the cycle will be a "left translation," which means it will spend more time going down in price than going up.

In actuality, you may not see all three characteristics of a bull or bear market present in a given cycle. Many cycles contain mixed signals. But the most important factor in determining a trend is where the cycle ends relative to where it began. *In a bull market, the lowest price will always be the beginning of the cycle. In a bear market, the lowest price will always be at the end of the cycle.* Thus once a market takes out the low that began the cycle, the trend is bearish, regardless of whether it has been a right translation pattern or with more instances of higher highs within that cycle. The end of the cycle determines the trend above all else. Until it takes out the price that started the cycle, it is still bullish. But once it breaks that starting point, it turns bearish. One must adjust his strategy quickly from bullish to bearish once the starting price of the cycle is violated.

Cycles

Let us now discuss the various cycles in stock indices, and see how to apply this concept of using multiple cycles for developing a trading plan. In this book, we will refer to three types of cycles: long-term, intermediate-term, and short-term. For our purposes, a **long-term cycle** will refer to the 4-year cycle and those that are longer than 4 years. These will include the following cycles, many of which were discussed within the first volume of this Stock Market Timing series:

90-year	
72-year	
45-year	(half cycle to the 90-year)
36-year	(half-cycle to the 72-year)
18-year	(half-cycle to the 36-year)
9-year	(half-cycle to the 18-year)
6-year	(one-third subcycle within the 18-year)
4-year	(may be two phases within the 6-year, or may include two or three phases within the 9-year)

The **intermediate-term stock market cycles** include all the phases of the 4-year cycle, plus the 50-week cycle. In other words, they include:

23-month	(half cycle to the 4-year cycle, or one-third phase to a 6-year cycle)
15.33-month	(one-third phase of the 4-year cycle; it may differ depending on which phase is in force, as the 1st phase is more of a 16.5-month periodicity)
50-week	(half the 23-month cycle; there are usually 3-5 of these 50-week cycles within a 4-year cycle, and mostly four phases)

10

The **short-term stock market cycles** include all the phases of the 50-week and primary cycles, as follows:

Primary cycle (17 weeks, usually two or three within the 50-week cycle)
Half-primary (9 weeks, half-cycle to the primary)
Major cycle (6 weeks, one-third phase to the primary)
Trading cycle (2-4 weeks, two or three phases within the major cycle)

These short-term cycles can be further broken down into 4-9 day alpha and beta cycles, which can then be broken down into hourly and intraday cycles, etc. The identification of primary, half-primary, trading, alpha and beta cycles was originated by legendary cycles' analyst Walter Bressert (www.walterbressert.com).

Regardless of what type of investor or trader one is (long-term, intermediate-term, or short-term), the rule for success with the use of cycles is the same. That is, *in order to understand trend and develop a sound trading plan, you must first learn to tie in your analysis of any given cycle with a cycle that is immediately above it and the one that is immediately below it, in length.* In other words, you need to understand which phase of the greater cycle your current cycle of study is in. Then you need to also understand which phase your current cycle is in, with regards to its subcycles. The idea is to make sure the greater cycle, the current cycle, and its current phase, are all pointed (or about to be pointed) in the same direction for maximum probability of profit potential.

Let us assume we are analyzing the 18-week primary cycle in U.S. stocks for a possible trading position (note: the primary cycle in the Dow Jones Industrial Average is 17 weeks, whereas in the S&P and NASDAQ Composite indices it is 19 weeks). To do this correctly, we need to first of all analyze where the market is in terms of the greater 50-week cycle. Is this the first, second, or third primary cycle phase within the greater 50-week cycle? If it is the first primary cycle within the greater 50-week cycle, then the appropriate strategy will be a bullish one. The trader will be looking to buy all corrective declines to the "phases" of the primary cycle that are above the price that started this primary and 50-week cycle. If it is the third (and last) primary cycle within the greater 50-week cycle, then the strategy will begin to shift to bearish. The trader will be looking for signs of a top to sell into, for even in bull markets, the rule is that the steepest decline will happen once the crest of this final primary cycle is completed. In the case of the second phase, it is a little more complex, because one does not yet know whether the 50-week cycle will consist of two or three primary cycle phases. That is, one does not know ahead of time if the 50-week cycle will be a two- or three-phase pattern – at least not without the help of weekly technical studies.

The next step is to analyze the phases within the primary cycle. Here too, the first phase of the primary cycle will almost always be bullish. One does not want to become bearish at the start of a primary cycle, even if it is the last primary cycle phase within the greater 50-week cycle. If it is to be a three-phase pattern, then it is most wise not to start looking for signs to go short until the second phase (the second 6-week major cycle within the greater 18-week primary cycle), and again in the third major cycle phase. If it is to be a two-phase primary cycle with two half-primary cycles, one may not want to start probing the short side aggressively until the crest of the second half-primary cycle is being realized. Once again, the understanding of technical studies will help determine whether it is to be a two- or three-phase primary cycle. These studies will be covered in great detail later on in this book.

Mastering the ability to tie in at least three types of cycles is essential for constructing a successful trading or investing plan via the methodology outlined in this five volume series of "The Ultimate Book on Stock Market Timing." With this understanding, one will be able to more accurately identify the underlying trend, the time bands when the trend is most likely to reverse, and the optimal trading strategy to employ for the most consistent profits. The next steps involve determining the most favorable price to enter or exit the trade, and recognition of both chart patterns and the set up of various technical studies that would support the timing of entry for maximum risk-reward ratios.

References:

1. Merriman, Raymond A., *The Ultimate Book on Stock Market Timing, Volume 1: Cycles and patterns in the Indexes,* W. Bloomfield, MI, USA, MMA, Inc, 2005.

CHAPTER TWO

INVESTORS, TRADERS, AND THEIR CHARTS

Throughout this book we will be referring to investors and traders. The majority of studies and techniques that will be presented in this book will be for traders, because for them, "timing is (almost) everything." They need all the tools available to gain an edge in perhaps the most difficult of all market tasks: trading.

Yet a number of readers will not be interested in short-term trading. It does not suit their temperament or life style. There are a number of tools associated with these market timing studies that can be invaluable for investors too. Therefore, let's refine this further into three categories of market participants, according to the strategies involving different cycles and different time frames for chart analysis. The reason for making this distinction is because investors and traders will use different technical studies and chart patterns to determine a favorable point to enter and exit a position.

Long-Term Investor

From a cycles' perspective, a long-term investor is one who will create an investment strategy with the four-year cycle as the central focus. That means the 4-year cycle will be used in tandem with a longer-term cycle, such as an 18-year cycle, a cycle that is "above" (longer than) the time frame of the 4-year. Additionally the investor will use the subcycles or phases that unfold within the 4-year cycle, as the next cycle of a lower degree. That will involve the two- or three-phase classical breakdown of the 4-year cycle, which may include two 23-month cycles (with a usual range of 19-27 months), and/or three 15.33-month cycles, with a range that varies according to whether it is the first, second, or third phase. As outlined in Volume 1, the mean average of each phase of a 46-month cycle would be 15.33 months. But historical studies show that the first phase has a mean cycle length of 16.5 months with a normal range of 13-20 months. The last phase, however, is shorter, with a mean cycle length of only 14.3 months, with a very wide range of 8-23 months. Because it is the last phase of a longer-term cycle, it is not surprising that 54% of the historical cases of this third phase occurred outside the "normal" range of 13-20 months that were observed in the first phase.

In my own practice, I use the 18-year cycle as the "greater cycle" containing four or five 4-year cycle phases. In other words, historically there are usually 4 or 5 four-year cycles within the greater 18-year cycle. There has been at least one instance of 6 four-cycle phases within an 18-year cycle (see Table 1). The "lesser degree" cycles I use in tandem with the 4-year cycle are the 2- and 3-phase subcycles within the 4-year cycle.

These are the 23-month and 15.33-month subcycles discussed previously. I will also use the 50-week cycle to help time a long-term entry or exit point. As demonstrated in Volume 1 of this "Stock Market Timing" series, there may be anywhere from three to five 50-week cycle phases within a 4-year cycle. Half of the time (50%) the 4-year cycle will contain four 50-week cycles. The other 50% of the time it will likely contain three or five 50-week cycle phases. Thus one starts with the idea that a 4-year cycle will contain four 50-week cycles, but at the same time be aware that it might contract to include only three, or expand to include as many as five 50-week cycles. The point to understand is that a long-term investor who is applying these methods to enhance investment performance will use a 4-year cycle and tie it in with at least one longer-term cycle and one shorter-term cycle.

The long-term investor will also examine charts of at least three different time frames. The primary time frame to be used for analysis might be the monthly chart. Above that, he may tie it in with the yearly or quarterly charts. Below that, he may tie in the monthly studies with the weekly and maybe also the daily charts. The point is that he wants to invest in the direction of what his monthly charts are telling him. But he wants to make sure this conforms to the trend direction suggested by the yearly or quarterly charts and their technical studies. He then wants to make sure that the weekly chart is at a point of reversal, and ready to move into the direction of both the monthly and longer-term charts.

Intermediate-Term Investor

In actual practice, quarterly and yearly charts are not that practical for investment purposes. An investor can do just fine by concentrating on the weekly and monthly charts, and then maybe using the daily chart to fine tune entry and exit points. A distinction may be made between a "long-term investor" and "intermediate-term investor." An intermediate-term investor, in this case, may use the monthly, weekly, and daily charts for applying technical studies in the pursuit of optimal investment entry and exit points. At the same time, he may use the 50-week cycle as his primary frame of reference, and tie it in with the 4-year cycle and its phases (a level above the 50-week cycle), and the primary cycle (one level below the 50-week cycle). This type of investor may be most comfortable holding a position for several months, and maybe even 1-3 years.

In terms of geocosmic studies, the long-term investor gives greater importance to not only longer-term cycles, but also longer-term planetary cycles that are in effect. As demonstrated in Volume 2 of this Stock Market Timing series, 4-year or greater cycles usually take place when there are major aspects unfolding between the planets Saturn, Uranus, Neptune and/or Pluto. If there are no major aspects between any two of these four planets, the probability of a 4-year or greater cycle unfolding is relatively small.

An intermediate-term investor may also apply some of the geocosmic studies discussed in Volume 2 of this "Stock Market Timing" series, which is subtitled: "Geocosmic Correlations to Investment Cycles." That is, he may add signatures involving Jupiter to the list of planetary cycles to be considered when preparing to enter or exit the market. A major aspect between Jupiter and one of the four most distant planets in the solar system (Saturn, Uranus, Neptune, and Pluto) is oftentimes present when a 50-week cycle, or one of the phases of the 4-year cycle, unfolds. In fact, it is highly unlikely that a 50-week or greater cycle will take place unless there is a major aspect involving one of these 5 planets, as demonstrated in Volume 2.

The basic rule in Financial Astrology, regarding the correlation of planetary cycles to financial market cycles, is this: *the longer the planetary cycle that is in effect, the longer the market cycle that is due to unfold. Or, longer-term market cycles require the presence of longer-term planetary cycles in order to culminate.* As above, so below. Or in other words, astrology is essentially the correlation of planetary cycles to cycles in human activity.

Position Trader, or "Trader"

Throughout this book, the term "position trader" will refer to one who intends to be in a position less than one year but usually at least two weeks. This trader will primarily be focused upon the daily chart. But in assessing an entry or exit point, he will tie this in with the weekly chart (one time frame above), and quite possibly an intraday chart (one time frame below the daily chart), such as a 60- or 30-minute type. In reality, it seems that most position traders are not concerned about intraday charts. They use mostly daily and weekly charts, and perhaps some will use monthly charts, just as investors will.

In terms of cycles, this type of market participant would be advised to use the primary cycle as the central point of analysis, and combine it with both the 50-week longer-term cycle (one level above the primary), and the major and/or half-primary cycle phases within the primary cycle (one level below the primary). If entering the first primary cycle within the greater 50-week cycle, the trader may elect to hold onto this position for several months. If entering the final primary cycle phase of the greater 50-week cycle, he may elect to hold onto the position for only 2-8 weeks.

Short-Term Trader

Most professional traders are short-term or even aggressive traders. Their basic goal is to enter a trade that – according to their studies – has *maximum profit potential with minimal market exposure.* Their average duration in a trade may range from one day to three weeks, sometimes more.

The short-term trader will use the same time frame charts as the position trader. But he will tie in different multiple cycles in choosing his entry and exit points. That is, the daily chart will likely be the primary chart for reference. Against that chart, he will integrate studies from the weekly chart (one level above) and perhaps a 30- or 60-minute chart (one level below the daily). He wants to trade in the direction of the trend indicated on the weekly chart. If the weekly chart studies suggest rising prices, then he wants to enter the market when the daily chart signals are bottoming and exhibiting signals that it is ready to turn up. He will then use the 60- or 30-minute charts to fine tune his entry point.

In terms of cycle studies, the short-term trader may use the 6-week major cycle as the central point of focus. The level above the major cycle to use in this endeavor would be the 18-week primary cycle, and the cycle to use on the next lower level would be the 2-4 week trading cycle, or even the 4-9 day alpha-beta cycles. If the primary cycle is in its early stages, the short-term trader will look to buy on any corrective decline to a major or trading cycle trough. He may use the alpha and beta cycles to help him make this decision.

In terms of Financial Astrology, the short-term trader will pay great attention to any grouping of multiple geocosmic signatures that unfold in a rather tight time band. These time bands are known as "geocosmic clusters," and are the basis for determining a critical reversal date, +/- 3 trading days. When a critical reversal date unfolds in a time band when a cycle trough or crest is due, it is a powerful leading indicator. It is a time when the trader wants to pay great attention to technical studies that will assist in determining the optimal price of entry, or exit, during this critical geocosmic and cyclical reversal time band. The precise rules for identifying these time bands were discussed at length in Volume 3 of this Stock Market Timing series. But in this book, the technical tools and setups that can support successful trading during these highly charged critical reversal zones will be discussed at great length. In fact, that is the major objective of this book.

Aggressive Short-Term Traders

In my daily and weekly market reports, parameters are provided for both "position traders" and "short-term aggressive traders." These suggestions for aggressive traders are for those willing to go against the trend of the primary cycle. Or, in some cases, it will refer to those who wish to be enter a trade for perhaps only 1-4 days on average.

An aggressive short-term trader is going to use a host of intraday charts to find the right technical set up for entry and exit. He may be most focused upon a 30- or 60-minute bar chart. The next level up to tie his analysis in with may be the daily chart. He should always try to trade in the direction of the daily chart, except when he believes the daily chart is about to reverse. Because he is willing to "bottom pick" or "pick the top" of a move before the reversal is confirmed, he is an aggressive short-term trader. Often he is picking the top or bottom of a move *before* it has actually reversed. He understands that the sharpest price moves in the shortest amount of time occur when the market reverses its trend and starts a counter-trend move. This is especially true in bull markets when prices are making a crest. The decline is usually sharp and vicious at the end of the rally to the cycle's crest. However, the decline is also brief in comparison to how long it took to reach the crest. That is why the most successful traders are willing to sell short at certain points in a bull market. Investors would (almost) never think of such an unconventional and risky approach. But aggressive short-term (and professional) traders know that the greater the risk, the greater the profit potential as well.

Below the 30- or 60-minute chart, this aggressive trader may use a 5- or even 1-minute chart to fine tune entry-exit points, and maybe even a "tick chart," which records each and every trade as it is being made. This trader studies the technical signals of these very short-term charts, and waits until they are also ready to turn against the trend of the daily chart, as well as the 30- and/or 60-minute charts.

There are no three cycles to tie in with one another for this type of aggressive speculator, unless one uses intraday cycles, like 50-minute, or 3-hour cycles, which are not within the scope of this book. However, an aggressive short-term trader may use the fast moving solar-lunar phases, within the field of geocosmic studies, to help determine days when 4% or greater reversals, lasting 1-4 days, are most likely. The Sun-Moon combination changes every 2-3 days, and many of these combinations have very high historical correlations to 4% or greater price reversals in various stock indices. These studies were reported in Volume 4 of this Stock Market Timing series, titled: "Solar-Lunar Correlations to Short-Term Reversals." For the aggressive short-term trader, the studies in this book are invaluable for knowing when to enter and exit a 1-4 day trade that has a higher than normal probability of success, assuming the very short-term technical studies are set up properly. Once again, the primary purpose of this book is to know how to identify such a compatible technical set up.

Summary

The importance of using multiple time frames and multiple cycles to establish a successful trading plan cannot be underestimated. It is the most important factor in determining the trend. It is only through an understanding of where the market is in terms of its trend that one can consistently realize profitable trades or investments. But trend means different things to different people. It means different things to a cycles' analyst too. The trend to a short-term trader may be completely opposite the trend to a long-term investor. The key to understanding trend is to focus on a particular time frame or cycle, and to tie it into a time frame or cycle that is "above" that level, and also one that is "below" that level.

The idea is to first of all determine when the "up one level" chart or cycle is in a clearly defined trend. Then patiently wait for the next lower time frame or cycle to finish a contra trend move (i.e. retracement) and indicate it is ready to begin a thrust in the direction of the "up one level" chart or cycle. When it appears the lesser cycle is ready to move in the direction of the greater cycle trend, then time the entry (or exit) to coincide with the "below one level" chart entering an oversold (if buying) or overbought (if selling) technical pattern. The central and "below one level" time frames or cycles should also be in a time band when a cyclical trough (if buying) or crest (if selling) is due, or recently completed. It should also be in a time band when appropriate geocosmic signatures correlating with a reversal are present. This concept will be repeated over and over again, for these are the steps within the methodology of this series that make the market timing studies work. These are the steps that provide the structure in which market timing can be a very valuable tool to the success of any investor or trader, regardless of one's market temperament. But as with all successful endeavors in life, it requires work. It requires planning and proper analysis, and the correct implementation of these rules, plus perhaps a few of the reader's own. But the rewards are worth it, and it is an exciting process.

The following list represents suggested time frames and cycles to use in this endeavor for each type of market participant. The first time frame or cycle listed in each group represents the next "higher level" type to use. The middle time frame given will be highlighted in bold. It represents the suggested primary time frame to use for trading or investing. The last time frame given represents the suggested "lower level" type to use to fine tune one's optimal entry and exit point for maximum profit potential.

Buy and Hold Long-Term Investor (6+ years)

    Cycle: 72- or 90-year, **18-year**, 4-year
    Charts: Yearly, **monthly**, weekly – concerned with percentages.

Long Term Investor (2+ years buy and hold):

    Cycle: 18-year, **4-year**, 50-week
    Charts: Yearly, **monthly**, weekly

Investor (1-3 year position):

    Cycle: 4-year, **50-week**, primary
    Charts: Monthly, **weekly**, daily

Position Trader (2 weeks – less than one year)

    Cycle: 50-week, **primary**, half-primary or major
    Charts: Weekly, **Daily**, 30- or 60-minute

Short-Term Trader (3 days – 3 weeks, sometimes as long as 6 weeks)

    Cycle: Primary, **major**, trading
    Charts: Daily, **30- or 60-minutes**, 5- or 15 minutes

Aggressive Short-Term Trader (1-4 days, sometimes longer, sometimes shorter)

    Cycle: None. This speculator looks for contra-trend moves based on technical set ups, but may use Sun-Moon studies as a leading indicator.
    Charts: Daily and perhaps 60-minutes, **30-minutes**, 5-minute or 1-minute, and even tick charts.

Determine which of these best fits your own psychological temperament and life style. It is possible to utilize more than one of these types. It is possible to utilize all of these types for various purposes and at various times. I do. But make the effort to define which approach you are taking with each investment, with each trade. Once that is determined, apply the suggested time frames to that type of investment or trade for the best and most consistent results.

CHAPTER THREE

SUPPORT AND RESISTANCE

The field of technical analysis can be defined as the study of market prices. According to the website wordnetweb.princeton.edu/perl/webwn, technical analysis is "… the analysis of past price changes in the hope of forecasting future price changes." The website en.wikipedia.org/wiki/Technical_analysis states "Technical analysis is a security analysis discipline for forecasting the future direction of prices through the study of past market data…" Another website, en.wiktionary.org/wiki/technical_analysis, defines this study as follows: "A stock or commodity market analysis technique which examines only market action such as prices, trading volume and open interest."

The one thing all definitions of technical analysis have in common is this: it is the study of price behavior in financial markets, with the idea of uncovering patterns or formulas that will help determine a future price. There are literally hundreds – maybe thousands – of different technical studies that aid one in determining the future course of a market's price activity. Many of these studies involve very complex mathematical formulas involving open, high, low, and/or closing prices, such as MACD (moving average convergence/divergence), RSI (Relative Strength Index), Stochastics, and other oscillators. Many involve simple mathematical formulas, like simple moving averages which take the closing prices of the certain number of days, weeks, months, or even minutes, and divide the total accumulation of those prices by the number of time frames involved to get a "moving average" for the current time frame. For a list of various books, just go to Google and type in "technical analysis for financial markets." Scores of books on this subject will appear. Many of these are excellent studies and compilations.

For this book, only a few technical studies will be discussed in detail and you will see how they may be used effectively in timing an optimal point of entry or exit into any market. The technical tools that will be used herein are not necessarily the most sophisticated ones available, or even the "best." But they work extremely well within the context of the market timing methodology developed in the first four volumes. How do I know this? Because I have been using them successfully to analyze, forecast, and trade financial markets for over 30 years. If they didn't work, I wouldn't use them, and I would not maintain a successful practice as a market analyst. Because if there is one thing the market doesn't tolerate, it is lack of adequate performance. Nevertheless, if the reader has other technical studies and tools that he finds valuable in identifying potential tops or bottoms in market prices, by all means use those in combination with the market timing tools presented in this Stock Market Timing series. For the record, my specialty is timing tops and bottoms in financial markets by means of cycle and geocosmic studies. That is my niche as a market timer. That is where my reputation has been built over many years of market analysis and trading. But I find the use of pattern recognition studies and technical analysis tools as excellent compliments to market timing methodology. Without a doubt, they enhance one's ability to forecast accurately with consistency. Thus they are the subject matter of this fifth and final volume in the Stock Market Timing series.

Let us now begin our journey into the field of technical analysis, which is the study of market prices.

INTRODUCTION TO SUPPORT AND RESISTANCE

At any point in time, a financial market is in one of three states. It is either in a trend run up (bullish), trend run down (bearish), or congestion (neutral, in a trading range). What determines a market's current status is the relationship of its current price to levels of support or resistance. In a trend run up, it will keep breaking above resistance and hold above the support zones. In a trend run down, it will keep breaking below support zones and stall on rallies into resistance zones. In a neutral or congestion market, it will trade between support and resistance. This rule can be applied by every type of investor or trader, and to every cycle or time frame being studied. Although I have not done a formal study, my observation is that about 70% of the time, the market is in congestion. The trend is uncertain or unclear, especially in the shorter time frames. To be a successful trader or investor, it is important to be patient until all of one's studies are setting up for a high probability successful trade. That means that approximately 70% of the time, there is no optimal traded to take. One has to patiently wait until the studies are in agreement.

Whether you are an investor, position trader, or short-term trader, you are concerned about the price of any financial vehicle you are about to buy or sell. Price is important for all types of buyers and sellers. In financial markets there are two pieces of conventional wisdom that are oftentimes spoken: in bull markets no price is too high to pay, and in bear markets no price is too low to sell. In spite of these maxims, everyone strives to buy low and sell high. However this is all relative to where prices have been, where they are, and where they are going to be in the future.

The study of price begins with an understanding of support and resistance. Support represents a price in which buyers will enter the market because they think the asset is of value at that time. It is also a point where sellers will no longer sell, because they feel the value is greater than this price, and if they wait, they will get a higher price. Thus it defines a low in price, a "floor" to the price of that asset. Every time prices decline, the asset finds "support' in this price range. It won't go below this price easily. When it does go below this price, it is referred to as "downside breakout." What was support is now broken, and it henceforth becomes resistance.

Resistance represents the price where sellers will emerge because they think the asset is becoming too pricey, too expensive. They may sell here because they believe they will be able to buy it back at a lower price in the future. It is also the point at which buyers stop buying. They too feel the cost of the asset is now too high. They won't pay more for it, and hence the rise in price stops here. It represents a top in the market, a ceiling in which prices cannot easily go any higher. Every time the market rallies to the resistance zone, the advance stops. When prices do exceed the resistance zone, it is said to be an "upside breakout." What was resistance now becomes support.

This, then, brings up another rule in technical analysis and market trading: once support is broken, it becomes resistance. Once resistance is broken, it becomes support. Sometimes a market will briefly break above resistance and then immediately trade back below it. Or sometimes a market will briefly trade below support, and then quickly trade back above it. These are known as "fake-outs." For this reason, it is oftentimes necessary to see two (or even three) consecutive daily (or even weekly and monthly) closes above resistance or below support before it is declared a real "breakout.' Until then, it may be just a "fake out." There are several geocosmic signatures that seem to have a higher than usual correlation to periods when fake outs are more likely, such as during periods of Mercury retrograde, or hard aspects between Uranus and other planets.

As an example, let's look at a monthly chart of the Japanese Nikkei index from 1990 through 2003, as shown below. You will notice that the 14,000 area defined support for over 8 years, except in one brief instance in late 1998. Once it penetrated below 14,000 in late 2000, that level then became resistance which turned back future rallies. You can also notice from this chart that the Nikkei defined resistance between 20,800 and 22,750 (A-B-C). Thus we could say that the market was neutral, or in congestion, between 14,000 and 22,750 for these eight years. Finally in late 2000, the Nikkei commenced a "downside breakout" of the 14,000 support level. It then became resistance to future rallies (4).

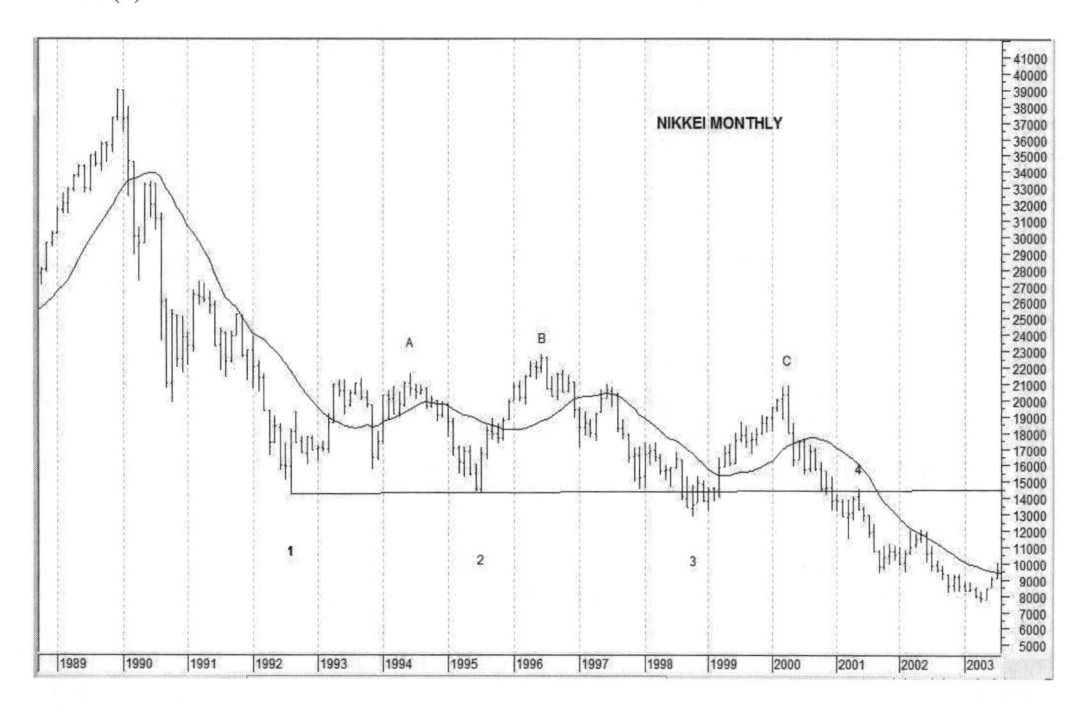

Figure 3: Example of support. Once it breaks, it becomes resistance. Note that the market found support around 14,000 in mid 1992 and mid-1995 (1 and 2). It broke below it temporarily in late 1998 (3), but then quickly rallied back to this 14,000 area. It finally closed well below this support level in late 2000. When it rallied again in 2001, the 14,000 area marked resistance. Support became resistance.

DETERMINING SUPPORT AND RESISTANCE BY CHART PATTERNS

There are many ways to determine price support and resistance. The easiest way is simply by viewing a chart (daily, weekly, monthly, or really, any time frame), and just noting instances of double bottoms or double tops. In the monthly chart of the Nikkei shown in Figure 3, the lows at 1 and 2 are an example of a double bottom. In other words, the market makes a clearly defined low that holds up over several days, weeks, or months. It then goes back to test that area again, and it holds. In this case, the Japanese Nikkei fell from an all-time high of 38,957 in December 1989 to an initial low of 14,194 in August 1992. It then rallied for nearly two years to 21,753 in June 1994 before falling again back to the 14,000 area. It declined to a low of 14,295 in July 1995, very close to the 14,194 low of three years earlier. Once again this level held. These two lows just above 14,000, in June 1992 and July 1995, qualify as a "double bottom," a chart pattern that defines a long-term support zone. The idea is that every time prices return near this area, one can buy with a stop-loss below there. However, once it breaks, it will be either a "downside breakout" or a "fake out."

After the double bottom in July 1995, the Nikkei again approached the low 14,000's at the end of 1997. Again it held, and then rallied above 17,000 in the next three months. Once again it fell back to the 14,000 area in August 1998. This time it closed below it. In fact, it sold off to 12,787 into October 1998. This was a "fake out," because it didn't stay below 14,000 for long. By November 1998, it was back above, and 14,000 was again an important support zone. The next time it broke below 14,000, it was a true "downside breakout." Why? Because after breaking 14,000 in late 2000, it fell all the way to 11,433 in March 2001. The rally that followed then tested the 14,200-14,300 area in May 2001. That former support area was now resistance. It could not close above there on the monthly chart. Instead it fell hard, falling all the way to the 7600 area in April 2003.

We can use this same chart to illustrate the effectiveness of a double top as well. After completing its first leg of the double bottom in August 1992 (1), the Nikkei soared to a high of 21,573 in June 1994, shown as A on the graph in Figure 3. It then declined back to the low 14,000's for the second leg of the double bottom in July 1995 (2). Following that, it rallied once again to test the 21,573 high. In fact, it went a little higher, to 22,750 in June 1996, thus forming a double top. This would now act as resistance to a congestion zone defined as a range of 14,000 on the low side and about 22,750 on the high side. The idea here is that investors can buy as the Nikkei tests 14,000, and sell when it approaches slightly over 20,000. You will note that the rally into April 2000 stopped just slightly short of 21,000, which is below this double top resistance area.

Thus the easiest way to spot support and resistance is to just look at a price chart for clearly identifiable lows and highs. If the low is tested again and holds, it is a "double bottom" chart pattern, which is an excellent area to buy. A double bottom defines support. But once it breaks, it becomes resistance – unless it was a "fake out." If a clearly defined high is tested again and holds, it creates a "double top," which is a bearish chart formation. It means that prices will decline when they approach this level, and investors and traders can be sellers. But once it starts closing above the double top resistance area, it usually becomes an "upside breakout." The range that defines the double top now becomes support.

Once a double bottom support area or double top resistance area is broken, one of two things tends to happen. It either becomes a legitimate "breakout," or a "fake out." You will usually know within the next few days, weeks, or even months, depending on how long the time is between these two double bottoms or double tops. In the case of the Japanese Nikkei monthly chart shown in Figure 3, one would know within the next 5 months. That is, the 14,000-14,500 support area of the 1992-1995 double bottoms broke twice. The first instance (1998) was a "fake out," because within five months, the Nikkei closed back above 14,000-14,500. It didn't just re-test the former support area and turn back down. It tested it and then started closing back above it. That is what happens in "fake outs." If it was a real "breakout," then the former support area would now become resistance. It didn't in the first break of the 14,000-14,500 area. But it did in the second case (late 2000). This time when it broke below, it rallied back and retested the old 14,000-14,500 support area a couple of months later, and this time it couldn't close above it. This time the former support area did act as resistance. It was therefore a legitimate downside breakout.

What can traders and investors learn from this example? When you have a double bottom formation, you can usually buy whenever that support area is tested. Once it breaks, however, you need to reverse to bearish strategies. Look for prices to rally and re-test that former double bottom support zone again within the next few months (or weeks, or days, depending on your time frame of chart analysis). If it is a legitimate breakout, it will not close significantly back above this former support zone that has now become resistance. The opposite is true in the case of double tops that are broken. Those resistance zones now become support. Within a few days, weeks, or even months after breaking out above a double top formation, prices will oftentimes go back and test that area again as support. If it is a legitimate upside breakout, the test to those former highs will hold. If it is a fake out, prices will soon start closing well below those former double top resistance zones.

Fortunately, double top and double bottom chart formations are quite common. In Volume 1 of this Stock Market Timings series, it was reported that 66.2% of primary cycle troughs in the U.S. stock market exhibited a double bottom formation within a time band extending six weeks before, through three weeks after, the correctly labeled primary bottom. In other words, if you missed the buy signal generated from the first bottom in a primary cycle trough formation, chances are 2:1 you have another chance to buy on a re-test of that bottom within the next 9 weeks. The same is true with regards to primary cycle crests. In the study discussed in Volume 1, there was a double top formation to the primary cycle crest in 64.7% of the instances observed. These double tops, however, had a much wider range of completion. They could unfold in a range extending from 10 weeks before to ten weeks after the correctly labeled primary cycle crest. In most cases, the range was six weeks before through six weeks after.

There is another fortunate feature of these studies related to "breakouts" that comes from the study of Geocosmic principles, or Financial Astrology. It is my observation that the support zones of double bottoms and resistance zones of double tops are more apt to be broken when a transit involving Uranus is taking place. That is, if prices are testing support or resistance at a time when Uranus turns retrograde, direct, or forms a major aspect with another planet, be careful. These are times when breakouts of support and resistance are more likely. Uranus has a dynamic of not behaving according to conventional rules. It is a rule-breaker. In markets, this means that support and resistance zones are oftentimes violated, or broken through.

Further Thoughts

The field of technical analysis uses only prices in its analysis. Many traders and analysts use only technical analysis in their trading and market analysis, which means they are constantly studying the mathematics derived from various price combinations. Since there are so many successful technical analysts, there is obviously something to be said about the credibility of this form of analysis.

But just as important as price (and more important, really, in my view) is time. This is the forte upon which market timing is founded. Markets go up and down. They reverse at consistent intervals of time, known as cycles. And sometimes – oftentimes – these cyclical turns are synchronistic with a confluence of geocosmic signatures, which is the basis for Financial Astrology, or Geocosmic studies. One who primarily uses Cycle or Geocosmic studies as the basis for their market analysis is known as a market timer. Unlike technical analysis, there are not so many market analysts who are market timers, which is odd.

Time and price are both important in successful trading. To use one without the other would be like using a partial set of tools to build a house. You can do it, but you could do a better job with all the tools at your disposal. Or, to an astrologer, it would be akin to doing an astrological analysis with only an entity's birth data (date and time) but not location of birth. Just as a complete astrological analysis is based upon both the factors of time and space, so is the most accurate market forecasting based upon the factors of both time and price. You may have quite a bit of success using one without the other, but the integration of each – and even the use of other tools like fundamental analysis, pattern recognition, and trend analysis - leads to even more accuracy and success as a market analyst, trader, or investor. The purpose of this book (Volume 5) is to now bring price analysis – technical studies – into our set of market timing tools (Volumes 1-4), in order to create the most optimal methodology for successful market analysis. Although each may be used successfully as a stand-alone system, the fact is that each enhances the other in a synergistic way. It is as if 1 + 1 = 3. Market analysis using both fields of study (technical analysis and market timing) has an exponential effect on results.

CHAPTER FOUR

PRICE TARGETS FOR LONG-TERM INVESTORS

Long-term investors are oftentimes referred to as "buy and hold" types. They buy a stock, commodity, bond, or some form of financial asset with the purpose of holding it for a very long time. The belief is that this purchase is indeed an investment that will appreciate over time. For them, owning stocks or bonds, or even Gold and Silver, is like owning a house. Although everyone likes a bargain when they purchase and a profit when they sell, the long-term investor isn't necessarily obsessed with buying at the absolute low or selling at the absolute high, with the sole objective of attaining the maximum profit. It is enough to buy when the financial climate suggests that this asset will appreciate smartly over a period of many years. It is enough to sell when the financial climate suggests that this asset will no longer appreciate smartly over the next several years. Therefore the rules for determining a favorable price to enter or exit are not as complicated or complex as in the case of traders. *In theory, the general principle is that the longer the term of expected ownership, the simpler the rules for price determination regarding entry and exit. Or, the shorter the expected term of ownership of a financial asset, the more complex and detailed the rules become for establishing a favorable price in which to buy and sell.*

For a long-term investor, there are basically three factors used in determining a favorable price to enter and exit a financial asset, such as a stock. They are:

1. Identify the time frame in which a long-term cycle is due to bottom or peak.
2. Identify long-term support or resistance by observation of double bottoms or double tops that extend over a long period of time, when this time band is entered.
3. Identify historical percentages of gains and losses in cycles lasting 4 years or greater.

When the value of a stock or asset has appreciated or depreciated percentage-wise within the historical norm, or has exhibited a double bottom or top during the normal time band for that cycle's high or low, it is time to buy or sell. That is all the long-term investor needs to know.

Since the other books in this series established rules for the timing of a cycle trough or crest, and the previous chapter covered double bottoms and tops, this chapter will focus on understanding the historical range of percentage declines and gains pertinent to long-term cycles. In particular, this chapter for long-term investors will examine the 4- and 18-year cycles and especially the range for historical percentages of increase and decrease. After all, long-term investors think in terms of percentages, not in terms of complex mathematical formulas to identify exact support and resistance, as traders require.

THE 72- AND 90-YEAR CYCLES

There are not many investors who are going to purchase a stock or commodity with the intent to hold it for the crest of the 72- or 90-year cycle. Yet it is important to understand the historical percentage gains and losses that occur with these cycles because they represent the next important level up from the 18-year cycle for purposes of applying these percentages. As discussed in the previous chapters, it is always important to tie any cycle to a greater cycle above it and to a cycle below it, in order to understand the status of a trend (i.e. "phase" of a cycle). Thus here too one is advised to use the concept of multiple time bands or multiple cycles when figuring out when to buy, and in what price range to make the purchase or sale.

Calculating the historical percentage of gain in a cycle this long is "off the charts." By this, I mean two things. First, there really is no limit as to how high a stock or stock index will go from the start (bottom) to the top of a 72- or 90-year cycle. A bullish trend that long will have a hard time being confined to a reasonably narrow percentage gain. For example, at the 72- and 90-year cycle convergence on July 8, 1932, the price of the Dow Jones Industrial Average was at 40.56. As this is being written the all-time high of the DJIA, reached on October 11, 2007, was at 14,279.96 (theoretical) or 14,198.10 (actual). Since all of the figures we used in previous volumes were expressed in theoretical prices (i.e. the price of the DJIA when each of the stocks that comprised it formed their highs of that day), we will use the 14,279.96 high. In that case, the market appreciated nearly 3500%! It would be useless to advise someone to purchase a stock or index at a 72- or 90-year cycle bottom with the pronouncement to hold it until it appreciated 3500%.

Secondly, there are only three or four cases of a 72- or 90-year cycle in the history of the U.S. and British stock markets. These are not enough cases to even consider a valid historical norm and not enough cases to consider either cycle as even existing. But since we do have many more cases of cycles with a multiple of 18 years, it is probable that one or both of these longer-term cycles are indeed valid, given a range of a few years (i.e. our rule is that most cycles may have an orb of approximately one-sixth their mean cycle length, hence a 90-year cycle might have an allowable orb of up to 15 years and a 72-year cycle an orb of up to 12 years).

In the possible case of the 90-year cycle, we can observe its presence in 1762, 1842, and 1932. These few instances cover a range of 80-90 years. In the case of a 72-year cycle, we note the historical lows of 1784, 1857, 1932, and possibly 2009. These instances have a range of 73-77 years so far. In all cases since 1857, the 72-year cycle has also exhibited a two-phase pattern of 36-year half cycles (1857, 1896, 1932, 1974 and possibly 2009), with an orb of six years either side of the mean due date.

Foundation Long-term Stock Index

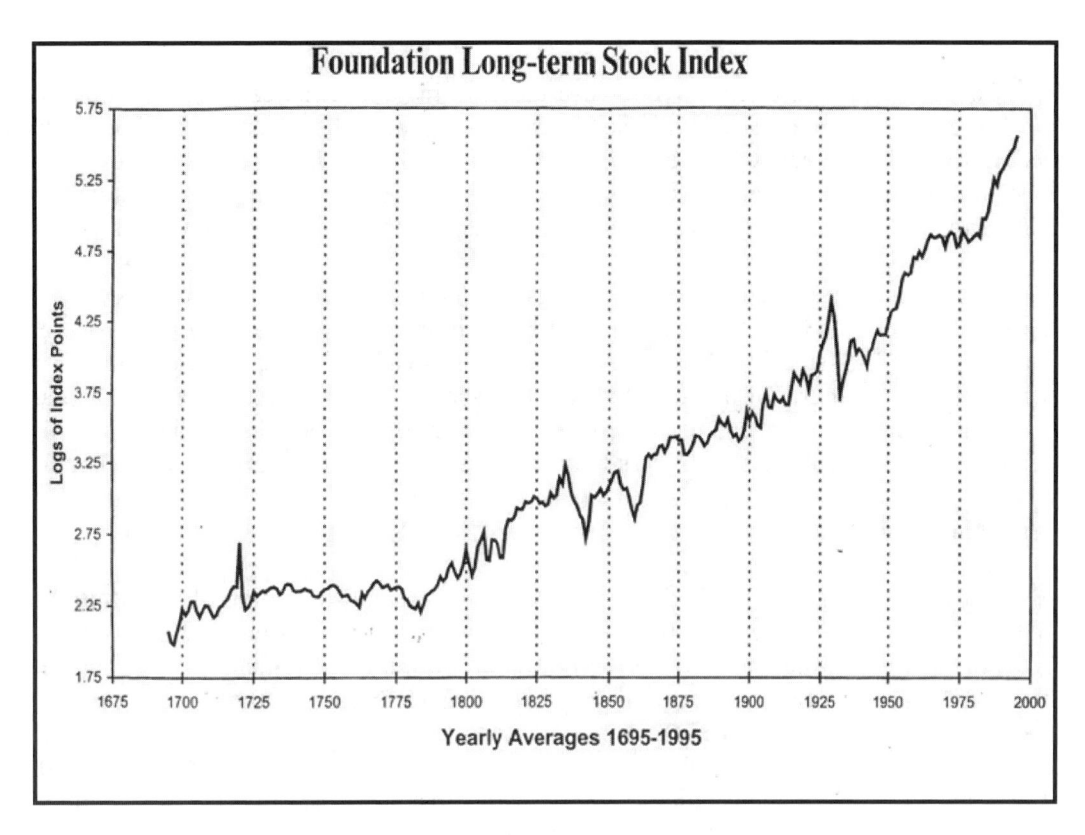

Figure 4: Long-term chart of the British and USA stock prices, since the late 1600's, in logarithmic form, from the Foundation for the Study of Cycles, and as printed in Volumes 1 and 2 of the Stock Market Timing Series.

Although it is of little use to project the percentage of gains from the trough to the crest of the 72- and/or 90-year cycles, it can be very useful to know the percentage of declines in these cases. In the case of the long-term cycle troughs in 1842 and 1932, the percentage of decline from the preceding crests of the same cycle type was approximately 80 and 90% respectively. In looking at major declines in various commodities like Silver and Crude Oil, we could make a case that very long-term cycles usually witness a decline in the range of 77-93% from their previous all-time highs. This can be a general point to keep in mind when it seems apparent that the stock market is going to fall into such a long-term cycle low.

However, the more outstanding rule to apply is this: if a market has been bullish and it is entering the phase of the cycle where its long-term cycle trough is coming due, then the decline into that trough will be the largest percentage decline of the entire cycle. That is, if one were to examine all the phases of that long-term cycle, it would be noted that the largest decline (percentage-wise) took place in the last phase. As an example, one can study all the longer-term cycles within the 72-year cycle that started in 1932. The 36-year subcycle bottomed in 1974. It represented a decline of 46.6% in the DJIA. Its second and final 36-year phase would be due 30-42 years later, in 2004-2016. According to the rule just given, the decline from the crest of this second 36-year cycle to its trough (which will coincide with the 72-year cycle trough) will be more than 46.6%. As of March 2009, that has already proven to be correct, as the DJIA fell 54.4% from its high of October 2007.

So how does a long-term investor use this information? It is really quite simple. If the 18-year cycle is to coincide with the 72- or 90-year cycle, the investor would patiently wait until the DJIA declined more than 46.6% from its all-time high before considering a long-term investment. Ideally this investor would like to see the decline be as great as 77-93%. But at 46.6% or more, he is starting to get interested in a long-term buying strategy.

The investor might do one of two things here. First, he might start to invest as the market declines to the 50% level. Why? Because in every case in history (that we can find), once the U.S. stock market has declined 50% from a prior crest, it always returns to that 50% mark within 5 years and usually much sooner. In nearly all cases, it will soar well above that 50% point and even appreciate another 50% beyond that. In actuality, this percent of decline may be slightly less than 50% (say 48%) and the ensuing rally may be slightly less than 50% above this mark (say 48% again), but more study is required to verify this observation.

For a recent example (as of this writing), consider the all-time high of 14,198 in the DJIA, recorded on October 11, 2007. The market would have realized a 50% loss at the 7099 mark. Let's assume an investor bought then, on the premise that once the market has lost 50%, it will soon afterwards rebound back to that point and even appreciate another 50%. In hindsight, we can now see that the market hit 7099 on February 27, 2009. It eventually bottomed a few days later at 6469.95 on March 6. By April 26, 2010, it was up to 11,258, an appreciation of 58.5% above that 50% mark of 7099. It has rallied even further by the end of 2010, and above 12,000 by early 2011.

To find another example of the market dropping at least 50%, one would have to go back to 1937-1938. From a high of 195.60 in March 1937, the DJIA dropped to 97.5 one year later, in March 1938. The 50% point would have been 97.8. By November 1938, just 8 months later, the DJIA was up to 158.90. From the 50% down mark of 97.8, this was an appreciation of 62.5% in just 8 months.

The time before that was a little more challenging. It corresponded with the start of the Great Depression, and the crest and trough of the previous 72- and 90-year cycle. In September 1929, the U.S. stock market, represented by the Dow Jones Industrial Average, reached a record high of 386.10. The 50% loss mark would thus be half of that, or 193.05. In November 1929, just two months after the crest, it fell to 195.40, a decline of 49.4%. Five months later, in April 1930, it was back up to 297.30, an appreciation of 52%. But then it fell much more than 50% (which would have been 148.65) as it plunged to its 72- and 90-year cycle lows of 40.60 in July 1932. It took 2-1/2 years to get to the 148.65 area again. It eventually rallied to 195.60, which was only 31.5% above the 50% mark of this instance. It took nearly 5 years – to the highs in March 1937 – before it made it back to the 50% mark from the high of September 1929, which would have been 193.05. But it did make it back - and then proceeded to fall 50% from that mark into March 1938, as described above.

Prior to that, we would have to go back to the end of the 19th century to see a 50% loss in the DJIA. The point is, it doesn't happen too often. Perhaps it is a phenomenon that happens only when 72- and/or 90-year cycle troughs are in process. But when the set up does occur, a long-term investor can start to buy once the stock market has lost 50% of its value at the high with a fair degree of confidence that the market will bounce back to that level and probably another 50% above that level, within a few months afterwards, according to this brief history. The exception might be in the final plunge down to the extreme low of the 72- and/or 90-year cycle bottom. But even then, it tends to make it back within five years.

THE 18-YEAR CYCLE

The longer-term 72- and/or 90-year cycles are too long for constructing a historical norm for price appreciation from cycle trough to crest. However, the 18-year cycle is more practical for this purpose. On the top of the next page is a listing of these cycles in the U.S. stock market since 1797. This is an update of the table presented in Volume One of this series on "The Ultimate Book on Stock Market Timing." The reader is encouraged to go back to that book and review the patterns and filtered wave graphs of this cycle.

Let's review the three factors for determining a favorable price to enter and exit the stock market for a long-term investor. They are: 1) identify the time frame in which a long-term cycle is due to bottom or peak, 2) identify long-term support or resistance by observation of double bottoms or double tops that extend over a long period of time, once this time band is entered, and 3) identify historical percentages of gains and losses in 4 year or greater cycles.

We will focus on points 1 and 3 here, for in the case of an 18-year cycle, prices will oftentimes fall well below a previously defined double bottom and rise well above a previously defined double top. Those chart patterns will be more valuable when we deal with the 4-year cycles.

In regards to the first point, one will note that all twelve of the 18 year cycles have a range of 13-21 years. There is a possibility that the last one, as of this writing, expanded to 22 years, although the probabilities are just as high that it fell on time in October 2002, the 15th year. The other possibility is that the expanded version of this cycle is still unfolding as of summer 2010 and it was not completed in March 2009.

Next, one is directed to note the number of years from the start of the 18-year cycle to its crest. The time band of the rally extends from a minimum of 6 years to a maximum of 20. If you omit the two longest and shortest durations of the rally, you will note a "normal" range of 9-19 years. Thus, in terms of timing long-term entry and exit strategies, the following can be deduced: *Long-term investors can look to purchase stocks for the long-term every 13-21 years when the 18-year cycle trough comes due. Long-term investors can look to hold those positions for 9-19 years afterwards, when this cycle is due to make its crest.* It should be pointed out that this is not necessarily in conformity to basic cycle rules, as discussed in Volume 1. But long-term investors are not interested in these rules, which apply primarily to shorter-term traders or intermediate-term investors. They are interested in actual results. What is the range of a normal rate of return one can expect by investing in the stock market near its 18-year cycle trough? How long will that take? What is the normal percentage of decline from a high into the 18-year cycle low, at which point an investor should prepare to enter the market?

TABLE OF 18-YEAR CYCLES

Cycle #	Trough	Crest	Trough	Yrs Up	Yrs Dn	Low*	High*	Low*	% Up*	%Dn*
1.	1797	1806	1813	9	7	3.0	8.0	4.0	166.7%	50.0%
2.	1813	1824	1829	11	5	4.0	15.0	10.5	275.0%	30.0%
3.	1829	1835	1842	6	7	10.5	25.0	5.0	138.1%	80.0%
4.	1842	1852	1857	10	5	5.0	22.0	8.0	340.0%	63.6%
5.	1857	1873	1877	16	4	8.0	36.0	22.5	350.0%	37.5%
6.	1877	1889	1896	12	7	22.5	50.0	27.0	122.2%	46.0%
7.	1896	1906	1914	10	8	27.0	102.0	52.0	277.7%	49.0%
8.	1914	1929	1932	15	3	52.0	386.1	40.6	642.5%	89.5%
9.	7/32	1/53	9/53	20	1	40.6	295.10	254.00	626.8%	13.9%
10.	9/53	1/73	12/74	19	2	254.00	1067.20	570.00	320.1%	46.6%
11.	12/74	8/87	10/87	12	1	570.00	2746.70	1616.20	381.9%	41.2%
12.	10/87	1/00	10/02	12	3	1616.20	11,908.50	7181.50	636.8%	39.7%**
12A	10/87	10/07	3/09	20	2	1616.20	14,279.96	6440.08	883.5%	54.9%

Table 2: List of 18-year cycles in U.S. stock market, showing number of years between trough and crest, then number of years between crest and trough and percentage of each move. * Means that up until 1932, all prices quoted here are approximations. Staring with cycle #9, prices and percentages are exact. ** Means 12 or 12A could be the correct 18-year cycle trough as of this writing. Prices are theoretical, not actual, which would be slightly less than shown above.

Now let's consider the third point by examining the historical percentage norms of price declines and appreciation for this cycle. The next to last column shows the percent of the up move from the 18-year cycle trough to crest. Here one will observe that the price appreciation has historically been in a range of 122-883%. If the last case is omitted – which assumed the last 18-year cycle expanded to March 2009 instead of forming on time in October 2002 – it will be seen that the range for appreciation has always been within 122-642%. And since 1896, it has always been 277-642%. In fact, in most instances, the DJIA has appreciated 275-382%. The times that it exceeded 382% have coincided with the first or last 18-year cycle phase of the greater 72- and/or 90-year cycles. Normally there will be four or five 18-year cycle phases within the 72- and/or 90 year cycles, so only in about half of those cases (first and last phase of the 72- and/or 90-year cycles) should one be prepared for rallies exceeding 382%.

From this study, we can add another rule: *Once an 18-year cycle has bottomed, one can expect an appreciation in stock prices of at least 122%, and more likely 275-382%, in the next 9-19 years.*

If, for instance, the last 18-year cycle trough as of this writing occurred in October 2002 at 7181.50, then the crest of the new 18-year cycle would be expected to attain at least 15,942.90 (122% increase) in 9-19 years, or 2011-2021. A "normal" appreciation of 275-382% would give an upside price target of 26,930-34,615 during this same period.

But something happened along the way, which needs to be discussed within the context of cycles' theory. The stock market fell to a lower low before attaining this upside target. This means one of three things: either the correct starting point of the 18-year cycle is the lower low attained on March 6-9, 2009 at 6440.10, or that 18-year cycle low is still unfolding as of this writing (and expanding), or this is a newer 18-year cycle trough following the low of October 2002, and it will not follow the historical norm. That is, this current 18-year cycle may be bearish and not due to bottom until 2015-2023. Its crest is already in (at 14,280 on October 11, 2007, theoretical value), and it will be the shortest and the weakest in history so far. The crest was only five years in the making (October 2002 to October 2007), and its appreciation was only 98.8%. If this later possibility is valid, then this will be the shortest and weakest rally in the history of the 18-year cycle to date.

In the case that this is a newer 18-year cycle that started on March 6-9, 2009 at 6440.10, the long-term investor could apply these rules of probability investing as follows: the stock market (as measured by the Dow Jones Industrial Average) would likely top out in 9-19 years (2019-2029) at a level equating to a 275-382% appreciation of that low, or 24,150 – 31,041, with a possibility of going much higher.

In the case that the 18-year cycle bottomed in October 2002, the market has already broken below the low of its starting point. That means the crest is already in, for one of the basic rules of cycles is this: once a market takes out the low that started its cycle, it will be bearish and not realize its lowest price until the cycle ends. There are some historical exceptions to this rule, but they are rare and far between. A rally above the 14,280 high of October 11, 2007 would negate this, but more than likely it would affirm that the 18-year cycle expanded by one year to bottom in March 2009. Until that happens, a labeling of an 18-year cycle low in October 2002 means 1) the high is in as of October 2007, and 2) the market has not yet seen its bottom and won't until before prices fall below 6440 in the DJIA, perhaps not until 2015-2023 when the next 18-year cycle trough would be due as measured from October 2002.

More important than determining the crest is to identify the bottom of the 18-year cycle. The first step to building a long-term portfolio of stocks is to make the purchase. Therefore one must look at the history of those cycle lows. From Table 2, it is already known that the historical time band for most 18-year cycle troughs is 13-21 years with a possibility of expanding slightly. One can also observe that historically the time of decline for the crest to trough of the 18-year cycle ranges from 1 to 8 years so far (in a database going back over 200+ years).

The last column in Table 2 shows the history of the percentages of those declines from crest to trough. Note that these declines have been as benign as 13.9% in 1953 to as much as 89.5% in the stock market crash coinciding with the Great Depression, from its high in September 1929 to its low in July 1932. If we take those two extreme cases out, we will see the range narrow to 30-80%. We already know from the early discussion on the longer-term 72- and/or 90-year cycles, that the decline is usually 77-93% when they come due. If we omit those extreme longer-term cycle lows of 1842 and 1932 plus the 13.9% of 1953, we get a "normal" range of decline of 30.0-63.3%. Even if we omit the 30% case that took place in 1829, we get an even more narrow and probable range for declines of 37.5-63.3%. As an analyst who continually observes the manifestation of Fibonacci ratios in financial market prices, I believe this is a useful range to apply when expecting a decline into an 18-year cycle trough that does not coincide with a greater 72- or 90-year cycle trough. That is, Mr. Fibonacci would expect declines of 38.2-61.8%. In comparison, the history of the 18-year cycle points to evidence of declines from 37.5-63.3%. That is close enough for Dr. Fibonacci's students to feel proud of his mathematical discovery.

Thus we can construct a guide for long-term investors using the 18-year cycle for entering and exiting the U.S. stock market and probably many other world stock markets.

1. Identify a time band for the 18-year cycle trough. It will usually be 13-21 years after the previous one and mostly only 15-21 years. It is possible to expand as much as 26 years, although so far there have been no confirmed historical cases in which this has occurred.
2. When entering this time band, prepare to buy stocks if the price has fallen 37.5-62.5% from the high (cycle crest) of at least one year before. If it is to coincide with a longer-term 72- or 90-year cycle, then the decline may be more, perhaps 77-93% as noted in cases of long-term cycle troughs in other financial markets. It will be the steepest decline since the longer-term cycle began, more than any of the other 18-years within the longer-term cycle.
3. If at any time the stock market falls 50% from a prior crest, the long-term investor can look to buy with the expectation that prices will soon thereafter return to that 50% level and appreciate even another 50% or more beyond it. The exception may be when the 18-year is coinciding with either 72- and/or 90-year cycle.
4. Once the 18-year cycle has bottomed, the long-term investor may buy, and stay in that position for at least 6 years and probably 9-19 years.
5. The market will likely appreciate at least 122% from that low in the next 9-19 years and usually more like 275-382%, with a possibility of exceeding even 600% if it is the first or last 18-year cycle phase to the greater 72- and/or 90-year cycles.
6. Once that time frame is entered and the price range of appreciation is realized, the investor needs to think about exiting, or hedging, and waiting for the market to decline over the next 1-8 years. The amplitude of the decline is likely to be 37.5-63.3% from those highs, at which time the investor may then plan to re-enter. If an even longer-term 72- and/or 90-year cycle trough is also due, then the decline may exceed 63.5%. It tends to plunge 77-93% from the prior all-time high.

TABLE OF 4-YEAR CYCLES

Cycle #	Trough	Crest	Trough	Mo Up	Mo Dn	Low*	High*	Low*	% Up*	%Dn*
1.	7/1893	9/1895	8/1896	26	11	44.0	63.0	27.0	43.2	57.1%
2.	8/1896	4/1899	9/1900	32	17	27.0	78.0	52.5	188.9%	32.7%
3.	9/1900	6/1901	11/1903	9	29	52.5	79.0	42.5	50.5%	46.2%
4.	11/1903	1/1906	11/1907	26	22	42.5	102.0	53.0	140.0%	48.0%
5.	11/1907	9/1909	9/1911	22	24	53.0	101.5	72.0	91.5%	29.1%
6.	9/1911	9/1912	12/1914	12	27	72.0	93.0	52.0	29.2%	44.1%
7.	12/1914	11/1916	12/1917	23	13	52.0	115.0	66.0	121.2%	42.6%
8.	12/1917	10/1919	8/1921	22	22	66.0	125.0	64.0	89.4%	48.8%
9.	8/1921	2/1926	3/1926	54	1	64.0	175.0	145.0	173.4%	17.1%
10.	3/1926	8/1929	11/1929	41	3	145.0	386.1	195.0	166.3%	49.5%
11.	11/1929	4/1930	7/1932	5	27	195.4	297.3	40.6	52.1%	86.3%
12.	7/1932	3/1937	3/1938	56	12	40.6	195.6	97.5	381.8%	50.2%
13.	3/1938	11/1938	4/1942	8	41	97.5	158.9	92.7	63.0%	41.7%
14.	4/1942	5/1946	10/1946	49	5	92.7	213.4	160.5	130.2%	24.8%
15.	10/1946	6/1948	6/1949	20	12	160.5	194.5	160.6	21.2%	17.4%
16.	6/1949	1/1953	9/1953	43	8	160.6	295.1	254.4	83.7%	13.8%
17.	9/1953	4/1956	10/1957	31	18	254.4	524.4	416.2	106.1%	20.6%
18.	10/1957	11/1961	6/1962	49	7	416.2	741.3	524.6	78.1%	29.2%
19.	6/1962	2/1966	10/1966	44	8	524.6	1001.1	735.7	90.8%	26.5%
20.	10/1966	12/1968	5/1970	26	17	735.7	994.7	627.5	35.2%	36.9%
21.	5/1970	1/1973	12/1974	32	23	627.5	1067.2	570.0	70.1%	46.6%
22.	12/1974	9/1976	3/1978	21	18	570.0	1026.3	736.8	80.1%	28.2%
23.	3/1978	4/1981	8/1982	37	16	736.8	1031.0	770.0	39.9%	33.9%
24.	8/1982	8/1987	10/1987	60	2	770.0	2746.7	1616.2	256.7%	41.1%
25.	10/1987	7/1990	10/1990	33	3	1616.2	3024.3	2344.3	87.1%	22.5%
26A	10/1990	1/1994	4/1994	39	3	2344.3	4002.8	3520.5	70.7%	12.0%
26B	10/1990	1/1994	11/1994	39	10	2344.3	4002.8	3612.1	70.7%	9.8%
27A	4/1994	7/1998	9/1998	51	2	3520.5	9412.6	7379.7	167.4%	21.6%
27B	11/1994	7/1998	9/1998	44	2	3612.1	9412.6	7379.7	160.6%	21.6%
28.	9/1998	1/2000	10/2002	16	33	7379.7	11,908.5	7181.5	53.2%	39.7%
29A	10/2002	5/2006	7/2006	43	2	7181.5	11,709.1	10,658.3	63.0%	8.9%
29B	10/2002	10/2007	3/2009	60	17	7181.5	14,280.0	6440.1	98.8%	54.9%
30A	7/2006	10/2007	3/2009	15	17	10,658.3	14,280.0	6440.1	34.0%	54.9%
30B	3/2009	????	????	26???	??	6440.1	????	????	????	???

Table 3: List of the dates of each 4-year cycle trough and its crest since 1893. It also shows the number of months the market rose from the beginning trough to the crest, and the number of months it declined into its next trough. It gives the low price at the beginning of the cycle (trough), the crest, and the end of the cycle (trough), and the percentage of each move up and down. The asterisks (*) above indicate that all prices prior to the 1929 crest are estimated. The grouping (between paragraph spaces) is based on 18-year cycles. Each group contains the 4-year cycles within each 18-year cycle. It is possible that the last grouping ended in March 2009, not October 2002, and contains 29 (A or B) and/or 30A. 30B is unfolding as this is being written and could be the start of a new 18-year grouping if the 18-year cycle ended March 2009. Prices of the DJIA are theoretical, not actual, which would be slightly lower.

THE 4-YEAR CYCLE

Within the 18-year cycle are either two half-cycles lasting 7-11 years each (also known as a 9-year cycle) or three 6-year cycles, which have an historical range of 5-8 years each. The first is known as a "two-phase cycle" and the second a "three-phase cycle." Sometimes both patterns are present in the same cycle. That is, there may be cases of 18-year cycles containing three troughs at the 5-8 year intervals, as well as a steeper decline than the first two at the 7-11 year interval. In these cases, it is referred to as a "combination cycle." These three patterns are present in all cycles in almost all cases. If I had to make a guess, I would say one of these three patterns occur in over 95% of all cycles throughout the modern history of financial markets.

Within most 6-year cycles, and almost all 9-year cycles, are two 4-year cycle phases. Sometimes a 6-year cycle will be exactly the same as the 4-year cycle, especially when the 6-year cycle is on the short side, say less than 6 years, and/or the 4-year cycle has expanded well beyond 4 years, as might be the case in 29B shown in the Table 3 of 4-year cycles on the previous page. It is the 4-year cycle that is important to a long-term investor, for here too one can find consistency not only in the length of time between trough to trough, trough to crest, and crest to trough, but also consistency in percentages of price appreciation and depreciation into the lows and highs respectively. With minimum time and price targets, one can make astutely calculated investment decisions, which is the objective of the long-term investor.

The 4-year cycle is also valuable to the long-term investor who would use the 18-year cycle as his core cycle for investing. If the concept of using at least three cycle periods ("tying in multiple cycles") is applied to the long-term investor, he may find it most useful to adopt the 72- and/or 90-year cycle as the higher level cycle, and the 4-year cycle as the lower one, with the 18-year cycle used as the core. This is the combination of multiple cycles to be advised in this book for the long-term investor. Since the 72- or 90-year cycle is not the immediate cycle above the 18-year cycle, nor is the 4-year cycle the immediate one below the 18-year cycle, it will require a modification of the rule given before. It requires an understanding that there can be other patterns within the 18-, 72-, and 90-year cycles beside the "two-phase," three-phase," and "combination" types. And even with this modification, it will still be very valuable to also use the two and three-phase intervals of each of these longer-term cycles for optimal understanding of where one is in each cycle, and hence which strategy to employ. For instance, one should still be cognizant of the 36-year half-cycle to the 72-year cycle, or the 45-year half-cycle to the 90-year cycle, when considering the cycles above the 18-year. Likewise one should also be aware of the 6- and 9-year subcycles within the 18-year cycle when considering the cycles immediately below it. Thus, in a sense, we are suggesting that most of the attention for long-term investing be directed at the 18-year cycle, with the higher cycle to be used as two levels above it (72- and/or 90-year) and the lower one to be used as two levels below it (the 4-year cycle) This is a variation of the normal cycle patterns based on the division of a cycle by the numbers 2 or 3, or both.

Table 3 on the prior page gives a list of all 30 of the 4-year cycles recorded since 1893 in the Dow Jones Industrial Average. The first point to note is that all of these cycles have lasted 32-68 months. An exception may be 29B (October 2002-March 2009), which may have lasted 77 months if it is valid. If all cycles other than 29B were used, then, the mean length would be 50 months. But in the study of cycles, we don't use all cycles to obtain the mean length. We use the middle 80+% of cases. Those that fall out of this 80% range are considered "distortions," which are given special significance as discussed in great detail in Volume 1 of this series, as well as the primer titled "Merriman on Market Cycles: The Basics." Since Table 3 identifies 30 instances of 4-year cycles, we will want to reduce it to at least the middle 24 cases to obtain the 80% "normal" range for this cycle's occurrence. That is done by omitting the 2 or 3 longest and shortest samples from our list (review Table 1 earlier in this book).

By adding the columns titled "months up" to "months down" in Table 3, one derives the length of each cycle (or go back to Table 1). One will note that there are three cases of only 32 months (#11, 15, and 30A). These are the shortest on record. The two longest shown here would be instances #12 and 24, which were 68 and 62 months respectively (again, if we omit 29B, which for purposes of this discussion we will assume is not to be included). The other 25 cases of the 4-year cycles unfolded at the 36-56 month interval. Thus the "normal" mean length would be 46 months with an orb of 10 months. Or, it could be said that in 83.3% cases of the 4-year cycle, the range was 36-56 months. Any 4-year cycle falling outside of this range will be referred to as a "distortion." If it occurs prior to 36 months, it is a distortion referred as a "contraction" of the cycle. If it occurs later than 56 months, it is a distortion known as an "expansion." You will notice that in the five cases of "distortion" shown in Table 3, four had exceptionally large price appreciations or declines, far more than the norm. The two longest ones, for instance (the "expanded" 4-year cycles) had the two largest price appreciations of all 4-year cycles. The 1932-1937 instance saw the DJIA appreciate 381.8% from low to high. The 1982-1987 instance, 50 years later, witnessed a price increase of 256.7% from trough to crest. Additionally, these two cases contained the longest periods of growth in the bull market phase of the 4-year cycle. In the former case, the market did not reach its crest until 56 months after the cycle began. In the later case, it took 60 months from the start of the cycle to its crest. The same would be true if case 29B is a valid "expanded' 4-year cycle. It too topped out in the 60th month.

So how can Table 3 be of use to a long-term investor? Let's start with a study of the length of time it takes the 4-year cycle to reach its crest, followed by an understanding of what type of increase the stock market tends to make during this period. From the column titled "Months Up," one can see a range of 5-60 months in which the DJIA rallied from the trough that started the 4-year cycle to its crest. That is, the shortest period for the bullish phase of a 4-year cycle has been 5 months (November 1929 through April 1930). The longest bull market within this cycle lasted 60 months (August 1982 through August 1987 and possibly October 2002-October 2007). Once again, we can omit the shortest and longest cycles until we get the middle 80% cases. The shortest rallies lasted 5-9 months. The longest ones lasted 54-60 months. If we eliminate those from the study, we will see that in 80% of the cases, the 4-year cycle rallied 12-51 months. In other words, it could be said that in 90% of instances (27 out of 30 times), the DJIA stock index rallied for at least one year after it completed its 4-year cycle trough. In fact, there have been no cases since 1938 where this has not been the case, as of this writing. In most cases, the duration of the bull market phase will last considerably more than one year. In 80% of the instances shown here (24 of 30), the stock market appreciated at least 20 months. In over half of the cases (16), the rally lasted at least 30 months.

Thus we come to our first rule for long-term investors. *Once the 4-year cycle bottoms, the ensuing rally will last at least one year (90% probability and usually at least 20 months (80% probability).*

The next matter of importance to the investor is the amount of appreciation that one can expect from an investment nearby to the 4-year cycle trough. If he is to hold the position for at least 20 months, what is the normal range that the price will appreciate? For this, we look to column titled "% Up." Here one will note that the stock market has appreciated anywhere from a low of 21.2% (October 1946 to June 1948) to a high of 381.8% (July 1932 through March 1937). If we omit the three lowest percentage increases, we will see that in 90% of these cases, the stock market appreciated at least 35%. Furthermore, there are only six cases where it did not appreciate at least 50%.

Thus we come to the second rule for long-term investors in regards to the 4-year cycle. *Once the 4-year cycle bottoms, the stock market will rally at least 35% (90% probability), and usually at least 50% (historical rate of frequency for this is 80% probability).*

The next step involves determining where, and at what price, to actually enter the market based on the four-year cycle. It has already been established that the normal interval between 4-year cycle troughs is 36-56 months. Once the stock market enters this time band, the investor begins looking for opportunities to buy. There are two columns in Table 2 that would appear to be helpful in this task. The first is titled "Months Down," or the time it took for the market to decline from its 4-year cycle crest to trough. The second would be the last column, titled "% Down." Unfortunately, the column titled "Months Down" will not be of much use, for the time bands of the bearish phase of the 4-year cycle have varied greatly, from as short as 1-3 months (in 7 instances, with five occurring only since 1987, thus making it a relatively more recent phenomenon), to over 2 years (there have been 6 instances in which the decline lasted 24-41 months). That would leave 17 instances in which the bear market lasted 5-23 months. It can also be observed that in 19 of these 30 cases (63.3%), the market declines 7-24 months. Perhaps that is the norm for the decline within the 4-year cycle, but it is not frequent enough to be of reliability for the long-term investor. It would be better for him to simply outline the 36-56 month time band from the start of the cycle, to identify the period of time in which the next bottom is due. Then apply the historical range of "percentage of decline" from the crest within that time frame in order to ascertain a favorable price in which to enter the market.

In the last column titled "% Down," it will be observed that the range of decline from crest to trough in four-year cycles has had a range of 8.9% to 86.3%. Upon closer inspection, one will note that in the two cases in which the decline was less than 12%, there is a possibility they were part of an ongoing cycle low in which the decline was more than 12%. If we remove these cases, we will see that the next three lowest percentage declines were 12-17.1%. There was another at 17.4%. After that, it jumps to 20.6%. Thus we can say that the bearish phase of the 4-year cycle will find stock prices declining at least 20% off its crest. The rate of frequency for this 20+% decline has been

86.7%. Likewise, if we remove the most extreme decline – the 86.3% loss from April 1930 - July 1932 (#11) – we would discover that in 25 of the 30 historical cases, the bearish phase of the 4-year cycle declined 20.6-57.1%. Or, said another way, the mean percentage of a decline into the 4-year cycle trough is nearly 40%. It is 38.85% +/- about 18%. This is about right, for one will note that in 14 cases (about half), the decline has been at least 39.7%.

Thus we come to the third rule for long-term investors. *Once the stock market enters the 36th month of its 4-year cycle (and even the 32nd month to be more certain) and the stock market has fallen at least 20%, investors can begin to look for opportunities to buy.* The exception to this rule would be when the 18-year cycle is also due. In those cases, the decline is apt to be at least 39.7%, as has been the case in at least six of the prior seven instances. The actual low for the 4-year cycle will usually be longer than 36 months (but not usually longer than 56 months), and the actual percentage of decline may be considerably more than 20% (the mean is 38.85%). But the long-term investor is not so concerned with getting in at the exact bottom (although that would be nice) in terms of time and price. He is simply concerned about recognizing when prices are in the area of a long-term low (i.e. good value) and thus represent a favorable investment probability over the long-term. These studies demonstrate that this type of environment usually comes around every 3-5 years, after a decline of at least 20%. And from that actual bottom, prices will usually appreciate at least 50% over the next 20 months.

These three rules are simple enough to be of immense use to an investor. In fact, they may be all that is required for those who prefer simplicity. Yet they can be refined to produce even greater probabilities of success. Let's now return to the concept of tying in multiple cycles in order to increase the probability for success.

We begin by once more asserting that the long-term investor will use the 18-year cycle as his "core cycle" for analysis and investment decisions. Although there is not enough history to validate this tenet, it appears that there are either four or five 18-cycle phases within the greater 72- or 90-year cycles. That has been the case since 1762, but in all, there are only three historical cases to draw from. In all 3 cases so far, the highest price of the longer-term 72- or 90-year cycles has been attained in at least the fourth 18-year cycle phase. In the two 90-year cycles (1762-1842 and 1842-1932) the crest occurred in the fifth 18-year cycle phase. In the three probable cases of the 72-year cycle (1784-1857, 1857-1932, 1932-2009), the crest has also been attained in the fourth 18-year cycle phase (twice the 72-year cycle has had four phases and once five). In looking at Table 2, it will be noted that as of this writing there have probably been four 18-year cycles completed so far since the 1932 low, as of this writing, if we assume the last was completed in March 2009. If there is yet to be a 90-year cycle, then it will contain five 18-year cycle phases.

Based on this idea that the 72- or 90-year cycles will usually not top out before the fourth 18-year cycle phase within them, the long-term investor will want to consider two things: 1) hold onto stocks until the fourth 18-year cycle phase of these longer-term cycles, and 2) plan to add onto positions at each of the first three 18-year cycle troughs within the 72- or 90-year cycles. As one can observe from Table 2, the last 18-year cycle phase of these longer-term cycles tend to decline 63.6-89.5% from crest to trough. But in the 18-year cycles before the fourth phase of either of these longer-term cycles, the decline from crest to trough is less, usually only 30-50%. In one instance, it was only 13.9%, but this is clearly a case of price distortion – it is not the norm.

The 4-year cycle can now be used to refine one's entry and exit. As evidenced in Table 3, the 18-year cycle has been comprised of as few as three 4-year cycle phases or as many as five, since 1893. In fact, it is more often comprised of five 4-year cycle phases. The 1974-1987 instance was the only one that contained just three 4-year cycle phases. All instances prior to 1974 contained five 4-year cycles. And the one since 1987 may have contained 4, if it ended in 2002 or 5 if it ended in 2009.

Perhaps the most important point that may be derived for the long-term investor from these studies is that the crest of the 18-year cycle is not achieved before the third 4-year cycle phase, according to Table 3. It is possible that the only time in history it was achieved before the third phase was in 1835. That would have been the second 4-year cycle phase of that shortened 13-year interval which qualified as the 18-year cycle. But in all cases since 1893, and probably all but one since 1797, the crest of the 18-year cycle has unfolded in the third (or later) 4-year cycle phase. In fact, with the exception of the 1974-1987 instance (in which there were only three 4-year cycles), the 18-year cycle crest has unfolded in the 4th or 5th phase. The 1896-1914 cycle produced a double top in the third and fourth 4-year cycle phases.

This information is valuable for the long-term investor because it means that 4-year cycles can be used to time additional purchases for the long-term. In other words, as long as it is not the fourth or fifth 4-year cycle phase within the 18-year cycle, the long-term investors can buy at the lows of the 18-year cycle and the first two or three 4-year subcycles within it. It is only after entering the third 4-year cycle phase that the long-term investor may consider exiting from long-term stock holdings. And although there may be substantial declines along the way, they will not take out the low that started the 18-year cycle, unless the longer-term 72- or 90-year cycles are unfolding. In fact, it is rarely the case that a 4-year cycle trough will take out its starting point unless it is the last phase of the 18-year cycle. That has only happened once since 1921 (it happened in 1970). In these cases, the stock market may decline 20-50% from the crest of their 4-year cycles, but 1) they do not take out the low that started the 18-year cycle, and 2) these are additional buying opportunities for the long-term.

Summary

Putting it altogether then, the following represents an investment plan for long-term "buy and hold" investors, using the concept of cycles as postulated here.

1. Identify the time band for an 18-year cycle trough.
2. When the market has declined at least 37.5% from its crest prior to this time band, prepare to buy. Usually this decline will be 40-50%. However, it will be more than 50% if it is the last 18-year cycle within the greater 72- or 90-year cycles. In that case, the decline may be as much as 77-93%.
3. Plan to stay in this position for 9-19 years, or at least until the third 4-year cycle phase within the 18-year cycle.

4. Plan for the market to have appreciated at least 122% from the start of the 18-year cycle and more likely 250-400%. This appreciation should not be completed before at least the third 4-year cycle phase. In cases where it is the first or last 18-year cycle within the greater 72- or 90-year cycle, the appreciation may exceed 600%. These will generally be realized after the third 18-year cycle phase of the longer-term cycles (i.e. fourth or fifth phases).
5. Additional long-term purchases may be made at the end of the first and second 4-year cycle phases within the 18-year cycle and oftentimes at the end of the third one too. In each case, the decline from the 4-year cycle crest will likely be at least 20% (usually 20-50%) and occur 36-56 months after the prior 4-year cycle trough. If it is the 5th (and sometimes even the 4th) four-year cycle within the greater 18-year cycle, then the decline is likely to exceed 40%.
6. It may be anticipated that in the rally to the crest of the new 4-year cycle, 1) the stock market will not take out the low that started the 18-year cycle, and 2) it will likely appreciate at least 50% over the next 20 months (80% historical frequency). The market has appreciated at least 35% for at least 12 months in 90% of the historical cases studied. The appreciation is usually more like 50-200%, and the duration of the rally is usually more than two years.
7. After nine years have elapsed since the start of the 18-year cycle, and after appreciation of over 122% (and preferably over 250%) in the value of the stock index (DJIA) has been attained, and after the market has entered the third 4-year cycle phase of the 18-year cycle, the investor may begin to take profits. His horizon for investing may now shrink to study only the 4-year cycle. That is, he can still buy the lows of the third and fourth 4-year cycle bottoms, but his position may only last 12-30 months, and the market may only appreciate about 50% from these lows. In fact, if the market is entering the time band for an 18-year cycle trough, the duration of the rally may be less than 20 months.
8. The price appreciation in the fourth or fifth 4-year cycle phase of the 18-year cycle may be extremely powerful (70-250%) or very anemic (only 20-50%). It may not make a new cycle high, or it may explode, and then be followed by a severe collapse.

TECHNICAL ANALYSIS

"Sometimes it is very difficult to ignore the news headlines and go about one's business in a routine fashion. Of course that is what a technician should ideally always do… One of the cornerstones in technical analysis is that price reflects all that is known, anticipated, and discounted by all market participants in exactly the right proportions on each and every day."

- Chief Market Technician at a major world bank (whose compliance department would not grant use of his name for this quote).

CHAPTER FIVE

PRICE OBJECTIVES:
BASIC METHODS OF CALCULATIONS

There are many methods used by traders, which are different from those used by long-term investors, to calculate a price objective for a stock, index, commodity, or financial asset. In this chapter, we begin with the simplest methods based on chart patterns. They are easy to see on a chart. Most "price objectives," as well as technical studies, are the result of mathematical calculations involving past prices, especially previous or historic highs, lows, and in some cases, closing prices.

We will start with basic price objective theories. These involve calculations used to project a "normal" price range for a cycle trough or crest for trading purposes. These calculations yield different results than the percentages of appreciation and depreciation used by investors. Then we will progress into the more complex methods of determining support, resistance, and narrower price objective zones. Just as it was important to use three types of charts or cycles to determine the underlying trend and the optimal strategy to utilize for successful trading or investing, it is also important to use more than one means for determining price support and resistance. When multiple studies yield price targets that overlap with one another, the probability of defining a solid support or resistance area - buy and sell points - becomes stronger. Then the challenge is to wait until prices fall or rise into this price range within the time bands identified for a market reversal. This is the art of integrating time and price factors for trading purposes.

To understand the basic price objective via the methods outlined in these books, one needs to know two things: 1) is it a bull or bear trend, and 2) what cycle or cycle phase will be used to calculate a price target? In a bull trend, we want to buy all corrective declines at the end of the "phases" of that cycle. We may also want to take profits when we reach a price target zone for the crest of that cycle. In bear markets, we want to sell all corrective rallies to the crest of those phases of the greater cycle. We may also want to take profits on shorts, or even reverse to the long side when we reach a price target for a cycle trough, especially if it is in within the time band for that cycle trough.

We will start this study by identifying the price of a correction within a trend.

50% "Normal" Corrections:

When a market is in a bull or bear trend, it will make "retracements" or "corrections" to that trend. Those corrections within the trend are usually around 50% of the previous thrust in the direction of the trend. Many technical analysts like to use Fibonacci retracement ratios to determine the price "range" of a retracement. Fibonacci (named after the Italian mathematician) is a sequence of numbers as follows: 0, 1, 1, 2, 3, 5, 8, 13, 21, 34, 55, 89, 144, etc. Each number in this sequence is the sum of the two preceding numbers and the sequence continues infinitely. One of the remarkable characteristics of this numerical sequence, according to www.investopedia.com, is that "… each number is approximately 1.618 times greater than the preceding number. This common relationship between every number in the series is the foundation of the common ratios used in retracement studies." The most common Fibonacci retracement percentages are 38.2, 50, and 61.8%. Others may include 23.6 and 76.4%.

To illustrate this concept, let us assume a stock is in a bull market. The first leg up has advanced from 10 to 20, or 10 points. The 50% retracement theory would suggest this stock would now give back about 50% of its gain, or about 5 points. A correction back to around 15 would be a "normal" price retracement.

Now let us assume we wanted to calculate a "normal" price range for this retracement. It would be 38.2-61.8% of the 10-point gain, or 3.82-6.18 points. If we subtracted this amount from the high of 20, we would get a "normal" price correction back to 13.82-16.18, which is "around" the 50% target of 15.

In the same way, one can calculate a retracement in a bear market. Assume the market topped out at 20, and then declined all the way back to 10. It lost 10 points before it found support. Assuming the trend is down, or bearish, a "normal" corrective retracement (rally) would take prices back up to 50% of its loss, or 5 points, to 15/share. Again, applying the "normal" Fibonacci ratios, the "normal" price target for this retracement would be 13.82-16.18.

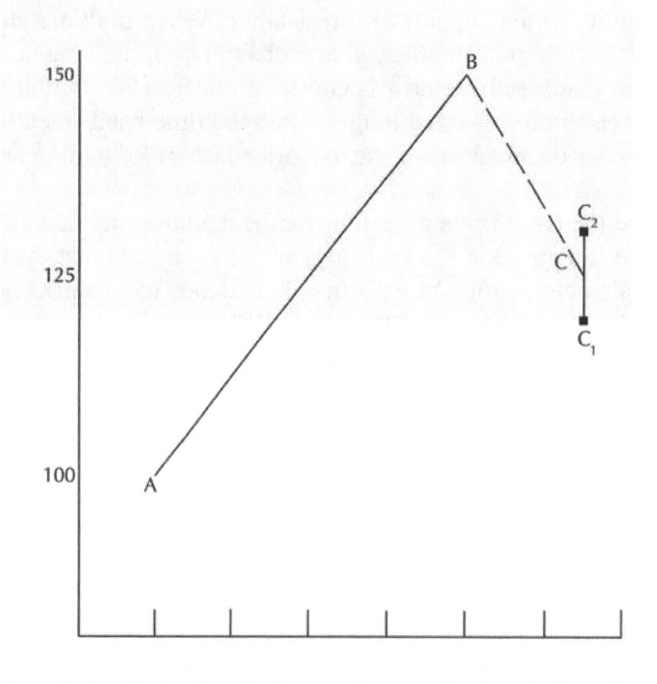

Figure 5: An illustration of a "normal" correction in a bull market

Bull Market "Normal" Corrective Declines

In bull markets, each crest of the same cycle type is higher than the previous one. Each low of the same cycle type is higher than the previous trough too. In other words, there are usually higher highs, and higher lows of the same cycle type, in typical bull markets. The decline to the phases within this cycle will tend to be 50% of the swings up within that cycle, with a range of 38.2-61.8% - *assuming it is a three-phase pattern.* A prototype of this market behavior is shown in Figure 5. The market goes up 50 points, and then has a corrective decline of 25 points, +/- 11.8% of the 50-point move, or +/- 2.95. Since the fundamental idea is to trade in the direction of the trend – and it is determined that the market is in a bull trend - traders will buy these corrective declines at the troughs of the sub cycles (or phases) within the greater cycle, in these price ranges.

The mathematical formula for determining a "normal" price corrective decline in a bull market is as follows: add the price that starts the cycle to the price that marks the crest of this phase of the cycle. Divide it by 2. This gives the 50% price target for the corrective decline.

To determine the "normal range" for this sub cycle trough, take the crest minus the trough that began the cycle, and multiple by .118. You will note that .118 + 50% (.50) = .618, or 61.8%. You will also note that 50% - .118 (or 11.8%) = .382, or 38.2%. These two normal limits define the Fibonacci levels of support in a corrective decline to a bull market.

Let us illustrate this calculation by referring to Figure 5. In this figure, the cycle started at point A, at a price of 100. It achieved the crest of its first phase at point B, which was 150. How far might it decline in a normal retracement? The formula is:
(A + B)/2 = 50% retracement, or, in this example, (100 + 150)/2 = 125.

What is the "range" for the expected corrective decline? The formula is:
(B-A) x .118, or, in this example, (150-100) x .118, or 50 x .118 = 5.90. We now add and subtract this to the 50% mark, which was 125. Therefore the range for the expected decline is 125 +/- 5.90, or 119.10-130.90.

Now let us apply this technique to a real example. Figure 6 depicts a daily chart of the Dow Jones Industrial Average. Specifically it identifies two 50-week cycle troughs. The first trough (1) occurs on July 18, 2006, at 10,683.30. It is not only a 50-week cycle trough, but it is also a 4-year cycle trough. Thus, it starts the first 50-week cycle within the new 4-year cycle. We know it will be a bullish cycle because it is the first phase of a longer-term cycle, and almost all first phases of cycles are bullish. Indeed this one is. It rallied to a high of 12,795 on February 20, 2007. It then commenced a decline of the entire rally. The calculation for this corrective decline of the 50-week cycle is:
10,683.30 + 12,795.00 = 23,478.30.
23,478.30 ÷ 2 = 11,739.15

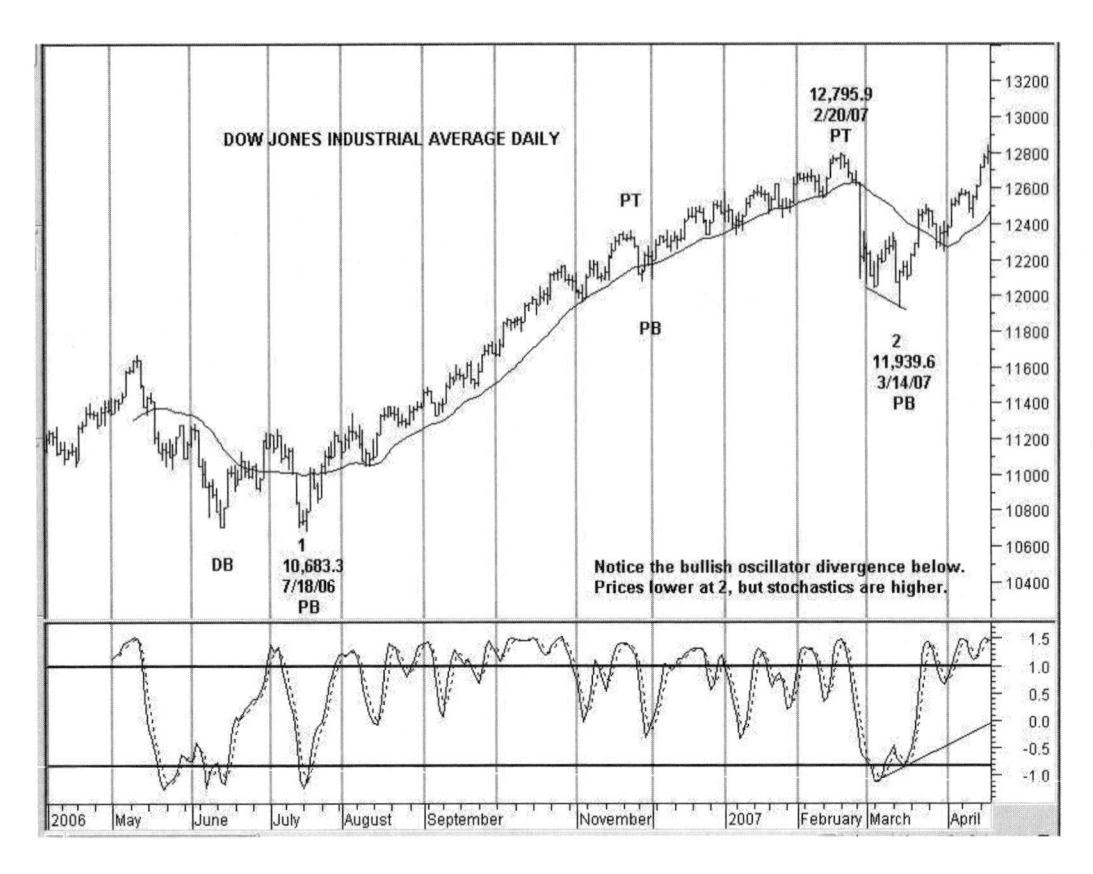

Figure 6: DJIA daily chart, showing the primary move up from the 50-week cycle trough on July 18, 2006 (1) through the crest of that cycle on February 20, 2007, and then the corrective decline to the 50-week and primary cycle trough (PB, 2)) of March 14, 2007.

The 50% retracement point is therefore 11,739.15.

Now we want to find the orb, or range, for this price target. To do that, take 12,795 – 10,683.30 = 2117.70. This is the amount of the price move from low to high. Now multiply it by .118 (2117.70 x .118 = 249.18). This is the orb from the 50% price target that constitutes the range for the corrective price decline. The price target is thus 11,739.15 +/- 249.18, or, 11,489.97-11,988.73.

As you will note from the chart in Figure 6, the actual 50-week cycle trough was 11,939.60, which is within the "normal" range of a corrective price decline for the 50-week cycle trough in a bullish market.

Bear Market "Normal" Corrective Retracements (Rallies)

In bear markets, each crest of the same cycle type is lower than the previous one. Each trough of the same cycle type is also lower than the previous trough. In other words, there are usually lower highs and lower lows of the same cycle type in typical bear markets. The rallies to the crests of the phases within this cycle will tend to be 50% of the swings down within that cycle, with a range of 38.2-61.8% - *assuming it is a three-phase pattern.* A prototype of this market behavior is shown below in Figure 7.

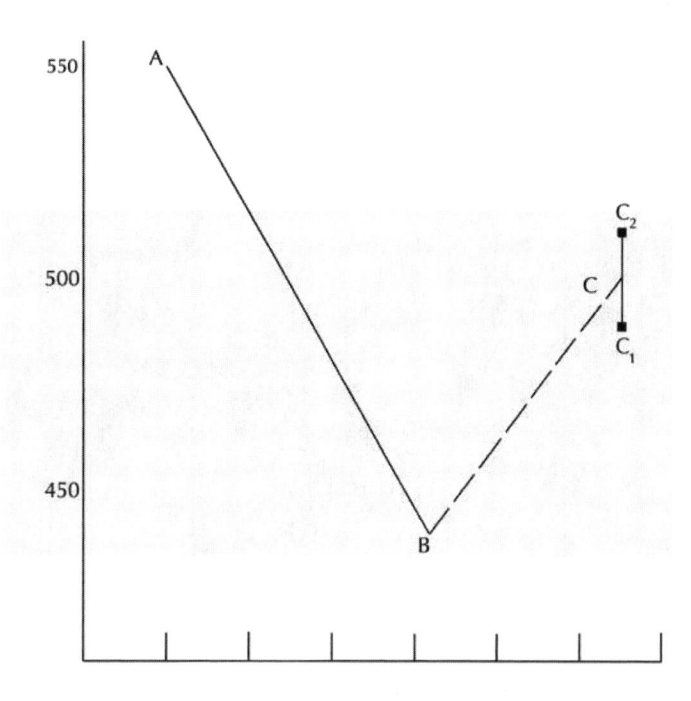

Figure 7: An illustration of a "normal" corrective rally in a bear market

In this example, the market declines 100 points (550-450), and then has a corrective rally of 50 points, +/- 11.8% of the 100-point move. Since the fundamental idea is to trade within the direction of the trend, and it is determined that the market is in a bear trend, investors or traders want to sell these corrective rallies to the crests of the sub cycles (or phases) within the greater cycle.

The mathematical formula for determining a "normal" price corrective rally in a bear market is as follows: add the price that starts the cycle (A) to the price that marks the trough of this phase of the cycle (B). Divide it by 2 to get the 50% price target.

To determine the "normal range" for this sub cycle crest, take the crest that began the cycle (A) minus the trough that ended the cycle (B), and multiple by .118. You will then add and subtract this "orb" to the 50% level, and that will give you the "range" of the projected correction.

Let us illustrate this calculation by referring to Figure 7. In this figure, the crest of the cycle started at point A, at a price of about 550. It then declined to the trough that ended its first phase at B, which was about 450. How far might it rally in a normal retracement to the crest of the next phase in a bear market? The formula is:

(A + B) ÷ 2 = 50% retracement, or in this example, (550 + 450) ÷ 2 = 500.

What is the "range" for the expected corrective rally? The formula is:

(A-B) x .118, or, in this example, (550-450) x .118, or 100 x .118 = 11.80. We now add and subtract this to the 50% mark, which was 500. That is, the range for the expected decline is 500 +/- 11.80, or 488.20-511.80.

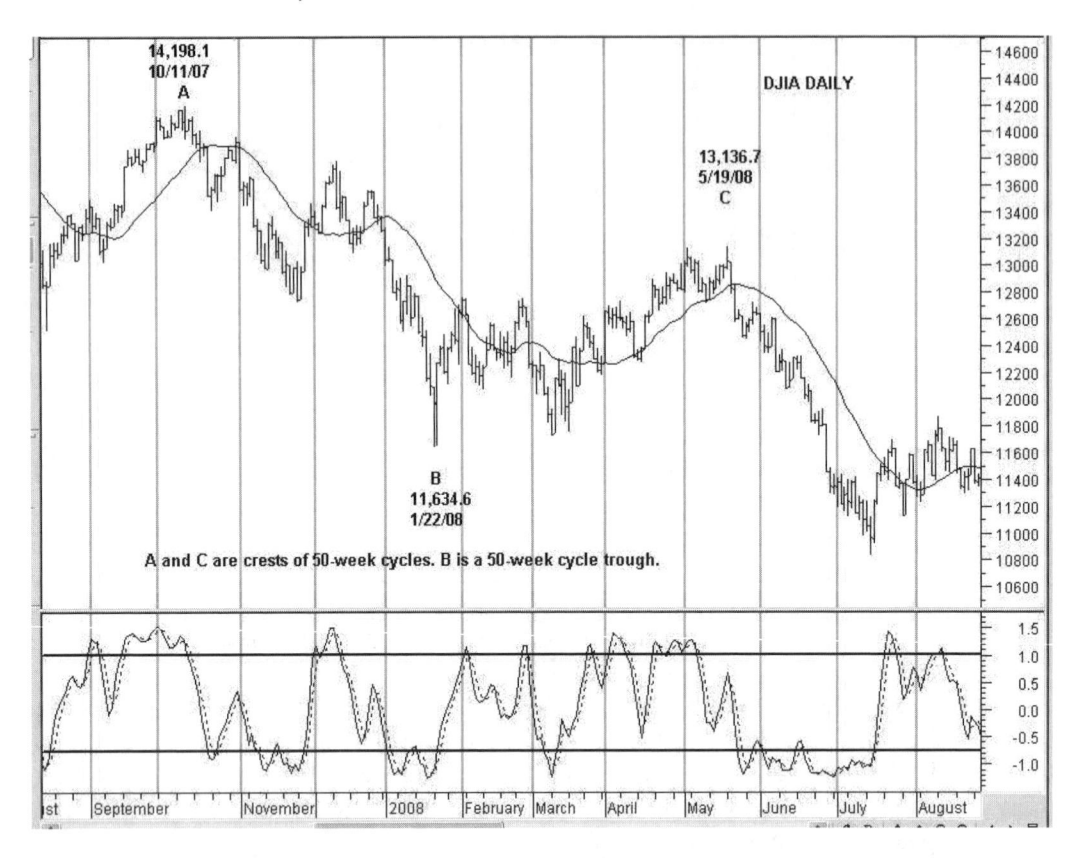

Figure 8: DJIA daily chart, showing the primary move down from the crest of the 50-week (and even greater) cycle on October 11, 2007 (A) to the 50-week cycle trough of January 22, 2008 (B), and then its corrective rally to the crest of the next 50-week cycle at C on May 19, 2008.

Now let us apply this technique to a real example. Figure 8 depicts a daily chart of the Dow Jones Industrial Average following its all-time high of 14,198.10 on October 11, 2007. This began a new bear market that would last 17 months. The first wave down ended with the 50-week cycle trough of 11,634.60 on January 22, 2008. For those who study Financial Astrology, this was the week that the 248-year Pluto cycle entered Capricorn.

The move down from the prior 50-week cycle crest to the 50-week cycle trough would represent the first step of the calculation for the projected crest of the next 50-week cycle. According to the formula given above, we add A + B and then divide by 2, in order to get the 50% level. Thus, (14,198.10 + 11,634.60) ÷ 2 = 12,916.35. That is the midpoint of the price objective target for the 50-week cycle crest, and represents a 50% corrective rally of the prior move down.

Now the range to this price target is determined by the formula (A-B) x .118. In this case, it is (14,198.10-11,634.60) x .118, or 2563.50 x .118 = 302.50. Thus our price target

46

for the crest of the 50-week cycle in this bear market would be 12,916.35 +/- 302.50. The range would therefore be 12,613.85-13,218.85. As one can see in the chart, the actual crest occurred on May 19, 2008, at 13.136.70. It was indeed in the "normal" price range for a corrective rally of the same cycle type (50-week cycle crest).

Price Targets for Crests in Bull Markets (MCP)

Calculating the 50% retracements, and their 38.2-61.8% Fibonacci ranges, is relatively easy. It is important to know this because it keeps one's mind focused on the trend. In bull markets, one wants to know where to buy any declines, and this formula is both simple and effective. The idea is to "buy low." In bear markets, one wants to know when to get out of holdings, or to establish new short positions in the direction of the bear trend. The idea is to "sell high." Once again, this formula of calculating "normal" corrective declines and rallies is a simple and effective means to establish where to sell in a bear market, and thus stay in a position that is headed in the direction of the trend.

What about identifying the price target for a *crest* in a bull market, or a *trough* in a bear market? There is a standard calculation for this as well that is relatively simple. It is known as the Mid-Cycle Pause (MCP) price projection. According to the HAL Bluebook by Walter Bressert and Jimmy Jones,[1] credit for the MCP calculation goes to William Jiler in his book, How Charts Can Help You in the Stock Market.

To calculate the MCP price objective of a crest in a bull market, the market must first complete a phase within the cycle. That is, it must have a cycle trough from which to begin, followed by the crest of the phase of that cycle, followed by a decline to the trough of that phase. The rally to the crest of the *next* phase will then be approximately equal to the rally in the first phase. The swing up in both phases is approximately the same.

This concept is illustrated in Figure 9. Here you see the first move up from the cycle low to the crest of the first phase as A-B. It is about 200 points from a price of 600 to 800. It then makes a normal corrective decline of 100 points to C (down to 700). If we add the amount of the move up (B-A, or 200 points) to C, we then get the MCP price target for the crest of the next cycle phase at D, or 900.

The mathematical formula that makes this computation very simple is: (B+C) – A = D, where B is the crest of the first cycle phase, C is the trough that ends the first cycle phase, and A is the trough that begins the cycle. D then becomes the projected crest of the second cycle phase. In this case, that would be (800+700) – 600 = 900.

To find the allowable orb for this MCP price objective crest, we take the distance between D and A (the crest of the second phase, minus the trough that started the cycle), and multiply it by .118. We then add and subtract this from the MCP to get the Fibonacci range for the projected price of this crest. In our example of Figure 9, the MCP price target for the crest of the second cycle phase at D would be calculated as follows:

(D-A) x .118, or (900-600) x .118 = 35.40. This is the orb. We could say the MCP price target for D is 900 +/- 35.40. The range for the crest of this price target would thus be 864.60 – 935.40.

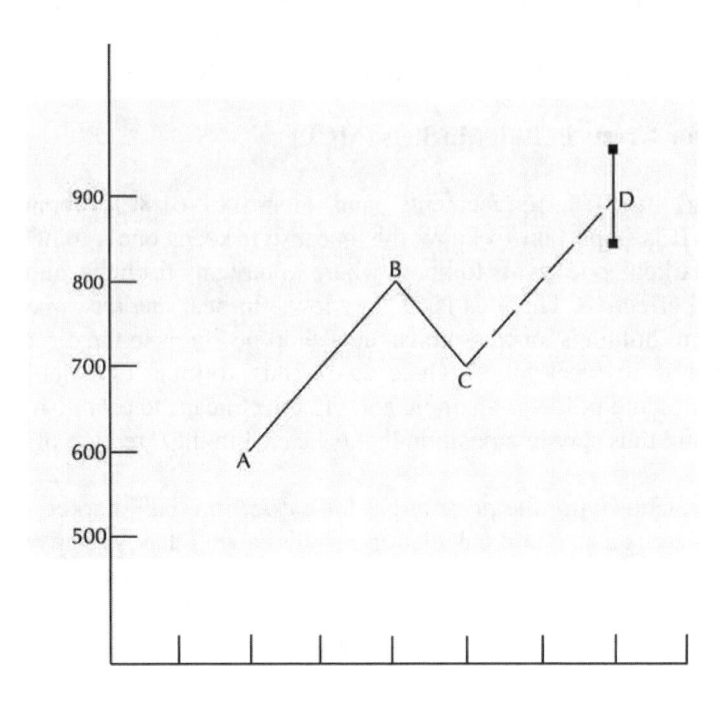

Figure 9: A diagram showing the form of a projected crest in a bull market. The cycle begins at A. It makes the crest of its first phase at B. It makes a corrective decline to the trough of its first phase at C. The projected crest of the next phase is shown at D.

Now, let's use a real example. Figure 10 on the following page is a daily chart of the Japanese Nikkei stock index from June 2006 through April 2007. On June 14, 2006, the Nikkei made a primary cycle trough at 14,045.50, designated on the chart as 'A.' It then rallied to a primary cycle crest at B, on October 24, 2006, at a price of 16,901.50. The rally advanced the index 2856 points (B-A). It then declined to its primary cycle trough at 15,615.60 (C) on November 27, which was within a normal price target for a corrective decline in a bull market of 15,473.50 +/- 337. That is, by adding the primary cycle trough that started the cycle (14,045.50) to the primary cycle crest that followed (16,901.50), you get a sum of 30,947. Divide that by 2 and the 50% correction for the next primary cycle trough would be 15,473.50. The orb of allowance would then be (15,473.50 – 14,045.50) x .236 = 337.

Our next task is to calculate the price range for the crest of the next primary cycle, or D. This formula is as follows: (B + C) – A = D, or (16,901.50 + 15,615.60) - 14,045.50 = 18,471.60.

The orb of this price target is then calculated: (D-A) x .118, or, 18,471.60-14.045.50) x .118 = 522.28. Thus we can say that the price objective for the crest of the next primary cycle (D) would be 18,471.60 +/- 522.28. The range for this price target would be 17,949.32 – 18,993.88. As shown on the chart in Figure 10, the actual crest occurred at 18,300.40 on February 26, 2007. That was easily within the MCP price target range just calculated.

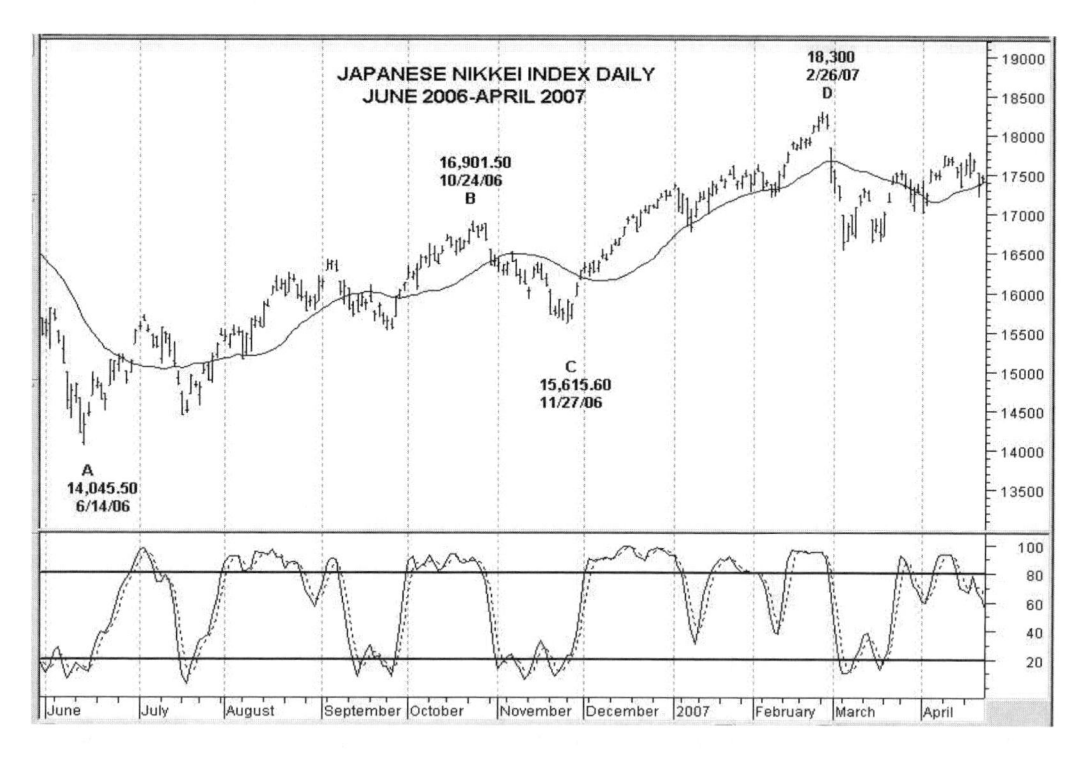

Figure 10: Example of the MCP predicting the price target of the crest at D.

Price Targets for Troughs in a Bear Market (MCP)

To calculate the MCP (Mid-Cycle Pause) price objective of a trough in a bear market, you need a cycle crest from which to begin, followed by the trough of that same cycle. You then need to see the completion of the corrective rally to the crest of the next phase of that cycle. The decline to the trough that ends the next cycle phase will be approximately equal to the decline witnessed in the prior phase. That is, the decline from the crest of the first cycle phase can be subtracted from the crest of the next cycle phase, in order to project the price target for the trough of the next cycle phase in a bear market. The swing down in both phases is approximately the same.

This concept is illustrated in Figure 11. Here you see the first move down from the cycle crest to the trough of the first phase as A-B. It is a decline of 60 points, from 350 down to 290. It then makes a normal corrective rally to C of 30 points, up to 320. We determine the amount of the move down (A-B, or 60 points) and subtract it from C, and get the MCP price target for the trough of the next cycle phase at D, which is 260.

A mathematical formula similar to that used in the bullish market trend can make the computation very simple. It would be: (B+C) – A = D, where B is the trough of the first cycle phase, C is the crest of the next cycle phase, and A is the crest of the first cycle phase. D then becomes the projected trough of the second cycle phase. In this case, that would be (290+320) – 350 = 260.

49

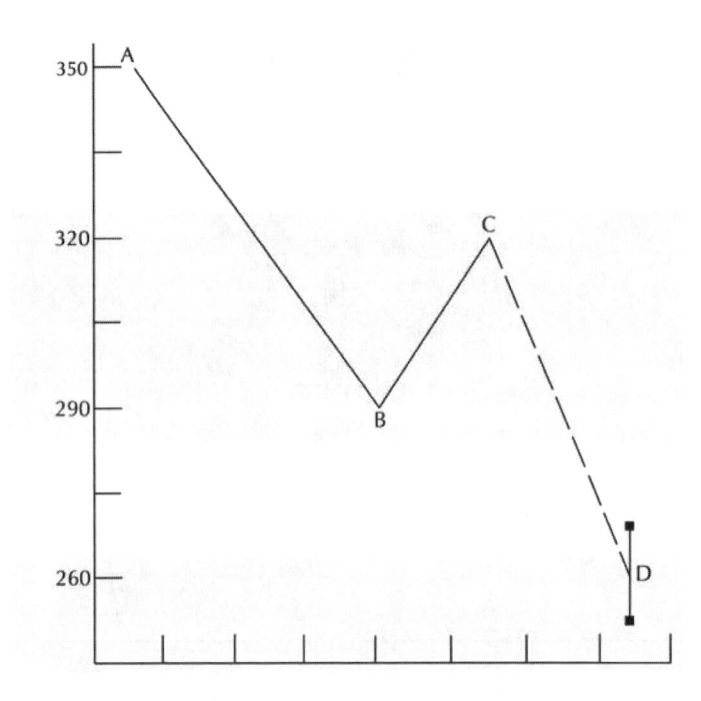

Figure 11: A diagram showing the form of a projected trough in a bear market. The cycle crest for this calculation begins at A. It makes the trough of its first phase at B. It makes a corrective rally to the crest of its next phase at C. The projected trough of the next phase is shown at D. The move from C-D is about the same as from A-B.

To find the allowable orb for this MCP price objective crest, we take the distance between A and D (the crest of the first phase, minus the trough of the second phase of the cycle), and multiply it by .118. We then add and subtract this from the MCP to get the Fibonacci range for the projected price target of this crest. In our example of Figure 11, the MCP price target for the crest of the second cycle phase at D would be calculated as follows: (350-260) x .118 = 10.62. Therefore the MCP price target for this cycle trough is 260 +/- 10.62, or 249.38 – 270.62.

Now let us observe this in a real example. Figure 12, shown on the next page, is another daily chart of the Japanese Nikkei stock index. In this chart, A represents the primary cycle crest at 10,767.00 on August 31, 2009. The market then declined to its second major cycle trough at B, on October 6, 2009, at 9628.67. It then rallied to the crest of the third major cycle phase at C, on October 27, 2009, at a price of 10,397.70. The decline to the third major cycle trough (which was also the primary cycle trough), is shown at D.

To calculate the MCP price objective of the trough at D, apply the formula given previously as: (B + C) – A = D. In this case, that is (9628.67 + 10,397.70) – 10,767.00 = 9259.37. To get the accepted orb of this MCP price target, we then take (A-D) x .118, or (10,767 – 9259.37) x .118 = 177.90. The MCP price target for this major (and primary) cycle trough is therefore 9259.37 +/- 177.90, or 9081.47 – 9437.27. The actual low, as shown in Figure 12, was 9076.41, which is very close to the lower end of this Fibonacci projected price range. It is not unusual to slightly overshoot a price target as a primary cycle trough (or crest) is forming. In fact, this leads to the understanding that multiple price targets are often necessary in forecasting any move in a financial market. It also enhances the understanding that all the technical tools available are simply good guidelines in helping one determine when to buy or to sell a financial vehicle. The market seldom stops exactly where a mathematical calculation says it should stop. If it did, everyone would be profitable all the time. Unfortunately, a silver platter of unlimited profits is never a given when you compete against the brightest minds in the world every day. You have to earn your rewards in the markets, just as you do with any endeavor in life and mastering the studies of market timing and price projections are important keys for those who trade or invest in financial markets.

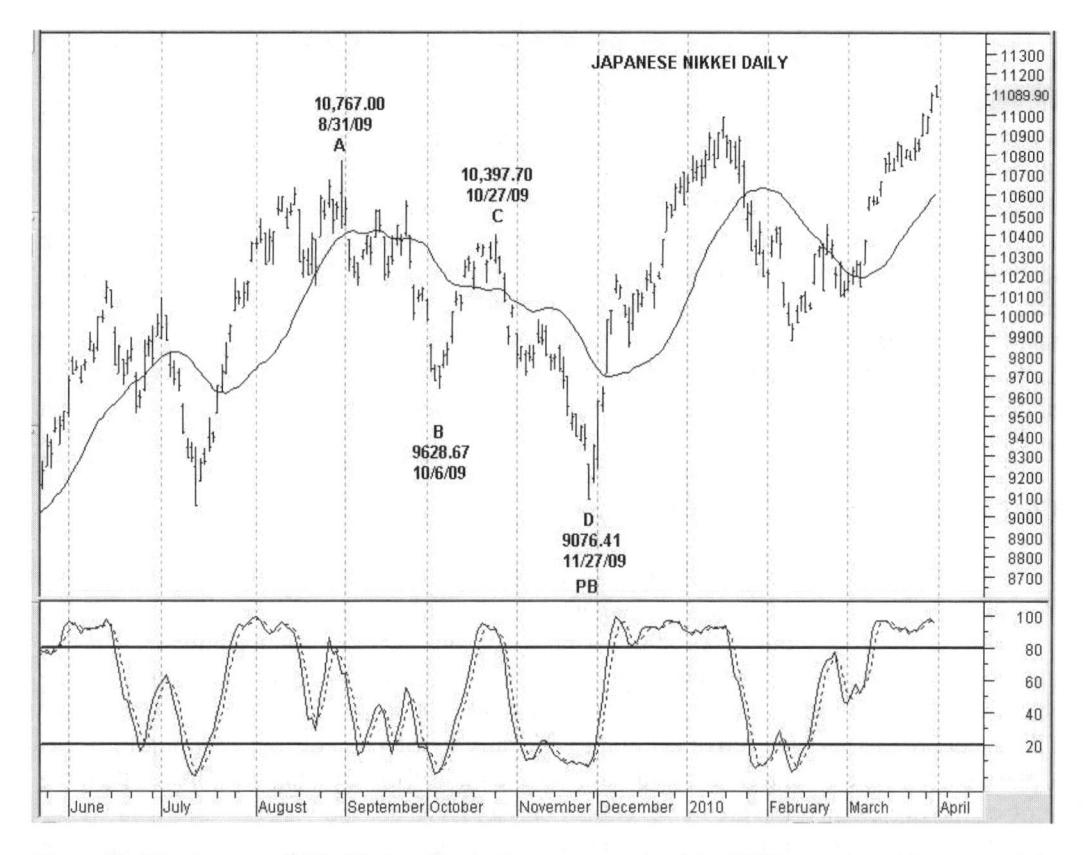

Figure 12: The Japanese Nikkei Index, illustrating an example of the MCP price target for a trough in a move down from primary cycle crest to primary cycle trough in late 2009.

References:

1. Bressert, Walter, and Jones, James. THE HAL BLUE BOOK, HALCO, 1981.

CHAPTER SIX

PRICE OBJECTIVES
MORE ADVANCED METHODS

The basic methods of calculating price objectives as given in the last chapter are very useful, especially with corrective retracements. However, they are only a few of the many mathematical formulas that are used to establish price targets. In real life trading, the basic methods given in the last chapter probably will accurately forecast price targets in less than half the cases one will encounter. They are most effective when markets attain these price objectives in time bands when cycle troughs or crests are due, or when technical studies indicate an overbought (high) or oversold (low) condition. To attain the price objectives by these methods before the "time" is right, usually means that the market move is going to exceed the basic price objective range. It is then that other methods of determining possible price targets for cycle highs and lows are required. To understand these new calculations, one must first identify various chart patterns, and what price targets would apply to each.

Corrective Declines That Exceed Normal Fibonacci Ratios

Let us review the three basic chart patterns within all cycles, as illustrated in Figure 1 earlier in this book. Regardless of whether it is a bull or bear market in terms of the longer-term cycle, we know that the first phase of any cycle is usually bullish. If it is a classical three-phase or combination pattern, the end of the first phase is usually higher than the trough that began the cycle. In fact, the end of that first phase is usually a normal Fibonacci 38.2-61.8% corrective decline of the rally to the crest of that first phase. If it is a classical two-phase pattern, then sometimes the end of the first phase is lower than the start of the cycle when the greater cycle is bearish. Even so, the biggest rally takes place in that first phase. Yet there are occasions when the trough of the first phase is more than a 61.8% correction. In fact, there are many cases when the trough of that first phase is a double bottom to the trough that began the cycle, and sometimes the second bottom is even slightly lower than the first, especially in a two-phase pattern.

In bull markets that exhibit a classical two-phase pattern, the decline to the half-cycle trough is not the usual 38.2-61.8%. It is more often a 45-85% correction of the swing up from the start of the cycle to its half-cycle crest. An illustration of this is shown in Figure 13. Because the correction is oftentimes more than 61.8%, it causes many technical analysts to pre-maturely announce that the market has changed from bullish to bearish. But it hasn't - at least not until and unless the decline takes out the low that started the cycle. That is the major determinant for the cycle to be labeled as bearish.

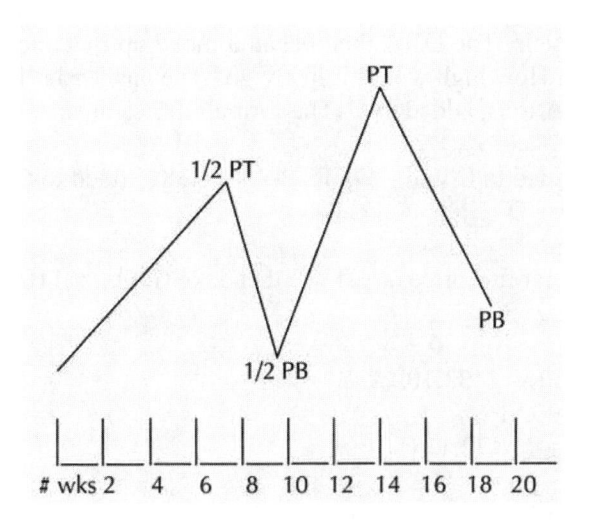

Figure 13: A typical two-phase primary cycle pattern in a bull market. Note that the half-primary cycle bottom (1/2-PB) is very close to the low that started the cycle, but still above it.

Nevertheless, this characteristic of two-phase cycles makes them the most difficult of all cycles to trade. Fortunately they only happen about 20% of the time.

Sometimes the trough of the first or second phase in a three-phase pattern also exceeds 61.8%. When it approaches, or even exceeds an 85% corrective decline, it will appear as a double bottom formation. This sets up a challenge in forecasting the price objective for the crest of the following phase. If it is to be a bullish cycle, the rally may exceed the price target generated by the Mid-Cycle Pause (MCP) price objective. If it is to be a bear market, the next rally may fail to meet the price target of the MCP calculation. It may even fail to exceed the crest of the previous (first) phase. Knowing the possibilities of the next move up can help the analyst determine the rest of the market behavior within that cycle. Let us discuss these possibilities.

In the case of a bull market, let us assume the end of the first cycle phase is a double bottom to the trough that started the cycle. It is higher in price than the low that started the cycle, so an MCP price objective can be calculated, but it will yield a price range that will essentially be a double top to the crest of the first phase. Yet in a bull market, that rally will usually exceed the area that would constitute a double top. In fact, the rally to that second crest will more often be about 1.236, 1.382, or 1.618 times the rally that defined the crest of the first phase. If it is a three-phase pattern, it may take until the third phase before that price target is hit.

Let's look at an example of how this works. In Figure 14, the Dow Jones Industrial Average (DJIA) made a primary and 50-week cycle trough at 11,634.60 on January 22, 2008. This is shown as 'A' on the chart. The crest of the first major cycle phase was 12,767.70 on February 1, represented as 'B' on the chart. Four weeks later, a double top formed at 12,756.60 on February 27 (not marked on the chart). The market then declined to the first major cycle trough (first phase of this new primary cycle) on March 10, 2008, at 11,731.60 (labeled as 'C' on the chart). This was more than the typical 38.2-61.8%

corrective decline of the move up from A to B. In fact, it is a double bottom to A, the start of the primary cycle. The DJIA then began a move up that exceeded the double top at 12,756 and 12,767. How high would it likely go? The answer is: 1.236, 1.382, or 1.618 of the move up from A to B, added to C. The formula for each is:

(B-A) x 1.236 added to C will = D, or (B-A) x 1.381 added to C will = D, or (B-A) x 1.618 added to C will = D

To get the range for this price target, we then take (D-A) x .118. So let's do each and see what we get.

(12,767.70 – 11,634.60) = 1133.10
1133.10 x 1.236 = 1400.51
11,731.60 + 1400.51 = 13,132.11 (D)

Then, D-A is 13.132.11 – 11,634.60 = 1497.51
The orb is thus 1497.51 x .118 = 176.70.

The price target for D is therefore 13,132.11 +/- 176.70. The actual high was 13,136.70, so this was a very accurate price projection for this crest, via this method.

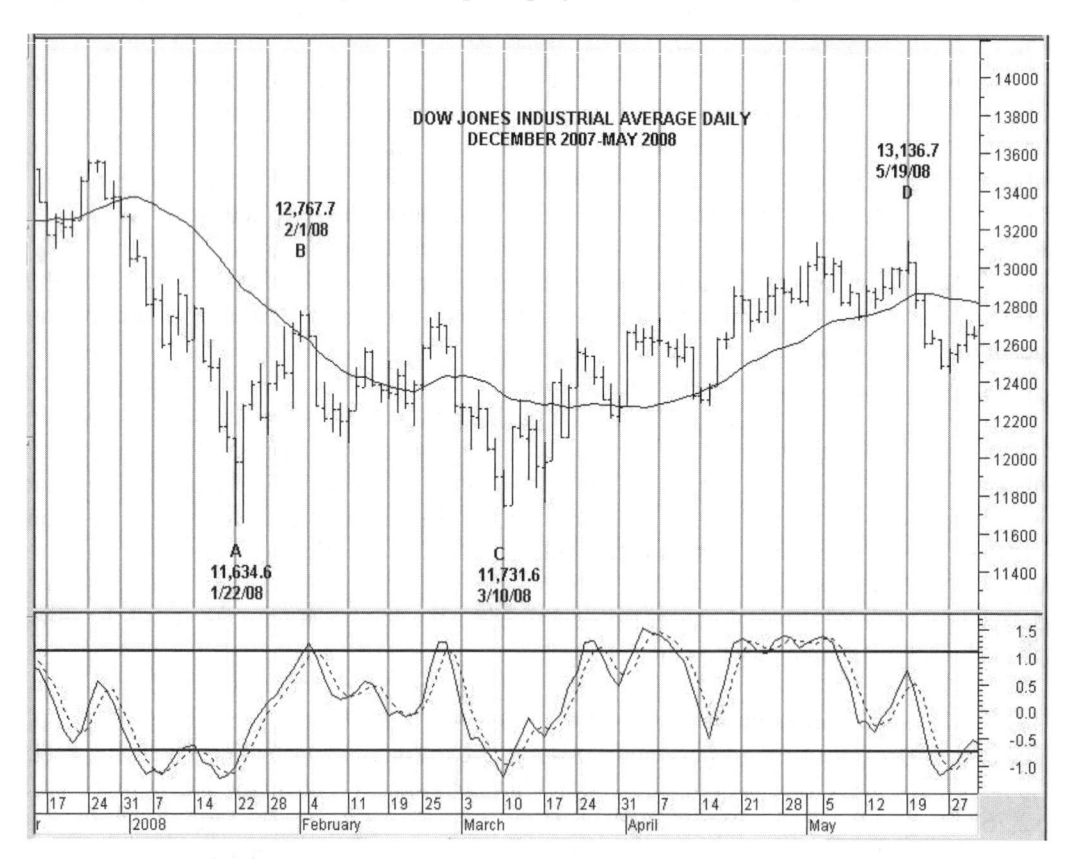

Figure 14: A case where the rally from C to D was 1.236 of the rally from A to B.

Had it gone much higher, we would then apply the 1.382 or 1.618 multiple to the rally in the first phase. In this price target, we would again take the price movement of A to B, or 1133.10. But this time we would multiply that by 1.382 or 1.618 and add it to C.

Let us illustrate with the 1.618 multiplier as follows:
1133.10 x 1.618 = 1833.35
11,731.60 + 1833.35 = 13,564.95. This would be our exact price target. But it has a range, so....

13,564.95 (D) - 11,634.60 (A) = 1930.35 x .118 = 227.78. The price target, had it gone higher, could next be 13,564.95 +/- 227.78.

Bear Market Price Objectives for Troughs

These same methods can be used for rallies and declines in bear markets too. That is, a normal bear market rally will be a 38.2-61.8% retracement of the prior swing down of the same cycle (or sub-cycle) type. But in the case of a two-phase cycle, the retracement rally can be as much as 45-85% of that swing down to the half-cycle trough.

But how do you project the price target for the next low in a bear market if the crest of the second phase in either a two- or three-phase pattern is a double top? Assuming the next leg down will exceed the low of the first phase, it will likely fall in the range of a 1.236, 1.382, or 1.618 multiplier of the first leg down (i.e. of the move from the first major cycle crest to the first major cycle trough).

Let us view an example of calculating a bear market price target for a cycle trough. For this illustration, let us use the chart of the Dow Jones Industrial Average following its then all-time high of 14,198.10 on October 11, 2007, shown in Figure 15. Here, the first crest occurs on July 17 at 14,022, as denoted by 'A'. This is the crest of the 50-week cycle, which is also the crest of the first primary cycle in a two-phase 50-week cycle that began March 14, 2007. Following the crest of the first primary cycle on July 17 (A), the DJIA fell for one month into its primary cycle trough at 12,517.90 on August 16 (B). That was above the level that began the primary and 50-week cycle of March 14, which was 11,939.60. Note that this decline to the trough of the first primary cycle phase of the 50-week cycle was more than the "normal" 38.2-61.8% correction. This alone is a clue that this 50-week cycle would likely be a two-phase pattern, consisting of two primary cycles and not a classical three-phase pattern. If it were to be a normal three-phase pattern, the decline would usually remain within the 38.2-61.8% retracement range. But the decline was 72.2%, more than the normal 38.2-61.8% corrective decline, but well within the norm for a 45-85% half-cycle retracement in a two-phase pattern.

The rally that followed to the crest of the second primary cycle took prices up to a new all-time high of 14,198.10 on October 11, 2007 (C). This was less than the normal price target of a Mid-Cycle Pause price objective, which would have been 14,600.30 +/- 313.96. This was yet another clue that the market was not as bullish as it had been over the past several years. Still, it was exhibiting higher highs and higher lows of the same cycle types, which is the basic pattern of a bull market. But now each rally was less than the normal price objective target for a bull market, and the declines were deeper than the price target for a "normal" retracement in a bull market. The confirmation that this was turning into a bearish cycle would come if and when prices took out the low that started the primary cycle first (12,517) and the 50-week cycle next (11,939). Both would happen within the second primary cycle phase, in early January 2008.

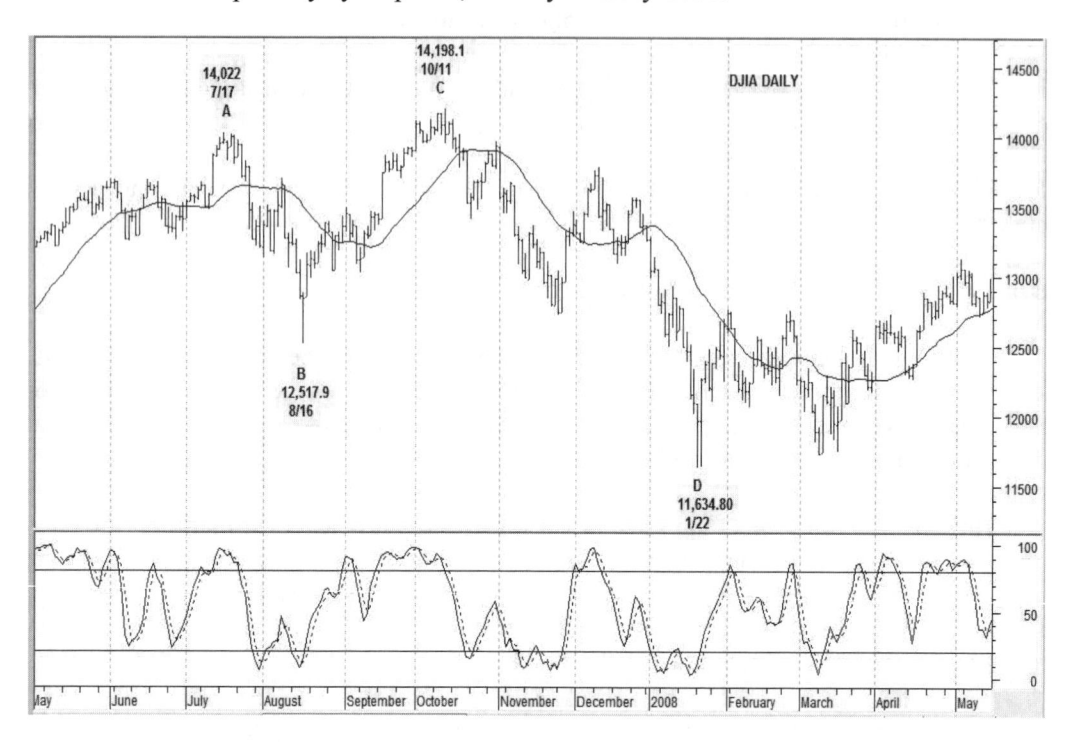

Figure 15: Illustration of a decline in a bear market that fell 1.618 of the first leg down.

The all-time high at C was essentially a double top to the crest of the first primary cycle at A. Now let's assume it would break below B, at 12,517. Where could this market fall to? The answer is that it could fall 1.236, 1.382, or 1.618 times the distance of A-B, subtracted from C. Or, in this case, let's take these steps using a 1.618 multiplier:

C - [(A-B) x 1.618] = D.
14,198.10 - [(14,022-12,517.90) x 1.618] = D.
D = 14,198.10 - [(1504.10) x 1.618]
D = 14,198.10 - 2433.63 = 11,764.46.

To get the range for this price objective, once again take the distance between the high and low of these numbers and multiply by .118. In this case, it is (C – D) x .118 = the orb of allowance for this price target, or (14,198.10 – 11,764.46) = 287.17. The price target for the trough of this primary and 50-week cycle trough, then, is 11,764.46 +/- 287.17, if the 1.618 multiplier is applied to the distance between A and B. This captured the actual low. The multipliers of 1.236 and 1.382 could also have been used, but the actual price was 11,634.80, which exceeded both the 1.236 and 1.382 calculations. As expected, the first phase of the new 50-week cycle was bullish. But the whole 50-week cycle turned bearish, and did not end until March 2009.

CHAPTER SEVEN

PRICE OBJECTIVES FOR THE LAST PHASE OF A THREE-PHASE PATTERN

By now, there is a basic rule about price objectives and market reversals that should start to be obvious. Once a market reverses, it will do one of three things:

1. If the greater cycle trend is intact, then a market reversal may have a price target that is a "normal" corrective calculation. This means it can retrace 38.2-61.8%, or 45-85% of the primary swing in a trend of a classical three-phase, or a rarer two-phase cycle type, respectively.

2. In many cases, the reversal may lead to a re-test of the prior cycle crest or trough, resulting in a double top or double bottom formation.

3. In the third case, the reversal may lead to the "breakout" of a defined support or resistance level, which in itself is often determined by a double bottom or double top formation. In these cases, the trend of that cycle will shift from bullish to bearish, or vice-versa and a slew of different calculations may be used to compute the next price target.

We have introduced many of the standard calculations used to project a price target at any time, in any market. However there are yet other calculations of the Fibonacci ratios that can be used for projecting the price of a crest or trough that completes a three-phase pattern in a bull or bear market respectively.

Calculating the Crest of the Third Phase in a Bull Market

Let us begin with a discussion of this "third phase price objective" for bull markets. For the purpose of this chapter, we will be referring to the model of the primary cycle. However, the concepts used to describe the parts within the primary cycle can be applied to any three-phase cycle pattern. In a classical three-phase bullish primary cycle, a pattern similar to Figure 16 occurs. The market starts at a low, then rallies about 3-5 weeks to the crest of its first major cycle phase. In many cases, this crest can be a re-test of the previous primary cycle crest, thus forming a double top chart formation. But if it is truly a bullish cycle, then a decline to the trough of that first major cycle (MB) will only last 1-2 weeks, and represent only a 38.2-61.8% retracement of the move up from the primary bottom (PB) to the first major cycle top (MT).

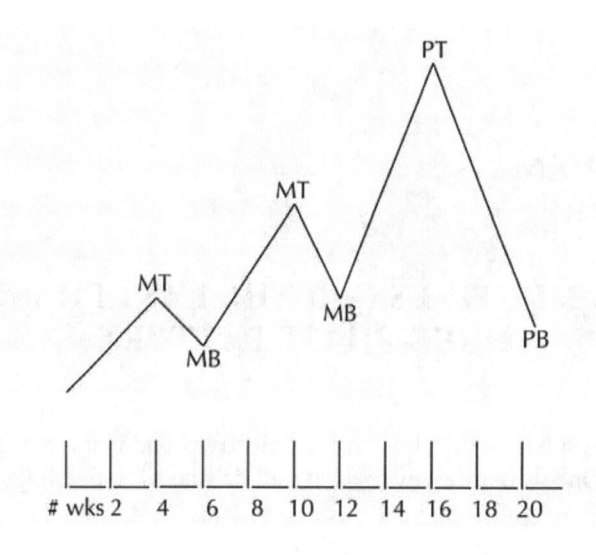

Figure 16: Classical three-phase primary cycle in a bullish market.

The move up to the crest of the second major cycle phase will usually be to a Mid-Cycle Pause (MCP) price objective level. It will be approximately equal to the move up in the first phase. In some cases, it may actually be much more. It can be as much as 1.618 times the move up to the crest in the first phase, and sometimes even more. This rally usually lasts about 3-5 weeks. Once the crest of this second major cycle is completed, the move down to the second major cycle trough is about 38.2-61.8% of that move up to the crest of the second major cycle. It lasts about 1-2 weeks.

Now we come to the third phase, where several different things can happen. We know from previous chapters that in a bull market the last phase of any cycle is the most bearish. This only means that the steepest decline of the entire cycle is likely to unfold in this last phase. Instead of correcting 38.2-61.8% of the rally from the start of this third phase, it will instead usually correct 38.2-61.8% of the move up from the start of the entire cycle. In terms of the primary cycle (as shown in Figure 16), the correction would be from the start of the primary cycle (PB, week #0) to its crest (PT, shown as week #16 in the graph above), which is usually the same as the crest of the third major cycle – but not always. In fact, there are at least four different paths that may unfold to the crest of the third or last phase in a cycle, such as the third major cycle phase within a primary cycle. They are as follows:

1. The rally to the crest of the third phase within a three-phase pattern can be corrective in nature. That is, it may only rally 38.2-61.8% of the move down in the second phase (from the second MT to the second MB). This is not very common, but theoretically it is possible because after all, the last phase of any cycle in a bull market is the most bearish. Therefore, the rally to the crest of this phase may only be corrective in nature, because it is a bearish characteristic. You can see this type of pattern in the diagram that follows, which is referred to as "Bull Market Phase 3 – Corrective Rally." The corrective rally is shown at 2-C.

Bull Market Phase 3 -- Corrective Rally

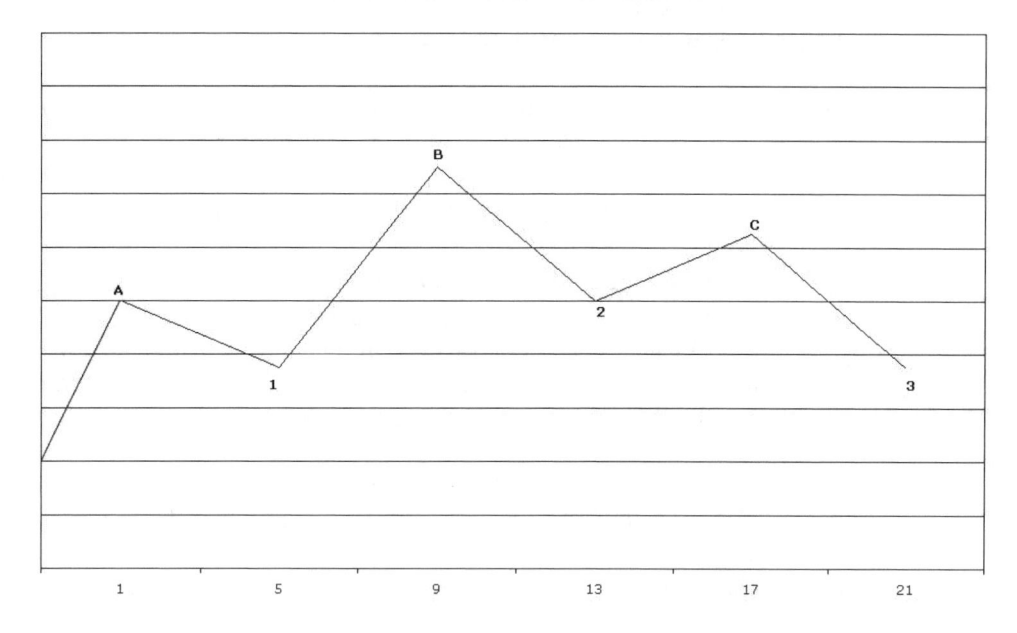

2. The rally to the crest of the third phase may be a re-test (double top) to the crest of the second phase. This is much more common. If a double top does not happen here in a primary cycle, then oftentimes it occurs in the first major cycle phase of the next primary cycle. That is, a double top can occur with the crests of the second and third phases, or it can occur with the crest of the first phase of a new primary cycle to the crest of the previous primary cycle. The diagram below shows illustrates this type of third phase pattern with a double top, shown as B-C.

Bull Market Phase 3 - Double Top

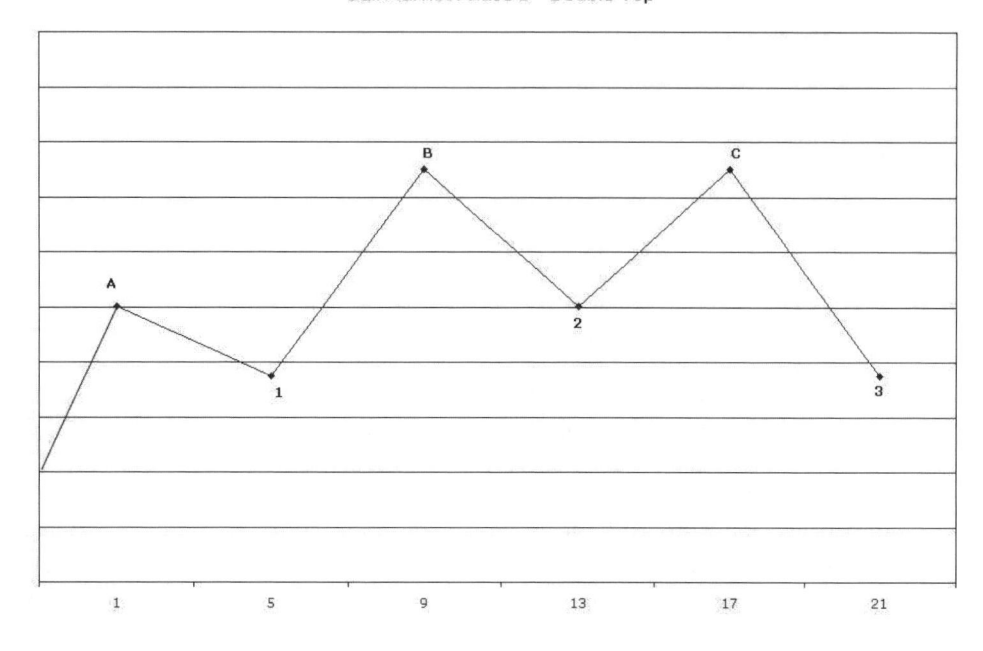

3. The crest of the third phase may be well above the crest of the second phase, but still within a well-defined price target. It usually unfolds one of three ways here, and often these will overlap with one another price-wise:

- It can be a normal MCP (Mid-Cycle Pause) price target based on the move up and corrective decline in the second phase.
- It can be a .618 multiplier of the rally from the start of the primary cycle to the crest of the second major cycle, added to the trough of the second major cycle.
- It can be a multiplier of 1.236 (and sometimes as much as 1.382) of the decline from the crest of the second major cycle to the trough of the second major cycle, added to the trough of the second major cycle. In Elliot Wave terminology, this third option might be referred to as an "irregular 'b' wave rally" to new cycle highs.

We will discuss these last two calculations shortly. A .618 multiplier of phases 1 and 2 for the crest of phase 3 is shown on the prototype graph below. This might also be the form if the crest of phase 3 is 1.236-1,382 of the move down in phase 2 (B-2). We will use 1.236 for our examples here.

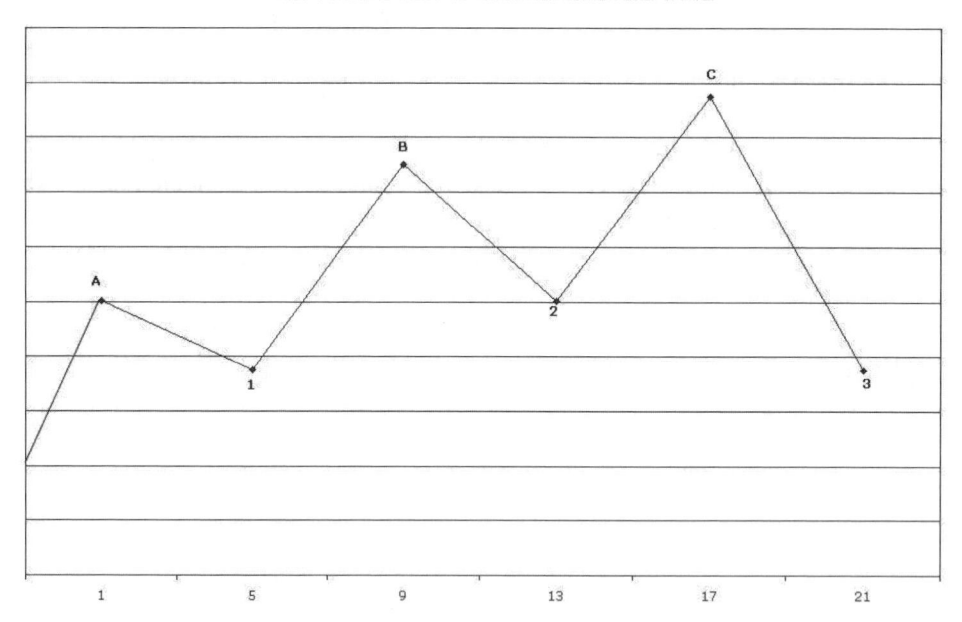

Bull Market Phase 3 - C is .618 of Phases 1 & 2

4. The third major cycle phase is also where "runaways," "blow-offs," and/or "bubbles" can occur. These are just some of the names given to markets that exhibit the "irrational exuberance" once ascribed by former Federal Reserve Board Chairman, Alan Greenspan. That is, powerful rallies can occur, especially if there is a well-defined resistance present and prices "break out" above this area. In fact, there are many chart patterns that can identify powerful resistance areas, such as double tops, triangles, wedge formations, and inverse head and shoulders formations (bullish).

That is why this book will also include a discussion of patterns. When certain patterns arise, it may indicate something spectacular is about to happen in that market. The point is that in the last phase – usually the third phase – of a cycle these types of "breakouts" tend to happen, although they can occur in the second phase as well. When they do occur, it is not easy to calculate where the "blow-off" will end price-wise. It may be 1.382 or 1.618 of the move up in the first or second phase, or 2.618 and even as much as 4.618. It may be a calculation that doubles the move up to the "break out" point from the prior cycle low. We never know for sure. However, we do know that when "bubbles" or "blow-offs" form in the third or last phase of a cycle, the decline that follows will usually be devastating. The cycle will not end well for investors, who usually suffer huge losses. It is not unusual for the decline in that third phase to come all the way back to the trough of the second phase, and even more. It should also be pointed out that when such a "blow-off" above a well-defined resistance level occurs, there is usually a powerful Level One geocosmic signature involving Uranus nearby. The prototype of a phase 3 blow-off in a bull market is shown below, where the crest of the third phase (C) represents a 1.618 of the move up witnessed in phase 2. However, it can be more.

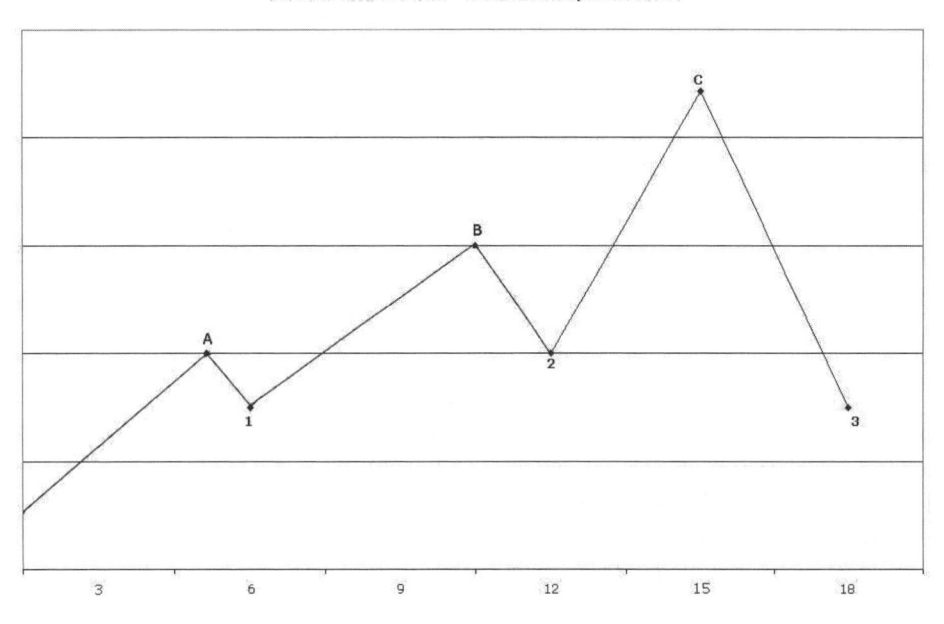

Bull Market Phase 3 - 1.618 of Rally in Phase 2

Let us look at some historical examples of these various third phase patterns, and how their price targets might have been calculated. For this example, we will use the chart of the weekly German DAX Index, shown in Figure 17.

Let us begin with the long-term cycle trough of March 2003, at 2188.75. That could have been either a 4- or 6-year cycle trough, maybe even longer. What we want to illustrate is how the then all-time high in July 2007, at 8151.57 might have been forecasted using some of the calculations described herein.

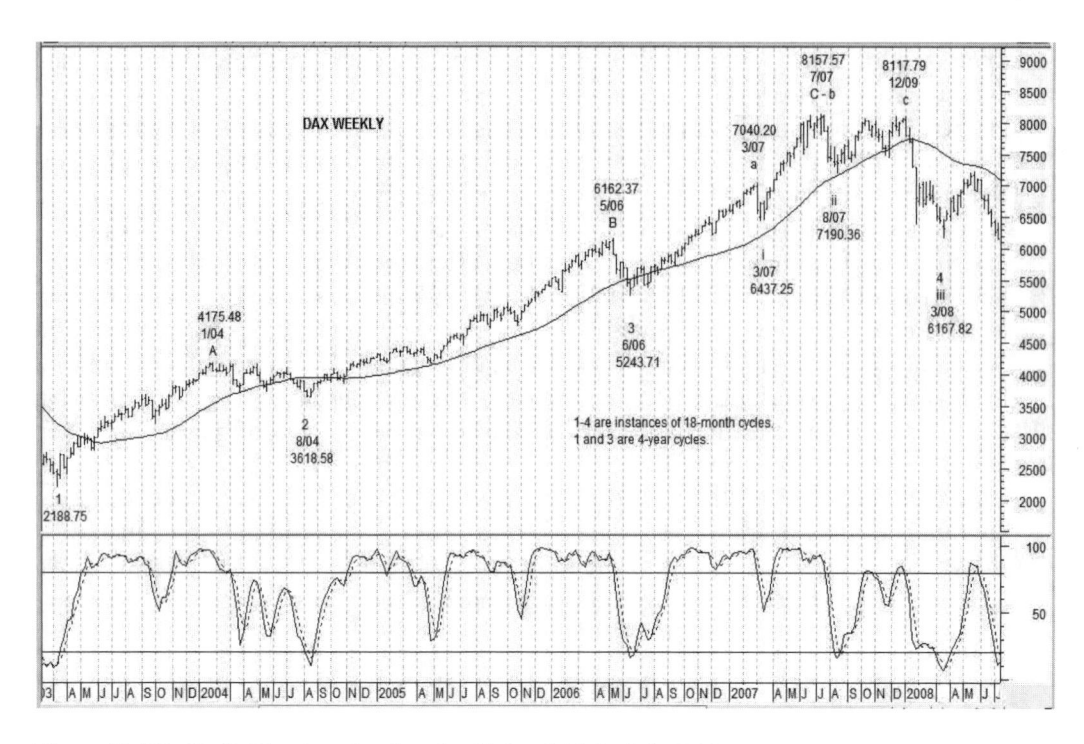

Figure 17: Weekly DAX prices showing the all-time high in July 2007.

First of all, let us assume that we expected this to be a 4-year cycle, comprised of three 78-week (or 18-month) sub-cycles, or phases. You can see the first two 78-week cycle troughs listed as 2 and 3 on the chart. Our first calculation for a crest of the third 78-week cycle phase would be the simple MCP method. In this case, it would be (B+3) – 2, or (6162.37 + 5243.71) – 3618.58 = 7787.50. The range would be (7787.50 – 3618.58) x .118 = 491.93, or 7787.50 +/- 491.93. The high of July 2007 was 8151.57, which is in the top part of this range.

We could have also made a calculation by multiplying the rally from the start of the cycle to the crest of the second phase by .618, and then adding it to the trough of the second phase. From the chart, that would be [(B – 1) x .618] + 3 = C, or [(6162.37 – 2188.75) x .618] + 5243.71 = 7699.41. Then, taking (7699.41 – 2188.75) x .118, we get an orb of 650.25, yielding a price target range for this crest at 7049.15 – 8349.66. The high of 8151.57 was also in this range.

Shorter-term, we could have also calculated the crest of the second phase within the 78-week cycle. That is, the German DAX has a 78-week cycle that sub-divides into a classical two-phase pattern of 39-week half-cycles. You can see this on the chart, where the third 78-week cycle begins at 3. The crest of the first half-cycle is at 7040.20 in early March 2007 (marked 'a' on the chart). The 39-week first half-cycle trough followed one week later at 6437.25, marked as 'i' on the chart. A simple MCP formula can then be constructed to calculate the crest of the next 39-week half cycle (and the crest of the entire 78-week cycle) as follows: (a + i) – 3 = b, or (7040.20 + 6437.25) – 5243.71 = 8233.74. Taking 11.8% of the distance between b and 3 gives us our range: (8233.74-

5243.71) x .118 = 352.82. Therefore the target of this second 39-week cycle crest becomes 8233.74 +/- 352.82. Again, the final high of 8151.57 was in this range.

In summary, we used three different calculations to identify a price range for a top. We can then take the overlap of all three and derive an "ideal" price target as follows:

1. 7787.50 +/- 491.93, or a range of 7295.57 – 8279.43
2. 7699.41 +/- 650.25, or a range of 7049.15 – 8349.66
3. 8233.74 +/- 352.82, or a range of 7880.92 – 8586.56

You can see that all three ranges overlap in the 7880.92 - 8279.43 price zone. The actual high of 8151.57 was in the middle of this "ideal" price target range.

Now let us apply these rules to a case when the third phase resulted in a "blow-off," a roaring bull market that far exceeded the norm for a rising market. For this, we go to the weekly chart of the Japanese Nikkei Index, leading up to its all-time high of 38,957.40 on December 29, 1989, as shown in Figure 18. We can consider the low in October 1986 at 15,819.50 as the start of a 4-year cycle trough. The first leg up in this 4-year cycle was from October 1986 to October 1987 (1 to A). 'A' was a 48-week cycle crest, the first phase of this longer-term cycle. The Nikkei topped out at 26,646.40. It then declined for 4 weeks to form its 48-week cycle trough at 21,036.80. Now let us apply a 1.618 multiplier to that first phase rally and add it to the low of that first phase. Remember that when we do this, it does not have to be realized in the very next phase. It may take a couple of phases before this price target is met, assuming it is to be a bullish cycle.

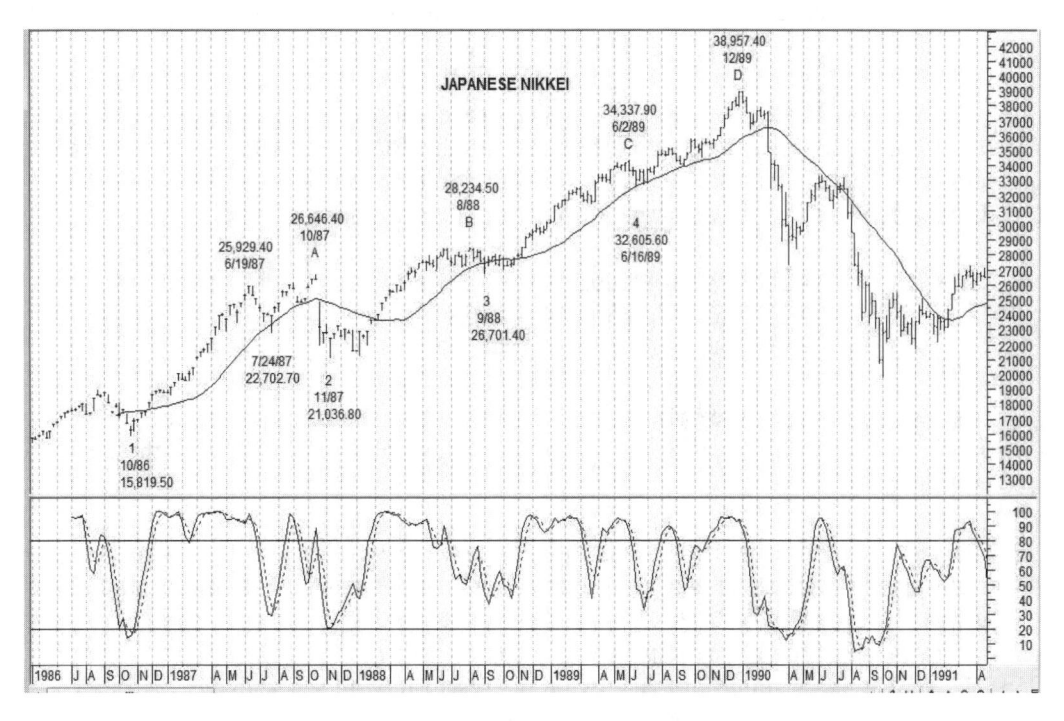

Figure 18: Weekly Japanese Nikkei Index, showing its "blow-off" bubble formation for an all-time high in late 1989.

The formula for this calculation would be: [(A-1) x 1.618] + 21,036.80. Or, [(26,646.40 – 15,819.50) x 1.618] + 21,036.80 = 38,554.720.

The orb would be (38,554.72 – 15,819.50) x .118, or 2682.76
The price target would thus be 38,554.72 +/- 2682.76.

Not bad, when you consider the actual top turned out to be 38,957.40. However, it would be another year before that price target was realized.

Now let us do the same thing with the second 48-week cycle. This one started with the low of 21,036.80 in November 1987, marked as '2' in Figure 18. From there prices rallied to the crest of this second 48-week cycle at 28,234.50 in August 1988, marked as 'B' in the chart. The size of the rally was 7197.70. Now multiply this by 1.618 to get a result of 11,645.87. This will then be added to the low of this 48-week cycle, which was 26,701.40, just four weeks later again, in September 1988. This gives us a price target of 26,701.40 + 11,645.87 = 38,347.27. If we take that figure, less 21,036.80 (the start of the second 48-week cycle), and multiply it by .118, we get an orb of 2042.63. The price target of this calculation is thus 38,347.27 +/- 2042.63. Again, this is within the range for the all-time crest, which was 38,957.40 on December 29, 1989.

We can go even one step further. The low of September 1988 (3) began a third 48-week cycle phase to the 4-year cycle. Usually there will be four of these 48-week cycles within a 4-year cycle, although there are several cases of three or five instances. The crest of this third 48-week cycle occurred the week of June 2, 1990 at 34,337.90 (C). Two weeks later, it bottomed at 32,605.60, shown as 4 in the chart. Now let us do an MCP calculation for the crest of the fourth and next 48-week cycle. The formula is (C + 4) – 3, or (34,337.90 + 32,605.60) – 26,701.40 = 40,242.10. If we then multiply that swing up (40,242.10 – 26,701.40) x .118, we get the orb of allowance to this price target as 1597.80. The MCP price target for the crest of the fourth 48-week cycle within the greater 4-year cycle is thus 40,242.10 +/- 1597.80. So here too we have three price targets that accurately identified the eventual all-time top in the Japanese Nikkei as follows:

1. 38,545.00 +/- 2681.60, or 35,863.40 – 41,226.60
2. 38,347.27 +/- 2042.63, or 36,304.64 – 40,389.90
3. 40,242.10 +/- 1597.80, or 38,644.30 – 40,242.10

The overlap of these three price targets is within this last calculation, or 38,644.30 – 40,242.10. The actual high was 38,957.40, right in this price range where all three targets overlapped.

There is one other calculation we would like to discuss in this section. This is where the crest of the third phase of a cycle is about 1.236 times the decline in the second phase. If you will observe the rally to the crest of the first 48-week cycle phase, from 1 to A, you will notice the crest of the second primary cycle occurred in the week of June 19, 1987, at 25,929.40. There were three primary cycle phases in this 48-week cycle, although you cannot clearly see the end of the first one on this weekly chart (you would need a daily chart to see it clearly). From the crest of this second primary cycle phase, the Nikkei declined to its second primary cycle trough during the week of July 24, to 22,702.70. This represented a loss of 3226.70 points. If we multiply that by 1.236 and add the result (3988.20) to that second primary cycle trough (22,702.70), we get an irregular 'b' wave price target of 26,690.90 for the crest of the third primary cycle phase. The orb of allowance to this price target would be (26,690.90 – 22,702.70) x .118 = 470.60. Thus, the price target would be 26,220.29 – 27,161.50. As you can see from the chart in Figure 18, the actual price for this 48-week and primary cycle crest was 26,646.40, very close to the exact price target via this calculation.

Calculating the Trough of the Third Phase in a Bear Market

The same rules for finding the crest of the third and/or final phase in a bull market, work in reverse for finding the trough of the third and/or final phase in a bear market. In a classical three-phase bearish primary cycle, a pattern similar to Figure 19 occurs. The market starts at a low, then rallies about 3-5 weeks to the crest of its first major cycle. In many cases, this crest will be the primary cycle crest, for in bear market cycles, a pattern begins to unfold of lower highs and lower lows of the same cycle type. Eventually, prices will break below the start of the cycle, thus confirming it is a bear market. Each successive rally will be to a lower high than the crest of the same cycle type, and will usually be a 38.2-61.8% retracement of the prior swing down. The lows on the other hand fall lower and lower until the cycle ends. The lowest price will be at the end of the cycle in a bear market. So what will that price be?

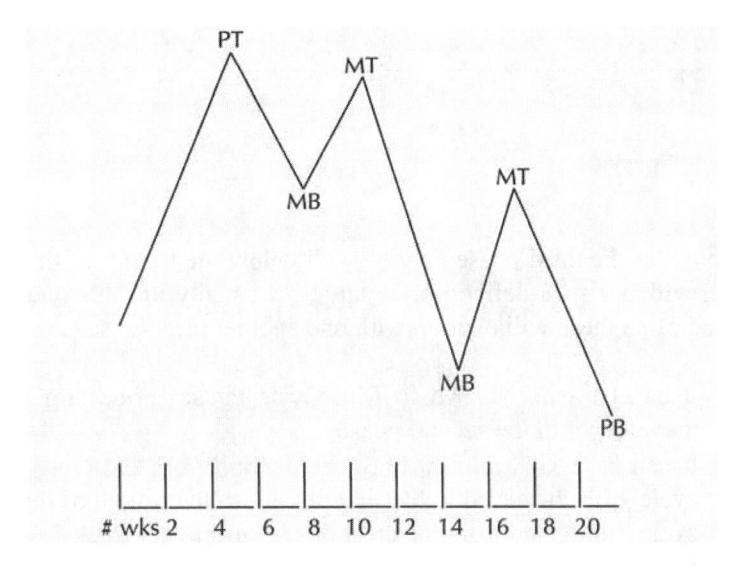

Figure 19: Classical three-phase primary cycle in a bearish market.

The move up to the crest of the second major cycle will usually last 3-13 days. It will then decline about 3-5 weeks to the trough of the second major cycle. The price of this trough will usually be to a Mid-Cycle Pause (MCP) price objective level. It will be approximately equal to the move down in the first phase. In some cases, it may actually be more. It can be 1.618 times the move down from the crest to the trough in the first major cycle phase. However, as demonstrated before, sometimes that 1.618 price target will not be seen for a couple more phases, and sometimes it will be more than 1.618.

Now we come to the third phase, where again almost anything can happen. Here too are three basic market moves that tend to unfold in this final phase.

1. The decline to the trough of the third phase can be a re-test (double bottom) to the trough of the second phase. This is a common pattern as the market prepares to enter the bullish first phase of the new cycle, as illustrated in the prototype graph shown below, at 2-3.

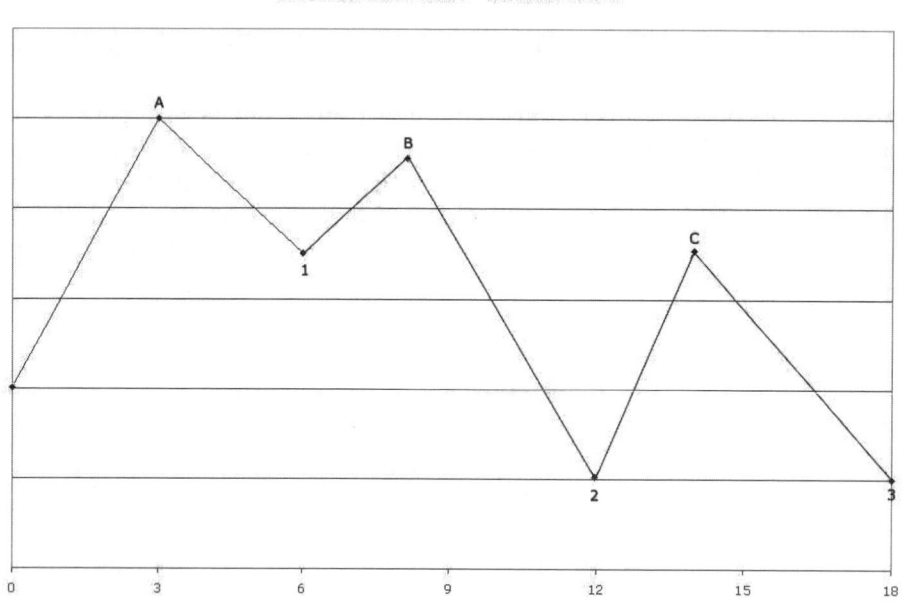

Bear Market Phase 3 - Double Bottom

2. The trough of the third phase may be well below the trough of the second phase, but still within a well-defined price target. It usually unfolds one of three ways here, and often these will overlap with one another price-wise:

    - It can be a normal MCP (Mid-Cycle Pause) price target based on the move down in the second phase.
    - It can be a .618 multiplier of the decline from the crest of the primary cycle – if it occurred in the first phase - to the trough of the second major cycle, subtracted from the crest of the third major cycle.
    - It can be a multiplier of 1.236 (and in some cases, as much as 1.382) of the rally from the trough of the second major cycle to the crest of the third major cycle, subtracted from the crest of the second major cycle. In Elliot Wave terminology, this third option might be referred to an "irregular 'b' wave decline" to new cycle lows.

    We will discuss these last two calculations shortly, but a prototype can be seen by two of the graphs that follow.

Bear Market Phase 3 - 1.236 of Rally in Phase 3

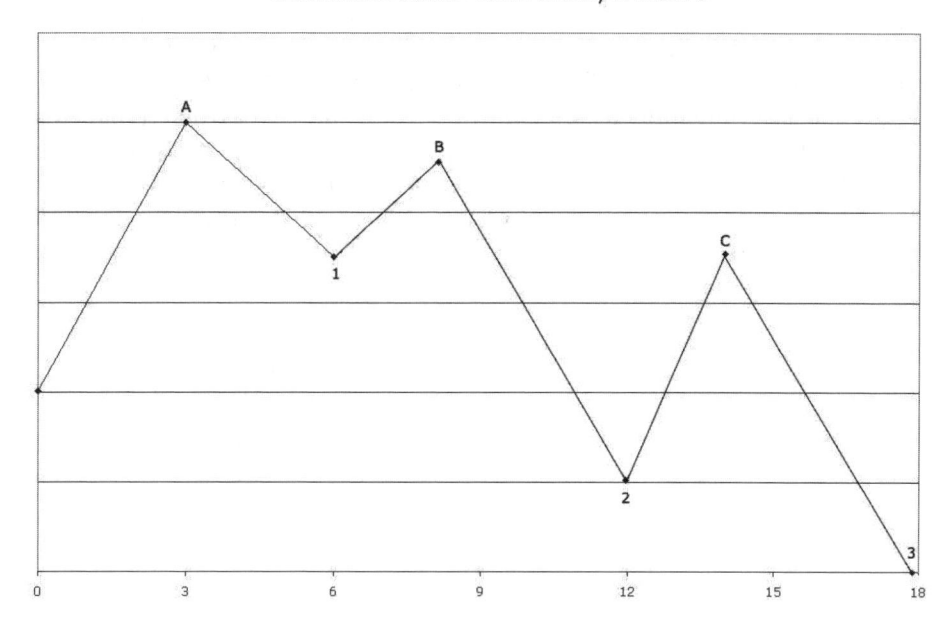

Bear Market Phase 3 - .618 of First Two Phases

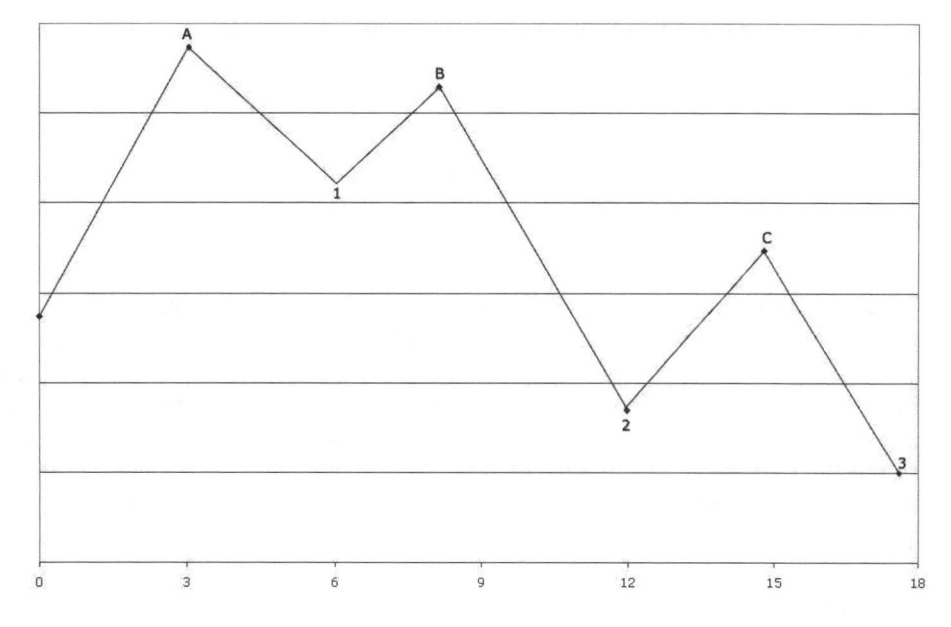

3. The third major cycle phase is also where very powerful declines (panic selling) can occur, especially if there is a well-defined support area present and prices "break out" below this support level. In fact, there are many chart patterns that can identify powerful support areas, such as double bottoms, downside channels, and necklines of head and shoulders formations (bearish). The point is that in the last phase (usually in the third phase, but sometimes in the second phase) of a

cycle is where these types of "breakouts" tend to happen, forming what is also referred to as a "spike" bottom. When such panic selling occurs, it is not so easy to calculate where the "breakdown" will end price-wise. It may be 1.382 or 1.618 of the move down in the first or second phase, even 2.618 or 4.618. It may be a calculation that doubles the move down of the "break out" point from the prior cycle high, especially if there is a "gap down" along the way (to be discussed later). We never know for sure. But this we do know: 1) it is usually followed by a powerful rally once the next cycle begins and 2) there is usually a powerful, Level One geocosmic signature involving Uranus nearby. Below is a prototype of a move down in phase three (C-3) that is 1.618 of the move down in phase 2.

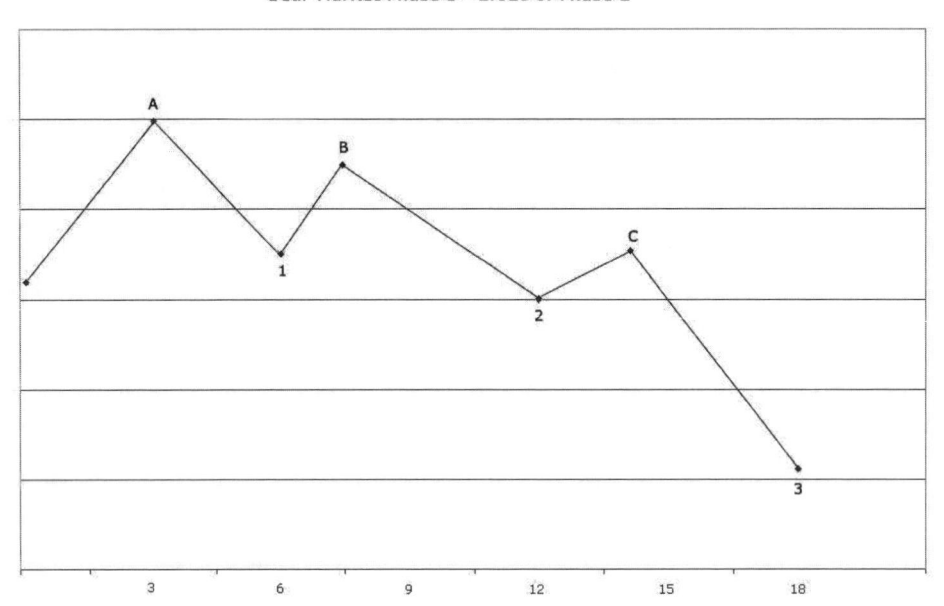

Bear Market Phase 3 - 1.618 of Phase 2

Let us look at some historical examples of these various third phase patterns in bearish cycles, and how their price targets may have been calculated. For this illustration, we will study the chart of the DJIA as it made its panic-selling low on March 6, 2009. We will examine this based on the final 50-week cycle that defined this low, and its three-phase structure consisting of three primary cycle phases. As a point of reference, this was also the final 50-week cycle phase of the greater 4-year and 6-year cycles, and possibly the third and final 6-year cycle within a greater 18-year cycle, and maybe even longer cycles.

For this illustration, we start with the 50-week cycle trough of January 22, 2008. The U.S. and world stock markets were in a free-fall at this time, following the all-time high of 14,198 on October 11, 2007. The sub-prime mortgage crisis was being exposed as much worse than anyone thought, and a rogue trader of a large bank in France caused a massive default through undetected large trading losses. Fears abounded that more banks would follow with similar losses. This was the week that Pluto moved into Capricorn for the first time since 1762 (along with Venus). This combination rules wealth (Venus) and debt (Pluto) in Capricorn (loss). Pluto also rules revelations, and these large losses and unexpected large debts were now being exposed after initially being covered up. Yet as this panic selling was taking place, the Federal Reserve Board made some spectacular decisions to add massive liquidity to the banking system, and the market rebounded sharply. However, in terms of our work, this was to be just a corrective rally at the beginning of a new 50-week cycle that was destined to be the last 50-week cycle within a bear market 4-year cycle (or longer) that would not bottom until its end. And, as the former 50-week cycle ended with panic selling on January 22, 2008, so would this 50-week cycle end with panic selling.

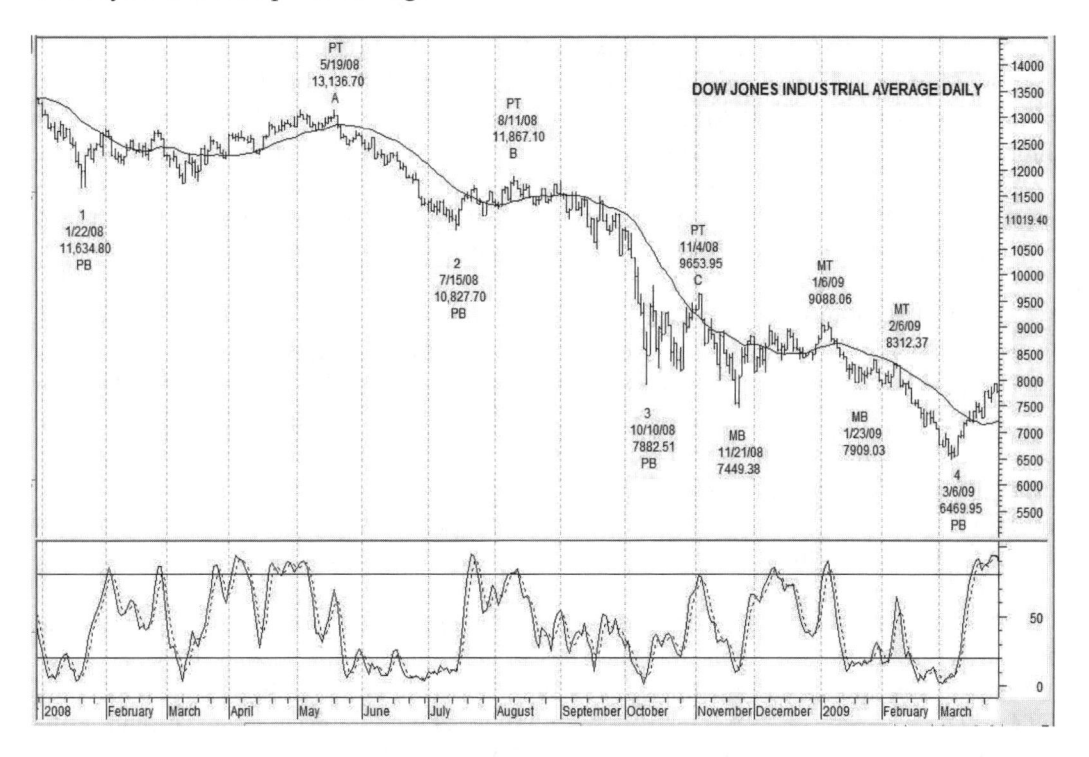

Figure 20: Daily chart of the DJIA as it fell to its "panic-selling" low of March 6, 2009, shown as point 4 on the chart above..

From the low of 11,634.80 that started this 50-week cycle on January 22, 2008, the DJIA rallied for nearly 4 months to its crest on May 19, at 13,136.70. That was also the crest of the first primary cycle phase of this new 50-week cycle. In bear markets, the crest of a cycle usually occurs in its first phase. This was no exception. In fact, after that crest, the market broke down below the low that started the 50-week cycle. It fell to its primary cycle trough on July 15, 2008 at 10,827.70. That was a clear sign that the stock market was in serious trouble, for once you take out the low that began the cycle, it means the lowest price will not be realized until the end of the cycle. And this was only the first primary cycle phase of the longer-term 50-week cycle. Let us begin by noting that the decline from May 19 (A) to July 15 (2) was 2309 points.

The rally to the crest of the second primary cycle phase was corrective in nature, which was to be expected since this was clearly to be a bearish 50-week cycle after falling below the start of the cycle. The crest of the second primary cycle was achieved 4 weeks later on August 11, 2008, at 11,867.10. This was not far from the low that started the 50-week cycle at 11,634.80 on January 22. However, it was a rally that regained only 45% of the decline, which is a "normal" corrective rally in a bear market (i.e. 38.2-61.8% retracement). A "normal" decline to the MCP price target for the next primary cycle trough would be (2 + B) – A, or (10,827.70 + 11,867.10) – 13,136.70, which is 9558.10 +/- 422.27. That range was determined by multiplying .118 of the difference between the previous crest (13,136.70) and the projected primary low (9558.10). But following the full-fledged banking crisis of September and October 2008, the market fell much further. It did not bottom until October 10, 2008, at 7882.51.

Now let us calculate other mathematical formulas that often apply to "panic-driven" markets. Let us take that first decline from May 19 (A) through July 15 (2) of 2309 points, and multiply it by 1.618. This gives a projected decline of 3735.96 points. Now subtract that from the 11,867.10 high of August 11 (B). This yields a "run away" price target to the downside of 8113.14. Applying our formula for the allowable orb to this price target (11.8% of the move down from 'A'), we get a price objective of 8113.14 +/- 590.65. The next primary cycle trough was in this price target range. It was 7882.51.

The bear market still was not over. After the primary cycle trough of October 10, 2008, the DJIA again rallied only 4 weeks, to the crest of a third primary cycle phase on Election Day, November 4, at 9653.95. This was a rally of 1771.44 points. But the prior primary swing down was 4044.59 points (from B to 3). Thus the rally was a normal corrective type in a bear market, recovering 43.8% of the swing down. From this we can calculate an MCP downside price target of 5669.36 +/- 731.33 for the trough of the third primary cycle phase. The final low of 6469.95 on March 6 was near the very top side of this MCP target. But there were other calculations that would get closer to the actual low.

One of the most accurate means to calculate the projected low for the third phase is to take .618 of the distance down from the crest to the trough of the second phase, and then subtract it from the crest of the third phase. In the case illustrated in Figure 19, that would be C - [(A-3) x .618] = 4, where '4' is the final projected low price target. Filling in the numbers, we would have 9653.95 - [(13,136.70 – 7882.51) x .618] = 4, or 9653.95 – 3247.09 = 6406.86. The allowable orb to this price target would then be (13,136.70-6406.86) x .118 = 794.12. But the actual low was 6469.95, very close to the exact price target calculated without much orb at all.

There was yet another calculation that came close to identifying this exact bottom. If we dissect the final primary cycle phases, we will see that the second major crest was 9088.06 on January 6 and the trough of the second major cycle phase was 7909.03 on January 23. If we take 1.618 times the difference, we get (9088.06 – 7909.03) x 1.618 = 1907.67. If we then subtract that from the crest of the third major cycle (8312.37 on February 6), we get a downside "panic-driven sell-off" to 6404.70 +/- 316.63. Again, the final low of 6469.95 was very close to this target. The fact that this level was attained as Venus turned retrograde (a powerful Level 1 signature as identified in Volume 3) exactly on March 6 was a strong clue that our time and price targets were converging. Another key was the rising stochastics as the market was making a low. This is a powerful technical indicator known as "bullish oscillator divergence," which will be discussed in a later chapter.

SUMMARY: INTEGRATING PRICE WITH TIME

With regards to price objective theory, the question invariably arises: With so many calculations, how do you know which price target will be the correct one? You don't know at first. If there was only one correct price target calculation for any given market or cycle, then everyone would be buying and selling at nearly the same price. Unfortunately the market is not so static and predictable.

This is why it is necessary to understand market timing principles before mastering price objective calculations. When a cycle begins, there are several price targets for the subsequent moves that are possible, as just outlined in the previous three chapters. One does not know if the next move will be to a price target that reflects a corrective retracement, a re-test of a former cycle top or bottom, or a "breakout." Furthermore, one does not know which price target to use for a corrective retracement or breakout, because there are several calculations that will yield different price targets for each type.

There is, however, a basic guideline to follow for price projections within the concept of cycle studies as the market unfolds. One may begin by calculating all of the price target possibilities, or at least the first few. That is, one may calculate a 38.2-61.8% "normal" price target for a corrective retracement. One may also calculate a 45-85% retracement zone, which is common in two-phase patterns. One should also always be aware of a price area for a double top or double bottom to a prior cycle crest or trough. And finally one may wish to calculate at least an MCP price target, if not some of the various Fibonacci multipliers (1.236, 1.382, 1.618, 2.618, etc).

As the cycle unfolds, more price targets will be calculated following the completion of each phase of the cycle. There will be times when two or more of these calculations overlap one another. These should be noted, for the more overlap there is between different calculations of potential price targets, the more likely the market will eventually get to the price range of these overlapping targets.

Yet that is not enough. It is not even the most important consideration in determining the most likely price target of a market move. The crux of these studies centers on the idea of market reversals, those points in time where a cycle or a phase of a cycle is completed, and the market reverses in the opposite direction. If the market has been rising, then we try to ascertain a time when it is mostly likely to complete the crest of the cycle or cycle phase. When the market is falling, then we try to determine the most likely time when it will complete its cycle trough, or the trough of this phase of the cycle. *Once we enter the time band for a cycle trough or crest, then we determine which price target is the most likely to halt the market move, and begin a reversal.* In other words, there is no one price target that will consistently identify where a cycle will end once it begins. There are several. But whichever price objective correlates with where the market actually is at a pre-calculated time band for a reversal, that is the price objective to use.

There will be some difficulties with this concept when longer-term cycles are used. From the studies in Volume One, "Cycles and Patterns in the Indexes," we know that cycles are not static. They have an orb of time when they can culminate. Generally this orb of time is about one-sixth of the mean cycle length. In other words, if we are trying to time the next 4-year cycle in stocks, we have to allow an orb of up to 10 months from the time the cycle is ideally due. That is a long time, and prices can change greatly during those 20 months. If we wish to identify an 18-week primary cycle trough in Gold, we have to allow a time frame of 15-21 weeks after the last primary cycle trough. That is more manageable than trying to pick the time and price for a 4-year cycle in stocks. Yet within that 6-week time frame, the Gold market may enter more than one calculated price target range. But that time frame can be narrowed as we complete the first two phases of a three-phase pattern, or the first phase of a two-phase pattern. It can be narrowed even further when we identify a geocosmic critical reversal date, which has an orb of three trading days (see Volume 3, "Geocosmic Correlations to Trading Cycles").

Once a market is within a time band for a cycle completion, and once the most likely dates within that cycle for the reversal to commence are identified (i.e. "geocosmic critical reversal dates"), we only need to wait until we get there, see what the price of the stock or commodity is trading at, and then determine if it satisfies one or more of the calculated price targets for that cycle. If it does, then we have the ideal set up where time and price targets are being met. A trade can be executed with greater confidence by knowing the time of a "low risk, high reward" set up. You know where your risk is, and you know the probability of a reversal commencing during this time band is at a peak. And even this set up can be maximized by applying just a couple of technical studies that measure market momentum, a subject that we will cover shortly.

These are important guidelines to understand in regards to projecting price targets. There are so many price targets that can be applicable, but in the end, the only ones that matter are those that are being realized when you enter a time band for a market reversal, or cycle completion. When a market enters a price target, and there are no cycles that are due to culminate, and no geocosmic critical reversal dates in effect, chances are that the market will just blow past that price target without any meaningful retracement or reversal. Therefore, despite the insistence of many market trading coaches to clearly identify a profit objective when entering a trade, the idea of exiting or entering a position based solely on price is not really a useful component in a market timer's trading plan. Getting out just because the market has reached a pre-determined price target, when in fact the market is not in a time band for a reversal, is in essence wasting an opportunity for greater profit. It is far better to wait until you enter the time frame for a cycle reversal, and then establish the price target for exiting a trade. In other words, in this methodology, price is important. But time is more important to us. Combining the two methods of study is even better.

CHAPTER EIGHT

PRICE TARGETS FOR BREAKOUTS OF HEAD AND SHOULDERS CHART PATTERNS

A chartist is one who studies charts. In their studies, chartists identify many "chart patterns." These chart patterns often coincide with certain market movements. For example, a "bullish" chart pattern will imply higher prices when its setup is activated. A "bearish" chart pattern will indicate lower prices when the criteria for its setup are activated. This field of market analysis is known as "Pattern Recognition." When certain chart patterns are activated, they can also yield accurate price targets.

This chapter will introduce some of those chart patterns from which various price targets can be calculated.

HEAD AND SHOULDERS PATTERN - BEARISH

The basic head and shoulders pattern is a bearish chart formation. We begin with this chart pattern, and see how it can establish a downside price target. An illustration of the basic head and shoulders pattern via filtered waves is shown in Figure 21.

This basic head and shoulders pattern begins with an isolated high, shown on the chart as LS, which stands for "left shoulder." From that crest, the market declines to a low, shown on the chart as 'A.' This is the first point of what is to be called the "neckline" of the head and shoulders pattern. The market then rallies to a price that is higher than the left shoulder (LS). This new price high is known as the "head" of the head and shoulders pattern, and is depicted as 'H' in the Figure 21. Prices then decline again back to the area of 'A'. This second low is denoted by 'B' and is the second point of the "neckline." A line connecting A-B thus becomes the neckline of this developing pattern. Following this low, the market rallies again, back to the area that defined the left shoulder (LS). It will however be below the head (H). This crest becomes the right shoulder of the head and shoulders pattern, as is identified as RS in Figure 21. If the right shoulder is higher than the left shoulder, it is considered a little less bearish. If it is lower than the left shoulder, it is considered "drooping," and a harbinger of a more serious decline about to occur. The pattern is now set up. The bearish head and shoulders formation becomes activated when prices start to close below the neckline (A-B). Prices will then be expected to fall equidistance down below the neckline, as it was between the head and the neckline, especially as measured from the neckline on the date that the head (H) of the head and shoulders pattern formed.

Head Shoulders - Bearish

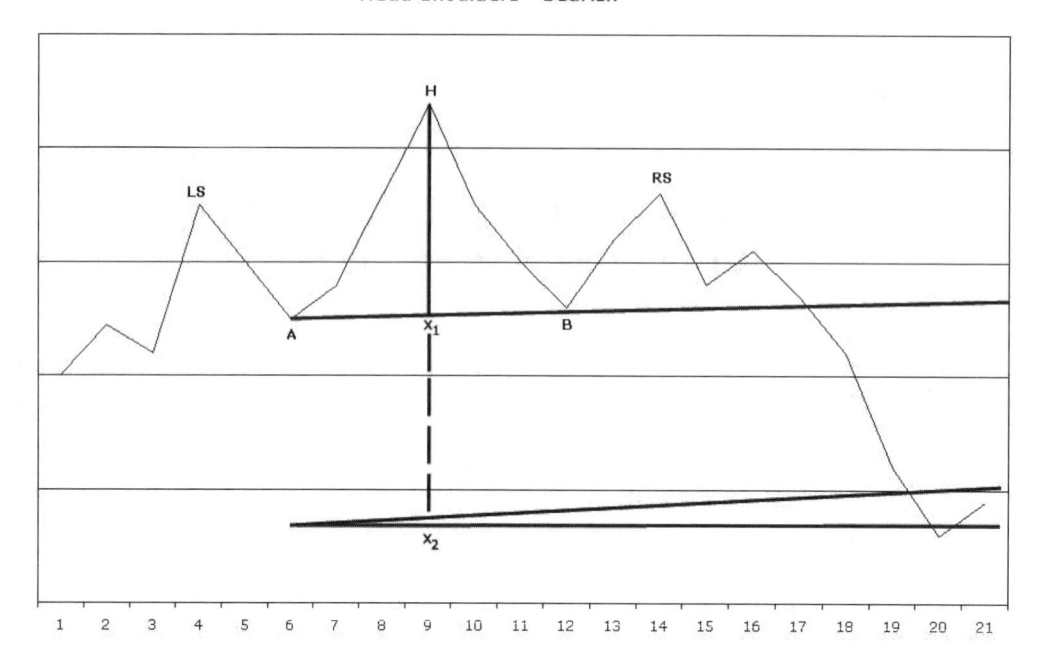

Figure 21: An illustration of a typical form for a bearish head and shoulders pattern.

You can see both the basic chart formation and subsequent market activity with the downside price targets, on Figure 21. The downside price target is represented as the distance between H and X_1, then applied (subtracted) to the neckline at that point (date of the head formation) to give a price target down to X_2. The usual rule for this calculation is to *take the difference between the price at the head (H) and the price at the neckline that was in effect on the day the head formed (X_1)*. Then subtract that same amount from the neckline that was in effect on the day the head formed. This gives the first price target for the ensuing decline, shown as X_2.

You can then take the difference between the price at the head and the price of this projected low, and multiply by .118 to get the range of the downside price target. If that fails to hold the decline, then you multiply the difference between the head and the neckline ($H - X_1$) by 2, then 3, 4, and 5 and so on (usually by 2 or 4 is sufficient) until you reach a price target that corresponds to the actual price of a falling market on a critical reversal date, and in a time band when a cycle trough is due.

In addition to the formula given above to calculate the downside price target of a bearish head and shoulders pattern, one can also construct a parallel line to the neckline of the head and shoulders pattern. This parallel line should be equidistant from head and the neckline, below the neckline, and sloped at the same angle as the neckline. You can see this line in Figure 21, in addition to the horizontal line at x_2. Both of these downside lines can represent support to a market that is falling hard after the neckline is broken.

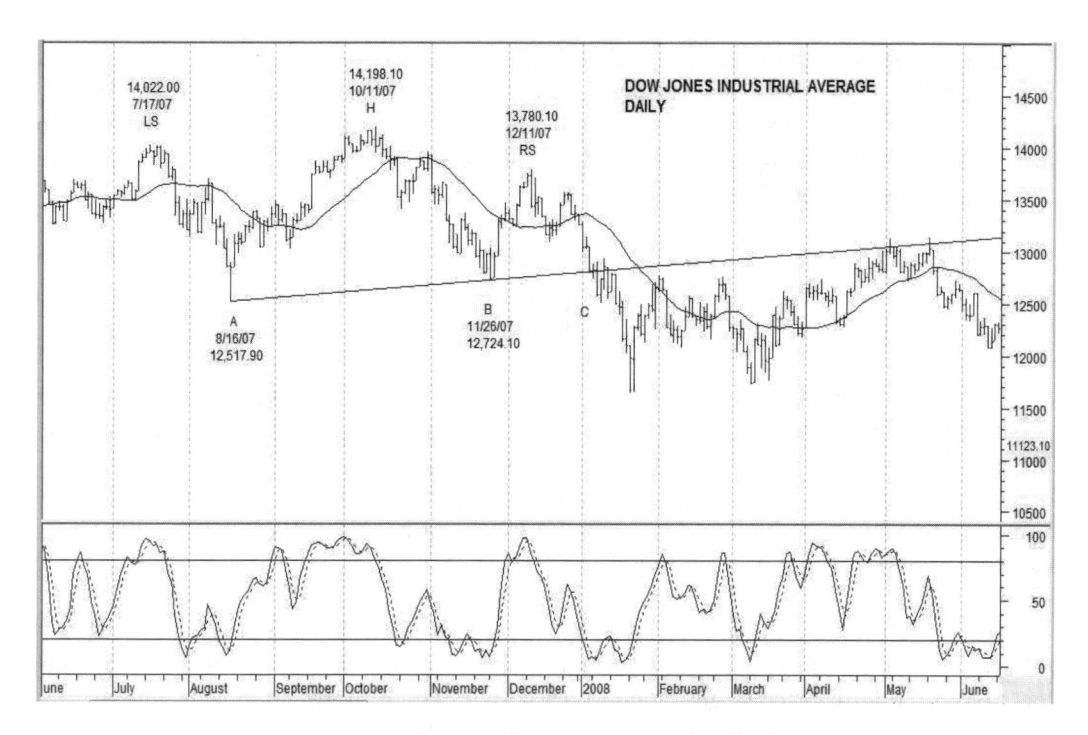

Figure 22: Example of a bearish head and shoulders pattern, where A-B is the neckline, LS the left shoulder, H the head, and RS the right shoulder.

Another point to remember is that once the neckline is broken, it then becomes resistance. The market can rally back to this area, and sometimes even trade slightly above it. Generally speaking, the market will not close above it more than 2-3 consecutive days or weeks. If it does, then the low may be in. Until then, the extension of that neckline represents major resistance to all rallies until this bearish pattern is negated. Until that happens, the decline will usually go to one of the two downside price targets just calculated, or else 2 or 4 times that distance, or 2 or 4 parallel lines below.

Let us now look at an historical example of this, as shown in Figure 22, which is the daily chart of the Dow Jones Industrial Average following its then all-time high on October 11, 2007. In this chart, the left shoulder (LS) formed at 14,022 on July 17, 2007. The market then declined for a month to form the primary cycle low at 12,517 on August 16. Then the market rallied to the all-time high, leading the DJIA to its historic crest on October 11, 2007, at 14,198. That became the head (H) of the formation. The ensuing decline took prices down to 12,724 on November 26, thus forming point B, and second part of the neckline. After the rally to the right shoulder on December 11, 2007 at 13,780 (RS), the pattern was set up, and the line connecting A-B would define the neckline. Note that the right shoulder (RS) was below the left shoulder. This is known as a "drooping shoulder," and is more bearish than if RS had been higher than LS. The DJIA then broke below the neckline (A-B) at C. This downside breakout "activated" the pattern, and provided downside targets that would equal the distance between the head and the neckline, subtracted from the neckline as it appeared on October 11, the day of the high, or head. That distance could be subtracted from the neckline, and then doubled or quadrupled and subtracted from the neckline, to get various downside price targets.

In this example, the head was 14,198.10. The neckline on October 11, 2007, would have been 12,633.06 (the value of line A-B on October 11). The difference is 1565.04. Thus, we can subtract that from the neckline at 12,633.06 to get our first downside price target. We can also multiple 1565.04 by 2 or 4 (or even other multiples), to get lower price targets. So let's do that:

First target is 12,633.06 – 1565.04   = 11,068.02 +/- 369.35
Second target is 12,633.06 – 3130.08 = 9502.98 +/- 554.02 (times 2)
Third target is 12,633.06 – 6260.16   = 6372.90 +/- 923.37 (times 4)

The first leg down took prices to 11,634 on January 22. That wasn't low enough to satisfy any of the downside price targets just calculated. However, what is interesting is the rally that followed over the next four months, taking prices back to 13,136.70 on May 19, 2008. That was back to the extension of the neckline of this head and shoulders formation that had been broken. Once support breaks, it becomes resistance, and this was a perfect example of that rule.

After the primary cycle crest of May 19, 2008, the DJIA then began its historic collapse. It finally bottomed nearly 10 months later on March 6, 2009 at 6469.95. This was within the third price target range given above, which represented a decline of four times the value of the distance between the head and the neckline on October 11, 2007. This is shown on the weekly chart in Figure 23. When the DJIA closes back above the extension of the former neck line, it will be a signal that the long-term bear market is truly over.

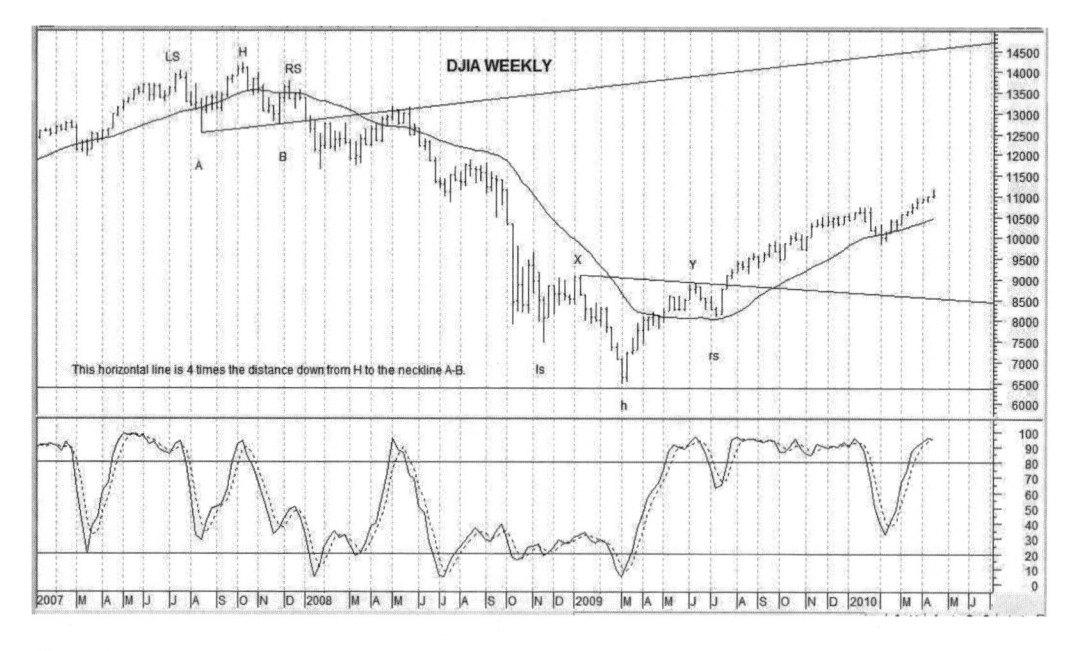

Figure 23, showing the collapse from the head and shoulders pattern that formed in late 2007 to its recovery rally back to A-B (May 2008), then final decline to the downside price target shown by the 4 x decline to the horizontal line shown on graph (around 6372). It then shows the reverse bullish head and shoulders that formed off that bottom (ls, h, and rs), as it broke above the new neckline at X-Y.

Reverse Head & Shoulders - Bullish

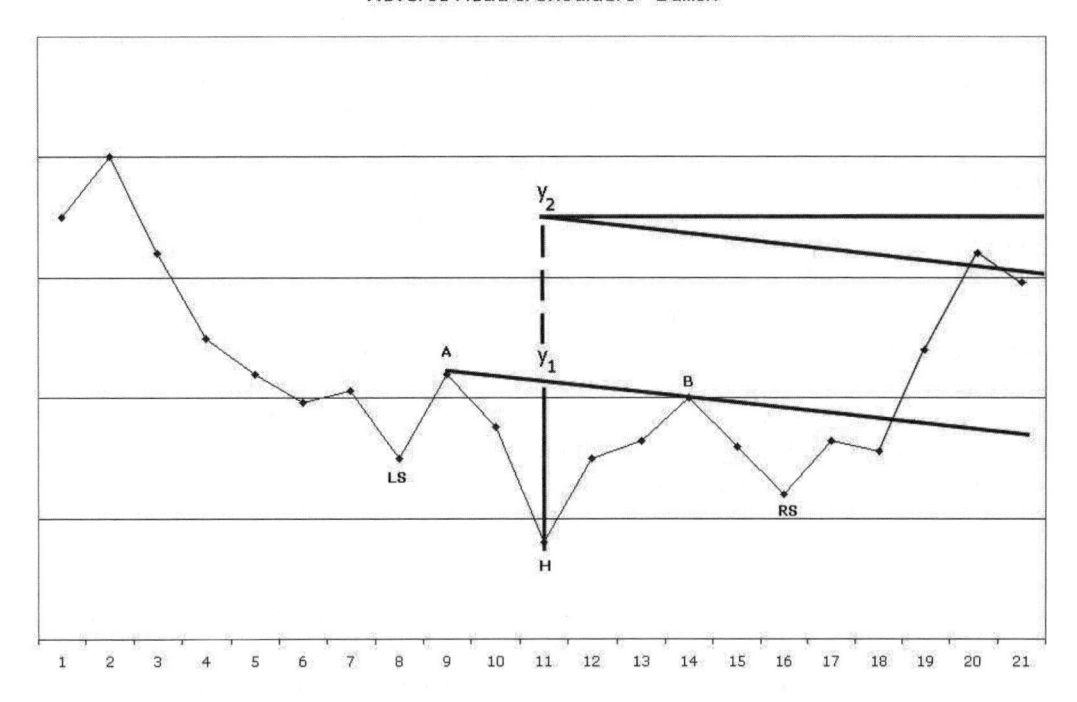

Figure 24: An illustration of an inverse (or reverse) head and shoulders pattern, which is bullish. LS is left shoulder, H is head, and RS is right shoulder. A-B is the neckline representing resistance. When it breaks, it projects a move up to the area of a parallel line to A-B that starts at Y2, or a horizontal line that begins at Y2 and is the same distance from the head to the neckline as above it (Y1-Y2 is same distance as H-Y1). The breakout above A-B usually goes at least into these two price areas.

BULLISH INVERSE (REVERSE) HEAD AND SHOULDERS PATTERN

A bullish "inverse" head and shoulders pattern is like an upside down conventional head and shoulders pattern. Sometimes this is referred to as a "reverse" head and shoulders pattern, but in either case, it means the same thing. This pattern begins with an isolated low, shown on the illustration in Figure 24 as LS. This also stands for "left shoulder," just as it was in the normal head and shoulders formation that is bearish. From that trough, the market rallies to a crest, shown on the chart as 'A.' This is the first point of what is to be called the "neckline" of the inverse head and shoulders pattern. The market then declines to a price that is lower than the left shoulder (LS). This new low is known as the "head" of the inverse head and shoulders pattern, and is depicted as 'H' in the Figure 24. Prices rally again back to the area of 'A.' This second high is denoted by 'B' and is the second point of the "neckline." A trendline connecting A-B thus becomes the neckline of this developing pattern. Following this crest, the market declines again back to the area that defined the left shoulder (LS). It will be above the head (H), however. This trough becomes the right shoulder of the head and shoulders pattern, and is identified as RS in Figure 23. If the right shoulder is higher than the left shoulder, it is considered a little more bullish, and a harbinger of a significant rally about to occur.

The pattern is now set up. When prices start to close above the neckline (A-B), this bullish chart formation is activated. At this point, the upside price target can be established. Prices are expected to rally equidistant above the neckline, as it was between the head and the neckline. You can see this on Figure 24 as the distance between H and y_1, which is added to the neckline at that point to give a price target up to y_2. The usual rule for this calculation is to *take the difference between the price at the head (H) and the price at the neckline that was in effect on the day the head formed (y_1). Then add that same amount from the neckline that was in effect on the day the head formed.* This gives the first price target for the ensuing decline, shown as y_2.

You can then take the difference between the price at the head and the price of this projected high, and multiply by .118 to get the range of the upside "breakout" price target. If that fails to stop the rally, then multiply the difference between the head and the neckline (H – y_1) by 2, then 3, 4, and 5 and so on (usually by 2 or 4 is sufficient) until a price target is attained that corresponds to the actual price of a rising market on a critical reversal date, and in a time band when a cycle crest is due.

In addition to the formula given above to calculate the upside price target of a bullish reverse head and shoulders pattern, one can also construct a parallel line to the neckline of this pattern. This parallel line should be equidistant from head and the neckline, above the neckline, and sloped at the same angle as the neckline. You can see this line in Figure 24, in addition to the horizontal line at y_2. Both of these upside lines can represent resistance to a market that is rising after the neckline is broken.

Another point to remember about a reverse head and shoulders pattern is that once prices break above the neckline, that neckline then becomes support. The market can decline back to this area again, and sometimes it even trades slightly below it. However, generally speaking, it will not close below it more than 2 consecutive days (best to allow maybe three consecutive days). If it does, then the high may be in. Until then, the extension of that neckline represents major support to all declines until this bullish pattern is negated. Until that happens, the decline will usually go to one of the two upside breakout price targets just calculated, or else 2 or 4 times that distance, or 2 or 4 parallel lines above.

Let us now look at an historical example of this, as shown in Figure 25, a daily chart of the DJIA. The weekly configuration of both a bearish and bullish head and shoulders pattern was shown in Figure 23, as a frame of reference, and an example showing both types of head and shoulders patterns, in the same market, relatively close to one another.

In Figure 25, the left shoulder of the inverse head and shoulders pattern was completed with the primary cycle trough on November 21 at 7449.38. The rally that followed took prices up to a primary cycle crest of 9088.06 on January 6, represented as 'A' on the chart, and also as the first point of the neckline to this pattern. From there the DJIA collapsed to its primary and long-term cycle low of 6469.95 on March 6, 2009 (as Venus turned retrograde, a very powerful Level 1 geocosmic signature). This became the head (H) of the inverse head and shoulders pattern. The market then rallied three months to a primary cycle crest on June 11, 2009, at 8877.93. This became the second point defining the neckline A-B.

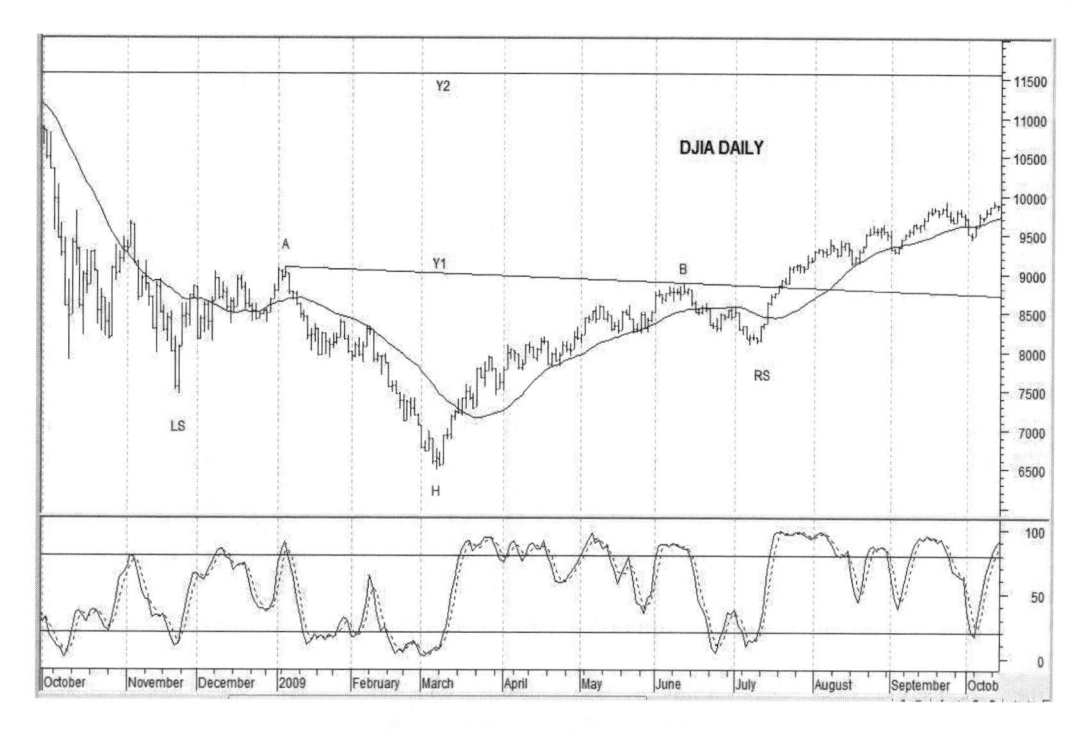

Figure 25: The inverse head and shoulders pattern shown in the DJIA following its long-term cycle low of March 6, 2009. Note that after the right shoulder formed at RS, prices "broke out" above the neckline A-B. If the distance between the head (H) and the price of the neckline on that day (Y1), is added to the neckline, we get the first upside price objective, shown as Y2. That price target range was achieved with the high of 11,258 on April 26, 2010. When it exceeds 11,800, we then take twice the value of Y1 – H and add it to Y1. After that, 4 times the value and add it to Y1.

The market then declined to the primary cycle trough on July 8, 2009 at 8087.19, which became the right shoulder (RS). This was also nearby to the conjunction of Jupiter and Neptune, another very powerful long-term Level 1 geocosmic signature, as discussed in Volume 3.

At this point, readers might notice two bullish characteristics as a clue the bear market was about to end. First of all, this second shoulder (RS) is higher in price than the first. Secondly, this primary cycle formed a bullish "right translation" pattern. Its crest was higher than the left shoulder and previous primary cycle crest (LS), and it occurred past the midway point in the cycle. That wasn't the case in the former primary cycle. That primary cycle was a bearish "left translation type," and the start of its primary cycle (LS) was lower in price than the start of this one. The setup was now indicating that the neckline would be broken, thus confirming the end to the bear market, and the start of a new bull market. Indeed, that "breakout" of the neckline happened on July 21.

The old neckline can now be extended to define new support. As long as prices remained above this extension, the new bull market would be intact. If prices started to close two or three consecutive days below, it may instead have indicated the rally was a "fake out." The market might be returning to its bearish trend. But that didn't happen, as one can see from the chart. In fact, the market did not decline to even re-test this extended neckline over the following year.

The next step is to calculate the upside price targets of this "breakout." To do that, one must first determine the price of the neckline as it would have been on the day the head (low) formed. That was March 6, 2009 and on that date, the value of the A-B line – as shown at Y1 – was 9007.40. The difference between 9007.40 (Y1) and 6469.95 (H) is 2537.45. If this distance is then added to 9007.40 (Y1), the first upside price target of this breakout becomes 11,544.85 (Y2, as shown on the graph).

The range to this price objective can then be calculated by taking the difference of Y2 and the head (H), and multiplying by .118. That is, (11,544.85 – 6469.95) x .118 = 598.83. Thus, the first price objective for an important crest to this new bull market would be 11,544.85 +/- 598.84, or 10.946.01-12,143.69. On April 26, 2010, an important crest formed in this range – the first leg up off this bullish pattern. In 2011, it exceeded 12,143, the upper end of this range. To find the next price objectives suggested by this pattern, one will take the difference of Y1 and H (2537.45) and multiply it by 2, and then again by 4. In this case, multiplying it by 2 gives an upside price target of 14,082.30. Multiplying it by 4 gives a target of 19,157.20. Each of these targets has a range that can be calculated using the formula given above.

First target is 9007.40 + 2537.45   = 11,544.85 +/-   593.83
Second target is 9007.40 + 5074.90   = 14,082.30 +/-   898.25 (times 2)
Third target is 9007.40 + 10,149.80   = 19,157.20 +/- 1497.10 (times 4)

CHAPTER NINE

GAPS, MEASURING GAPS, AND ISLAND REVERSALS

Once a market breaks out above or below a well-defined resistance or support area, it is necessary to use different mathematical formulas than standard Fibonacci ratios for determining the price objective of the ensuing move. This was observed in the last chapter, as multipliers of the distance between the head and neckline of a head and shoulders formation were added or subtracted from the neckline price to determine the next price targets.

The same mathematical calculations can be used for other chart patterns that indicate that a "breakout" is underway. But in all cases, the first step is identifying the point of a breakout. Once that point is determined, the distance between that "breakout" point and a previous trough or crest is calculated. That distance is then added or subtracted to the point of the breakout. Multiples of that distance can be further added or subtracted if the market exceeds the first price target.

At this point, it is useful to reiterate two basic rules for price objective calculations. First, they are most important when they are achieved in a time that coincides with both a cycle culmination and a geocosmic turning point. Price must coincide with time to attain the highest probability of accuracy. If a price objective is being realized at a time that does not coincide with a projected cyclical high or low, or at a time in which there is not a geocosmic critical reversal date in effect, then the probability increases that the move will continue to the next multiple for that price target. One has to wait until a price target is being realized within a time band for a projected market reversal, for optimal success. Second, it is most effective when there is an overlap of multiple price target calculations. That means the market is more likely to reverse from a well-defined price target if the range of a price target was determined via more than one calculation. If three or more calculations all overlap, then chances are greater that the market will at least pause in the overlap of those price targets, if not make a substantial cyclical reversal from there.

Let us assume we are in the time band for a 15-21 week primary cycle trough. Let us also assume there is a cluster of geocosmic signatures present that centers on the 18th week. We now have a time frame identified for a primary cycle trough and a subsequent reversal. Next, let us say we are able to calculate a Fibonacci price target for this low. We may also calculate an MCP price objective, and we note that there is some overlap in these two price ranges. We might also notice a bearish head and shoulders pattern from before and the calculated price target from the breakout below the neckline of that pattern also overlaps these two previously calculated price targets. Now we have a case of time (cycles and geocosmics) coinciding with price (the overlap of three price target calculations). If the market falls to the price range overlapping these three price targets during the time band of this cyclical and geocosmic reversal, it presents an exceptional risk-reward set up. That is, one is able to buy low with a well-defined price point that would negate this setup. If correct, then the potential for reward is great, compared to the monetary risk of loss. Usually, in setups like this, the risk-reward is at least 1:4. That is, your profit potential is at least four times your stop-loss risk.

In the last chapter, we covered one type of measurement based on a breakout of support and resistance - the break of the neckline of a head and shoulders formation or a reverse head and shoulders pattern. In this chapter, we want to examine other types of patterns and breakouts that can yield certain price targets for a big move, as suggested by the breakout. We will start this discussion with the phenomenon of "gaps."

GAPS

A "gap" is created when the price of a market trades entirely outside the range of its previous time frame. Usually "gaps" refer to daily or weekly time frames, although there is no reason why it couldn't also pertain to monthly or hourly bars as well. By "bars," we mean the chart notation (vertical line) that identifies the high and low of that time frame. Thus, when the high and low price of one day is entirely above or below the high and low price of the previous day, it becomes a "gap" day. This has importance to a market technician, because it often means a big move is underway. If so, then it becomes a "measuring gap." If not, it ends up being an "exhaustion gap," or "fake out." Examples of various "gaps" are shown in the prototype of Figure 26.

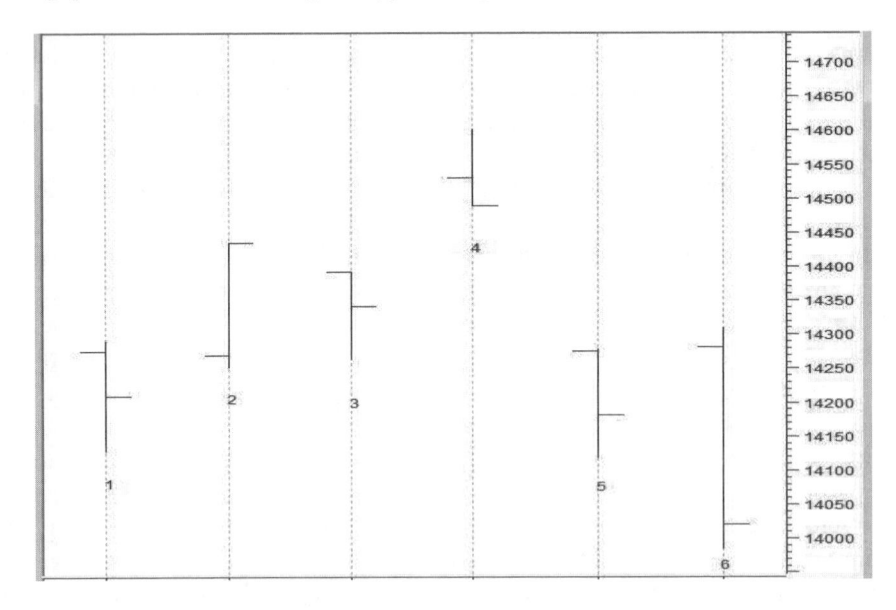

Figure 26. Examples of various "gap" days. Note that day 4 is a "gap up" above day 3. Note that day 5 is a "gap down" below day 4. Days 3-5 therefore create a "bearish island reversal" chart pattern where one day (4) is completely above the range of the prior day (3) and the day after (5). Day 4 would also be an example of an "exhaustion gap," because the next day's trading (5) was below the gap up on 3-4.

A "measuring" gap means the market price will continue in the direction of the "gap" until it reaches a certain price target. In other words, it is the start or middle of a rather sizeable move in that direction. If it is a "gap up," then a measuring gap means prices will continue to rally until its upside measuring gap price target is achieved. If it is a "gap down," then it means prices will continue to fall until a level is reached that satisfies its downside measuring gap price target. In both cases, prices will not turn back and fill in the empty price area created by the 'gap' for quite some time - usually not before the measuring gap price target is achieved.

An "exhaustion gap," on the other hand, is a "gap up" or "gap down" day where the empty price area is soon filled. In other words, the "gap" area gets filled soon after the gap formed. And instead of making a big move in the direction of the gap, the market move fizzles, prices quickly fill the gap and go the opposite way that the gap had suggested. An "exhaustion gap" is thus a "fake out." This happens quite often, for instance, when Mercury is retrograde, which fits with Mercury's reputation as a "trickster."

Many technicians and chartists don't know if and when a "gap" is a "measuring" or "exhaustion" type until after the fact. Cycle analysts have an advantage here because "exhaustion gaps" happen near the end of a cycle, whereas "measuring gaps" tend to happen earlier in a cycle. That is, the later in a cycle, the more likely that a "gap" up or down is a fake out. If a market is making new highs and it is late in the cycle and there is a "gap up" day, there is a good chance that gap will get filled soon afterwards, thus negating its bullish signal. The same is true if the market is in the time band for its cycle trough, and prices are falling to new lows, and there is a day in which that market "gaps down" below the low of the prior day. Chances are that the primary bottom will be reached quickly, and prices will soon fill that gap down as the new primary cycle gets underway, since the first phase of every cycle is bullish.

MEASURING GAP TARGETS FOR "GAPS UP"

For this part of the book we will only use gaps as they pertain to daily or weekly charts, since they are the most useful for calculating price objective targets. In fact, unless otherwise noted, we will refer to gaps only in terms of daily charts, since weekly gaps are rather rare. However, readers should know that weekly gaps do occur and are even more powerful and meaningful than daily gaps.

A "gap up" occurs when the lowest price of a day's range is *above* the high of a prior day's range. There is thus a "gap" between the high of the prior day and the low of the current day. In Figure 26, this can be seen in the price range between days 3 and 4. Day 4 is a "gap up" above the entire range of day 3. As long as prices do not close that gap, i.e. do not fall back to the high of the day before, this is a "measuring gap" and points to higher prices. If they do fall below that gap range, then it is an "exhaustion gap." In Figure 26, the gap up on day 4 was an "exhaustion gap." But if it were a "measuring gap" up, how high would the price be expected to rally? This is determined by a specific calculation, much like that used in calculating the price target for a breakout of the neckline of a reverse and head and shoulders formation. In other words, one will take the difference between the high of the prior day and the cycle low that preceded it, and then add that difference to the low of the day on the "gap up." This gives the upside measuring gap price objective. The distance between that price target and the previous cycle trough can then be multiplied by .118 to determine the range for this upside price target.

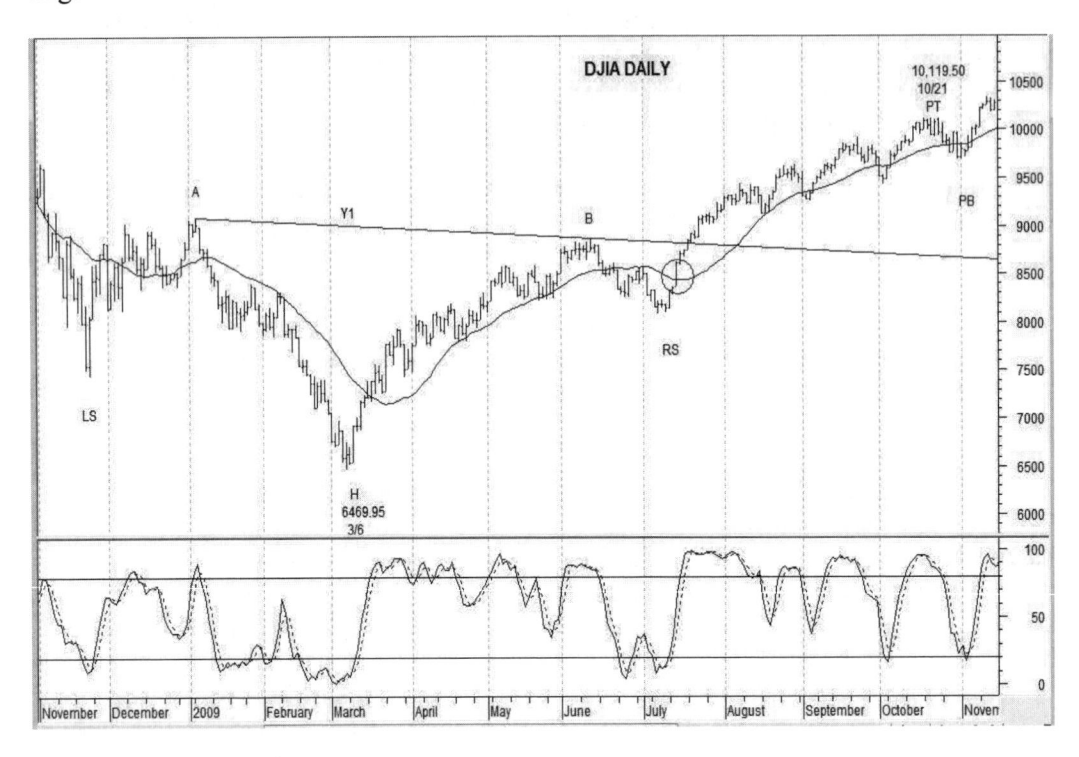

Figure 27: The circle above identifies the gap up in the DJIA on July 15. On July 14, the high of the day was 8361.23. On July 15, the low of the day was 8363.95.

The best way to understand measuring gaps and their price targets is to show examples. For this, let us look at the daily chart of the DJIA on July 14 and 15, 2009, as illustrated in Figure 27. A long-term cycle trough occurred at 6469.95 on March 6 as discussed previously. The market rallied to a primary cycle crest on June 11, followed by a corrective decline to its next primary cycle trough on July 8. This was in a time band for both a primary cycle trough as well as a geocosmic critical reversal date according to the rules outlined in Volume 3. One of the main points to remember is that measuring "gaps up" tends to occur most frequently at the beginning of new primary cycles. But when they happen extremely close to the start of the primary cycle, the appropriate preceding low to use for the measurement of upside price targets will be the previous primary cycle trough (if it was lower), and not the one that just unfolded. Why? Because the distance from the high of the day before the "gap up" to the low of the just-formed primary cycle trough is probably not very substantial. It is not likely to produce a price target that will overlap with a Mid-Cycle Pause (MCP) price target or a Fibonacci-related price target based on other price breaks. But if one uses the price of the previous primary cycle trough that was lower, it will likely produce a more probable upside price target for the next primary cycle crest.

After the primary cycle trough of July 8 at 8087.19, and a re-test of that low on Friday, July 10 at 8093.31, the DJIA started to move up (as a side note, a re-test of an important low two trading days later is not uncommon). Two trading days later (July 14), the DJIA closed near its high of the day at 8361.23. The following day (July 15), the DJIA "gapped up." The range for that day was a low of 8363.95 to a high of 8626.83. Note the low was higher than the high of July 14. Therefore July 15 was a "gap up" day.

The "gap up" on July 15 can be seen in the ellipse (circle) on the chart in Figure 27. If we subtract the low of the primary cycle trough on July 8 (8087.19) from the high on July 15, the day before the "gap up" (8361.23), we get a difference of 274.04. If we then add that to the low of the "gap up" day on July 15 (8363.95), we get a measuring gap upside price objective of 8637.99. Applying our .118 multiple of this distance between the July 8 primary cycle trough (8087.19) and the upside price target of the measuring gap (8637.99) gives us an orb of 64.99 to this upside price target, or 8637.99 +/- 64.99. The range via this calculation would be 8573.00-8701.98. The market soared above that range the very next day, which simply demonstrates the importance of using the previous primary cycle low instead of the one just formed in a bull market. So let's do that.

Let us subtract the price of the previous primary cycle trough on March 6, 2009, at 6469.95, from the high of July 14 (8361.23), the day before the "gap up," or 8361.23 − 6469.95 = 1891.28. Let us then add that to the low of the "gap" day of July 15, which was 8363.95, to get the upside price target for this "measuring gap up." The calculation is 8363.95 + 1891.28 = 10,255.23. Next, to find the range, multiply .118 times the difference between this price target and low of March 6, or (10,255.23 − 6469.95) x .118 = 446.66. Thus, the range for this upside measuring gap is 9808.57- 10,701.89. A look at the chart in Figure 27 will show that the next primary cycle crest occurred on October 21, at 10,119.50, which is within the measuring gap price target range.

Now we check to see if there are other price target calculations that overlap with this "measuring gap up" price range. We could do a Mid-Cycle Pause (MCP) calculation, for instance, and see that it overlaps this range. In this case we would subtract the primary cycle low of March 6 (6469.95) from the primary cycle crest of June 11 (8877.93). That gives a value of 2407.98. Add this to the primary cycle low of July 8 (8087.19) and an MCP price target of 10,495.17 is achieved. To get the range for this MCP, simply take (10,495.17 − 6469.95) x .118, and that gives an orb of 474.97. Thus the MCP price target for the next primary cycle crest was 10,495.17 +/- 474.97, or 10,020.20-10,970.15. If we compared this to the upside "measuring gap" price target range of 9808.57- 10,701.89, we see that both of these price objectives overlap at 10,020.20-10,701.89. The actual price of the primary cycle crest on October 21 was 10,119.50.

Until prices fill that gap up at 8361.23, there is a possibility that the DJIA could go up two or even four times the 1891.28 distance between the high of July 14 and the low of March 6. For example, a multiplier of 2 (2 x 1891.28 = 3782.56) could be added to 8363.95 to give an upside target of 12,145.51, with an orb of 669.83. This produces a range of 11,475.68-12,815.34. A multiplier of 4 times 1891.28 would equal 7565.12. Adding that to 8363.95 gives the next higher price objective at 15,929.07, +/- 1116.17. Eventually, those levels could also represent important future resistance, as long as the gap up on July 15, 2009 is not filled.

MEASURING GAP TARGETS FOR "GAPS DOWN"

In a similar manner, a downside price target can be calculated following a "gap down" day (or week). A "gap down" occurs when the highest price of a day's range is *below* the low of a prior day's range. In other words, the entire day's trading range is below the trading range of the prior day. Thus, there is a "gap" between the low of the prior day and the high of the current day. This can also be seen in Figure 26, using days 4 and 5. Day 5 had a range completely below the range of Day 4. Its high was lower in price than the low of day 4. Therefore day 5 is a "gap down" day. As long as prices do not close that gap, i.e., do not rally back to the low of the day before, this creates a downside "measuring gap" and points to lower prices. If the market were to rally and fill that "gap down," then it would be an "exhaustion gap," which is a "fake out." Assuming the gap down was not filled, then the extent of the projected low is determined by taking the difference between the low of the prior day and the cycle crest that preceded it, and then subtracting that difference from the high on the day of the "gap down." In the case of bear markets, it is often necessary to use the cycle crest preceding the most recent one if the "gap down" is very soon after a cycle crest. This difference gives the downside measuring gap price objective. The distance between that price target and the cycle crest used for the calculation can then be multiplied by .118 to determine the range for this downside measuring gap price target.

Once again, this setup and calculation is best illustrated with an example. Let us look at the chart of the Japanese Nikkei stock index during the "Panic of 2008," as shown in Figure 28. First of all, notice that the primary cycle crest that preceded the market collapse occurred on June 6 at 14,601.30. This was a "gap up" from the day before. The "gap" was between 14,329.60 (high of June 5) and 14,489.40 (low of June 6). But the very next day, which was Monday, June 9, the Nikkei gapped down. The high that day was 14,278.80. When a "gap up" day is followed by a "gap down" day, it is known as a "bearish island reversal." As the name implies, this is a very bearish signature, especially when it occurs off of a primary cycle crest. As you can see from the chart, this was indeed the case, as the market had a prolonged decline following this "bearish island reversal" at the primary cycle crest. However, since the "gap down" occurred the day after the primary cycle crest, it was too soon to construct a downside measuring gap. Measuring gaps need some time to elapse between the "gap" day and the cycle low or high that is being used to calculate a measuring gap price objective. The "gap down" on June 9 was just one day after the primary cycle crest, so it could not be used to calculate a reliable downside measuring gap price target. Yet the fact that it happened the day after the primary cycle crest was a strong indication that a sharp down move would now commence, especially since it was an even more bearish pattern known as the "bearish island reversal."

The more important "gap down" to use for the downside measuring gap occurred several weeks later, on October 6, 2008. In fact, that was a Monday and the gap down became a weekly gap, which is even more important. On Friday, October 3, the low of the day (and week) was 10,938.10. The high of the next day (Monday, October 6) was 10,839.50 and that was also the high of that new week. Thus the Nikkei had a "gap down" week from 10,938.10 to 10,839.50.

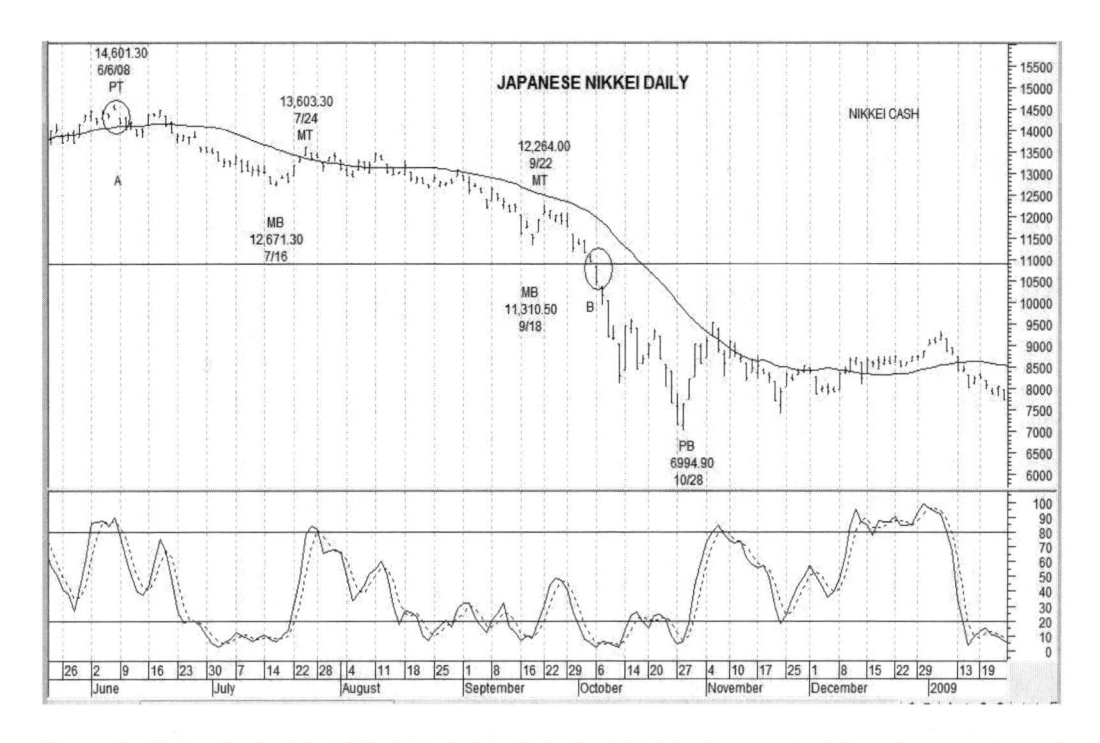

Figure 28: Daily chart of the Nikkei, depicting 1) the bearish island reversal at the primary cycle crest June 5-9, 2008, shown as A, and 2) the "measuring gap down" at B. In fact, the gap down at B was a weekly gap down, which produced a downside measuring gap target around the PB of October 28.

To calculate the downside measuring gap price target, subtract the low of the day before the gap (10,938.10, October 3) from the previous primary cycle crest, which was 14,601.30 on June 6, or 14,601.30 - 10,938.10 = 3663.20. Next, subtract this from the high of the "gap down" day, which was 10,839.50. The calculation for the downside measuring gap price objective is thus 10,839.50 - 3663.20 = 7176.30. If we multiply the difference between this and the 14,601.30 primary cycle crest by .118, we get an orb of 876.15 to the price target, or, (14,601.30 - 7176.30) x .118 = 876.15. Thus the range for this downside measuring gap is 7176.30 +/- 876.15, or 6300.15 - 8052.45. You will note that the low of the move was 6994.90 on October 28, which was in the middle of the downside measuring gap price range.

A variation of a Fibonacci downside price calculation for the primary cycle trough of October 28 could be constructed too. One could take the distance down from the high of June 6 (14,601.30) to the major cycle trough of September 18 (11,310.50), and multiply that difference by 1.618. The calculation would thus be (14,601.30 - 11,310.50) x 1.618 = 5324.51. Subtract that amount from the major cycle crest of September 22 (12,264). This price objective would thus be 12,264 - 5324.51 = 6939.49. The orb of this price objective would then be (14,601.30 – 6939.49) x .118 = 904.09. Thus the downside price target range for this calculation would be 6939.49 +/- 904.09, or 6035.40 - 7843.58.

If we take the ranges of these two downside price targets just calculated (the measuring gap and the 1.618 Fibonacci calculation), we get an overlap of 6300.15-7843.58. The actual low was 6994.90, right in the middle of these two price objectives.

ISLAND REVERSALS

Although this book is primarily about prices, the entire series of these five volumes is about market timing. And one of the most important factors involved in successful market timing is the recognition of certain patterns that indicate a market is headed up or down. In this regard, gaps can be very useful. For instance, once a market is in the time band for its primary cycle trough, it is not unusual for the market to start having "gap up" days shortly after that bottom is completed. The same is true in reverse at a primary cycle crest (or any cycle trough or crest, and not necessarily just primary types, although they are the most important for trading strategies). In other words, once the primary cycle crest is completed, it is not uncommon for markets to exhibit "gap down" days shortly after. However, because these "gaps" occur so close to the actual primary cycle trough or crest, they cannot usually be used to calculate a "measuring gap" price target. They are simply an important chart pattern that alerts the trader that a move is beginning in the direction of that gap, and that the primary cycle trough or crest is probably completed. This assumes that these gaps take place in a time band when the primary cycle trough or crest is due and ideally near (or immediately after) a geocosmic critical reversal date.

One of the most powerful chart patterns involving "gaps" is known as the "island reversal." A "bearish island reversal" was illustrated in Figures 26 and 28. It occurred with the primary cycle crest of June 6, 2008 (day 4 in Figure 26). That was a "gap up" from the prior day's range of June 5. That is, the entire range of June 6 was above the entire range of June 5. And the following day (Monday, June 9) was a "gap down" day. That is, its high was below the low of June 6. So June 6 was a "gap up" of the day before and followed by a "gap down" the day after. Thus, June 6 is an "island" day. In this case, it is a "bearish island reversal" because it stands as an isolated high between the two days surrounding it, and is both preceded and followed by "gap" days. It usually means a top of significance has just been completed. The market will now trend lower and lower, unless that last "gap down" is filled. "Bearish island reversals" that occur in the time band for a primary cycle crest - and especially if nearby to a geocosmic critical reversal date - are exceptional sell signals. One can go short with a stop-loss above that gap zone or at least above the close of the day of the high. The times that bearish (or bullish) island reversals should not be taken quite so seriously are when they happen outside of a time band for a cycle crest or when Mercury is retrograde. The later is a three-week phenomenon that occurs 3-4 times per year and usually denotes a market climate in which there is propensity for numerous false technical and chart pattern signals.

It should also be pointed out that bearish or bullish island reversals do not have to involve only a single day that is preceded and followed by gaps. It is possible to have a bearish island reversal if the market has had several days trading above a "gap up" day that is then followed by a "gap down day" below the low of this group of days. Let us say, for example, that on July 1 the market "gaps up" above the high of June 30. It then stays above here for the entire next week. But the following week, it gaps down below the low of these days of the past week. That is also a "bearish island reversal." It may be more powerful because it broke the gap support of several days with a gap down. An example of a bearish island reversal covering several days can be seen in Figure 29 of the Japanese Nikkei in 2008, on the way down to "Panic" bottom low of October of that year.

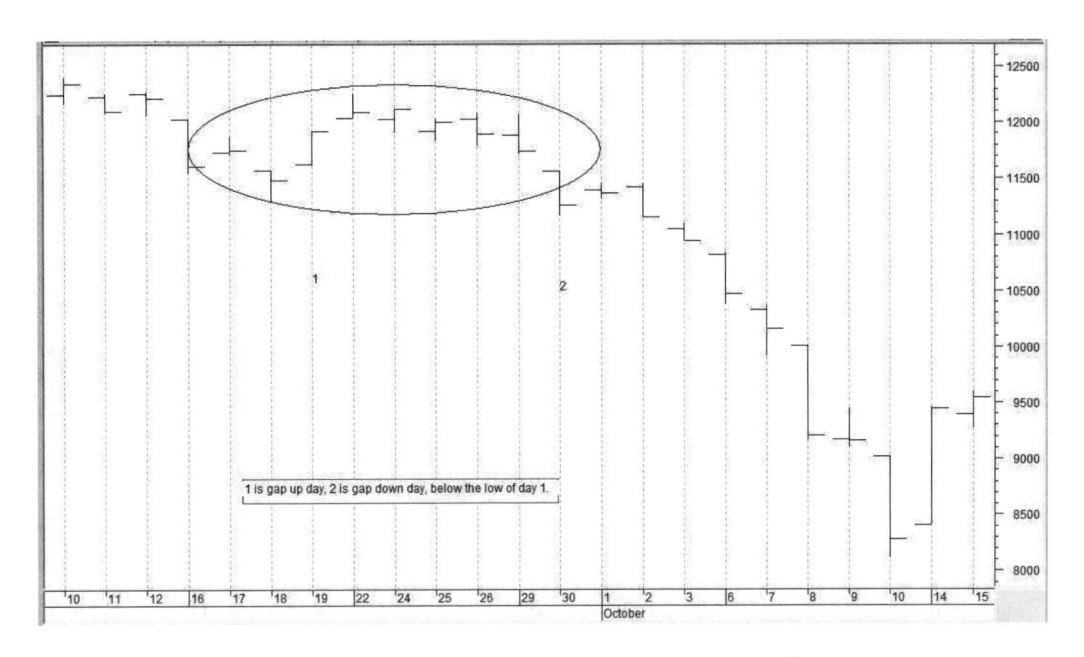

Figure 29: Illustration of a "bearish island reversal" in the Japanese Nikkei Index that covered several days. Note that the market "gapped up" on day 1 (September 19). The low of that day was 11,615. That low held for the next 6 trading days. Then on September 30, shown as '2' in the chart above, the market "gapped down" below the lowest price since the "gap up" occurred. Thus all the days from September 19 through September 29 are part of an "island." When it "gapped down" on September 30, this became a "bearish island reversal" and led to a steep sell off.

A "bullish island reversal" usually happens shortly after a primary cycle trough has been completed. It can actually happen after any type of cycle low has just formed, but for our purposes as traders, we are mostly interested in primary cycles, for they provide the best times for initiating position trades that may be held for several weeks. A "bullish island reversal" occurs when market "gaps down" from its prior day's range and then "gaps up" the next day. The low of the move is an isolated low (lower than the low of the day before and day after). But not only that, it is the middle day between first a "gap down," and then a "gap up." It usually leads to a powerful rally that lasts for several days, even weeks or months.

Sometimes the "gap down" day in a "bullish island reversal" pattern can be followed by several days of trading below the low of the day that preceded the "gap down." In other words, the price that created the "gap down" is not filled for several days. Then, the market suddenly "gaps up" above the range of these days, and fills the "gap down" mark created earlier. This too is a pattern known as a "bullish island reversal." It usually means the market is starting a torrid rally over the next several days, weeks, even months, as long as a the "gap up" is not filled on any decline. An example of a "bullish island reversal" pattern is shown in Figure 30 of the market behavior in the German DAX in the summer of 2005.

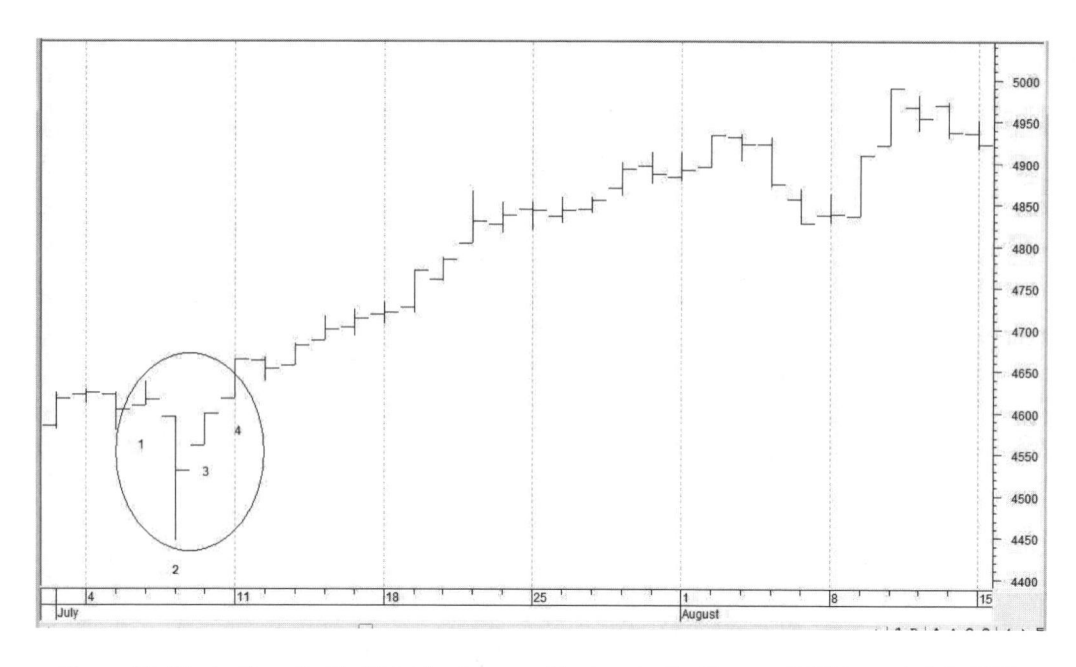

Figure 30: Illustration of a "bullish island reversal" set up in the German DAX in early July 2005.

Note in Figure 30 how the DAX had a gap down between July 6 and 7, listed as '1' and '2' in the graph. The low of July 6 was 4607.57. The next day, July 7, it gapped down to form a primary cycle trough at 4444.94. The high of that day was 4595.23, which was below the low of the prior day, thus making it a "gap down day." The next day, July 8, the market traded up as high as 4597.97 (see 3). This was still below the gap down day of July 6. But on the next trading day, July 11 (Monday), the market "gapped up" above the highs of July 7 and 8 (see 4). Its low was 4616.36, which also filled the "gap down' of July 6-7. Thus we have a "bullish island reversal," where the island was comprised of two days (July 7 and 8), between a "gap down" and a "gap up." An impressive rally followed for the next several weeks, as seen in this chart.

CHAPTER TEN

TRENDLINE ANALYSIS (AND GAPS THAT FOLLOW)

Gaps are important, but not all gaps result in bullish or bearish moves. Many are "fake outs," as in "exhaustion gaps." But as seen previously, many gaps can be followed by impressive moves in the direction of the gap if they occur at critical times in a market cycle or in combination with certain types of chart patterns. For example, a gap above or below the neckline of a head and shoulders pattern can lead to a very powerful move. So can a bullish or bearish island reversal nearby to a primary cycle trough or crest.

There are other chart patterns that can be broken by a "gap," that can also possibly lead to powerful price moves. For instance, a "gap up" above a downward trendline can signal that the bearish trend down is over and the market has commenced a new bullish trend. Likewise a "gap down" below an upward trendline can occur when the market is commencing a new bearish trend. The same is true when a market gaps above a double top resistance area or below a double bottom support area. It is also important if the gap is above or below an important moving average, such as one that is one-half or one-quarter of a cycle length. Each of these technical studies defines an important support or resistance zone. When a market gaps below or above them, it is much more powerful as a reliable indicator that the market is beginning a strong move in the direction of the gap, which means it can be a confirming signal that the previous trend has reversed. These gaps are especially useful in calculating measuring gap price objectives, because they usually occur well after the completion of a primary cycle trough or crest, but not at the end of those cycles.

In real life experience, however, gaps above or below trendlines, double bottoms or tops, and moving averages, are rare. This is especially true when using cash indices, like the Dow Jones Industrial Average, which rarely ever exhibits gaps. You will find gaps much more common in commodity indices, or futures. They are also more common in non U.S. stocks indices, or even individual stocks. But when they happen to occur above or below a well-defined resistance or support zone, they are usually worth trading in the direction of that gap.

More often than not, a market will close above or below one of these important resistance or support zones without a gap. But shortly afterwards, gaps begin to happen. Sometimes a market will have a retracement below or above that breakout point for a day or two (even three) and then a gap in the direction of the breakout. That is when one knows that the trend has reversed, and the new trend is really underway. In other words, it doesn't require a gap beyond these support or resistance points to signal that the new move has begun. The gap can happen shortly afterwards. The primary cycle that preceded these gaps can be used to calculate measuring gap price targets. If the gaps occur shortly after a primary cycle trough or crest, it may be necessary to go back to the prior primary cycle for the calculation, just as we did in the previous chapter on gaps. We will examine this phenomenon of chart patterns and their subsequent gaps throughout this book. But primarily this and the following chapters will introduce the concept of other chart patterns that can aid the trader in understanding their importance - which in turn indicate that a market is "breaking out" of an old trend - and suggest that a new trend is underway.

TRENDLINE ANALYSIS

Trendline analysis is one of the most basic tools used by chartists. But not all chartists use the same points to construct a trendline, and not all trendlines are valid or useful, especially for the purpose of calculating price objectives.

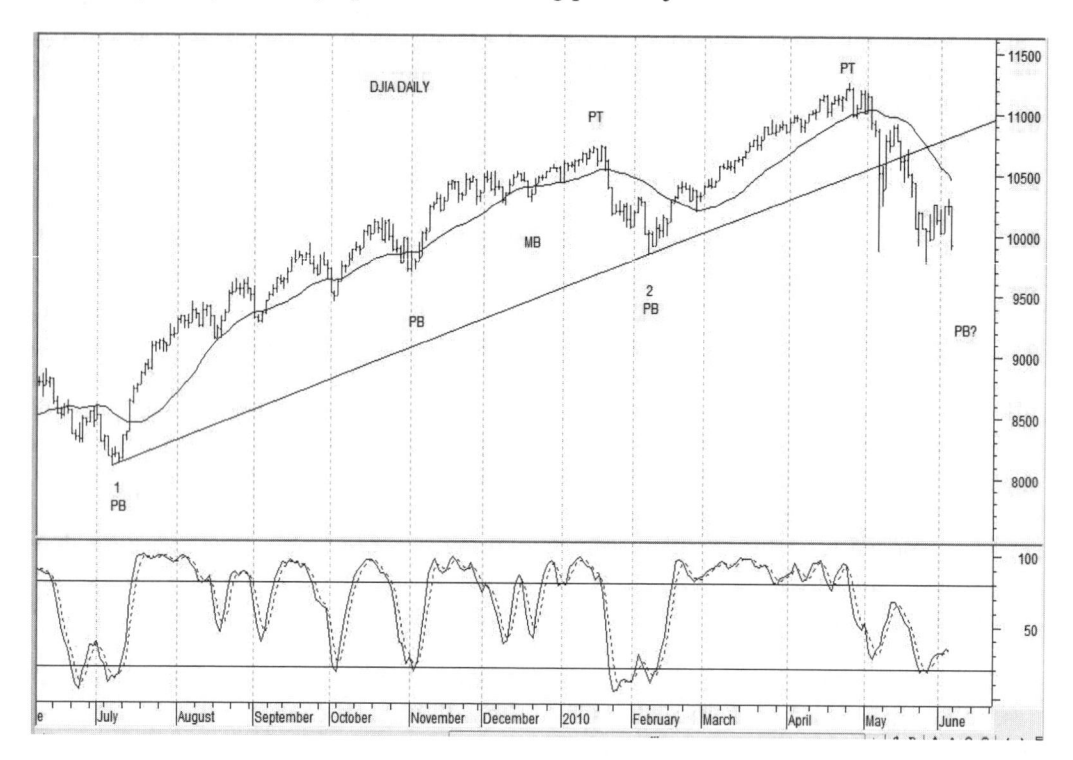

Figure 31: 1-2 (and both are PBs, or primary cycle bottoms) is an example of an upward trendline that was broken in early May 2010. Because it connects two primary cycles, this is known as a "primary trendline up." When a primary trendline is broken, it usually confirms the end of the next highest cycle, or in this case, the 50-week cycle. The trend is now down until a new trendline down forms, especially if it connects two primary cycle crests.

A trendline connects at least two isolated highs or lows to one another. When two lows are connected, and the second low is higher than the first, it is known as an *upward trendline*. The market is considered bullish until it breaks below this trendline. You can see an example in Figure 31. Conversely, when two highs are connected, and the second high is lower than the first, it is known as a *downward trendline*. The market is bearish until prices close above this trendline. You can see an example of this in Figure 32.

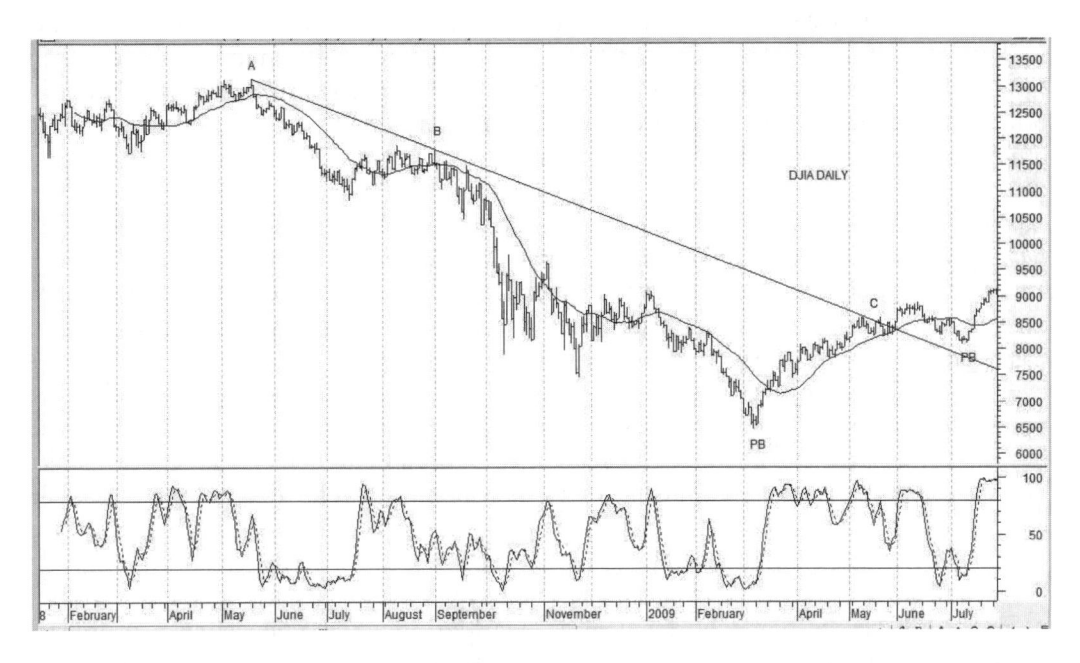

Figure 32: Example of a downward trendline, A-B-C, that broke after third point C. Three-point or greater trendlines are very powerful indicators of a trend reversal when broken. Still, there is usually a pullback shortly afterwards that will test the extension of that former trendline. As long as that extension holds on the attempted pullback, the market's new bullish trend is reconfirmed and all the more likely to continue for some time.

Occasionally there will be instances when the price breaks slightly above or below a trendline. These are "fake outs." You can see an example of a "fake out" in Figure 33. Usually a "fake out" will not violate a trendline with two consecutive closes beyond it. If that happens, then the trend represented by the trendline is considered over.

Sometimes analysts connect two or more lows that are successively lower, or two or more crests that are successively higher. This too represents support and resistance. However, these types of trendlines do not identify new trends in the market. They only identify support and resistance areas to the trend already underway, or points at which an accelerated breakout may occur. In many cases, these types of trendlines are part of other chart patterns such as "channel trends" or "triangles." You can see an example of a channel trend in Figure 34. Yet the trend isn't really broken until either a *downward* line connecting tops, or an *upward* line connecting lows, is broken. And to be certain, this break should occur on the closes of at least two consecutive time frames (i.e. two consecutive days on the daily chart or two consecutive weeks on a weekly chart, etc.).

As suggested above, not all trend lines are equal or useful. In the study of cycles, a valid trendline should connect at least two lows or highs of the same cycle type. In applying this rule, keep in mind that every cycle is comprised of smaller cycles or phases. Thus an upward trendline connecting a primary and major cycle trough is valid because a primary cycle is also a major cycle (three 6-week major cycles make up an 18-week primary cycle). Nevertheless, in the study of cycles as used in this series of books, a trendline is identified according to the second shortest cycle that makes it up. A trendline between a major cycle trough (6-week cycle) and a primary cycle trough (18-week cycle) is thus referred to as "the major trendline" or "major upward trendline" if it connects lows that are successively higher in price. A trendline connecting two successively higher primary cycle troughs will be referred to as "the primary trendline" or a "primary upward trendline," even if it connects with a third point that is a major cycle trough.

But the important rule is this: *when a trendline connecting two cycles of the same type is broken, it strongly implies the next longest cycle has just been completed.* Thus if an upward trendline connecting two major cycle troughs is broken, it means the next longest cycle (the primary cycle) has probably topped out. If an upward primary trendline has been broken (i.e. connecting two primary cycle troughs), it means the next longest cycle - the 50-week cycle - has topped out. This is important to note, because when one knows the type of cycle just completed, one has a better understanding of how long and how far the ensuing move will go. A break of an upward trend line connecting two major cycles means the market is moving lower to a primary cycle trough. A break of an upward trendline connecting two primary cycles means the 50-week cycle has topped out, and the market is moving to its 50-week cycle trough. If the breakout was of a downward trendline connecting two major cycle crests, then it is starting a move towards its primary cycle crest. If a breakout of a downward trendline connecting two primary cycle crests occurs, it means the next longest cycle - the 50-week cycle trough - has probably been completed, and the rally to the 50-week crest is well underway.

Also very powerful are trendlines that connect at least three points. Three-point or greater trendlines usually represent strong support to declines or resistance to rallies. Sometimes trendlines contain 4, 5, even 6 or more points, as in Figure 34. The market just can't close beyond it. But when it does, the move in the direction of the breakout can be substantial, especially if at least two of those points involve primary cycles. But what is even more powerful is when the break beyond a trendline happens on a gap up or down day, or if a gap above or below the trendline happens shortly after the trendline was broken. That gap, then, gives an upside measuring gap price objective for the move.

Let us look at examples of valid trendlines that were broken and followed by "gaps" in the direction of the breakouts. Figure 33 shows a daily chart of the Japanese Nikkei Index in the middle of 2003. In this example, the trend was bearish from the primary cycle crest (PT) in early December 2002. A half-primary cycle crest (1/2-PT) occurred in mid-February 2003. A downward trendline connecting these two crests is thus a downward "half-primary cycle trendline," because the second longest cycle is a half-primary cycle crest. When prices break above it on two consecutive days, it means that the next longest cycle - the primary cycle trough - is completed.

On April 28, the primary cycle bottomed at 7603.76. Of course, one does not know this at the time. The first sign of this possibility would have been when the market rallied and broke above this trendline, which took place on May 13 as prices rallied to 8339.07. But it closed at 8190.26 that day, back below the trendline, so it's not confirmed. In fact, it may have been a "fake out." The next day it closed at 8244.91, which was above the trendline, suggesting again the breakout to a new trend may be underway. But it was not to be, for the following six days it was back below it again, which means that the high of May 13, the day it first went above the downward trend line, was indeed a "fake out."

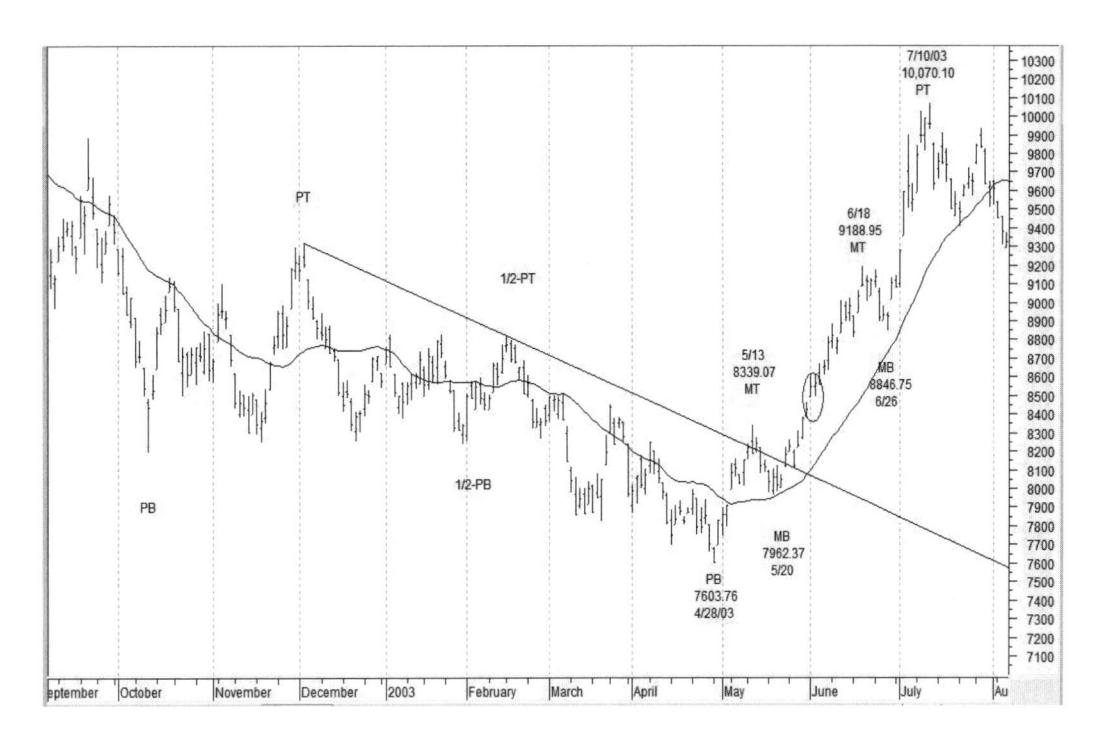

Figure 33: Example of a downward trendline in the Japanese Nikkei Index, broken with a "gap up" and followed by another "gap up" above the recent high, creating an upside measuring gap target near the primary cycle crest.

On May 20, it completed a major cycle trough. Then on May 23, it "gapped up" above the trendline. That gap held and was a strong signal that the primary bottom was in, because it closed above the trendline for the next two consecutive days (and more). The move up was now looking like it might be underway.

On May 29, the Nikkei closed above the major cycle crest of May 13. This was a further sign the primary cycle trough was in. The next day, May 30, the Nikkei rallied to a high of 8461.74. The next trading day, June 2, it "gapped up" with a low of 8488.89, which is completely above the prior day's trading range. The move up is now truly underway. This gap up becomes the basis for calculating an upside measuring gap price target. It is shown on the graph with a circle around those days. If we take the low of the primary cycle trough on April 28 (7603.76) and subtract it from the high of May 30 (the day before the gap up at 8461.74), we get a difference of 857.98. The first upside measuring gap price target then becomes 857.98 added to the low on the "gap up" day, which was 8488.89. That calculation is 8488.89 + 857.98 = 9346.86. By multiplying the difference between that price target and the primary cycle trough of 7603.76 by .118, the range for this projected crest is determined. The price orb is (9346.86 – 7603.76) x .118 = 205.68. The price target is thus 9346.86 +/- 205.68, or the range is 9141.18 - 9552.54. The chart indicates that the Nikkei rallied to a major cycle crest on June 18 at 9188.95, which is within our price target for the measuring gap up.

However, the market can go higher as a long as 1) the original gap up is not taken out on the next decline, and 2) the high of the first price objective zone is taken out afterwards. Both of those conditions were met. Therefore we can multiply the original distance between the primary cycle trough and the high of the day preceding the gap, by 2. We know that distance was 857.98. Doubling that distance gives us a greater move up of 1715.96. If we add that to the low of the "gap up" day, we get 8488.89 + 1715.96 = 10,204.85. We can calculate the orb to allow for this price target as follows: (10,204.85 – 7603.76) x .118 = 306.93. Thus, the next upside measuring gap target is 10,204.85 +/- 306.93, or 9897.89 - 10,511.78. The primary cycle crest was completed at 10,070.10 on July 10, which is within the calculated price objective range.

This price range becomes more significant because it is supported by other methods that were described earlier. For instance, we know that this crest is occurring in the third major cycle phase of the primary cycle. An MCP upside price target could be calculated from the move up in the second phase. In other words, the crest of phase two was 9188.95 on June 18. The major cycle trough that preceded it was 7962.37 on May 20. The move up in phase two was thus 9188.95 – 7962.37, or 1226.58. If that is then added to the major cycle trough that ended phase two at 8846.75 on June 26, an MCP price target can be calculated for the crest of the third major cycle phase at 10,073.33. The orb to this price target would then be (10,073.33 - 7962.37) x .118 = 249.09. The range would have been 9824.24 - 10,322.42. The actual crest was right there, almost an exact MCP price target.

A third calculation could also provide a price target range that was met with this primary cycle crest. If the rally to the crest of the second major cycle (9188.95 on June 18) from the primary cycle low of April 28 (7603.76) was multiplied by .618 and then added to the trough of the second major cycle (8846.75 on June 26), the calculation is: (9188.95 - 7603.76) x .618 = 979.64. Then, 8846.75 + 979.64 = 9826.40. The orb of this price target would then be (9826.40 - 7603.76) x .118 = 262.27. The price target of this .618 calculation for the crest of phase three would thus be 9826.40 +/- 262.27, or a range of 9564.13 - 10,088.67.

Thus, three price targets for the primary cycle crest have been calculated as follows:

Measuring gap upside target	=	9897.89 - 10,511.78
MCP upside price target	=	9824.24 - 10,322.42
Phase 3 is .618 of phases 1 & 2	=	9564.13 - 10,088.67

They all overlap at 9897.89 - 10,088.67. The actual high of the primary cycle crest was 10,070.10, which is within the ideal price target range where all three studies overlapped.

Although this was an example of a breakout above a downward trendline that was followed by a measuring gap up, readers should understand that the importance of trendline studies is the idea that they confirm a new trend is underway. The old trend is over, at least until the crest or trough of that new cycle is completed. That could be relatively soon afterwards, or it may take several weeks or even months, depending on 1) the type of trendline that was broken (i.e. a major cycle, primary type, or something else) and 2) the pattern that is forming in this new cycle (i.e. left translation, right translation, etc.).

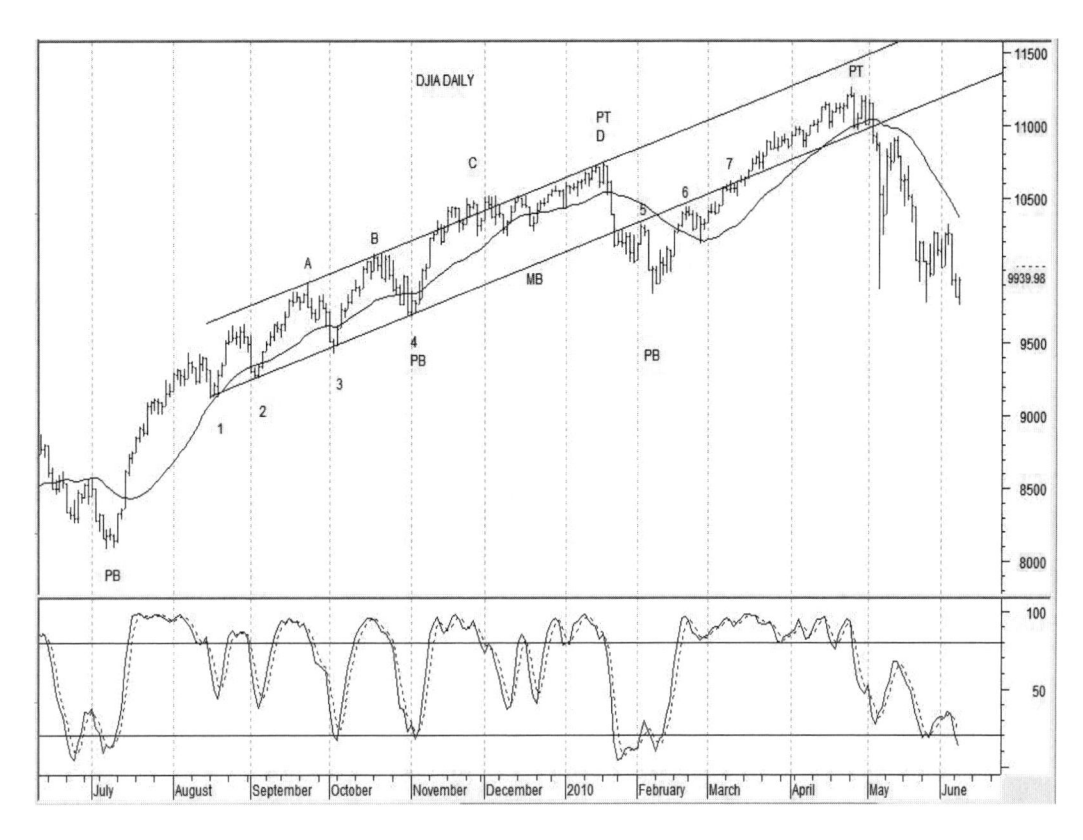

Figure 34: Note the 4-point trendline up (1-4) and the upward channel it forms also connects the highs of A-D (it went slightly above at C). When the lower line (1-4) of the channel broke after D, it formed a primary bottom. But even then the rally failed several times (5-7) after pulling back to the extension of the former upward trendline.

Let us look at yet another trendline example (Figure 34), this time of an upward trendline (1-4) connecting more than two lows (and is also part of an upward channel where the highs can be connected, too). On this chart, you will note the upward trendline connects lows at 1-4. The third point (3) poked slightly below this trendline, which will sometimes happen, perhaps due to scalpers recognizing that there are resting stop-loss orders there. They try to "run the market down," to set off those stop-losses and see if some momentum can be generated for a sharp sell-off. In this case, it did not work, as the DJIA recovered quickly and continued back above the trendline that started at 1-2.

We can see this dynamic at work on the highs, which also can be connected to one another, thus forming what is called an "upward channel." You can see the upper line of this channel at A-D. Every time the market falls to the lower channel (the trendline connecting more than one low), it finds support, and rallies. The rally carries it to the line connecting the highs, which is parallel to the line connecting the lows, thus it is also sometimes referred to as a bullish "parallel channel line." Theoretically, one buys every time it touches the lower end of the channel, and takes profits (even sells short) when it touches the upper line. However, since it is an upward or bullish channel, the position trader is only interested in buying and taking profits and not selling short against the trend, which is clearly up in this channel.

97

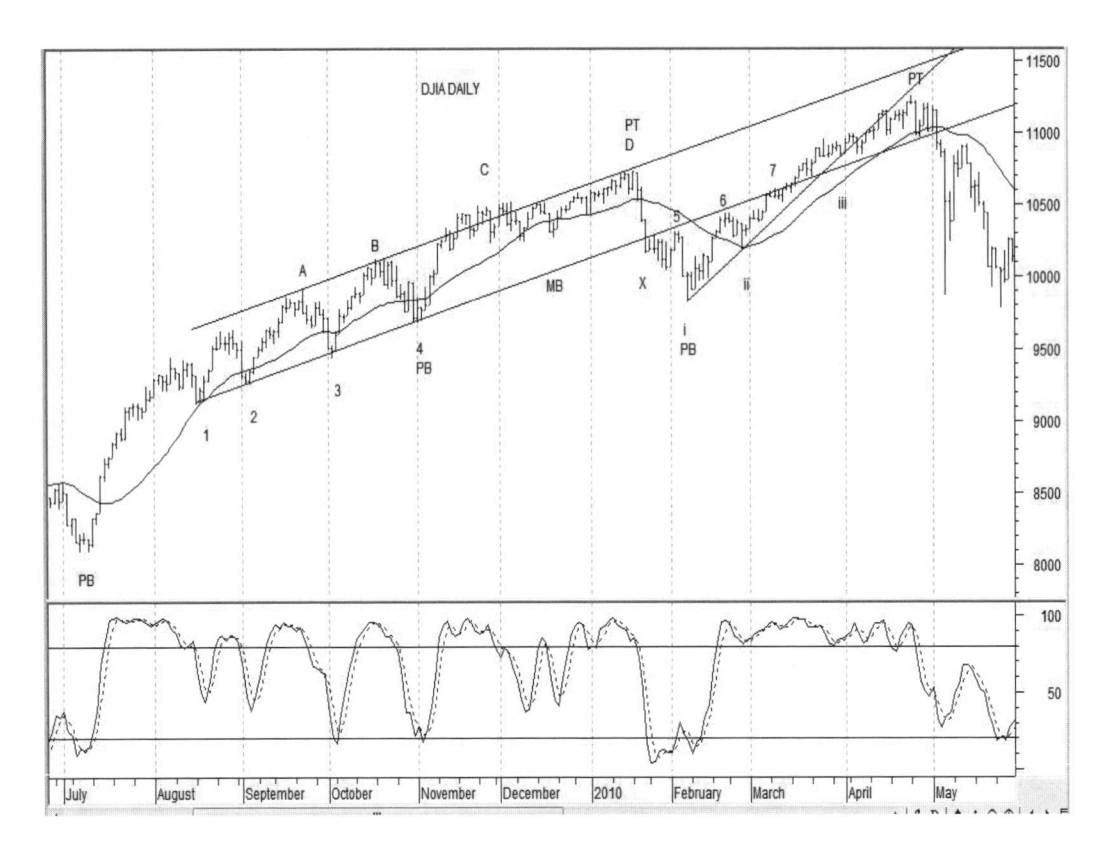

Figure 35: After the DJIA rallied back above the extension of the former upward trendline 1-4, it then created a new three-point upward trendline (i-iii). Once it broke below there, the extension of that shorter upward trendline (i-iii) then became resistance, which ended nearby to the final move up at PT (Primary Top) on April 26.

Once again, we see that prices slightly exceeded the upper line of a channel at C. Usually this means the market will soar upwards much higher, or else it is a "fake out." In this case, it didn't run away to the upside. Instead, after a few days of trading slightly above, prices returned into the channel, remaining there for several days. Finally the market touched the upper channel again at D to complete its primary cycle crest. The DJIA sold off to the primary cycle trough in February 2010, breaking below the upward trendline 1-4 and thus breaking out to the downside of the channel. This confirmed the primary cycle crest was in and prices were falling to the primary cycle trough.

But then an interesting thing happened, which demonstrates why trendlines yield important price targets even after they are broken. As with all charting indicators, once support breaks it becomes resistance. Once the support of an upward trendline breaks, that former trendline can still be extended. The extension then represents resistance to future rallies. These rallies are known as "pullbacks" and identify resistance to all future rallies until the market can close back above the extension of that former trendline. In Figures 34 and 35, one can see that several rallies "pulled back" to the extension of the former upward trend line (see 5, 6, and 7). In those three cases, the rally was halted at the extension of the former trendline. Finally prices broke above the extension of this former trendline, on the way to the crest of the new primary cycle (PT, on April 26, 2010).

A new upward three-point trendline can now be constructed. It is a shorter trendline identified as i, ii, and iii in Figure 35. And after it broke, prices then rallied back ("pulled back") to the extension of this former upward trendline i, ii, iii, topping out right at the primary cycle crest denoted as PT on April 26, 2010.

This is one of those rare examples where the usual corrective decline to the primary cycle trough in February 2010 failed to work. The decline to the primary cycle trough in February was more than the usual range of 38.2-61.8% of the primary swing up. That happens occasionally; it is simply a fact of life. Nothing works all the time, and market forecasting is in many respects based on probabilities, which themselves are determined by historical rates of frequency. You try to get the historical odds (i.e. we use mostly historical rates of frequency of 80% or more) in your favor.

However, there was another calculation that did work in identifying the low of February 2010. This was calculated from the point where the trendline was broken at X. If you take the point where an upward trendline is broken, oftentimes the market will continue to fall to a point that is equidistance below that trendline as the crest was above it. In this case, the break of the trendline at X was about 10,262.65. The prior high was 10,729.90. The distance from PT to the break at X was thus 10,729.90-10,262.65 = 467.25. If we then subtract that from the trendline break (10,262.65 – 467.25) we get 9795.40. Another way to calculate this is to multiply the break point (10,262.65) times 2, and subtract it from the high, or 10,262.65 x 2 = 20,525.30. Then 20,525.30-10,729.90 = 9795.40. Again, we can find the range of allowance by multiplying the difference by .118. Thus (10,729.9 - 9795.40) x .118 = 110.27. The range for the expected line, based on this formula for price objectives via trendline breakage is 9795.40 +/- 110.27, or 9685.13-9905.67. The low was 9835.09, which is in this range for the primary bottom of February 5, 2010.

But what also worked in this example were the price targets established by trendlines and the pullbacks to their extensions after they broke. The pullback to the extensions of former upward trendlines (one long, one short) defined both of the primary cycle crests shown in these graphs (Figure 34 and 35). We also know from previous chapters that the crest on April 26, 2010 (11,258 in the DJIA) was an almost exact 61.8% corrective rally of the bear market from its start on October 11, 2007 to its low on March 6, 2009. We could also calculate that the rally to the crest of April was within the range of a 1.236 multiple of the previous primary swing up (from 4 to D), added to the primary cycle low of February 5, 2010. Thus we had at least three studies indicating resistance there on April 26, 2010, and it just happened to also be in a very important critical reversal zone defined by geocosmic signatures. In fact, that was the exact date of the 45-year Saturn–Uranus opposition, the fourth in a series of five passages (between November 4, 2008 and July 26, 2010).

Since this example used the cash Dow Jones Industrial Average, we had no "gaps up" or "gaps down" following the break of the trendlines as we note in many other markets. The cash DJIA just doesn't do that very often because all the stocks start trading at different times. Hence the opening is usually not too far from the prior day's close. But this particular example served the purpose of demonstrating how trendlines, channel lines, and breakage of trendlines can be used to calculate yet other price targets. Trendline analysis is also important because it helps one establish 1) which type of cycle has just formed, 2) which type of cycle is next to unfold and hence how long the new trend is likely to last, and 3) what type of trading strategies should now be employed (bullish or bearish). *In bullish strategies, the trader is primarily looking to buy corrective declines. In bearish strategies, the trader is primary looking to sell all corrective rallies.* To be a successful position trader via the methods outlined in these books, one must abide by this principle with only a few exceptions (selling sometimes at the crest of primary or greater cycles in bull markets, or buying sometimes at the trough of primary or greater cycles in bear markets), depending on the presence of certain technical conditions outlined in this book.

CHAPTER ELEVEN

STOCHASTICS AND THEIR PATTERNS: IDENTIFYING CYCLE TROUGHS AND CRESTS

Up until now, this book has focused on the task of determining price objectives for optimal buying and selling. In the last chapter, we introduced trendlines, a technical study that aids in determining when a trend has changed and a contra-trend has started. It can also be used to identify certain price targets for lows and highs, as well as identifying prices of near-term support and resistance that will often result in a crest or trough from which prices then reverse. We will now move into the field of other technical studies and patterns that will help you to time or confirm a cycle reversal. These involve stochastic oscillators, bullish and bearish divergence patterns, and moving averages. It is not so much that these studies will yield specific price targets, but mainly that they will identify when price targets are valid. For instance, if a market has achieved a price objective target, but one of these technical studies strongly implies the move is not yet over, then that price target is not likely valid. On the other hand, if the market does stop there, it is only a short time before it continues its trend, until the technical study indicates that the momentum has finally reached an overbought or oversold level.

My first experience with oscillators like stochastics came from legendary cycles' analyst Walter Bressert (www.walterbressert.com), back in 1980-1982. Although Bressert is most noted for his pioneering work in cycles, he is often overlooked for his pioneering work with oscillators in technical analysis. He was a master at using these oscillators to determine more precisely when to buy or sell when a cycle time band for a bottom or top was in effect. However, the market analyst most noted for his work on stochastic oscillators, which are used in this book, is George Lane (1921-2004).

In his book titled Using Stochastics, Cycles and RSI, Lane described his famous indicator as follows: *"Stochastics measure the momentum of price. If you visualize a rocket going up in the air - before it can turn down, it must slow down. Momentum always changes direction before price."*[1] Often referred to as "The Father of Stochastics," Lane once stated in a lecture, titled Getting Started with Stochastics, *"As prices move down, the close of the day has a tendency to crowd the lower portion of the daily range. Just before you get to the absolute price low, the market does not have as much push as it did. The closes no longer crowd the bottom of the daily range. Therefore, stochastics turn up at or before the final price low."*[2] For a calculation of stochastics, please refer to the glossary of terms at the beginning of this book. For further information on the works of George and Caire Lane, the reader may go to www.lanestochastics.com.

There are many different time frames that traders use in their application of stochastics. The one that I use most frequently - and hence the one that will be used throughout most of the discussions on stochastics referred to in this book - is known as a 15-bar (hour, day, week, etc.) slow stochastic, with a three-bar moving average of the 15-bar stochastic. Most market charting software programs have a toolbox where one can input parameters for a stochastic, like the one shown below from MetaStock, one of the market charting software programs that I personally use.

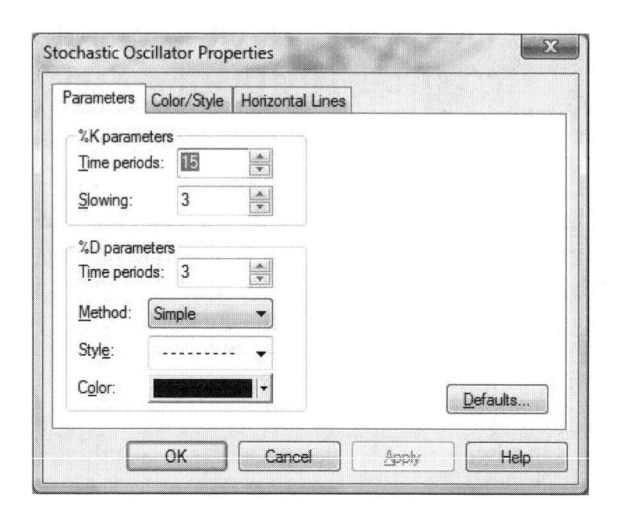

Figure 36: The set up page for stochastics in MetaStock software.

Notice that there are two values, one known as %K (faster) and the other as %D (longer, or slower moving) line. D is slower because it is a 3-day average derived from K. When viewing charts in this book, you will notice the stochastics on the bottom of many of these graphs. You will notice two lines: a solid line (%K), which moves faster and with greater amplitude and a dotted line (%D), which moves with less amplitude over a longer period of time. The default setting for the Stochastic Oscillator used herein is 15 periods (days, weeks, months, or an intraday timeframe). A 15-day %K, for instance, would use the most recent close, the highest high over the last 15 days and the lowest low over the last 15 days. %D is a 3-day simple moving average of %K. %K is plotted alongside %D and acts as a signal or "trigger."

Stochastics seem most useful on daily and intraday charts. They can be valuable on weekly charts too. However, my experience is that they are not so useful on charts of time frames longer than weekly charts. For instance, I do not use them for monthly, quarterly, or yearly charts. I find that it takes too much time for these longer-term stochastics to unfold in a clearly defined buy or sell set up. From the time it is overbought or oversold until the time it takes to develop a bullish or bearish pattern, too much time has elapsed in these longer time frames for trading purposes. During that time the market will yield many favorable shorter-term buy and sell signals. Which would you use? The answer would be in the shorter-time frames. Therefore, it is the weekly, daily, hourly, and even 30-minute time frames that I find most effective for the use of stochastic indicators. When certain stochastic patterns form in these time frames, converging with other market timing and technical studies, it yields a very reliable buy or sell signal.

OVERBOUGHT AND OVERSOLD

On the chart itself, the stochastic values are displayed in a range between 0% and 100%, where 0% is the extreme oversold condition and 100% is the extreme of overbought. This book will refer to any stochastic level below 20% as oversold and any reading above 80% as overbought. A reading between 42 and 58% may be considered as "neutral," which is important in identifying the extent of many corrective rallies or declines against the basic underlying trend. If the stochastics start to move through the 42-58% neutral area, they will usually continue until reaching below the 20% oversold or above the 80% overbought levels. Thus, if a market has a certain price objective target and it reaches that target when stochastics are between 20 and 42% and headed down, or 58-80% and headed up, the chances are great that it will exceed that price objective target and continue to the next lower or higher one.

STOCHASTIC "BUY" PATTERNS

There are two set ups to initially look for. The first occurs when the stochastics reach an oversold level (below 20%). The second is when they fall back to the neutral 42-58% range after having been above 80%. In the first case, it is best to see an oversold condition when a primary cycle trough is due, especially if the longer-term cycle is still pointed up (in its earlier phases). However, just because it is oversold - below 20% - does not mean that it is time to buy. One must first determine if the time band for a cycle low is in effect. It is also important to determine if a geocosmic critical reversal time band is present as well, according to the market timing methods outlined in this work. Then one must determine if prices have yet attained a calculated price objective range. If these factors are not present, then buying (going long) just because stochastics are below 20% will usually be pre-mature. In most cases, the market will continue to fall lower in price until these other factors are also in place.

In the second case, if the market is bullish, we of course want to buy all corrective declines to phases (subcycles) within that cycle. For example, if the market is only in the middle two-thirds of its cycle, the trader should be prepared (and willing) to buy any corrective declines to a major and trading cycle trough. In these cases, the 15-day slow stochastics may never decline as low as 20%. But they will usually fall back to 42-58%. If they do that in the time band for a trading or major cycle trough, and if the price at that time is in the price range for a normal corrective decline to these subcycles, then one can start to probe the long side of that market. Sometimes these subcycles will not retrace even 38.2-61.8%. An example of this is shown in the chart in Figure 37.

Let us begin our analysis of Figure 37 by looking at the upward trendline 1-2-3. Note that 2 was probably a short primary cycle trough. The DJIA was 10,368.60 on January 24, 2005. It ran up to 10,853.40 on February 16 for a major cycle crest, the end of its first phase in this new primary cycle. In the fifth week, on February 23, it declined into its major cycle trough at 10,609 shown as "3" in the chart. It was the 5th week of the cycle, so a major cycle trough was due. A normal corrective decline at this point would have been 10,611 +/- 57.20, following the rules of earlier chapters. Therefore the market had made a normal corrective decline for a major cycle trough. Note that the 15-day slow stochastics indicted %K was at 46.05% and below %D at 56.26%. Both were in the neutral 42-58% range. It is not necessary for both K and D to be in this range, but it is best if both are.

We will come back to this chart in a moment, for it displays many of the important points to consider when studying the slow stochastics for optimal buy and sell points, especially when used in combination with cycle studies and price objective calculations.

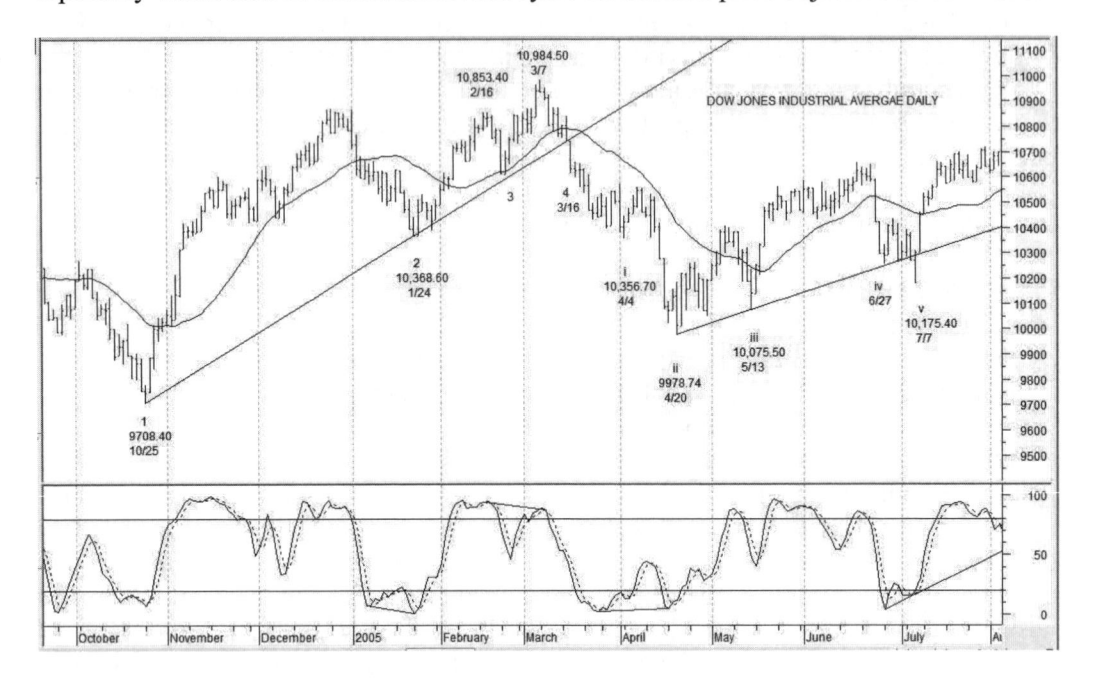

Figure 37: Illustration of the Dow Jones Industrial Average depicting examples of stochastics falling to neutral (3 and iii), exhibiting bullish looping formations (2 and iv-v), bullish oscillator divergence (i-ii), and bearish oscillator divergence (2/16 and 3/7, as well as the highs in May and June 2005).

Bullish Looping and Bullish Oscillator Divergence Patterns

Now let us consider cases where stochastics are oversold and exhibit patterns that indicate it is close to the time to buy. There are two patterns of importance to consider here. The first is known as the "bullish looping pattern," where stochastics fall below 20%. The %K value (the solid line that moves more sharply) is below %D. K then curls up and either touches D or rises slightly above it (but not above the neutral 42-58% area and it is best if not much above 25%). K then turns back below D and crosses back under 25% and preferably even below 20% again. This is the "looping pattern." K is below D, and then it crosses back above, then back below again. When K crosses back above D the next time, it is setting up for a bull run. But to confirm this, it needs to cross back above 20% (and preferably 25%), with K widening its distance above D. That is then a buy signal, especially if it happens in a time band when a primary cycle trough is due. On the graph shown in Figure 37, you can see cases of a "bullish looping pattern" in the stochastics at 2, i-ii and iv-v.

The second bullish stochastics pattern of importance is known as "bullish oscillator divergence." Oftentimes this will occur along with a "bullish looping" pattern. When it

104

does, it is a very powerful buy signal - if a primary cycle trough is due. A bullish stochastic oscillator divergence happens when the price falls to a low, rallies a little bit, and then falls to a lower low. But the stochastics do not make a lower low on the second move down. In other words, the price is lower but the stochastics are higher. Think of it like this: the price is the weight of an object and the oscillator (stochastics) represents the number of people holding that weight up. If you have more people (stochastics) holding up less weight (market price), it is a case of bullish oscillator divergence. Figure 37 shows an example of bullish oscillator divergence at the first primary cycle trough on October 25, 2004 (shown as 1 in the graph). Note that the price was lower than it was in late September. But at the low in late September, the 15-day slow stochastics were lower than on October 25 (when prices were lower). Lower prices with higher stochastics are a buy signal, especially if a) they are below 20% at the first low, and b) a primary cycle trough is due. You can also see cases of bullish oscillator divergence at the primary cycle trough on April 20 (ii, which was a lower price than i, but a higher stochastic reading) and on July 7 (v, which was a lower price, but higher stochastic reading than the low of June 27). In each case, the stochastics were below 20%, then rose a bit, then fell back to the 20% or lower level, but in the second move down, they did not fall as far as the first low. Yet prices were lower in the second move down. When they moved back above 25%, and K widened its distance above D, a strong rally followed.

This chart also illustrates the more powerful impact of a bullish looping formation when the low of the second loop is higher than the first. Or, when a bullish looping pattern also contains a pattern of bullish oscillator divergence, it is also usually more powerful. Look at the primary bottom and bullish looping pattern that formed at 2. It was a bullish looping pattern, but it was not a case of bullish oscillator divergence too. As the price made a new low at the second loop, so did the stochastics. Still, the market rallied to a higher high on March 7. But the rally was then followed by a decline that took out the low that began the primary cycle. That didn't happen so fast in the cases of a bullish looping pattern combined with a bullish oscillator divergence. It is interesting to note that in this instance, the rally following the bullish looping stochastics (without the bullish oscillator divergence signal), was followed by a rally to a primary cycle crest that contained both a bearish looping pattern and bearish oscillator divergence (to be covered next). These crests and bearish stochastic patterns were evident on the highs of February 16 and March 7.

If you look at the two primary cycle troughs in this chart (2 and ii), you will see that not only did they indicate the primary bottom coincident with bullish stochastics, but they also fell into price targets that could have been calculated from formulas given previously. From the primary bottom of 9708.40 on October 25, the DJIA rallied to a primary cycle crest of 10,868.10 on December 27. Using the formulas given in earlier chapters (50% correction, +/- 11.8%), a normal 2-5 week corrective decline from the primary cycle crest to trough could be calculated to take prices back to 10,288.25 +/- 136.85. The low on January 24, four weeks later, was 10,368.60, which is within the price target range. The stochastics were under 20% before that, and prices had entered the price objective range a little before that. But it took the bullish looping pattern on stochastics to finally lift prices up afterwards.

At the second primary cycle trough (ii), the issues were a little different. From the primary cycle crest of March 7 at 10,984.50, the DJIA started to fall sharply. In fact, it gapped down below an upward trendline on March 16 (shown as 4 on the graph). As discussed in the previous chapter, this is a very bearish development. Because it was a primary trendline that was broken, it meant that March 7 was a 50-week cycle crest (the top of the next biggest cycle), and prices would now be down until the 50-week cycle bottomed, which was due later that year. By April 4, the DJIA was down to 10,356.70 and stochastics were well below 20% even the week before. But this was too early for a primary cycle trough, because it was only the 11th week, and the primary bottom is normally 13-21 weeks in length. Yet this was a re-test of where the cycle started 11 weeks earlier at 10,368.60 on January 24, so there was support there. The DJIA rallied to 10,557.10 on April 7. It then broke below the double bottom one week later, on April 14. Now an MCP (Mid-Cycle Pause) price target can be calculated for a low, using the high of March 7, the low of April 7, and the high of April 14. The MCP price target was 9923.30 +/- 125.22. It achieved this range on April 18 as stochastics were forming a bullish looping pattern below 20% and a possible bullish oscillator divergence. Two days later, on April 20, it bottomed at 9978.74 with bullish oscillator divergence. On April 22, the K line crossed above 25% and was widening its distance above D, a confirming buy signal (see Figure 38 below, a zoom-in of Figure 37.). That is, the market was now in a time band for a primary cycle trough. It was in a price range for a primary cycle trough, and the stochastics were exhibiting both a bullish looping formation below 25% with the second loop higher than the first - as prices were lower - and a case of bullish oscillator divergence. That's as good as it gets.

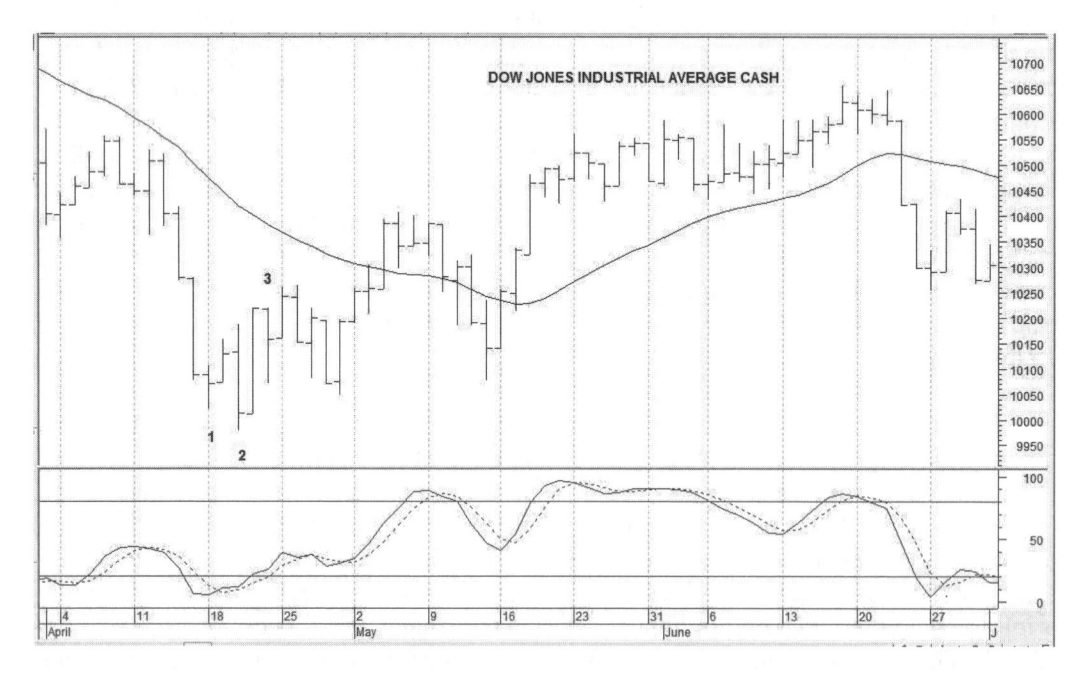

Figure 38. Note that stochastics made a low at 1, on April 18. But two days later, at 2 (April 20), prices dropped to a new intraday low, but stochastics did not make a new low. Two-three days after that, April 22 and 25, the %K line widened its distance above the %D line, as it surpassed the 25% level, thus giving a buy signal.

STOCHASTIC "SELL" PATTERNS

There are two set ups to initially look for here as well. The first occurs when stochastics reach an overbought level (above 80%). The second is when they rally back to the neutral 42-58% range after having been below 20%. In the first case, it is best to see an overbought condition when a primary cycle crest is due, especially if the longer-term cycle is still pointed down (in its later phases). But just because it is overbought - above 80% - doesn't mean that it is time to sell. One must first determine if the time band for a cycle crest is in effect, which itself is not always as easy as identifying a time band when a cycle trough is due. But the matter is helped if a geocosmic critical reversal time band is present and prices are rising into it. Then one must determine if prices have yet attained a calculated price objective range. If these factors are not present, then selling (going short) just because stochastics are above 80% will usually be pre-mature. The market will, in most cases, continue to rally further in price until these factors are also in place.

In the second case, if the market is in the bearish part of its cycle, the trader will want to sell all corrective rallies to the crest of phases (subcycles) within that cycle. For example, if the market is only in the middle two-thirds of a bearish cycle, the trader should be prepared (and willing) to sell any corrective rallies to major and trading cycle crests. In these cases, the 15-day slow stochastics may never rise as high as 80%. But they may rise to the neutral 42-58% in many instances. If that happens in the time band for a trading or major cycle crest and if the market at that time is in the price range for a normal corrective rally to the crest of these subcycles, then one can start to probe the short side of the market. Sometimes these subcycles will not even retrace 38.2-61.8% of their prior move down.

Bearish Looping and Bearish Oscillator Divergence Patterns

When a market is in the time band for its primary cycle crest (and often other types of crests, like a 50-week cycle crest), the stochastics will not only be well above the overbought 80% level, but they will form a bearish looping pattern or display a case of bearish oscillator divergence.

A bearish looping pattern happens when stochastics are over 80%, and the K line begins to cross below the D line. Prior to falling below 71% (a level that has been determined simply by personal observation and has not been formally tested by this author), the K line turns back up and crosses back above D, thus creating the "loop." Now when the K line crosses back below D, the market may turn down. But it is not really a valid bearish looping pattern until K falls below 71% and widens its distance below D. Once that happens, the crest is confirmed. If the market then falls below the neutral 42-58% level, we can assume the market will continue lower until the stochastics fall below 25% and usually even below 20%.

A bearish oscillator divergence pattern is exhibited when there are two or more crests that form close in time to one another. The second (or later) crest is higher in price than the first. But the stochastics are at a lower level than they were at the former (and lower) price high. When prices are higher and stochastics are lower, it is like having fewer people holding up a greater weight. Eventually the weigh is too much, and the object collapses. This condition is known as bearish oscillator divergence and portends an almost imminent decline in prices or at least a pause in the upward trend.

Both of these patterns are very important to recognize when a primary cycle crest is due. It is also important to recognize if one of these patterns is present when a geocosmic critical reversal zone is also in effect and furthermore if prices are trading within a calculated price objective range (or an overlap of several price target ranges) for a crest. When all of these factors are in place, one can start to sell short. The confirmation then comes when the stochastics drop below 71% with K widening its distance below D. It is further confirmed if the stochastics drop below 42%, but by then one needs to start preparing to buy the market as it will soon be under the oversold level of 25%.

The most effective sell pattern of all for stochastics is when it forms a double looping pattern above 80%, and the second stochastic high is also a case of bearish oscillator divergence. That is, the second high is higher in price, but lower in its stochastic reading. If this happens in a geocosmic reversal zone, when a cyclical crest is also due and when the price is within a calculated price objective for a top, then it presents a favorable risk-reward ratio to sell short.

Let us analyze an example that demonstrates these principles. Figure 39 is a weekly chart of the Dow Jones Industrial Average from late 2001 through mid-2005, showing the 4-year cycle trough of October 2002 and its half-cycle trough (22.5-month) in October 2004. The first instance of bearish oscillator divergence is shown at the highs of A-B. On the week of January 11, 2002 (shown as A), the DJIA topped out at 10,300. Stochastics were at 96% for K and 91% for D, so they were overbought. Prices fell and so did stochastics, down to about 60% in February as the primary cycle bottomed. But then the DJIA rallied to a higher high in the next primary cycle, touching 10,673 during the week of March 22, shown as B in the chart. On this second high, the 15-week slow stochastics got to 95% (K) and 89% (D). This was slightly lower than its levels of January 11. Therefore this is a case of bearish oscillator divergence (higher high, but lower stochastics). Three weeks later, the stochastics fell below 71%, with K widening its distance below D, suggesting that at least a 50-week cycle crest had been completed. Prices in fact were headed down into the 4-year cycle trough, not to be realized until October 10, 2002.

The next instance involved a long series of bearish looping patterns starting in mid-2003. Note that the first stochastic high was attained the week of May 16 as K reached 96.32% while D was at 84.04%. There was a temporary high a month later (9th week of June 20), but the stochastics never fell below 71%. They kept finding support around the 80% level and eventually a second stochastics top was realized the week of December 26, 2003, when K reached 97.48% and was above D at 94.64%. About 8 weeks later, during the week of February 20, 2004, the DJIA topped out at 10,753. However, by this time, the weekly stochastics were registering K at 89.37% and slightly above D at 88.15%. They were lower than they were a few weeks earlier, and they were looping. This was a case of bearish looping stochastics above 80% *and* bearish oscillator divergence. Four weeks later, the crest could be confirmed as stochastics fell below 71% with K widening its distance below D. February 22 would mark the crest of the 22.5-month cycle in stocks, the half-cycle crest to the 4-year cycle. The DJIA would continue to fall to its 22.5-month cycle trough in October 2004.

The next instance of a bearish stochastic pattern would occur at E-F in December 2004 and March 2005. This one was at first a bit of a fake out, for after the first high (E) in the week ending December 31, 2004, when stochastics were at 93.86% (K) and 92.70% (D), the market fell for 4 weeks. The stochastics fell below 71% with K widening its distance below D. K at least fell below 71%, declining to 64.75%, while K held at 71.88%. But then it reversed, and over the next five weeks the DJIA soared to a new cycle high the week ending March 11 at 10,984. As it rallied, the stochastics curled back up too. K climbed to a high of 91.79% and was above D at 89.96%. But this was lower than the stochastic readings of December 31 and thus a case of bearish oscillator divergence *and* a case of a bearish looping pattern as well. The very next week, stochastics were in a free fall, declining below 71% with K widening its distance below D. This confirmed that at least a 50-week cycle crest had formed.

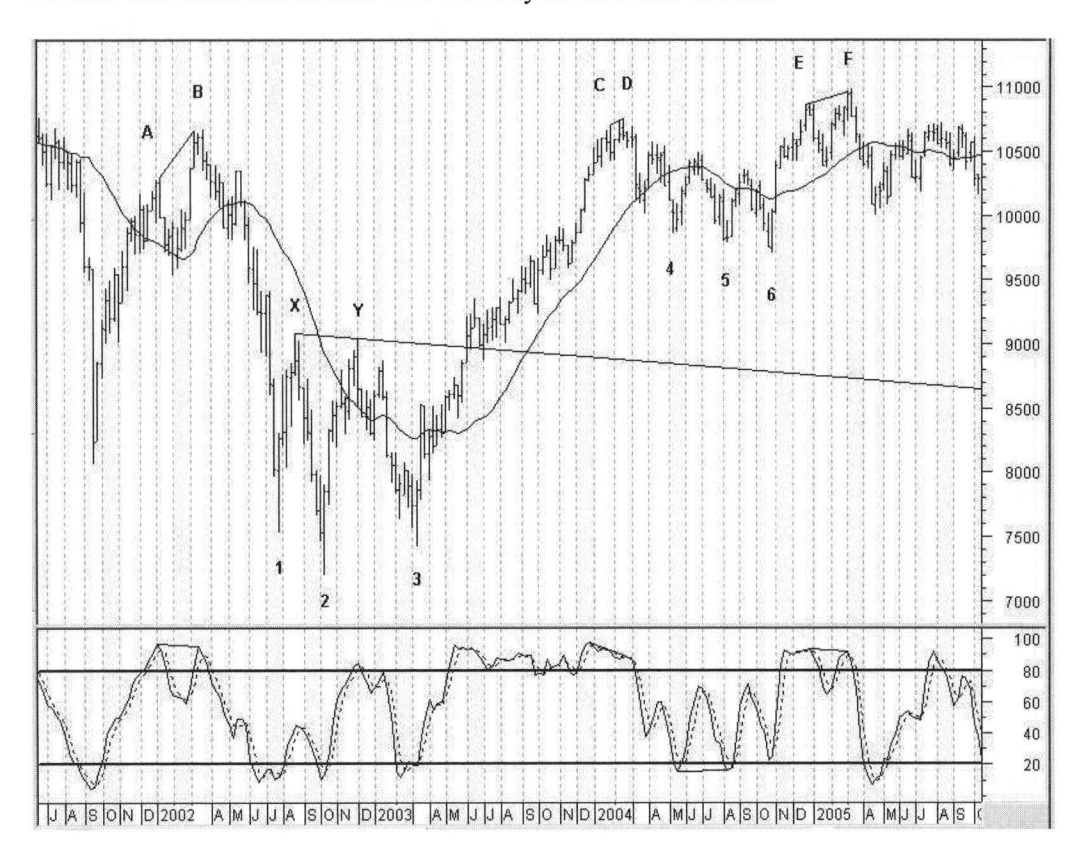

Figure 39: A weekly chart of the Dow Jones Industrial Average, showing several cases of bearish and bullish stochastic patterns, as well as neutral 42-58% corrective retracements.

This chart also illustrates a bearish case of stochastics retracing from an oversold level to the neutral 42-58% area, with prices then falling again. This can be shown in combination with a bullish reverse head and shoulders pattern at 1-2-3. After the cycle crest was achieved at B and under a bearish oscillator divergence sell signal, the DJIA fell to the left shoulder of this bearish pattern, at 7532.66 on July 26, 2002 (1). One can see a bullish looping formation and a bullish oscillator divergence pattern as this low formed at 1. For 4 weeks the market rallied strongly back to 9077 (the week ending August 23, 2002, denoted as X, which would be the start of the neckline). But a look at the stochastics pattern at this time revealed that K was at 44.88%, in the neutral range. It was above D at 38.45%. Additionally, the 9077.10 high at that time was in a normal corrective retracement range of the move down from B (10,673.10) to 1 (7532.66). That price target would have been 9102.88 +/- 370.57, so there was bound to be some resistance there. Nevertheless, this is an example of stochastics only getting back to a neutral 42-58% range in a bear market rally.

But let us continue the analysis, even though the issue of a neutral stochastic reading ending a corrective retracement has been demonstrated. In this chart, other important factors can be observed. After the corrective rally to X, the market then fell to a lower low, the 4-year cycle trough on October 10, 2002 (as Venus turned retrograde, which is one of the most powerful level 1 signatures as reported in the studies of Volume 3 of this series). The DJIA was down to 7197.43 that day (shown as 2 on the chart), thus lower than the 7532.66 low of the week of July 26. This formed the head of the inverse head and shoulders pattern. Yet the weekly stochastics were slightly higher than during the low of July 26, for a case of bullish oscillator divergence. A couple of weeks later the market rallied back to 9043.37, thus completing the second part of the neckline during the week of December 6. The weekly stochastics got slightly above the critical 80% overbought level and immediately turned down from the double top and neckline (X-Y).

At the time, the U.S. military commenced its Iraqi War assault preparations. Stock markets all over the world began to fall as the U.S. issued an ultimatum to Saddam Hussein to give up his non-existent weapons of mass destruction. (It was not known at the time he did not have any. The issue became a point of intense political tensions). Nevertheless, many stock markets of the world fell to new 4-year cycle lows in March 2003, whereas the DJIA did not make a new low. It fell to 7416.64 on March 12, which was above the low of October 10 and completed the right shoulder of the reverse head and shoulders pattern. This is shown as 3 in the chart of Figure 39. Notice at this low how the weekly chart again displays a case of bullish looping stochastics and bullish oscillator divergence. The market is turning bullish as K rises above D just one week later, and widens its distance above D.

The bottom was then confirmed further when the DJIA closed above the neckline X-Y during the week of June 6. An upside price objective could then be established. The neckline was at 9061.34 on the day the head formed, October 10, 2002. If we take the distance between that and the actual low (9061.34 - 7197.49 = 1863.85) and add it to the breakout of the neckline, we get an initial upside price target of 9061.34 + 1863.85 = 10,925.19, +/- 439.86. The high that followed, shown on this graph as F, was 10.984.50 during the week of March 11, 2005. That high would hold until January 2006. It also represented at least a 50-week cycle crest (and possibly a 4-year cycle crest), until the DJIA fell to its 50-week cycle trough (and possibly a 4-year cycle trough, depending on how one starts the count) in October 2005. Therefore Figure 39 is an excellent chart to study in regards to many of the technical studies and price objective theories introduced in this book.

SUMMARY

Stochastics may not be a study used for obtaining potential price objective targets, which is the primary purpose of this book. But they are important to study when they exhibit certain patterns within previously calculated price objective ranges and time bands for cyclical troughs and crests. In other words, when time and price objectives are being realized, it is important to also recognize if a stochastic pattern signaling a possible reversal is occurring too. If so, then the probability of an excellent risk-reward situation is presented.

Of most importance to buyers is the recognition of bullish looping patterns below 20% and/or bullish oscillator divergence patterns in which prices fall to a lower low than witnessed just a few days or weeks before, but stochastics do not make a lower low. Shortly after, stochastics rise above 20 and even 25%, with K widening its distance above D. Buyers can also take note when stochastics drop back to 42-58% after being above 80%. This is a neutral area, but can indicate a corrective decline is about to end a phase of the greater cycle, which is still bullish.

To sellers, it is important to recognize bearish looping patterns above 80% and bearish oscillator divergence setups in which prices rise to a higher high than witnessed just a few days or weeks before, but stochastics not reaching a higher level than at the previous high. Shortly after, stochastics decline below 80% and even 71%, with K widening its distance below D. Sellers can also take note when stochastics rally back to 42-58% after first being below 20%. This is a neutral area, but can indicate a corrective rally is about to end a phase of the greater cycle, which is still bearish.

There are many other stochastics parameters that can be applied than discussed here. And there are hundreds of other oscillators that can be used in combination with the market timing indicators and price objective calculations given in this chapter. Two others that I would highly recommend studying are the Commodity Channel Indicator (CCI), using a standard calculation of 18 days or time frames, and an RSI (Relative Strength Indicator). In my own trading, I might use both of these. But my favored one for stock indices is the 15-bar slow stochastics and the patterns formed as described herein - especially when cycles and geocosmics point to a time frame for a reversal. If a market is not in such a time frame for a reversal, I do not pay a great deal of attention to these technical studies, for they can give false buy and sell signals when the time for a reversal or cycle culmination is not yet ready.

References:

1. Lane, George, *Using Stochastics, Cycles, and RSI*, Watseka, IL., Investment Educators, 1986.
2. Lane, George, from lecture entitled, "Getting Started with Stochastics," 1998, confirmed in conversation with Caire Lane of Investment Educators.

CHAPTER TWELVE

INTERMARKET BULLISH AND BEARISH DIVERGENCE

Markets behave in strange ways. One of the more unusual patterns that can occur is when one stock index makes a new multi-week, multi-month, or multi-year low or high, while other indices in the same region (or sector) do not. Market analysts are divided over what this means. In some cases, it indicates the first market to exhibit the new high or low is simply the leader, and others will follow shortly afterwards. But in many cases that is not the case, especially when primary or greater cycles are unfolding. And it doesn't matter if the interval between these new lows or highs lasts weeks, months, or even several years.

In this chapter we will study this phenomenon, which is known as "intermarket bullish or bearish divergence." We then use it as an indicator - not so much to predict prices - but rather to recognize that an important trough or crest is forming, what to do about it, and what risks are involved in taking action as a result.

For our purposes, intermarket divergence refers to stock indices in the same region of the world (Europe, Asia, United States, etc.) as well as cash versus futures indices. For instance, intermarket divergence can be noted when either the Dow Jones Industrial Average, S&P, or NASDAQ Composite indices make a new high or low - but not all three at once. It can be noted when the cash or futures index of one makes a new high or low, but not both (such as cash S&P versus S&P futures or even cash DJIA versus S&P futures). In Europe, there may be times when the German DAX makes a new high or low, but the Swiss SMI, Netherland's AEX, or London FTSE indices do not. In Asia, the Japanese Nikkei may make a new high or low, but the Japanese Topix (TPX) does not. The same can be true between the Hang Seng stock index of Hong Kong and the Shanghai (SSE) Stock index of China. When this happens, it either means the others will soon follow or else they won't. When others do not follow, the market reverses and this becomes a reversal indicator. But it is only valid at certain times, such as when a cycle low or high is due. When a cycle high or low is not due, it usually means the others will soon follow and make new cycle highs or lows.

INTERMARKET BULLISH DIVERGENCE

When a primary or greater cycle trough is due, the market will often exhibit a double bottom. In Volume 1 of this Stock Market Timing series, studies showed that in 66.2% of cases dating from 1982 through 2005, a double bottom pattern formed from a time band 8 weeks before through 6 weeks after a primary cycle trough in the cash DJIA.

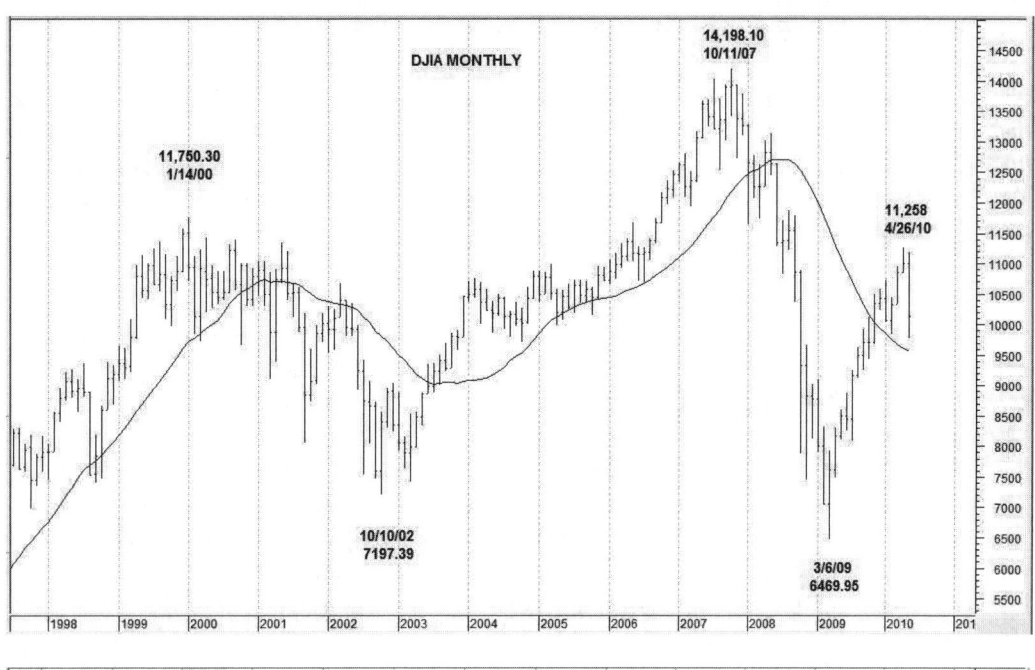

Figure 40: Note the bullish divergence at the lows in 2002 and 2009. The low in March 2009 was lower in the DJIA than the low in October 2002. It was not lower in the NASDAQ Composite. There was also a bearish intermarket divergence at the highs in 2000 and 2007. The DJIA made a new all-time high in October 2007, taking out its high in early 2000, but the NASDAQ Composite did not.

In about 70% of those instances (or about 45% in all instances), it was also a case of intermarket bullish divergence to the S&P futures. If the NASDAQ cash or futures were included, the rate of incidents would have been higher. That is, at the time of a double bottom to a primary cycle trough, there were many cases where not all three of these indices made a low during the same week (it is most effective when intermarket divergence between markets does not occur during the same week - at least one week apart is more valid). For some, the low was on the first leg of the double bottom, and for others it occurred on the second leg down. Sometimes the second low is not actually a double bottom. It may be too high or too low in price compared to the first low. However, of most importance are those times when one of the legs occurs when the time band for the primary cycle trough is in effect AND a geocosmic critical reversal date time band is also in effect. To be most valid, the market must then close in the upper third of a day's (or week's) range before both take out those lows.

Although the use of intermarket bullish divergence is most valuable during the completion of primary cycles, they are often noted during the completion of longer-term cycles too. Therefore, they can be used by long-term investors as well as position traders, providing that other factors are in place for the culmination of those cycles as described elsewhere in this book and other volumes in this series. For example, consider the two possible 18-year cycle troughs of October 10, 2002 and March 6, 2009 (see Figure 40). These were double bottom formations in the cash NASDAQ Composite, in which the first leg in October 2002 was lower than the second in March 2009. In the Dow Jones cash market, the low in March 2009 (second leg) was considerably lower than its first low in October 2002. In both cases, geocosmic critical reversal dates were in effect. However, that is not so important to a long-term investor. What is more important is 1) the NASDAQ fell nearly 80% from its high in March 2000 to its low in October 2002, qualifying it as a long-term cycle trough, and 2) it did not take out that low in March 2009, whereas the DJIA did, falling more than 50% from its all-time high of October 2007 (the largest decline since the Great Depression), thus forming a case of intermarket bullish divergence. That is one of the reasons that made the low in March 2009 an excellent time for an investor to buy.

As stated previously, cases of intermarket bullish divergence are most useful during primary cycle troughs. To have the DJIA, S&P, or NASDAQ Composite make a low in that time band (but not all three making a new low below a previous and recent low), is the set up that has to unfold. It is important that one or both of these lows occurs within the time band for a primary cycle trough. It is more effective when one, or both lows, happens during a geocosmic critical reversal date time band. And it is even more effective if the market(s) making the lower low do so with a bullish stochastic pattern. Figure 41 shows an example of this ideal set up in the U.S. stock markets.

In this example, the stock market was falling sharply following the all-time high on October 11, 2007. The threat to banks around the world, related to the sub-prime mortgage fiasco in the USA, spread to Europe in January 2008. It was the first wave of the crisis after the all-time highs had been realized. The Dow Jones Industrial Average bottomed at 11,634.80 on January 22, 2008. The S&P bottomed a day later, at 1270.05. Both markets then rallied strongly as the Federal Reserve Board hastened to add liquidity to the financial system and lowered interest rates dramatically to 0-.25% for member banks. That only worked for a little while. By the end of February, another wave down started. It would take the S&P cash to 1256.98 on March 17, a lower low than realized in January. However, the DJIA did not fall quite as hard. It formed a secondary bottom on March 10 at 11,731.60, clearly a double bottom to the low of January 22, but this second leg was higher, for a case of intermarket bullish divergence between the two indices.

Figure 41: Note the case of intermarket divergence between the cash DJIA and cash S&P at 1 and 2. The DJIA made its primary cycle trough on January 22, 2008 as both markets formed a bullish looping stochastic pattern (but the second stochastic low was lower than the first in both cases, which suggested another decline would likely happen soon). On March 10 and 17, both markets made a double bottom, but in the case of the S&P, the second low (2) was lower than the first (1). This makes it a case of intermarket bullish divergence. Furthermore, the March 10-17 period was a three-star geocosmic critical reversal zone and a case of bullish oscillator divergence in the S&P, which made this an excellent buy signal.

In this example, the March 17 low in the S&P provided two cases of intermarket bullish divergence to the DJIA. First, it was lower than the low of March 10, whereas that was not the case in the DJIA, and they were at least one week apart. Secondly, the low of March 17 in the S&P took out its low of January 23, whereas the DJIA did not, which is yet another - and stronger - case of intermarket bullish divergence between these two markets. Additionally, March 17 was within the time frame of a geocosmic three-star critical reversal date for U.S. stocks, AND the stochastic pattern in the S&P exhibited a classical case of bullish oscillator divergence. You can see that both markets then rallied for several weeks, reaching a primary cycle crest on May 19. At that time, the DJIA especially exhibited a very strong bearish oscillator divergence stochastic pattern, leading to the next wave down in the financial and banking crisis of 2008.

INTERMARKET BEARISH DIVERGENCE

According to the studies presented in Volume 1 of this series, there were 44 cases out of a possible 67 instances, when a primary cycle crest was accompanied by a double top from 1982 through 2005. In 39 of those cases, the double top was between six weeks before through six weeks after the primary cycle crest. This study furthermore determined, "Intermarket bearish divergence also occurred frequently at primary cycle crests - in fact, more frequently than at primary cycle troughs. In 39 of 67 instances of primary cycle crests (58.2%) the S&P futures topped out slightly before or slightly after the Dow Jones Industrial Average. In the majority of cases, the two tops were five or fewer weeks apart from one another.

An intermarket bearish divergence occurs when the DJIA or S&P cash or futures (or even the NASDAQ Composite cash or futures) makes a new high unaccompanied by one of the other indices. The pattern is validated when each of the markets then closes in the lower third of a day's (or week's, or month's) range before all make new highs. If this happens in a time band for a primary (or greater) cycle crest, it often marks the culmination of the cycle crest. This is further supported if the high of either one of these indices (and best if both) occurs within three trading days of a geocosmic critical reversal date, as outlined in Volume 3 of this series. When this set up unfolds, it is usually a strong signal to sell, as a significant decline to a primary or greater cycle low is vulnerable to commencing.

As in the case of intermarket bullish divergence, cases of intermarket bearish divergence can also be noted in cycles longer than primary cycles. If you look at the monthly charts of the DJIA and NASDAQ Composite shown in Figure 40, you will see two cases of intermarket bearish divergence. In the first case, the DJIA made a long-term cycle crest (perhaps an 18-year cycle crest) on January 14, 2000. But on March 10, 2000, the NASDAQ made a higher all-time high, and the DJIA failed to do the same. This was a case of intermarket bearish divergence and led to both indices falling hard to their 6- or even 18-year cycle lows of October 10, 2002. But an even greater case of intermarket bearish divergence was realized on October 11, 2007 when the DJIA made its new all-time high, but the NASDAQ Composite was well off its high from March 2000. This case of intermarket bearish divergence led to an even greater decline in the DJIA into March 2009 (but the Composite did not make a greater decline then).

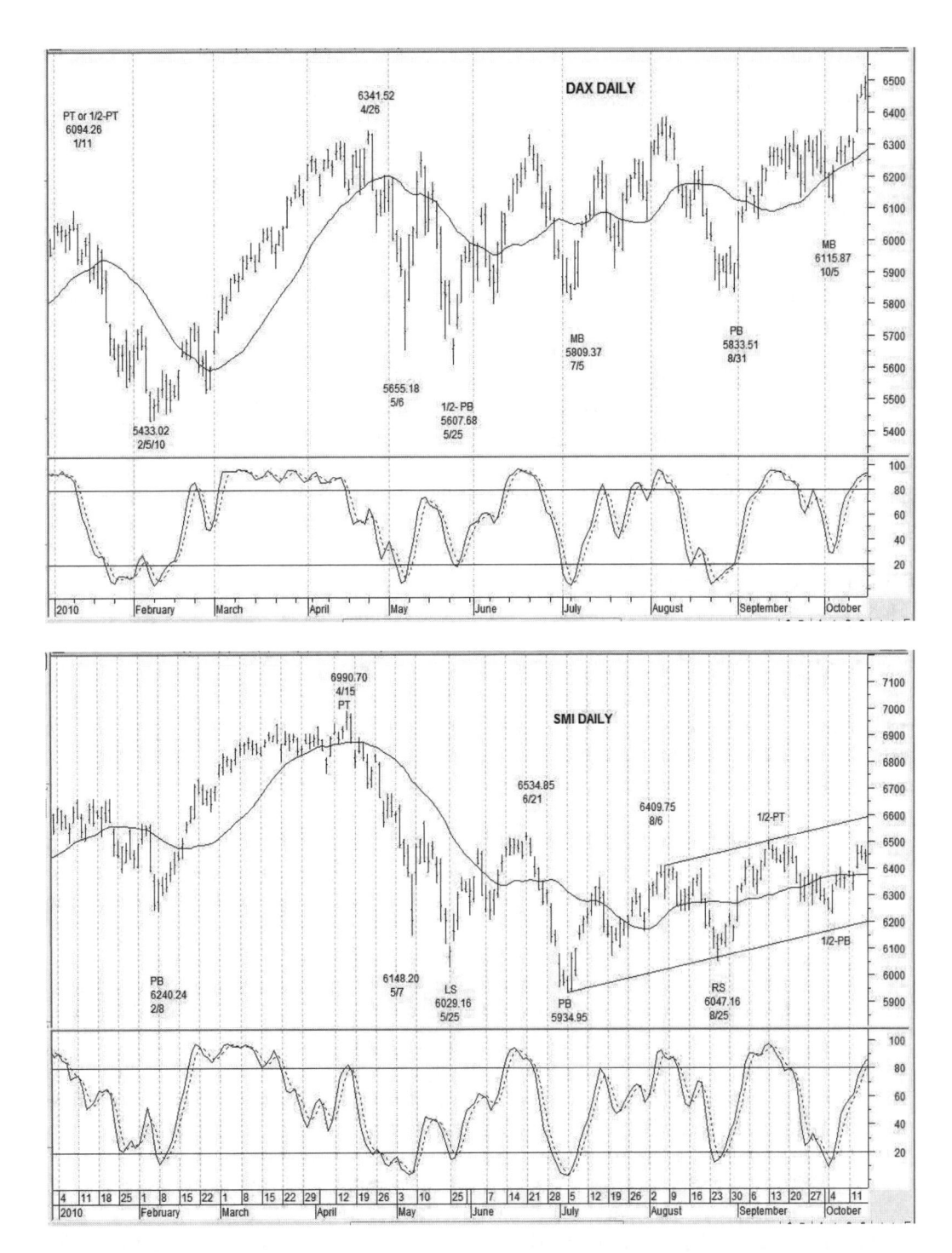

Figure 42: Illustrating intermarket bearish divergence in the same region. The German DAX and Swiss SMI stock indices both made new yearly highs on April 15, 2010. On April 26, the DAX made a higher high, but the SMI did not. By the next day, both closed in the lower third of the day's range, thus creating a valid case of intermarket bearish divergence. Note that the DAX also exhibited bearish oscillator divergence at the high on April 26 (as well as bullish oscillator divergence on the low of May 25 in both indices). Both also exhibited a bullish island reversal at the low on May 25.

Yet, the concept of intermarket bearish and bullish divergence is more useful to position traders than to longer-term investors, for by the time the set up is realized in a long-term chart, the opportunity to take advantage of this pattern has already largely passed. In the case of primary cycles accompanied by supporting geocosmic signatures of a reversal (critical reversal zone), a favorable risk-reward trading opportunity can be taken advantage of in a fairly timely manner. Let us look at a case of this as shown in Figure 42.

On April 15, 2010, both the German DAX and Swiss SMI stock indices made a new yearly high. They are in the same region (Central Europe), so these are two markets that track fairly close to one another. After a slight decline, the DAX soared to a higher high on April 26 (as did most world stock indices on this date, as Saturn was in exact opposition to Uranus). But the SMI was well off its high of April 15. Additionally, as the DAX made a new high, it was under much lower stochastic readings, creating a case of bearish oscillator divergence. April 26 was also within three trading days of a three-star geocosmic critical reversal date (April 22) and late enough in the cycle where a primary cycle crest could occur. The next day, both indices closed in the lower third of the day's range, thus validating this as a case of intermarket bearish divergence. Both markets then fell hard into May 6, finally finding their cycle troughs on May 25 (in the case of the DAX) and July 5 (in the case of SMI) for a new case of bullish oscillator divergence.

SUMMARY

Intermarket bullish or bearish divergence patterns represent favorable opportunities to trade if certain conditions are met. The following is a list of some of the factors that strengthen (or weaken) the argument for a case of intermarket divergences.

1. There should be at least one week between the two highs or lows that make up the intermarket divergence pattern. The highs or lows should not occur in the same week. However, it is OK if one occurs on a Friday and the other on the following Monday.
2. The market should be in a time band when a primary cycle trough or crest is due.
3. The market should be in a time band when one of the lows or highs occurs during which a geocosmic critical reversal date is also in effect, +/- 3 trading days. Sometimes it can expand to as many as five trading days.
4. If it is a case of intermarket bullish divergence, then both markets need to close in the top third of a day's trading range that day or very soon afterwards (before the lows are taken out), which would then be bearish and negate the signal.
   - Oftentimes this will be a case of a double bottom.
   - Oftentimes this will be a case of bullish oscillator divergence on the second bottom with the market that makes the lower low.
5. In the case of intermarket bearish divergence, both markets need to close in the lower third of a day's trading range that day or very soon afterwards (before the highs are taken out), which would then be bullish and negate the signal.
   - Oftentimes this will be a case of a double top.
   - Oftentimes this will be a case of bearish oscillator divergence on the second crest with the market that makes the higher high.

CHAPTER THIRTEEN

THE MOVING AVERAGE AS A TREND INDICATOR AND CONFIRMATION SIGNAL

Not all technical studies involve complex mathematical calculations. The previous chapters outlined several techniques used to calculate price targets, which are necessary to provide an idea of when to buy or sell in the future. Like cycles and geocosmic studies, these calculated price targets are akin to "leading indicators," because they address the future of the market. Several technical studies and chart patterns were also discussed, like stochastics and intermarket bullish or bearish divergence signals. These are known as "coincident indicators" because they frequently coincide with important highs or lows from which reversals occur, especially when they unfold in the time and price target zones of a reversal indicated by market timing and price objective studies.

But in many cases, a cycle doesn't end when a market timing signal is in effect, or a pre-calculated price objective is attained, even if coincident technical studies of a reversal are also present. Instead of reversing at that point, the market may simply pause and go sideways. Sometimes it even "breaks out" and accelerates in the direction of the trend already in force. In other words, it doesn't reverse as these signals suggested. This is where the use of other technical studies known as "lagging" or "confirming" indicators can be very valuable. They identify certain price areas that must be attained *after* the reversal has taken place to affirm that a cycle high or low has indeed culminated. Until prices decline (or rally) to these pre-determined price levels, the cycle high or low cannot be confirmed. The purpose of this chapter, then, is to understand these "confirming" indictors, and to establish price levels that need to be met before one can assume that the cycle did culminate, as the leading and coincident indicators suggested. Furthermore, these confirming indicators may also act as "triggers." That is, they can provide the trader with minimum price targets that will likely be met once a reversal has indeed taken place, even without exhibiting the necessary "confirming" criteria.

Simple Moving Averages

One of the most useful of the "confirming" or "lagging" indicators is the simple moving average. If a particular moving average relevant to a particular cycle is touched or broken after a cycle has culminated, then it "indicates" that cycle's completion. If it closes two consecutive time periods below or above this moving average, it "confirms" that the cycle crest or trough has been completed. This is not a 100% reliable indicator, but it is valid often enough that it can be a valuable tool for market analysis, especially when used in combination with cycle time bands and other technical studies.

According to Investopedia.com, *"A simple, or arithmetic, moving average, is calculated by adding the closing price of the security for a number of time periods and then dividing this total by the number of time periods."* But the question for analysts and traders is: what moving average is most useful to use? Here we have the same situation as discussed between long-term investors and short-term traders regarding theory and practice. That is, there is a *theory* as to which moving averages should work best, and then there is the *actual practice* of which works best. The *theory* in regards to optimal moving averages to use with cycle analysis is this: *A moving average that is half the length of the mean cycle is most optimal.* The reality in practice is that moving averages other than *half the length of the mean cycle* are sometimes more useful indicators as to how a market behaves, especially during a trend run. Not always, but sometimes.

Another distinction that is important to note is the difference between the moving average as an "indication" that a market cycle has topped or bottomed, versus the moving average as a "confirmation" of a cycle completion. The difference is this: once a market cycle has been completed, it will generally return to at least "touch" the relevant moving average associated with that cycle. This is an "indication" that the cycle has topped out or bottomed. But it is not a confirmation. It is only a minimum requirement of a cycle completion. A "confirmation," on the other hand, occurs when the market has two consecutive closes back above (in the case of confirming a trough) or below (in the case of confirming a cycle crest) this moving average. Thus, once a market returns to its appropriate moving average, we have to consider that the recent cycle top or bottom is in. Once a market exhibits two consecutive closes beyond this moving average, we can be more certain, for that is considered the confirmation of the cycle completion, and the move to its next trough or crest is well underway. This will be demonstrated shortly.

In the effort to identify the moving average(s) that best meets what one needs for accurate analysis, an analyst or trader is advised to consider the following points: *When a cycle low is due, the price is usually below this moving average (but not always, as in the case of the early phase of a strong bull market cycle). Once you enter the time band for the cycle low and prices are below this moving average, then that cycle trough will be confirmed when prices close back above this moving average. Ideally the price will close above this moving average on at least two consecutive days (or weeks or months). Sometimes it may require three consecutive closes back above it to confirm.*

When a cycle crest is due, the price is usually above this moving average (but not always, as in the case of a strong bear market cycle). Once you enter the time band for the cycle crest and prices are above it, then that cycle crest will be confirmed when prices close back below this moving average. Ideally that will happen on at least two consecutive closes (daily, weekly, or monthly, depending on which type of chart is being analyzed). Sometimes it may require three consecutive closes back below it to confirm.

Theoretical Versus Form Fitting

What moving average should be used? Which are most useful? The theoretical rule is this: use a moving average that is half the mean length of the cycle you are trying to identify. For example, if you want to identify the completion of a major 6-week cycle in stocks, then use a 15-day moving average. That is, there are 30 market days in 6 weeks (5 market days/week times 6 = 30 days). Of course there are exceptions when holidays take place. The theoretically correct moving average to use to measure the 6-week cycle, then, is 15 days (one-half of 30 market days in 6 weeks). If an 18-week cycle is being studied, then the correct theoretical moving average to use is 45 days. That is, in 18 weeks there are 90 market days. One-half of 90 days is 45 days.

But sometimes other moving averages are valuable for determining support, resistance, or minimal price objectives to a reversal of a trend. They may not be the same as the theoretically correct moving average to use based upon cycles. These moving averages are based upon "form fitting." That is, one may find a moving average that consistently stops all rallies or declines based on personal studies. This moving average seems to "fit the form" of that market's movements, so it is a "form fitting" moving average. For instance, in many stock markets, a 25-day moving average has been used to identify support and resistance consistently. But unless there is a consistent 10-week cycle phase to that market, it is not the theoretically "ideal" moving average to use.

In actual practice, one will often find that the moving average of half a cycle's length is the best 'form fit' to that market. Therefore, the theoretical moving average and the ideal "form fitted" moving average are often the same or very close to one another.

Long-Term Cycles and Moving Averages

Moving averages are most useful when a market is first in a time band for a particular cycle trough (or crest). In the case of a cycle trough, we want to see the actual price *at least touching (*and preferably *below*) a moving average that is associated with that particular cycle. In the case of a cycle crest, we want to see the actual price *at least touching* (and preferably *above*) a moving average that is associated with that particular cycle. As stated before, this criterion for a cycle trough or crest does not work 100% of the time. But it happens often enough that it can be considered a reliable indicator of a minimum price move that a market will make as it heads to its cycle trough or crest. Breaking above this moving average on two consecutive closes also serves as a confirming indicator that the cycle associated with it has indeed bottomed. As it breaks below this moving average in two consecutive time periods, it serves as a confirming indicator that a cycle crest associated with that average has topped out.

To illustrate these points, let's address two long-term cycles (cycles longer than the primary cycle). For this exercise, we will examine the 4-year and 50-week cycles in the Dow Jones Industrial Average.

We will start with the 4-year cycle in U.S. stocks, via the DJIA. As discussed in an earlier chapter, the 4-year cycle in the Dow Jones Industrial Average is actually a 46-month mean cycle. That is, in over 80% of cases examined, the range of this cycle has historically lasted 36-56 months (trough to trough). The midway point between the extremes of this 80% range is thus 46 months with an orb of 10 months either side. Theoretically, then, the appropriate moving average to use in order to determine 1) the completion of this cycle's high or low, as well as 2) the minimum price target for the next high or low, is one-half of the mean's cycle length, or 23 months. In the case of the 4-

year cycle trough, we expect to see the DJIA trading below this moving average *after the 36th month* (unless it contracts to 32-35 months, which is rare). In the case of the crest of a 4-year cycle, we expect to see the DJIA trading above this moving average at least 5 months after the trough has been realized (and ideally, much longer than 5 months afterwards). Furthermore, once the 4-year cycle trough or crest has been realized, we then anticipate that the reversal will find prices rising or falling to at least this moving average in the future. It becomes a minimum price target for the new trend.

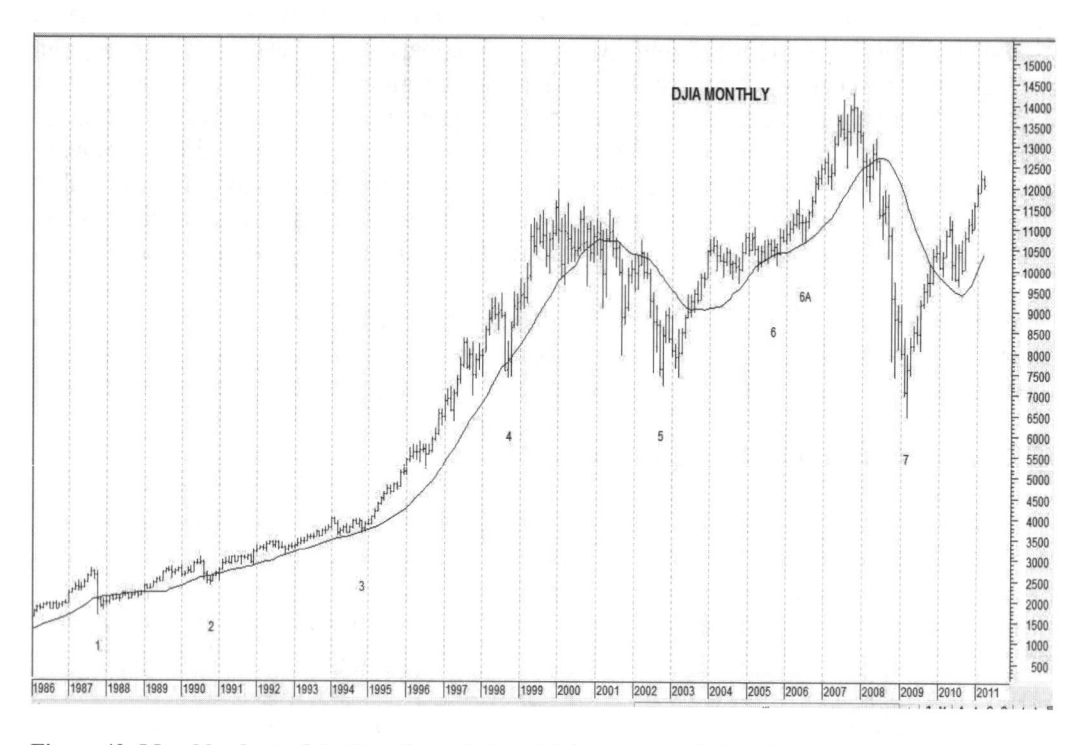

Figure 43: Monthly chart of the Dow Jones Industrial Average, depicting the 4-year cycle troughs (1-7) and the 23-month simple moving average.

Let us look at the long-term monthly chart of the DJIA, as shown in Figure 43, and see how this has worked out between 1987 and 2010. We will begin with the 18-year cycle trough of October 1987. Notice how the DJIA was above the 23-month moving average prior to October 1987 after attaining an all-time high just two months before. From its high in late August 1987, the DJIA plummeted 40% to its 4-year (and greater) cycle low just two months later, on October 20, 1987. Such a short decline into a 4-year cycle trough is very unusual. As one can see from Table 3 (page 32), that was one of the shortest declines ever for a 4-year cycle trough. But prices broke below the 23-month moving average, which is one of this signal's criteria for confirming that the crest of the 4-year cycle had been attained. Two consecutive closes below this average is a stronger criterion for confirmation. It meant that prices were headed into the 4-year cycle trough. That happened the next month, November 1987, even though the low was not lower in price than October. That trough of October 1987 would nonetheless be confirmed when the DJIA had two consecutive monthly closes back above the 23-month moving average, assuming that happened at least 5 months past the low.

The DJIA had its first monthly close above the 23-month moving average in June 1988, eight months after the low. Therefore June 1988 was an initial signal that the 4-year cycle trough occurred in October 1987. But by the next month, it was back below it again, so it wasn't a confirmation. It did, however, serve as initial resistance, and a minimum price target following the 4-year cycle trough. Finally in January and February 1989, it closed two consecutive months above this average, thereby fulfilling the moving average criterion that the 4-year cycle had bottomed in October 1987. Now prices would head to the crest of the new 4-year cycle.

We can establish a minimum price range for this crest based on the history of prior 4-year cycles, as discussed in Chapter 4. *In over 80% of cases studied, the minimum price appreciation between the 4-year cycle trough and the crest of the next 4-year cycle was at least 50%.* The 4-year cycle low in October 1987 was at 1616. Therefore the minimum price target for the crest of the new 4-year cycle would be 2424. That is, once the DJIA exceeds the 23-month moving average in two consecutive months, we would look for prices to continue higher (to at least 2424) before the new 4-year cycle crest was attained. In February 1989, the 23-month moving average was 2179. The close that month was 2258. There was still room and time for the DJIA to rise further, before it closed two consecutive months below this moving average and thus confirmed the crest.

In fact, the DJIA continued higher into July 1990, when it finally topped out at 3024, an appreciation of 87%. This was in the normal range of historical appreciation. The crest would be *confirmed* when prices closed below the 23-month moving average in two consecutive months. But even touching this moving average would be an *indication* that the crest might already be completed. The first close below this moving average following the high of July 1990 occurred in September 1990. This was the first *indication* that the crest had been attained. The close of October 1990 was the second consecutive month below this moving average, thus *confirming* that the 4-year cycle crest was in.

The DJIA was now headed to the 4-year cycle trough. The next challenge would be to confirm that the 4-year cycle had bottomed. We know from previous chapters that 4-year cycles will bottom in 36-56 month intervals in over 80% of cases studied. Measured from the start of the 4-year cycle in October 1987, the next trough of this cycle would be due October 1990-June 1992. *We also know that in over 80% of the cases studied, the decline would be at least 20% off of the highs of that cycle.* The crest of this particular 4-year cycle in July 1990 was at 3024. During the time band in which this cycle was due (October 1990-June 1992), our minimal price target for the 4-year cycle trough therefore would be at least 2419 (20% loss from the high). That level was reached in September 1990. Thus, by October 1990, as prices fell lower, the DJIA had already fulfilled the minimum time and price objectives for the trough of this 4-year cycle.

The next step was to confirm the October 1990 low as the 4-year cycle trough. With the use of the 23-month moving average, this confirmation signal would occur once 1) the market was at least 5 months past the low and 2) it completed two consecutive monthly closes above the 23-month moving average. The reader should understand that this confirmation becomes invalidated if at any time the market declines back below the start of the cycle during the time band in which the cycle low could still be unfolding, or if it falls lower during the 36-56 month interval when the 4-year cycle trough is due. That is a scenario not likely to happen, but it must always be understood as a possibility.

In our continuing example, it didn't take long for the DJIA to close two consecutive months above this moving average. It did so in December 1990 and January 1991. In March 1991 (the fifth month following the low), it was still closing above the 23-month moving average, so the 4-year cycle trough could now be confirmed with the low in October 1990 at 2344. It was more than 20% off the prior high (actually a decline of 22.5%), and it was in the time band for the 4-year cycle trough (October 1990-June 1992), and there were at least two consecutive monthly closes back above the 23-month moving average after the 5th month following the low. Therefore October 1990 was confirmed as the 4-year cycle trough. The next step, then, was to confirm the crest of the new 4-year cycle.

Once again, the two minimum criteria are that prices 1) test the 23-month moving average after the fifth month, and 2) appreciate at least 50% off of the cycle low. Keep in mind that there are exceptions to this latter rule, but it has been the case in over 80% of historical instances studied between 1893 and 2009 and these forecasts (and rules) are based on historical rates of frequency like these. Since the market bottomed at 2344 (a 50% appreciation), it means that the minimum price objective for the crest of the new 4-year cycle would be 3516. This would represent another new all-time high for the DJIA. It didn't take long for the DJIA to close back above the 23-month moving average. It did it in December 1990, just two months later. But our 50% appreciation level was not attained until May 1993. The setup then began to confirm the crest of the 4-year cycle. That is, we waited for two consecutive months of closing below the 23-month moving average to confirm that the crest was in and a decline of at least 20% was attained. This instance would not fulfill these particular criteria. But it would fulfill some of the other minimum criteria for a 4-year cycle crest, such as touching the 23-month average.

First of all, note that the high of this new 4-year cycle occurred in January 1994 at 4002. This was a 70.7% increase in prices off of the 2344 low of October 1990, so it fulfilled the minimum price target for a 4-year cycle crest (50% appreciation). Three months after the high, in April 1990, the DJIA declined to the area of the 23-month moving average. It did not close below it, which would have been a stronger signal that the top was in if it happened over two consecutive months. Nor did this decline represent a 20+% depreciation of prices off the high of that cycle. But this brings up a very important point about moving averages, and in particular between *confirming* criteria and *minimum* criteria for establishing the culmination of a cycle. Even though the *confirmation* requires two consecutive closes below the moving average to confirm a cycle crest, that doesn't always happen. The *minimum criterion* is simply that the price touches (or comes very close to) the moving average. In other words, a 4-year cycle crest may never be followed by two consecutive closes below the 23-month moving average (which would be the confirming signal). But prices might only touch (or come very close to touching) this moving average when the low of that cycle actually unfolds. That was the case this time, and that is why the moving average would also serve as a minimum price criterion for a cycle trough (or crest).

In April 1994, the DJIA dropped to 3520. The 23-month moving average was 3506. It was close, but it did not close the month below this important moving average. Therefore, we conclude only that it *might be* the 4-year cycle trough, and *it might mean* the crest of the 4-year cycle was in, because the minimum criterion was achieved (test of the moving average). But this low could not be *confirmed* as the 4-year cycle trough since there were not two consecutive closes below this moving average.

In November 1994, the DJIA traded below the 23-month moving average, which was a stronger signal than that of April 1994. But once again it didn't close below this average, so it wasn't confirmed. In December 1994 (second consecutive month), it again traded below this moving average, but again it didn't close below. So once more the DJIA yielded a signal that the 4-year cycle might have topped out in January 1994, and bottomed in April or November 1994, but still no confirmation.

Unfortunately, the confirmation of both the 4-year cycle crest and trough did not come about until 1) prices exceeded the crest of January 1994, and 2) after it passed beyond the time band for a 4-year cycle trough (the 56th month) without lower prices unfolding below the 23-month moving average. That is, we were not able to *confirm* the 4-year cycle crest at 4002 in January 1994, or its trough in April 1994 or November 1994 at 3520 and 3612 respectively, until February 1995, when the monthly close was above 4002. In fact, these cycles could not be confirmed until after the 56th month (or June 1995), when the market exited the normal time band for the 4-year cycle trough without making a lower low and without ever closing below the 23-month moving average. Thus, the important point to note here is that 1) the market did touch (or came close to touching) the 23-month moving average as the 4-year cycle bottomed, and 2) it happened within the normal 36-56 month time band for a 4-year cycle trough (October 1993-June 1995). That is, the minimum criteria and the confirming criteria are different. In this case, the minimum criteria for a 4-year cycle crest and trough were met, but the confirming criteria were not met until after the time band elapsed for the 4-year cycle.

In the next 4-year cycle, the confirming indicators were once again achieved for a 4-year cycle trough and crest. The DJIA continued soaring to new record highs after the 56th month and never (during that time band) went back to the 23-month moving average. From a double bottom low of 3520 in April 1994 and 3612 in November 1994, the DJIA exploded to its 4-year cycle crest of 9412 in July 1998. This represented an appreciation of over 160%, well above the minimum standard of 50%. This crest was then almost confirmed when the DJIA closed below the 23-month moving average in August 1998. It went lower in September 1998, down to 7379, for a loss of 21.6% off the high of July 1998. This satisfied the 20% loss of value criterion for a 4-year cycle trough. Even though prices then rallied to close the month back above the 23-month moving average, they then fell again into October 8, 1998 to 7399 for a double bottom. Consequently, the DJIA never fulfilled the criterion of two successive monthly closes below the 23-month moving average, but it satisfied the other minimum criteria for this to be the 4-year cycle trough. It was off by over 20% from the high. It occurred exactly in the 46th month of the cycle, and prices at least touched the 23-month moving average and even closed below it once while trading below it for three successive months. By January 1999, the DJIA was making new all-time highs, well above the 9412 high of July 1998, thus confirming that the 4-year bottom was in with the 7379 low of September 1, 1998.

The next 4-year cycle low would thus be due 36-56 months later, or September 2001-May 2003. But prior to that, the crest would occur. We knew that this crest would likely be at least 50% higher than the low of 7379 that started the cycle, or 11,068 (80+% probability). A look at the monthly chart in Figure 43 shows that this cycle topped out with another new all-time high of 11,908 on January 14, 2000 (that was the theoretical high; the actual high was 11,750, and from this point onwards, we will use actual prices unless identified otherwise). The DJIA suggested that this was the high when it declined back to the 23-month moving average. It first did this one month later, in February 2000. It went even lower in March 2000, but neither of these forays were below the 23-month moving average witnessed a close below there. Thus, even though prices started back up again, it was unlikely that March 2000 was the 4-year cycle trough because it was much too early. It was not due until at least September 2001, the 36th month. We really needed to get to September 2001 before considering that the bottom was in.

In September 2001, following the 9-11 attack on the World Trade Center, the DJIA fell sharply to 7926 on September 21, 2001. This was the 36th month, so it was entering the time band of the 4-year cycle trough. Thus, it represented a decline of 33.4% off the all-time high of January 2000. Thus two important criteria for a 4-year cycle were being met. It looked very promising by March 2002 when prices closed above the 23-month moving average. However, the very next month the DJIA closed well below this moving average, so the bottom could not yet be confirmed. As one can see from the monthly chart, the DJIA then declined even further, to 7197 (actual) on October 10, 2002. This was an even better fit, for it was closer to the middle of the normal time band for this trough (October was the 49th month). It also occurred on the day of Venus retrograde, one of the most powerful and consistent geocosmic signatures correlating to significant market reversals as outlined in Volume 3 of this series.

This 4-year cycle trough would be confirmed when prices closed back above the 23-month moving average in two consecutive months and continued closing above it past the 56th month. Two consecutive monthly closes above this average occurred in July and August 2003. This was also well past the 56th month of May 2003. The DJIA was now well into its new 4-year cycle and headed for the crest of this new cycle.

The minimum price target for the crest of this new 4-year cycle would be 50% above the low of 7197. That means we would now look for a multi-month (even multi-year) rally to at least 10,795. That was attained by December 2004. The challenge now would be to confirm the crest of this new 4-year cycle and look for the low that would define the next trough, due 36-56 months after October 2002, or October 2005-June 2007. The first step would be to see prices decline back to the 23-month moving average, preferably in October 2005 or later (the 36th month of the 4-year cycle). This would not actually confirm the 4-year cycle crest, but it would be a minimal criterion for a 4-year cycle trough. On October 13, 2005, the DJIA broke slightly below the 23-month moving average when it plummeted to 10,098 in the theoretical price, and 10,156 in the actual price. Besides not closing below the 23-month moving average for two consecutive months, here was another problem with this low. It was only 7.5% down from the high (actual) of the cycle at 10,984 on March 7, 2005. That would make it the smallest decline in history. Yet in retrospect, that would be the case.

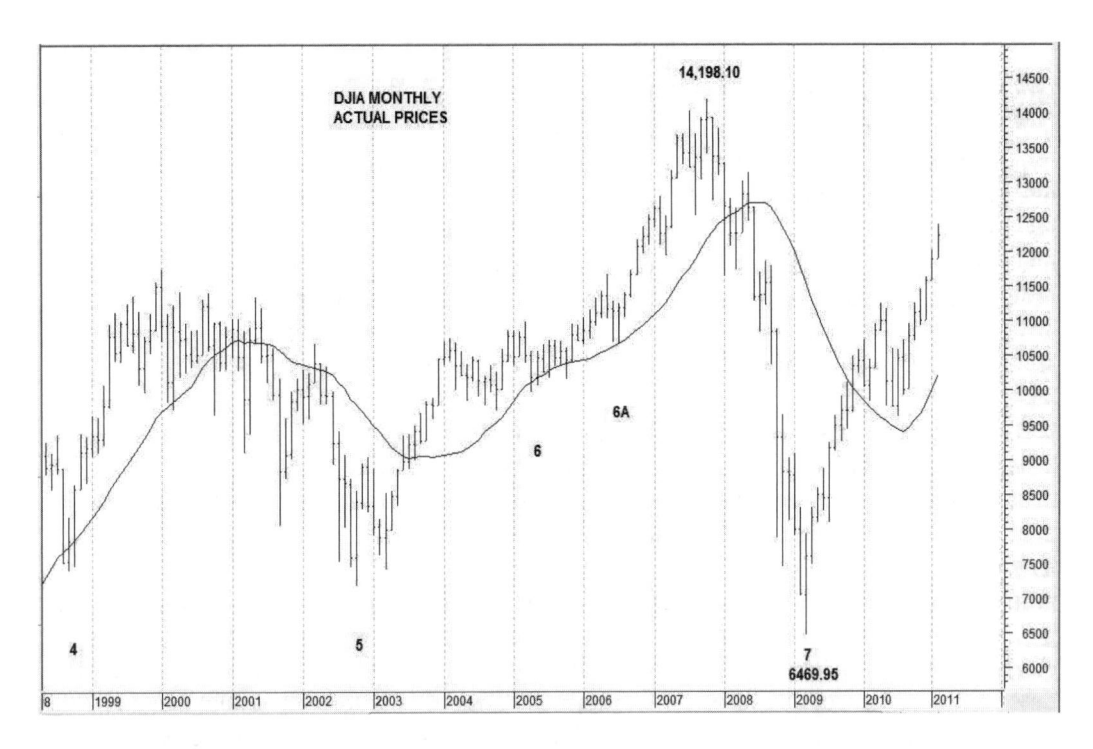

Figure 44: A replica of Figure 43 in actual prices and with less months showing. Note the lows of 6 and 6A as possible 4-year cycle troughs. Neither witnessed two consecutive closes below the 23-month moving average, nor a 20% decline from the prior high, but ultimately the low was one of these, for the DJIA soared to a new high after the time band ended for a low.

There are actually two possibilities for the 4-year cycle trough in this instance. The first was on October 13, 2005, as just described. The second would be July 18, 2006, at 10,683 (actual), or 10,653 (theoretical) the month before (June). The crest that preceded this one was at 11,670 (actual) on May 10, 2006. Time-wise, this was a better fit for the 4-year cycle trough because it occurred in the 45th month, much closer to the mean of this 46-month cycle. Also, the decline represented a loss of 8.45% - still well short of the 20% minimal level sought, but a little better price-wise than the 7.5% of October 2005. The 23-month moving average in the actual market was 10,674, so the low of 10,683 was close enough to be considered "touching it." In retrospect, one could consider either October 2005 or July 2006 as the 4-year cycle trough. Both were in the time band for this low, but in neither case did prices fall at least 20%, nor close two consecutive months below the 23-month moving average. But by the time the DJIA completed its 56th month (June 2007), there were no other options available. The DJIA was on its way to another new all-time high in October 2007, thus confirming one of these prior dates (October 2005 or June-July 2006) as the 4-year cycle trough.

The next 4-year cycle would be due 36-56 months following October 2005 or July 2006. The first case would equate to October 2008 - June 2010; in the second case, it would equate to July 2009-March 2011, assuming they were to unfold in their "normal" cycle time bands. But this case could be distorted, for the even longer-term 72-year cycle was also due (2004 +/- 12 years, as measured from the last instance in July 1932). In retrospect, we know this was the case if July 2006 was the start of the 4-year cycle.

The first step now is to identify the completion of the crest to this new 4-year cycle. If we take a 50% appreciation of the low of October 2005, we get 15,234. If we take a 50% appreciation of the low of July 2006, we get 16,025. Those become minimum price targets. But remember: when a market is in its last phase of a bull market cycle, the most bearish characteristics of the entire cycle will usually unfold. In this case, it could be the last 4-year cycle phase of the 72-year cycle, which had been decidedly bullish. Therefore, this 4-year cycle might 1) turn into a left translation pattern, 2) fail to meet its upside price target, 3) distort from its normal time band, and/or 4) experience its sharpest decline since 1932. All four of these characteristics happened in the 4-year cycle that started in July 2006. (Two of them applied if October 2005 was the correct starting point.)

This particular 4-year cycle topped out on October 11, 2007 at 14,198 in the DJIA. This period coincided with Jupiter in Sagittarius, forming a 270° square to Uranus - one of the strongest geocosmic correlations to a market reversal as demonstrated in Volume 3 of this series. Also, Saturn formed a conjunction to the South Node of the Moon (with Venus) during this time. The first indication that this was the crest of the 4-year cycle (and even greater) via our moving average theories occurred when the DJIA fell to the 23-month moving average. This happened in January 2008. However, there were not two consecutive closes below this moving average until May and June 2008. The initial downside price target would be a minimum 20% of the 14,198 high of October 11, 2007, or 11,358. That was achieved in June 2008. This was still too early for the bottom, so it was likely to fall lower. And it did - all the way to 6470 on March 6, 2009 - when Venus again turned retrograde. From the high of 14,198, this represented a loss of 54.4%, the steepest decline since the 1930's. We could therefore now confirm that the crest of the greater 72-year cycle was also completed in October 2007. Time-wise, the low of March 6, 2009 was the 41st month following the low of October 2005, or 32 months following the low of July 2006. The first case would make it a normal time band for the 4-year cycle trough. The second case would be a 32-month interval, which would represent a distortion, known in this case as a "contraction." Since distortions are more common when longer-term cycles unfold, this is certainly a possibility. There have been two previous cases of 32-month contractions for the 4-year cycle in the past (October 1929 - July 1932, and October 1946 - June 1949). But since 1893 (when these studies commenced) there have been no cases of 4-year cycles lasting less than 32 months.

As the cycle bottomed March 6, 2009, the DJIA was well below the 23-month moving average. If that was the 4-year bottom, then we would expect to see 1) prices appreciate at least 50% from that low, and 2) at least touch the 23-month moving average after the 5th month. To confirm it as the 4-year cycle trough, the DJIA would need to close above this moving average for two consecutive months. From a low of 6470, a 50% appreciation would give an upside minimum price target of 9705. That was attained in September 2009. However, at that time the DJIA had still not recovered enough to test the 23-month moving average. That would happen in November 2009. In fact, it closed above this average in November and December 2009, thus *confirming* March 6, 2009 as the 4-year cycle trough. As of this writing in early 2011, it has not been back to test this moving average. When it does, it will be an initial indication that the 4-year cycle has topped out. That will then be confirmed on two successive monthly closes below the 23-month moving average. For those who like to look ahead, the "normal" time band for this

4-year cycle trough would be 36-56 months following March 2009, or March 2012 - November 2013. At that time, we will anticipate a decline of at least 20% from the crest or at the very minimum, prices touching the 23-month moving average.

The 50-Week Cycle and 25-Week Moving Average

When the DJIA is in the last 50-week cycle phase of a bullish 4-year cycle, one does not have to wait for the 23-month moving average to be broken to confirm the 4-year cycle crest has been completed. It can be confirmed when the 25-week moving average of the last 50-week cycle phase has been broken. That is, once the appropriate moving average of the last phase of a cycle is broken, it also indicates that the crest of the greater cycle has been completed. Prices will then continue to trend lower and lower until both the 50-week and 4-year cycles are completed. The final 4-year cycle trough, however, will not usually be realized until 1) the market enters the time band where both the 50-week and 4-year cycles overlap, and 2) the DJIA also falls to (or below) the 23-month moving average. Keep in mind that the trough of the last phase of a cycle will always coincide with the trough of the greater cycle itself.

Conversely, after the 4-year cycle trough has been attained, one of the first stages of confirmation will come when prices exceed the 25-week moving average. That is, the appropriate moving average for the first phase of a new cycle will often be exceeded before the appropriate moving average for the greater cycle is even touched. However, that is not always the case. Sometimes the moving average of the greater cycle is lower than the moving average of the subcycle. The more valid confirmation that the 4-year cycle has bottomed will take place after monthly prices start to close above *both* the 23-month and 25-week moving averages. It is even stronger if the 25-week moving average was below the 23-month one and has reversed to rise above the 23-month average, with actual prices trading above each. That may or may not happen in the first 50-week cycle phase, but it will eventually happen. When it does, it means the market is starting a powerful trend up and those moving averages become support for the bull trend.

Let us demonstrate this principle by examining the weekly chart of the DJIA with a 25-week moving average, the theoretical "ideal" moving average to use with the 50-week cycle (It is not just theoretically the "ideal" to use in my opinion; it actually works very well for our purposes.). We will do this with an example that takes into account the later 50-week phases of a 4-year cycle, the weekly chart of 2005-2009, as shown in Figure 45.

In a previous chapter (and in Volume 1), our research studies showed that there are three, four, or five 50-week cycle phases within the 4-year cycle. Since 1893, this pattern has failed only once, and that was in the longest 4-year cycle observed, which extended from July 1932 through March 1938. There were six 50-week cycle phases then, as that was the first 4-year cycle following the 72- and 90-year cycle lows of the Great Depression. In the majority of cases, there will be four or five 50-week cycles within the greater 4-year cycle. Thus, when trying to confirm the end to a four-year cycle, we want to study closely the third, fourth, and even fifth 50-week cycle phase for signs of a completed trough. Our attention, however, will be most acute in the fourth and fifth phases. In fact, it has been the fourth phase that appeared most often to end the 4-year cycle, and we should be most alert to the end of that 50-week cycle.

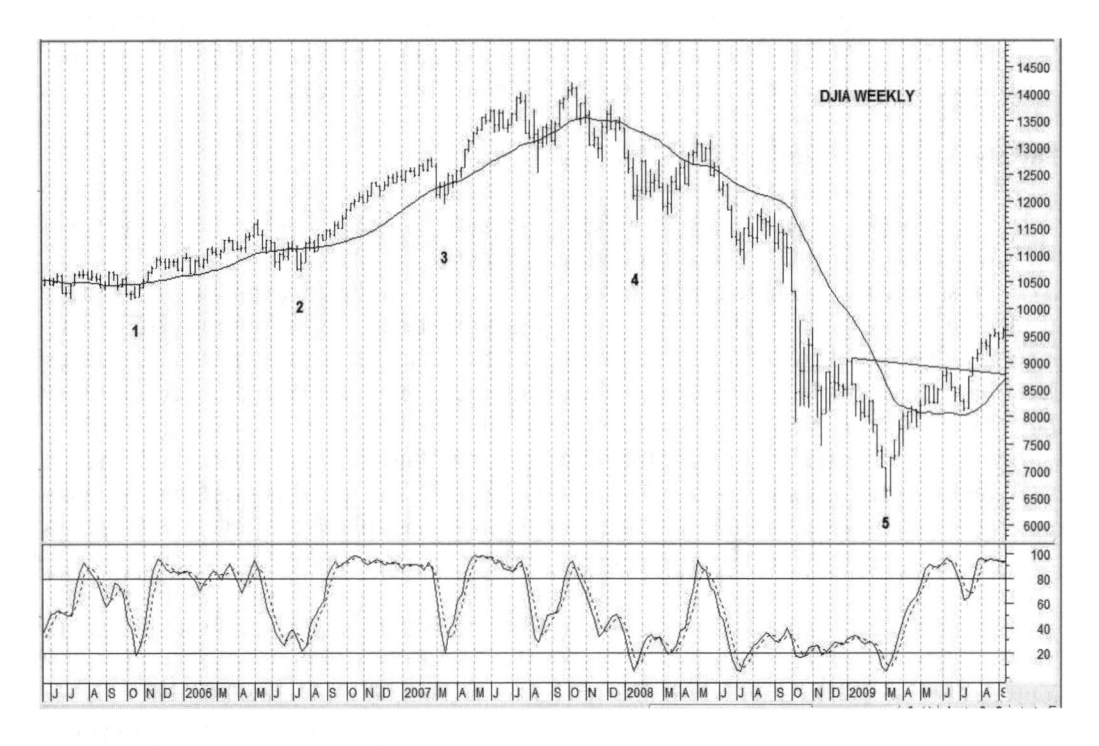

Figure 45: Weekly chart of the DJIA, identifying the 50-week cycle phases within the 4-year cycle (1-5). Shown here is the 25-week moving average.

In the example above (Figure 45), the 50-week cycles are identified in a 4-year cycle that began on October 13, 2005. As stated before, it is also possible to start this 4-year cycle with the lows of June or July 2006. Either one could be used, but for purposes of showing how the latter phases of the 50-week cycle are usually used to confirm a 4-year cycle trough, let us assume this 4-year cycle began in October 2005. This starting point is depicted as "1" in the chart above. The subsequent 50-week cycles occurred at 2, 3, 4, and 5. That is, the third 50-week cycle began at 3 and ended at 4. This is where our analysis begins in the quest to confirm the 4-year cycle trough, for the earliest we expect a 4-year cycle to begin is when the third 50-week subcycle within it comes to an end. The third 50-week subcycle ended at 4 in this example, or with the low of January 22, 2008.

Now, what else do we know about 4-year cycles from a timing point of view? We know they generally last 36-56 months, with the shortest on record being 32 months. From a starting point of October 2005, we would not expect a low for at least 32 months (June 2008) and more than likely at least 36 months (October 2008). Since the end of the third 50-week subcycle occurred on January 22, 2008, we know that was too early for the 4-year cycle. So our attention shifts to the fourth 50-week subcycle that began at that time.

As we study this 50-week cycle, first of all note that it was confirmed for January 22, 2008, when the DJIA closed two consecutive weeks above the 25-week moving average. That happened the weeks ending April 18 and 25, 2008. This 50-week cycle will now confirm its crest upon two consecutive closes back below the 25-week moving average. This will be important, because if it is indeed the last 50-week cycle phase of the greater 4-year cycle, the steepest decline of the 4-year cycle will likely be in force.

The 25-week moving average was taken out on two consecutive weekly closes on June 6 and June 13, 2008. This confirmed that the 50-week cycle crest was completed on May 19, 2008 at 13,136. Note that this high was lower than the previous 50-week cycle crest (14,198 on October 11, 2007), and if valid, would represent a left translation 50-week cycle. A more important confirmation that the 50-week cycle had topped out would occur when the DJIA closed below the price that started this 50-week cycle, which was 11,634 on January 22, 2008. Hence, once prices take out the low that starts a cycle, its trend will be bearish (prices will continue lower and lower) until the end of the cycle. That happened during the last week of June 2008. This 50-week cycle would now be bearish, with the lowest price not due until the end of the cycle. And since this was the fourth 50-week cycle phase of the greater 4-year cycle, there was good reason to anticipate that its low would also be the 4-year cycle trough.

The next step now was to identify the likely time band for this 50-week cycle trough, knowing that it must also overlap the time band for the 4-year cycle trough. As reported in Volume 1, 50-week cycles have a 90% probability of bottoming at the 34-67 week interval. That translates into about 7.8-15.5 months. In this case, we would anticipate the low of this cycle to unfold September 2008-May 2009.

Once the market entered this time band for the fourth (and possibly last) 50-week cycle phase of the greater 4-year cycle, we watched for several bullish technical signals and chart patterns to suggest a low was in, as discussed in the prior chapters. But the confirmation wouldn't arise until the DJIA closed above the 25-week moving average for two consecutive weeks. That is our primary challenge - to identify a new trend is underway - based on the purpose of this chapter. If the weekly close is above this moving average prior to entering this time band, we ignore it. It is only after this time band has been entered that we pay attention to consecutive weekly closes above it.

Looking at the weekly chart in Figure 45, it will be seen that the DJIA never closed, or even touched, the 25-week moving average after breaking below it in early June 2008. That is, it didn't rise to the average until well after the low on March 6, 2009.

It first poked above the 25-week moving average in the week ending April 17, 2009, six weeks after the low. However, it didn't complete two consecutive weekly closes above it until the week ending May 8. This then, confirmed the completion of the 50-week cycle low on March 6, 2009. It was the first signal, via moving averages, that the 4-year cycle was also completed, for this was the fourth 50-week cycle phase of the 4-year cycle. There was now ample reason to think this was the last 50-week cycle within the 4-year cycle, since it was the fourth such phase. Therefore it would now be worth the risk of establishing a long-term long position.

Of course, there was still the possibility of a fifth 50-week cycle phase to complete the 4-year cycle. But several chart patterns soon negated that possibility. From the point of view of moving average studies, the first thing that negated the possibility of a five-phase 4-year cycle pattern was the consecutive monthly closes above the 23-month moving average, which occurred in November and December 2009. By that time, the DJIA was already more than halfway through the new 50-week cycle, so it would be a bullish right translation pattern. In the last phases of longer-term cycles, we are more likely to see left translation bearish patterns, especially if the prior phase was left translation and bearish (which it was, in our case). As it turned out, the market never fell back below the 25-week moving average for the rest of 2009, another sign that this was to be a bullish 50-week cycle, which is a characteristic of the first phase of a new longer-term cycle, and not the last phase of an older one.

Primary and Shorter-Term Cycles

Every cycle trough has a time band when it is normally due. An 18-week primary cycle, for instance, may be normally due 15-21 weeks after its current cycle begins. This is the case in many commodity cycles, like Gold and grains. In the case of the Dow Jones Industrial Average, the primary cycle is actually 17 weeks, and its "normal" historical range is 13-21 weeks, established by studies covering over 70 years (1928-2005) as reported in Volume 1 of this series. Of course, it can distort. But we are working with the middle 80% probabilities, so we will first focus on the 13-21 week time frame for the primary cycle in the DJIA. But note that this varies for other stock indices. For example, it is 15-23 weeks in the S&P and the NASDAQ Composite, 13-19 weeks in the Japanese Nikkei, 15-26 weeks in the German DAX and the Swiss SMI, and 17-27 weeks in the Netherlands AEX, to name just a few.

Once the DJIA enters the 13th week, we expect prices to at least test - and preferably to break below - a moving average that has been defined as appropriate for the confirmation of a primary cycle crest. Theoretically, that would be a moving average that is half the mean length of the primary cycle. Since the mean primary cycle for the DJIA is 17 weeks, it means a moving average of 8.5 weeks, or 42.5 days. In many cases, it is usually a little less than 42.5 days because of holidays. Also, we don't use half-days. Therefore 42 days – or even 40 days – is a good figure to use for a moving average to correspond with the primary cycle in the DJIA.

In fact, the 40-day moving average is very popular and used by many market analysts, because it works so well in understanding their concepts of a "market trend." If the market is in a longer-term bear trend, then it will almost always be below this 40-day moving average at some point in the 13-21 week time band when the DJIA primary cycle trough is due. But if the longer-term cycle is bullish, there will be times in which prices may not fall below here. In these cases, the 40-day (or 42-day) moving average may act as support to any corrective declines. At a primary cycle trough, prices might only touch this moving average, so it provides a minimal price target for a decline. In order to confirm a primary cycle trough, however, it needs to close below here on at least two consecutive trading days once the time band for the low is entered. If it doesn't, but instead only tests the moving average, then the primary bottom cannot be confirmed until the market exits the time band in which the cycle low is due and starts making new highs. These, then, are the steps to confirming that a primary cycle trough has been completed, via the moving average.

After a market has entered a time band when its primary cycle crest could unfold, we use the moving average of half its cycle length to confirm that the crest has been completed. *That confirmation comes if and when prices drop below this average on two consecutive occasions.* As suggested before, the price may never drop below this average if the longer-term cycle is in a very bullish phase. Therefore there may never be a confirmation of the cycle trough in these cases via this rule. The important point to note is that the market must be in (or past) the time when a cycle crest is due before a drop below that moving average becomes significant. Why? Because as a cycle bottoms, prices may rise and fall sharply for a few days or weeks, and they may rise above and fall below that moving average several times. The market must at least get to the point where it is most probable for a cycle crest to occur, which means at least 1/8 into the mean cycle length. In the case of a primary cycle, for instance, we would not consider a primary cycle crest as having occurred if the market is not at least 2-5 weeks removed from the start of that primary cycle. In those first 2-5 weeks, it is not uncommon for a market to trade above and below a critical moving average several times. But if it has been above the 40-day moving average for several days, and the market is well past the second week, then a drop below can indicate that the primary cycle crest is completed.

The same is true in regards to confirming cycle troughs. In fact, moving averages are even more important here, because troughs occur at regular intervals of time. Crests do not. As a market enters the time band for a primary cycle trough, it is most important if prices close below the appropriate moving average and better yet, if it happens on two or more consecutive trading days. Prices may not fall below this moving average if the market is very bullish and in the early stages of a longer-term bull market. But when they do (and they usually do) then it is a confirming signal that the cycle trough is unfolding.

The moving average can also be used to confirm that the primary cycle trough has been completed. This happens when prices form a low in the time band for a cycle bottom, and preferably within a price target range for that bottom, and more ideally at a time when there is a geocosmic critical reversal date. When all of those factors are in place, a move above this moving average will confirm that the cycle trough is over, and a new cycle is underway. To be valid, it should register at least two consecutive closes above this moving average. Until that happens, the cycle low is not confirmed, and there is nothing to say the market will not have another decline to lower prices as long as the time band for the cycle low is still in effect. Furthermore, if it closes above that moving average in the first 1/8 of that new cycle, it may still fall back below it again without making a new low. When prices fall back below the moving average that early in the primary cycle, it does not confirm that the new cycle has already topped out. The point is a technical analyst need not pay much attention to the moving average until the market is entering the time band for the primary cycle trough.

It is at this point that we want to introduce the 25-day moving average, because it is one of those "form fitted averages" that works well for our purposes. In other words, this is a case where actual practice will often supersede theoretical considerations. It is especially useful in confirming a primary cycle trough after prices have entered the time band for that cycle low and are under the 25-day moving average. As they then start to close back above this 25-day moving average, it usually confirms that the first phase of a new primary cycle is in force.

The same concept can be applied to a bullish primary cycle once it enters its last major cycle phase (i.e. the third 5-7 week major cycle within the greater 17-week primary cycle). That is, if prices are trading above the 25-day moving average, and the market has completed two 5-7 week major cycle phases, then it will likely fall below this moving average as the primary cycle trough unfolds. In any event, that is what we anticipate to happen when the primary cycle trough comes due, and we use that as an important indicator in the setup for attempting to buy the primary cycle trough.

To illustrate these concepts, let us look at a daily chart of the DJIA that depicts the primary cycle of July 2, 2010 through November 29, 2010, as shown in Figure 46. This is a typical 3-phase bullish primary cycle. That is, it contains three major cycle troughs, identified as MB (major cycle bottom) with the last being the primary cycle bottom (PB). The greater cycle type is always used to identify a cycle, thus the last major cycle low is also a primary cycle low, but it is referred to as a primary bottom (PB) and not MB. PB means it also contains the lesser cycles, such as a major cycle trough or half-primary cycle trough. The chart also shows a 25-day moving average (solid line) and 40-day moving average (dotted line). As discussed above, theoretically the 40-day moving average is appropriate because it is approximately half the length of a normal primary cycle. But in actual practice, I find the 25-day moving average to be more useful in the process of confirming primary cycles in many cases.

As expected, prices fell well below both the 40- and 25-day moving averages at the start of the primary cycle on July 2, 2010. On July 8, just three trading days later, the DJIA closed above the 25-day moving average, the first sign that the primary bottom might be in. The next day, it closed above the 40-day moving average, which denoted the same thing. But this was the second consecutive day above the 25-day average, so it was more of a confirming signal, although it could still fall back and forth (below and back above) several times in the first 2-5 weeks. On Monday, July 12, it closed a second consecutive day above the 40-day moving average, thus issuing its confirming signal of a primary cycle trough. Two weeks after the low, it did indeed fall back below both moving averages slightly. It was too early for a primary cycle crest, so this was nothing to worry about, unless it actually fell below the start of the primary cycle (It did not.).

The DJIA rallied back above both moving averages again, as it should, by July 22, on its way to the crest of the first major cycle. This crest culminated on August 9, after which it again fell below both moving averages. This was a signal that the primary cycle crest may have also been completed on August 9. However, that would not be confirmed until prices actually took out the low that started the cycle back on July 2. That never happened. In fact the two moving averages intersected on September 3, and the DJIA closed well above both, thus confirming August 27 as either a major or half-primary cycle trough. It could be either type, because that low was in the 8th week of the primary cycle. Most major cycles last 5-7 weeks, but they can expand to 8 weeks. Most half-primary cycles last 7-11 weeks, so this low could be either type, and it wouldn't be known until it was determined that this would be a two or three-phase primary cycle. It turned out to be a three-phase type, and hence that low of August 27 would be labeled a major cycle trough (MB).

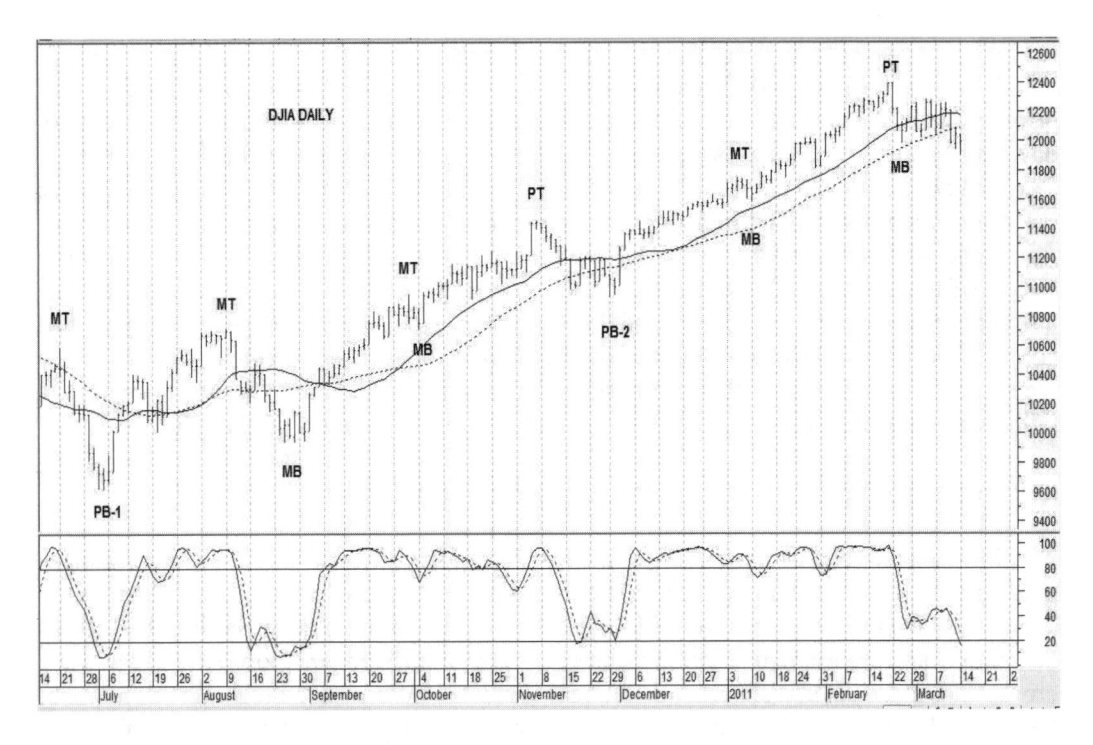

Figure 46: Daily chart of the DJIA, showing the primary and major cycles between July and November 2010, along with the 25-day moving average (solid line) and 40-day moving average (dotted line).

By the end of September, prices were above both moving averages, and the 25-day was above the 40-day, indicating a trend run up was in force. This signaled that a new bull market was underway, one we would call part of the "Asset Inflation Express" because it was taking place when both Jupiter and Uranus were in the very early degrees of Aries, a very speculative combination from the studies of geocosmic signatures.

Because it was such a strong bullish technical setup, prices stayed well above both the 25- and 40-day moving averages through the second major cycle trough (MB), which took place on October 4. That also began the third and final major cycle phase.

Now, this is where it gets interesting via the use of moving averages combined with cycle patterns. It was a bullish primary cycle because it clearly exhibited a bullish right translation pattern (pPrices made new highs after the halfway point.). Thus, once this cycle completes its crest, the steepest decline of the cycle would likely unfold. That is, once the crest of the third major cycle was attained, a sharp 2-5 week decline to both the major and primary cycles would take place. As this happened, we would now expect to see prices fall below the 25-day moving average (but not necessarily the 40-day). They might only touch the 40-day average, since it had been such a bullish primary cycle.

The primary cycle crest culminated on November 5. One week later, on November 12, prices touched the 25-day moving average, the first sign via this study that the primary cycle may have topped out on November 5. Two trading days later, on November 16, it closed below the 40-day moving average, a stronger signal that the top was in. The next day confirmed this with its second consecutive close below.

Now we look for confirmation that the primary cycle has bottomed and a new primary cycle has started. On November 18 and 19, the DJIA closed back above the 40-day moving average. This was a strong signal that the market bottomed on November 16. But it didn't close above the 25-day moving average, which is our moving average indicator of a primary bottom once we reach the time band when a primary bottom is due. As can be seen in Figure 46, prices fell to a lower low on November 28 (PB-2). It was a couple of trading days afterwards that prices closed two consecutive days above both the 25- and 40-day moving averages. That was a better signal that a new primary cycle had commenced. It was further supported by the double looping daily stochastics, in which the second loop was higher than the first (bullish oscillator divergence). Subsequently the bull market resumed, carrying the DJIA to a new 2-year high into February 2011.

Using Multiple Moving Averages for Identifying Trend Runs

Most traders can be classified as one of two types, and each base their trading plans on distinctly different temperaments. The most common type of trader is the trend trader. These individuals enter a market in the direction of that trend only when it either breaks out above an important resistance zone or below significant support zones. They are buyers in bull trends and short sellers in bear trends based on these breakouts. Sometimes they are referred to as "breakout" traders. Their psychology is to attain consistent profits, to experience a high percentage of winners versus losers. Before they go long, they want to have a high degree of confidence that an important low has already been attained, and the trend is up. Or before they go short, they want a relatively high probability that an important crest has been completed, and the trend will now be down.

The other type of trader is more concerned with risk-reward opportunities. These individuals are more focused on trying to pick bottoms and tops nearby to important support or resistance zones. They will buy low - near support zones - and risk a small fraction of what they consider a reasonable profit objective if they are correct. They will also sell short on highs - near resistance zones - with a stop-loss just above those resistance zones. If they are correct without getting stopped out, they make a very handsome return on their investment. But by trying to pick bottoms and tops, this trader is going *against* the immediate trend, whereas the trend trader is going *with* the immediate trend.

The trend trader will likely miss a good portion of the initial move. However, he will often capture the middle third of a move in the direction of a trend with a high level of consistency. His percentage of gains versus losses will be high in comparison to the one who is more concerned with risk-reward parameters (or bottom and top pickers).

Thus, one can see the dilemma facing every trader before a trade. The two questions to ask are 1) what is the probability of being right on this trade, and 2) is it a favorable risk versus reward ratio? The trend trader, or breakout trader, has a higher probability of being right on the trade, but will likely have to assume more risk in the event he is wrong. The bottom and top picker is going to achieve a lower percentage of winners versus losers, but when he is wrong, his loss is much less (assuming both use stop-losses after entry based on recent highs or lows), and when he is right, his gain is likely to be much greater as a percentage of his investment. Since the trend trader has a higher percentage of gains versus losses, it is no wonder that most books on technical analysis are heavily weighted to this type of trading.

However, trend trading is not the dominant approach of these books. The methodology outlined here is heavily weighted with tools that help one to identify the times and the prices of potential troughs and crests and thereby to find a very favorable place (location) to enter or exit a market for the greatest risk-reward ratios. But having said that, there are times when one may exclusively trade in the direction of the trend, and even upon breakouts, and those times can be identified by the use of multiple moving averages. In fact, during these trend runs, it is possible to make a large fortune by pyramiding upon a core position. Of course, if wrong, then one's large fortune may turn into a smaller fortune very quickly, or worse.

As suggested before, multiple moving averages can be used to identify trend runs, especially when used in combination with cycle studies. For trading purposes, this can best be illustrated with the primary cycle. We know, for instance, that the first phase of every cycle is bullish. We also know that the middle phase will also be bullish if the longer-term cycles are in their earlier stages. Thus, we look for signs of a trend run up in the first two-thirds (or longer) of a bullish primary cycle. Expressed in another way, a bullish primary cycle will likely top out after the second (of three) major cycle phases has been completed. The converse is true with bearish primary cycles. That is, they will top out in the first major cycle phase and then turn bearish, not to bottom until the entire primary cycle ends.

How do we handle this with moving averages? The basic premise is this: In a trend run up, the price of the market will be above the moving average that applies to both the major and primary cycles (have their mean length). Furthermore, the moving average associated with the major cycle (the faster moving, or changeable, one) will be above the moving average associated with the primary cycle (the slower moving, or smoother, one).

In this practice it is best to use moving averages that are half the length of the primary cycle and a second or third shorter moving average that is half the length of the major and/or half-primary cycles. In other words, the moving average of the primary cycle should be two or three times the length of the moving average associated with the major or half-primary cycle. The proportions are important if the purpose is to establish the likely trend of the primary cycle, which in turn is important if one wishes to be on the right side of the market for large and longer-lasting price moves in most cases.

Let us apply this rule to the Dow Jones Industrial Average and see how it works. If the primary cycle has a mean periodicity of 17 weeks, then the theoretically correct moving average to use is 42 days (i.e. 8.5 weeks x 5 days). If the major cycle (one-third of the primary cycle) has a mean interval of 6 weeks, then the theoretically correct moving average to use is 15 days (three weeks, of five days each). But for the purpose of trend analysis, we want to use moving averages that are in a direct proportion to one another by either a multiple of two or three. Therefore, since we chose a 42-day moving average for the primary cycle, we will use a 14-day moving average for the major cycle's appropriate major average.

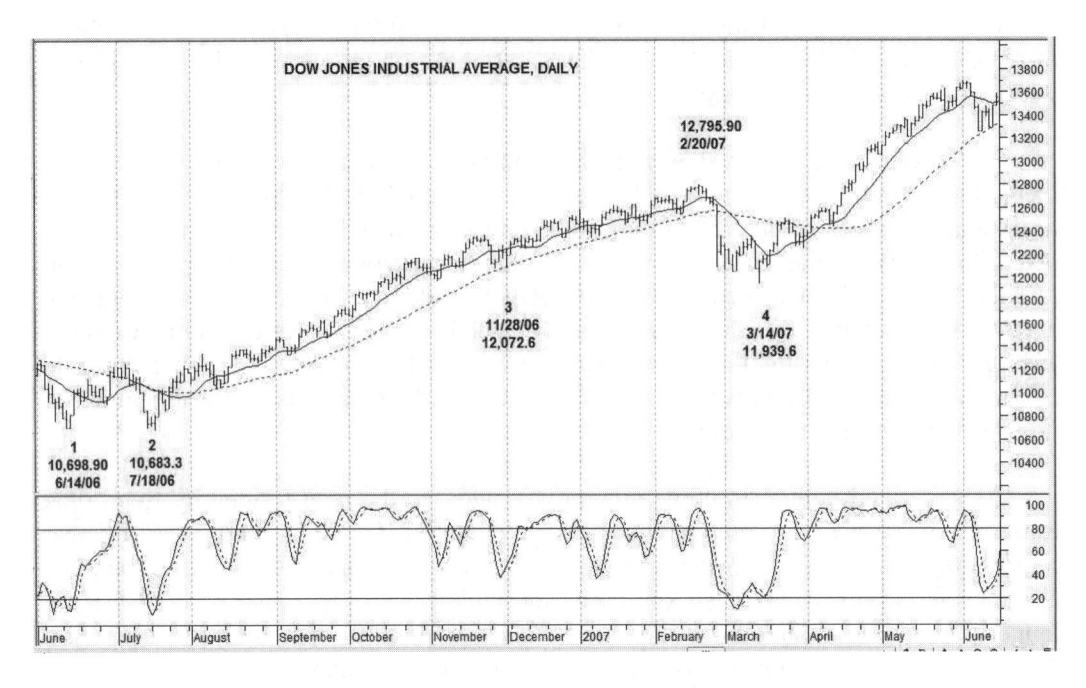

Figure 47: Daily chart of the DJIA following the possible 4-year cycle low at the double bottom of June 14 and July 18, 2006. The solid line is the 14-day moving average, pertinent to the 6-week major cycle. The dotted line is a 42-day moving average, relevant to the 17-week primary cycle. 2, 3, and 4 are primary cycle troughs.

This example begins with the double bottom lows of June 14 and July 18, 2006. This was cited earlier as two of the possible starting points for a 4-year cycle trough. Therefore we expect the early stages of this new cycle to exhibit a trend run up pattern, especially in the first primary cycle phase of this new 4-year cycle. One will notice that during the low of June 14, the DJIA was below both moving averages, and the shorter one (solid line, 14-day moving average relevant to major cycle) was also below the longer one (dotted line, 42-day moving average relevant to primary cycle). On June 29, the DJIA rose above both moving averages, which was a signal that the primary cycle low may have formed June 14 (It did in the theoretical DJIA prices.). But the 14-day moving average couldn't quite get above the 42-day average, which is necessary to confirm that a new trend run up was in force. As one can see, the DJIA then fell once more to a lower actual low on July 18. By this time, the 14- and 42-day averages were virtually together.

On July 24, the DJIA rallied sharply to close above both of these moving averages again - yet another sign that the bottom may be in. However, it wasn't until August 2 that the 14-day moving average turned above the 42-day. The DJIA closed at 11,199.90 that day (above both moving averages), so this was a confirmation sign that the primary cycle trough had been completed, and the trend run up was in force. The idea now would be to adopt bullish strategies until 1) prices entered the time band for a primary cycle crest, 2) prices would break below the 42-day moving average, especially on two consecutive closes, or 3) the 14-day moving average turned below the 42-day average, and prices fell below each. Since we are now more concerned about trends than trading opportunities, let's just see how this measured the trend run up by looking only at the last two points.

On November 28 and December 1, the DJIA declined very close to the 42-day moving average, but it never closed below (it touched it on December 1). Furthermore, the 14-day moving average never fell below the 42-day average and even though November 28 was a primary cycle trough, it never turned the trend down. It remained bullish into and following the primary cycle trough.

In fact, it was not until February 27 of 2007, over six months after it gave a trend run up signal that the DJIA closed below the 42-day average. It closed at 12,216 that day. On March 5, the 14-day MA (moving average) also crossed below the 42-day moving average, thus confirming the trend run up was over (via this signal). It closed at 12,050 that day. Whether one exited on the first or second signal, the gain was 800-1000 points.

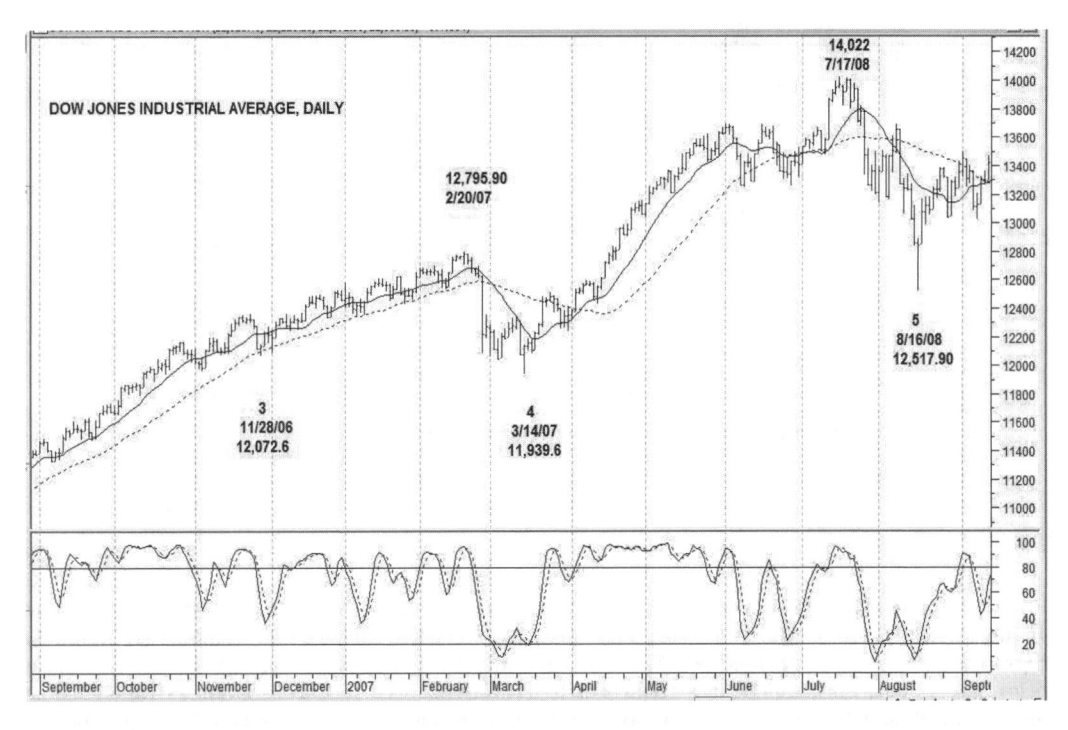

Figure 48: Daily chart of the DJIA with the same 14- and 42-day moving averages.

You can see the same trend run up in effect in the next primary cycle, shown in Figure 48. Once the 14-day moving average curled back above the 42-day average, and prices were above both, another bull run was in force. It too lasted until the 14-day moving average moved back below the 42-day one, and prices were below each (August 9). This was another 900+-point advance measured by the difference in closing prices at each of these signals. In both of these examples, the primary cycles were bullish, and the moving average rules defined the greater body of the trend run up. During these periods, trend traders could have remained long, and risk-reward traders could have bought any corrective declines back to the 14-day moving average with a stop-loss on closes below the 42-day average, or at a time when the 14-day average turned below the 42-day one. In both cases, these trading strategies would have been very profitable. This is usually the case when you have trend runs up like these. In fact, pyramiding one's long position on every new high after a 3-day or greater decline took place during these trend runs up, would have been extremely profitable. However, one can also see that when the 14-day turned below the 42-day average, it wasn't necessarily a profitable time to be short. In these examples, traders entering the short side of the market on the basis of moving average theory alone would have suffered modest losses. Yet, if there were to be a big move down, utilizing these principles of moving averages would likely capture a good part of that move. One could see this in the bear market of late 2007 through March of 2009, as shown in part in Figure 49.

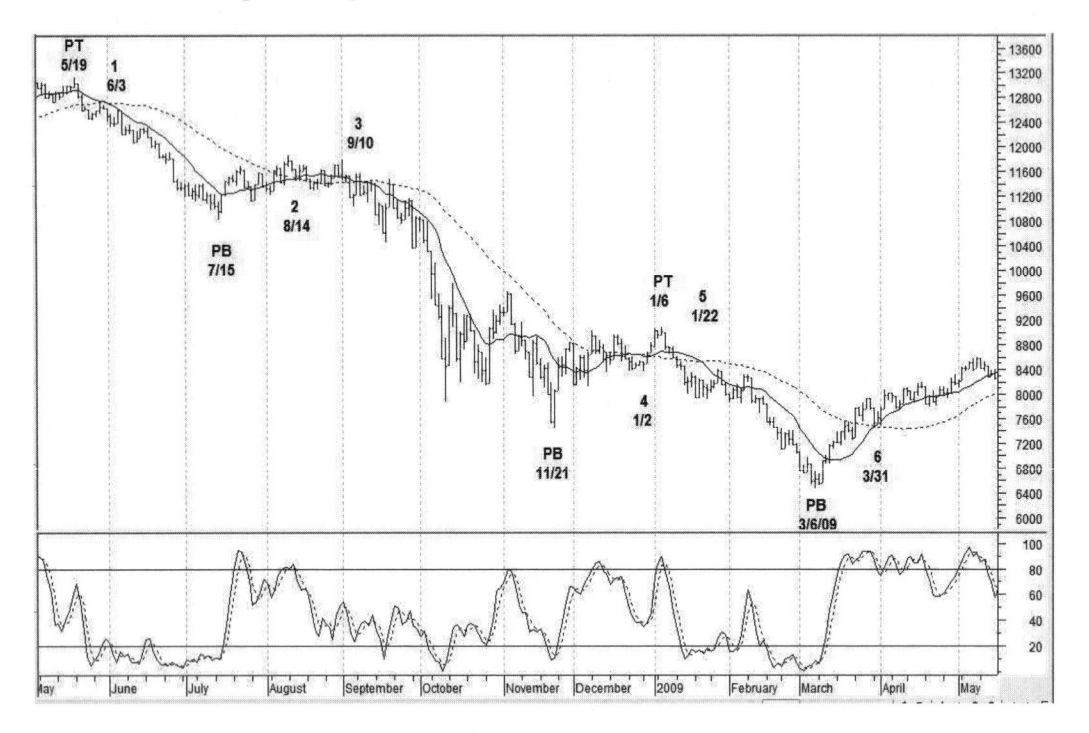

Figure 49: The daily DJIA from the primary cycle crest of May 19, 2007 through the 4-year (or greater) cycle trough of March 6, 2009. This was a bear market, and the odd numbers (1, 3, and 5) represent points at which prices were below the 14- and 42-day moving averages, and the 14 was also below the 42-day, thus indicating a trend run down was in force. The even numbers (2, 4, and 6) indicate the dates when the trend run down was negated, and a trend run up was in force (but not for long, because this was a bear market period).

In this example of a bear market, you can see how all of the points where the bear trend went into effect (all the odd numbers) yielded handsome profits from a short sale. When the moving averages turned bullish, there were losses, but they were minimal. Therefore the "trend following" method utilizing moving averages can be useful for identifying long bull or bear trend runs during which all traders can adopt bullish or bearish trading strategies until negated.

There are several ways you can trade with the use of multiple moving averages, but primarily you want to trade in the direction of a trend, once it can be identified. One way to do this in a bull market is to initiate the long position as the 14-day moving average turns above the 42-day one. Then after every decline of at least three days, you can add on to the long position whenever it makes a new high for the cycle. This is known as "pyramiding," and is the basis by which many position traders build handsome fortunes. Your stop-loss is either on a close below the 42-day moving average, or when the 14-day turns below the 42-day average, with prices below each. Of course you can take profit positions along the way, depending upon your trading style. But basically one remains long and adopts bullish strategies until the trend changes via these rules.

In the same way, one can make a small fortune by selling the market in bear runs. That is, once the 14-day moving average turns below the 42-day average, and prices are also below both, one can initiate a short position with a stop-loss based on a close back above the 42-day average, or when the 14-day average turns back above the 42-day one, and prices are above both. Until that happens, one can wait for minimal three-day rallies, then "pyramid" the short position (i.e. add on to short positions) every time the market breaks to a new low in the cycle. Continue doing this until the bearish trend run down is negated by a close above the 42-day average or a move above the 42-day average by the 14-day average with prices above each. Of course when the market is in a time band for the primary cycle trough, one may (and should) start to take profits too, especially if clearly defined support levels are being tested and hold.

Summary

Moving averages are very useful as confirming indicators of a cycle completion (and the start of a new cycle). They are also useful as trend indicators (identifying trend run ups and trend run downs), as well as identifying minimal price objectives for counter-trend moves. The following represent key points to remember in the use of moving averages:

1. Apply a moving average that is half the length of the cycle being used. This is the theoretical "ideal" moving average to apply. However there may be other moving averages that are a better "form fit," and if you identify those (like a 25-day one), use them as well (or instead of) the half-cycle length.

2. This moving average will indicate a minimal price objective for a reversal into that cycle's trough or crest.

3. This moving average will represent a confirmation that the cycle crest has been completed when the market closes two consecutive time periods below it, or a cycle trough when it closes two consecutive time periods back above. To be valid, the market must bottom or top out in a time band when the particular cycle's trough or crest is possible.

4. If the market closes two consecutive time periods beyond the moving average, and it is immediately after a cycle top or trough has formed, it does not mean the counter-trend move (or reversal) is over. For instance, assume a primary cycle trough is due, and prices are below the 40- or 42-day moving average. They then close back above this average in the next week, but immediately close back below the average again in that same week. Does this mean the primary cycle has already formed? No. It is too early. In those first couple of weeks, it is not unusual to see prices go back and forth over the 40- or 42-day moving average. As long as it doesn't take out the low, it could still be a new

primary cycle. If it does take out the low, it means that previous low was not the bottom, but it is still forming. Once you get past the second week and prices start closing consecutive days above this moving average, then the primary cycle trough is confirmed.

5. Multiple moving averages involving half the cycle length, and others that are half the length of its subcycles, may be used to identify trend runs. When prices are above all these moving averages, and the shorter-term moving average is above the longer-term one, then a trend run up is in force. One can adopt bullish strategies and even "pyramid" additional purchases from the long side until negated, according to the rules given in this chapter. When prices are below these moving averages, and the shorter-term one(s) is below the longer-term average, one can adopt bearish strategies, selling all rallies that remain below the longer-term moving average. Or one may pyramid additional short positions during this trend run down, until negated by a close above the longer-term average, or a time when the shorter-term average rises above the longer-term one. These strategies should be used in combination with an understanding of the phases of both the greater cycle and its subcycles. That is, the early phases of cycles are bullish, and the later ones are mostly bearish.

Once all these principles involving price projections are understood, it is time to learn the rules for short-term trading. Consider everything up until this point as "the greater picture," the proverbial "forest" that you are entering. You need the context of the background in order to be successful. With that, you are now ready to learn short-term trading methods, which are like the proverbial "trees within the forest." It is time to bring the microcosm into alignment with the macrocosm to enhance your probabilities of consistent success in the markets. After all, this is why you purchased this book and why I wrote it.

SUPPORT AND RESISTANCE STUDIES: SHORT-TERM TRADING TOOLS FOR THE PROFESSIONAL TRADER

So, you really want to be a trader?
Start here.

But if you really want to become skilled
at trading, study the works of Charles Drummond.

CHAPTER FOURTEEN

THE FORMULAS FOR SHORT-TERM TRADING

One of the problems with learning a new set of skills is that it can be costly in the beginning. If you aspire to be a trader, you simply have to think like a politician. That is, instead of considering losses as "losses," you have to translate those early experiences as "investments." You are investing time and money in developing a skill. There is a cost to learning that skill as a student, and then there is the cost of developing that skill through actual trading experience, which is vastly different from the intellectual challenge of "paper trading." Learning these techniques is difficult enough, but nothing compares to the challenge of actual trading where all the tools must be coordinated in real time experience all at once. One error, one omission of an important point, can be costly.

The journey to become a successful trader is no less difficult than the journey to "know oneself." In many ways, it is equivalent to psychotherapy or learning a new language. It is a long process, and there will be many moments when you feel like quitting and going back to your "old habits" and familiar language. But at a certain point, this new skill or language becomes a part of your natural thinking process. You begin to instantly recognize words, signs, and patterns. When you look at a chart, you see it in terms of the new skills you have acquired and not as a maze of random lines without order or meaning.

The reason why this book addresses long-term, intermediate-term, short-term, and aggressive investors and traders is that because everyone has a different temperament. There is no right or wrong when it comes to trading and investing temperaments, despite the fact that many investment advisers are highly critical of traders, and many short-term traders are equally critical of those who are too conservative in their investment approach to markets. It all depends upon one's psychological makeup, or in popular terms, one's "comfort zone" in how active to be involved in the buying or selling of financial markets.

In this final section of the book, very short-term trading tools will be introduced that will be invaluable to the aggressive, short-term trader. I am completely aware that this is the reason many of you bought this book. The original source of some of the formulas used in this section is hard to determine. You pick up an idea from this teacher, that book, this seminar, that lecture, etc., etc. But in most cases, those traders and analysts who introduced you (me) to these formulas and strategies were unaware of how they first came into contact with them. So if I cite the work of someone in this field, it is not with conviction that they created these formulas or strategies, for many are "obvious understandings" and cannot be patented, like moving averages - or the averages of highs, lows, and/or closing prices over any period of time.

What is important is the application (the use) of the values generated by these formulas. How does one use them in a trading plan? How does an analyst use them to generate trading strategies for the next week, next day, or even the next hour? That is what separates this book from the works of others in this field. The applications of these formulas - their relationship to market timing principles, and the strategies employed based on the numbers generated from these calculations - are to my knowledge unique and original, except where otherwise mentioned. They are the result of over 30 years of research in financial markets, of which much has been dedicated to the study of technical, cyclical, and geocosmic analysis.

With this understanding in mind, let us proceed to learn some valuable trading tools. Combined with the market timing methods of Volumes 1 through 4 in this series, as well as with the technical studies already discussed in prior pages, you will soon have at your disposal some very powerful tools for short-term trading. But remember: you are about to learn a new skill. In fact, you are about to learn a new language, for after all, the community of traders is like a whole other world. It will take time to become proficient at both the new language and the new skill sets you are about to learn. Thus, like everything else in one's successful quest of markets, it takes patience, persistence, and hard work.

The Formulas

Our short-term trading approach will be based on weekly and daily numbers. It can also employ longer-term monthly numbers and short-term intraday time band numbers, like 60- and 30-minute price bars. As stated in the beginning chapters, it is always advisable to coordinate multiple time frames, or cycle lengths. In this case, we will utilize multiple time frames, and especially the comparison of daily and weekly numbers, for these are the time frames I find most useful in combination with our other studies. In fact, it would be quite dangerous, in my opinion, to use these formulas solely on their own. They work best when our market timing studies indicate a change of trend is likely, and when prices are within the ranges calculated by previously discussed price target formulas. This section of the book produces a more specific time and price range − within the greater time and price frame of our other studies − in which to enter or exit a trade. I point this out because I know that once you learn these formulas and strategies, you will be tempted to use them immediately and without regard to the bigger picture. Consider this a warning not to do that, for almost as certain as night follows day, you will lose sight of the greater trend and encounter losses by focusing too much on the details and not enough on the bigger picture. For that reason, readers are encouraged to always keep in mind the market timing (cycles and geocosmics) bands for reversals and the price targets for cycle highs and lows as discussed previously, and then to apply these shorter-term calculations and strategies to refine your shorter-term trading plan.

With that in mind, here are the basic formulas we will be using in these chapters.

Pivot Point (PP):

PP = (H+L+C) ÷ 3, where H is the high, L is the low, and C is the close of the time frame you are studying (such as weekly, daily, hourly, etc).

Resistance 1 (R₁):

R₁= C + (H-L)/2, where H represents the high, L represents the low, and C represents the close of the previous time frame being studied.

Resistance 2 (R₂):

R₂ = (PPx2) – L, where PP represents the pivot point of the current time frame being studied and L represents the low of the prior time frame.

Resistance Zone:

The range of R₁ and R₂ represents the *resistance zone* of the next time frame from which these numbers were calculated. If using a particular day's high, low, and close, then R₁ and R₂ would yield the resistance zone for the next day's trading. There are other formulas for determining other resistance zones, but these are the two for short-term trading that we will be using throughout the remainder of this book.

Support 1 (S₁):

S₁ = C - (H-L)/2, where C is the close, H is the high, and L is the low of the previous time frame being studied (such as weekly, daily, hourly, etc).

Support 2 (S₂):

S₂ = (PPx2) – H, where PP represents the pivot point of the time frame being studied and H represents the high of the previous time frame.

Support Zone:

The range of the S₁ and S₂ represents the *support zone* of the next time frame from which these numbers were calculated. If using a particular day's high, low, and close, then the S₁ and S₂ would yield the support zone for the next day's trading. There are other formulas for determining other support zones, but these are the two for short-term trading that we will be using throughout the remainder of this book.

CHAPTER FIFTEEN

THE PIVOT POINT (PP)

The Pivot Point Calculation is PP = (H+L+C) ÷ 3

"Pivot Points" are the basis for many (but not all) of the calculations that short-term traders use to determine daily or weekly (or any time frame's) support and resistance. Short-term traders need to determine support and resistance in order to construct useful trading strategies. And as mentioned before, it is best to utilize multiple time frames for optimal results. Therefore, in this section of the book we will use these formulas for determining weekly and daily pivot points and support/resistance zones.

My first introduction to the pivot point (PP) came from a speaker at a conference my company (MMA, Inc.) hosted in New York City in 1981. The speaker did not invent the formula, nor did he cite the source of where he learned it. The pivot point formula has been around for a very long time, and a check on internet search engines will reveal thousands of references to the pivot point, but again, I found no original source cited. Later on (in other seminars and workshops), I discovered that other technical analysts used this same calculation as part of their short-term trading methodology and oftentimes with a different name than the pivot point. For instance, noted market technician Charles Drummond refers to it as the "1x1 point." But "pivot point" is an appropriate name for this indicator, because various support and resistance areas "pivot" around it.

The pivot point (or PP) is the average of the high, low, and close for a given time period. The formula is simple: H+L+C/3 = PP. That is, add the high, the low, and the close of the time frame being studied, and divide it by three. That number is then the pivot point for the *next* time period. In fact, this will be the case in most of the studies introduced in this section of the book: they apply as pivots, support, or resistance for the *next* time period. If, for example, one takes the high, low, and close of last week's market trading, and divides it by three, that yields the pivot point for this week's current trading. This is done for daily charts as well in order to derive the *next* day's pivot point. It can also be done for 60-minute and 30-minute (or any time) intervals if you are a day trader.

Let us use a real-time example. Figure 50 is a daily chart of the Dow Jones Industrial Average. The last day of trading here is shown as March 25, 2011. On the upper left hand corner of the chart, the open, high, low, close, and change of the day are identified. We are only concerned with the high, low, and close. On March 25, the high was 12,259.80, the low was 12,170.70, and the close was 12,220.60. To find the pivot point for the next trading day, March 28, add all three and divide by 3. Or, (12,259.80 + 12,170.70 + 12,220.60) ÷ 3 = 12,217.03. This price (12,217.03) is thus the pivot point for March 28.

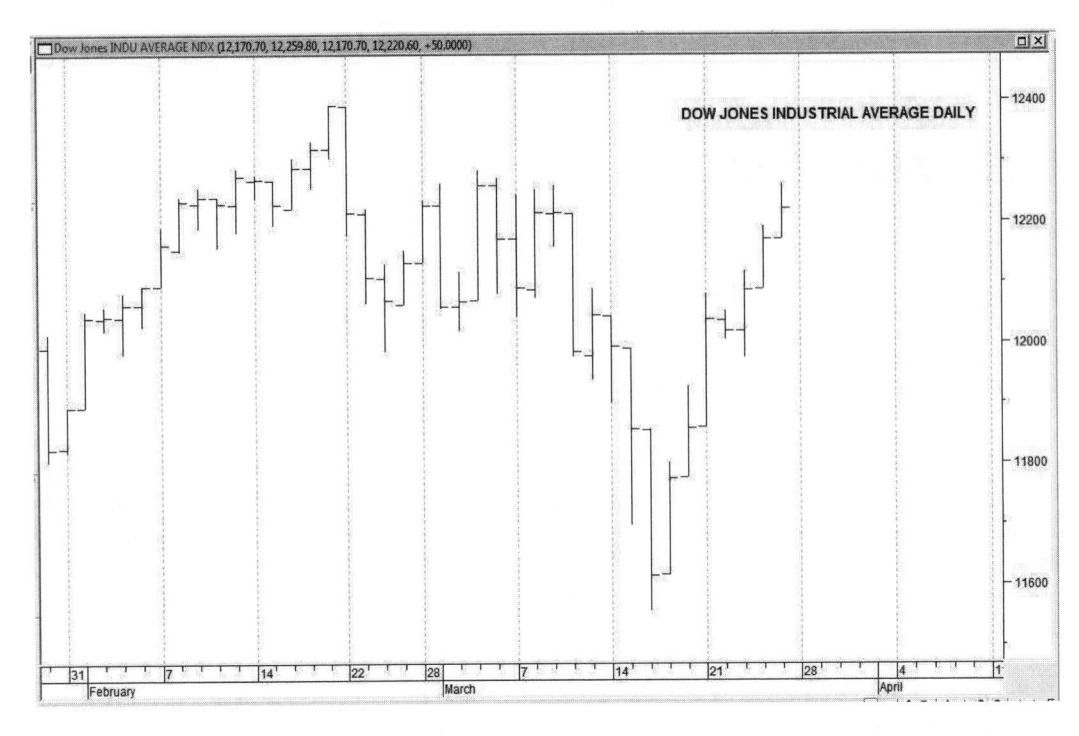

Figure 50: Daily chart of DJIA, ending on March 25, 2011. The open, high, low, close and change for the day is listed on the upper left hand corner, from which the next day's pivot point can be calculated.

Function of the Pivot Point

By itself, the pivot point has limited use for trading purposes. However, it is necessary to calculate because from the pivot point, several support and resistance areas plus trend indicator points may be derived from which a variety of trading strategies can be employed. Our particular use of these will be discussed in the following chapters.

By itself, the pivot point of a day's trading range (high, low and close) represents the neutral price area of the next day's trading of that market. If the close of the day is above it, or if the opening of the next day to which it applies is above it, that means the market is more bullish than bearish for the start of that next day. If the close is below it, or if the opening of the next day is below its pivot point, it means the market is more bearish than bullish for the start of that next day. Of course, that can change depending upon any events or economic reports that may be announced prior to the next day's opening.

In our example of March 25, the close at 12,220.60 was slightly above the next day's pivot point of 12,217.03. This suggests the market closed slightly bullish, and so the next trading day (March 28) may have a slightly bullish bias as it opens. Indeed, on the next day, March 28, 2011, the market opened higher and continued higher for the first hour of trading. This is common and to be expected. But it should not be expected that the market will remain bullish all the next day.

By itself, the pivot point is not a powerful level of support or resistance. Generally speaking, the next day's trading will be below and above this point. In a preliminary study of the next day's trading range in relationship to the pivot point over an 8-year period, I found that the next day's trading range would indeed be both above and below the pivot point in about two-thirds of the cases. The other one-third of the days found prices entirely above the pivot point (bullish) or below it (bearish). This can be somewhat useful in those cases where a trader ended the day on the wrong side of the market. If he wants to exit the position the next day at a slightly better position than where the market closed, there is a two-thirds probability that he can do so at the pivot point or better.

Of course there are exceptions to this rule, such as when a market gaps up or down. In those cases, the market won't trade on both sides of the pivot point. It will either trade the entire day above it (gap up) or below it (gap down). If it fills the gap, then often it will find support or resistance at the pivot point. If it closes on the other side of the pivot point, then it is probably extremely bullish or bearish. For example, if a market opens with a gap up, but then fills that gap *and* closes the day below the pivot point, it is probably commencing a sharp decline. That's a bearish signal for the next day. Conversely, if a market opens with a gap down, but then closes above the pivot point for that day, it is probably starting a healthy rally. That's a bullish signal for the next day. When this happens, one can usually put on a trade in the direction of the break of the pivot point, with a stop-loss above or below the opening range of that day, or pivot point.

Pivot points may act as support or resistance in lower time periods. For instance, the daily pivot point may act as support or resistance in the 30- or 60-minute charts of that day. Likewise, a weekly pivot point may serve as support or resistance in a daily chart. Let's view an example of this occurrence on the weekly chart of the DJIA for the week ending March 4, 2011, in Figure 51, shown on the next page.

The high of the week ending March 4 was 12,283.10. The low of that week was 12,018.60, and the close was 12,169.90. Thus the pivot point (PP) for the next week would be (12,283.10 + 12,018.60 + 12,169.90) ÷ 3, or 12,157.20.

Now let us look at the daily chart for that next week, as shown in Figure 52, also on the next page. Notice that the market moved back and forth over this pivot point on March 7 and 8. But on March 9, the low of the day was 12,156.60, which was almost exactly on the weekly pivot point. Once again, this is not usually a powerful support or resistance level. But the weekly pivot point can act as support or resistance at times in the lower time frames (like the daily), especially if it converges with other support or resistance points pertinent to that day.

The three main things to remember about pivot points are:

1. They are used to calculate more powerful support and resistance areas, as well as Trend Indicator Points, as will be discussed shortly.
2. A market will trade to the level of the pivot point calculated for the next time period in approximately two-thirds of cases.
3. Pivot Points may act as support or resistance in lower time periods.

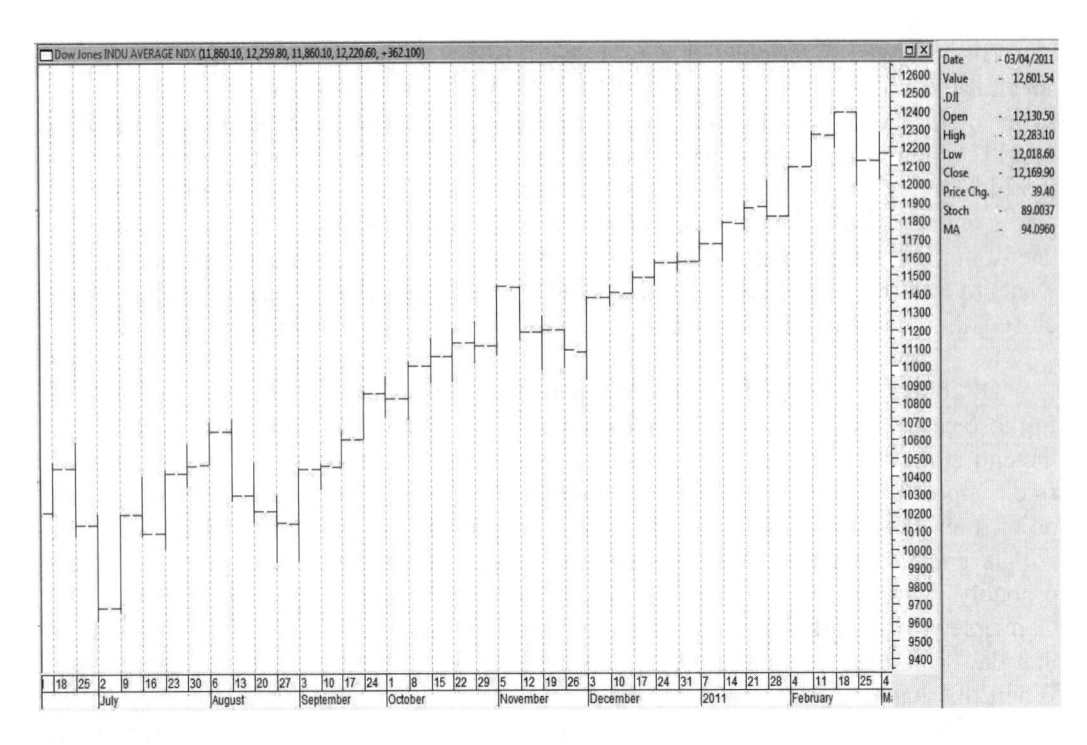

Figure 51: A weekly chart of the DJIA (above). Note the high, low, and close for March 4 as listed in the upper right hand part of this chart.

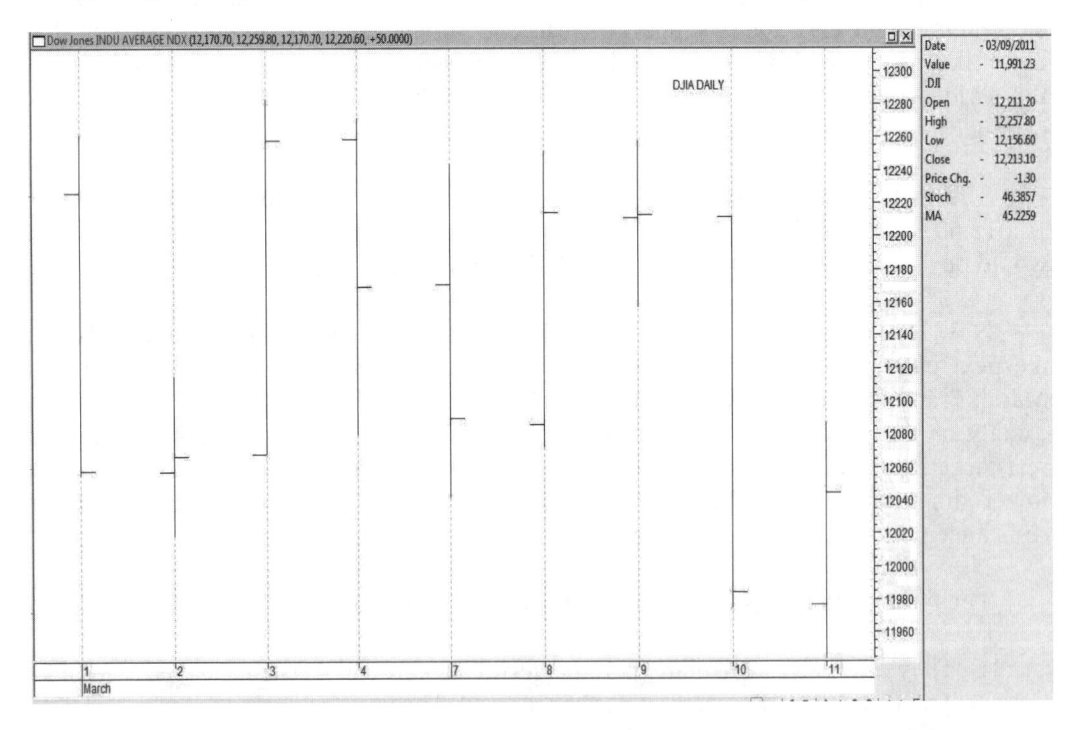

Figure 52. The daily chart of the DJIA from March 1-11. This shows that on March 9, the low of the day was almost exactly on the weekly pivot point at 12,157.20, based on the week's trading ending March 4.

CHAPTER SIXTEEN

THE TREND INDICATOR POINT (TIP)

In the chapter on moving averages, the concept of "trend runs" was introduced. Basically, when prices are above two moving averages that apply to a cycle and one of its phases, and the shorter moving average is also above the longer one, it is known as a "trend run up." When prices are below these two moving averages, and the shorter average is also below the longer average, it is known as a "trend run down."

However, this is not the only use of these terms in the field of technical analysis. In fact, there is an entire branch of technical analysis that uses these terms differently. This branch of technical analysis has been constructed by one of the most rigorous, inventive, although relatively uncited market analysts of modern times. His name is Charles Drummond, and his contribution to this field is known as "Drummond Market Geometry."

By way of background, I had the privilege of meeting Drummond in the mid-1980's. I learned about his work through clients and colleagues who had studied with both Drummond and myself. It was well after I learned about pivot points and the basic floor trader calculations for support and resistance (that I will discuss shortly). After hearing about some of Drummond's impressive market calls, I decided to purchase his workbook titled "P and L Labs"[1]. I believe it cost $2000.00 at the time, so for me in 1985, it was "an investment" in the development of my own trading skills.

Over the next few years, I became both a fan and friend of Charlie. I attended some of his students' seminars, such as market analyst Patrick Shaughnessy in Scottsdale, Arizona, where Charlie would also participate. He also came to one of my seminars on market timing in the early 1990's. I admired the wealth of useful ideas and formulas Drummond put into his work and the sheer ingenuity of his market geometry from the "price" point of view. I knew "market timing" as well as anyone (or so I believed, with the exception of Walter Bressert, my own mentor into markets), based on my knowledge of geocosmic and cycle studies. And I knew several of the floor trader calculations for support and resistance, around which I developed my own trading plans in combination with market timing factors, as you will learn shortly.

I soon realized that no one knew "price geometry" quite like Drummond. Yet he is seldom cited for his remarkable contributions to this field of study. You can go to internet search engines and type in terms like "bullish triggers," "bearish triggers," "bullish and bearish crossover zones," and "trend run ups and downs." These are just some of the many market terms that Drummond used in his works. And yet you won't find him cited for the way he used these terms in market analysis, which is every bit as valuable as the way others apply these terms. So it is my hope that this section of Volume 5 will correct that lack of credit given to this remarkable technician who has contributed so much to the field of technical market analysis and price objective studies.

Drummond applied some of the same floor trader calculations that I had learned from others as referenced earlier, and which I will discuss again in the following chapters. Druumond used a great deal more than the points I will be discussing. He would take the high, low, and closing prices of any time frame he found pertinent. With those prices he created an entire mathematical system of analysis that pinpointed several key support and resistance levels. He would use daily, weekly, and monthly prices. For long-term analysis, he would use quarterly and yearly prices. For very short-term trading, he would use intraday time frames like 30- and 60-minute prices, although he used other intraday time frames too that are unique to him. In short, he created an eclectic system of calculating support and resistance points from which he constructed a variety of specific trading plans. His market geometry and short-term trading strategies are very comprehensive – more than will be discussed here. So if you wish to truly enhance your trading skills, the study of his courses on market geometry is highly recommended. You can obtain further information on his works at www.DrummondGeometry.com.

It is Drummond's use of the terms "trend run up," "trend run down," and "congestion" that will be introduced in this chapter. These "trend analysis" terms are not used in quite the same way as discussed in the chapter on moving averages. Nonetheless, their use as short-term trend indicators is extremely valuable to the aggressive, short-term trader. They are valuable for position traders too. However this section of the book will primarily address their usage in short-term trading.

In order to understand Drummond's use of these terms, we have to first understand the "Trend Indicator Point" (TIP), or "Dot," as Drummond calls it. I prefer the term "Trend Indicator Point" because that is its function. It is the basis for understanding whether the market is in a short-term trend run up, neutral (congestion), or trend run down. The Trend Indicator Point (TIP, or Dot) is a three-day, or three-week (or 3 of whatever time frame one wishes to use) moving average, or the average of the high, low, and closing prices over the previous three time periods. More specifically, it is the sum of the last three Pivot Points divided by three. Or, TIP = $(PP_1 + PP_2 + PP_3) \div 3$, where PP_1 represents the pivot point of the first day, and PP_2 and PP_3 the pivot points of the second and third days used in the calculation. Like the Pivot Point itself, the Trend Indicator Point applies to the next time frame's trading.

Let us do a sample calculation to show how the TIP (or Dot) is derived. Let us assume the last 3 days of trading figures for stock XYZ are as follows, where H represents the high of that day, L represents the low, and C represents the close:

Day	H	L	C
1	75.50	71.20	73.75
2	77.00	73.25	76.80
3	79.20	75.50	76.20

Our first step is to calculate the pivot point (PP) for each day. As discussed before, this is simply the average of the high, low, and close for each day, applied to the next day. In other words, today's high, plus low, plus close, divided by three, gives us the pivot point (PP) for the next day's trading. Or, PP = (H + L + C) ÷ 3.

Now, let us calculate the Pivot Point for each of the following days:

Day	H	L	C	PP
1	75.50	71.20	73.75	
2	77.00	73.25	76.80	73.48
3	79.20	75.50	76.20	75.68
4				76.97

Notice how the pivot point for day 2 is based on the daily high, low, and close of day 1. The PP for day 3 is based on the trading range and close of day 2, and the PP for day 4 is calculated for the high, low, and close of day 3. Whatever happens in the current time frame creates the numbers for the next time frame of the same duration. In this case, we are using a daily chart. However, the same calculations can be constructed from weekly, monthly, and yearly charts, or 60-minute and 30-minute charts, as well.

Once we have three pivot points, we can calculate the trend indicator point (TIP) for the time frame pertaining to that third pivot point. In this case, TIP = (73.48 + 75.68 + 76.97) ÷ 3, or 75.38. The trend indicator point for the fourth day is 75.38. On our table, it would look like this:

Day	H	L	C	PP	TIP
1	75.50	71.20	73.75		
2	77.00	73.25	76.80	73.48	
3	79.20	75.50	76.20	75.68	
4				76.97	75.38

Trend Run Up, Trend Run Down, and Neutral

We discussed trend runs in Chapter 13 on moving averages. As mentioned earlier, when prices are above two moving averages that apply to a cycle and one of its phases and the shorter moving average is above the longer one, it is known as a trend run up. Since the trend indicator point is based on a 3-bar moving average, its relationship to prices and trend indictor points *of different time frames* can also be used to identify a market that is in a trend run. For instance, if the price of a market is above both the daily and weekly trend indicator point, and the daily is above the weekly, one could surmise that the market is in a trend run up, just as discussed in the chapter on moving averages. Conversely, if prices are below both the daily and weekly trend indicator points, and the daily is lower than the weekly, one could conclude the market is in a trend run down. Drummond, however, offered other approaches to trend runs using the relationship of prices to these trend indicator points, or "Dots," as he referred to them.

First of all, he advised simply to "follow the Dot." If it is rising from one time frame to the next, the market is moving up. It is bullish. If the Dot (or TIP) starts to decline, then the market may also be starting to reverse downwards. If it continues moving down, then the market trend is bearish. That's the most simple and practical way to use the three-day moving average, known as the "Dot," or trend indicator point (TIP).

Drummond also discussed another way to view the trend based on the relationship of closing prices to the Dot. If the market closed three consecutive periods above the trend indicator point (TIP), Drummond considered the market as being in a new "trend run up" for the time period being examined. If it closed three consecutive periods below the TIP, it was considered a "trend run down." At all other times, the market was considered neutral, or in congestion.

Thus the first step to establishing the short-term trend status of a market via use of the trend indicator point (TIP) is to identify the relationship of at least the last three closing prices to the TIP. To illustrate how this works, let us return to our prior example and add more daily prices in order to achieve at least three days of trend indicator points.

Day	H	L	C	PP	TIP	STATUS
1	75.50	71.20	73.75			
2	77.00	73.25	76.80	73.48		
3	79.20	75.50	76.20	75.68		
4	78.15	76.25	78.00	76.97	75.38	
5	79.50	77.95	79.45	77.47	76.70	
6	80.50	79.55	80.25	78.97	77.80	UP
7				80.10	78.85	

Notice on days 4, 5, and 6 that prices closed above the TIP for that day. In other words, there were three consecutive daily closes above the TIP. You can also see that the TIP was rising each day above the prior day's level. Therefore this market can be assigned a "trend run up" status on the daily chart as of the sixth day of trading. We will designate that status as UP, or U. As long as prices continue to close above the TIP, and especially if the TIP is rising each day, this market is in a *trend run up*, via these rules. As soon as it closes below the TIP, it is downgraded to *neutral*. And should the market close three consecutive days below the TIP, it will be downgraded further to a *trend run down*. In this case, the value of the TIP may also be declining over consecutive days, although that is not always the case. Additionally we should be aware of instances in which the rate of change in TIP from one period to the next begins to diminish. This is a warning that the trend may be about to change. In any event, we will designate the status of these changes in the column marked STATUS. In this column, a trend run up status is shown as U, a trend run down as D, and neutral as N. And there may be exceptions to this assignment of trend indicator status that will be introduced shortly, as a result of my own observations regarding this indicator since 1985.

Before getting to those exceptions and other possible ways to rate the trend, let us construct closes that are now below the TIP. Let us have day 7 close below it.

Day	H	L	C	PP	TIP	STATUS
1	75.50	71.20	73.75			
2	77.00	73.25	76.80	73.48		
3	79.20	75.50	76.20	75.68		
4	78.15	76.25	78.00	76.97	75.38	U
5	79.50	77.95	79.45	77.47	76.70	U
6	80.50	79.55	80.25	78.97	77.80	U
7	80.00	77.15	78.75	80.10	78.85	N
8				78.63	79.23	

In this example, the seventh day closed at 78.75, which was slightly below the TIP that applied to that day at 78.85. Therefore, after closing above the TIP for three consecutive days, it then closed below it on the fourth day. Hence the short-term trend of this market was downgraded from a trend run up to neutral. Notice that the TIP itself did not decline from the prior day, so it was not necessarily the start of a reversal. It may just be pausing or entering into a short-term congestion. Nevertheless it will stay in a neutral status until it closes three consecutive days below the trend indicator point, at which time it will then be downgraded further to a trend run down (D). It could also resume its uptrend by closing three consecutive days above TIP, in which case it would be upgraded back to a trend run up. In fact, it may be upgraded to a trend run up if it closes back above the TIP the very next day, given that TIP itself never turned down.

Let us return to the example and demonstrate how a trend run down would look.

Day	H	L	C	PP	TIP	STATUS
1	75.50	71.20	73.75			
2	77.00	73.25	76.80	73.48		
3	79.20	75.50	76.20	75.68		
4	78.15	76.25	78.00	76.97	75.38	U
5	79.50	77.95	79.45	77.47	76.70	U
6	80.50	79.55	80.25	78.97	77.80	U
7	80.00	77.15	78.75	80.10	78.85	N
8	79.20	76.50	78.80	78.63	79.23	N
9	78.50	74.95	75.00	78.17	78.96	D

Notice that after day 7 closed below TIP, this downgraded the market to neutral. Day 8 also closed below TIP. It remained neutral. Notice also that the TIP itself has not yet started to decline from the prior day. We see that on day 9, the market closed below TIP for the third consecutive day. Thus the status of the short-term market trend is now downgraded further, to a trend run down (D). The TIP had also declined from the prior day, supporting this downgrade in trend. In these 9 days, the market changed from trend run up (day 6) to neutral (days 7 and 8) to a trend run down (day 9).

These, then, represent the basic principles or rules of trend analysis on a short-term basis as introduced by Charles Drummond.[2]

COROLLARIES TO BASIC SHORT-TERM TREND ANALYSIS RULES

Knowing Drummond, it is entirely likely that he has added corollaries to these basic rules of trend analysis centered around his "Dot," or what we call TIP, the "trend indicator point." Nevertheless, I present my own corollaries to his principles that I have evolved after applying these rules for the past 25 years, knowing that several of these corollaries may have also been considered by Drummond in his later works.

"Trend Run Up" Corollaries

1. **Non-confirmed trend run up:** If the close is above the TIP for three consecutive days (weeks, months, or whatever time frame is being analyzed), it is not necessarily upgraded from neutral to a trend run up unless the close of the third day is also an "up" day from the close of the prior day. That is, if the market closes down from the previous day, it remains neutral, even though that close was above the TIP for the third consecutive day. This is true even if it happens on the fourth day. That is, the close may be above the TIP for four consecutive days, but if the close on the third and fourth days was below the close on each of those prior days, it still remains neutral. The trend run up is thus not yet confirmed.
2. **Confirmed trend run up on fourth or fifth day**: If the close is then above the prior day's close and TIP on the 4th or even 5th day (but not the third), it is then upgraded from neutral to a trend run up. That is, if the close was above the TIP for three consecutive days, but on the third day the market closed down, it remained neutral. If on the fourth day the close was up from the prior day and still above the TIP, it is upgraded to a trend run up. If the close was above the TIP on the fourth day, but it was still a down day, it can be upgraded to trend run up if the close is up on the fifth day and also above the TIP that day.
3. **Trend run up resumed after a one-day interruption:** Once the market is in a trend run up, it is downgraded to neutral on the first day it closes back below the TIP. However, if the close of the next day is back above the TIP and also an up day, it is upgraded again and the trend run up is resumed. It does not require three *new* consecutive days above the TIP to be upgraded back to a trend run up.
4. **Downgrade to neutral after an interrupted trend run up:** However, if after an interruption of the trend run up and then the resumption of it again, the market will revert back to neutral once more if it closes below the TIP again in the next two days. That is, in order to maintain its trend run up status, it must continue to close above the TIP point for the next two consecutive days (three consecutive days in all) even after a temporary interruption where it closed below the TIP for one day. If the next day (after the interruption) it closes above TIP, it resumes its trend run up. But if the following day (or even two days after that) it closes below the TIP, it is downgraded to neutral again.

5. **On edge, trend run up:** Sometimes a market can be upgraded from neutral even when it hasn't closed three consecutive days above the TIP. For instance, the market might have such a powerfully strong rally that it closes not just above the TIP, but also above the high of the cycle so far. It forms a new cycle high on a powerful up day. However, it is only the first or second day above the TIP. In this case, the TIP may be upgraded from neutral to "on edge, trend run up." When it exhibits three closing days above the TIP, and the third day is also an up day, it can be upgraded further to a trend run up from an "on edge, trend run up."
6. **Pause in the trend run up:** There will be cases where a market closes right on the TIP. In these cases, the trend run up that was in effect remains intact. This is a warning that it may be about to change. For example, if the market has been in a trend run up, and then the close of the current day is exactly on the TIP, it remains in a trend run up. If on the next day it closes below the TIP, it reverses from trend run up to neutral. Furthermore this means that the market has not closed above the TIP for two consecutive days. If the next day is a down day and also below the TIP, it will be downgraded from neutral to trend run down.
7. **Overextended, exhaustion:** Trend runs up can last for several days (or weeks, months, whatever your time frame is). Yet at some point there will be a close below the TIP, and it will change from trend run up to neutral and eventually trend run down. How long do trend run ups last? Later on we will present a study on the weekly Dow Jones Industrial Average from June 3, 2002 through May 20, 2011 that attempts to identify how many weeks a trend run up or down tends to last. From this we will determine a length of time that we will consider overextended or exhaustion, from which a reversal or pause tends to follow.

Now, let us see how these corollaries might work in actual practice. Let's take the following example from our XYZ Corporation, as used before, to show how an interruption in a trend run up might look, as well as a pause in that trend run up:

Day	H	L	C	PP	TIP	STATUS
1	75.50	71.20	73.75			
2	77.00	73.25	76.80	73.48		
3	79.20	75.50	76.20	75.68		
4	78.15	76.25	78.00	76.97	75.38	N
5	79.50	77.95	79.45	77.47	76.70	N
6	80.50	79.55	80.25	78.97	77.80	U
7	80.00	77.15	78.75	80.10	78.85	N
8	81.10	77.60	80.65	78.63	79.23	U
9	82.00	79.45	79.50	79.78	79.50	U*
10	81.15	79.25	80.80	80.33	79.58	U

Notice on day 6 that the close was above the daily trend indicator point (TIP) for the third consecutive day. Thus it was in a trend run up as of the close that day. The next day (day 7) it closed below TIP, and thus it was downgraded back to a neutral status. On day 8 it closed back above TIP. It was thus upgraded back to a trend run up after the one-day interruption when it closed below and was temporarily downgraded to neutral. On day 9, it closed exactly on the TIP. It was still considered a trend run up (U*) because it didn't close below TIP. The trend didn't change here, although it was a warning that it could change. However the next day (day 10) the close was well above the TIP. We now consider that the close has been above (or on) the trend indicator point for 6 of the past 7 days. It is in a trend run up that was interrupted back on day 4, but it resumed its uptrend the very next day. There was also a pause on day 9 when prices closed right on the TIP. But the trend run up does not change then unless the next day closes below TIP.

Now let us show how an unconfirmed trend run up might look for XYZ Corporation, using the same starting prices for the first five days, but with different prices afterwards.

Day	H	L	C	PP	TIP	STATUS
1	75.50	71.20	73.75			
2	77.00	73.25	76.80	73.48		
3	79.20	75.50	76.20	75.68		
4	78.15	76.25	78.00	76.97	75.38	N
5	79.50	77.95	79.45	77.47	76.70	N
6	80.50	79.15	79.35	78.97	77.80	N*
7	80.00	77.15	79.10	79.67	78.70	N*

Notice that the close on day 6 was above the TIP for the third consecutive day, but the close of that day was lower than the close of day 5. Therefore it was not a confirmed trend run up (N*). On day 7, the close was again above the TIP, but again it was a lower close than the prior day. Therefore, even though prices had closed above the TIP for four consecutive days, it was still not a confirmed trend run up because XYZ had not exhibited a close above the prior day (in this case, not above the prior two days). It was still in neutral. In cases like this, the market can still go either way. If it can close up the next day, and above the TIP, it will then be upgraded to a trend run up.

Let us continue with the above example and show how an "on-edge trend run up" would look like. Let us assume that a couple of weeks ago XYZ rallied to 82.00, its highest price so far in this primary cycle. If at any time XYZ closes above 82.00 before closing three consecutive days above the TIP, it will be considered an "on edge, trend run up." Once it closes the third day above the TIP - and if that day is a higher close than the prior day - then it will be upgraded further from an "on edge, trend run up" to a full trend run up. An example of how this would look is shown in the continuation of XYZ, shown in the table below.

Day	H	L	C	PP	TIP	STATUS
1	75.50	71.20	73.75			
2	77.00	73.25	76.80	73.48		
3	79.20	75.50	76.20	75.68		
4	78.15	76.25	78.00	76.97	75.38	N
5	79.50	77.95	79.45	77.47	76.70	N

6	80.50	79.55	80.25	78.97	77.80	U
7	80.00	77.15	79.10	79.67	78.70	U
8	79.40	78.50	78.85	78.63	79.23	N
9	80.00	78.85	79.95	78.92	79.21	N
10	82.50	80.00	82.45	79.60	79.05	OEU

Note that on day 8 the close was below the TIP after being above it four of the previous five trading days. Thus it was downgraded back to neutral. On day 9 it closed back above the TIP, so it remained neutral. On day 10, it gapped up and closed sharply higher, at 82.45. It was far above the TIP, and also closed at a level above the highest price so far in this primary cycle. It was only the second consecutive day above the TIP, and because it was a new cycle high and above the TIP, it would be upgraded from neutral to an "on edge, trend run up" (OEU). If it closes up the next day (above the close of day 10), it will be upgraded to a full trend run up, as that would also represent three consecutive closes above the TIP.

"Trend Run Down" Corollaries

The same corollaries apply in reverse to trend run downs. We will repeat them here, except we will make changes to reflect the trend run down condition.

1. **Non-confirmed trend run down:** If the close is below the TIP for three consecutive days (weeks, months, or whatever time frame is analyzed), it is not necessarily downgraded from neutral to a trend run down unless the close of the third day is also down from the close of the prior day. That is, if the market closes up from the previous day, it remains neutral, even though that close was below the TIP for the third consecutive day. This is true even if it happens on the fourth day. The close may be below the TIP for four consecutive days, but if the close on the third and fourth days are above the close on each of the prior days, it still remains neutral. The trend run down is thus not yet confirmed.
2. **Confirmed trend run down on fourth or fifth day**: If the close is then below the prior day's close and TIP on the 4th or even 5th day (but not the third), it is downgraded from neutral to a trend run down. That is, if the close was below the TIP for three consecutive days, but on the third day the market closed up, it remained neutral. If on the fourth day the close was down from the prior day and still below the TIP, it is downgraded to a trend run down. If the close was below the TIP on the fourth day, but it was still an up day, it can be downgraded to trend run down if the close is down on the fifth day and also below the TIP.
3. **Trend run down resumed after a one-day interruption:** Once the market is in a trend run down, it is upgraded to neutral on the first day it closes back above the TIP. However, if the close of the next day is back below the TIP and also a down day, it is downgraded again to trend run down. The trend run down resumes. It does not require three *new* consecutive days below the TIP to be downgraded back to a trend run down.
4. **Upgrade to neutral after an interrupted trend run down:** However, if after an interruption of the trend run down, followed by the resumption of it the next day, the market will be upgraded back to neutral again if one of the following two days finds the market closing above the TIP. That is, in order to maintain its

trend run down status, it must continue to close below the TIP point for the next two consecutive days (for a total of three consecutive days) even after a temporary interruption. If the next day (after the interruption) it closes below the TIP, it resumes its trend run down status. If on the following day (or even two days after that) it closes above the TIP again, it is upgraded to neutral again.

5. **On edge, trend run down:** Sometimes a market can be downgraded from neutral even when it hasn't closed three consecutive days below the TIP. For instance, the market might have such a powerfully strong decline that it closes not just below the TIP, but also below the low of the cycle so far. It forms a new cycle low on a powerful down day, although it is only the first or second day below the TIP. In this case, we can downgrade the TIP from neutral to "on edge, trend run down." When it exhibits three closing days below the TIP, and the third day is also a down day, it can be downgraded further to a trend run down from an "on edge, trend run down." This is a strong sign that the trend status is changing.

6. **Pause in the trend run up:** There will be cases where a market closes right on the TIP. In these cases, the trend run down that was in effect remains intact. This is a warning that it may be about to change. For example, if the market has been in a trend run down, and then the close of the current day is exactly on the TIP, it remains in a trend run down. If it closes above the TIP the next day, it reverses from a trend run down to neutral. Furthermore this means that the market has not closed below the TIP for two consecutive days. If the next day is an up day and also above the TIP, it will be upgraded from neutral to trend run up.

7. **Overextended, exhaustion:** Trend runs down can last several days (or weeks, months, whatever time frame used). However at some point there will be a close above the TIP, and it will change from trend run down to neutral and eventually to a trend run up. How long do trend run downs last? Later on we will present a study on the Dow Jones Industrial Average from June 3, 2002 through May 20, 2011 that identifies how long a trend run up or down tends to last. From this we will determine a length of time that we will consider overextended or exhausted, from which a reversal of the trend (or more likely just a pause) tends to follow.

Now, let us see how these corollaries might work in actual practice. Let us take the following example from our XYZ Corporation, as started out before, to show how a non-confirmed trend run down might look, followed by a confirmed trend run down.

Day	H	L	C	PP	TIP	STATUS
1	75.50	71.20	73.75			
2	77.00	73.25	76.80	73.48		
3	79.20	75.50	76.20	75.68		
4	78.15	76.25	78.00	76.97	75.38	
5	79.50	77.95	79.45	77.47	76.70	
6	80.50	79.55	80.25	78.97	77.80	U
7	80.00	77.15	78.75	80.10	78.85	N
8	79.50	78.00	78.25	78.63	79.23	N
9	79.00	78.00	78.50	78.58	79.10	N*
10	78.45	77.00	77.10	78.50	78.57	D

On Day 6, XYZ closed above the TIP for the third consecutive day, and it was an up day, which meant it was upgraded to a trend run up. That didn't last. The next day (day 7) it closed below the TIP, downgrading its status from trend run up to neutral. Day 8 also closed below the TIP for the second consecutive day, so it remained neutral. Day 9 also closed below the TIP, but it was an up day. Therefore, even though it closed below the TIP for three consecutive days, it was not confirmed as a trend run down because the third day was not a down day from the previous day's close. Thus it remains neutral (N*). However the next day (day 10) it closed down from the prior day's close, and it was below the TIP point for the fourth consecutive day, which meant XYZ was now in a confirmed trend run down.

An example of an interrupted trend down that is then resumed is shown below. Also shown here is a case where the interrupted and resumed trend run down is then upgraded back to neutral.

Day	H	L	C	PP	TIP	STATUS
6	80.50	79.55	80.25	78.97	77.80	U
7	80.00	77.15	78.75	80.10	78.85	N
8	79.50	78.00	78.25	78.63	79.23	N
9	79.00	78.00	78.50	78.58	79.10	N
10	78.45	77.00	77.10	78.50	78.57	D
11	78.00	76.50	77.10	77.52	78.20	D
12	78.50	77.40	78.25	77.20	77.74	N-I
13	78.20	76.90	77.00	78.05	77.59	D
14	77.50	76.50	77.40	77.37	77.54	D
15	78.50	77.25	78.45	77.13	77.52	N

Here N-I means neutral, but it is an interruption of a trend run up or down. In this case, it interrupts the trend run down, which then resumes after this one-day interrupt. This is different than N*, which means the close was above below the TIP for three straight days, yet the third day closed up, so it was not a confirmed trend run down,

Note that on day 11, XYZ has closed below the TIP for the 5th consecutive day. It is clearly in a trend run down. However on day 12, it closed above the TIP, thereby upgrading its status to neutral. It will remain neutral if the next day also closes above the TIP for the second consecutive day. In fact, it could even be upgraded to an "on edge, trend run up," if prices closed sharply higher and above the high of the primary cycle up to this point (assuming the primary cycle has been underway for a few weeks). On the other hand, if XYZ closed back below the TIP, then the trend run down would resume after the one-day interruption. In this example, the following happened on day 13: it closed back below the TIP, and it closed down from the prior day's close, so the trend run down was resumed. It continued that way on day 14, since that day also closed below the TIP. On day 15, just two days after it resumed its trend run down status, it closed again above the TIP. The trend run down thus came to an end, and its status was upgraded to neutral.

Now let us see what an "on edge, trend run down" (OED) might look like. In this set up, the market needs to be neutral for one day, although there are exceptions where prices can just suddenly collapse to a new cycle low from a trend run up. Let us assume the primary cycle low started on day 1 at 71.20. The following daily prices for XYZ were:

Day	H	L	C	PP	TIP	STATUS
1	75.50	71.20	73.75			
2	77.00	73.25	76.80	73.48		
3	79.20	75.50	76.20	75.68		
4	78.15	76.25	76.25	76.97	75.38	N
5	76.00	73.50	73.50	76.88	76.51	N
6	73.20	70.70	71.00	74.33	76.06	OED
7	71.70	70.50	71.20	71.63	74.28	N
8	71.00	69.00	69.40	71.13	72.36	D

Notice on day 4 that the market closed above the first TIP calculated for this example. It was thus neutral. On day 5 it closed below the TIP again, so the status was neutral again. On day 6 it closed sharply down below the TIP for the second consecutive day. It also closed below the primary cycle low that started the cycle on day 1 at 71.20. Normally this would be considered neutral as it was only the second consecutive day down. This was sharply lower and below the low that started the cycle, so it is downgraded to an "on edge, trend run down." This is shown as OED in the "status column." This means the trend is pointing lower and prices are expected to fall further.

On day 7 it again closed below the TIP, but it the close was higher than the prior day's close. Thus, even though XYZ closed below the TIP for the third consecutive day, we have to upgrade it back to neutral because it was an up day. However, the next day (day 8) it closed lower than the prior day and well below the TIP, so it is fully downgraded to a trend run down status.

These are all hypothetical examples, designed to illustrate how these terms are used. Once these concepts are understood, we have a language by which to convey what the trend status of the market is at any given point, depending on the time frame traded. According to Drummond Market Geometry, this manner of looking at the market is known as "following the Dot," or in our terminology, it is studying the relationship of closing prices to the TIP (trend indicator point).

TIP Studies

Conducting special studies can show more clearly how certain principles have worked historically, while at the same time yield additional insights into the nature of these concepts. For instance, a study can reveal the range of time frames a market remains in a trend run up or down. A study can provide a guideline as to when a trend run is extremely long and due for a reversal or pause. Or a study can provide an understanding of the different paths a market may take after its trend run is interrupted.

In order to find insights into some of these questions, I did a study of nine years of weekly data on the Dow Jones Industrial Average. I assigned the trend status of each week during the time period of this study in order to determine information about the length of time the DJIA tended to remain in a trend run on a weekly basis.

Weekly DJIA Studies on TIPs

The weekly study of the DJIA covered the period from June 3, 2002 through May 20, 2011, or 467 weeks. The initial purpose was to see how long trend runs up and trend runs down tend to last on a weekly basis, as per the Drummond rules. One objective was to determine how long it took for a trend run to become overextended or exhausted before it paused or reversed. I also wanted to see how often a market closed above or below a weekly trend indicator for three consecutive weeks, and when the third week was a non-confirmed trend run, as per the corollaries added. Then I wanted to see how often a market confirmed, or failed to confirm, the trend run by the fourth week. And finally I wanted to see what historically occurred after trend interruptions. Did trend runs really resume after a one-week interruption? Or were they apt to stay in neutral and/or move towards a trend run in the opposite direction?

In the first part of the study, no interrupted cases were used. If, for instance, a market closed above the weekly trend indicator for three or more consecutive weeks and then closed below it, the trend run up was ended. It was downgraded to neutral. If it then resumed weekly closes above the TIP the next week, it was not considered a resumption of the trend run up for this study. It was still in neutral. The number of weeks closing above the TIP was reset at 1 week. It would not be considered a new trend run up until it exhibited three new consecutive weekly closes back above the weekly TIP, even though in actual practice we would consider it a resumption of the trend run up even after the first week closed back above the TIP following an interruption.

Below are the results of the study.

Week #	UP	Non-Confirm 3rd Week	DOWN	Non-Confirm 3rd Week
3	15	6	6	3
4	6	1	13	0
5	5	0	4	0
6	4	1	3	1
7	2	1	2	0
8	1	0	1	0
9	1	0	2	1
10	4	0		
11	3	0		
12	1	0		
14	1	1		
Totals	43	10	31	5

The first column is titled "Week #" and represents the number of weeks involved in consecutive closes above or below the weekly trend indicator point (TIP or Dot). The second column is titled "UP" and represents the specific number of times it closed above the TIP those exact number of weeks. The third column is titled "Non-Confirm 3rd Week" and indicates the number of instances in which the third week closed above the TIP, but at the same time it closed below the close of the second week. In other words, it was a down week, even though it closed above the TIP. Therefore it was not a confirmed trend run up. The fourth column is titled "DOWN" and represents the number of consecutive weeks it closed below the TIP. The fifth column is titled "Non-Confirm 3rd Week" and indicates the number of instances in which the third week closed below the TIP, but at the same time it closed above the close of the second week. In other words, it was an up week, even though it closed below the TIP. Hence we would consider the trend status still neutral, or an "unconfirmed trend run down."

As the table indicates, there were 43 cases in which the market closed above the weekly trend indicator point for at least three consecutive weeks during our study of 467 weeks. Of those, 10 were non-confirmed trend run ups at the end of the third week (see totals at bottom of the third column titled "Non-Confirm 3rd Week"). That is, the weekly close was above the weekly trend indicator point in the third week, but the weekly close was lower than the prior week's close. It closed down. Of those 10 non-confirmation cases, 4 continued higher the following week. That means in 60% of these cases studied, a non-confirmed trend run up in the third week would be followed by weekly closes back below the weekly TIP. It did not become a weekly trend run up the following week.

The results were similar for trend run downs. There were 5 cases of non-confirmed trend run downs at the end of the third week. That is, the weekly close was below the weekly trend indicator point in five cases, but the weekly close was above the prior week's close each time. It closed up. Of those five non-confirmed cases, 2 continued higher the following week. That means in 60% of these cases, a non-confirmed trend run down in the third week would be followed by weekly closes back above the weekly TIP. It did not become a weekly trend run down the following week 60% of the time. This study supports the importance of not necessarily assuming the market is in a trend run up or down just because it closed three consecutive weeks above or below the weekly TIP respectively. If the weekly close isn't up or down respectively from the prior week as well, chances are slightly greater that a new trend run status will not be confirmed.

With these considerations, the study shows that there were 43 cases of trend run ups over this 9-year period, of which 37 were confirmed cases (6 remained non-confirmed after the third week). There were 31 instances of trend run downs during the same time frame, of which 28 were confirmed cases. In all, there were 74 cases of trend runs up and down, of which 65 were confirmed. As can be seen in the table, the majority of these cases lasted 3-7 weeks, and mostly only 3-5 weeks. That is, 32 of the 43 cases of trend runs up lasted 3-7 weeks. That is nearly a 75% rate of occurrence. If we remove the unconfirmed cases, we find 26 of 37 instances that lasted 3-7 weeks (70% occurrence). In the trend run down column, we find 28 of 31 cases lasted 3-7 weeks (90% occurrence). If we remove the unconfirmed cases, we still find 25 out of 28 instances apply at the 3-7 week interval, or 89% frequency. If we reduce the field to only cases lasting 3-5 weeks, we find 26 of 43 total cases of trend runs up (60.5%), of which 20 of 37 were confirmed cases (54%). And there were 23 of 31 total cases of trend run downs (74%), of which 20 of 28 were confirmed cases (71.4%). The majority of trend runs will last only 3-5 weeks.

There is yet another way to view these results too. If we remove the non-confirmed cases of the third week that did not make it past the third week as a trend run, then we have 37 cases of confirmed trend runs up and 28 cases of confirmed trend run downs. Now if we subtract the cases of confirmed trend run ups that ended the third week, we find that in the remaining 28 cases the market continued to trade above the TIP in the next weeks (weeks #4-14). That means there is a 75.67% probability that a confirmed trend run up by the third week will not end in the third week. It has a 75% probability of continuing to close above the weekly TIP in the next week. The ratios are even higher in the cases of confirmed trend run downs in the third week. Here we find 28 such cases of confirmed trend run downs after three consecutive weeks. And of those, 25 continued to close below the TIP in the following weeks. This represents a nearly 90% probability that if the market closes below the TIP for three consecutive weeks (and the third week is also a down week), the following week(s) will also find prices closing below the TIP.

However there were still cases where the market had consecutive closes above or below the TIP considerably longer than three weeks. One of the objectives of this study was to determine how long trend runs last before they are exhausted and overextended. In the trend run up column, we see four cases where the weekly close was above the weekly TIP for 10 consecutive weeks, three cases where it lasted 11 consecutive weeks, one case where it continued 12 consecutive weeks, and one other case where it lasted 14 straight weeks. Therefore one can deduce from this study that once a trend run up reaches its 10th consecutive week of closes above the TIP, it is overextended, exhausted, and vulnerable to a reversal or a pause at any time, usually by the 12th week. In the trend run down column, there were no cases in which the weekly close was below the weekly trend indicator point for more than 9 consecutive weeks. Once it reaches the ninth week, one should be prepared for a pause or reversal of the trend from down to at least neutral.

An interesting phenomenon was observed in the cases of exhaustion and overextension (not shown in the table). In many cases where the trend run up entered the 10th week or more of consecutive closes above the TIP, the following decline was modest. It was perhaps only 3-5% off the crest that coincided with the end of the trend run up (that week, the week before or after the last close above the weekly TIP). The decline to neutral status only lasted 1-2 weeks. It didn't go into a trend run down mode. However there were two cases (of the nine) where the DJIA did in fact turn into a trend run down. In those cases the decline was more substantial (800-1500 DJIA points) and lasted 5-6 weeks. In one case, the DJIA actually traded slightly higher one week after the week in which the trend run topped out. In the second case, the DJIA topped out in the week that the trend run up ended. However, the next week it came within just two points of that high again (other indices were higher, for a case of intermarket bearish divergence).

Thus the end to a long (overextended) trend run up does not always presage a powerful decline. To the contrary, the market is more likely to enter a period of congestion for 1-2 weeks and then proceed to even higher levels. If, however, the following week the market does make a slightly higher high or exhibits intermarket bearish divergence to other stock indices, then the decline can be more powerful and it can last more than 1-2 weeks. In fact, over the past nine years, the decline has been sharp and lasted 5-6 weeks. However, the same was not true in cases of overextended trend runs down. In the three cases of 8-9 consecutive weekly closes below the TIP, all were followed by powerful rallies of 600-1500 points. Two of the cases took 5-6 weeks before they topped out. The third case resulted in a change of 1500 points, and it only took two weeks to accomplish (it was during the financial panic of September-October 2008). What is perhaps just as interesting is that the low of the trend run down in those cases did not occur in the week that the trend run down ended. The actual low was the week before or the week after. In the one case where the low occurred the week before the trend run down ended, the low of the following week was very close to the actual low of the preceding week.

We also examined the cases of interruptions to the trend run in an effort to determine how many times it resumed the same trend run and for how long. If, for instance, a trend run up was interrupted by a weekly close below the TIP, and then the next week it closed back above the TIP, we would consider that a resumption of the trend run up. But what is the history of such cases actually continuing the trend up for more than one week?

In our sample of 467 weeks over nine years, the DJIA exhibited an interruption to the Drummond trend run in 19 cases. That is, only cases were used in which the DJIA had closed a minimum of 3 consecutive weeks above the TIP (trend run up) or below (trend run down). Yet during its trend run, there was one weekly close that was on the other side of the TIP for one week and then the following week it closed back above the TIP in the resumption of a trend run up, or below the TIP in the resumption of a trend run down. Only cases in which the interruption lasted just one week were used in this study.

Weeks	Trend Runs Up — Cases Above TIP Before Interrupt	Trend Runs Up — Cases Above TIP After Interrupt	Trend Runs Down — Cases Below TIP Before Interrupt	Trend Runs Down — Cases Below TIP After Interrupt
1		2		2
2		2		0
3	6	7	0	1
4	1	2	3	2
5	0	0	1	0
6	3	0	0	0
7	0	0	0	0
8	0	0	1	0
9	1	0	0	0
10	1	1	0	0
11	1	0	0	0
12	0	0	0	0
13	0	0	0	0
14	1	0	0	0
Totals	14	14	5	5

In this table, the far left hand column represents the number of weeks that applied to each category. The next two columns pertain to trend run up cases. The first column here (2nd overall) is titled "Cases Above TIP Before Interrupt." It identifies the number of cases in the study in which the market closed above TIP 'x' number of consecutive weeks, where 'x' refers to the number of weeks in the far left column. Since we only examined cases of trend run up or trend run down, this column showed no cases before the row beginning with the third (3) week. Trend runs must have a minimum of three consecutive weeks of closings above or below the TIP. At 3 weeks, one can see six (6) cases where the market interrupted the trend run that was in force. The next column refers to the number of cases in which the trend run then resumed for 'x' number of weeks after the interrupt. Here you can have as few as just one week afterwards, which simply means that the close was above the weekly TIP for just one more week after the interrupt. In the first row, marked "1" under "Weeks," we see two (2) cases where the trend run up resumed for only one week after an interrupt occurred to the trend run up.

The next two columns represent the interruptions that occurred during a trend run down. The first column here (4th column on the table) is titled "Cases Below TIP Before Interrupt." Once again there will be no cases involving only weeks #1 or 2, because it takes three consecutive weekly closings below TIP to constitute a trend run down. We note from this table that there were no cases of interruptions to trend run downs after three consecutive weekly closings below the TIP. However, after four consecutive weekly closings below TIP there were three (3) cases of a trend run down that was interrupted. The last column to the right refers to the number of weeks in which the trend run down continued after the interrupt. Here there are cases lasting 1 or 2 weeks. In fact, we see two (2) cases where the trend run down resumed for only one week after the interrupt.

The results of this study support our corollary that one-week interrupts do not necessarily derail the trend run that was in force. Of the 19 cases of an interrupt in a trend run, only six (6) failed to resume the trend for at least the following three weeks. Although this study covered 9 years and 467 weeks, it only produced 19 interrupt examples, which is a very small sample from which to draw strong conclusions. So far we find that in 68.4% of cases studied in which a one-week interruption of the weekly trend run occurred, the market resumed weekly closes in the direction of that trend again for the following three weeks or more. In fact, it becomes even more interesting than that. In these 13 cases of a resumption of the trend run lasting at least three additional weeks, only 1 lasted more than 4 weeks. In other words, if a trend run is resumed after a weekly interrupt, chances are it will not continue to exhibit weekly closes above or below the TIP (in the direction of the trend) for more than 4 additional weeks. The resumed trend run ends within the next 4 weeks in 92.3% of cases studied. If we include the cases where the interrupt was followed by only 1 or 2 weeks of trend resumption, then we observe 18 of these 19 cases ended by the 4th week, or a 94.7% rate of occurrence. Thus we conclude that the concept of a one-week interrupt is important. If this happens, the market is likely to continue closing back above or below the TIP point, but only for 3-4 weeks in most cases. It seldom continues the trend run past the 4th week following an interrupt.

As mentioned, some of these qualifications yielded very small sample sizes from which to draw any definitive conclusions. They point to a possible correlation that needs more study. For the record, this study of 467 weeks contained 199 weeks when the trend status was neutral (42.6%), 185 weeks when it was in a trend run up (39.6%), and only 83 weeks of being in a trend run down (17.8%). Thus one can see that this time band contained many more bullish weeks than bearish weeks. In fact, if one looks at the weekly chart from June 3, 2002 through May 20, 2011, it is apparent the DJIA spent more time in a bullish trend than bearish one.

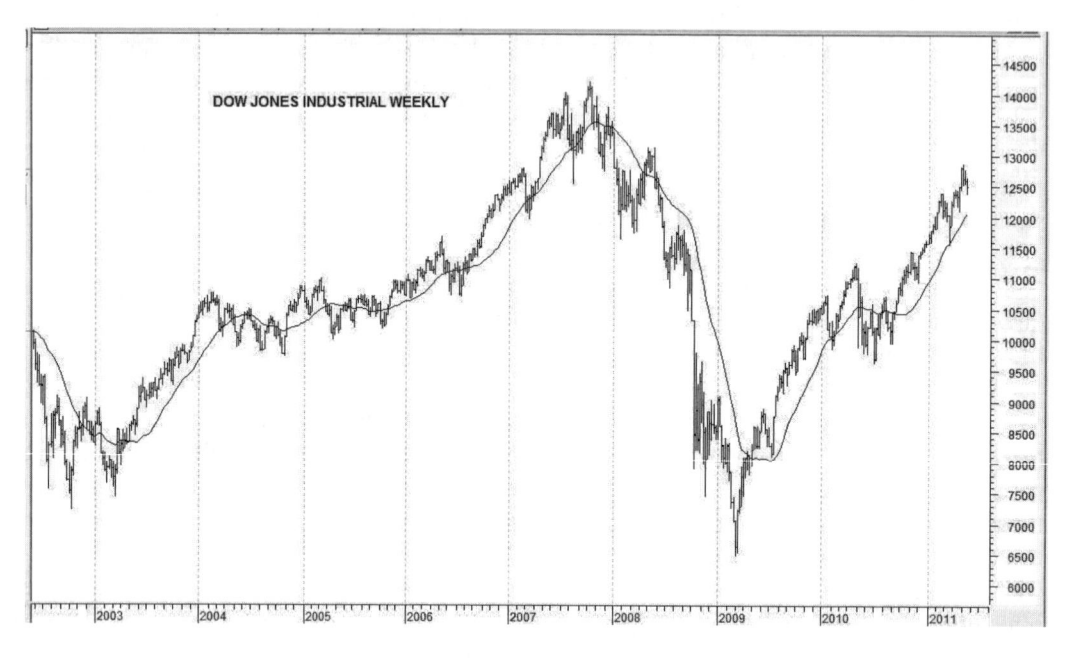

Figure 53: Weekly chart of the Dow Jones Industrial Average from June 3, 2002 through May 20, 2011, with a 25-week moving average. Note that it spent more time in a bull market (October 10, 2002 through October 11, 2007, and then again since March 6, 2009), than in a bear market (June 3, 2002 through October 10, 2002 and October 11, 2007 through March 6, 2009).

Illustrations of Weekly Trend Runs Down and Trend Runs Up

Let us now examine an actual case of a weekly trend run down in the DJIA and see how these principles worked. We will take the period from August 5, 2002 through November 8, 2002, which covers the 4-year (and possibly longer) cycle trough of October 10, 2002. This example will demonstrate how the DJIA exited from a trend run up into congestion that quickly became a powerful trend run down. It also demonstrates how it exited that trend run down to a long-term cycle trough and entered congestion before commencing a trend run up. As we consider the technical picture via the Drummond Market Geometry rules (and our corollaries to them), keep in mind that the bottom of October 10, 2002 was a geocosmic critical reversal period, as per the rules presented in Volume 3 of this series. On October 10, the very powerful Venus retrograde occurred. The next day a powerful Saturn direct unfolded. And on Monday, October 14, transiting Mars formed a waxing square to Saturn. Each of these is a powerful Level 1 geocosmic signature. Each has a 70-80% correspondence to primary or greater cycles within 9-12 trading days. A powerful trend reversal was thus due via these studies.

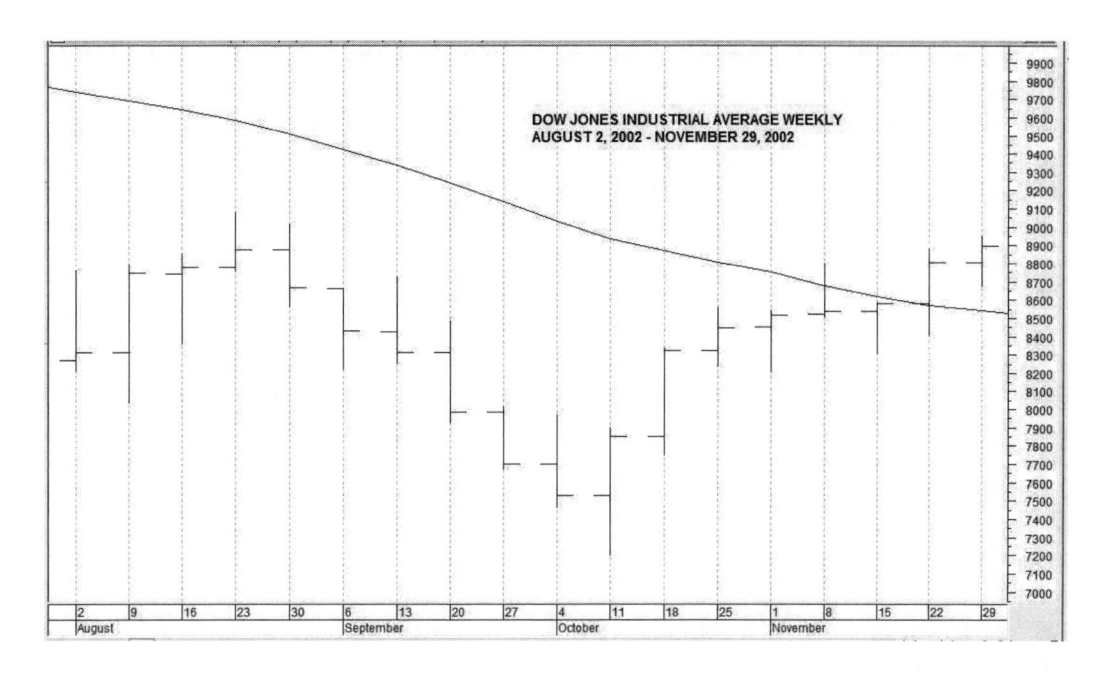

Figure 54: Weekly chart of the DJIA from August 2, 2002 through November 29, 2002. This chart depicts the trend run down into the 4-year (and maybe greater) cycle low of October 10, 2002 and the rally that commenced right afterwards. The 25-week is also displayed on this chart.

The following represents the weekly high, low, close, PP, TIP, and trend status for this period. Prices are rounded off to the nearest point. The PP, TIP, and STATUS of the first three weeks are carried over from the calculations of previous weeks not shown here.

WEEK ENDING	H	L	C	PP	TIP	STATUS
2002/08/02	8762	8204	8313	8035	8390	D
2002/08/09	8796	8031	8745	8426	8232	N
2002/08/16	8854	8353	8778	8524	8329	N
2002/08/23	9077	8753	8873	8662	8537	U
2002/08/30	9017	8558	8663	8901	8696	N
2002/09/06	8659	8217	8427	8746	8710	N
2002/09/13	8727	8248	8313	8434	8694	D
2002/09/20	8482	7922	7986	8429	8536	D
2002/09/27	8012	7666	7701	8130	8331	D
2002/10/04	7964	7461	7528	7793	8117	D
2002/10/11	7901	7197	7850	7651	7858	D
2002/10/18	8331	7745	8322	7650	7699	N
2002/10/25	8558	8228	8444	8133	7811	N
2002/11/01	8542	8198	8518	8410	8064	U
2002/11/08	8800	8499	8537	8419	8321	U

August 2, 2002 ended a trend run down in which prices had closed below the TIP in 8 of the prior 9 weeks (there was a one-week interrupt the week ending July 5, 2002). But in the week ending August 2, the close was 8313, which was below the TIP. However, the previous week (not shown), July 26, the close was 8264. That too was below TIP. Yet the week of August 2 was an up week, which was a sign that the trend run down might be ending. This was further reinforced by the fact that the close was above the TIP of the next week. It would have been an even stronger signal of an impending trend change if the close would have also been above the PP (pivot point) of the next week, but it wasn't.

Still, the next week of August 9, 2002 was a change of trend status. The close of that week was 8745, which was well above the TIP at 8232. Therefore the market exited its trend run down (D) status and entered congestion, or a neutral (N) status. It is interesting to note that the low of this week was 8031, which was lower than the prior week when the trend run down ended. That often happens. The actual low of a trend run down doesn't always occur in the last week of the trend run down. Sometimes it occurs in the week before, and sometimes it occurs in the week after. When the lowest price of the decline occurs the week after the trend run down ends and the close of that week is also above the close of the prior week, it is referred to as a "key reversal up" signature. This is a common signature that many technical analysts consider important. Thus in the week ending August 9, the DJIA changed its trend status from a trend run down to neutral, and the close of that week exhibited a "key reversal up" signature.

The next week ending August 16 also closed above the TIP. It was the second consecutive week up, so the trend status remained neutral. The following week, ending August 23 also closed above the TIP, and the close was above the prior week's close. Thus the status was upgraded to a trend run up (U).

The trend run up did not last long. The very next week, ending August 30, the DJIA closed below the TIP. Thus its status was downgraded back to neutral. The following week ending September 6, it again closed below the TIP, so it remained neutral. One week later, ending September 13, the DJIA closed below the TIP for the third consecutive week, and the close was also below the close of the prior week. Thus the trend was now downgraded to a trend run down (D). The trend run down will continue as long as prices continue to exhibit weekly closes below the TIP.

The week ending October 11, 2002 ended the trend run down in this example. It was the seventh consecutive week of closes below the TIP. As stated before, this week coincided with the 4-year cycle trough on Thursday, October 10, at 7197. It was an important geocosmic critical reversal zone. Note that after Thursday's low of 7197, the market reversed sharply to the upside. It closed the week at 7850, near the weekly high. That close was also 322 points above the close of the prior week, after taking out the low of the prior week, so it also qualified as another "key reversal up" technical signal for the week. It was only 8 points below the TIP at 7858, so it remained in a trend run down. Not only was it a "key reversal up" week, it also closed above both the PP (pivot point) and TIP of the *next* week. All of these factors (the weekly key reversal up, the close above the prior week's close, the close above the next week's PP and TIP) combined to produce a strong argument that the trend was about to change. It in fact did change.

The next week, ending October 18, was another strong up week. The DJIA closed at 8322, up nearly 500 points above the prior week's close and already more than 1200 points (over 15%) above the low of October 10, just six trading days earlier. It was the first weekly close above the weekly TIP in 8 weeks, thus its status was upgraded from trend run down to neutral. The next week, ending October 25, continued to close above the TIP, so the DJIA continued in its neutral status. The week after that, ending November 1, was yet another weekly close above TIP, and the close was also above the close of the prior week, and thus it was upgraded from neutral to a trend run up. It continued in the trend run up through the week ending November 29. It closed above the weekly TIP for seven consecutive weeks following the week ending October 11.

This was a fairly simple example of how the trend is determined using these basic principles of Charles Drummond. Now let us look at an example of a trend run up that contains a non-confirmed trend in the third week, as well as one interrupt week. For this we will go to the weeks ending November 24, 2006 through January 26, 2007.

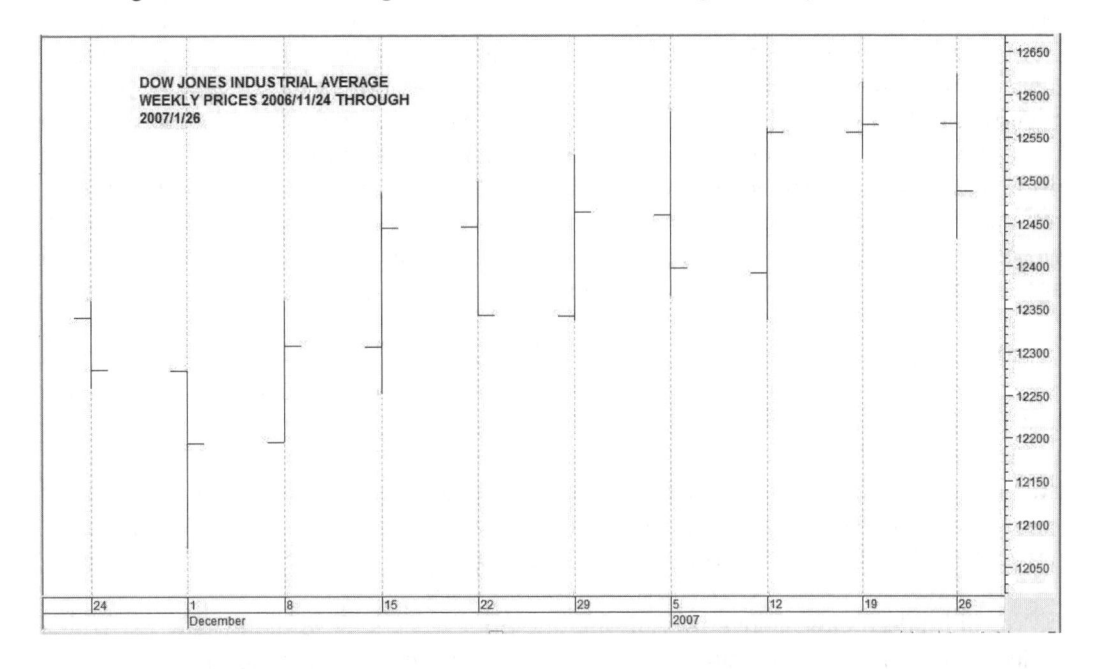

Figure 55: Weekly prices of the DJIA, the week ending November 24, 2006 through January 26, 2007. The chart depicts a trend run up that is unconfirmed in the third week (week ending December 22) and an interrupt to the trend run up that took place the week ending January 5, 2007.

As one can see, the DJIA was in a bullish trend during this period. It was mostly higher after the low during the week ending December 1, and prices continued higher throughout the period shown in this chart. Yet it wasn't an easy period to forecast because there was a case of both an unconfirmed trend run up in the third week, as well as an interruption to the trend run up in the fifth week (week ending January 5).

Let us examine the weekly high, low, close, pivot point, and trend indicator points during this period in the quest to understand how these principles work in real cases.

WEEK ENDING	H	L	C	PP	TIP	STATUS
2006/11/24	12,361	12,259	12,280	12,256	12,126	N
2006/12/01	12,279	12,072	12,194	12,300	12,217	N
2006/12/08	12,361	12,195	12,307	12,182	12,246	N
2006/12/15	12,486	12,252	12,445	12,288	12,256	N
2006/12/22	12,498	12,342	12,343	12,394	12,288	N*
2006/12/29	12,530	12,337	12,463	12,394	12,359	U
2007/01/05	12,580	12,365	12,398	12,443	12,411	N-I
2007/01/12	12,581	12,337	12,556	12,448	12,428	U
2007/01/19	12,614	12,523	12,565	12,491	12,460	U
2007/01/26	12,622	12,431	12,487	12,567	12,502	N

This example begins simply enough with a weekly close above the TIP for the week ending November 24, followed by a weekly close below the TIP in the week ending December 1. The market's trend status is thus neutral (N). It then closes above the TIP in the following three weeks. The third consecutive week that closed above the TIP occurred in the week ending December 22, 2006. Normally that would be considered a trend run up (U). However that week's close (12,343) was lower than the close of the prior week ending December 15, which was 12,445. Therefore it is an unconfirmed trend run up, which means its status remains neutral. This is designated as N*. If the next week closes below the TIP, it will remain neutral. But if the next week closes above TIP and above the prior week's close, it will be upgraded to a trend run up.

The next week ending December 29 did in fact close above the TIP and it was a higher close than the prior week. Therefore the trend status is upgraded from neutral (N*) to a trend run up (U). It has now closed above the TIP for four consecutive weeks. The following week, January 5, 2007, it closed at 12,398. This is below the TIP for the first time in 5 weeks, so it is downgraded from trend run up to neutral. If the next week's close is also below the TIP, it will remain neutral. However if the next week's close is both above the TIP and above the prior week's close, it will resume its trend run up (U) status.

It did indeed close above the TIP and the prior week's close the next week, which ended January 12. Thus it is upgraded back to a trend run up, and the prior week's status is noted as "N-I," which stands for "Neutral-Interrupted." In other words, it was downgraded from a trend run up to neutral for one week. It was a week in which the trend run was interrupted. Moreover, since it then closed back above the TIP the following week, the trend run up resumed. However that previous week is considered an interruption (N-I) week to the trend run up that was in force prior to the week ending January 5. You may remember from a previous discussion on interrupts, that a resumption of the trend does not usually last more than the next 4 weeks before returning to neutral. Yet in that time the market tends to make new highs for the cycle if it is a trend run up.

The trend run up resumed in the week ending January 12. The following week, January 19, it again closed above the TIP and again above the close of the prior week.

The next week, ending January 26, it closed below the TIP and below the close of the previous week. Thus the resumed trend run up lasted only two weeks after the interrupt week, which is not unusual, before returning to neutral. Yet in those two weeks, and even the week after, the DJIA rose to higher prices in the cycle. If we count the interrupt week, we will see that this trend run up saw prices closing above the TIP in 6 of 7 weeks, and the price continued rising throughout this entire period.

Daily Studies on TIPs

A study was also conducted on the daily prices of the DJIA, covering the period November 25, 2002 through May 20, 2011. In this study, the same criteria was used as implemented on the weekly research studies. That is, we recorded the number of consecutive days in which the daily close was above or below the daily TIP, starting with three consecutive days, for that was the minimum number of consecutive daily closes that would qualify as a trend run. Once again, we identified those cases in which the third week of a consecutive close above or below the daily trend indicator point was not confirmed with a daily close that was above or below the prior day's close respectively (confirmed versus unconfirmed trend runs at the end of the third day). In the first table (shown below) are the results of these cases, which do not include the interrupt instances.

Day #	UP	Non-Confirm 3rd Week	DOWN	Non-Confirm 3rd Week
3	40	19	41	17
4	24	6	33	8
5	23	5	15	3
6	21	1	18	5
7	18	2	9	1
8	10	2	6	1
9	8	1	9	0
10	7	2	1	1
11	2	0	0	0
12	5	1	1	1
13	1	0	1	1
14	0	0	1	1
15	2	1	0	0
16	0	0	0	0
17	1	0	0	0
18	1	0	0	0
19	1	0	1	0
Totals	164	40	136	39

The results of the study on daily prices and trend runs are similar to those obtained in the study of weekly prices, except the trend runs generally lasted longer in the daily study. In all, there were a total of 300 instances of trend runs (how convenient to have such a round number), where the daily close was above or below the TIP for at least three consecutive days. There were 164 instances of trend runs up (54.7%) and 136 instances of trend runs down (45.3%). Albeit, 36 of these cases (12%) were never confirmed trend runs. This was virtually the same rate of frequency of non-confirmed trend runs observed in the weekly studies. That is, at the end of the third consecutive day of closes above or below the TIP, 36 also did not also close above or below the prior day's close respectively, and then the DJIA failed to do so the next day as well. Therefore, of the 300 cases of three consecutive daily closes above or below the TIP, 264 were confirmed trend runs. We will return to the unconfirmed part of the study shortly.

Let us look at the cases of trend runs up. In all, there were 164 cases in which the DJIA closed at least three consecutive days above the daily TIP. There were 19 unconfirmed cases in this category, which means 1) they did not close above the prior day's close on the third day, and 2) they did not close above the TIP on the next day (fourth day). They never confirmed the trend run up. In the final tally, there were 145 confirmed cases of trend runs up in this study.

There were 40 cases in which the DJIA closed up only three consecutive days before reversing back to neutral. Of these 40 cases, only 21 also closed above the prior day's close, which qualified them as confirmed trend runs up. That means approximately half the cases of trend runs up that lasted only three days were confirmed. If we look only at confirmed cases of trend runs up, we will notice the vast majority (107 of 145) ended their trend run up by the seventh consecutive day of closes above the TIP (73.8% frequency). There were 30 cases (20.7%) in which the consecutive string of daily closes above the TIP lasted 8-12 days. There were only 6 cases in which the DJIA closed above the daily TIP more than 12 consecutive days (4% frequency of occurrences at the 13-19 day interval). Thus we can conclude that a trend run up on the daily time frame tends to reach its exhaustion point after 12 consecutive daily closes above the TIP. There were no cases in which the daily DJIA closed above the daily TIP for more than 19 consecutive trading days. It only happened once during the 17, 18, and 19-consecutive day intervals.

It is also interesting to note the number of cases in which the trend run up was interrupted when it lasted a long time (not shown in the table). Of the 20 cases in which the market closed above the TIP for at least ten consecutive days, 14 exhibited an interrupt. The trend run up then resumed in these 14 cases (70% frequency) as the following day(s) witnessed closes back above the daily TIP. Half of these resumptions (7) lasted at least 5-7 days. Four lasted only one day, and three of those cases occurred in the 10-consecutive-days-up category.

Now let us look at the cases where the market exhibited a non-confirmed trend run up at the end of the third consecutive day. That column in the table shows this phenomenon occurred 40 times in this study (see "totals" at the bottom of the third column). That means that in about half the cases where a market closed above the daily TIP on the third day - but it wasn't a close up from the prior day's close - it did not enter a trend run up by closing above it the next day. In the other half of the cases, it did. Even if it did close above the daily TIP and the prior day's close on the 4th day, chances were still great that it would not do so beyond the 5th day. As one can see from the table, there were 19 instances when the trend run up was not confirmed on the third day, and it ended right there. There were 6 instances where it did close above the TIP on the 4th day, but then the trend run up was halted. There were 5 additional instances where a non-confirmed trend run up occurred on the third day, and then the market continued to close above the daily TIP for five consecutive days before the trend run ended. That means that in 30 of these 40 cases (75%), an unconfirmed trend run up on the third consecutive day led to an end of the trend run up by the fifth consecutive day. An unconfirmed trend run up is signal that the market's advance is likely to end by the 5th day.

Now let us examine the 136 cases of daily trend run downs. Here we find 17 instances where the market closed below the daily TIP for three consecutive days, but the third day closed higher than the prior day's close, which were thus unconfirmed trend runs down. Once again, this yields approximately a 12% rate of frequency (actually 12.5%), which is similar to daily trend runs up and even weekly trend runs of both types. Thus we see 119 cases of confirmed trend runs down in this study.

There were 41 cases in which the DJIA closed down only three consecutive days before reversing back up to neutral. Of these 41 cases, 24 also closed above the prior day's close. This qualifies them as confirmed trend run downs. That means 58.5% of the cases of trend runs down that lasted only three days were confirmed. If we look only at confirmed cases of trend runs down, we will notice the vast majority (90 of 119) ended their trend run down after the sixth consecutive day of closes below the TIP (75.6% frequency). If we expanded that to seven consecutive days, as we did in the study on trend runs up, we find 99 cases ended their trend run by then, or 83.2%. There were 15 cases (12.6%) in which the consecutive string of daily closes above the TIP lasted 8-9 days.

There were only 5 cases in which the DJIA closed above the daily TIP more than 9 consecutive days (4% frequency of occurrences, at the 10-19 day interval). Four of those cases were at least 12 consecutive weeks. In fact, there was only one case where a trend run down witnessed more than 14 consecutive closing days below the TIP. Thus we can conclude that a trend run down on the daily time frame tends to reach its exhaustion point after 9 consecutive daily closes below the TIP. There were no cases in which the daily DJIA closed above or below the daily TIP for more than 19 consecutive trading days. In fact it only happened once that the DJIA closed below the TIP more than 14 consecutive days, and that was the one occurrence at the 19-consecutive day mark.

Unlike the trend run up cases, there were very few instances of interrupts to the trend run down when it reached the exhaustion stage after 9 days. Of the 14 cases in which the market closed below the TIP for at least 9 consecutive days, only 6 ended with an interrupt. The trend run down then resumed in these 6 cases (42.8% frequency), as the following day(s) witnessed closes back below the daily TIP. Five of these six resumptions lasted only 1-2 days. The other instance lasted 5 additional days in a trend run down. Thus it appears that when an interruption occurs in an overextended trend run down, the trend will *not* resume, as it often does in the case of interrupted trend runs up. And if it does resume its downward trend, it does not last more than 1-2 additional days.

Now let us look at the cases where the market exhibited a non-confirmed trend run down at the end of the third consecutive day. The last column in the table shows that this occurred 39 times in this study (see "totals" at the bottom of the last column). This means that in 43.5% of the cases where a market closed below the daily TIP on the third day, but it wasn't a close down from the prior day's close, it did not enter a trend run down by closing below it the next day. In the other 56.5% of the cases, it did. However, even if it did close below the daily TIP and the prior day's close on the 4th day, chances were still very great that it would not do so beyond the 6th day. As one can see from the table, there were 17 instances when the trend run down was not confirmed on the third day, and it ended right there. There were eight instances where it did close below the TIP on the 4th day, but then the trend run down was halted. There were three instances where a non-confirmed trend run down occurred on the third day, and then the market still continued to close below the daily TIP for five consecutive days before the trend run ended. Finally, there were five instances where a non-confirmed trend run down occurred on the third day. The market still continued to close below the daily TIP for six consecutive days before the trend run down ended. That means that in 33 of these 39 cases (84.6%) an unconfirmed trend run up on the third consecutive day led to an end of the trend run up by the sixth consecutive day. An unconfirmed trend run down is a signal that the market's decline is likely to end by the 6th day.

Using Multiple Time Frames

You may be asking yourself at this point: "What is the purpose of these studies on trend runs? How are they to help me become a more skilled short-term trader?" It goes back to two basic principles discussed earlier. The first is, "The trend is your friend." You make the highest percentage of successful trades when you trade in the direction of the trend. However determining the trend is no easy matter, for as discussed before, the trend depends upon which time frame, or cycle, is being examined. The second principle is to trade in a time frame, or cycle, that is moving (or about to move) in the direction of the trend of the greater time frame or cycle. It is even more effective when you use a shorter time frame, or cycle, to help you pinpoint a corrective low or high that anticipates the reversal in the direction of the greater time frames or cycles. For short-term traders, this is known as taking a favorable "risk-reward" position. And as explained in Volume 4 of this series, titled "Solar-Lunar Correlations to Short-Term Trading Reversals," the goal of every short-term aggressive trader is to attain maximum profit potential with minimal market exposure.

Yet the concepts discussed in this section of the book work well for any type of trading. It may not work so well for the long-term buy and hold investor. Yet whether one wishes to trade every day (short-term aggressive), every week (short-term), or every couple of weeks (short-term position), or even every month or two (position trader), the principles of Drummond Market Geometry combined with technical analysis studies outlined in this book, plus the market timing studies presented in Volumes 1-4, will prove to be both reliable and powerful tools for today's modern trader.

In terms of cycles, we have demonstrated over and over again that the start of every cycle is bullish. That is, the first phase of every cycle will be bullish. Its trend is more up than down. And in the rare event that this first phase takes out the low that began the cycle, it will still turn out that the highest price (the biggest rally) most frequently (almost always) occurred in that first phase of the cycle. Thus it is very valuable to recognize 1) when a cycle trough or crest is due, and 2) when the Drummond trend indicator studies are exhibiting a trend run up or down in that time band. For example, if the market is in a time band for a primary cycle trough and the price has been declining into this time band, it is most likely that prices are closing below the daily and weekly TIP. However, as the cycle bottoms, the price will begin to close above the daily TIP first. Soon the market will exhibit a trend run up status with three consecutive daily closes above the TIP with the third day (or next) also closing above the close of the prior day. It will thus confirm - via the rules of Drummond Market Geometry - a new trend run up is underway following a new low for the cycle that was within the time band when the cycle trough was due. This will be one of the early signs that the trend is reversing to the upside, and a smart rally is commencing to the crest of at least the first phase of this new cycle.

The weekly close will do the same, although perhaps a week or so later. The longer time periods will almost always lag behind the shorter time periods in producing a new trend run. And that brings us back to the importance of tying in multiple time frames, a concept that is important to us as cycles' analysts, and also reflects the work of Charles Drummond for technical market analysts.

Basically, for our trading purposes in this section of the book, there are three main steps to follow:

1. Determine the weekly trend.
2. Trade the daily in the direction of the weekly trend. In other words, if the weekly is in a trend run up, then wait for the daily to 1) exit a trend run down and enter congestion or 2) commence a trend run up. If the weekly is in a trend run down, then wait for the daily to 1) exit a trend run up and enter congestion or 2) commence a trend run down.
3. Use intraday time frames, such as the 60-, 30-, 15-, and/or 5-minute bars (high, low, and close) to pick the bottom of a corrective decline in a trend run up (buy point) or the top of a corrective rally in a trend run down (sell point).

Let us look at an example of how the concept of tying in multiple time frames involving the weekly and daily trend indicator points works with the knowledge of cycle studies. For this illustration, let us examine the weekly and daily charts of the DJIA for the last confirmed primary cycle trough prior to the writing of this section of the book. That would be the primary cycle trough of March 16, 2011, which just occurred after the tragic earthquake-tsunami that struck the northeast coast of Japan on March 11 and on the day that Uranus - planet of earthquakes - moved from Pisces into Aries. You can see the weekly and daily chart of the DJIA for this period on the next page.

In reviewing these charts, note that the primary cycle began with the low of 10,929 on November 29, 2010. According to our knowledge of cycles, we would expect the next primary cycle trough to occur 13-21 weeks later, or February 28 to April 29, 2011. We would expect the DJIA to be declining rather sharply into this low with weekly closes below the TIP and probably in a weekly trend run down. We would certainly expect the daily closes to be in a trend run down during the week, or just before that low was completed. We would expect the daily and then the weekly prices to exit the trend run down with closes above the TIP shortly after the low was completed. Now let us see what happened.

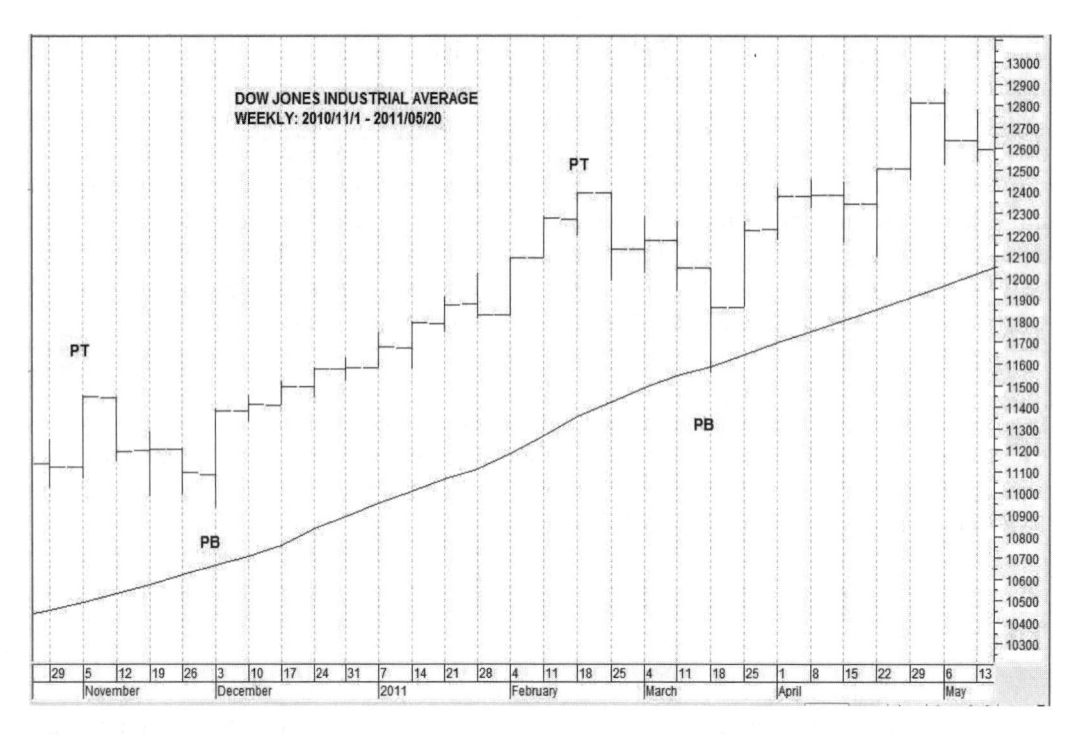

Figure 56: Weekly chart of DJIA from November 1, 2010 to May 13, 2011. PT represents primary cycle top, or crest, and PB represents primary cycle bottom or trough. Also shown here is the 25-week moving average.

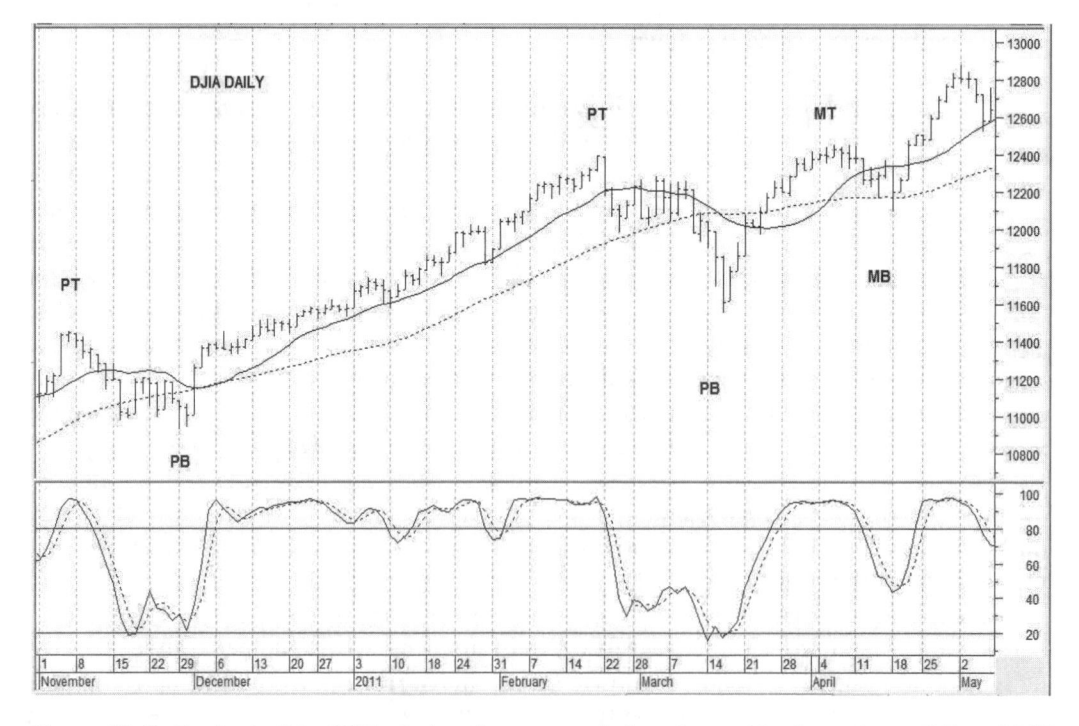

Figure 57: Daily chart of the DJIA during the same period as the weekly chart above. MB and MT refer to the major cycle bottom and major cycle crest within the primary cycle. Also shown here are 15-day and 40-day moving averages.

Let us begin by examining the weekly high, low, close, pivot points (PP), and trend indictor points (TIP) following the primary cycle crest of 12,391 on February 18, 2011. That crest occurred in the 11th week of the primary cycle. In bull markets, we look for declines from the primary cycle crest to the primary cycle trough to last 2-5 weeks. Sometimes they last longer. However, the majority of cases will find the decline lasting 2-5 weeks. We already know that the 13-21 week primary bottom is due February 28 to April 29, 2011. If February 18 was the primary cycle crest, then the primary bottom would likely be completed in 2-5 weeks, or February 28 - March 25. This overlap to the original calculation helps narrow that time frame. The use of geocosmics would also alert us to a potential reversal on Monday, February 21, +/- 3 trading days, and March 18 - 21 (a weekend), +/- 3 trading days, as per the instructions given in Volume 3 of this series. For now, we will apply the Drummond rules for trend analysis to get an indication when the new primary cycle would be underway in this time band of February 28 - March 25.

Below we provide the weekly numbers for this analysis. Numbers are rounded off to the nearest whole number, and therefore the PP or TIP may appear to be off by 1 point.

WEEK ENDING	H	L	C	PP	TIP	STATUS
2011/02/18	12,391	12,193	12,391	12,217	12,033	U
2011/02/25	12,389	11,983	12,130	12,325	12,181	N
2011/03/04	12,283	12,018	12,170	12,168	12,237	N
2011/03/11	12,258	11,936	12,044	12,157	12,217	D
2011/03/18	12,042	11,556	11,850	12,089	12,135	D
2011/03/25	12,260	11,860	12,220	11,806	12,014	N
2011/04/01	12,420	12,173	12,376	12,113	11,999	N
2011/04/08	12,451	12,321	12,380	12,323	12,081	U
2011/04/15	12,444	12,164	12,342	12,384	12,273	U
2011/04/22	12,506	12,093	12,506	12,317	12,341	U
2011/04/29	12,833	12,446	12,810	12,369	12,456	U
2011/05/06	12,876	12,521	12,639	12,696	12,460	U
2011/05/13	12,781	12,537	12,596	12,678	12,581	U
2011/05/20	12,643	12,379	12,512	12,638	12,671	N

The weekly analysis begins with the week ending February 18. On that day, Friday, February 18, the DJIA completed its primary cycle crest at 12,391. It was the 11th week of the primary cycle, and it was a geocosmic critical reversal zone, and prices were making a new high for this cycle. We would therefore be on alert to the possibility that a primary cycle crest could be unfolding. The next week (week ending February 25) found the weekly high on Tuesday, February 22 (Monday was a holiday) at 12,389, only two points lower than the prior day (and prior week) high. This alone was a reason to be alert that a primary top (PT) might be forming, for often primary cycle crests occur when the current week's high is slightly above or slightly below the high of the prior week. Additionally, a check of other world stock indices would reveal that many made a higher high on February 21. Thus there was a case of intermarket bearish divergence on a weekly basis, where one index made a new cycle high, but others did not, and then all closed in the lower half of the weekly range. More importantly for purposes of this section of the book, the weekly close was below the weekly trend indicator point (TIP) for the first time in 13 weeks. It thus exited out of its trend run up status (U) and was downgraded to neutral (N).

If the next week's close was above the TIP at 12,237, it would be upgraded back to a trend run up. The week ending February 25 would be considered an "interrupt week" and the trend run up would then resume. According to our historical studies on the weekly DJIA, we would then anticipate that the resumption of the trend run up would end within the next 4 weeks, but at prices higher than 12,391.

Prices did not close above the TIP in the week ending March 4. They closed at 12,170, below the TIP of 12,237. Even though this close was up 40 points from the prior week, the fact is that it closed below the TIP for the second consecutive week, and thus the market remained in a neutral (N) status.

The market was now poised to exit the neutral status and commence a new trend run down. All it had to do was 1) close again below the TIP (12,217) for the third consecutive week and 2) have a weekly close lower than that of the prior week (12,170). If both of these conditions did not occur, then it would remain in a neutral status. In this case, the market closed at 12,044 on March 11. It was below the weekly TIP and the prior week's close. It was thus downgraded to a trend run down.

The week ending March 11 completed the 14th week of the primary cycle. It was now in its time band for a 13-21 week primary cycle trough. It was also the third week following the crest of February 18. The low of the week ending March 11 was 11,936, which was the lowest price since the crest. Therefore the market had been in decline for 2-5 weeks, and thus the two minimum time requirements criteria for a primary cycle trough were being met. What we wanted to see at this point was a close back above the weekly TIP. That would upgrade the weekly trend status from trend run down to neutral. That would be the first sign via the weekly studies that a primary bottom may have been completed.

The next week, which ended March 18, witnessed a new low at 11,556 and a weekly close at 11,850. This was still below the weekly TIP, which was 12,135, for the 4th consecutive week. The weekly status still remained in a trend run down (D). However, the following week ending March 25 produced a weekly close above the TIP. The TIP was 12,014 and the weekly close was 12,220. The weekly trend was thus upgraded to neutral, the first weekly sign that the market was exiting its trend run down status and in a time band in which a primary cycle trough was due. The low as of that point was 11,556 on March 16. It was the 15th week of the 13-21 week primary cycle time band, and it was 4 weeks following the primary cycle crest. The market timing conditions were right for a primary bottom. This would be confirmed if the following two weeks also closed above the weekly TIP, with the third week also an up week for the close of the prior week. Those conditions were indeed met by the third week, which was the week ending April 8. According the rules of the Drummond Market Geometry method of trend analysis, combined with the principles of cycle studies, this was now a new confirmed primary cycle, and the market was thus bullish.

However, one need not wait three weeks for the weekly chart to enter a trend run up in order to start employing bullish strategies, especially if we are looking for the most favorable risk-reward ratios prior to entry. Initial indications of a trend reversal would show up even earlier on the daily calculations. So let us examine the price activity of the daily DJIA leading into - and out of - the primary cycle trough of March 16.

DAY ENDING	H	L	C	PP	TIP	STATUS
2011/03/10	12,211	11,974	11,984	12,209	12,173	N
2011/03/11	12,087	11,936	12,044	12,057	12,150	N
2011/03/14	12,042	11,897	11,993	12,023	12,096	D
2011/03/15	11,989	11,696	11,855	11,977	12,019	D
2011/03/16	11,857	11,556	11,613	11,846	11,949	D
2011/03/17	11,800	11,615	11,774	11,675	11,833	D
2011/03/18	11,927	11,777	11,850	11,730	11,751	N
2011/03/21	12,078	11,860	12,036	11,852	11,752	N
2011/03/22	12,051	12,003	12,018	11,992	11,858	N*
2011/03/23	12,116	11,973	12,086	12,024	11,956	U
2011/03/24	12,191	12,088	12,170	12,058	12,025	U
2011/03/25	12,260	12.171	12,220	12.150	12,072	U

We start the daily analysis as the market began closing below the daily TIP on March 10. It had been in congestion (neutral readings, with closing prices vacillating back and forth above and below the daily TIP) since March 3. On Monday, March 14, the DJIA closed below the daily TIP for the third consecutive day, and the close was down from the prior day's close. Thus its trend status was downgraded from neutral to a trend run down. Keep in mind that the weekly was already in a trend run down status, so the daily is just confirming the weekly, which suggested that prices were falling even lower into the primary cycle trough that was due at any time that week or the next, as it was already the fourth week of declining prices since the primary cycle crest of February 18.

The trend run down on the daily chart continued through the close of March 17. That was the 6th consecutive day in which the DJIA closed below the daily TIP. The lowest price had occurred the day before, March 16, at 11,556. On Friday, March 18, the close was finally above the daily TIP, which upgraded the daily trend from trend run down to a neutral status. This was the first sign, via the daily chart, that the bottom might be in. That possibility would be strengthened if 1) the next two days also exhibited closes above the daily TIP, with the third day an up day, and 2) if the following week's close would also be above the weekly TIP, thus upgrading its status from a weekly trend run down to neutral. The progression of upgrades on both the daily and weekly trend numbers would be a strong sign that the primary bottom was completed on March 16.

As can be observed on the table of daily prices, the DJIA did in fact close above the daily TIP over the next two days. However that third day of daily closes above the TIP - March 22 - was not a confirmed trend run up because it was a lower close than the day before. Thus it remained neutral, but with an asterisk (N*). What do we know about the historical correlation of unconfirmed trend runs up on the third day? We know that nearly 50% of the time the market will not confirm a new trend run up. So we do not want to become bullish just yet.

The next day, March 23, the DJIA closed at 12,086. This was above the TIP for that day at 11,956, and it was 68 points higher than the close of the prior day. Now the daily trend would be upgraded from neutral to a trend run up. However, the weekly was still down, so caution was still warranted. On Thursday March 24, it closed above the TIP for the fifth consecutive day, and Friday, March 25, it did the same. More importantly, Friday's (March 25) close of 12,220 was above the weekly TIP at 12,014 for the first time in 5 weeks. The weekly trend status was upgraded from trend run down to neutral, and the daily trend status was already in a trend run up from March 23. The energy of the market can be seen as shifting from bearish to neutral on the weekly and from neutral to trend run up on the daily, and this positive shift occurred following a low in a time band when a primary cycle trough was due. One could now approach the next week with a greater confidence that the low was in and start looking for a point to buy with a stop-loss on a close under the 11,556 low of March 16. Position traders could buy the close of March 25 with a stop-loss below 11,556. Short-term aggressive traders would need to look for better risk-reward possibilities in the days that followed. The point is that all traders could start to adopt more bullish strategies at this point, for the trend status was being upgraded on both the weekly and daily time frames.

The next chapter will introduce further tools that will enhance the short-term trader's ability to find favorable locations for market entry and exit, once the trading strategy becomes clear via the shift in trend analysis.

SUMMARY

The following represent the key points to remember about trend analysis utilizing the core principles of Drummond Market Geometry in combination with market timing indicators (or even other technical tools).

1. A market's trend status is neutral until there are three consecutive closes above or below the trend indicator point (TIP), which Drummond refers to as the "Dot."

2. Once a market closes three consecutive times above the TIP, it is upgraded to a trend run up. However, if the third close is not also higher than the close of the previous period's close, the trend run up is not confirmed. It remains neutral. It will be a confirmed trend run up when the following period's close is higher than the prior bar's close, assuming the price still closes above the TIP.

3. Once a market closes three consecutive times below the TIP, it is downgraded to a trend run down. However, if the third close is not also lower than the previous period's close, the trend run down is not confirmed. It remains neutral. It will be a confirmed trend run down when the following period's close is lower than the prior bar's close, assuming the price still closes below the TIP.

4. Most weekly trend runs up and trend runs down end after the 7th consecutive week of closes above or below the weekly TIP.

5. Most daily trend runs up end by the 10th consecutive day of closing above the daily TIP. Most daily trend runs down end by the 9th consecutive day of closes below the daily TIP.

6. Weekly trend runs up become exhausted after 11 consecutive weeks of closing above the weekly TIP. There were only two cases (out of 43) of trend runs up in which the DJIA closed above the weekly TIP for more than 11 consecutive weeks, according to studies done on the weekly DJIA as reported in this chapter. It is considered exhausted even after 10 weeks.

7. Weekly trend runs down become exhausted after 9 consecutive weeks of closing below the weekly TIP. There were no cases (out of 31) of trend runs down in which the DJIA closed below the weekly TIP for more than 9 consecutive weeks.

8. Daily trend runs up become exhausted after 12 consecutive days of closing above the daily TIP. There were only six cases (out of 164) of trend runs up in which the DJIA closed above the daily TIP for more than 12 consecutive days.

9. Daily trend runs down become exhausted after 9 consecutive days of closing below the daily TIP. There were only five cases (out of 136) of trend runs down in which the DJIA closed below the daily TIP for more than 9 consecutive days.

10. A weekly trend run up or down may be interrupted for one week and then resume its prior trend. When that happens, the resumed trend run up or down tends to end within the next 4 weeks. In only one case (out of 19) did the resumption of the trend last more than 4 weeks after the interrupt week.

11. A daily trend run up may be interrupted for one day and then resume its trend run up status by closing above the daily TIP the next day. When that happens, the resumed trend run up tends to end within the next 7 days, with most ending after just one day. In only 8 cases (out of 56) did the resumption of the trend run up last more than 7 days after the interrupt day. In 19 cases it lasted only one day.

12. A daily trend run down may be interrupted for one day and then resume its trend run down status by closing below the daily TIP the next day. When that happens, the resumed daily trend run down tends to end within the next 3 days. In only 2 cases (out of 21) did the resumption of the trend run down last more than 3 days after the interrupt day. It never lasted more than 6 days in this study.

13. A market may be upgraded to an "on edge trend run up" even before it exhibits three consecutive closes above the TIP. That happens when the close is so sharply higher that it is above the prior high of the cycle, even though it may only be the first or second time frame in a neutral status. It is fully upgraded to a trend run up if the next bar is a higher close than the prior bar.

14. A market may be downgraded to an "on edge trend run down" even before it exhibits three consecutive closes below the TIP. That happens when the close is so sharply lower that it is below the prior low of the cycle, even though it may only be the first or second time frame in a neutral status. It is fully downgraded to a trend run down if the next bar is a lower close than the prior bar.

15. It is best to trade with multiple time frames and in the direction of the trend status for the higher two frames. For best risk-reward ratios, the lower (shorter) time frame can be used to enter the market shortly after the bottom or top of a counter-trend move is suggested. For example, one can trade the daily chart in the direction of the weekly trend status or the direction of a change in the weekly trend status. One can use a lower time frame, such as the 30- or 60-minute bars, to pinpoint a corrective retracement against that trend to identify a time and price at which to enter the market after the trend has begun. This process will be discussed shortly.

References:

1. P&L Labs: Introductory Manual, Point and Line Charting, Charles Drummond, 1981, Toronto, Ontario, Canada.
2. Classic Drummond Market Geometry lessons, Ted Hearne and Charles Drummon, www.drummondgeometry.com.

CHAPTER SEVENTEEN

SUPPORT AND RESISTANCE FOR SHORT-TERM TRADING

Now it gets interesting.

It also gets a little dangerous because there is the temptation to forget all the other calculations and methods of market analysis presented in this book to determine price targets for cyclical highs and lows. Nevertheless, keep one thing in mind: the calculations presented in this chapter for support and resistance levels are most valuable when they overlap with the price targets from formulas given in prior chapters. They are even more valuable when calculated for time bands in which our market timing signals indicate a market reversal is most likely, *and* when they fall within the price targets established for a cyclical trough or crest as identified in earlier chapters.

The prior chapter on Trend Indicator Points (TIPs) was important because it established the basis for one's trading strategy at any given time. When the trend is up, we know we want to buy on corrective declines. When the trend is down, we want to sell on corrective rallies. Corrective declines and rallies are known as *retracements* to the basic trend. Yet just as cycles have time bands in which a trough or crest is due to occur, so also do price retracements have a range in which a corrective decline can bottom or a corrective rally can peak. Just as we use geocosmic studies and solar-lunar phases to help narrow a time band when a cycle trough or crest is more likely to occur, so also do we use other calculations and studies to help narrow down the price range that will define support or resistance to a retracement. In some cases, we use these mathematically calculated support and resistance zones to identify when the retracement is over, or when it is safer to enter the market with a higher probability of being on the right side of the resumed (or new) trend.

As short-term aggressive traders, our challenge is to identify when and where a short-term market move is likely to bottom or peak. And although this is contrary to what most market analysts would recommend, our goal is to pick bottoms and tops as close as possible to the actual time and price in which they occur. One who chooses to enter the market at those projected lows or highs is known as a "bottom picker" or "top picker." Often those terms are used in a derogatory way by the market community, implying the notion that traders who do this are doomed to lose over time. But this is not always the case, and when it is, it is more a result of the trader's lack of discipline than it is to a fallacy in the concept. Being able to forecast lows and highs extremely close to their exact time and price provides a means to keep the risk-reward parameter at a most favorable ratio, which is essential to short-term aggressive traders. The biggest problem with being a bottom or top picker isn't that one suffers losses, for the losses with this type of trading are very modest compared to any other trading approach. The bigger problem is that there will be far more losses - small losses, but losses nonetheless - than from a trading approach that waits until a new trend is more firmly established before entering a new position. The problem is ultimately more psychological than financial, for a number of even small losses can affect one's confidence in trading. As much as anything else, one needs to have confidence when trading in order to be successful. You simply cannot succeed at trading if you are constantly filled with doubt before putting on trades. On the other hand, success at trading may be very fleeting if one is overconfident to the extent that if he believes so strongly in the position taken, he cannot adapt when the market goes against that position, thereby turning what should have been a small loss into a large loss.

Thus we begin this final section on support and resistance. For short-term traders, this is quite possibly the most important chapter of the book, whether you are a bottom-top picker or someone who prefers to first see evidence that the market is holding (or breaking) support and resistance. The first step is to revisit the formulas for support and resistance, and then explain how they are used to pick bottoms and tops, as well as to identify signals that bottoms and tops have been completed, at least on a short-term basis. This process will thus address the needs of both types of traders: those who prefer to pick the bottoms and tops of market moves and those who prefer to see the lows and highs established before entering a position in the direction of the reversal, i.e. new trend or resumed trend.

Formulas

There are many formulas for calculating a support or resistance level for any time frame. If one explores the internet search engines for support and resistance formulas, hundreds of web sites will come up, and they will provide dozens of different formulas, interpretations, and uses. The one thing they will not do is to cite the originator of these formulas, other than to sometimes say they are "Floor Trader Formulas" for support and resistance. From this I can only conclude that most of these formulas have been around a very long time. But how one uses the numbers derived from these calculations is more important. What signals do they generate that leads one to become a buyer or seller of a particular stock or commodity? This is what separates one system, one analyst, from another.

In Chapter 14, the following formulas for support and resistance were given that will be used from this point forward. But as mentioned before, there are literally dozens of other support and resistance formulas that traders use. Charles Drummond proposed several other support-resistance calculations, around which he built numerous trading plans. But for our needs, we use two formulas for determining short-term support and two for short-term resistance. Drummond also uses one of these formulas (in addition to his several other formulas), which we will note herein. Once we understand support and resistance on the daily and weekly time frame, we can incorporate these numbers - along with the TIP - to determine strategies and trading plans for buying and selling. We can determine the price at which to enter or exit the market when a tradable top or bottom is forming or has just formed. For this we will also need a listing of terms we apply to these "set ups" based on support and resistance.

Support 1 (S$_1$)

S$_1$ = C - (H-L)/2, where C is the close, H is the high, and L is the low of the time frame being studied (such as weekly, daily, hourly, etc.). Sometimes this is referred to as the "Predicted Low" of the time frame being used.

Support 2 (S$_2$)

S$_2$ = (PPx2) - H, where PP represents the pivot point and H represents the high of the time frame being studied. This is one of the classical "floor traders" formulas for determining daily, weekly, or whatever time frame of support one is calculating. Charles Drummond refers to this as the "1x1 up" point.

Support Zone

The range of the S$_1$ and S$_2$ represents the *support zone* of the next time frame from which these numbers were calculated. If using a particular day's high, low, and close, then the S$_1$ and S$_2$ would yield the support zone for the next day's trading. There are other formulas for determining other support zones, but these are the two for short-term trading that we will be using throughout the remainder of this book.

Resistance 1 (R$_1$)

R$_1$ = (H-L)/2 + C, where H represents the high, L represents the low, and C represents the close of the time frame being studied (such as weekly, daily, hourly, etc.). Sometimes this is referred to as the "Predicted High" of the time frame being used.

Resistance 2 (R$_2$)

R$_2$ = (PPx2) - L, where PP represents the pivot point and L represents the low of the time frame being studied. This is one of the classical "floor traders" formulas for determining daily, weekly, or whatever time frame of resistance one is calculating. Charles Drummond refers to this as the "1x1 down" point.

Resistance Zone

The range of R$_1$ and R$_2$ represents the *resistance zone* of the next time frame from which these numbers were calculated. If using a particular day's high, low, and close, then R$_1$ and R$_2$ would yield the resistance zone for the next day's trading. There are other formulas for determining other resistance zones, but these are the two for short-term trading that we will be using throughout the remainder of this book.

Simple Examples of Calculating Support/Resistance Zones

Let's do some simple calculations to show how the support or resistance zones of a day are derived. Let's assume we have the last 3 days of trading figures for stock XYZ as follows, where H represents the high of that day, L represents the low of that day, and C represents the close:

Day	H	L	C
1	75.50	71.20	73.75
2	77.00	73.25	76.80
3	79.20	75.50	76.20

Our first step is to calculate the Pivot Point. As discussed before, this is simply the average of the high, low, and close for each day, applied to the next day. In other words, today's high, plus low, plus close, divided by three, gives us the pivot point (PP) for the next day's trading, or, PP = (H + L + C) ÷ 3.

Now, let's calculate the Pivot Point for each of the following days:

Day	H	L	C	PP
1	75.50	71.20	73.75	
2	77.00	73.25	76.80	73.48
3	79.20	75.50	76.20	75.68
4				76.97

Notice how the pivot point for day 2 is based on the daily high, low, and close of day 1. The PP for day 3 is based on the trading range and close of day 2, and the PP for day 4 is calculated for the high, low, and close of day 3. Whatever happens in the current time frame creates the numbers for the next time frame of the same duration. In this case, we are using a daily chart. But the same calculations can be constructed for weekly, monthly, quarterly, and yearly charts, or for 60-minute and 30-minute charts as well.

Once we have the pivot point, we can calculate the support and resistance zones for the next day's trading. On our table, the support zone for day #2 would be the range between S_1 and S_2. The range for the next day's resistance would be determined by R_1 and R_2. It would look like this:

Day	H	L	C	PP	S_1	S_2	R_1	R_2
1	75.50	71.20	73.75					
2	77.00	73.25	76.80	73.48	71.60	71.46	75.90	75.76
3	79.20	75.50	76.20	75.68				
4				76.97				

S_1, or predicted low, would be the high of the prior day minus the low, divided by 2. That amount is then subtracted from the close of the previous day (day 1). In this case, it would be (75.50 - 71.20) ÷ 2 = 2.15, or 73.75 - 2.15 = 71.60. This is the S_1, or the first support point, for day 2.

S₂ would be (PP x 2) - the high of the prior day, or (73.48 x 2) - 75.50 = 71.46. This is the second support point, or S₂, on day 2.

The range for support on day 2 is thus the combination of S₁ and S₂, or 71.46-71.60. We will refer to this as the *daily support range*.

R₁, or predicted high, would be calculated as the high minus the low of day one, divided by 2, and then added to the close of day 1. In this case, that would be (75.50-71.20) ÷ 2 = 2.15. And then, 73.75 + 2.15 = 75.90. This is the first resistance (R₁) point for day #2.

R₂ would be (PP x 2) - the low of the prior day, or (73.48 x 2) - 71.20 = 75.76. This is the second resistance point (R₂) for day 2.

The range for resistance on day 2 is thus 75.76-75.90. We will refer to this as the *daily resistance range*.

Day traders will often find that intraday prices bounce off of these two ranges. In other words, when prices fall to the daily support zone, the market will frequently stall and then commence a rally. When it reaches the daily resistance zone, it will often stall and then commence a decline. In many cases, these support and resistance zones will mark the low or high of the day's trading to which they apply. Sometimes both ranges will define the day's trading range, which makes it an ideal day for day trading.

Now let's calculate the support and resistances zones for days 3 and 4. Try to do it on your own, and then check it against the figures below.

Day	H	L	C	PP	S₁	S₂	R₁	R₂
1	75.50	71.20	73.75					
2	77.00	73.25	76.80	73.48	71.60	71.46	75.90	75.76
3	79.20	75.50	76.20	75.68	74.92	74.36	78.67	78.11
4				76.97	74.35	74.74	78.05	78.44

In day 2, the low of the day (73.25) was well above the daily support zone (71.46-71.60). The high (77.00) and close (76.80) were above the daily resistance zone (75.76-75.90). This is a classic "bullish" day. The market ended the day "bullish" because it closed above daily resistance.

Day 3 found the market once again trading above daily resistance (78.11-78.67). The high was 79.20. The low (75.50) was also above daily support (74.36-74.92). But the close (76.20) was below daily resistance (78.11-78.67). When the market trades above daily resistance but then closes back below, it is known as a "bearish trigger." It is not bearish because it did not close below daily support. But it is not bullish, because it didn't close above daily resistance. It took out resistance, which at the time was bullish. But then it closed back below it, which meant resistance failed. Remember: when resistance is broken, it becomes support. When support breaks, it becomes bearish. However, in this case, daily resistance broke, but daily support did not. Yet because resistance broke during the day, it became support on a smaller intraday time frame. The fact that it closed below this daily resistance level, after trading above it intraday, means there is a bearish quality to the close. But the decline into the close was not bearish enough to break the daily support zone. It was not a "bearish close" day. It is thus referred to as a "bearish trigger" day.

We will define these types of market behavior shortly, for every day the high, low, and close - relative to daily support and resistance - creates a type of trading label for that day. And that either supports our trading plan or causes us to alter it. Another important rule to always keep in mind about trading is this: when the market isn't doing what it is supposed to do (by these studies and their signals), then it is probably doing the opposite. So if you are wrong, don't be wrong for long, or it will hurt.

Before introducing the terms that describe market action and the strategies they produce, there is one minor point to make. The distance in the range of daily (or weekly, or whatever time frame) support and resistance should be the same. If their distance is not the same, check your calculations. In the example before, the support range was 71.46 to 71.60. The distance in this range is 71.60 - 71.46 = .14. The range in the daily resistance should be the same. For that day, the resistance zone was 75.76 to 75.90. The difference is once again 75.90 - 75.76, or .14. In day 3, the distance in the range of support and resistance was the same as well. Daily support was 74.36 to 74.92, which was a range of .56. Daily resistance was 78.11 to 78.67. The difference was once again .56. This should always be the case if your calculations are correct. In fact the range between S_1 and R_1 should be the same as the range between S_2 and R_2 as well as the range between the high and low of the prior day (to which these calculations apply). This is market geometry.

Terms Used To Describe Market Activity

In order to understand how these calculations are used effectively for short-term trading with both market timing principles as well as other technical studies presented in this book, it is necessary to understand the terminology used for this type of analysis. Some of these terms were first introduced (to me) by Charles Drummond, and others I originated. Some of the applications are similar to those used in parts of the Drummond Market Geometry methodology. Others are applications that I constructed. Once again, I chose the terms, calculations, and applications used in this book because they have been found to work very effectively with the market timing studies introduced in the first four volumes. But if the reader wishes to further his/her understanding of more advanced trading plans based on a multitude of other support and resistance calculations without the market timing indicators as presented herein, please refer to the "30 Lesson Course on Classic Drummond Geometry" by Charles Drummond.[1]

For the sake of convenience, these terms will be used to describe daily market activity. However the reader should understand that they can also be applied to weekly and monthly charts, as well as to intraday charts, such as 30- and 60-minute charts.

1. **Neutral:** A market is neutral when the trading range of the day (low and high) does not exceed daily support and resistance. The entire range of the day was between support and resistance. It is a purely neutral close if the day's high was

below daily support and the low was above daily resistance. If the high was into resistance, or the low was into support, but the close was between the two, it is still a neutral day, but with a bullish (if support held) or bearish (if resistance held) bias.

2. **Bullish:** A market is bullish if it closes above daily resistance. This is a signal to look for after a cycle low is completed, as an indication that a reversal or new upward trend is beginning. It frequently occurs during trend runs up, but the first one to occur after a trend run down is an especially important signal of a change.

3. **Bearish:** A market is bearish if it closes below daily support. This is a signal to look for after a cycle crest is completed, as an indication that a reversal or new trend down is beginning. It is common during trend runs down, but the first one to occur after a trend run up is especially important.

4. **Very bullish:** A market is very bullish if it trades into or below daily support, but then closes above daily resistance. This is also known as an "outside day," or week, or whatever time frame is being used. But it is the bullish type of an outside day because it closes above resistance. Not all "outside days" close above resistance or below support.

5. **Very bearish:** A market is very bearish if it trades into or above daily resistance, but then closes below daily support. This is also known as an "outside day," or week, or whatever time frame is being used. But it is the bearish type of an outside day because it closes below support. Not all "outside days" close above resistance or below support.

6. **Mostly bullish:** A market is mostly bullish when it closes in daily resistance.

7. **Mostly bearish:** A market is mostly bearish when it closes in the daily support.

8. **Bullish trigger:** When a market trades below both daily support and resistance, but then closes back above the daily support zone, this is known as a "bullish trigger." As the name implies, the market may be setting up for a rally off the low of that day, which now becomes another important support zone, at least on a closing basis. A bullish trigger is more powerful when it also closes above the daily pivot point (PP). It is more powerful if it also closes above the daily TIP (trend indicator point). This is a signal to look for as - or soon after - a cycle low is completed, assuming the lowest price of the cycle occurred that day. Or this may happen on a secondary low that shortly follows the actual low of the cycle and it is still a bullish development.

9. **Bearish trigger:** When a market trades above both daily support and resistance, but then closes back below the daily resistance zone, this is known as a "bearish trigger." As the name implies, the market may be setting up for a move down off the high of that day, which now becomes another important resistance zone, at least on a closing basis. A bearish trigger is more powerful when it also closes below the daily pivot point (PP). It is more powerful if it also closes below the

daily TIP (trend indicator point). This is a signal to look for as - or soon after - a cycle crest is completed, assuming the highest price of the cycle occurred that day. Or this may happen on a secondary high that shortly follows the actual high of the cycle and it is still a bearish development.

10. **Bullish bias:** This occurs when the market trades into - but not below - daily support and then closes above that support zone. Support held, which is a bullish sign. For this to be the case, the market should not touch daily resistance, but only support. It is a stronger signal if the close is also above the daily pivot point (PP). This is another signal to look for as - or soon after - a cycle low is completed, assuming the lowest price of the cycle occurred that day. Or this may happen on a secondary low that shortly follows the actual low of the cycle and it is still a bullish development.

11. **Bearish bias:** This occurs when the market trades into - but not above - daily resistance and then closes below that resistance zone. Resistance held, which is a bearish sign. For this to be the case, the market should not touch daily support, but only resistance. It is a stronger signal if the close is also below the daily pivot point (PP). This is another signal to look for as - or soon after - a cycle crest is completed, assuming the highest price of the cycle occurred that day. Or this may happen on a secondary high that shortly follows the actual high of the cycle and it is still a bearish development.

12. **Mixed:** The market is considered "mixed" when it trades below daily support *and* above daily resistance, but closes back between the two. The market is neither bullish nor bearish, but volatile. This is also called an "outside day," although it is not clearly bullish or bearish because it did not close into or above daily resistance (very bullish) or into or below daily support (very bearish). It may be slightly more bullish if the close was above the daily pivot point (PP). It may be slightly more bearish if the close was below the daily pivot point (PP).

13. **Bullish sequence:** When the market closes on a "bullish trigger" or "bullish bias," and the next day it closes "bullish" (the close is above daily resistance), it is referred to as a "bullish sequence." Going from a bullish trigger or bullish bias to an outright bullish close is a sign the trend is up or turning up. The low of the prior move should now serve as strong support to the new bullish trend that this indicator signals. A close into or below daily support (bearish or mostly bearish close) would negate this bullish sequence signal.

14. **Bearish sequence:** When the market closes on a "bearish trigger" or "bearish bias," and the next day it closes "bearish" (the close is below daily support), it is referred to as a "bearish sequence." Going from a bearish trigger or bearish bias to an outright bearish close is a sign the trend is down or turning down. The high of the prior move should now serve as strong resistance to the new bearish trend that this indicator signals. A close into or above daily resistance (bullish or mostly bullish close) would negate this bearish sequence signal.

15. **Bullish Crossover Zone:** A condition in which daily support is above the prior day's resistance. For our purposes, this specifically occurs when the highest price of the daily support zone is above the lowest price of the previous day's resistance zone. That "range" between the current day's support and the previous day's resistance becomes very strong support in the days ahead. It will usually hold on the first attempt into it, and often it will hold on future attempts as well. There will be times where the market trades below this bullish crossover zone (support), but then closes back above. That works in much the same way as a bullish trigger. There are times when the market will close within the bullish crossover zone. This means the market is vulnerable to breaking down, especially if that close was near the low of the day. Therefore the market is bullish until prices close below its nearest bullish crossover zone. There is no time limit as to how long this support remains valid. It remains in effect until the market closes below it. And until it is broken, other bullish crossover zones may occur. The nearest one is always the most important. When there are several bullish crossover zones in effect, the market becomes extremely bearish when two or more are taken out on a single day's close. In these cases, it is not unusual for the market to find support at the third or fourth lower bullish crossover zone, if they exist.

16. **Bearish Crossover Zone:** A condition in which daily resistance is below the prior day's support. For our purposes, this specifically occurs when the lowest price of the daily resistance zone is below the highest price of the previous day's support zone. That "range" between the current day's resistance and the previous day's support becomes very strong resistance in the days ahead. It will usually hold on the first attempt into it, and often it will hold on future attempts as well. There will be times where the market trades above this bearish crossover zone (resistance), but then closes back below. That works in much the same way as a bearish trigger. There are times when the market will close within the bearish crossover zone. This means the market is vulnerable to an upward breakout, especially if that close was near the high of the day. Consequently the market is bearish until prices close above its nearest bearish crossover zone. There is no time limit as to how long this resistance remains valid. It remains in effect until the market closes above it. And until it is broken, other bearish crossover zones may occur. The nearest one is always the most important. When there are several bearish crossover zones in effect, the market becomes extremely bullish when two or more are taken out on a single day's close. In these cases, it is not unusual for the market to find resistance at the third or fourth higher bearish crossover zone, if they exist.

It should be pointed out that many of these terms are used in Drummond Market Geometry.[2] Charles Drummond introduced several of these terms in his works, such as bullish and bearish triggers, and also bullish and bearish crossover zones. There are some subtle differences with our use of these signals in this section of the book, however, that are due to the fact that we are using different support and resistance zones. Of the two support and resistance points that we calculate for every time period - and thus use for our application of bullish and bearish triggers as well as bullish and bearish crossover zones - Drummond Market Geometry uses but one of each: S_2 and R_2, which he refers to as the "1x1 up" and "1x1 down" respectively. In addition, Drummond uses many other support and resistance zones from which he devised several trading plans that are not covered in this book, but which can also be used effectively with the methods of analysis described in this five-volume series.

The idea for the use of these signals is very simple. When the market is in a time band for a cycle trough, you look for one (or several) of these bullish indicators to take place. When the market is in a time band for a cycle crest, you look for one (or several) of these bearish indicators to take place. Of course you need to use these signals in combination with geocosmic signals and the various technical studies and price objective calculations too, for optimal setups. It is very seldom that all signals point in the same direction. After all, most technical signals are lagging - or at best, coincident - indicators. But with the use of these support and resistance signals, combined with our market timing studies, one's skill at identifying lows or highs in the market before or as they happen is increased significantly.

Hypothetical Examples

Now let's create examples to illustrate how these signals are generated. We will show how these signals are generated without the concern of any other market timing or technical factors. Once we understand how they unfold, we will then begin to integrate other studies to enhance our ability to spot lows and highs as they occur or very shortly afterwards. For this example, we will add the TIP. You will then begin to see how it works in combination with the signals unfolding from the daily support and resistance calculation, as well as the relationship of closing prices to these numbers.

Day	H	L	C	PP	S_1	S_2	R_1	R_2	TIP
1	75.50	71.20	73.75						
2	77.00	73.25	76.80	73.48	71.60	71.46	75.90	75.76	
3	79.20	75.50	76.20	75.68	74.92	74.36	78.67	78.11	
4	78.00	74.20	74.25	76.97	74.35	74.74	78.05	78.44	75.38
5	75.75	73.10	74.60	75.48	72.35	72.96	76.15	76.76	76.04
6	75.40	73.25	74.00	74.48	73.27	73.21	75.92	75.86	75.64
7				74.22	72.92	73.04	75.07	75.19	74.73

Previously we determined that day 2 closed "bullish" and day 3 closed with a "bearish trigger" (the high of the day was above daily resistance, but then it closed back below). Day 4 then closed below daily support, which is a "bearish" signal. Not only that, but it followed a "bearish trigger" day, which meant a "bearish sequence" was now in effect. The market will be bearish until it closes above resistance, or until the daily TIP is upgraded to a trend run up, whichever comes first. The first daily TIP of this example showed up on day 4. It was 75.38. The close was below it, but it won't have a trend status until there are three consecutive closings above or below this point. This was only the first day of closing below it, so the TIP was considered in a neutral status. Do not confuse the TIP's neutral status with a neutral close based on the daily high and low being between support and resistance. The former relates to trend, and the latter simply to the labeling of the day's activity or the close relative to the support and resistance zones of that particular day.

Nevertheless, the market closed "bearish" on day 5 and also exhibited a "bearish sequence." This was an alert that the market would likely head lower, at least until it could close back above daily resistance or the TIP for three consecutive days. Either of those events would negate the bearish sequence.

On day 5, the high of the day was below daily resistance and the low was above daily support. It traded between each. Therefore this was a "neutral" day. However, it did not negate the bearish sequence of the prior day because it did not close above daily resistance. It did close below the TIP at 76.04, but this was only the second consecutive day of closing below this point. Therefore the TIP too remains neutral. If the next day finds prices closing down on the day and still below TIP, it will be downgraded to a trend run down status.

The next day, day 6, XYZ had its daily low in daily support. Daily support held. It closed back between daily support and resistance. And it never touched resistance, so the close was "neutral but with a bullish bias." This was a positive sign. However, it was not a very strong positive sign because the close was below the pivot point (PP). Additionally it also closed below the daily TIP for the third consecutive day and was down from the close of the prior day. Hence the trend indicator point (TIP) was downgraded to a trend run down.

But traders must be alert now to a possible reversal occurring because support held. If the next day XYZ can close above the daily TIP, its status will be upgraded from "trend run down" to "neutral." If it closes above resistance, a daily "bullish" signal will be generated. In fact, it would be a "bullish sequence," having moved from a "neutral with a bullish bias" close to a "bullish" close. This would be a much stronger buy signal than the prior day's "neutral with a bullish bias" close. On the other hand, failure to close above the TIP and daily resistance would mean the TIP will remain in a trend run down, and the daily bearish sequence generated two days earlier would remain intact. Prices would be expected to continue lower.

Let's assume the market reversed now and started a new bullish move. On Day 7, let's have the market close above both the daily TIP and daily resistance, as shown below.

Day	H	L	C	PP	S_1	S_2	R_1	R_2	TIP
1	75.50	71.20	73.75						
2	77.00	73.25	76.80	73.48	71.60	71.46	75.90	75.76	
3	79.20	75.50	76.20	75.68	74.92	74.36	78.67	78.11	
4	78.00	74.20	74.25	76.97	74.35	74.74	78.05	78.44	75.38
5	75.75	73.10	74.60	75.48	72.35	72.96	76.15	76.76	76.04
6	75.40	73.25	74.00	74.48	73.27	73.21	75.92	75.86	75.64
7	76.00	74.20	75.90	74.22	72.92	73.04	75.07	75.19	74.73
8	77.50	75.50	76.80	75.37	75.00	74.74	76.80	76.55	74.69
9	78.00	75.50	76.50	76.60	75.80	75.70	77.80	77.70	75.40
10	77.80	74.80	74.90	76.67	75.25	75.34	77.75	77.84	76.21

You will remember that day 6 closed "neutral, but with a bullish bias." The seventh day found XYZ closing above daily resistance. This is "bullish," and since it followed a "neutral but with bullish bias" day, it became a new "bullish sequence." The close was also above the TIP, which meant its status was upgraded from trend run down to neutral. The upward change in the status of both of these studies was a bullish sign. The market would now be expected to trade higher. A close below daily support or the daily TIP would instead negate the bullish sequence of XYZ and coincide with the market entering a more bearish outlook.

Day 8, however, continued the bullish sequence. The market traded above daily resistance and then closed back into it. This was a "mostly bullish" close. If it had closed below daily resistance, it would have been a "bearish trigger." But it closed "mostly bullish," and it was also above the TIP for the second consecutive day, which meant that indicator remained neutral.

Day 9 witnessed the market trading above daily resistance, but also below daily support. This is known as an "outside day." The close was back between the daily support and resistance, which meant the close of the day was "mixed." The market was becoming volatile. It closed above the TIP for the third consecutive day, but it was a down day, which meant the TIP remained neutral. It was not a confirmed trend run up. These were signals that the market could be reversing to the downside again, although the bullish sequence was not yet negated.

On day 10, the high was into daily resistance. It stopped there. It then closed back below daily support, which was "very bearish." It also closed below the TIP for the first time in 4 days, which meant it never became a trend run up. It remained neutral with this close. But one can see that the momentum of the market was turning down as the bullish sequence was negated on this day.

Our final discussion in this hypothetical example will focus on bullish and bearish crossover zones: how they are formed and how they serve as additional powerful support and resistance areas. One point to understand is that a market is usually very bullish immediately after a bullish crossover zone has formed. Often this will take place on a "gap up" day in which the market closes in the upper half of the day's range. Or it can be just a "big range" day where prices stay above support but then close near the highs of the daily range - a considerably larger range than the prior day. In other words, the day exhibits an explosive rally and closes sharply higher. Likewise, a market is usually very bearish immediately after a bearish crossover zone has formed. Often this will take place on a "gap down" day in which the market closes in the lower half of the day's range. Or it can be just a "big range" day where prices stay below resistance but then close near the lows of the daily range - a considerably larger range than the prior day. In other words, the day exhibits a serious selloff and closes sharply lower. Although my experience is that these crossover zones hold on the first challenge about 80-90% of the time. I have also seen cases where the market has flipped-flopped from a bullish crossover zone one day to a bearish crossover zone the next, or vice-versa. This is a very rare occurrence that indicates a particularly volatile market, but one must go in the direction of the most recent crossover zone. That is, if the last crossover zone was a bullish one, then the strategy for the next day(s) must be bullish. If the last crossover zone was bearish, then the strategy for the next day(s) must be bearish. But there will be some rare times when this strategy may quickly be invalidated.

Now let us see how a bullish and bearish crossover zone might look. Let us resume the daily activity of XYZ stock following the tenth day discussed before. This time we are going to change the setup a little bit to list the TIP after PP and we are going to start at Day 6. The reason for doing this is so that we may more easily see when the TIP converges with daily support or resistance, a condition that is important and will be discussed shortly.

Day	H	L	C	PP	TIP	S_1	S_2	R_1	R_2
6	75.40	73.25	74.00	74.48	75.64	73.27	73.21	75.92	75.86
7	76.00	74.20	75.90	74.22	74.73	72.92	73.04	75.07	75.19
8	77.50	75.50	76.80	75.37	74.69	75.00	74.74	76.80	76.55
9	78.00	75.50	76.50	76.60	75.40	75.80	75.70	77.80	77.70
10	77.80	74.80	74.90	76.67	76.21	75.25	75.34	77.75	77.84
11	74.50	71.00	71.00	75.83	76.36	73.40	☐73.86☐	76.40	76.86
12	72.50	69.50	70.90	72.17	74.89	69.25	69.84	☐72.75☐	73.34
13	73.35	71.15	72.50	70.97	72.99	69.40	69.44	72.40	72.44
14	75.80	73.00	75.70	72.33	71.82	71.40	71.31	73.60	☐73.51☐
15	76.00	73.60	74.50	74.83	72.71	☐74.30☐	73.86	77.10	76.67
16	75.90	74.30	75.80	74.70	73.95	73.30	73.40	75.70	75.80
17				75.33	74.95	75.00	74.75	76.60	76.36

Starting with day 10, the market closed very bearish. The high of the day was into daily resistance, but the close was below daily support. XYZ closed below the daily TIP for the first time in 4 days, so it remained neutral since the prior day - the third consecutive close above TIP - was down from the prior day's close. Day 9 was not a confirmed trend run up. Thus XYZ's trend indicator point remained neutral, but the close was very bearish, so our outlook would be more bearish than bullish heading into day 11.

Sure enough, day 11 closed bearish. It was a "gap down" day, and the close was below daily support. It was below the daily TIP as well for the second consecutive day, which would normally mean its status remained neutral. However in this case, the close was below the low that started the cycle on day 1, so its status was downgraded to an "on edge, trend run down." If the next day's close would be down, the TIP status would be downgraded to a full trend run down. If the close would be up from the previous day, its status would likewise be upgraded to neutral, for it would not yet be a confirmed trend run down even if it closed below the daily TIP. It must also close down from the prior day after three consecutive closes below TIP to be downgraded to a trend run down.

But there was something more important to notice after the close of day 11. The resistance zone generated for day 12 was below the support zone of day 11. This created a bearish crossover zone for day 12. The support zone of day 11 was 73.40-73.86. The resistance zone for day 12 was 72.35-73.34. One can see that this resistance zone was entirely below the support zone of the prior day. It doesn't have to always be entirely below to create a bearish crossover zone, but in this case it was. Thus a new bearish crossover was now in effect between the lowest resistance price on day 12 and the highest support price on day 11, or 72.75-73.86. On the table, these prices are marked with a border around the highest support level of day 11 and lowest resistance level of day 12. This represents the range to the crossover zone. This new bearish crossover zone now becomes very strong resistance into the future, until prices close back above it.

Day 12 then closed down from the prior day, and of course it was also below the TIP for the third consecutive day, so the TIP was now downgraded to a trend run down. However the low of day 12 (69.50) was held by daily support (69.25-69.84). It didn't close below daily support, which would have been a bearish close. It didn't close into daily support, which would have been a "mostly bearish" close. It closed back between daily support and resistance, which meant it closed "neutral but with a bullish bias." This was an alert that the move down might be ending already, for support was starting to build. One of the signs that a trend run down may be ending arises when the prices start to hold support. Another is when it starts to take out resistance.

The next day (13) found prices rallying to a high of 73.35. Note that this was into the bearish crossover zone that formed after day 11. This was the first challenge to that bearish crossover zone, and it held the rally, as it should on the first attempt. Although the market closed up on the day, it continued to close below the daily TIP for the fourth consecutive day. It was already in a trend run down from the prior day, so it continued with this status on day 13. But there was a new concern here. The close of day 13 was above daily resistance, which meant it closed bullish. The prior day closed "neutral but with a bullish bias," and this day closed bullish. This created a "bullish sequence" and a further alert that the trend of XYZ was shifting from bearish to bullish. All it would take now is a close above the resistance of the bearish crossover zone to propel this market upwards. Note that on the next day (14) the resistance zone of 73.51-73.60 overlapped with the bearish crossover zone (72.75-73.86). When such an overlap occurs, it represents powerful resistance. If XYZ could close above these areas of resistance, it would be considered very bullish. One's trading strategy would immediately become bullish, looking for opportunities to trade from the long side.

On day 14, XYZ did exactly that. It exploded up to close at 75.70, well above both daily resistance and the recent bearish crossover zone. The bearish crossover zone was thus negated as the market turned bullish here. Note also that activity of day 14 created a new bullish crossover zone for day 15, as shown by the borders around the prices that make up the new bullish crossover zone. The support zone for day 15 (73.86-74.30) was above the resistance zone of day 14 (73.51-73.60). The new bullish crossover zone is defined as the range between low the end of the resistance on day 14 and the high end of support on day 15, or 73.51-74.30. The close of day 14 was also above the daily TIP for the first time in 5 days. Therefore its status was upgraded from trend run down to neutral.

XYZ then traded down below daily support (73.86-74.30) on day 15, but into the new bullish crossover zone (73.51-74.30). The low of the day was 73.60. The bullish crossover zone held on the first challenge, as it normally does. Since the low of the day was below daily support and the close was back above, day 15 produced a "bullish trigger." The TIP status remained neutral, however, because the close was above it for only the second consecutive day. If it closed above the TIP the next day, and the close would be up on the day, it would be upgraded to a trend run up.

Day 16 did close up, and it was above the TIP for the third consecutive day. The trend status of TIP was thus upgraded to a trend run up. The stock traded slightly above daily resistance (75.70-75.80) but then closed back into it at 75.80, which meant it closed "mostly bullish."

Before we close this example, let's look at day 17. There is something different here that would be instructive to discuss. The daily TIP is at 74.95. Daily support is 74.75-75.00. The daily TIP is within the range of daily support. This increases the strength of the daily support zone, especially when the market is in a trend run up. In cases like this, the market will usually be up the next day. Support usually holds, and is not even touched in most cases when the TIP and daily support overlap. In those instances where the market breaks below this support area, it is usually followed by a further decline. The market plummets. Thus heading into day 17, one would adopt bullish strategies and trade from the long side unless (or until) prices start to break below support. In that case, one would switch to bearish intraday strategies unless it closed the day back above.

This then concludes our hypothetical examples of how markets generate daily buy and sell (bullish and bearish) signals from the daily support and resistance zones. The primary purpose of this exercise was to familiarize you with the language and concepts used in our approach to short-term trading and the quest to identify cycle lows and highs as soon as possible in order to maximize the most favorable risk-reward ratios for initiating new trades.

Our next and final steps involve how to integrate these short-term trading signals with the other tools discussed in this book and the prior four volumes. That is, once the time band in which a market has a high probability of reversing (via market timing studies, such as cycles and geocosmics) has been determined, and once the price targets for a trough or crest have been met while simultaneously technical studies show an overbought or oversold condition, then we apply the short-term studies related to Drummond Market Geometry as introduced here:

1) to pick the high or low of the move
2) to show evidence that support or resistance is holding or breaking
3) to confirm that a reversal is in fact commencing.

These steps will provide the means for getting into the market at, or near the low or high of a move. And when each of these studies lines up properly, that is as good as it gets.

References:

1. *Charles Drummond and Ted Hearne, "30 Lesson Course on Classic Drummond Geometry," https://www.drummondgeometry.com/learning_center; email: ted@DrummondGeometry.com, phone 1-800-552-2317.*
2. *Ibid.*

CHAPTER 18

AS GOOD AS IT GETS: POSITION TRADING

"In his semi-annual monetary policy testimony to the Senate Banking Committee, Fed chairman Ben Bernanke assured that the central bank would remain flexible in light of the 'unusually uncertain' economic outlook." – Wall Street Journal, July 22, 2010.

We now come to the end of this 14-year effort to show how market timing studies can be integrated with cyclical and technical studies to produce a powerful market analysis tool for forecasting and trading stock markets - or for any financial market in the world. Through these five books, the necessary tools to succeed in this task have been introduced. Now, let us complete this journey by creating a step-by-step process for both position and short-term traders that identifies favorable trading opportunities as close as possible to cycle lows and highs in any market. We will conclude this book by creating trading plans based on these methods in order to attain maximum profit potential with minimal market exposure, which is, of course, the ultimate goal of all short-term traders.

Timing is Almost Everything

Our methodology for position and short-term trading begins with market timing studies. By determining a time frame in which a market has a high probability of reversing, one can closely observe how the market behaves going into that time period and apply an appropriate trading strategy. If a cycle low is due, one can readily observe if prices are declining into a pre-calculated downside price objective range for this time band. One can also observe if certain technical studies are becoming oversold and exhibiting patterns such as bullish oscillator divergence. One can judge if certain chart patterns are in effect, such as intermarket bullish divergence. And last but not least, one can watch the progression of daily and weekly trend indicator points (TIPs), support and resistance zones, and see how the market closes relative to these critical price points.

In the trading methodology outlined in these books, the analysis starts by defining a time band in which a cycle trough or crest is due. For this we use market timing studies because they are the leading indicators that alert traders as to WHEN a tradable top or bottom is due. Once we know WHEN a market is most likely to reverse, we can then start to determine at WHAT PRICE to buy or sell. In this regard, the process logically begins with a market timing approach. For us, that means the application of cycles and geocosmic studies. Some readers may use additional market timing approaches, such as Gann studies or even some form of Fibonacci studies applied to time periodicities.

Simply using market timing studies doesn't end the process of determining when and where to enter a market. Market timing is not everything. It is only the first step, the starting point for this methodology of market analysis and trading. Market timing may be *almost* everything. But there is more to do if one wishes to increase accuracy in timing important lows and highs, and thereby increase the probability of being on the right side of a trade. When used in combination with technical analysis and price objective studies, market timing does become "everything" to this effort, with the understanding that we cannot predict UFO's (Unforeseen Fundamental Occurrences) or the effect upon markets when UFO's hit the news. We can only forecast prices and create trading plans based upon factors that are within our control, such as the price of a market on a day or in a week that has already occurred, which then sets up a series of numbers - prices - for future support and resistance zones, or for price objective targets. If market timing is a leading indicator to which we accord great weight, then it is to be understood that chart patterns, technical studies, and trend analysis studies represent the coincident and lagging (or confirming) indicators that we also consider important.

To our grouping of market timing studies, we may also add price objective studies as yet another leading indicator. Like market timing studies, these calculations anticipate the price ranges that financial markets are most likely to attain in the future. And once there, we prepare to take action, just as we would do when a market enters a time band for cycle trough or crest. In fact, it works best to take action when both market timing and price objective studies simultaneously indicate the potential for a reversal simultaneously.

Using Multiple Cycles: Start With the Next Larger Cycle

Short-term trading is enhanced by knowledge of cycles if for no other reason than that the structure of a cycle can provide guidance as to when a market is in its bullish or bearish phase. Knowing what phase a market is in determines what type of trading strategy to employ: bullish, bearish, or congestion.

We begin our analysis by identifying a primary cycle and its subcycles, or phases. But utilizing the principle of multiple cycles, we must first start this process by also identifying which phase of the greater cycle (i.e. 50-week cycle) that a given primary cycle is in. For here too, we need to know whether a particular primary cycle is in the first phase within a new 50-week cycle (bullish), the second, or the last (more bearish).

Thus these first steps are actually more for position traders than short-term traders. Yet even short-term traders must be cognizant of where in the greater cycle a market is at any given time. Otherwise it is like being a traveler driving to a faraway location for the first time without a road map or GPS system. You may have a "sense" of where you are going - in this direction or that - but if you don't have a map (or GPS system), you cannot have knowledge of which path to take when you come to a fork in the road. It won't do to follow the instructions of Yogi Berra, who said, "When you come to a fork in the road, take it." Standing at a crossroad, the map or the GPS system can instruct you on the path that is most likely to get you to your destination by the most direct route possible and with the least amount of obstacles along the way.

And so it is with short-term trading. You may have an "intuitive sense" of where the market is going, but it is best if that "sense" is supported by other non-subjective factors. You are going to have several experiences where the market seems indecisive. You will ask yourself many times: "Will it turn here and go down, or will it just pause and then resume up?" If you know where the market is in the greater cycle, you know when the probability is highest that the underlying trend is up or down. If you are not sure, it is better to choose in the direction of that underlying trend, according to the next longest cycle. And cycles are very useful in determining which trend is in effect. Remember: the first phase of any cycle is almost always bullish, and the last phase is usually bearish or exhibits the sharpest decline within an otherwise bullish cycle.

Since our trading plans revolve around the primary cycle and its phases, we begin by utilizing cycle studies to determine which phase of the greater 50-week cycle a given primary cycle is in. We will illustrate these market timing principles by examining an actual case involving the U.S. stock market, specifically the Dow Jones Industrial Average, during an extraordinary period in which a multitude of long-term planetary (geocosmic) signatures occurred in a short span of time. This example will demonstrate how the use of technical and price objective studies could have helped navigate one through a difficult period of time, one that Ben Bernanke, Federal Reserve Board Chair, called "unusually uncertain." Indeed it was, for that is the nature of time bands that contain a slew of contradictory long-term geocosmic cycles all unfolding at once.

The astrological midpoint of one of the most powerful configurations of a lifetime - known as the "Cardinal Climax" - was just beginning to unfold in mid-2010. This rare planetary phenomenon involved Saturn, Uranus, and Pluto, all in the early degrees of cardinal signs (Aries, Libra, and Capricorn), making a very close T-square to one another. This celestial pattern hasn't happened since 1930-1931. The current "Climax" was at its closest proximity around August 1, 2010. Jupiter and Mars also entered cardinal signs around that time, with Mars conjunct Saturn, and Jupiter conjunct Uranus, and both sets of planets in opposition to one another and also in T-square to Pluto in early Capricorn. This astrological configuration was similar to the alignment of June 1, 1931. It was therefore expected to coincide with a time of extraordinary economic and financial market activity *and* uncertainty. And indeed this was the case in many financial markets. But how would our studies identify the movements that were to unfold in stock indices?

Let us apply the methods outlined in these books to the primary cycle that began with the low of July 2, 2010 in the Dow Jones Industrial Average. I chose this period because it was an exceptionally difficult one for anyone to trade, and not because it would demonstrate a perfect illustration of how the principles outlined in these volumes work. I intentionally chose a period in which the trader would come up against the reality of many conflicting signals at once. And yet the example would demonstrate how cycles combined with technical studies and chart patterns would have enabled him to recognize when the "unusual uncertainty" of the period would give way to a more "normal" trading environment. Thus his risk would be limited and his potential for profit increased by eventually getting on the right side of the correct underlying trend. In retrospect, the cycles' labeling and trend assumption, via the market timing methods outlined here, was initially incorrect. But ultimately the market data corrected this incorrect assumption via these analytical methods, kept losses limited, and then led to huge profit opportunities.

Figure 58: **Weekly chart of the Dow Jones Industrial Average from March 2007 through November 2010. 1, 2, and 3 or 3A are the 50-week cycle lows. 2 was also a 4-year or greater cycle. The moving average is a 25-week simple average.**

The first step in this case was to determine which phase of the 50-week cycle the DJIA was beginning on July 2, 2010. Here is what one would have known at the time:

1. The 4-year (and greater) stock market cycle bottomed on March 6, 2009, identified as "2" in Figure 58 of the weekly chart of the DJIA.
2. The first 50-week cycle of the new 4-year cycle was expected to be bullish, as are all first phases of any cycle.
3. The 50-week cycle has a 90% historical rate of frequency of unfolding at the 34-67 week interval. Following the 4-year cycle trough of March 6, 2009, the first 50-week cycle phase would thus be due **October 26, 2009-June 18, 2010.**
4. The 50-week cycle low would likely coincide with the end of the 2nd or 3rd primary cycle phase of this greater cycle.
5. The 50-week cycle low would very likely see prices drop to or below the 25-week moving average.
6. On February 5, 2010, the DJIA fell to 9835 (point 3 in Figure 58). That was below the 25-week moving average for the first time since early May 2009. It was also the 48th week of the 50-week cycle, and the third primary cycle of this 50-week cycle. It was thus "on time" via cycle studies, it fulfilled the minimum price criteria (below the 25-week moving average), and it was structurally correct (third primary cycle phase) for a 50-week cycle trough.
7. Following that assumed 50-week cycle trough of February 5, 2010, the DJIA commenced another big rally. This was to be expected since it was thought to be

the first primary cycle phase of a new 50-week cycle - the second 50-week cycle within the even greater 4-year cycle. On April 26, 2010, the 12th week of the new primary cycle, prices topped out at 11,258. It was the highest price since October 2008. Everything was behaving exactly as it should in the first primary cycle phase of a new 50-week cycle. It was up for more than 8 weeks, it was forming a 'right translation" primary cycle, and it was already making new highs, even above the crest of the former 50-week and primary cycles.

8. But on May 25, 2010, the DJIA broke below the 9835 low of February 5, 2010. It fell to 9774 intraday, but closed well above there at 10,043. This was also a geocosmic three-star critical reversal zone, it was in the time band for a primary cycle trough (16th week), and it was in the price range for a double bottom to the low of February 5. It was also still in the 90% time band for a 50-week cycle trough (64th week), even if it was forming a rare "4-phase" pattern, i.e., this would be the 4th primary cycle within the 50-week cycle.

9. The rally did not last. After two strong rallies, it started to fall lower and lower until the final bottom at 9614 on July 2, 2010. That was the 21st week of the primary cycle which began on February 5. However, it was 69 weeks following the start of the 50-week cycle if measured from March 6, 2009.

These were the conditions that were in effect in early July 2010, a time which the chairman of the Federal Reserve Board branded "unusually uncertain." Indeed that would prove to be true. As cycle's analysts, we could look at this in one of two ways:

1. This was the end to the first primary cycle phase of a new 50-week cycle, and it was going to be a bearish 50-week cycle because the DJIA already took out the low that started the cycle on February 5, 2010, i.e., once the start of a cycle is taken out, it will be bearish until the cycle ends for the lowest price in a bear market cycle is always at its end. The second primary cycle phase of this 50-week cycle would now begin, and it would be bearish since the 50-week cycle had just turned bearish. The rally would most likely only last 2-5 weeks, with a possibility of lasting as long as 8 weeks, but no longer than Tuesday of the 9th week (the "8-week" bullish rule). The high would not exceed the previous high of 11,258, and the low would fall below the 9614 level of July 2. This cycle analysis has a 90% probability based on the history of the 50-week cycle bottoming at the 34-67 week interval, or,

2. The low of July 2 was a distorted 50-week cycle, expanding to 69 weeks, and it was actually part of a longer-term cycle trough - one that was greater than the 50-week cycle (the first 15.5-month phase of the greater 4-year cycle). Thus this would be the first primary cycle phase of a longer-term cycle and also an expanded 50-week cycle. This outlook had a probability of less than 10%, based on the historical rate of frequency of the 50-week cycle within a 34-67 week range. The low of July 2 was 69 weeks, which was outside of the normal range.

Since our strategies are based on historical probabilities, the logical judgment was the first option - at least until data proved that it was incorrect. As it would turn out, the second option – the "less than 10% probability" - would be operative. The 90% probability was incorrect. At that time, however, this would not be known, which is why I this example was chosen. How would we handle such a case when our assumption of the longer-term cycle labeling was incorrect, and thus our bearish expectation of the primary cycle pattern would be wrong?

In retrospect, we can now see that July 2, 2010 was indeed a longer-term cycle trough. It was the end of the first phase (of three) within the greater 4-year cycle. With 4-year cycles, you never know if they will sub-divide into a classical three-phase pattern of approximately 15.5-month subcycles or two half cycles of approximately 23 months, or both. The two-phase pattern is more common in the 4-year cycle, as reported in the studies of Volume 1. But in early July 2010, the pattern of the stock market implied that the 50-week cycle was now bearish, and this new primary cycle - the second within the greater 50-week cycle - was most likely to be bearish. Still we would expect the first phase of this new primary cycle to be bullish, as are first phases of nearly all cycles. But after the completion of its first major or half-primary cycle trough (phase) we would expect a rally, followed by the market turning bearish and eventually taking out the low that started this primary cycle at 9614 on July 2.

Thus our analysis of this primary cycle begins with a bearish bias until proven otherwise.

Identifying the Time Bands for Market Reversals within the Primary Cycle

Let us start this section with a review of the primary cycle in stock markets. In the United States, the primary cycle varies slightly between indexes. For instance, as reported in Volume 1, the primary cycle in the Dow Jones Industrial Average has a historical range that varied from 13-26 weeks in 92% of instances studied between 1928 and 2006. If that range was reduced to 13-24 weeks, then primary cycles were observed in 84% of cases studied. At the 13-21 week interval, the primary cycle trough was observed in 73% of cases examined. If we use the 92% interval of 13-26 weeks, a mean primary cycle of 19.5 weeks would be derived, with an orb of 6.5 weeks. If we use the 84% grouping, the mean primary cycle lasted 18.5 weeks, with an orb of 5.5 weeks. And if we chose to use a primary cycle with a range of 13-21 weeks, the mean periodicity would be 17 weeks, +/- 4 weeks orb. Throughout these five volumes, we have used the later period for the primary cycle in the DJIA. That is, we based our analysis on the idea that a "normal" primary cycle interval lasts 17 weeks, +/- 4 weeks, or 13-21 weeks. Anything beyond that range is considered a distortion. However, our studies of the S&P and NASDAQ 100 futures' contracts suggest both have a 19-week cycle, +/- 4 weeks, with a "normal" range of 15-23 weeks. One can thus see there is a slight difference from one index to another.

But this is not the case in other stock markets of the world. Indeed, some are comparatively shorter, such as in Japan, while others are comparatively longer, such as in Europe. In the Japanese Nikkei stock index for instance, the studies in Volume 1 demonstrated that the "normal" primary cycle lasts 16 weeks, +/- 3 weeks. The range for the vast majority of primary cycles in the Nikkei has been 13-19 weeks. However there have been a few cases of expansion where the cycle lasted 20-23 weeks and even a couple that lasted longer (one lasted 28 weeks). There have been instances when it contracted to as short as 11 weeks.

In Europe, preliminary studies (not reported yet) indicate primary cycles lasting 15-26 weeks in the German DAX and Swiss SMI, to a slightly longer primary cycle of 17-27 weeks in the Netherlands AEX index. If valid, these studies imply that the primary cycle in Japan's Nikkei index is shorter than that of the USA stock indices, while Europe's leading indices have longer periodicities for their primary cycles.

Our studies in this final chapter will use examples from the Dow Jones Industrial Average (DJIA). We will focus on their cycles to illustrate how these timing principles work. These same principles may be applied to Japanese and European markets (or any financial market). However the time length of each cycle and subcycle (or phase) has to be extended or contracted proportionately when applied to European or Japanese stock indices or any financial market that has a mean primary cycle outside of 17 weeks.

For this section of the book, we begin with the premise (based on historical studies) that the DJIA exhibits a "normal" 17-week primary cycle with a range of 13-21 weeks, consisting of three major cycle phases lasting about 5-7 weeks each, or two half-primary cycles lasting 7-11 weeks each, or a combination of each. These cycle lengths can contract or expand slightly, depending on the patterns that form in each one. For example, in a three-phase primary cycle pattern that lasts more than 21 weeks, at least one of the 5-7 week major cycles will have to expand to 8 weeks.

Timing the Phases and Other Possible Turning Points in a Primary Cycle

1. **Locate the time band for a primary cycle trough.** Count 13-21 weeks following a primary cycle trough and highlight the time band when the next primary cycle trough is due in the DJIA (or 13-19 weeks later to highlight the time band when the next primary cycle trough is due in the Nikkei, or 15-26 weeks later for the German DAX or Swiss SMI index, or 17-27 weeks later for the Netherlands AEX index).
2. **Calculate the upside price targets for the crest of this new primary cycle.** The first calculation will be a simple 38-62% retracement of the recent move down from the prior primary cycle crest. The second would be an MCP (Mid-Cycle Pause) price target if this primary cycle trough was *higher* than the prior one. If it wasn't - that is, if this current primary cycle low is below the prior one - then there is a greater probability the 38-62% retracement area is all the first 2-5 week rally will attain. If it is higher, then there may be other upside targets that can be calculated based on other methods listed in Chapter 6 of this book.
3. **Identify the time band for the first major cycle trough.** Measure out 5-7 weeks from the start of the primary cycle to identify the time band when the first major cycle trough is due to unfold in a classical three-phase primary cycle pattern, or even a "combination" pattern. One of these two patterns occurs in about 80% of all instances. Thus the probability of a major cycle trough occurring is about 80% and it will usually be at the first 5-7 week interval. This major cycle trough time band would mark the end of the first phase of the new primary cycle, which in most cases will be a bullish phase. It is rare to find the first major cycle trough taking out the low that started the primary cycle. Once a market falls below the low that started a cycle, it is bearish. But even in bear markets that it not very likely to happen in the first major cycle phase of a

primary cycle. The first phase of all cycles tends to be more bullish than bearish, which means its low does not take out the low that started the cycle. *Hence our strategy in this phase is always bullish.* It only changes when the price falls below the start of the primary cycle. In the Japanese Nikkei index, one would mark out 4-6 weeks after the primary cycle low, to determine when the first major cycle trough of this primary cycle is due. In the S&P and NASDAQ, the normal major cycle lasts 5-8 weeks. In the German DAX and Swiss SMI, it is 5-9 weeks, and in the AEX, it is 6-9 weeks.

4. **Identify time bands for first half-primary cycle trough.** Also measure out 7-11 weeks from the start of the primary cycle. Then mark the time band in which the first half-primary cycle trough is due to unfold in a classical two-phase primary cycle pattern or even a "combination" pattern. These two patterns have a 60% historical rate of occurrence. It is the same range in the Japanese Nikkei, S&P, and NASDAQ indices. It is slightly longer in the European indices.

5. **Identify geocosmic critical reversal dates in first half-primary cycle.** Now, with the use of an ephemeris or a geocosmic (astrological) computer program, look to identify groupings of geocosmic signatures unfolding during the first half of the primary cycle - known as a "cluster." Determine the midpoint of each of those clusters (if there is more than one). The steps for this were provided in Volume 3, but it is very simple: the point midway between the first and last signature of a cluster is the geocosmic "critical reversal date." Allow a 3-trading day orb to this reversal date. Mark this time frame on your charts. See if these critical reversal dates overlap with the time bands when both the first 5-7 week and 7-11 week major or half-primary cycle troughs are due. It is possible there is more than one grouping that intersects the time bands for a major or half-primary cycle trough. Understand that it is possible that these critical reversal periods could also coincide with the crest of a major or half-primary cycle, especially if they occur in the first 5 weeks of the new primary cycle. They may also coincide with trading cycle troughs or crests from which the market reverses at least 2.5%, and usually at least 4% of the lowest price in this cycle.

6. **Identify specific solar-lunar reversal dates within the first phase of the primary cycle.** If the market forms an isolated low in these short-term time periods, they present favorable opportunities to go long too. These dates can be calculated from the studies given in Volume 4 of the "The Ultimate Book on Stock Market Timing: Solar-Lunar Correlations to Short-Term Trading Reversals." This study is not so important for position traders. However, they can be very valuable for very short-term aggressive traders, once they understand the phasing of the primary cycle and the appropriate trading strategy to employ. Until the major cycle crest is achieved, the appropriate strategy in the first phase of the primary cycle is to be bullish and buy the dips.

These are the first steps towards identifying the *time* of the culmination of the first phases within a new primary cycle and the points to buy since the first phase is usually bullish. This is how one starts by analyzing markets and preparing a trading plan. When is the market most likely to make its first major and/or half-primary cycle crest, and when is it most likely to make its first major and/or half-primary cycle trough? Until the first major or first half-primary cycle crest is completed, one can buy all corrective declines or trading cycle troughs (there are two or three trading cycles within a major cycle).

Against this background of cycles, we then plot the geocosmic signatures that indicate the possibility of a turning point. In reality, we don't really know yet whether the market will form a trough or crest at these geocosmic critical reversal dates. However, we do know that if the market is declining into these geocosmic points that overlap with a time band for a major or half-primary cycle trough (or even a trading cycle trough), the chances are great that it will identify the timing of that cycle low correctly. The same is true if prices are rising into these periods, and the cycle structure suggests it could be a major or half-primary cycle crest.

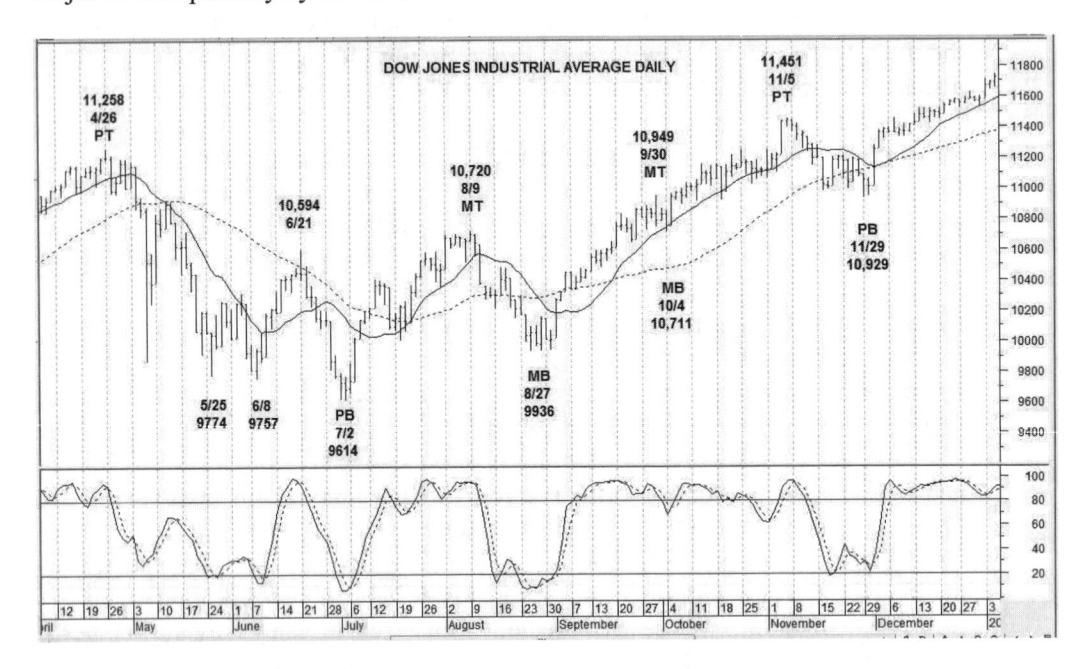

Figure 59: Daily chart of the DJIA from April 2010 through December 2010. Included are the 14- and 42-day moving averages. The 14-day is the solid line; the 42-day is the dotted line. The final cycle labeling is provided in this chart, along with the price and date of those cycles or important isolated lows or highs. However, at the time, the labeling of the first major cycle (8/27) was different.

We begin our example with a market timing analysis of the primary cycle trough of July 2, 2010 in the Dow Jones Industrial Average, as shown in the chart of Figure 59. We will apply only cycle and geocosmic studies for this period, in an effort to show how they help identify potential primary cycle troughs. Also, note that this particular primary cycle trough (July 2) was a classic example of *intermarket bullish divergence* to other indices. For example, it occurred on May 21 in the Australian All Ordinaries and May 25 in the German DAX, Netherlands AEX, and Hong Kong's Hang Seng. It took place on June 9 in the Japanese Nikkei and July 5-6 in the Swiss SMI and USA's S&P indices.

The previous primary cycle (not shown here) had occurred on February 5, 2010 at 9835 in the DJIA. Once February 5 was confirmed as the primary bottom, the first step would be to identify a time band 13-21 weeks later when the next primary cycle trough would be due. That equated to the period of **May 3 through July 2, 2010.**

Below is a list of the major geocosmic clusters between May 3 and July 2 in which the normal primary cycle trough would be due.

Date	Signature	Aspect Degree	Value	Level
May 4	☉□♂	270	8.56	3
May 11	☿SD		8.88	3
May 17	♀□♃	90	8.83	3
May 18	☉△♄	240	9.26*	1-2
	♀□♄	270	9.17*	1-2
	♀△♆	120	8.87	3
May 19	☉□♆	90	9.59**	1
	♀□♅	90	8.98	1
May 23	♀☍♇		9.20*	2
	♃☍♄		8.78	3
May 30	♄SD		9.43**	1
May 31	♆SR		9.52**	1
June 4	♂☍♆		9.17*	2
June 8	♃☌♅		9.73**	1
June 14	♀△♅	120	9.25*	2
June 15	♀△♃	120	9.26*	2
	♂△♇	240	9.07*	2
June 19	☉□♄	270	9.15*	1-2
	☉△♆	120	9.28*	1-2
June 21	☉□♅	90	9.70**	1
June 23	☉□♃	90	9.10*	1-2
June 25	☉☍♇		9.29*	1
July 5	♅SR		9.52**	1
July 8	♀☍♆		8.94	3
July 13	♀△♇	240	9.06	2

The first column lists the dates of geocosmic signatures taking place May 2-July 2, 2010, the time band that was calculated for a normal 13-21 week primary cycle trough. The second column gives the geocosmic signature in effect for each date. (Note: if you are unfamiliar with planetary glyphs, please refer to the "Geocosmic Abbreviations and Symbols" given in the preliminary pages of this book). Next to the geocosmic symbols are the degrees of separation involved in square aspects (90° and 270°) and trine aspects (120° and 240°). The next column is entitled "Value" and represents the C/S value of each signature according to the studies reported in Volume 3. The values can range from 0-10. The greater the value, the more consistent (C) and powerful its strength (S) has been in relationship to the cycle types it has coincided with historically. The final column is entitled "Level." This pertains to the three groupings of geocosmic signatures in terms of their correlation to primary or greater cycles. A Level 1 signature, for example, means it has a high C/S rating (9.40 or higher) and/or it has a high historical correlation (i.e. above 67%) to primary cycles nearby. A "1-2" means it has a C/S value less than 9.40, but its correlation to primary cycles historically is still at least 67%.

As you can see, we have segregated these signatures into five groups. The first group just contains two signatures: the Sun/Mars waning square of May 4 and Mercury turning direct on May 11. Both are Level 3 signatures, which are rather weak and not expected to coincide with a primary cycle trough, although we note the huge down day on May 6 when the DJIA sold off over 1000 points in about 25 minutes, but then recovered 800 of those points by the close. This was a very freakish day and perhaps it coincides with some of the rather "strange market behavior" that sometimes happens under a Mercury retrograde. It is a time when communication systems can break down, as was the case at this time. A large but wrong sell order was given to the market and it triggered many stops in the process of selling off before the market found support.

The other four geocosmic groupings are based on the fact that there were no more than 5 calendar days before any two consecutive signatures. Usually six calendar days is allowable between any two consecutive signatures that make up a geocosmic cluster. But when such a series of signatures extends over a month, the rule is to try and identify tighter clusters in which the distance is reduced to no more than 5 or even 4 days (or less, if applicable) between any two consecutive signatures within that cluster. Thus we find the following geocosmic clusters in effect during this period and their midpoints, or critical reversal dates, +/- 3 trading days:

	Cluster	Critical Reversal Date
1.	May 17-23	(May 20, Thursday)
2.	May 30-June 8	(June 3-4, Thursday, Friday)
3.	June 14-25	(June 19-20, Saturday, Sunday)
4.	July 5-13	(July 9, Friday)

In determining a critical reversal date that is apt to be most valid, it is important to remember that it is most effective if a Level 1 signature is within 4 calendar days of the reversal date as well. Thus a critical reversal date that does not have a Level 1 signature nearby may not coincide with the critical reversal date as shown by the midpoint of a cluster. It may need to be adjusted to occur closer to a Level 1 signature, if there is one in the cluster. This corollary is important in this case, for the primary cycle trough of the DJIA occurred on July 2, just one trading day before the only Level 1 signature in the cluster of July 5-13. In fact, July 5 was a holiday. July 2 was on a Friday, and the last trading day before the Level 1 signature of Uranus retrograde took place. Uranus retrograde is a powerful Level 1 signature with a C/S value of 9.52. It has a huge 77% historical correlation to primary or greater cycles within 11 trading days.

It is significant to note that the dates of the primary cycle in other world stock indices also showed up here. The May 20 critical reversal date was within the allowable orb of three trading days to the May 25 primary cycle trough in the DAX, AEX, and Hang Seng indices. It was only one day prior to the primary cycle trough in the Australian All Ordinaries index. The June 4-5 critical reversal date was just three trading days prior to the primary cycle trough in the Japanese Nikkei and only two days prior to an important bottom in many other indices (June 8), such as the DJIA. Note that June 8 was the exact date of the Jupiter-Uranus conjunction, the strongest of all Level 1 signatures taking place in this cluster. It was no wonder that it coincided to primary cycle troughs in some markets. It was even more pronounced in the Euro currency market, where it coincided with a 4-year cycle trough one day earlier, on June 7.

The next critical reversal date was during the weekend of June 18-21. June 21 was the end of the first leg up of this new primary cycle in many markets. It also marked an important trading crest in the DJIA, from which this index reversed and fell sharply to its primary cycle trough on July 2. June 21 was an effective turning point in other markets too. Gold, for instance, formed a primary cycle crest exactly on that day.

As pointed out before, the primary cycle trough low on July 2 in the DJIA was not accompanied by many other leading stock indices, and hence it became a case of intermarket bullish divergence. This is an important technical indicator that frequently takes place at primary cycle troughs. That is, one stock index makes a new low but it is not accompanied by others, which bottom earlier or later. July 2 was also the last trading day before the powerful Level 1 signature of Uranus turning retrograde.

If one views the chart of Figure 59, it will be noted that the faster 14-day moving average never moved above the longer 42-day moving average until *after* the bottom of July 2. In fact it wasn't until July 22 that the price of the DJIA was above both the 14- and 42-day moving averages, and the 14-day was above the 42-day, thus confirming a new bullish trend. At that point (July 22), one was able to confirm July 2 as a primary cycle trough. Yet it would not be confirmed as a bullish primary cycle until September. We were still working on the assumption that the primary cycle would be bearish, based on the idea that this was the second primary cycle within a 50-week cycle, and prices had already taken out the low that began this cycle on February 2. It was well after the middle of this primary cycle before one would know that this would be a bullish "right translation" primary cycle. It was not until then that we would have to re-label both the primary and longer-term cycles. In retrospect, this would also confirm July 2 as both the 50-week cycle trough and the end of the first phase (13-20 months) of the 4-year cycle that began on March 6, 2009. It was therefore likely that this 4-year cycle would be either a classical three-phase pattern (three sub-cycles of 15.5-months, +/- 3 months) or a combination pattern, consisting also of an 18-27 month half cycle to the 4-year cycle.

So let us now begin the analysis and trading strategies that would be applied to this new primary cycle that began on July 2, 2010, following our first steps outlined earlier.

1. **Locate the time band for the next primary cycle trough.**

We do that by counting forward 13-21 weeks after July 2 for a normal primary cycle trough. In doing so, we are aware that such primary cycles occur with a 73% frequency in this time frame, but 84% of the time it will expand up to expanded 24 weeks, and there is a 92% frequency if the primary cycle is expanded to 26 weeks. Nevertheless, the time band in which a normal 13-21 week primary cycle would be due is **September 27-November 26.** There is a possibility it could expand to December 31, but we always start with the idea that it will be a "normal" primary cycle and not an expanded (or "distorted") one.

2. Calculate the upside price targets for the crest of this new primary cycle.

The last primary cycle was bearish, so the first price target would be a 38.2-61.8% retracement of the prior move down from primary cycle crest (April 26) to primary cycle trough (July 2). Or, it could be stated that it would be a 50% retracement, +/- 11.8%. The calculation is simple either way and yields the same result. Add the price of the previous primary cycle crest of April 26 (11,258) to the low of the July 2 primary cycle trough (9614) and divide the total by 2, or, (11,258 + 9614) ÷ 2 = 10,436. The orb is 11.8% of the difference between 11,258 and 9614, or 194. Thus the price target for the rally to the crest of the new primary cycle would be 10,436 +/- 194. The price range would be **10,242-10,630**. If this primary cycle was to be bearish, that would most likely be achieved at the first 2-5 week interval.

Although our bias was that this would be a bearish primary cycle, we also knew there was a 10% possibility it could be the start of a new longer-term cycle - the second phase of the 4-year cycle. If that was the case, then the rally could be more substantial. Even though the 50-week cycle indicated just a 10% probability of being bullish, we had to consider that it was possible, that this primary cycle could be the first phase (15.5-month subcycle) to the 4-year cycle. Therefore we should also calculate higher upside targets, such as the MCP (Mid-Cycle Pause) price objective for the crest of a bullish 50-week cycle, which would be the same MCP price projection as the crest for the second phase of the 4-year cycle.

For the MCP price of the new 50-week cycle crest, we add the high for the crest of the just completed 50-week cycle (11,258 on April 26, 2010) to the low of the just completed 50-week cycle (9614 on July 2). We then subtract the low of the prior 50-week cycle (6470 on March 6, 2009) from this, or (11,258 + 9614) – 6470 = 14,402. This would be the MCP price target for the crest of the new 50-week cycle and second phase of the 4-year cycle. It would have a range of 11.8% of the difference between the projected high (14,402) and the low of 6470 that started the cycle. In this case that would be (14,402-6470) x .118 = 936. The range for the MCP calculation of the crest of the new 50-week cycle, if bullish, would thus be **13,466-15,338**. Other price targets would be calculated along the way.

We also knew that the crest of the previous primary (and 50-week) cycle could act as resistance. Normally a variance of 2% is allowed from a previous high to serve as the range for a double top. In this case, the previous crest was 11,258 on April 26. Giving that a range of 2% yields a double top resistance zone of 225 points, or **11,033-11,483**.

Thus we have three price targets to the upside to watch for in this primary cycle: **10,242-10,630, 11,033-11,483, and 13,466-15,338**. There may be others, but we start with these three price targets for the primary crest. In fact, more price targets will unfold as each phase of this new primary cycle is completed. Additionally there may be upside measuring gap price targets, breakouts of bullish inverse head and shoulder patterns, and a host of other upside targets that may unfold from various chart patterns along the way, as described in the earlier chapters of this book.

3. Identify the time band for the first major cycle trough.

Count out 5-7 weeks following the start of the primary cycle on July 2, 2010. This gives a time band of **August 2 through August 20, 2010**.

4. Identify the time band for first half-primary cycle trough.

Count out 7-11 weeks following the beginning of the primary cycle on July 2, 2011. This yields a time band of **August 16-September 17, 2010**.

5. Identify geocosmic critical reversal dates in the first half-primary cycle.

Below is the list of the major geocosmic signatures in effect July 2-September 17, 2010. They are separated out in groups comprising a geocosmic cluster.

Date	Signature	Aspect Degree	Value	Level
July 5	♅SR		9.52*	1
July 8	♀☍♆		8.94	3
July 13	♀△♇	240	9.06	2
July 23	☉△♅	120	9.14*	2
	♃SR		9.14*	2
July 24	♃□♇	90	8.90	2
July 26	♄☍♅		9.40**	1
	☉△♃	120	9.15*	2
July 30	♂☍♅		9.39**	1
July 31	♂☌♄		9.18*	1-2
Aug 3	♂☍♃		9.20*	1-2
	♃□♇	90	8.90	2
	♂□♇	270	8.95	3
Aug 7	♀☍♅		9.42**	1
Aug 8	♀☌♄		8.67	3
Aug 9	♀□♇	270	9.45**	1
	♀☍♃		8.98	3
Aug 16	♃☍♄		8.78	3
Aug 20	☉☍♆		9.57**	1
	♀☌♂		9.47**	1
	☿SR		9.15*	2
Aug 21	♄□♇	270	8.91	1-2
Aug 26	☉△♇	240	8.90	2
Sep 4	♀△♆	240	9.26*	2
Sep 9	♂△♆	240	9.33	1
Sep 12	☿SD		8.88	3
Sep 13	♇SD		8.80	3

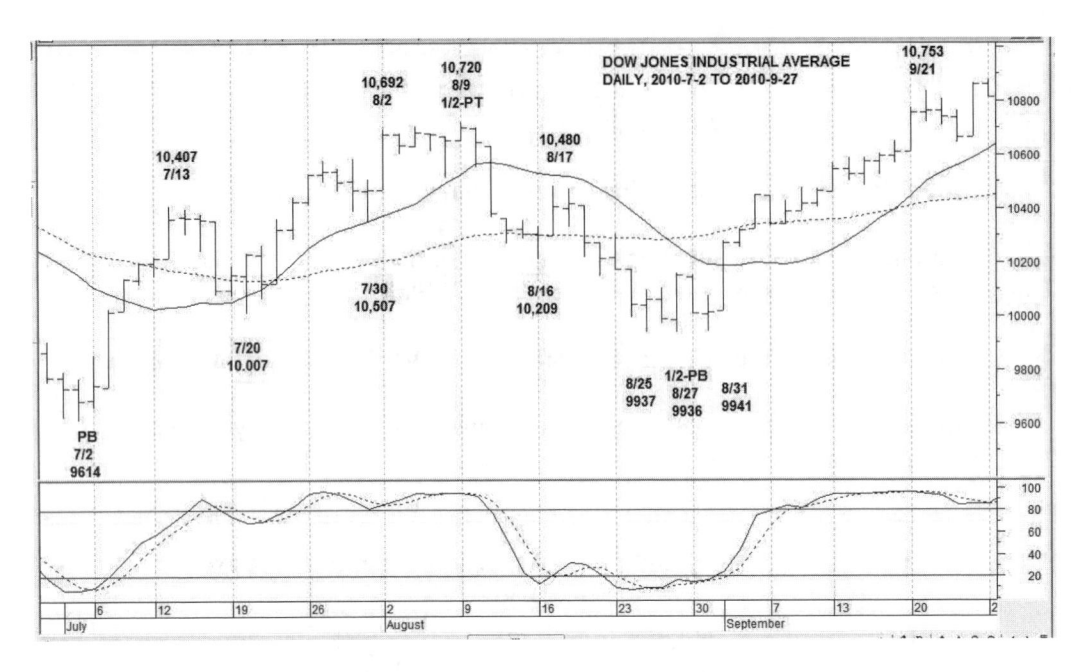

Figure 60: Daily chart of the Dow Jones Industrial Average during the height of the Cardinal Climax.

The two most important time bands defining a geocosmic cluster are **July 23-August 9 and August 16-26**. The first one overlaps with the time band for a 5-7 week major cycle trough (August 2-20), which means that if a major cycle trough occurs, it would most likely unfold August 2-9, for that is the overlap period. The second cluster overlaps with the time band for the 7-11 week half-primary cycle trough due August 16 - September 17. The overlap here is August 16-26. The geocosmic critical reversal dates pertaining to these two clusters are July 31-August 1 (Saturday and Sunday), +/- 3 trading days and August 21 (a Saturday), +/- 3 trading days. When a critical reversal date occurs on a weekend, we assign that Friday and Monday as the reversal dates. In this case, the reversal dates would be **July 30 - August 2 and August 20-23**. However, keep in mind that reversals can occur 1) if there are even tighter clusters than the 5 or 6 consecutive-day interval between any two signatures, and 2) the most effective reversals occur when a critical reversal date is also nearby to a Level 1 signature.

Let us take a closer look at what happened during these periods when a major and/or half-primary cycle trough was due, as shown on the daily chart in Figure 60 on the top of this page.

The first critical reversal date was July 30-August 2, a Friday through Monday. You will note that July 31-August 1 was the actual midpoint of the July 23 - August 9 cluster. On August 2, the first trading day following this midpoint, the DJIA jumped to 10,692. This was very close to its eventual major cycle crest at 10,720 recorded five trading days later, on August 9. However, this was another case of intermarket bearish divergence to other indices. The nearby S&P futures contract, for example, topped out on August 5, just three trading days later. Furthermore, all the stock indices were basically in a topping pattern August 2-9, with the final high in stock indices being posted August 5-9. It is interesting to note that Gold and Silver made primary cycle troughs on July 28, just two trading days before. It reinforces the idea that 1) critical reversal dates potentially affect all financial markets and 2) some may make new two-week or greater highs and others may make two-week or greater lows. Crude Oil, for instance, made its primary cycle crest on August 4, along with stock indices, but precious metals made primary cycle troughs.

Now back to the timing of the stock market. The entire period of August 2-9 can be considered a topping formation of the crest that actually fell on August 9 in the DJIA. This date itself stands out by virtue of the fact that there was a very tight cluster of signatures on August 7, 8, and 9, including two Level 1 signatures on August 7 and 9. Financial markets that were still rising or falling would be vulnerable to a reversal on the midpoint of this very tight cluster of three signatures in which no more than one calendar day separates any two consecutive ones. The midpoint of this very tight cluster equates to August 8, +/- 3 trading days.

6. Identify specific solar-lunar reversal dates within the first phase of the primary cycle.

A review of the solar-lunar cycles for that period would reveal that the Sun and Moon were both in Leo on August 9-10. From studies reported in Volume 4 on "Solar-Lunar Correlations to Short-Term Trading Reversals," the weighted value of that combination is a very strong 159.4. The only other very strong solar-lunar cycle during this month was the Sun in Leo with the Moon in Aquarius, July 28-30, which had a weighted value of 146.5. Any weighted value above 120 has the potential of a reversal from an isolated high or low of that day(s). That coincided with the trading cycle low of July 30 at 10,507. In the case of the Sun-Moon in Leo on August 9, the DJIA formed an isolated high and as can be seen from the chart in Figure 60, it was to be labeled a half-primary cycle crest at the time. Ultimately it would be re-labeled as a major cycle crest (see Figure 59). It was the 6th week of the primary cycle, so it was late in the time band for a major cycle crest, which is ideally due 2-5 weeks into the new primary cycle. This was a sign the primary cycle might skip its normal 5-7 week interval for a major cycle trough and instead move directly to a 7-11 week half-primary cycle trough. So in this case, the geocosmic critical reversal date that was in effect during the time band for a major cycle trough turned out instead to be a half-primary (or major) cycle crest. Geocosmics don't care whether it is a crest or trough, but only that it is one or the other from which a reversal follows. But it is best when geocosmic critical reversal dates coincide with the expected cycle type that is due, which is usually the case. But this primary cycle was no "normal" cycle type. It was destined to distort in many ways due to the confluence of so many long-term planetary cycles that were in force July 26 - August 21.

The next geocosmic critical reversal date applied to the normal time frame for a 7-11 half-primary cycle trough. The midpoint of the August 16-26 geocosmic cluster fell on August 21, a weekend. Thus we assign the critical reversal date to Friday and Monday, August 20-23. As one can see on the charts in Figures 59 and 60, the DJIA was falling into that period as would be expected. By Tuesday, August 24, it broke below 10,000, its lowest level since the start of the primary cycle on July 2. At this point it was already the 8th week of the primary cycle, so a price target could be calculated for this expected half-primary cycle trough. The primary cycle could still be bullish if the decline was 45-85% of the move up from the July 2 primary cycle trough at 9614 to the half-primary cycle crest on August 9 at 10,720. That swing up was 1106 points. A retracement of 45-85% would mean a decline of 498-940 points was likely for the half-primary cycle trough in this case. But keep in mind that our bias was still that this primary cycle would be bearish. It could fall below 9614, the start of the primary cycle. Subtracting this from the crest would yield a price target of 9780-10,222 for that low. It turns out the DJIA bottomed in this range, at 9936-9941 between August 25 and August 31, with the actual low at 9936 on August 27. Once again it was slightly outside the orb of 3 trading days we prefer to see (it was four days after August 23) for an actual reversal to the geocosmic critical reversal date. But the low of August 25 was just one point higher and only two days after the August 20-23 geocosmic critical reversal date. It was close enough, especially considering that it never closed below the low of August 25. And the fact that the decline did not take out the low that started the primary cycle kept the 10% probability alive that this could still be a bullish primary (and longer-term) cycle.

This concludes our section on market timing for this example, which is the first step to undertake in a trading plan based on the start of a new primary cycle.

The Second Step: Calculating Additional Price Targets Along the Way

In the first step of developing the trading plan for the primary cycle, we identified the price targets for the first major, half-primary, and/or primary cycle crests. We performed three calculations, which we can do once we know that a primary cycle trough has been completed. These three initial calculations are:

1. 38.2-61.8% retracement of the move down from the former primary cycle crest to the primary cycle trough that begins the new primary cycle.
2. A 2% range of the former primary cycle crest, which would equate to the range of a double top formation.
3. An MCP upside price target if the new primary cycle is at a higher level than the prior primary cycle trough. The rules for this calculation are given in Chapter 5.

These price objectives, and the time bands for the major and half-primary cycle troughs, should be placed on your charts for reference during the entire primary cycle. When these price ranges are attained and when these time bands for reversals and/or cycle completions are entered, the trader prepares to take action.

However, as the primary cycle unfolds, there will be other highs and lows formed along the way known as trading cycles. From these trading cycle troughs and crests, additional price objectives can be calculated for both crests and troughs of the major cycle type and greater. Additionally the market might exhibit certain chart formations, such as head and shoulder patterns or measuring gaps (up and down) that yield more price targets. When these price targets overlap with the price objectives calculated in the first step, they become very important as support and resistance zones from which cycles are completed.

Thus, once a primary cycle is underway, we look for three factors that might provide additional price targets for the cycle crests and troughs within this primary cycle:

1. **Trading cycle troughs and crests**. These occur every 2-4 weeks, and in many financial circles they are referred to as "swing" highs and lows. They can be very valuable in calculating new and accurate price targets for major cycle troughs or crests (or greater), either via MCP or normal price retracement calculations.
2. **Head and shoulders formations** (bearish) or inverse head and shoulders formations (bullish). When these patterns form, there will be a neckline that represents support below the market or resistance above the market. When the neckline is broken, it yields a new downside or upside price target, per the instructions given in Chapter 8.
3. **Measuring gaps**. A gap up can yield a new upside price objective, whereas a gap down can yield new downside price objectives. If these overlap with previously calculated price targets, they become very important. It is important to note that the DJIA seldom has a gap up or gap down day.

Returning to our example in Figure 59 and 60, we can see a couple of these factors would have applied to the first phase of this new primary cycle.

1. **Trading cycle troughs and crests.**

On July 13, the first trading cycle crest of the new primary cycle was completed at 10,407. One week later, on July 20, the first trading cycle trough was completed at 10,007. This was a perfectly normal "first trading cycle" within a new primary cycle. That is, it was bullish in form and price structure. The crest of 10,407 was right in the middle of a 38.2-61.8% retracement of the primary cycle swing down from 11,258 (April 26) to 9614 (July 2), as calculated in our first steps. That corrective price retracement target was 10,436 +/- 194. The fact that it was achieved so early in the primary cycle (second week) suggested two possibilities: 1) if the primary cycle is to be bearish, this might be the primary cycle crest already, or 2) this primary cycle will be more bullish than would be the case in a bear market retracement.

It could be anticipated that the following decline would be a corrective retracement because it was only the first trading cycle in a new primary cycle, and the early stages are (almost) always bullish. Indeed, the decline that followed was well within the normal 38.2-61.8% retracement zone. That price target was (10,407 + 9614) ÷ 2, or 10,010 +/- 94. The actual low was 10,007 on July 20. This was a perfect example in terms of our time and price studies. The trading cycle was three weeks into the primary cycle (its normal range is 2-4 weeks). A normal price corrective decline would have been 10,010 +/- 94, and the actual low was 10,007. That was "as good as it gets" for the start of a new primary cycle and would represent the first "buy point" in the bullish trading strategy that was in effect at this time.

With the completion of a 3-week trading cycle trough, it was now possible to calculate an MCP price objective for the crest of this first major cycle phase. Since the first trading cycle lasted 3 weeks, we could assume there would be two trading cycle phases within this first 5-7 week major cycle. If the first thrust up was 793 points (10,407 high on July 13, less the 9614 low of the primary bottom on July 2), then the next rally would be expected to be about the same amount. The MCP (Mid-Cycle Pause) price objective for the crest of the second trading cycle (which would also be the crest of the entire first major cycle) would thus be calculated as follows: (10,407 + 10,007) – 9614 = 10,800 +/- 140. The orb was determined by the following formula: (10,800 – 9614) x .118 = 140. Thus the MCP price target range for the crest of the first major cycle was 10,660-10,940. That range was entered on August 2, the critical reversal date, when prices rallied to 10,692. They remained in that range until the major cycle crest was finally completed on August 9 at 10,720. If you sold short on August 2 with a stop-loss above this range as the bearish trading strategy in effect at this time would dictate (i.e. end of first major cycle phase), you did quite well. You weren't stopped out, and shortly afterwards the decline proved to be rewarding.

Now that we had the first major cycle crest with which to work, the price target for the first 5-7 week major cycle trough could be calculated. Time-wise, we knew it would be due the next week, for the crest of August 9 occurred in the 6th week, and normally the major cycle trough unfolds in the 5-7 week time period. Since it was only the first major cycle phase of the new primary cycle, it would not be expected to take out the 9614 low that started the primary cycle on July 2. In fact, it would most likely be just a normal corrective decline of the swing up from the July 2 bottom to the major cycle crest of August 9, because it was apparent the whole major cycle would be a bullish "right translation" pattern. That is, the high was already past the midway point of 5-7 weeks. It happened in the 6th week. The calculation for this major cycle trough was thus a simple (10,720 + 9614) ÷ 2, or 10,167. The orb of allowance to this price target was (10,720 – 9614) x .118, or 131. The price range for the major cycle trough due the next week would thus be 10,036-10,298. If the DJIA fell to this price level, it would represent a "buy," the third tradable point in this new primary cycle. The market complied nicely by falling to 10,209 one week later, on August 16, which was in the middle of this price target for another excellent trade. The trader would exit shorts taken on August 2 and go long with a stop-loss below this major cycle trough. So far, the first phase of this primary cycle performed exactly in textbook-perfect fashion from the viewpoint of cycle studies and price objective calculations. But this last trade - going long the week of August 16 - would require great caution, for we were still under the assumption that this would be a bearish primary cycle. Thus the next rally would not likely make a new cycle high. And if it did, it would likely not exceed the crest of the major cycle (August 9) by more than 2%. It could be a double top, although it should not continue up to an MCP price target above that 2% double top range.

We now come to the first fork in the road where a decision has to be made. Would this be a "classical three-phase" primary cycle pattern, consisting of three 5-7 week major cycle troughs or would it become a "combination" pattern consisting also of two 7-11 week half-primary cycle phases? In the first case, the market could be a little more bullish. It could challenge the 10,720 high of August 9, even in a bearish primary cycle. And if it went higher, it would become a bullish primary cycle, thereby negating our bearish bias based on the phasing of the 50-week cycle. In that case, an MCP price target for the crest of the next major cycle could be calculated as 11,315 +/- 201. But our bias was that the primary cycle would be bearish, which would mean the crest of the next major cycle would not attain an upside MCP price objective. More than likely it would form a double top to the first major cycle crest of 10,720, i.e., within 2% of that mark - or even less. It might rally only 38.2-61.8% of the move down from the major cycle crest (10,720) to the major cycle trough (10,209). Adding those two prices together and dividing by 2 would yield a corrective rally only back to 10,464 +/- 60. However, such a weak recovery might imply that the market would be forming a half-primary cycle trough, especially if it happened quickly. If we were bearish (and we should have been based on the 50-week cycle phasing), this is what we should have expected - and indeed, that is what actually happened.

One day after the August 16 major cycle trough, the DJIA rallied to 10,480 and stopped. It was already in the 38.2-61.8% corrective price retracement range of the prior swing down. One could cover longs and/or go short here with a stop-loss on a close above the major cycle crest of 10,720. That would be the correct action in a bearish strategy, as was now the case. Three days later, on August 20, the DJIA broke below the 10,209 major cycle trough of August 16.

Now we would have to consider the possibility that the market would form a 7-11 week half-primary cycle trough. Previously we had calculated its price target as 9780-10,222 (45-85% retracement of the swing up from 9614 on July 2 to 10,720 on August 9). And here we could also perform an MCP calculation to the downside based on the swing down from August 9 (10,720) to August 16 (10,209). The difference of 511 points can be subtracted from the rally to 10,480 on August 16 to get the price target for this current decline to a half-primary cycle trough. Thus, (10,480 + 10,209) – 10,720 = 9969 would be the new downside price objective. The orb would be (10,720 – 9969) x .118 = 89. The price range for the half-primary cycle trough would be 9880-10,058. Note that this overlaps the previous calculation for a half-primary cycle trough at 9780-10,220. It is thus important support. We also know that this half-primary cycle low would most likely occur within three trading days of August 20-23. On August 24 the DJIA fell into this range. The next day it fell lower, to 9937, and two days later it finally bottomed at 9936, just one point lower, for the half-primary cycle trough in the 8th week of the primary cycle. This was yet another excellent example of time and price coming together with geocosmics to produce an accurate cycle completion. One could take profits on shorts now and if aggressive, could even go long with a stop-loss on a close below this low or the range calculated for the half-primary cycle trough.

2. **Head and shoulders formations.**

As the new primary cycle got underway, it would be important to note if any head and shoulders, or inverse head and shoulders patterns, were forming. If so, additional price targets could be calculated from the breakout above or below the necklines of these formations (see Chapter 8). There was indeed a bearish head and shoulders formation that developed in this primary cycle, as shown on the chart below, connecting the lows of July 20 (1) and August 16 (2). This trendline (neckline) was broken the following week, and after a failed one-day attempt to get back above it, prices broke lower, thus displaying the importance of consecutive closes above it to negate the pattern. Had it closed two consecutive days back above this neckline, it would have been a bullish sign.

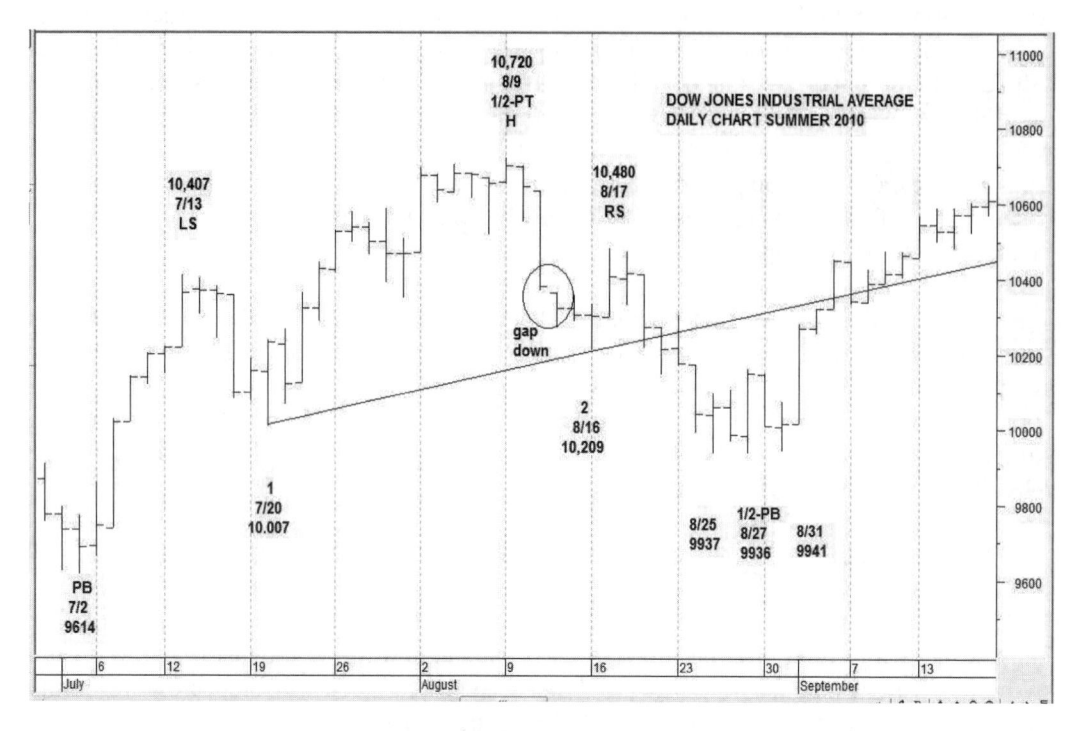

Figure 61: Daily chart of the DJIA in the summer 2010, depicting a head and shoulders formation. The left shoulder is marked LS, the head is H, and the right shoulder is RS, The neckline connects the two lows at 1 and 2. When prices broke below 1-2, it created a downside price target. This price target was not achieved before prices rallied back above 1-2, thus negating that price target. This chart also shows a gap down on August 12 (see circle, titled "gap down"), which created a downside measuring gap price target.

In this case, the neckline connecting the lows of July 20 and August 16 (1-2 in the graph of Figure 61) came in about 10,156 on the day of the head (or high), which was August 9. Therefore a downside price objective could be calculated once prices closed below this neckline. The calculation would be (10,156 x 2) – 10,720, or 9592 +/- 133. This did not overlap any prior price target range, and so it was not surprising that the decline did not fall that far. The head and shoulders downside price target was thus negated when prices started to close back above the extension of this neckline on September 3. It is instructive to point out that once prices broke back above the neckline, it then became support over the next few days. It fell back to the extension of this neckline for the entire next week, thus providing multiple opportunities for traders to buy there.

3. Measuring gaps.

When a new primary cycle gets underway, there will often be cases of "gaps up," where the market trades entirely *above* the prior day's trading range. After a cycle crest is completed, there will sometimes be "gaps down," where the market trades entirely *below* the prior day's range. In each case, a measuring gap price target is created, according to the instructions given in Chapter 9.

In the summer of 2010 there was a gap down from August 11 to August 12. The low on August 11 was 10,367. The high on August 12 was below this, at 10,362. This can be seen in Figure 61 where the price bars are circled. This created a downside measuring gap price target. To determine that price target for a low, take the difference between the preceding crest, which was 10,720 on August 9 and the low of the day before the gap down, which was 10,367. In this case, that difference was 10,720 – 10,367, or 353 points. Now subtract this from the high of August 12, which was 10,362, or 10,362 – 353 = 10,009. The orb for this price target is (10,720 – 10,009) x .118, or 84, and the range is then 9925-10,093. This measuring gap price target did overlap with two prior price targets that were also in effect at 9880-10,058, thus making the ideal price target for the half-primary cycle trough at 9925-10,058. This downside measuring gap price target was negated when prices rallied to fill this gp down on August 17, well before the final low was realized at 9936. Nonetheless, it turned out to be a correct price target.

The Third Step: Coincident and Lagging/Confirmation Indicators

When major, half-primary, and full primary cycle troughs and crests are due, there are a host of technical indicators that will let one know when a cycle is close to completion. These are known as coincident indicators. Then there are other technical signals, known as lagging indicators, which confirm the culmination of that cycle low or high. Even though these indicators imply it is already too late to buy or sell the exact trough or crest, they are important because they provide the correct trading strategy to employ in order to maximize profit potential. They can indicate if a trend run up or down is in force and thereby dictate whether one should be focused mainly on buying the corrective declines or selling the corrective rallies. This is very important to the longer-term goal of trading profitably. Thus, even though the cycle has been completed, there will be many points within the new trend where one can enter the market in the direction of the trend run. Before we can discuss these shorter term buy and sell points, we need technical indications that imply that 1) the cycle is being completed and 2) a new trend run is due to commence. For this we employ the following technical signals:

1. Stochastic patterns.

Please review Chapter 11. At primary cycle troughs, the 15-day slow stochastics are usually below 20% (oversold) and the weekly below 25%. Ideally there is also a double looping pattern where K is at first below the D line, then rises above it, but then falls back below it again before rising up once more to start a strong rally. This is verified when the second loop finds K below D and below 20% (sometimes even 25% if the first loop was below 29%), but then crossing back above D and widening its distance above D. The opposite pattern is usually exhibited in the case of primary cycle crests. That is, both the K and D lines are above 80%, with K above D, which represents an overbought condition. Then a bearish looping pattern often forms where K falls below D temporarily and then rises back above it. When K falls below D again and below 80% (even better if below 71%), with K widening its distance below D, the stochastics indicate a primary crest has been completed. In the case of weekly stochastics, a move above 75% is sufficient for an overbought condition leading into these patterns.

During the subcycles within the primary cycle, these overbought and oversold conditions may not materialize, such as during a major cycle trough or crest. In these cases, the daily stochastics may only retrace to a neutral 42-58%.

2. Bearish and bullish oscillator divergence.

The ideal stochastic pattern for a primary cycle trough or crest occurs when there is divergence to price as the cycle culminates. For example, if a primary cycle trough is forming, it is best to see a double looping pattern below 20% (25% on weekly is sufficient), but one in which the low stochastic reading of the second loop is at a higher level than the first, while the price is lower. This is known as *bullish oscillator divergence*. Conversely on a primary cycle crest, it is ideal when there is a bearish looping pattern above 80% (75% on weekly is sufficient), but also one in which the second loop is at a lower stochastic value than the first, while the price is now higher. A higher price with a lower stochastic reading than at a previous crest is known as *bearish oscillator divergence*. This is a powerful sell signal if it happens when a primary cycle crest is due and within the time band of a geocosmic critical reversal date.

3. Intermarket bullish and bearish divergence.

This occurs when a market makes a new cycle high or low, but other markets in the same category (or region of the world, in the case of stock indices) do not. It is especially important when this happens during the time band for a primary cycle trough or crest, as well as when a geocosmic critical reversal date period is in effect at the time one of those markets is making a primary cycle high or low.

4. Trendlines.

These are important confirming indicators that a cycle high or low has been completed. The idea here is to connect the lows or highs of the same cycle type. When prices break below an upward trendline or above a downward one, it is a confirmation that the lowest cycle type on the trendline has been completed, and the next highest cycle is in the process of unfolding. Also important are cases where there are at least three points on the trendline. A three-point (or greater) trendline offers powerful support or resistance to the market. When it breaks, it usually means a powerful contra-trend move is in progress.

5. Moving averages.

These are important in projecting minimum price moves for cycles, based on a moving average that is half the length of the cycle being studied. For instance, a 6-week major cycle is comprised of 30 trading days (6 weeks, with 5 trading days each, equals 30 trading days). When the major cycle low is due in a bullish primary cycle, the price will usually decline to at least the 15-day (half the cycle's length) moving average. In actual practice, we use a 14-day moving average for the DJIA since its primary cycle is 17 weeks, and not 18. Usually the price will fall below this average as the major cycle trough forms. Conversely, even in bearish primary cycles, the price will move up to at least the 14 or 15-day moving average as the major cycle crest unfolds.

Moving averages are also important because they define the more conventional trend runs. If one uses moving averages that are half the cycle length for the primary and major cycles, and the shorter one representing the major cycle is above the longer one represented by the primary cycle, and the price is above each, the market is in a trend run up. Conversely, if the moving average for the major cycle is below the moving average relevant to the primary cycle, and the price is below each, the market is in a trend run down. In trend runs up, one adopts bullish trading strategies and buys all corrective declines. In trend runs down, one adopts bearish trading strategies and sells all corrective rallies.

Let us now return to the weekly and daily charts of the summer of 2010 and see how these indicators could have helped one identify key turning points in the first phase of the new primary cycle that started July 2, 2010. Let us start by examining the weekly chart of that time, as shown in Figure 62.

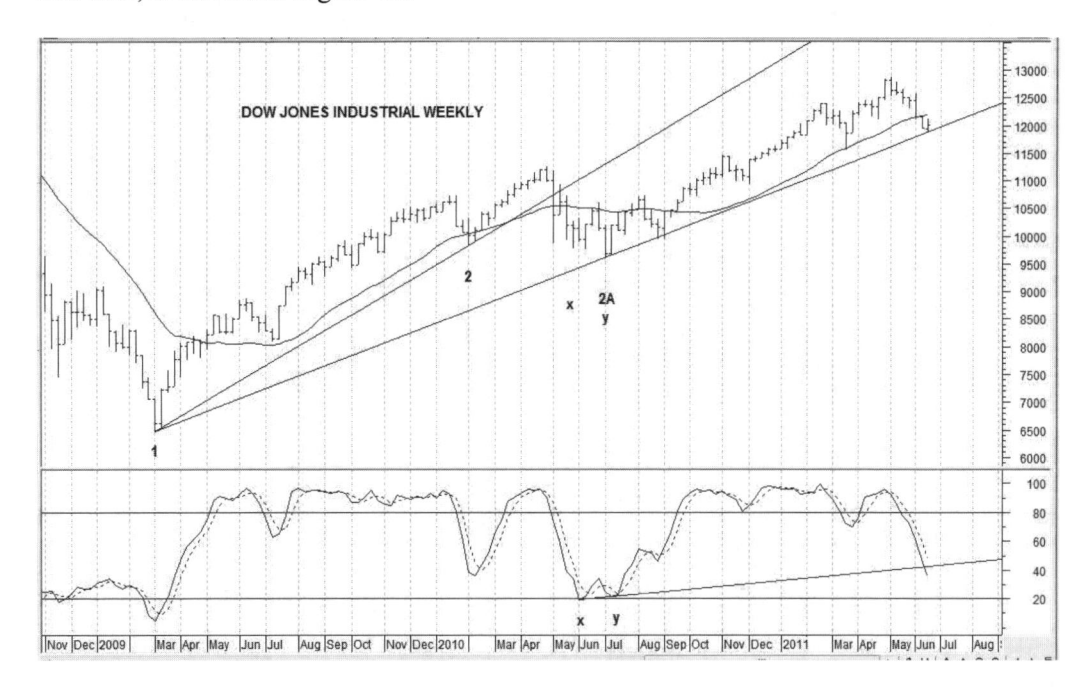

Figure 62: Weekly chart of the DJIA, 2009-2011. 1 represents start of 4-year cycle. 2 represents the "normal" 50-week cycle trough, yet it expanded to 2A to coincide with the first phase (15.5-month) of the greater 4-year cycle. The 15-bar stochastics (bottom of the chart) show a double looping pattern at x-y, with y lower in price but slightly higher in the stochastic level, for a case of bullish oscillator divergence. The trendline connecting the 50-week cycle lows at 1-2 turned out to be incorrect, as 2 was not the 50-week cycle low. But this would not be known until prices made a new high. The real 50-week cycle trendline is shown as 1-2A. Also shown here is a 25-week moving average.

1. Stochastic patterns, looping formations, oscillator divergence.

On the low of July 2, 2010, the 15-week stochastic pattern showed a classic bottoming pattern for a primary and longer-term cycle low. The actual stochastic low occurred on the week of June 4, when K dropped to 19.36% and was below D at 30.89%. This is shown as 'x' on the chart in Figure 62. It was below 25%, so it was oversold. Both

223

the price and stochastics rose the next three weeks. But then the DJIA suddenly reversed and fell to a new low on July 2 - lower than the low nearby to June 4. However, the weekly stochastics did not make a new low (at least not %K). On the week beginning July 9, K was back below D, bottoming at 21.76%, while D was at 26.87%, shown as 'y' in Figure 62. D was not as low as it was during the week of June 4. Thus it was a case of a double looping formation (K was below D, then rose above D, then fell back below D again). It also exhibited bullish oscillator divergence (D was higher at 'y' than at 'x,' when the price was lower). Two weeks later, K was back above D, and both were above 25%, with K widening its distance above D, for a confirmation that a new primary or greater cycle was underway.

On the daily chart, these stochastic patterns did not show up at the primary bottom of July 2. The stochastics were at deeply oversold levels (K was down to 7.29% and below D at 19.86%), as shown in the daily chart below (Figure 63), from which powerful rallies can begin. They did not exhibit either of the other two major patterns (bullish looping pattern, bullish oscillator divergence) that we like to see at important lows.

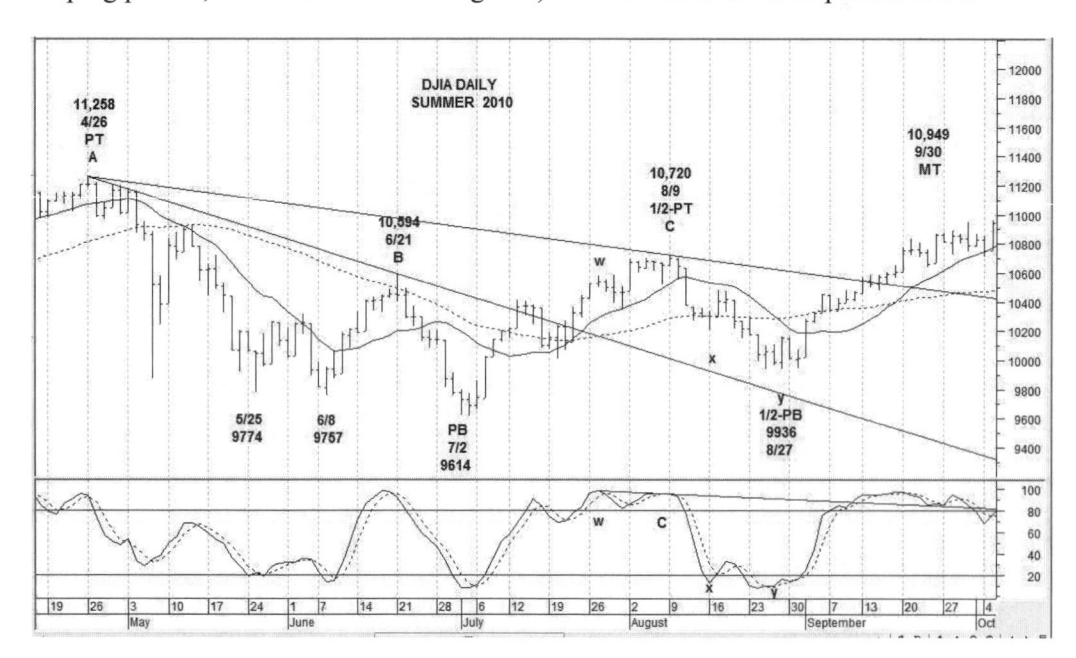

Figure 63: Daily chart of the DJIA in the summer of 2010, depicting the 15-day slow stochastics and two downward trendlines at A-B and A-C. The stochastics show a bearish looping pattern at the C, the half-primary cycle crest (at the time), and as well as bearish oscillator divergence. A double looping bullish pattern shows up at x and y, where y is the half-primary cycle trough (at the time... later it would be changed to a major cycle trough due to the primary cycle pattern that formed).

The daily chart, however, shows a case of bearish oscillator divergence with a bearish looping stochastic formation at the high on August 9. The actual stochastic high occurred on July 27 ('w' on the chart in Figure 63). K then fell below D, but never got below 71%. It then rose back above D to form a bearish looping pattern above 80%. On August 9, two weeks after the highest stochastic reading of this move, the DJIA completed its half-primary cycle crest. The stochastics were slightly lower for a case of bearish oscillator divergence, shown as 'C" on the chart. This was confirmed when the stochastics then fell below 71%, with K widening its distance below D, a confirmation that a cycle crest had been completed. Based on our bearish bias of the 50-week cycle, there was reason to believe that the high at C could also be the primary cycle crest. This was a strong signal to be short.

The move down continued into the half-primary cycle trough of August 27, which was near the next reversal period as indicated by the stochastics. The DJIA reached an oversold stochastic level on the low of August 16, marked as 'x' on the chart in Figure 63. You may remember we first thought that this might be the 5-7 week major cycle trough (it was the 7th week of the primary cycle, and it was in the price target range of a corrective decline for a major cycle trough). The 15-day slow stochastics showed K at 12.61% and below D at 29.17%. The following rally started a bullish looping pattern as K rose back above D. But it didn't last. Both the price and the stochastics fell again to new lows, as K bottomed at 7.62% on August 24, below D at 12.65%. The actual price low was August 25 and 27. By September 1, K was well above D again and widening its distance above D and above 20%, for a confirmation of the cycle low on August 27. There was not a clear case of bullish oscillator divergence, as the second loop was slightly lower than the first. Yet the stochastics did form a bullish looping pattern with both below 20%, which was in the oversold territory from which strong rallies can commence.

Therefore, we see three examples of stochastics assisting in the determination of important cycle completions. The weekly stochastics accurately coincided closely to the primary cycle trough of July 2, and the daily stochastics accurately identified the half-primary cycle crest of August 9 and the half-primary cycle trough of August 27 within just a couple of days, which was close enough to enter into profitable trades as the DJIA reversed sharply in each case.

2. Intermarket bullish and bearish divergence.

This signal is most effective when there is at least one week separating an important cycle trough or crest between two related markets. In this case we are discussing the Dow Jones Industrial Average, which is an American stock index. Therefore it is best when it is compared to the S&P or NASDAQ Composite indices, or their nearby futures contract.

Examples of intermarket bullish divergence at the primary cycle low of July 2 have already been discussed. As a review, the DJIA and NASDAQ Composite made their primary cycle lows on July 2 and July 1 respectively. This is only one day apart, and during the same week, so it is not really a case of intermarket bullish divergence between the two. However, the nearby S&P futures bottomed on July 6, one week later, and so this was a case of intermarket bullish divergence, where one index made a new cycle low (S&P on July 6), in a different week than other indices in this region. It was also nearby to a Level 1 geocosmic signature (July 5), and was thus a signal that a primary cycle trough could be forming.

The same combinations of indices were involved in an intermarket bearish divergence signal at the half-primary cycle crest of August 9 in the NASDAQ Composite and DJIA. The nearby S&P futures did not top out that week. This index completed its half-primary cycle crest one week earlier, on August 5, which was within the three-day orb to the critical reversal date of August 9. One could therefore sell short at this time with a stop-loss above the previous week's high in the S&P futures, or at a time that all three made new cycle highs, which never happened during this period.

The same divergence in the same three indices also happened on the half-primary cycle trough of Friday, August 27 in the case of the DJIA and NASDAQ Composite. However, the nearby S&P futures did not complete its half-primary cycle trough until Tuesday, August 31, in the following week. Thus once again position and short-term traders had a signal to enter the market, this time from the long side. Since it was still uncertain that this primary cycle would be bullish, it was probably a trade more for the short-term trader. The stop-loss on a new long position could be based on a time when all three indices made new cycle lows. That never happened during this period after the intermarket bullish divergence signal was generated on August 31. The market would now commence its rally to the crest of the next phase of this primary cycle.

Just as the stochastic studies yielded three tradable instances for entering the market in the first half-primary cycle phase of this primary cycle, so too did the intermarket bullish and bearish divergence indicator at virtually the same places. And each of these signals occurred when a cycle trough or crest was due, nearby to a geocosmic critical reversal date. Therefore these were two very important 'coincident" indicators, signaling a reversal in the U.S. stock market at a very "unusually uncertain" time in the American economy. Still, we had no compelling reason to think this primary cycle would become bullish yet, other than perhaps the fact that the half-primary cycle trough did not take out the low that started the primary cycle. That needed to happen to fully confirm a bearish primary cycle.

3. Trendline Studies

In Figure 62, one can see a trendline connecting the lows of March 6, 2009 and February 5, 2010. At the time, this was viewed as the 50-week cycle trendline, because March 6 was a 50-week cycle trough (and even the greater 4-year cycle trough), and February 5, 2010 was believed to be a 50-week cycle trough, since it occurred in the 48th week of the cycle and it was also the end of the third primary cycle phase of the greater 50-week cycle (usually there are only 2 or 3 primary cycles within the 50-week cycle). That upward trendline (1-2 on the chart) was broken in the first week of May 2010, which suggested that not only had the 50-week cycle topped out, but the next longer one as well, which would be either the 15.5-month (first third) phase of the 4-year cycle or possibly the 23-month half-cycle phase to the 4-year cycle. Only a close above the 11,258 high of April 26 (the prior 50-week cycle crest assumed at this point) would negate that labeling. Thus one's bias would be bearish, for the trendline supporting the assumed 50-week cycle was broken.

Prices did indeed fall to new lows. On May 25 they took out the lows of February 5. The 50-week cycle was now bearish according to these studies (90% probability based on the history of the 50-week cycle), or a bigger cycle low was forming (10% probability based on the 50-week cycle history), as turned out to be the case. By July 2, the market had fallen to a new low of 9614.

In retrospect, we now know July 2 was the 15.5-month cycle trough, and a case of the 50-week cycle expanding to 69 weeks, which has a historical frequency of actually occurring less than 10%. Nevertheless, it was in the time band for that first phase low of the 4-year cycle, which occurs at the 13-20 month interval, and July 2 was the 16th month (the second and third phases are more like 15.5-month mean cycles, while the first is more often a slightly longer 16.5-month subcycle). One could now draw a trendline connecting the low of the 4-year cycle trough of March 6, 2009 to the low representing the trough of its first phase on July 2, 2010 (line 1-2A on the graph in Figure 62). This would now be the 15.5-month cycle trendline. A break below that would be a signal that the crest of the next highest cycle was completed, which would be the 4-year cycle crest. The confirmation of that analysis, however, would only come about when prices took out the low at 2A. You will notice at the half-primary cycle trough of August 27, prices dropped back to this upward trendline, thus making it a powerful "3-point" trendline. A weekly close below there could signal a major trend change in the longer-term cycle.

The daily chart exhibited some useful downward trendlines that helped in one's shorter-term analysis of the situation. From the primary (and possible 50-week) cycle crest of April 26, 2010, a downward trendline could be constructed that connected several highs prior to the low of July 2. This is shown as A-B in the graph of Figure 63, with the most important highs being April 26 and June 21. But it also captured the highs just after April 26, so it was at least a "3-point trendline," which meant it was strong. You can see that the price of the DJIA closed above A-B for three straight days beginning July 13th. This strongly suggested that the primary cycle trough was in as of July 2.

Even though the DJIA dropped back below this trendline shortly afterwards for four days, it eventually climbed back above on its way to the half-primary cycle crest of August 9. A new trendline could now be constructed, connecting the previous primary cycle crest of April 26 to the new half-primary cycle crest of August 9. If indeed this primary cycle was going to be bearish, this new trendline would act as important resistance, for a close above it would mean that not only had the half-primary cycle bottomed, but probably the next higher cycle had bottomed too (which would be the primary cycle). It would suggest that this market was no longer bearish, but instead was turning bullish. As you can see from the chart in Figure 63, the DJIA did break above this trendline A-C during September 13-15, the first point at which our bearish bias for the 50-week cycle became suspect.

These examples show clearly how trendlines serve as useful guides to understanding the underlying trend of a market. They do not coincide with cycle lows or tops, but rather they act as lagging or confirming indicators to the stronger underlying trend. They help one to adopt the correct trading strategy (bullish or bearish), as they assist in determining the completion of a recent and important cycle.

4. Moving averages.

The last technical indicator that we will examine in this section of our analysis of the summer of 2010 is the moving average, or multiple moving averages.

In the weekly chart, we use a 25-week moving average to identify the status of the 50-week cycle. You will see from the weekly chart shown in Figure 62 that the 25-week moving average was taken out in the first week of May 2009. This confirms March 6, 2009 as at least a 50-week cycle trough. It stayed above this important average all the way until the week ending February 5. It broke below this average as the assumed 50-week cycle bottomed on February 5 at 9835. Two weeks later it was back above this average, suggesting that the 50-week cycle trough had been completed, for it was in the 48th week, which meant it was "on time."

The DJIA remained above this 25-week moving average until the first week of May, when it broke not only below this average, but also the upward 50-week cycle trendline. This was a signal that an important crest had just formed (11,258 on April 26, 2010). If it was the 50-week cycle crest, then the market would be bearish for several more weeks. If it was to be a decline to the first phase of a 3-phase four-year cycle, it might only be down a few weeks. As it turned out, the market did fall to a new multi-month low on July 2, 2010 at 9614. But just 5 weeks later (the week ending August 9), it closed back above the 25-week moving average, giving support to the idea that perhaps July 2 was a longer-term cycle trough.

These hopes were temporarily dashed as the DJIA fell back below this average the very next week, lending support again to the idea that this would be a bearish 50-week cycle that started back on February 5, 2010. However, in the week starting September 17, the DJIA closed back above the 25-week moving average for the second consecutive week, strongly suggesting that the 50-week cycle had bottomed July 2, 2010, and not February 5, 2010, as per our bias. Our bearish longer-term bias about the 50-week cycle needed to change in mid-September, according to these "confirming" signals, or lagging indicators (trendlines and moving averages). It was now clear that the "Asset Inflation Express" of Jupiter and Uranus having entered Aries in May and June was now firmly underway and could last into mid-2011 or even longer.

We can also glean insight from examining the 14- and 42-day moving averages in the daily chart during this period. The 14-day would guide us through the 5-7 week major cycle phases, while the 42-day would strike boundaries defining the greater primary cycle. Following the primary cycle crests of April 26, the DJIA dropped below the 42-day moving average on May 5, one day before the historical 1000-point intraday 25-minute drop in the DJIA on May 6 (it recovered 800 of those points by the close). This break of the 42-day moving average signaled that the primary cycle crest was completed. You can see how the next rally was stopped at its test of this average on May 13, after which the DJIA turned lower again. That average served as resistance, which is not so unusual.

On June 21, the DJIA broke above the 42-day moving average, a sign that the primary cycle might have been completed on June 8 at 9757. But it couldn't close above this average, and therefore the bottom could not yet be confirmed. Prices did in fact fall to new lows on July 2 without ever closing above this average first. You can see that prior to June 21, the DJIA did close above the 14-day moving average, suggesting that the lows of May 25 and/or June 8 was a major cycle trough, but not necessarily the primary cycle trough. All during this time (late April through early July), the 14-day moving average remained below the 42-day moving average, which indicated the market was in a trend run down.

Finally on July 12 the DJIA closed above the 42-day moving average. It had a second daily close above this average the next day (July 13), as an important trendline down was also broken. These were two very strong signals that the primary cycle trough had been completed on July 2. But given that our bias was bearish for the greater 50-week cycle, how long would it be before the primary cycle topped out? In bear markets the crest of the primary cycle tends to unfold before Tuesday of the 9th week and usually only 2-5 weeks into the new cycle. July 12-13 was already the second week. This cycle could top out at any time if the pattern was to be bearish.

By July 16 the DJIA was closing back below the 42-day moving average, but not the 14-day one. In fact it never closed below the 14-day average before resuming its march up to the half-primary cycle crest of August 9. It is important to note that prices were above both the 14- and 42-day moving averages, and the 14-day crossed above the 42-day one on July 22. The market was now in a confirmed trend run up. But how long would it last?

On August 11, two trading days after the half-primary cycle crest of August 9, prices broke below the 14-day moving average. This confirmed that the high of August 9 was at least a major cycle crest. For the next three days it traded to and slightly below the 42-day average, but never closed below it. The DJIA then rallied slightly into August 17-18 but could not close back above the 14-day average. It then fell sharply into the half-primary cycle low of August 27, closing well below both the 14- and 42-day moving averages, with the 14-day also moving back below the 42-day one. This was a signal supporting the historical probabilities that the 50-week cycle was bearish, and soon this primary cycle would fall to a new low.

However it was not to be. Up until this point, the market timing and technical indicators were working very well, as they normally do. But something radically changed after the low of August 27. A UFO - an Unexpected Fundamental Occurrence - had exploded onto the world with the Federal Reserve Board's surprising decision to implement QE2 just a couple of weeks earlier and thereby guide long-term interest rates lower. This is exactly the type of decision that was necessary for the launch of the "Asset Inflation Express." On September 1, the market was up 254 points and closed well above the 14-day moving average, indicating that the half-primary cycle trough of August 27 was completed. On September 3 it was up another 127 points, and closed above the 42-day moving average. It was the first moving average signal that maybe this primary cycle would be bullish. However it hadn't yet closed above the downward trendline, so the signals were now mixed.

The uncertainty gave way on September 20, just a few days after the close above the downward trendline. This was when the 14-day moving average moved back above the 42-day average, and the price of the DJIA was above each. Thus the market was back into a trend run up. September 20 was important for another reason too: the DJIA closed up 145 points at 10,753, taking out the first half-primary cycle crest of 10,720 back on August 16. This would now become a bullish "right translation" primary cycle. The evidence was now mounting that the 50-week cycle was not pointed down and bearish from February 5, but instead it was pointed up and bullish from its expansion to July 2, 2010. Position traders could now forfeit the bearish strategies and adopt new bullish strategies as long as 1) prices remained above the 25-week moving average, and 2) certainly as long as prices remained above the 42-day moving average with the 14-day also above the 42-day one. In fact, the first case would remain in force through the first week of June 2011, nearly 9 months. The second condition (the 14-day average above the 42-day average) would remain operative until March 2011. Thus, even though one may have gotten whipsawed in early September 2010, the rewards that followed more than made up for this via the coincident and confirming indicators just described.

We will come back to the later stages of this primary cycle shortly. For now, it is time to show how the short-term trading indicators would be used not only in the bullish first phase of any primary cycle, but in any phase.

CHAPTER NINETEEN

AS GOOD AS IT GETS: SHORT-TERM AND AGGRESSIVE TRADING

The stage is now set for zooming in and making a trade. The time band for the start of the primary cycle has been identified. Once confirmed, the time bands for the first major and/or half-primary cycle trough have also been determined. Geocosmic critical reversal dates and Solar-Lunar reversal dates within this first phase of the new primary cycle have been identified. Price targets of support and/or resistance have been established or will be established as trading cycles unfold. Technical studies will be used to identify trading cycle lows, as well as other support areas in which to buy during this first phase of the primary cycle. Other technical studies and chart patterns will be used to determine when a particular move up or down has been completed.

Now it is time to apply the short-term trading tools of Chapters 14-17, which include the Drummond Market Geometry methods, to pinpoint optimal times of entry and exit. For this we use the weekly and daily trend indicator points (TIP, or DOT), as well as daily and weekly "floor trades" support and resistance zones. For this, we employ the following steps in the first phase of the primary cycle.

1. **Start with the Weekly TIP.** Please review Chapter 16. Usually a market is in a weekly trend run down when a primary cycle trough is unfolding. The actual low most often occurs the week before, the week of, or the week after a trend run down has ended. When the market is upgraded from a weekly trend run down to neutral via the Drummond Market Geometry methodology, during (or shortly after) the time band when the primary cycle trough is due, it is a signal that the trend is changing. However, it takes three consecutive weekly closes above the TIP, with the third week (or after) also closing above the prior week's close to confirm. Still, when looking for a primary cycle trough, the first step is to see a change in the trend status (TIP) via these studies.

2. **Look for bullish signals related to weekly support and resistance zones.** Please review Chapter 17. As the primary cycle trough unfolds, look for the weekly close to exhibit a bullish trigger, bullish bias, or outright bullish close. That is, if the weekly low is into or below the weekly support zone, but the close is above weekly support, this is a signal that a new primary cycle may be starting. Additionally, if the weekly close is above weekly resistance or a bearish crossover zone, that too is a signal that the primary cycle trough may be ending, especially if the market is in the time band for a primary cycle and even more so if a geocosmic critical reversal time band is in effect. The market needs to follow

through with a further rally ending the next week to confirm. That is, a bullish trigger or bullish bias close on the weekly chart, followed by a close above the next week's resistance, is a bullish sequence and a confirming signal that a new primary cycle is underway, especially if the low occurred during the normal time band when it was due. Expanded time bands for primary cycles are also acceptable, and they are perhaps even a stronger time in which to buy when they happen.

The weekly TIP and support-resistance studies are more important for position traders. For short-term traders, we need to examine the daily TIPS and support-resistance zones. For very aggressive short-term traders, we could also utilize hourly or 30-minute signals. Aggressive short-term traders could also use intraday technical signals like stochastics or other oscillators, moving averages, trendlines, and even volume studies to help pinpoint the precise bottom.

3. **Look for buying signals generated by the daily TIP.** The daily chart and the short-term signals generated therein are most important for the short-term trader. They can be used to probe the long side when a primary cycle trough is due. Not only that, but they may also be used to pinpoint buying opportunities all through the first phase of the new primary cycle, at least until the first major cycle crest is confirmed. In this application, we look for signs that any daily trend run down is being upgraded to neutral. Or if prices have closed three consecutive days below the TIP, but the third day is up and therefore not a confirmed trend run down, this can be a signal that a low is being completed as well, especially if the next day also fails to close down. Daily trend runs down tend to reach an exhaustion point after 9 consecutive days of closing below the TIP. Daily trend runs up tend to reach an exhaustion point after 12 consecutive days of closing above the TIP. If a trend run down is interrupted for one day, the resumed trend run down tends to end within the next three days. Trend runs up, on the other hand, may be interrupted for one day, but then the resumed trend run up tends to last no more than 7 days, with most ending just one day after resumption.

4. **Look for buying signals generated by the close relative to the daily support and resistance zones.** Of all the methods to enhance short-term trading, this is probably the most important. When a primary cycle trough is due, and especially after it is confirmed and the market is in its first phase (bullish), one can probe the long side on any bullish signal, such as:

    - a bullish trigger (intraday price drops below the daily support zone but then closes back above)
    - a bullish bias (low of the day goes into support and it holds)
    - a bullish close (close above daily resistance).

Very aggressive traders can buy daily support, or any decline into a bullish crossover zone, with stop-losses on a close below here. The idea in the first phase of a new primary cycle is to see support zones start to hold, and/or resistance zones start to break. These are signals to get long with stop-losses below recent lows, weekly (or even daily) support, or a nearby bullish crossover zone.

Now let us see how these signals would have worked as the primary cycle low of July 2, 2010 unfolded and all during the first phase of the new primary cycle that followed. Even if the primary cycle is to be bearish, we still take the approach that the first phase (2-5 weeks, maybe even 8) will be bullish. The bearish signals would not be expected to unfold until after the first phase in a bearish primary cycle and not until the last phase in a bullish primary cycle. So in the first phase, our approach is mostly bullish, even if we believe the primary cycle itself will ultimately end up bearish.

1. Start with the weekly trend indicator point (TIP, or Dot)

At the primary cycle crest of 11,258 on April 26, 2010, the weekly TIP had topped out the prior week. The DJIA had closed above the weekly TIP for ten consecutive weeks, so it was exhausted. The studies provided in Chapter 16 showed that weekly trend runs up are considered exhausted after ten weeks and would be due for a pause - if not a complete reversal - at any time after that. On the week ending April 30, the weekly close was below the weekly TIP for the first time in 11 weeks. It proceeded to close below the weekly tip for the next six weeks. It ended its trend run down in the week ending June 11. We will pick up the weekly numbers as they applied to the end of this trend run down to illustrate how to use this weekly indicator. Below are the weekly high, low, and closing prices, along with the weekly PP and TIP for reference, as the DJIA completed its primary cycle trough on July 2, 2010.

WEEK ENDING	H	L	C	PP	TIP	STATUS
June 4, 2010	10315	9890	9931	10058	10326	D
June 11	10216	9757	10172	10071	10135	N
June 18	10483	10186	10451	10048	10059	N
June 25	10594	10081	10144	10373	10164	N
July 2	10201	9614	9686	10273	10231	N
July 9	10201	9660	10198	9834	10160	N
July 16	10407	10079	10098	10019	10042	N
July 23	10442	10007	10424	10195	10016	U
July 30	10585	10347	10466	10291	10168	U
Aug 6	10703	10468	10653	10466	10317	U
Aug 13	10720	10268	10303	10608	10455	N
Aug 20	10480	10147	10213	10430	10501	N
Aug 27	10304	9936	10150	10280	10440	D
Sept 3	10451	9942	10448	10130	10280	N
Sept 10	10476	10332	10462	10280	10230	N

The weekly trend indicator will be the slowest signal to be generated of the four steps used in this part of the trading plan. At the low of July 2, the weekly TIP was in a neutral status. The prior week had closed below the weekly TIP, so this was the second consecutive week of closes below the weekly TIP. The DJIA was poised to be downgraded to a trend run down if the week ending July 9 simply closed lower than the close of the prior week, which was 9686. But it didn't. In fact the close was 512 points higher than the prior week's close, and it closed above the weekly TIP at 10,160 for the first time in three weeks. It could still become a trend run down, after this one week interrupt, if the week ending July 16 would close below the new weekly TIP at 10,042. But it didn't. It closed at 10,098, above the weekly TIP for the second consecutive week. Now it was poised to be upgraded to a trend run up if it would close above the prior week's close (10,098). It did that. It closed at 10,424 on Friday, July 23. Now it was upgraded to a trend run up. Via this method, the primary cycle trough was finally confirmed for July 2 at 9614. The confirmation came three weeks later. The weekly TIP studies now gave the green light to adopt bullish strategies until the next weekly close below this indicator.

The weekly TIP remained in a trend run up until the week ending August 13. By that time, the DJIA had closed above the weekly TIP for 5 consecutive weeks. It was finally downgraded from a trend run up to neutral on the week ending August 20. That was just following the week in which the half-primary cycle crest occurred at 10,720 on Monday, August 9. The market proceeded to fall to a half-primary cycle trough of 9936 on August 27. At the close of Friday, August 27, the DJIA exhibited three consecutive closes below the weekly TIP and the third week was a down week from the prior week. It was now downgraded further to a trend run down (D). But that turned out to be the low as the very next week (September 3) it was upgraded back to neutral. The TIP that week was 10,280 and the close of the week was higher, at 10,448. This ended the first phase of the primary cycle that commenced July 2.

In retrospect, the weekly TIP was a 3-week laggard in identifying the primary cycle trough of July 2. It was one week late in identifying the half-primary cycle crest of August 13 and one week late in identifying the half-primary cycle trough of August 27. Although this signal will work fine for position traders looking to participate in long trend runs, it wasn't close enough for shorter-term traders to capture any short-term profits. The buy signal on July 22 resulted in a small loss when it turned to a sell signal (neutral actually) on August 13. The sell signal didn't arise until the week ending August 27, which just happened to be the low. By the next week this signal was also negated when the weekly close was back above the TIP, resulting in another small loss. But then the buy signal would emerge when the market's weekly TIP status was upgraded to a trend run up on September 17 (not shown), which lasted several weeks and resulted in very large profits (to be discussed shortly).

And so this signal is actually more conducive for longer-term position trading than short-term trading. As one can see, the weekly TIP is more of a trend following system. It doesn't usually get one into the market as an important cycle low or high is forming. It gets one in a little later, and oftentimes a trader will get whipsawed for usually small losses by trading solely on the basis of this signal. It is however very effective in capturing the long trend runs when they occur, which means longer-term profits.

2. Look for bullish signals related to weekly support and resistance zones.

Once again we are dealing with weekly indicators, so the buy and sell signals generated here will lag behind those of the daily studies. Nevertheless, they are useful for short-term traders as well once a trend run is underway.

Below is a listing of weekly support and resistance zones for the same period used in the TIP studies. We will now demonstrate just how the weekly support and resistance zones confirmed the primary cycle trough of July 2 and as a result led to trading opportunities from the long side within the first phase of the new primary cycle. We provide these calculations in a table format instead of applying them right onto the charts because many readers will not have the software programs to do that. Hence they are depicted in table format here for easier reference and application by all readers.

Week	H	L	C	PP	TIP	S_1	S_2	R_1	R_2
Jun 4	10315	9890	9931	10058	10325-D	9891	9852	10381	10342
Jun 11	10216	9757	10172	10071	10135-N	9718	9826	10143	10252
Jun 18	10483	10186	10450	10048	10059-N	9943	9881	10401	10339
Jun 25	10594	10081	10143	10373	10164-N	10302	10263	10560	10599
Jul 2	10201	9614	9686	10273	10231-OD	9887	9951	10400	10465
Jul 9	10201	9660	10198	9834	10160-N	9392	9466	9980	10054
Jul 16	10407	10079	10098	10019	10042-N	9927	9838	10468	10374
Jul 23	10442	10007	10424	10195	10016-U	9932	9982	10262	10310
Jul 30	10585	10347	10466	10291	10168-U	10207	10141	10575	10641
Aug 6	10703	10468	10653	10466	10317-U	10347	10348	10584	10585
Aug 13	10720	10268	10303	10608	10455-N	10536	10513	10770	10748
Aug 20	10484	10147	10213	10430	10501-N	10077	10141	10528	10592
Aug 27	10304	9936	10150	10280	10440-D	10047	10080	10380	10413
Sep 3	10451	9942	10448	10130	10280-N	9966	9956	10334	10325
Sep 10	10476	10332	10463	10280	10230-N	10193	10109	10618	10702

The trend status is indicated under the TIP column, whereby D stands for trend run down, U represents trend run up, N means neutral, and OD means "on edge, trend run down." This pertains to the trend indicator studies discussed in Chapter 16. We will also refer to the closing price relative to support and resistance as either bullish, bearish, or neutral closes as discussed in Chapter 17. Our task here is to identify buy signals in the time band for a primary cycle trough, and once it is in, further buy signals for the entire first phase of the new primary cycle. Keep in mind this was an "unusually uncertain" time, when many false signals would be generated before the trend up was finally established by most of the methods outlined in this book.

We start this analysis of weekly support and resistance with the week ending June 4. Notice that the trend indicator point is in a trend run down. As stated before, this was the sixth consecutive week of closes below the TIP, or Dot. However, it is the 17th week of the primary cycle, a geocosmic critical reversal period (June 4, +/- 3 trading days) with three Level 1 signatures present between May 30 and June 8. From the table above, we notice that the weekly low of 9890 was into weekly support (9852-9891). Support held, and that is one of the signals to look for when a primary cycle trough is due. And so even though the TIP was in a trend run down, the weekly close was neutral, with a bullish bias. This is a signal for short-term traders to probe the long side. You would place a stop-loss on a weekly close below the support zone of the next week (9718-9826) or the low of the week ending June 4 (9890), depending on your risk allowance.

235

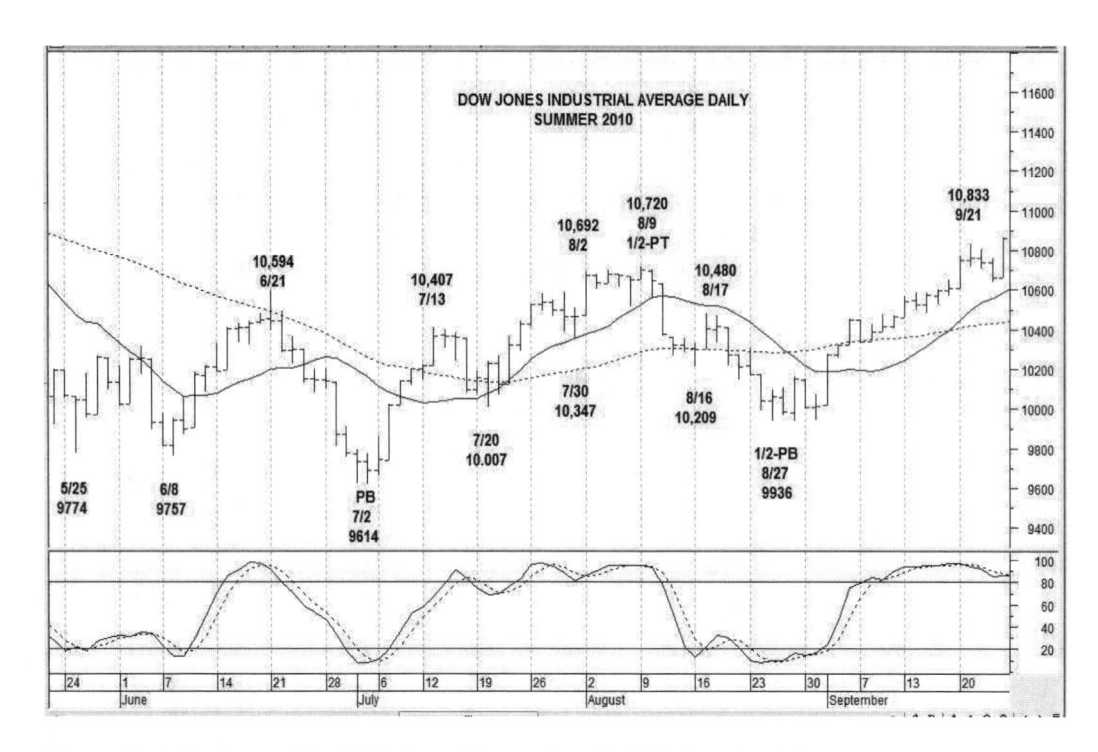

Figure 64: Daily chart of the DJIA, June 1-September 24, 2010. The dates listed here are on Mondays, like June 7, 14, 21, etc.

The following week ending June 11 (beginning June 7), the DJIA once again dropped to weekly support. The low was 9757 on June 8, the day of the Jupiter-Uranus conjunction, one of the most powerful geocosmic signatures of a reversal. Even though the market fell below the low of the prior week, there were several bullish signals again. First, weekly support held, but so did weekly resistance. The high of the week was 10,216 on Friday June 11. Weekly resistance was 10,143-10,252. Consequently this was an excellent week for trading as prices went right into weekly support and weekly resistance and both held. However the close was between the two, which meant it closed neutral. The balance of weight was more to the upside because the close was above both next week's TIP and pivot point (PP). The close above the current weekly TIP meant the trend status was upgraded from a trend run down to neutral. This is a positive (bullish) sign and yet another reason to be long. And now the stop-loss can be raised to a close below the low of June 8 (9757) or next week's support (9881-9943), depending on one's risk tolerance.

As we approach the next week ending June 18, we must calculate a price target for a corrective rally, based on the possibility that June 8 may have been the primary cycle trough. If so, a 38.2-61.8% corrective retracement would take prices to this first resistance zone, which would be 10,507 +/- 177. If this was the start to a new primary cycle, and the market was bearish, then the crest would be due 2-5 weeks after June 8, or June 21-July 16. During this time band we note that a geocosmic critical reversal date is in effect the weekend of June 18-21, +/- 3 trading days. We can assume that if it is a crest, it would be June 21-24, for the second week would not start until June 21.

The DJIA indeed rallied sharply the next week, which ended June 18 (it began June 14 as shown on the chart in Figure 64). The high of the week was on Friday, June 18, at 10,483, already into the price objective range of a possible primary cycle crest, but a week too early. Perhaps it would be a trading cycle crest from which prices then drop 4% or more, or make a 38.2-61.8% corrective decline of the move up so far. The DJIA closed at 10,450 that next week, which was above weekly resistance. This was a bullish weekly close, following the bullish bias closes of the prior two weeks. That was a "bullish sequence" pattern, which normally means a new primary cycle is underway. The close was also above the weekly TIP for the second consecutive week. It was on the verge of being upgraded again, to a trend run up, if the next week closed up from the prior week. Notice that on June 18, the DJIA still hadn't closed above the 42-day moving average, which from our moving average studies would be necessary to confirm a new trend run up. It was close, and a close up this week would probably do it. It was possible that the Drummond Market Geometry studies would be upgraded to a trend run up, and the moving average study would issue a confirmation of a new primary cycle, if the week ending June 25 was just higher than the close of the week ending June 18.

It didn't happen. What did happen was that the DJIA rallied to a new multi-week high on the June 21 critical reversal date, at 10,594. That was into our price objective zone calculated for a primary cycle crest in a bearish primary cycle. Time and price studies were converging on a critical reversal date. Since the high of that date was 10,594, above the 42-day moving average, but the close was well below it at 10,442, it would be wise for position traders to take some profits. Aggressive short-term traders, on the other hand, could take profits on all longs and even sell short, but we would need to consult the daily numbers before doing that since weekly studies are not the source for aggressive short-term trading. The weekly numbers are best used for position trading.

The market began selling off after the 10,594 high of June 21. That high of the week was into weekly resistance, which held. By the end of the week, the market closed at 10,143, below weekly support. This was a very bearish weekly close. The close below weekly support was bearish, but because the high was into or above weekly resistance first, it became a *very bearish* close. This would be a sign to exit all longs and even go short, for the market failed to be upgraded to a trend run up when it had the chance, and instead it closed neutral on the TIP indicator and very bearish based on the weekly support and resistance numbers. It was more bearish than bullish headed into the next week. If one did go short, the stop-loss would be placed above the 10,594 high of June 21, or on a close above weekly resistance of the next week (10,400-10,465), depending on one's risk tolerance.

As suggested by the very bearish weekly close of June 25, the market fell hard the following week. The high was only 10,201, far below the prior week's high of 10,594. The low was attained on Friday, July 2, at 9614, which was well below weekly support. This meant the market closed the week bearish for the second consecutive time. It also closed below the weekly TIP for the second time, but it was also a new cycle low. This downgraded its status from neutral to an "on edge, trend run down." A close down the next week would make it a full trend run down, whereas a close up would upgrade it back to neutral.

The next week's trading started on Tuesday, July 6 due to the Independence Day holiday. On Monday's trading holiday, July 5, a powerful Uranus retrograde took place, an important Level 1 geocosmic signature that would begin a cluster extending from July 5 through July 13. However, this was the only Level 1 signature within that cluster, which meant that if it were to be valid, the reversal would likely happen closer to July 5 than to the actual midpoint of the cluster, which was July 9.

There were other things to note about this new low of July 2. If it was an older primary cycle, it was the 21st week. Therefore this could be the completion of a primary cycle trough, based on cycle timing studies. However, it was lower than the prior lows of June 8 and February 5, which meant the 50-week cycle was turning bearish, assuming this was not an expanded 50-week cycle beyond 67 weeks. July 2 was the 69th week, so the probability was high that a primary cycle trough could be forming here, but it wasn't also a 50-week bottom. The other option that looked very possible was that this was only the 3rd week of a newer primary cycle off the low of June 8. After all, the high was June 21, the second week, and if indeed the 50-week cycle was bearish, the primary cycle could become a severe left translation pattern. In this outlook, the market could be down the next 10-18 weeks. The MCP downside price target for the next primary cycle trough in this case would be 9093 +/- 256. The calculation would be (9757 + 10,594) – 11,258. That is, the sum of the current primary bottom of June 8, plus the primary cycle crest of June 21, minus the prior primary cycle crest of 11,258 recorded on April 26. Either way, the most likely scenarios were for a bearish primary cycle. The only difference was whether the primary cycle started June 8, in which case it would continue falling for several weeks, or it was forming right now - July 2-6 - from which a 2-5 week rally would commence.

The next week would provide clues to that dilemma. If the market was bearish, it would likely close lower the next week starting July 6. If it was the start of a new primary cycle, then it would have to close up this week. But even that wouldn't confirm a new primary cycle. It would just mean it was *possible* to be a new primary cycle.

The week of July 9 did close up. In fact it closed at 10,198, which was up 512 points (over 5%) from the prior week's close. It was also above weekly resistance, which was 9980-10,054. Resistance was breaking, which is a positive sign of a new primary cycle, especially following a critical reversal zone with a strong Level 1 signature (Uranus retrograde). The close was also above the weekly trend indicator point, which was on the verge of being downgraded to a trend run down. Instead it was upgraded from "on edge, trend run down" to neutral. Just as important, the DJIA closed above the 14-day moving average, confirming that the low of July 2 was at least a major cycle trough. It was probably the primary cycle trough as well, since it was so late in the primary cycle, assuming this was an older primary cycle.

The high of the week ending July 9 was 10,201 and the close was 10,198. Suddenly the market was beginning to look bullish, but the 42-day moving average was right there at 10,199. It couldn't quite close above it, thus withholding yet another bullish signal that the primary bottom was in. Nevertheless, the bullish weekly close (above resistance) was a sign to cover all shorts and even go long with a stop-loss on a close below the 9614 level of July 2, or the next week's support, depending on one's risk allowance.

3. Look for buying signals generated by the close relative to the daily support and resistance zones and daily TIP

Although there was no confirmation at the week ending July 9 that the primary cycle had been completed as of July 2, several bullish signs were starting to emerge. Let us now introduce the daily numbers for the TIP, support, and resistance and see how they would work well together in revealing an even more opportune time to start buying this market, especially if one is a short-term, aggressive-type of trader - which this section of the book is designed to address. In the tables below, we will also include the weekly PP, TIP, support and resistance zones, all highlighted in bold, above the start of each week. We also provide the daily bar chart for this period in Figure 65.

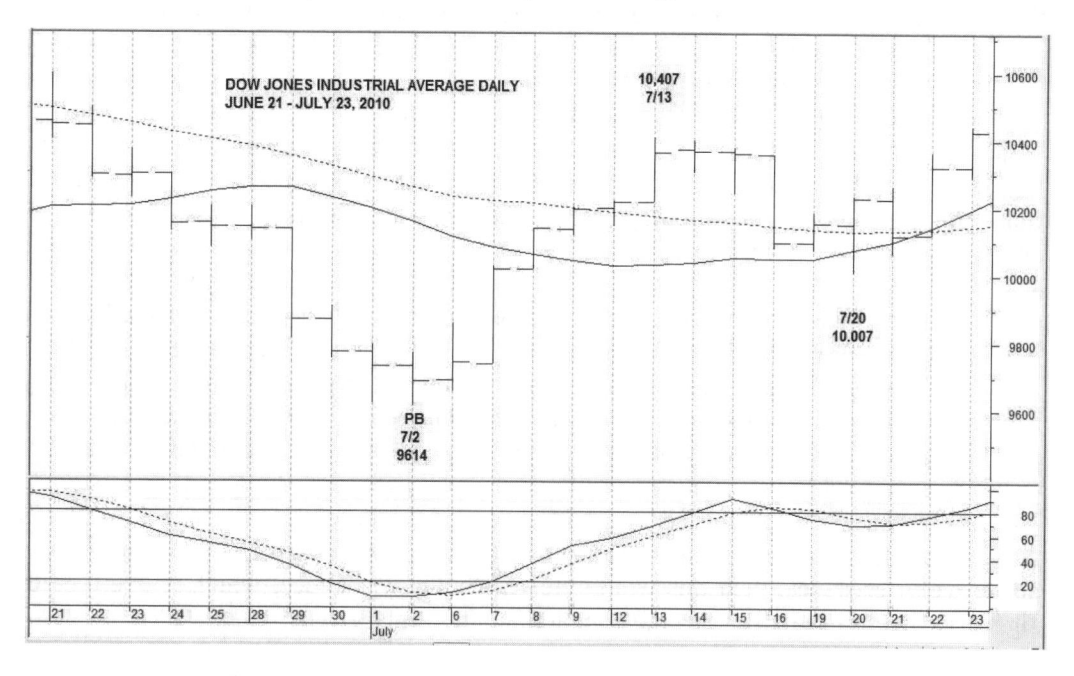

Figure 65: Daily chart of DJIA, pertaining to the time of the primary cycle trough on July 2 and related to the daily support, resistance and trend indicator point numbers below.

Day	H	L	C	PP	TIP	S₁	S₂	R₁	R₂
				10273	**10231**	**9887**	**9951**	**10400**	**10465**
Jun 28	10202	10101	10138	10142	10214-D	10083	10082	10205	10204
Jun 29	10136	9812	9870	10147	10164-D	10088	10093	10188	10193
Jun 30	9909	9753	9773	9939	10076-D	9708	9743	10032	10067
Jul 1	9795	9622	9732	9812	9966-D	9696	9715	9851	9870
Jul 2	9771	9614	9686	9716	9822-D	9645	9637	9811	9810
				9834	**10169**	**9392**	**9466**	**9980**	**10054**
Jul 6	9851	9689	9743	9690	9739-N	9608	9610	9764	9767
Jul 7	10026	9736	10018	9761	9723-N	9647	9671	9839	9863
Jul 8	10140	10019	10139	9927	9793-U	9827	9873	10163	10117
Jul 9	10201	10118	10198	10099	9929-U	10078	10058	10180	10199

239

The weekly PP, TIP, support, and resistance numbers appear in bold on the line above June 28. They provide support and resistance for the entire week and should be used in combination with the daily numbers (i.e. tying multiple time frames). The numbers in boxes represent cases of bullish or bearish crossover zones.

The daily numbers begin on Monday, June 28. The close of that day was 10,138, which was below the daily trend indicator point (TIP) for the 5th consecutive day, which meant its status remained in a trend run down (D). We expect this to be the case when the market is falling into a primary cycle trough, although there are exceptions to this rule. In fact you will note that it stayed in a trend run down all week, right into Friday, July 2. The TIP never gave a signal that a low might be forming this week. On Monday, June 28, the high and low of the day were between support and resistance, which was neutral. On June 29, the close was below daily support, which is bearish. It was also below weekly support, which only added to the idea that prices were still trending down into the primary cycle trough. On June 30, the range was again between support and resistance, which was neutral. On July 1, the first bullish trigger signal materialized. The low of the day (9622) was below daily support (9696-9715), and the close at 9732 was back above. Since this was only two trading days before the Level 1 geocosmic signature of July 5, and it might be the end of the 21st week of an older primary cycle, this could signal the start of a bottoming process, especially if Friday, July 2, held above support and/or broke above daily resistance. On July 2, however, yet another bullish trigger emerged, as the low of the day (9614) fell below daily support (9637-9645), but then closed back above (9686). These were signs that the market was trying to recover. It broke below daily support but it couldn't close below it. Remember that when support breaks, it becomes resistance, so this was a case where resistance intraday was actually breaking, although prices were not yet breaking above daily resistance. Aggressive short-term traders could have started buying in these daily support zones, or on the close, with a stop-loss on a close below the next day's support zone (9608-9610). Once again, if prices can close above daily resistance, then this would create a bullish sequence, which is one type of signal one likes to see following the completion of a primary cycle trough.

It almost happened the first trading day of the next week, July 6. The DJIA did trade above daily resistance (9764-9767), but then closed back below at 9743. The intraday trade above daily resistance, followed by a close back below daily resistance, created a bearish trigger. However, after nine consecutive closes below the daily TIP, the DJIA finally closed above it (9739). And so the trend status on the daily numbers was upgraded from a trend run down to neutral. An aggressive trader could still remain long from the prior day with a stop-loss below daily support, because if prices now closed below daily support, it would also become a bearish sequence (bearish trigger followed by a bearish close). As can be seen from the table (and the chart in Figure 65), that didn't happen. On Wednesday, July 7, the DJIA closed at 10,018, up 275 points, and well above daily resistance and the daily TIP. This was the first truly bullish close on the daily numbers during this period. More importantly, it now formed a bullish crossover zone at 9839-9873. That is, the resistance zone of July 7 was now lower than the support zone created for July 8. The market was now bullish until it closed back below here. Additionally, this bullish crossover zone offered strong support to any declines in the new primary cycle. If not long previously, one could now go long and place a stop-loss either below the low of the move on July 2 (9614) or on a close below the new bullish crossover zone (9839). This bullish crossover zone is in the boxes under R_1 of July 7 (the lowest end of resistance) and S_2 of July 8 (the highest end of support).

On July 8, the DJIA closed up 119 points. This was above weekly resistance and also above the daily TIP for the third consecutive day, thus upgrading its status from neutral to trend run up. The close was into daily resistance, which is "mostly bullish." The close was also above the 14-day moving average (see Figure 65), yet another sign that this could be a new primary cycle. The next day (Friday, July 9), it again closed into daily resistance (mostly bullish) and was above the daily TIP for the fourth consecutive day, which meant the trend run up was intact as the week ended. The weekly close was also above weekly resistance, which meant the weekly chart finally closed bullish as well. These were all excellent signs for the aggressive short-term trader to remain long, for most of the signals indicated July 2 was an important trough. As it would turn out, that was the primary cycle trough, so the stock market was now in the bullish phase of a new primary cycle for at least 2-5 weeks. July 12 would be the beginning of the second week. Both position and aggressive traders could now be long, looking for higher prices as this first phase - the bullish phase - of the primary cycle was in force. One's strategy was now bullish and all corrective declines could be bought until signs emerged that the major cycle crest was being achieved. It was still possible, of course, that the major cycle crest would also be the primary cycle crest, for the expectation was that this primary cycle would be bearish, as it was believed the 50-week cycle was pointing down.

Before proceeding with the analysis of daily and weekly support-resistance and TIP signals, let us pause and consider what one should be looking for the next week starting July 12. We stated that this was probably a new primary cycle, based on the market behavior of the prior week. It had gone from breaking below daily and weekly support prior to Uranus turning retrograde on July 5, to breaking above daily and weekly resistance in the days following this signature, which itself was in the 21st week of a 13-21 week normal primary cycle time band. A new bullish crossover zone had formed. The market had closed above the 14-day moving average on July 8, a confirmation signal that July 2 was at least a major cycle trough, but because it was so late in the primary cycle, it could also be a sign that the primary cycle trough had been completed. It was pressing up against the 42-day moving average, where a close above would be another sign that the primary bottom was in as of July 2. Even if the primary cycle was to be bearish, the "normal" upside price target would be at least 10,436 +/- 193 (and maybe higher), and the high of the prior week was only 10,201. The cycle was only one week old as of July 9, so there was time for it to go higher, and there was room for prices to go higher. If the market reached the price target zone this coming week (July 12-16) and started issuing signs of resistance holding and readiness to pull back, traders would want to cover at least some positions. Aggressive short-term traders would even consider selling short, especially if there was a geocosmic critical reversal date in effect, as the DJIA was making new highs for this new cycle. A look at the ephemeris would reveal that a Level 2 geocosmic signature was in effect July 13. It was the only geocosmic signature in effect that week, and it was not a Level 1 type. The last Level 1 unfolded on July 5, which was getting out of the 4-trading day orb of influence by July 12, so the probabilities were not high that a primary cycle crest would be forming this week. Let us now look at the weekly and daily numbers for July 12 through July 23.

Day	H	L	C	PP	TIP	S₁	S₂	R₁	R₂
				10019	10042	9927	9834	10468	10374
Jul 12	10220	10146	10216	10172	10066-U	10156	10143	10239	10227
Jul 13	10408	10217	10363	10194	10155-U	10179	10168	10253	10242
Jul 14	10400	10303	10366	10329	10232-U	10267	10251	10458	10441
Jul 15	10379	10240	10359	10356	10293-U	10318	10313	10415	10412
Jul 16	10356	10079	10098	10326	10337-N	10289	10273	10429	10412
				10195	10016	9932	9982	10262	10310
Jul 19	10187	10073	10154	10178	10287-N	9959	9996	10236	10276
Jul 20	10236	10008	10230	10138	10214-N	10097	10089	10211	10203
Jul 21	10265	10065	10120	10158	10158-N	10015	10080	10344	10308
Jul 22	10363	10121	10322	10150	10149-N	10020	10035	10220	10235
Jul 23	10442	10287	10424	10269	10192-N*	10201	10175	10443	10416

On July 12, the DJIA closed at 10,216, above the 42-day moving average, a confirmation signal that a new primary cycle trough was underway. The close was above the daily TIP for the 5th consecutive day, which meant it remained in a trend run up. The low was into daily support, which held, and the close was back between support and resistance, which was a neutral close but with a bullish bias. There was no need to change the long positions yet, as support was still holding on declines.

On July 13, the market was up 147 points, with an intraday high at 10,408. The close was still above the daily TIP, so the market remained in a trend run up. The close was above daily resistance, so it was a bullish close. Since this followed a bullish bias close in a bullish sequence, it was a further indication that a new primary cycle was underway. However, warning signs emerged on this day. The high was into weekly resistance and the close fell back below it. Resistance at the weekly level was holding the rally. Additionally the high of the day was now into the price objective zone for a primary cycle crest of a corrective bear market rally. That range was 10,436 +/- 194. This high was also happening on the day of a Level 2 geocosmic signature (Venus trine Pluto). It was not likely that a primary cycle crest was forming yet, for this signature alone is not strong enough to be overly concerned about that. However, it could be a trading cycle crest from which prices might drop back 38.2-61.8% of the swing up off of the July 2 primary bottom. Therefore it would be prudent to calculate a normal corrective decline and have a plan to buy if prices dropped back to that level and held for a trading cycle trough. That corrective decline price range would be (10,407 + 9614) ÷ 2. This would show a support zone of 10,010 +/- 94.

The next day, July 14, the DJIA traded between daily support and resistance, which was neutral. The close was still above the daily TIP, which meant the trend run up status remained unchanged. There was still no need to exit the long position, as both support and resistance were still holding

On July 15, the DJIA broke below support intraday, down to 10,240. It then closed back above daily support for a bullish trigger. The close was still above the daily TIP for the 8th consecutive day, so it remained in a trend run up. One would note that daily support was starting to break and resistance was holding. It was a concern, but not enough to exit the long position yet. On July 16 the market did close below both daily support and the daily trend indicator point. The close was bearish and the daily TIP was now downgraded to neutral. Additionally a bearish crossover formed between the lower end of Monday's resistance zone (10,236) and the higher end of Friday's support zone (10,289). This would act as formidable resistance, and one would be advised to exit all longs now. Aggressive traders might even sell short with a stop-loss on a close above this new bearish crossover zone.

This was the end of the week, so an analysis of the weekly numbers would be important. The close was above the weekly trend indicator point for the second consecutive week, so the TIP remained neutral. Yet the weekly high was held by weekly resistance, and the close was back between weekly support and resistance, which was a neutral close with a bearish bias. It was beginning to look like a reversal might be in process. However, the low of Friday was just beginning to fall into the price range calculated for a corrective decline to a trading cycle trough. The daily and weekly numbers were flashing caution and even a signal to exit from the long side. However, the cycle studies and price objective calculations were suggesting that a trading cycle trough was forming. Hence another buying opportunity was developing if that price target range for a trading cycle trough would hold. Here was a 'fork in the road." When confronted with a fork in the road (mixed signals), it is wise to choose in the direction of the underlying trend. The fact that this was still the first phase of a new primary cycle dictated that one should be looking for new signals to buy.

The next week began neutral. The high and low of Monday, July 19, were between daily support and resistance. The close was below the daily TIP for the 2nd consecutive day, which left it in neutral. A close down the next day would downgrade it to trend run down. Still, the market was in the upper end of the corrective decline price target zone, and it was still the first phase of a primary cycle. There was reason to believe that a bottom was close at hand and another rally to the major cycle crest - or a re-test to the 10,407 high of the prior week - could still unfold. Short-term traders could still look for a signal to get long.

On July 20, that buy signal came. The intraday low was 10,007, very close to an exact 50% corrective decline of the prior move up (the price target was 10,010 +/- 94). That low was below daily support, but the close at 10,230 was above daily resistance, which was not just bullish, but a *very bullish close*. The high of the day was 10,236, which was into the bearish crossover zone of 10,230-10,289. It held as it should on the first challenge. The close was also back above the daily trend indicator point for the first time in 3 days. Its status remained neutral, but it didn't turn into a trend run down, which could have been the case had it closed lower. One could now enter the market again from the long side with a stop-loss below the 10,007 low of July 20. It was possible that the trading cycle trough had just been completed, and the next leg up to the major (or even primary) cycle crest was underway. An MCP price objective could be calculated above the market for this crest. It was (10,407 + 10,007) – 9614, or 10,800 +/- 140. We would now record this upside price target range and watch for signs to sell if the DJIA got there and stalled, especially if the high formed nearby to a geocosmic critical reversal date.

The next day tested one's resolve to stay with this new bullish strategy as prices dropped below daily support during the day. The low was 10,065 and daily support was 10,079-10,115. However the close was back above at 10,120 for a bullish trigger. At the same time, it closed back below the daily TIP for the third time in 4 days, and the close was below the daily pivot point (PP), so it wasn't looking as promising as it had the day before. Aggressive traders may have elected to exit here, yet position traders would stay with it since the 10,007 of the prior day's *very bullish close* was holding. And for that they were rewarded because July 22 was a big up day. The market closed at 10,322, up 202 points from the prior day and well above daily resistance, which was bullish. It also closed above the bearish crossover zone of 10,236-10,289.

The week ended on July 23 with the DJIA up another 102 points, closing at 10,424, and into daily resistance, which was a mostly bullish close. It also closed above the weekly TIP for the third consecutive week, which meant its status was upgraded from neutral to trend run up. It also closed above the daily TIP for the 2nd consecutive day, which was neutral. Nevertheless it would be upgraded even higher - to an "on edge, trend run up" - because the close formed a new high for this primary cycle. Perhaps more importantly, the 14-day moving average had closed above the 42-day average for the second consecutive day, and the daily close was above both on each day, for a trend run up via that technical study. All of these studies suddenly looked very bullish, and the DJIA seemed destined to reach 10,800 +/- 140 for a major and even primary cycle crest. Therefore the forthcoming week would be very important: would this be a bullish or bearish primary cycle? There was still no convincing evidence to suggest that it wouldn't be bearish, with a primary cycle crest due at any time as the DJIA started the fourth week of this rather new primary cycle, and primary cycle crests were usually due by the fifth week in bear markets.

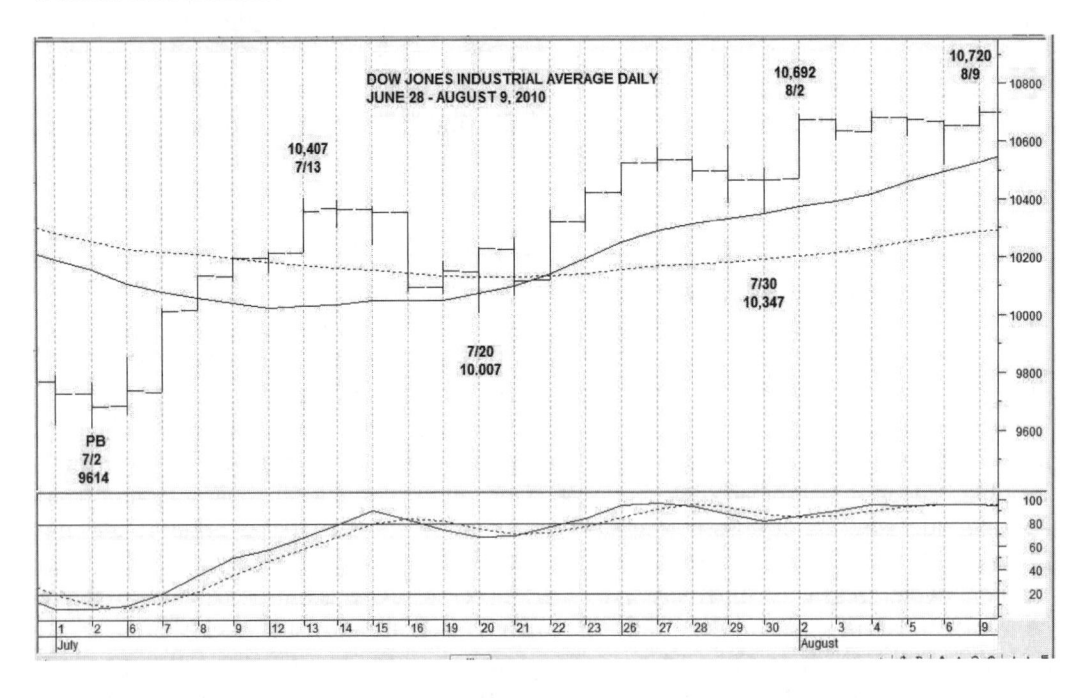

Figure 66: Daily chart of the DJIA, June 28-August 9, 2010, following the primary cycle trough of July 2, 2010.

Day	H	L	C	PP	TIP	S₁	S₂	R₁	R₂
				10291	**10168**	**10207**	**10141**	**10641**	**10575**
Jul 26	10527	10414	10525	10387	10268-U	10347	10331	10502	10486
Jul 27	10578	10495	10538	10189	10381-U	10469	10451	10581	10563
Jul 28	10548	10463	10498	10537	10471-U	10495	10496	10579	10580
Jul 29	10585	10387	10467	10503	10510-N	10455	10458	10540	10543
Jul 30	10507	10347	10466	10480	10506-N	10566	10572	10368	10375
				10466	**10317**	**10347**	**10347**	**10584**	**10585**
Aug 2	10692	10468	10674	10440	10474-OU	10386	10373	10545	10532
Aug 3	10677	10601	10636	10611	10510-OU	10562	10551	10786	10754
Aug 4	10703	10627	10680	10638	10563-U	10598	10599	10674	10675
Aug 5	10680	10613	10675	10670	10640-U	10642	10637	10718	10713
Aug 6	10668	10515	10653	10656	10654-N	10641	10632	10708	10699

The next week started out strong, with the DJIA up another 100 points on Monday, July 26. The close was above daily resistance, which was bullish. It was above the daily TIP for the third consecutive day, so that was also upgraded to a trend run up status. On Tuesday, July 27, resistance held, which was a cautionary sign. The high was 10,578, right into daily resistance of 10,563-10,581. However the close was back between support-resistance, which was a neutral close, but with a bearish bias. Still, it was above the daily TIP for the fourth consecutive day, so the trend run up was still in force.

On July 28, the DJIA fell to 10,463 - below daily support - but it closed at 10,498, back above it for a bullish trigger. This close was above the daily TIP for the 5th consecutive day, so it was still in a trend run up. On July 29, the high of the day was above daily resistance, and the low of the day was below daily support, but the close was back between the two, which is "mixed." Yet the close was back below the daily TIP for the first time in 6 days, so its status was downgraded to neutral. This was a concern because a powerful geocosmic cluster was now in effect, lasting from July 23 through August 9. The midpoint was July 31 - August 1, which was a weekend. So the critical reversal date was July 30-August 2, +/- 3 trading days. The DJIA was entering this time frame. It was making new highs for the primary cycle at 10,585 on Thursday, July 29, and its daily trend status had just been downgraded from trend run up to neutral. Yet prices were still above the 14-day moving average, and that was above the 42-day average, so the moving average studies were still in a trend run up.

On Friday, July 30, the DJIA traded as low as 10,347, below the daily support zone of 10,368-10,375, but it closed back above at 10,466 for a bullish trigger signal. Furthermore the weekly close was above the weekly trend indicator point for the fourth consecutive week, so it remained in a trend run up. A glance at the chart in Figure 66 will show that the low of that day was held by the 14-day moving average. It challenged it, but it held. It was still not a sell signal, although aggressive short-term traders might have exited longs the day before when the TIP status was downgraded. The daily close was below TIP again for the 2nd consecutive day, so it was not upgraded back to a trend run up, even though the weekly TIP remained in a trend run up. The bearish concern was that the high of the cycle occurred July 29, just one trading day before the July 30-August 2 critical reversal date. However the market was not yet into our MCP price target zone for the major cycle crest. As it started the next week, August 2, the DJIA was poised to go in either direction. All traders would now be looking for stronger signs of a top to sell into as a critical reversal zone was in effect, and it was the fifth week of a primary cycle (when primary cycle crests are due in bear markets). Additionally, the daily stochastics were overbought and starting to exhibit a bearish looping formation, plus prices were testing the 14-day moving average. A break below there could be damaging.

Monday, August 2, was yet another powerful up day. The close (10,674) was above both daily and weekly resistance, and a new bullish crossover zone formed at 10,532-10,562. The high of this day was 10,692, which was in the price target zone for the MCP of the major cycle crest. Was this it? After all, it was a critical reversal date. The leading market timing indicators said to be alert for a sell signal to be generated at any time, but the daily/weekly numbers were giving bullish signals. A close below this new bullish crossover zone would have to take place to give a sell signal now. In the meantime, the close was back above the daily trend indicator point for the first time in 3 days, which is neutral. However it would actually be an on-edge trend run up because it was a new high for this primary cycle.

The next day, August 3, was neutral as prices traded between the daily support and resistance zones. The close was above the daily TIP for the second day, but it was a down day, so it was downgraded to neutral from an on edge, trend run up. August 4 would thus be very important, for a close up would be an upgrade to a trend run up and a close down would certainly solidify it as neutral. It closed up, and so the daily TIP was indeed upgraded to a trend run up. The close was also above daily resistance, which was bullish. The high of the day was 10,703, well within the 10,800 +/- 140 price range for a major cycle crest (and perhaps primary). It was still within three trading days of the geocosmic critical reversal date of July 30-August 2.

On Thursday, August 5, the DJIA fell below daily support, but closed back above, for a bullish trigger. The close was also above the daily trend indicator point for the 4th consecutive day, so it remained in a trend run up. However there was a concern now because daily support started breaking during the day. A close below daily support on Friday, August 6, would create a bearish sequence. That didn't happen. The DJIA did trade below daily support again, but once more, it closed back above for yet another bullish trigger. And the close was above weekly resistance, which meant that weekly prices closed bullish. The weekly close was also above its TIP for the fifth consecutive week, which meant it remained in a trend run up. However the close was below the daily TIP for the first time in 5 days, so its status was downgraded from trend run up to neutral. Since the high of the week was 10,703 on Wednesday, August 4, and that high was in the geocosmic critical reversal zone, and it was the fifth week of a primary cycle that was assumed to be in the bearish phase of the 50-week cycle, it was time to exit from all longs. Aggressive traders could even look to sell short with a stop-loss on a close above 10,703 (the high of August 4), or daily or even the next week's resistance.

The next week began strong with a rally to 10,720, a new high for this cycle as it began its sixth week of the primary cycle. That high was into daily resistance (10,709-10,730), but it closed back below at 10,698. And so the close was neutral, with a bearish bias. If aggressive traders hadn't sold short the prior week, they could now.

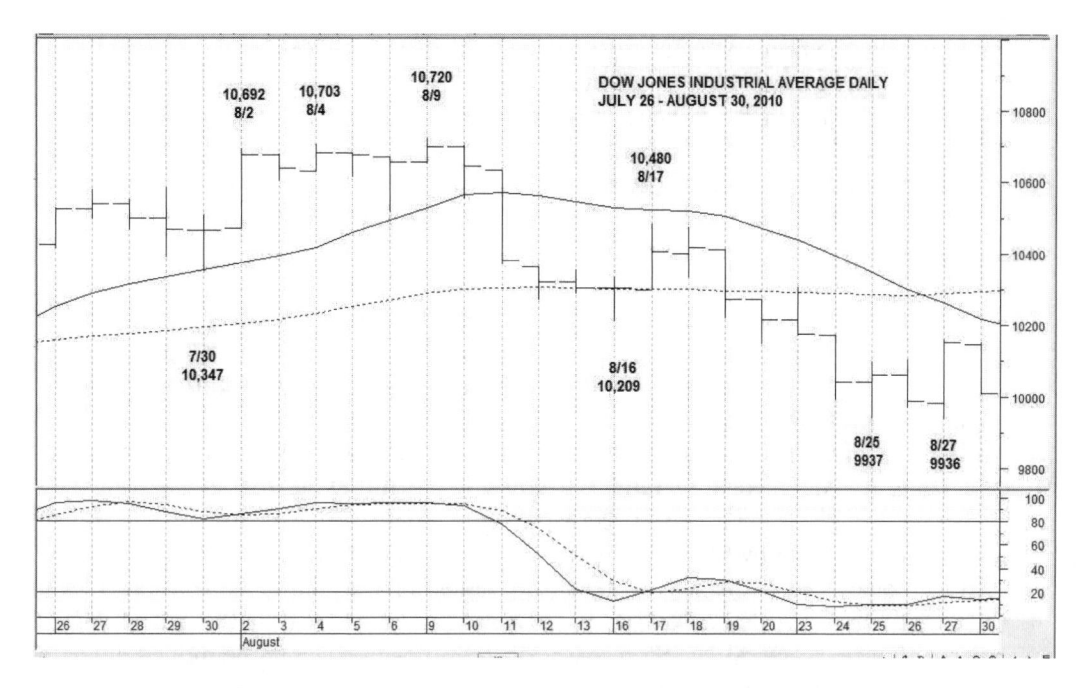

Figure 67: Daily chart of the DJIA from July 26-August 30, 2010. Notice the crest of August 9, and then the decline which broke below the 14- and 42-day moving averages into the end of the month. Notice also the bearish looping pattern of stochastics into August 9 and the bullish oscillator pattern at the low of August 27.

Day	H	L	C	PP	TIP	S₁	S₂	R₁	R₂
				10608	10455	10536	10514	10770	10748
Aug 9	10720	10649	10699	10617	10646-U	10570	10556	10730	10709
Aug 10	10701	10557	10644	10689	10652-N	10663	10659	10734	10729
Aug 11	10632	10367	10379	10632	10644-N	10570	10563	10719	10713
Aug 12	10361	10288	10320	10459	10593-D	10246	10286	10511	10551
Aug 13	10355	10285	10303	10316	10468-D	10273	10272	10366	10364
				10430	10501	10077	10141	10528	10592
Aug 16	10333	10209	10302	10314	10363-D	10268	10274	10338	10343
Aug 17	10480	10297	10405	10281	10304-N	10240	10230	10364	10353
Aug 18	10472	10330	10415	10394	10330-N	10314	10308	10497	10491
Aug 19	10411	10216	10271	10406	10360-N	10344	10339	10486	10482
Aug 20	10271	10147	10213	10299	10366-N	10173	10188	10368	10383

On August 10, the DJIA closed below daily support, which was bearish. It also closed below the daily TIP after being above it five of the prior six days. It had a one-day interruption to the trend run up on Friday, August 6. Typical of most interrupted trend runs, the resumption of the trend run up ended within the next 7 trading days, and most of the time just one day later, as was the case here. If short-term traders were not short yet, based on the geocosmic signatures and cycle phasing, they could go short now on the change of TIP status and the fact that the market closed bearish. The stop-loss could be placed above the high of the move so far (10,720), daily resistance (10,719), or weekly resistance (10,770), depending on one's risk allowance. Notice that the DJIA was testing the 14-day moving average. A break below would confirm August 9 as a major cycle crest and possibly the primary cycle crest since it was the sixth week, and the assumption is still that this was a bearish 50-week cycle. So the top was due before Tuesday of the ninth week. Ideally the primary cycle crest in a bear market is due 2-5 weeks after the primary cycle trough. But that primary trough occurred on a Friday, July 2, and this crest was attained on the first trading day of the sixth week. It was very close to the ideal range for a crest - and still before Tuesday of the 9th week - after which a new high would confirm the primary cycle would be bullish.

The DJIA then plummeted, as expected. On Wednesday, August 11, it closed at 10,379, down 265 points from the prior day. It closed well below the 14-day moving average, confirming a crest of importance had been realized two days earlier. It closed below daily support, which meant it was a bearish close again on the daily. It closed below the daily TIP for the second consecutive day, which was still neutral, but on the verge of being downgraded to a trend run down if the following day closed down. It closed below weekly support. And perhaps most importantly, it formed a bearish crossover zone as shown by the boxes under S_1 on August 11 and R_1 the following day, August 12. In other words, the support level for August 11 was above the resistance level for August 12, which created a bearish crossover zone at 10,511-10,570. That served as powerful resistance to any rallies. Stop-losses on short positions could be moved down to a close above this new bearish crossover zone.

That day, August 12, was another down day, which confirmed the downgrade of the TIP status from neutral to trend run down. The range of the day however was between support and resistance, which meant it was a neutral close. The next day was Friday, August 13, and once again the DJIA traded between daily support and resistance, which is neutral. However, its close below the daily TIP for the fourth consecutive day kept its status at trend run down. The weekly close at 10,330 was below weekly support, which was bearish. Not only that, but it formed a weekly bearish crossover zone, as one of the resistance zones for the next week (R_1) at 10,528 was below one of the support zones (S_1) for the current week at 10,536. Therefore the bearish crossover zones were in force on the daily at 10,511-10,570 and the weekly at 10,538-10,536. This development strongly supported the view that the DJIA had topped out and the primary cycle was turning bearish at last.

The one concern right now was that the market was entering the 7th week of the primary cycle, and a 5-7 week major cycle trough was due. Since it was only the first major cycle phase of the new primary cycle, there was a strong possibility that the decline could find support this week at a normal corrective decline price target. The price range for a major cycle trough would be a 38.2-61.8% retracement of the entire move up from the primary cycle trough at 9614 on July 2 to the major cycle crest of 10,720 on August 9. This retracement zone would be 10,167 +/- 131, or 10,036-10,298. Note that this was further buttressed by weekly support, which was 10,077-10,141. There were also a number of geocosmic signatures in effect August 16-26. The midpoint would be August 21, a Saturday. The geocosmic critical reversal date was August 20-23, +/- 3 trading days. Would the major cycle trough occur this week, or would prices just continue down into a 7-11 week half-primary cycle? And if it did occur, would the rally to the crest of the next major cycle be higher than 10,720, the crest of the first major cycle? These were the questions to be answered as the week of August 16 began.

On Monday, August 16, the DJIA fell to an intraday low of 10,209, well below daily support and into the price target zone of a normal corrective retracement for a major cycle trough. But the close was 10,302, back above the daily support zone of 10,268-10,338, which meant it closed on a bullish trigger. This could be the major cycle trough as it fulfilled the minimum criteria of a normal corrective decline, was below the 14-day moving average, and closed with a bullish trigger. The DJIA also traded below the 42-day moving average, but then closed back above it, which was a sign that a bottom could be forming here. The close was still below the daily TIP for the 5th consecutive day, so it remained in a trend run down. This would be enough for aggressive traders to go long, but not for short-term position traders. Aggressive traders who covered shorts and went long here would have to place their stop-loss on a close below the low of Monday (10,209) or below weekly support (10,077), depending on risk allowance. If Monday was the first major cycle trough, and the primary cycle was bearish due to the bearish 50-week cycle, then a corrective rally would show resistance at 10,465 +/- 61. Position traders expecting the market to be bearish would have a stop-loss on a close above that range, or the prior week's high at 10,720 since the crest of the second major cycle phase can be a re-test of the crest of the first major cycle.

The next day, August 17, the DJIA closed at 10,405, above daily resistance, which was bullish. It also closed above the daily TIP for the first time in six days, which upgraded its status from trend run down to neutral. The high of the day was 10,480, which was now in the price objective zone for a major cycle crest in a bearish primary cycle. Yet there was no sign that this move up was over yet. Prices were also still below the 14-day moving average. It would have to close above that to confirm Monday's low was a major cycle trough.

On August 18, the DJIA traded between daily support and resistance, which was neutral. It closed above the daily TIP for the second consecutive day, which meant its status also remained neutral. On Thursday, August 19, the DJIA plummeted again, down 144 points to close at 10,271, well below daily support, which was bearish again. The close was also below the 42-day moving average, a sign that the primary cycle was turning bearish. The close was below daily TIP for the first time in 3 days, and so it was not upgraded. It remained neutral.

The DJIA was down again on Friday, August 20, to 10,147 intraday, thereby taking out the 10,209 low of Monday, August 16. This was now the middle of the geocosmic critical reversal time band (August 20-23, +/- 3 trading days), and it was a new low. That low was below daily support, and the close was back above it, which created a bullish trigger. It was still possible the major cycle trough was forming at this time, for it was the last day of the 7th week, a geocosmic critical reversal date was in effect, and the new low was still within the price range for the major cycle trough. An aggressive short-term trader would see this as a signal to get long. However, position traders would either still be short, or waiting for the next rally to sell short, as the bias was still that this would become a bearish primary cycle. Yet the idea that this was an "unusually uncertain" time was very much apparent on August 20 - not just from the point of view of fundamental economists like Fed Chair Ben Bernanke, but also for those who study financial markets from a technical or cyclical point of view. Cycle and geocosmic studies suggested it was time to look for a short-term buying opportunity, but longer-term it looked more bearish. The daily technical picture was flashing bullish triggers, but the weekly charts still had a powerful weekly and daily bearish crossover zone above the market, adding pressure downward on any rallies that might begin, and the DJIA was closing below the 42-day moving average, signaling that the primary cycle was turning bearish. These mixed signals would get even more conflicting the next week, before clearing up and leading to more normal market behavior and exceptional profit opportunities for all types of traders.

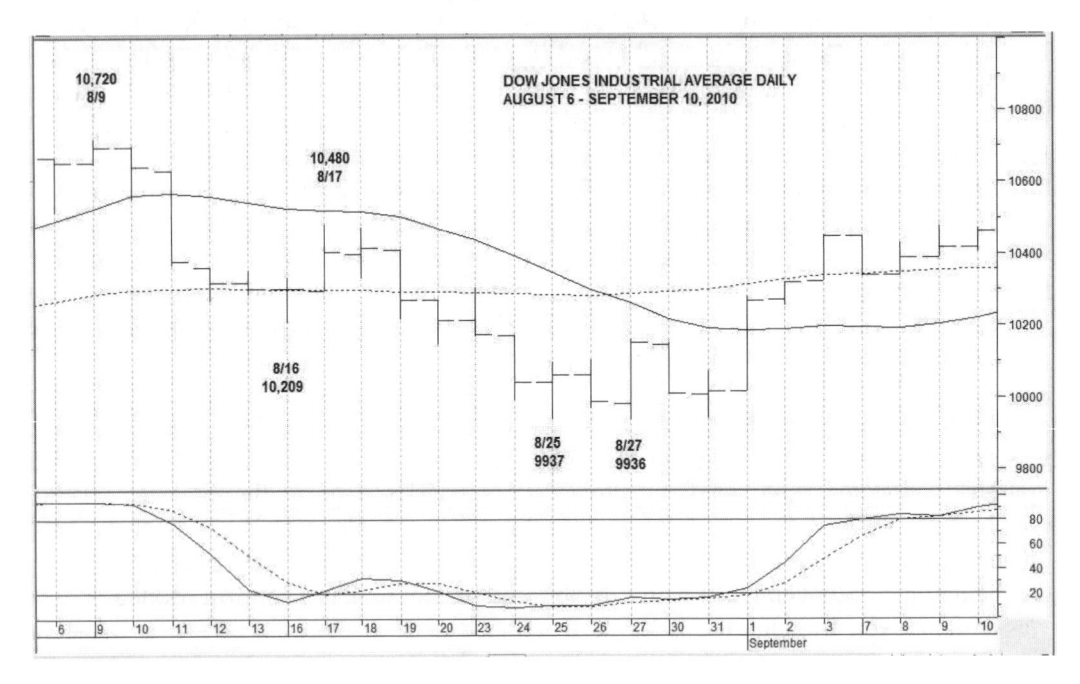

Figure 68: Daily chart of the DJIA, August 6-September 10, 2010.

Day	H	L	C	PP	TIP	S_1	S_2	R_1	R_2
				10280	**10440**	**10047**	**10080**	**10380**	**10413**
Aug 23	10304	10170	10174	10210	10305-D	10151	10150	10275	10274
Aug 24	10173	9991	10040	10216	10242-D	10107	10128	10241	10250
Aug 25	10097	9937	10060	10068	10165-D	9949	9963	10131	10145
Aug 26	10104	9968	9985	10031	10103-D	9980	9966	10140	10125
Aug 27	10159	9936	10150	10019	10040-N	9917	9934	10054	10071
				10130	**10280**	**9966**	**9956**	**10334**	**10324**
Aug 30	10150	10007	10009	10082	10044-D	10039	10005	10262	10228
Aug 31	10073	9941	10014	10056	10052-D	9938	9961	10081	10104
Sept 1	10279	10016	10269	10010	10050-N	9949	9946	10080	10078
Sept 2	10320	10254	10320	10187	10084-N	10138	10099	10401	10357
Sept 3	10451	10322	10448	10298	10165-U	10287	10276	10353	10342

Ultimately one realizes that there is no market signal or analysis that is 100% accurate in its ability to forecast every major move in any financial market. There are usually some indicators in contradiction to others, and the analyst must discern which to give the greater weight to. It varies from case to case. As the reader has witnessed so far in the first part of this primary cycle, the methods employed herein are about 'as good as it gets.' Every trading and major cycle trough and crest was captured perfectly after the primary cycle of July 2, until we reached the latter half of August. And then the market timing signals that had been given the greatest weight began to give way to patterns within the primary cycle that confirmed the longer-term cycle analysis was bullish, and not bearish, as had been assumed since after the DJIA broke below the lows of February 5, 2010. Let us now review the market activity that followed August 20.

On Monday, August 23, the DJIA closed below the daily TIP for the 3rd consecutive day, and it was a down day, which meant its status was downgraded to a trend run down. The high of the day was above daily resistance and the close was back below, which meant it was also a bearish trigger.

The following day the DJIA was down 134 points. It closed below the daily TIP for the fourth consecutive day. It also closed below the weekly TIP. The close was furthermore below daily support, which was bearish. Since this followed a bearish trigger day, it meant that the market was now in a bearish sequence. Time-wise, however, this was the 8th week of the 13-21 week primary cycle. A 5-7 week major cycle trough was never confirmed as the DJIA never traded back to the 13-day moving average, and now it was taking out the low of August 16, which had originally appeared to be a major cycle trough in the 7th week. It now looked like the DJIA was forming a 7-11 week half-primary cycle trough, and a "normal" price target for that low was already calculated as 9780-10,222 (45-85% retracement of the move up from July 2 at 9614 to August 9 at 10,720). Furthermore, August 20-23, +/- 3 trading days, was an important geocosmic critical reversal period. The DJIA was in the time band and the price objective range for a half-primary cycle trough as these technical signatures were all bearish. Aggressive traders would now be vigilant for a buying opportunity to emerge.

On Wednesday, August 25, the DJIA fell to a new multi-week low of 9937. This was below daily support (9949-9963), but the close was 10,060, back above support, for a bullish trigger. The close was still below the daily TIP for the 5th consecutive day, but the bullish trigger within the critical reversal zone would be enough for aggressive short-term traders to get long, with a stop-close below the 9937 low of that day. One would also note that the daily stochastics were deeply oversold and were in the process of making a bullish double looping formation below 20%. Since our longer-term view of the market was bearish, and this was now getting into the middle of the primary cycle, position traders would not be going long. They would wait for a corrective rally to the crest of the next half-primary cycle, due 1-3 weeks after the half-primary cycle trough, and then look to sell short.

On Thursday, August 26, the DJIA fell into daily support (9966-9980) with a low of 9968. Support held, and the market then closed back between support and resistance, which was neutral, but with a bullish bias. It was looking promising, as support held, but the close was still below the daily TIP for the 6th consecutive day. It was still in a trend run down.

On Friday, August 27, the DJIA fell to 9936, one point below its low of August 25 (9937). Then it rallied smartly to close the week at 10,150, which was above daily resistance. This was not only bullish, but created a bullish sequence. The close was also above the daily TIP for the first time in 7 days, which upgraded its status to a neutral. These were very positive signs, which were furthermore supported by the weekly numbers, which closed on a bullish trigger. Aggressive short-term traders who went long on August 25 never got stopped out. Those who did not go long then would have more signals to get long now, with a stop-loss on a close below the new low at 9936. Position traders would be waiting for the rally and a sign to sell short, based on the idea that this was the second primary cycle in a bearish 50-week cycle. If so, then the market would fall hard after the corrective rally to the crest of the second half-primary cycle.

At this point, the analyst could construct price target zones for the crest of the second half-primary cycle, based on the idea (valid at that time) that the double bottom lows of August 25 and 27 were indeed half-primary cycle troughs. A "normal" 38.2-61.8% corrective rally would yield a price target of 10,328 +/- 93. A 45-85% retracement (more typical of half-primary cycle corrections) would be 10,288-10,602. Time-wise, the rally would likely last only 1-3 weeks if the primary cycle was to be bearish, as expected, based on the 50-week cycle being bearish.

On Monday, August 30, the DJIA closed at 10,009, down 141 points. The close was in to daily support, which was "mostly bearish." The close was back below the daily TIP for the seventh time in 8 days, which meant the trend run down was resumed after the one day interrupt. At this point, one might have asked: "What do we know about markets after a one-day interrupt in a trend run down?" As stated in Chapter 16, *"A daily trend run down may be interrupted for one day and then resume its trend run down status... When that happens, the resumed trend run down tends to end within the next 3 days. In only 2 cases (out of 21) did the resumption of the trend run down last more than 3 days after an interrupt day."* Therefore, this new trend run down was due to end by Wednesday, September 1, three trading days after the interrupt of August 27.

On Tuesday, August 31, the DJIA dropped to a low of 9941 intraday, virtually a triple bottom to the 9937 and 9936 lows of August 25 and 27. But the test held. That low was into the daily support zone of 9938-9961 and held. The close was back above, which meant the close was neutral but with a bullish bias. The close was below the daily TIP again, for the eighth time in 9 days, which was also the second consecutive day after the interrupt on August 27.

The next day, September 1, the DJIA exploded up 255 points, thus rewarding those who went long the prior week with a stop-loss on a close below those lows. The close was 10,269, well above daily resistance, which was not only bullish, but following the prior day's bullish bias, it created a bullish sequence, strongly suggesting the half-primary cycle trough did unfold the prior week at 9936. This was confirmed by the close above the 14-day moving average as well. The huge rally also created a new bullish crossover zone at 10,078-10,138. Stop-losses could be moved up to a close below this new crossover zone. The market would now be bullish unless it closed back below. The close was also above the daily TIP after the two-day interrupt, which is normal. It was upgraded to neutral. Aggressive traders who were long would now begin to look for this rally to top out at 10,328 +/- 93 or 10,288-10,602 at any time. Ideally the later price range would be the target to look for in this run. That top was normally due 1-3 weeks after the half-primary cycle trough if this market was bearish, and this was the first week.

The DJIA entered this ideal price zone the next day, September 2. The high of that day was 10,320. The high and low of the day was between daily support and resistance, which is neutral. The close was above the daily TIP for the 2nd consecutive day, which is neutral as well. What was most important was the daily stochastics. They came off their double looping pattern, and K moved well above D and above 25%, widening its distance above D, which was a confirmation signal that this was a new half-primary cycle. The low of the first half-primary cycle was completed as of August 27.

The week ended on Friday, September 3, with the DJIA up another 128 points. The close at 10,448 was above both daily and weekly resistance, which was bullish. The close was above the daily TIP for the third consecutive day, so its status was upgraded from neutral to a new trend run up. The close was above the weekly TIP for the first time in 4 weeks, so its status was also upgraded from trend run down to neutral. The close was also above the 42-day moving average, which would be a concern to bears because that would suggest that the lows of August 25-31 may have been a half-primary cycle trough in a *bullish* primary cycle. This was the first new signal to suggest that the market may not be *bearish*. Everything had suddenly shifted from bearish at the close of the prior week to bullish at the close of September 3. And once again these market timing and technical studies caught the low very nicely.

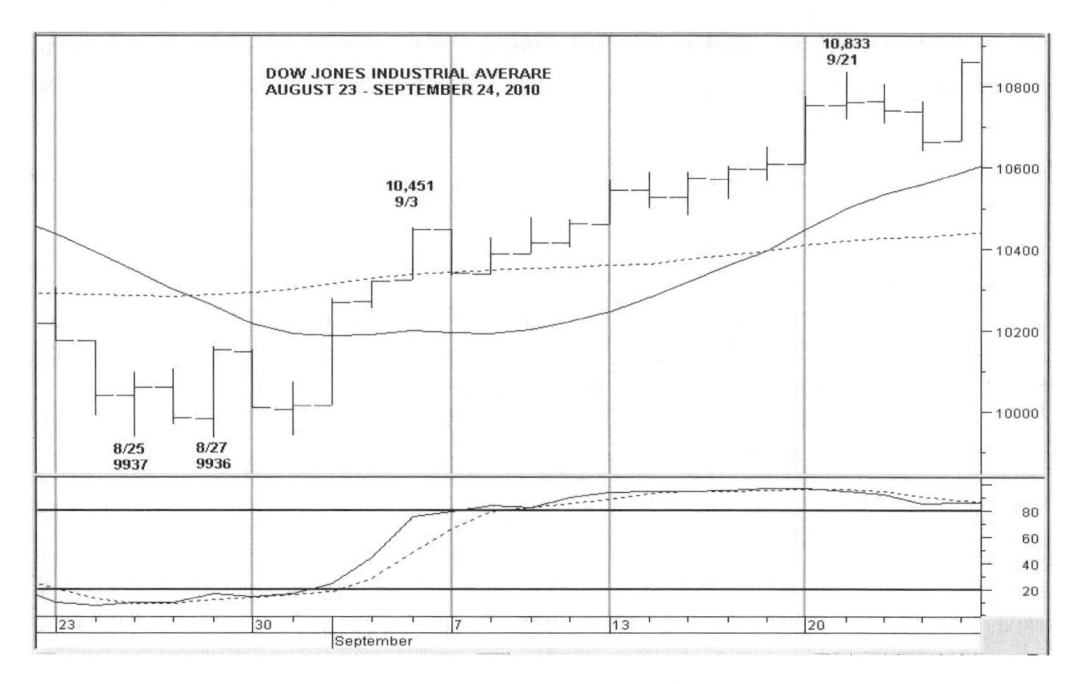

Figure 69: Daily chart of the DJIA, August 23 - September 24, 2010.

The high of September 3 was 10,451. It was still in the time band and price range of a normal half-primary cycle crest in a bearish primary cycle. This was also the start of another time band containing several geocosmic signatures that correlate with market reversals, lasting September 4 through October 8. The midpoint would be September 21, +/- 3 trading days. Although this is important, let us continue the exercise of seeking signs of a half-primary cycle crest in the 1-3 week period following the low of August 27.

Day	H	L	C	PP	TIP	S₁	S₂	R₁	R₂
				10280	**10230**	**10193**	**10109**	**10702**	**10619**
Sept 7	10446	10332	10340	10407	10297-U	10383	10362	10512	10492
Sept 8	10426	10335	10387	10373	10359-U	10283	10300	10398	10415
Sept 9	10476	10386	10415	10383	10387-U	10341	10339	10432	10430
Sept 10	10471	10403	10463	10426	10394-U	10370	10375	10460	10465
				10423	**10278**	**10390**	**10370**	**10535**	**10515**
Sept 13	10567	10458	10544	10446	10418	10427	10419	10498	10490
Sept 14	10588	10499	10526	10523	10465	10489	10479	10598	10588
Sept 15	10587	10480	10572	10538	10502	10482	10488	10570	10576
Sept 16	10603	10522	10595	10547	10536	10519	10506	10626	10613
Sept 17	10650	10567	10608	10573	10553	10554	10543	10635	10625
				10572	**10425**	**10512**	**10494**	**10703**	**10685**
Sept 20	10774	10608	10753	10608	10576	10566	10567	10649	10650
Sept 21	10833	10717	10761	10712	10613	10670	10649	10815	10836
Sept 22	10808	10708	10736	10770	10697	10703	10708	10818	10823
Sept 23	10762	10641	10662	10751	10744	10686	10693	10786	10793
Sept 24	10865	10664	10860	10688	10736	10602	10615	10723	10736

Monday was the Labor Day holiday and markets were closed. On Tuesday, September 7, the DJIA closed below daily support, which was bearish. The close was also below the 42-day moving average. Support was breaking and the market was in the time band for a half-primary cycle crest after having already achieved the price target for that crest. It was a signal for short-term aggressive traders to cover longs and reverse to the short side, with a stop-loss on a close above the 10,451 crest of September 3. Note however, that the daily TIP was still in a trend run up.

On Wednesday, September 8, prices rallied to a high of 10,426, which was above daily resistance, but the close was 10,387, back below resistance, which was a bearish trigger. The close was still above the daily TIP for the 5th consecutive day, so it remained in a trend run up. There was no trend change by this signal yet. Furthermore, the close was back above the 42-day moving average, a sign that perhaps the rally to the half-primary cycle crest was still unfolding.

On September 9, the DJIA rallied to 10,476, taking out the 10,451 high of September 3. This confirmed the half-primary cycle crest was still unfolding, yet still in the price target zone of 10,288-10,602. The high of the day was again above daily resistance (10,430-10,432), but the close at 10,415 was back below it. Since the close was below the high of September 3 (10,451), aggressive traders may have still remained short. The close was above the daily TIP for the 6th consecutive day, which meant it remained in a trend run up. The short side of the market was not very secure yet. To become secure, it needed three things: 1) a close below daily support, 2) a downgrade in the TIP status, and 3) a close back below the 42-day moving average.

That was not to happen. On Friday, September 10, the DJIA closed at 10,463, up again and above the 10,451 high of September 3. The close was above the daily TIP for the 7th consecutive day, so its status remained in a trend run up. The close was into daily resistance, which was mostly bullish. The close was also above the weekly TIP for the 2nd consecutive week, so it remained in neutral. A look at the chart in Figure 69 will show that prices were still above the 14-day moving average, which was still *below* the 42-day average, and the market was now about to begin its third week past the low of August 27. If indeed the 50-week cycle was bearish, then this rally was due to end by the end of the next week and ideally at a price below 10,602. Any move above the 10,720 high of August 9 would mean this was a right translation primary cycle and a signal that the 50-week cycle labeling was wrong. The trading strategy was still to sell short during this time band until prices rallied above these areas and thereby disproved the assumption that the longer-term cycle was bearish. The week beginning September 13 would therefore be very critical to this cycle labeling.

On Monday, September 13, the DJIA was sharply higher, closing at 10,544, its highest level since the low of August 27, but still in the normal price range for a half-primary cycle crest in a bearish primary cycle. The close was above daily resistance, which was bullish, and it was also above the daily TIP for the 8th consecutive day, maintaining its status as a trend run up.

The next day, September 14, the DJIA traded up into daily resistance of 10,588-10598, but closed back between support and resistance, which was neutral, but with a bearish bias. The close was also above the daily TIP for the 9th consecutive day, which remained in a trend run up. Yet resistance was starting to hold again, and prices were still in the normal price range for a half-primary cycle crest, so aggressive traders could probe the short side again with a stop-loss on a close above the 10,588 high of that day. Position traders would still need stronger signals before going short.

On September 15, the DJIA fell below daily support at 10,482-10488. The low was 10,480. But then it turned around and closed at 10,572, above daily resistance, which negated the sell signal of the prior day as this was a very bullish close. For the 10th consecutive day, the close was above the daily TIP. It was now entering a point where the trend run up was in the realm of exhaustion. Anytime the close is above the TIP for 10 or more consecutive days, it is ready to start closing back below it. It doesn't necessarily mean the ultimate high will be completed yet, but at least the market is readying for a pause and perhaps a modest pullback. Since we were looking for a half-primary cycle crest this week and prices hadn't yet exceeded 10,602 or even 10,720, it was still possible that a top was forming, and traders would still be looking to sell short.

The next day, September 16, the DJIA rallied to just one point above our price target of 10,288-10,602. The high was 10,603. This was important because it was also 3 trading days before the September 21 critical reversal date. The market was now in the allowable orb of the critical reversal date time band. Yet the range of September 16 was between daily support and resistance, which was neutral. The close was 10,595, above the daily TIP for the 11th consecutive day. It was well into the overbought (or exhaustion) zone now.

On Friday, September 17, the DJIA soared to 10,650 intraday and closed at 10,608, slightly above the ideal price target zone for a half-primary cycle crest, but still not above the 10,720 high of the first half-primary cycle on August 9. That high was above daily resistance (10,625-10,635), but the close was back below it, for a bearish trigger. The close was above the daily TIP for the 12th consecutive day, which was still a trend run up, but reaching the point of exhaustion. The close was above both the weekly TIP and weekly resistance, which meant its status was upgraded to trend run up and bullish.

This was the situation traders faced heading into the week of September 20. It was a three-star critical reversal zone (September 21 +/- 3 trading days). It was the end of the third week following the half-primary cycle trough, and in a bearish primary cycle, the crest of this half-primary cycle was now due. The powerful Jupiter-Uranus conjunction occurred September 18 - a Level 1 geocosmic signature with one of the highest correlation of all geocosmic signatures to primary cycle completions. (In this case, it would be a crest if it were to correlate with a primary type of cycle). Yet at the same time, all the technical studies were bullish, except the fact that the 10,720 high of the first half-cycle was still above the market. One other thing was important to note here as well. As the week ended on September 17, the 14-day moving average was rising and just about even with the 42-day moving average. If it went above, and prices remained above both, this would be a trend run up signal from the moving average studies.

Based on the market timing studies and the fact that the daily closed on a bearish trigger, aggressive short-term traders could sell short with a stop-loss either above 10,650 (Friday's high) or 10,720 (the crest of the first half-primary cycle). However the next day, September 20, that position would be stopped out as prices closed at 10,753, well above daily resistance, weekly resistance, and the first half-primary cycle crest. This changed everything. It was now apparent that this would be a bullish primary cycle, for the DJIA was making a new high in the second half of the primary cycle (right translation) and in the 12th week of the primary cycle (past Tuesday of the 9th week, putting into play the "8-week bullish rule"). The 50-week cycle would now have to be labeled as an expanded 69-week cycle that bottomed on July 2, 2010, along with the first of three phases of the 4-year cycle. In retrospect, this primary cycle would be the first phase of the new 50-week cycle, and hence it was bullish - as is usually the case in the first primary cycle phase of a new 50-week cycle. The 10% probability was now confirmed: July 2 was the end of an expanded 50-week cycle that began March 6, 2009.

As we look back on that time of "unusual uncertainty," we can see that our studies still did very well from a short-term trading point of view. Aggressive traders suffered some minor losses right at the end. Prior to that, position traders and short-term traders did very well trading from the long side through the first six weeks, and from the short side for the next couple of weeks. Aggressive short-term traders also did well, even going long during the half-primary cycle trough period. It was after that in which the losses from probing the short side occurred.

Before we leave this example and proceed to the next section of the book (with a couple more examples of trading under more "normal" circumstances), let us take a final look at this primary cycle, for there were to be even more distortions to the normal primary cycle structure. Up until now, we had labeled the low of August 27 as an 8-week half-primary cycle. Therefore the week beginning September 20 would start the 4th week of the second 7-11 week half-primary cycle. A top was therefore due at any time, and September 21 was a three-star critical reversal date, and the DJIA was rising into it. We could now calculate an MCP upside price objective target for this primary cycle crest based on the prior half-primary cycle. By adding the high of the first half-primary cycle crest (10,720) to the low of the half-primary cycle trough (9936), and then subtracting from this sum the low that started the primary cycle on July 2 (9614). This gives us a price target of 11,042 +/- 169. It was also possible that this price could halt within 2% of the 10,720 high of August 9 for a double top. That would give an upside resistance up to 10,934 (just add 2% to the 10,720 prior high).

On September 21, the DJIA soared to a new cycle high of 10,833. This was into daily resistance (10,815-10,836), and the close was back between daily support and resistance, which was neutral with a bearish bias. The close was above the daily TIP for the 14th consecutive day (that was a very long time ago and way overdue for a correction or pause). An aggressive short-term trader could sell short once again with a stop-loss on a close above the 10,833 high. The market did start a decline here. The next day, September 22, it fell into daily support at 10,703-10,708 and held, and then closed at 10,736, which was neutral but now with a bullish bias. Support still wasn't breaking, and the close was above the daily TIP for a most unusual 15 consecutive days.

On September 23 it finally closed below daily support for a bearish close. It also closed below the daily TIP for the first time in 16 trading days, thereby downgrading its status to neutral. This was now a sell signal, following the new high for this primary cycle on the September 21 critical reversal date. Once again, that sell signal was negated the very next day as the DJIA turned around and closed at a new cycle high of 10,860, closing above the daily trend indicator point and both daily and weekly resistance. After the one-day interrupt, the market resumed its trend run up. But remember: after a one-day interrupt, the resumption of the trend run tends to end within the next 4 trading days, and this one did exactly that. The resumed trend run lasted until September 29, four trading days later (not shown).

As one reviews the primary cycle of that time (Figure 70), it will be seen that it was necessary to re-label the phases within it, based on the actual structure that took place. Instead of an 8-week half-primary cycle trough, the low of August 27 would be re-labeled as the first of three major cycle phases that lasted 5-8 weeks and not the usual 5-7 weeks. The primary cycle would end up lasting 22 weeks, which meant it was an expansion of the normal 13-21 week periodicity.

It is also noteworthy to mention that this market behavior was ultimately consistent with the geocosmic combination of Jupiter and Uranus moving into Aries, a combination that would be termed the "Asset Inflation Express." This meant that assets like precious metals and stocks would likely inflate as these two speculative planets moved into the speculative sign of Aries in late May, early June 2010. Although each would move temporarily back into Pisces, they would remain close to the Aries cusp, forming a conjunction to one another two more times (September 18, 2010 and January 4, 2011) before returning to Aries until Jupiter left for the next sign of Taurus in the first week of June 2011. Even after that, Jupiter would return to the cusp (border) of Aries and Taurus again in late 2011 through early 2012, close enough for the Asset Inflation Express to possibly maintain its bullish influence. As one can see from Figure 70, the DJIA price and moving averages stayed mostly in a trend run up until the primary cycle topped out.

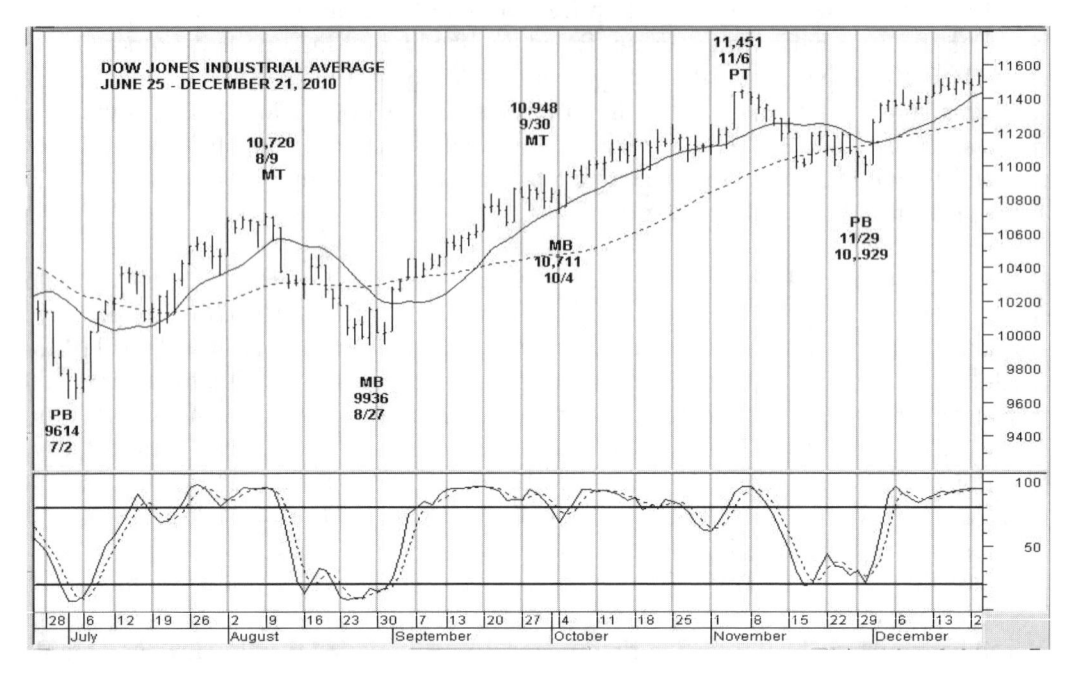

Figure 70: Daily chart of the DJIA showing the primary cycle of July 2, 2010 through November 29, 2010. Note that after September 20, the 14-day moving average (solid line) did not fall below the 42-day moving average (dotted line), and prices did not close below either, until the primary cycle crest was completed on November 6.

Now that the primary cycle had turned bullish and the 50-week cycle was re-labeled accordingly, the trading strategies for both position and short-term traders would change to bullish. That is, position traders would now look to buy all primary, half-primary, and major cycle troughs. The only time bearish strategies might be employed would be at the primary cycle crest, at least until the third phase of the 50-week cycle. Short-term traders would look to buy these same cycle lows, as well as all trading cycle troughs. However, they would be more willing to sell short on major cycle crests, especially in the last phase of a primary cycle. Aggressive traders would trade both sides of the market, especially after the first phase of each new primary cycle was completed. Yet in the first phase, even aggressive traders would employ mostly bullish strategies. As one would have experienced in the remainder of the July - November 2010 primary cycle, following the "breakout" to new highs of the primary cycle on September 20, bullish trading plans worked out very well. As this book is being written in the summer of 2011, position traders who subscribe to the MMA Cycles daily and weekly reports have remained long since the end of November 2010. Short-term traders have been in and out several times, but mostly from the long side for healthy profits. Aggressive short-term traders have traded many times from both sides, coincident with geocosmic critical reversal dates within time bands for trading cycle troughs or crests, as well as solar-lunar reversal periods suggesting a 1-4 day reversal of 4% or more, consistent with the status of daily stochastics, TIP points, and daily close indicators related to support and resistance.

CHAPTER TWENTY

CONSTRUCTING THE TRADING PLAN

We have now provided the formulas and rules for trading based on several market timing and technical indicators. Yet as demonstrated in the previous chapter, even with all of these tools, no one will ever be 100% correct in their analysis and profitability for each trade. It is very important to understand that each of these studies identifies probabilities, via "rates of frequency" based on the past, or the history of these markets correlated to the results of these studies. Our goal is to identify high probability setups and then to initiate the trade when a predominance of high probability setups arise. More importantly, exactly how and when do we initiate the trade? After all, once a market starts to rise or fall into a time and price target zone, the psychology seems to change. It is not easy to bring oneself up to the task of putting on a trade when the market is going in the opposite direction, as the trade setup dictates. Thus all that is left now is to impress upon the trader the importance of creating a trading plan based on one's particular temperament and then the discipline to follow it. In a very real sense, success in this field is dependent upon four factors:

1. Knowledge of what works with the greatest consistency
2. A trading plan based on that knowledge
3. The discipline to execute and stay with the trading plan until it is obvious that the market is not going according to plan any longer, and
4. The flexibility to exit and/or adjust the trading plan when the probabilities shift in the opposite direction. If it turns out the trading plan isn't going according to plan, you don't want to be wrong for long!

In this chapter we will outline trading plans for both the position trader as well as for short-term and even the aggressive short-term trader. The difference is this: the position trader looks to establish positions only in the direction of the primary trend, except perhaps at the primary cycle trough in a bear market or primary cycle crest in a bull market. A short-term trader is willing to go against the primary trend at the culmination of major and half-primary cycles if he thinks there is a reasonable possibility of a 4% or greater counter-trend reversal (retracement), according to the market timing studies of these books. The aggressive short-term trader is willing to go against the primary trend at any time if he thinks there is a reasonable possibility of a 4% or greater counter-trend reversal (retracement). In many cases, even a 2.5% reversal is attractive enough to encourage a trade. Such a possibility might show up due to the presence of a geocosmic critical reversal date, a solar-lunar reversal date, and/or a particular setup via technical studies.

The Trading Plan Begins with Trend Analysis

The very first question to ask in establishing a trading plan is whether the primary cycle is likely to be bullish or bearish. This depends upon which phase of the longer-term cycles are in force. The general rule espoused through each of these books is this: the first phase of every cycle (including a primary cycle) is bullish. The last phase is either bearish or contains the steepest decline within a bullish primary cycle.

Now what about the entirety of the primary cycle itself? Will it likely be a bullish right translation or bearish left translation cycle? You seldom know for certain. However, the understanding of "cycles within cycles" is a great aid to this task. And that brings us to market timing and understanding the structure of cycles, especially the primary cycle.

Fundamentally, the trading plan takes into account the following questions regarding the status of the primary cycle and considers the following factors:

1. Is the primary cycle likely to be bullish or bearish? If the primary cycle is the first phase of a greater 50-week cycle, it will likely be bullish. The crest will not be due until after Tuesday of the 9th week. If it is the last phase of a bearish 50-week cycle, the primary cycle will be bearish. It will usually top out before Tuesday of the 9th week and probably 2-5 weeks after the primary cycle trough that began the cycle.
2. As the primary cycle unfolds, the trading plan needs to identify which type of cycle is likely to be unfolding: a three-phase, two-phase, or combination pattern. In the first few weeks, one does not know the answer to that question, but there is an 80% probability that there will be a 5-7 week major cycle phase following the start of the primary cycle, for that is part of the three-phase and combination patterns, and each of those has an approximate 40% rate of occurrence. Thus the trader starts with the idea that the first phase will contain a major cycle trough at the 5-7 week interval. This assumption may be modified after the 7th week has passed.
3. The correct structure of the primary cycle pattern becomes known after the 11th week. By that time one can see if there is a clear 8-11 week half-primary cycle trough. If not, then one knows this will be a classic three-phase pattern. If there is a clearly identifiable half-primary cycle trough, then one knows this will be either a classical two-phase or combination pattern.
4. Based on the trend of the primary cycle, and the understanding of what type of pattern is unfolding within the primary cycle, one can determine the current status of the primary cycle at almost any time. One can then outline the steps to take within each phase of the bullish or bearish primary cycle.

Let us give a couple examples of how a trading plan begins for a position trader (this should also include short-term traders), based upon these two understandings:

1) Is the market bullish or bearish, and
2) What type of pattern is unfolding within the primary cycle?

If the primary cycle is expected to be bullish and...

1. It is to be a three-phase pattern. The trading plan of the position trader (and short-term trader) will be to buy every corrective decline until well into the third major cycle phase. That is, he attempts to buy every major and trading cycle low until at least two weeks into the third and final major cycle phase of the primary cycle. The only time his trading plan will attempt to sell short is when the market appears to be making a primary cycle crest (or double top) in that third phase, based upon other factors to be discussed shortly.
2. It is to be a two-phase pattern. The trading plan of the position trader (and short-term trader) will be to buy every corrective decline until well into the second half of the primary cycle phase. That is, he attempts to buy the half-primary cycle trough and every trading cycle low until after the DJIA (or whatever market) makes a new high for the primary cycle in the second half of that cycle. He may look for signs to go short after the highest price is being made in the second half of the primary cycle, in anticipation of a sharp 2-5 week decline into the primary cycle trough.
3. It is to be a combination pattern. The trading plan of the position trader (and short-term trader) will be to buy every corrective decline until well into the third major cycle phase. That is, he attempts to buy every half-primary, major, and trading cycle low until at least two weeks into the third and final major cycle phase of the primary cycle. The only time his trading plan will attempt to sell short is when the market appears to be making a primary cycle crest (or double top) in that third phase, based upon other factors to be discussed shortly. In that case, he looks for a sharp 2-5 week decline into the primary cycle trough.

If the primary cycle is expected to be bearish and...

1. It is to be a three-phase pattern. The trading plan of the position trader (and short-term trader) will be to sell every corrective rally until well into the end of the third major cycle phase, which is also when the primary cycle trough is due. That is, he attempts to sell every major and trading cycle crest until the time band for the end of the third and final major cycle phase of the primary cycle is entered. The only time his trading plan will attempt to buy is when the market is completing the primary cycle trough (or double bottom) in that third phase, based upon other factors to be discussed shortly.
2. It is to be a two-phase pattern. The trading plan of the position trader (and short-term trader) will be to sell every corrective rally until well into the second half of the primary cycle phase. That is, he attempts to sell the first half-primary cycle crest, the second half-primary cycle crest, and every trading cycle crest following that second half-primary crest until after the DJIA (or whatever market) makes a new low for the primary cycle in the second half of that cycle. Usually that second low is 7-11 weeks after the first half-primary cycle trough, and at least 2-5 weeks following the crest of the second half-primary cycle. He may look for signs to go long after the lowest price is being made in the second half of the primary cycle, and within a time band when the primary cycle trough is due, in anticipation of a sharp 2-5 week rally into the crest of the next primary cycle.

3. It is to be a combination pattern. The trading plan of the position trader (and short-term trader) will be to sell every corrective rally until the end of the third major cycle phase. That is, he attempts to sell every half-primary, major, and trading cycle crest until the time band for the third and final major cycle phase of the primary cycle is due to be completed. The only time his trading plan will attempt to buy is when the market appears to be making its primary cycle trough (or double bottom) at the end of that third phase, based upon other factors to be discussed shortly. When that happens, he looks for a sharp 2-5 week rally into the next primary cycle crest.

In summary, the first steps to constructing a trading plan is to anticipate whether the primary cycle is most likely to be bullish or bearish and then to ascertain which type of pattern is forming. You do not know these answers at first. However, you have a strong idea as to whether the primary cycle will be bullish or bearish depending on its phasing within the greater cycles, like the 50-week and 4-year cycles. You do not know which of the three basic chart patterns will be exhibited for any given primary cycle. However you do know the first phase will be bullish and that there is an 80% probability that a 5-7 week major cycle trough will occur. There should be very few problems encountered in these first 5-7 weeks of any primary cycle. After that, it may get unclear until after the 11th week of the primary cycle has passed. By that time, you should have an idea as to what type of pattern will be exhibited (three-phase, two-phase, or combination pattern), and from that you will know which type of trading strategy to employ.

Once we know the probable trend, and as we proceed through the primary cycle deciphering the pattern, we can then apply the next steps in constructing an effective trading plan. It starts with our market timing studies, for they are the leading indicators. And if the market is setting up for a high or low into these time bands, and we know what the trend and the pattern of the primary cycle is, we will know what type of trading plan to construct and therefore what action to take.

Market Timing

Where is the market in terms of its primary cycle? What phase is it in, and is this primary cycle bullish or bearish? These are the first questions each type of trader must ask when constructing a monthly, weekly, or daily trading plan. In reality, a weekly and daily trading plan is sufficient for traders. Monthlies would be more useful for investors.

The process of establishing the market's status in terms of its cycle is simple. You start from the longer-term cycles and work down to the trading cycles, always keeping in mind that the first phase of every cycle is bullish, and the last phase is either bearish or contains the steepest declines of the entire cycle if it has been bullish. The following represents the cycle labeling and phasing each trader is advised to monitor every week.

1. The four-year cycle. What phase of the 4-year cycle is the market in? When is the 4-year cycle next due to bottom? Which phase is likely to contain its crest?
2. The 23-month cycle if the 4-year cycle is to be a two-phase or a combination pattern (60% approximate probability), consisting of two 19-27 month phases.

3. The 15.5-month cycle if the 4-year cycle is to be a three-phase or combination pattern (80% approximate probability). Which 15.5-month cycle phase of the 4-year cycle is the market in? When is this phase due to bottom?
4. The 50-week cycle. There are usually four or five 50-week cycles within a 4-year cycle (77% historical rate of frequency). Sometimes there are only three 50-week cycle phases within the 4-year cycle (about 17% frequency). We will enter each 4-year cycle anticipating four or five 50-week cycles with a range of 34-67 weeks. Determine which 50-week cycle phase the 4-year cycle is currently in. When are its crest and trough due?
5. The 13-21 week primary cycle. There are usually two or three primary cycle phases within the 50-week cycle (over 90% historical frequency). Sometimes there are four primary cycles within the 50-week cycle (less than 10% frequency). We enter each 50-week cycle anticipating that there will be two or three primary cycle phases within it. Determine which primary cycle phase is currently in force within the 50-week cycle. Based on the 50-week cycle phasing, when is the crest of the primary cycle due,? When is its trough due?
6. The 8-11 week half primary cycle if the primary cycle is to be a two-phase or a combination pattern (60% approximate probability). Sometimes this cycle will contract to 7 weeks or expand to 12 weeks.
7. The 5-7 week major cycle if the primary cycle is to be a three-phase or combination pattern (80% approximate probability). Sometimes these can contract to 4 weeks or expand to 8 weeks. Which major cycle phase of the primary is the market in? What is the appropriate trading strategy for that major cycle? When is the crest of this major cycle due? When is its trough due?
8. The 2-4 week trading cycle. Within each major cycle are usually two or three of these 2-4 week trading cycles (usually only 2-3 weeks).

Every week these 8 steps in cycle analysis should be updated so that you know where you are within each cycle. Knowing where you are will help you to determine which trading strategy to employ, and that is essential to constructing a trading plan.

Geocosmic Critical Reversal Dates Refine the Market Timing

A market trend can be interrupted and reversed under certain geocosmic signatures, and even certain solar-lunar combinations, as detailed in Volumes 3 and 4. It is therefore important for traders to identify the following situations when constructing a trading plan for a given week or day:

1. Is there a geocosmic critical reversal date in effect? Outline its time band. This is done by identifying a cluster containing multiple geocosmic signatures, taking its midpoint, and allowing an orb of three trading days either side of that midpoint date as a potential market reversal zone.
2. Determine if there are any Level 1 signatures within 4 trading days of this geocosmic critical reversal date. If there are, the reversal is apt to be much sharper than otherwise.
3. Determine if this time band for a geocosmic critical reversal date overlaps with the time band in which a cycle crest or trough is due. Identify the boundaries (dates) of this overlap.

4. Identify any 1-2 day time bands in which a solar-lunar reversal is due in any given week. Does it coincide with a time frame for a cycle crest or trough?
5. If either a geocosmic critical reversal time band or a solar-lunar reversal time is in effect and overlaps with the time band for a cycle crest or trough, the trading plan should specify what action to take given certain technical setups that arise with a rally or decline into this reversal zone.

As one can readily see, the primary purpose of geocosmic and solar-lunar reversal periods is to help narrow down the time band when a cycle trough or crest is most likely to take place. Therefore, it is used as a tool within our understanding of cycle studies and not usually as a stand-alone indicator, except for more aggressive traders.

Establish Price Targets

Every month and every week, and even every day, in the case of short-term traders, price targets should be calculated for potential crests and troughs. When the market enters the time band for a reversal, traders need to determine if any price targets are being realized. If so, then the trading plan should indicate what action to take. The following represent some of the price targets that can indicate the opportunity to take action:

1. Normal "retracements" in a trending market. It doesn't matter what type of trader you are. If there is a trend underlying the primary cycle, all traders will want to trade 38.2-61.8% corrective retracements to any primary swing. If the primary cycle is bullish, then one must calculate 38.2-61.8% corrective declines to any swing up within the cycle. If the primary trend is bearish, then one must calculate 38.2-61.8% corrective rallies to any swing up within the cycle. There may be several of these, depending on which phase the primary cycle is in (the older the cycle, the more such price target zones will be present below or above the market).
2. Mid-Cycle Pause (MCP) price targets. This is used for trending markets to establish upside price targets in bull markets or downside price targets in bear markets.
3. Other Fibonacci price target zones, as explained in Chapter 6. These may involve 23.6% retracements, or 1.236 or 1.382 multiples of primary swings recently completed. They may also include taking .618 of a primary swing in the first two phases of a primary cycle, added to the low of the second major cycle trough in bullish primary cycle, or subtracted from the second major cycle crest in a bear market.
4. Measuring gap price targets. If there is a gap up, the trading plan should identify the upside price target of this breakout. Likewise, if there is a gap down, the trading plan should identify the downside price target of this downside breakout.
5. Head and shoulders price targets. The neckline identifies a support zone in a bull market. Your trading plan does not want to allow a long position when prices break below the neckline of a head and shoulders pattern. However, your trading plan needs to include the calculation for the downside price target in that event, for it may represent a point at which to buy if other bullish conditions are then in place.

6. Inverse head and shoulders price targets. The neckline identifies a resistance zone in a bear market. Your trading plan does not want to be in a short position when prices break above the neckline of an inverse head and shoulders pattern. However, your trading plan needs to calculate the upside price target in that event, for it may represent a point at which to sell short if other bearish conditions are then in place.
7. Moving averages may act as support or resistance. The most important moving averages to watch for in the DJIA are the 14-day, 42-day, and 25-week ones. If the market is declining into one of these moving averages when a cycle low is due, or rallying into one of these when a cycle crest is due, the trading plan needs to take this into account when considering what action is to be taken.

These are the first steps to enact in the creation of any trading plan, based on the methodology presented in these five volumes. That is, establish when the cycles are due to culminate, when reversals are most likely possible within the primary cycle, and the price targets that are in effect for the completion of any phase of the cycle. When these conditions are being realized, your trading plan should outline steps for taking action. These steps can be further refined with the aid of technical factors (to follow). However, keep in mind that the additional technical factors to be discussed next will often be in conflict with the timing and price objective studies just discussed. They will be lagging - or at best, coincident - indicators, and if given equal or greater weight as the parts of the trading plan involving our timing and price factors, you will miss several potentially profitable trading opportunities. This is why these books stress the greater importance on market timing studies - with price objective studies - above all other forms of technical analysis.

The Technical Setup for the Trading Plan

Once the optimal time frame and price target for a market reversal has been identified in the trading plan, the market must either rally or decline into this time band. In most cases, that means the market will be recording either a new two-week high or low and usually longer than that. If not a new two-week high or low, then the market should at least re-test the high or low of the past two weeks (i.e. double top, double bottom, perhaps with intermarket bearish or bullish divergence to another related market).

Whether the reversal will be strong or modest will depend to a large extent upon various technical studies and chart patterns, such as the following:

1. The daily and weekly stochastic pattern. When the market is rallying into a time band for a cycle crest and geocosmic reversal period, it is best if the stochastics are in overbought territory (i.e. above 80%). In cases of severe bearish trends, the stochastics may only recover to the neutral 42-58% area. Your trading plan needs to identify such a scenario if it occurs. It is also important to note if the stochastics are forming a bearish double looping pattern above 75% (the higher the better) or if there is a case of bearish oscillator divergence emerging. These latter two conditions support the trading plan of going short.
2. When the market is declining into a time band for a cycle crest and geocosmic reversal period, it is best if the stochastics are in oversold territory, i.e., above

80%. In cases of strong bullish trends, the stochastics may only fall to the neutral 42-58% area. Your trading plan needs to identify if this is happening. It is also important to note if the stochastics are forming a bullish double looping pattern below 25% (the lower, the better) or if there is a case of bearish oscillator divergence emerging. These latter two conditions support the trading plan of going long.

3. When the market is rallying into a time band for a cycle crest and geocosmic reversal period, note if a case of intermarket bearish divergence is unfolding. For instance, is the DJIA, S&P, or NASDAQ Composite taking out the high of the past few weeks? but they are not all doing that at once? If not all are making new highs at this time, are they closing in the lower third of a day's range after the divergence signal has formed? If so, the trading plan should allow for a short position (at least for short-term traders, whereas position traders only do this in bearish primary cycles or at the end of bullish primary cycles).

4. When the market is declining into a time band for a cycle trough and geocosmic reversal period, note if a case of intermarket bullish divergence is unfolding. For instance, is the DJIA, S&P, or NASDAQ Composite taking out the low of the past few weeks, but they are not all doing that at once? If they are not all making new highs in this time frame, are they closing in the upper third of a day's range after the divergence signal has formed? If so, that validates the intermarket divergence signal, and the trading plan should allow for a long position (at least for short-term traders, whereas position traders only do this in bullish primary cycles or in the first phase of a bearish primary cycle).

5. There are many other technical tools one may use to complement the market timing studies used in this methodology. For example, one might use RSI (relative strength indicators), or a CCI (Commodity Channel Index), or any other oscillator in much the same manner as stochastics are used. That is, they can register overbought or oversold readings in these critical reversal periods, or they can exhibit oscillator divergence patterns as cycle lows or highs form. Other types of technical tools that can be used to support a change of trend during this time bands are volume studies, or candlestick patterns. If you have your favorite technical tools, this methodology does not require you to give them up. But use them when the market enters a time band for reversal, for they will enhance the probability of getting into the market at a favorable price and time as described herein.

Short-Term Trading Signals

Once the market enters the time band for a market reversal or cycle culmination, and once the minimal price objective has been attained for the move up or down, then the trading plan looks to utilize the short-term trading signals discussed in Chapters 14-19. Specifically, an effective trading plan will outline setups to buy based on declines relative to daily and/or weekly support zones and the closing prices that follow, or setups to sell based on rallies relative to daily and/or weekly resistance zones and the closing prices that follow. Here are some of the factors to consider in your trading plan, once the market enters a time band for a reversal or cycle culmination, but let us separate these trading plan rules based on buy versus sell signals.

Buy Signals

1. When the market is declining into a time band for a cycle low, look to buy on a daily or weekly bullish bias or bullish trigger. You could also look to buy daily or weekly support if it appears to be holding intraday, with a stop-loss on a close below it.
2. You may buy if prices decline into a bullish crossover zone, but don't close below there.
3. You may buy if the daily or weekly trend indicator point (TIP) is upgraded from trend run down to neutral.
4. If the market starts to break above daily resistance following a low in the time band for a reversal, you may buy on an intraday pullback into that resistance zone, with a stop-loss on a close back below it for that day.
5. If the market closes above daily resistance following a low in the reversal time band, then look to buy on a pullback the next day to the pivot point, with a stop-loss below the support zone for that day, or the low of the move.

Sell Signals

1. When the market is rallying into a time band for a cycle crest, look to sell on a daily or weekly bearish bias or bearish trigger. You could also look to sell daily or weekly resistance if it appears to be holding intraday, with a stop-loss on a close above that range.
2. You may sell if prices rally into a bearish crossover zone, but don't close above.
3. You may sell if the daily or weekly trend indicator point (TIP) is downgraded from trend run up to neutral.
4. If the market starts to break below daily support following a high in the time band for a reversal, you may sell on an intraday pullback into that support zone (which is now resistance), with a stop-loss on a close back above it for that day.
5. If the market closes below daily support following a high in the reversal time band, then look to sell on a modest rally the next day to the pivot point, with a stop-loss above the resistance zone for that day, or the high of the move.

Pyramiding

When the 14-day moving average is above the 42-day average, and prices are above both, the market is in a trend run up, via moving average studies. Position traders may adopt bullish "pyramiding" strategies until the market reaches the third week of the third phase of the primary cycle. This strategy will identify any 2-day or longer decline (i.e. the lowest price in at least two days) and then will buy at the point where the market makes a new cycle high. Keep in mind the market has been registering new highs for this bullish primary cycle right along, so it won't take much to make a new high. The stop-loss should be placed just below the most recent primary or major cycle trough, or even trading cycle trough. Once the market enters the time band and price objective range for a primary cycle crest, it is time to take profits or move one's stop-losses up substantially, i.e., "trailing stop."

When the 14-day moving average is below the 42-day average, and prices are below both, the market is in a trend run down, via moving average studies. Position traders may adopt bearish "pyramiding" strategies once the market passes the first major cycle phase. This strategy will identify any 2-day or longer rally (i.e. the highest price in at least two days) and then will sell at the point the market makes a new cycle low. Keep in mind that if the primary cycle is indeed bearish, it has probably been registering new lows for this bearish primary cycle by the time the second major cycle phase is well underway. The stop-loss should be placed just above the most recent primary or major cycle crest, or even trading cycle crest. Once the market enters the time band and price objective range for a primary cycle trough, it is time to take profits or move one's stop-losses down substantially, i.e., "trailing stop".

The objective of "pyramiding" is to increase profits by going in the direction of a strong underlying trend. The difficulty is in knowing when and where to exit, for once the trend run is over, a very sharp counter-trend move usually occurs. The general rule in bull market trend runs up is, "The higher they go, the harder they fall." But this is where market timing studies can be very valuable. One of course wishes to capture as much profit as possible from a pyramid strategy. However in many cases, big fortunes that were made on paper suddenly become small fortunes and even losses in one's trading account. That is why successful trading plans must also contain stop-loss points.

Stop-Losses

The last part of the trading plan is to establish stop-loss points at which it is no longer wise to remain with the position. For many traders, this is a very difficult step, because very few people like to be taken out of trade, especially for a loss, even if it is a small loss. Furthermore, the shorter-term your perspective as a trader, the more losses you are likely to encounter, and that can prove to be frustrating. Yet frustration is a more tolerable emotion to go through than the despair that comes from remaining on the wrong side of a losing trade for too long. For this reason, every trading plan should contain at least a mental stop-loss point - a level in which the trader simply says, "This is not working as expected, so, let us abandon the position and start with a new mental slate."

Once you have entered into a position, your stop-loss may be based on one of many factors, depending on your personal risk tolerance. Once again, let us separate these trading rules for our trading plan based on whether we have established a long or short position.

Buy Signals, or Getting Long

Our suggested stop-losses on long positions are based on the lowest level up to the highest level, or the greatest loss potential to the least loss potential. Always remember that the lower the potential loss, the more likely you are to get stopped out. Conversely, the deeper from the market that you set your stop-loss, the more likely you are to remain in the position before being stopped out, but the greater your loss will be if and when you are stopped out. It is yet another factor that illuminates every trader's dilemma: do I reduce my risk of loss by increasing my probability of being taken out? Or do I increase my probability of being right over the long haul, while increasing my potential loss if I am wrong? Effective stop-losses find the balance point between these two issues.

1. Position traders will want to initially establish their original stop-loss below the low of the primary cycle. Once the low of a primary cycle is taken out, you know the trend is bearish until it ends, so you do not want to remain long once that happens. The stop-loss may be raised upon the completion of the first major or half-primary cycle trough in a bullish primary cycle.
2. The next level up for a stop-loss may be on a close below a primary or three-point upward trendline. Once that trendline is broken, it usually signals that the primary cycle crest has been attained, and the trend will be down until the primary cycle ends.
3. The next level for a stop-loss on a long position may be based on a close below the 14- or 42-day moving average, or even the 25-week average if it is the start of a new 50-week cycle, whichever is lower.
4. Next would be on a close below a weekly bullish crossover zone, weekly TIP, or weekly support, whichever is lower.
5. Next, the stop-loss can be set on a close just below a daily bullish crossover zone, daily TIP, or daily support, whichever is lower.
6. Last but not least, you could move your stop-loss up, based on an intraday move below any of these points that is followed by a close back above.

Sell Signals, or Getting Short

Our suggested stop-losses on short positions are based on the highest level above the market to the lowest level, or the greatest loss potential to the least loss potential.

1. Position traders will want to initially establish their original stop-loss above the crest of the primary cycle (or highest price of the primary cycle so far, which is usually in the first phase of a bearish primary cycle or the last phase of a bullish one). If the primary cycle is a bearish one, the stop-loss may be lowered upon the completion of the second major or half-primary cycle crest, assuming it is lower than the first crest of these cycles.
2. The next level up for a stop-loss may be on a close below a primary or three-point downward trendline. Once that trendline is broken, it usually signals that the primary cycle trough has been attained, and the trend will be up until the next primary cycle tops out.
3. The next level for a stop-loss on a short position may be on a close above the 14- or 42-day moving average, or even the 25-week average if it is the end of an older 50-week cycle, whichever is higher.
4. Next would be on a close above a weekly bearish crossover zone, weekly TIP, or weekly resistance, whichever is higher.
5. Next, the stop-loss can be set on a close just above a daily bearish crossover zone, daily TIP, or daily resistance, whichever is higher.
6. Last but not least, you could move your stop-loss down, based on an intraday move above any of these points, and followed by a close back below.

These are the considerations taken into account in the formulation of a trading plan. The actual rules for buying and selling, i.e., the trading plan, depends upon what type of trader one is (position or short-term), whether the primary cycle is expected to be bullish or bearish, and what phase of the primary cycle the market is in at any given point. The rules for the position trader were given in the first section of this chapter titled "The Trading Plan Begins with Trend Analysis."

Yet the first step is the same for each type of trader at the beginning of each primary cycle. That is, whether one is a position or short-term trader, the trading plan incorporates a bullish buying strategy at the start of every primary cycle. This was demonstrated in great detail in the prior chapter. The first phase is almost always bullish, and one looks only to buy between the primary cycle trough and the crest of the first major cycle phase. Whenever the market makes a 38.2-61.8% corrective decline in the first phase following the primary cycle trough, one is looking to buy. One may also look to buy if the market is making a double bottom to the primary cycle trough in that first phase, as long as prices do not fall below the start of the primary cycle *in all other related markets*. That is, cases of intermarket bullish divergence are allowable in the first phase of a primary cycle and may be bought by both short-term and position traders. However, after this point, the strategies between position and short-term traders part ways.

After the first phase is completed, the trading plan may differ for each type of trader as well.

Position Trader

In bullish primary cycles, position traders will create bullish trading plans until at least the second week of the third major cycle phase or well into the second phase in a two-phase primary cycle pattern. That is, the trading plan attempts to buy every half-primary, major, and/or trading cycle low until new cycle highs are realized in the last phase of the primary cycle. It is acceptable to look for shorting opportunities if a market is making a double top at the crest of the third phase of a primary cycle. Then, and only then, does the trading plan consider going short in anticipation of a sharp 2-5 week decline into the primary cycle trough, according to instructions and considerations given earlier in this chapter.

In bearish primary cycles, the position trader is still looking for opportunities to buy during the first 2-5 weeks of a new primary cycle; that is when the crest of the primary cycle is due. Once the market is in that time band for a primary cycle crest (2-5 weeks into a new primary cycle), the position trader switches from a bullish to a bearish trading plan. The intent now is to sell short the crest of that first major cycle, which is likely the crest of the entire primary cycle. From that point onwards, he will look to sell every corrective rally that retraces 38.2-61.8% of any swing down. He will look to sell every half-primary, major, or trading cycle crest until the market enters the time band for a primary cycle trough and after prices have made new lows for the primary cycle. At that point, and only at that point, will the trading plan switch to bullish strategies, seeking to buy the primary cycle trough in anticipation of a sharp 2-5 week rally to the crest of the new primary cycle. Then the process repeats.

Short-Term Trader

The short-term trader is primarily focused on buying any corrective retracements of the primary cycle trend. However, he will also consider going against the trend at major or half-primary cycle troughs or crests if it appears there is a reasonable chance of a 4% or greater reversal then.

For instance, let us say the market has rallied sharply for three weeks after a primary bottom. Maybe it has soared 10% very quickly. But after three weeks, this market is already in a price target for a primary cycle crest, the daily stochastics are in overbought territory, i.e., say about 90%, and there is a three-star critical reversal date in effect. Furthermore, the market cannot close above weekly resistance, and daily resistance starts to hold as well during this time band. When so many signals are present for a correction, the short-term trader may elect to take profits from the long side and sell short, looking for a 4% or greater pullback (say 38.2-61.8% retracement) of the whole move up from the primary cycle low, even if the primary cycle is expected to be bullish. When going against the primary trend, the trading plan should be very specific as to when to sell short, what stop-loss to put in above the market to keep the risk exposure tolerable, and then the price target zone, i.e., profit objective, in which to cover and reverse back to the long side. Obviously, there is more danger of loss when trading against the trend. But short-term traders - and especially aggressive short-term traders - seem to like a little danger. Perhaps it is because they know that the quickest profits are realized from being on the right side of a counter-trend move. The market moves sharply and quickly in these cases, But this type of activity is not for everyone, for it is difficult to be right on both the entry and exit position when going counter-trend in the middle of a primary cycle.

The short-term trader must be very nimble when going against the underlying trend, such as shorting in bull market primary cycle. He must adhere to a strict stop-loss policy in case the market starts running back up, as well as being very disciplined to cover those shorts and take a profit - and reverse to the long side - when the time and price targets for the decline are met. As an example, the stop-loss should be above the price target range for the major cycle crest when trying to short a major cycle crest. Once the market appears to be falling, that stop-loss should be adjusted to slightly above the high of the move so far, because once the market starts to take out the low of a prior day, then any move to a new cycle high can be construed as a breakout and a reason to get long again or even start to pyramid from the long side if one never got short. This is especially true if prices are above the 14- and 42- day moving averages, and the 14- is above the 42-day (trend run up based on moving average studies). But of course he may not be stopped out. The trade may go quickly in his favor if all the other conditions described work out as expected. Once the market starts falling into the price target of a corrective decline, the short-term trader can follow all the instructions given for covering those shorts, and then buying, as outlined in the case of the position trader.

Aggressive Short-Term Trader

It does not matter which type of primary cycle pattern is in force here, because aggressive short-term traders will trade in both directions depending on the market timing indicators in effect, as well as certain technical conditions that imply a possible 4%

reversal. For example, even if it is a bullish primary cycle, an aggressive trader may look to sell short at any phase within a primary cycle if a geocosmic critical reversal date is in effect, and prices are rising into it. He will be more inclined to sell short if this rally:

1) enters into a price objective zone for a crest
2) exhibits intermarket bearish divergence to related markets
3) exhibits a bearish stochastic pattern, or
4) exhibits certain types of bearish signals on a weekly or daily TIP or in relationship to the weekly or daily support-resistance zones.

It is best, of course, if several of these signals are present.

Aggressive short-term traders tend to be in the market less than 5 days. In many cases, they are day traders not wishing to take the risk of carrying a position overnight and coming in the next day to find that the market opened sharply against their position. For that reason, the aggressive short-term trader is advised to use intraday technical studies (like stochastics or other oscillators) to help pick the low or high of the day from which to trade. Even so, an awareness of the underlying primary cycle trend, and the phase of the primary cycle currently in effect, plus the level of various technical studies on a daily chart, can help position the aggressive short-term trader in the right direction.

Let us now look at an example of how to construct a trading plan for buying a primary cycle trough. For this example, we will go back to the primary cycle that started on July 2, 2010, the one we covered in great detail in the last chapter up until the 8-week low on August 27, 2010. At the time, we labeled that a half-primary cycle trough. But now we will show why it was later re-labeled as an 8-week major cycle trough.

Figure 71 is a classical three-phase bullish primary cycle, even though the first major cycle trough of August 27 lasted 8 weeks, as did the last major cycle phase that bottomed November 29. Each was one week longer than the normal 5-7 week interval between major cycle troughs. In retrospect, we can see that this was a 22-week expanded primary cycle, which means it was a distorted primary cycle since the norm is 13-21 weeks. In this case, 22 weeks means that the primary cycle was expanded by one week.

How do we know this is the correct labeling for this primary cycle? It is due to the fact that there was no criterion met for a primary cycle trough before November 29. There were no 2-5 week declines. There were no tests of the 42-day moving average before then. There was no oversold stochastics or bullish stochastics patterns before then. And once November 29 was determined to fulfill those criteria for a primary cycle trough, it was simply a matter of going back and identifying the pattern type. It couldn't be a two-phase pattern with August 27 as a half-primary cycle trough because the second half bottom on November 29 would have been 14 weeks later, which was too long. Assigning the low of October 4 as the second major cycle phase works well because 1) it was six weeks after August 27 and therefore in the "normal" time band for a 5-7 week major cycle trough, and 2) it was the only time in the 5-7 week interval in which prices touched the 14-day moving average, which is the minimum criteria for a major cycle trough. It was also near the midpoint of two Level One geocosmic signatures: Venus conjunct Mars on October 3 and Venus retrograde on October 8.

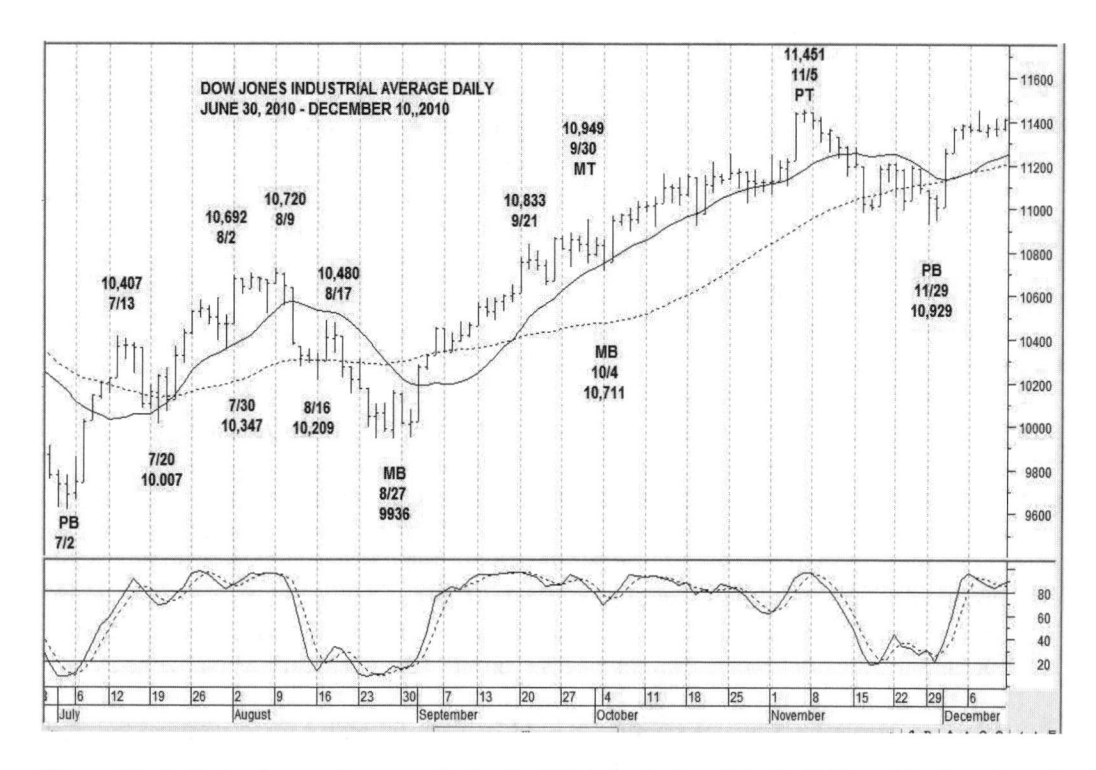

Figure 71: A three-phase primary cycle in the DJIA beginning July 2, 2010 and lasting through November 29, 2010.

This distorted primary cycle was an excellent example of the type of market in which a position trader can apply a "pyramiding" buying strategy, or trading plan. That is, after the market made a new high for the primary cycle on September 20, well past Tuesday of the 9th week, the 14-day moving average moved above the 42-day moving average, and the price was above each. This is the type of market environment where one can buy every new high *after* the market first declines for at least two days. This is also considered "breakout buying" and is usually a profitable trading strategy until the market enters the last phase of the primary cycle and starts to exhibit bearish signals. One's stop-loss can be placed just below the last isolated low or on a close below the 14-day moving average, depending on one's risk allowance.

The trading plan of the position trader would be to buy any corrective decline prior to the crest of the third major cycle phase. Also in this particular case, the trading plan would be to buy any new high after a 2-day or greater decline ("pyramiding up"). Once the market enters its third phase and is making new highs, the position (and short-term) trader may look for signs to take profits on all longs, and even to sell short, as a rather steep 2-5 week decline would be expected into the primary cycle trough.

In this example, we would expect the primary cycle crest to ideally unfold 2-5 weeks into the third major cycle phase. As you can see in Figure 71, that indeed happened. The primary cycle crest was on November 5 as the DJIA reached 11,451, which was four weeks after the major cycle trough of October 4. This high was within the range of a 1.382 multiple of the first leg up from the low of July 2 (9614) to the crest of the first major cycle at 10,720 on August 9, added to the 9936 low of August 27. Or, (10,720-9614) = 1106, and then 1106 x 1.382 = 1528. If one adds 1528 to the 9936 low of August 27, the result is 11,464. The high of the primary cycle was 11,451, which is very close to this upside price target and within the range for such a top (11,464 +/- 218).

The sell signal would not have been apparent on the high of Friday, November 5. It would be more apparent the next week when the nearby S&P futures made a new cycle high on November 9, but the DJIA did not, thus exhibiting a case of intermarket bearish divergence. There was also a bearish looping stochastic pattern in both markets at the time. On November 9, the daily TIP was downgraded from trend run up to neutral, and the daily close was below daily support (bearish). By the end of that week, the DJIA would also close below weekly support and a bullish crossover zone, strongly suggesting the primary top occurred November 5 in the DJIA and November 9 in the nearby S&P futures. However, this was a case where there was no compelling support from geocosmic studies to expect a crest. The only geocosmic signature in effect was Neptune turning direct on November 5. The more important geocosmic signatures were coming up after November 15, and they would fit the time band for a primary cycle trough. Thus it is doubtful if the position trader would have gone short as the primary cycle topped out November 5-9. It is more likely he would have taken profits, allowed the market to stop him out, and then waited for a 2-5 week decline into the next critical reversal zone to buy.

Now let us see how that buy signal would have unfolded. All types of traders will look for signs to get long on any primary cycle trough, and this particular primary cycle provides a good illustration on how to do that (as do most primary cycles). First of all, we know a primary cycle trough would be expected to occur 2-5 weeks after the primary cycle crest of November 5. In other words, it would be due November 15 - December 10. Ideally it would also be 5-7 weeks after the last major cycle trough, which occurred on October 4. This would yield a time band of November 9-26. The ideal overlap for this primary cycle trough would therefore be November 15-26. We begin our market timing studies by identifying geocosmic reversal signatures that were present November 15-26. The following represents the list of geocosmic signatures that was in effect at the time.

Date	Signature	Aspect Degree	Value	Level
Nov 15	☉△♃	240	8.94	3
Nov 18	☉□♆	270	9.30	1
Nov 18	♀SD		9.50	1
Nov 18	♃SD		9.29	2
Nov 19	☉△♅	240	9.42	1
Nov 29	♂□♃	270	9.29	1
Dec 3	♂□♅	270	9.59	1
Dec 5	♅SD		9.54	1

The most heavily populated time band of geocosmic signatures extended from November 15 through November 19. So the geocosmic critical reversal date would be November 17, +/- 3 trading days, which fell right in the cycle time band for a primary trough that was projected for November 15-26. All traders, therefore, would be looking for signs of a primary bottom November 12 - November 22 (three trading days each side

274

of November 17). Based on the idea that the low would unfold 2-5 weeks after the primary cycle crest, we can narrow this down to the week of November 15-22.

Let us now go through our list of indicators to watch during this period in an effort to determine when to buy, regardless of whether one is a position trader, short-term trader, or even aggressive shorter trader.

We have just established the time band for this primary cycle trough, so now we look at price targets. A normal 38.2-61.8% corrective decline of the entire primary cycle would yield a price objective of (11,451 + 9614) ÷ 2 = 10,532.50 +/- 217, or **10,315-10,749**. We could also do the same calculations based on the move up from the 8-week low of 9936 on August 27, since there were no impressive corrections after that. This would be (11,451 + 9936) ÷ 2 = 10,693.50 +/- 179, or **10,514-10,872**. Both of these overlap the low of the previous major cycle trough on October 4 at 10,711. The overlap would be **10,514-10,749**. This would be our ideal target for a primary bottom.

However, we know we don't always get the ideal. The minimum criteria for this cycle low would be a test or penetration below the 42-day moving average, assuming it is above the corrective price range for a low. Going into the week of November 15, that moving average was 11,043 and moving up about 10 points per day. If the DJIA touched that line (or fell below) and was followed by a change in status on the daily or weekly TIP, or some other powerful bullish signal, one could buy with a reasonable stop-loss below the market. At the same time, we would check to see if there was a case of intermarket bullish divergence to any market, or a case of bullish oscillator divergence, or a bullish looping stochastic pattern below 20%.

So let us see how the weekly and daily numbers looked going into the weeks of November 15 and November 22, as well as how the chart patterns were developing. Those numbers are shown in the table on the next page. Entering the week of November 15, the 20th week of the primary cycle and the 2nd week following the primary cycle crest, the DJIA was still trading above the 42-day moving average, and well above our price targets for a primary bottom. The market had closed above the weekly TIP for the 11th consecutive week, so it was in a trend run up. But that weekly close of November 12 was 11,192, which was below a weekly bullish crossover zone at 11,231-11,249 (not shown in the table), which was bearish. The market was in the process of falling to a primary cycle trough, just as we would have expected. However a primary cycle trough time band was in effect, and ideally that primary cycle trough would form this week beginning November 15, or the following week. Our task was to find a point to buy, somewhere below 11,043 (the 42-day moving average) and ideally down to 10,514-10,749 - an overlap of two price target zones. We would like to see a case of bullish intermarket divergence to the S&P or NASDAQ cash or nearby futures contract as this low forms, or a case of bullish stochastic divergence or a bullish looping pattern below 20% in the stochastic oscillator. We would also like to see weekly or daily support tested or broken, with a close back above that level, accompanied by a change in the status of the daily or weekly TIP. The chance of seeing all of these signals occur was remote, but possible. The probability of seeing several of these signals unfold was great and as traders, we have to decide if there are enough of these "high probability" signals to get long.

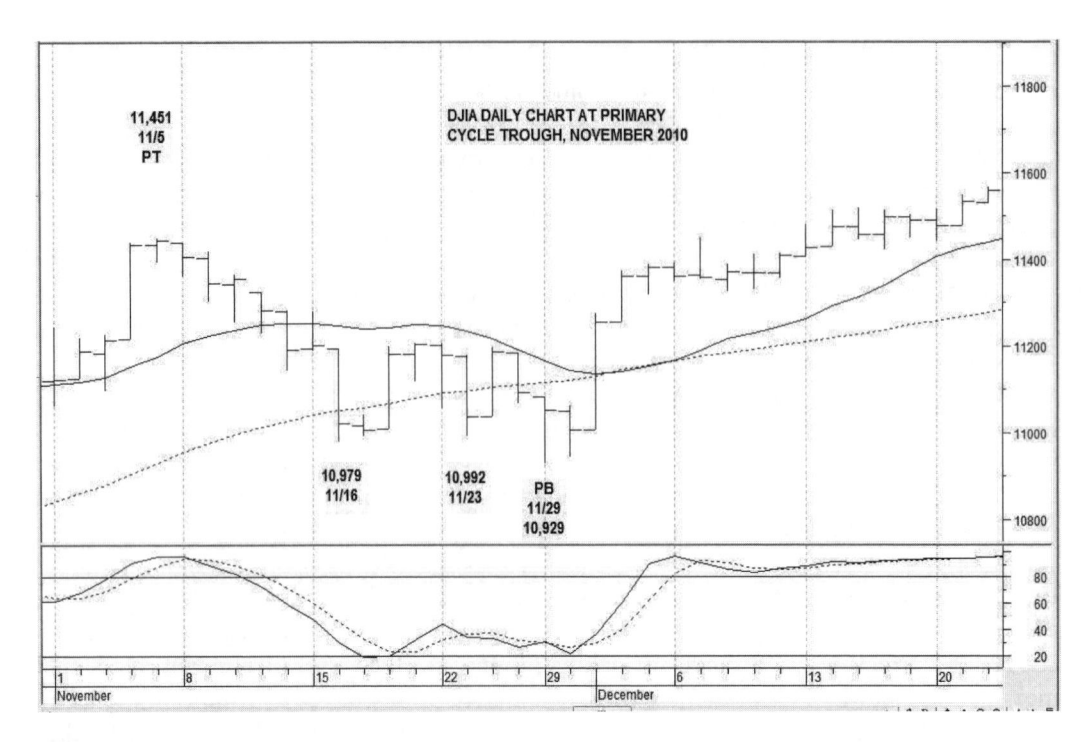

Figure 72: DJIA daily chart surrounding the primary cycle trough of November 29, 2010.

Day	H	L	C	PP	TIP	S₁	S₂	R₁	R₂
				11258	**11235**	**11044**	**11077**	**11340**	**11373**
Nov 15	11281	11189	11202	11206	11271-D	11127	11129	11267	11209
Nov 16	11194	10979	11023	11224	11237-D	11156	11167	11248	11259
Nov 17	11047	10991	11008	11065	11165-D	10915	10936	11131	11152
Nov 18	11199	11010	11181	11013	11101-N	10982	10985	11033	11036
Nov 19	11206	11119	11203	11130	11070-N	11086	11061	11276	11250
				11154	**11294**	**11052**	**11078**	**11354**	**11330**
Nov 22	11206	11054	11178	11176	11106-N*	11160	11146	11247	11233
Nov 23	11180	10992	11036	11146	11151-N	11103	11087	11254	11238
Nov 24	11196	11037	11187	11069	11130-N	10942	10959	11130	11147
Nov 26	11183	11067	11092	11140	11118-N	11108	11084	11266	11243
				11096	**11170**	**10985**	**10987**	**11199**	**11201**
Nov 29	11084	10929	11052	11114	11108-N	11033	11045	11150	11161
Nov 30	11062	10943	11006	11021	11092-D	10975	10960	11129	11114
Dec 1	11276	11067	11256	11004	11046-N	10946	10945	11066	11065
Dec 2	11373	11255	11362	11179	11068-N	11121	11083	11390	11352
Dec 3	11389	11319	11382	11330	11170-U	11303	11287	11421	11406

The trading plan for this week, might read like this: *"A primary cycle low is due, ideally November 15-22. Look for a break below the 42-day day moving average at 11,043. Weekly support is there at 11,044-11,073. If prices fall below weekly support and then close back above, get long with a stop-loss below 10,500 or on a close below weekly support Also look for a day in which the daily TIP is upgraded from trend run down to neutral as a signal to go long if prices are below 11,043."*

Heading into November 15, the market had closed below the daily TIP for 4 consecutive days, so it was in a trend run down. On Monday, November 15, the market traded above resistance, but closed back below, which was a bearish trigger. It closed below the daily TIP for the 5th consecutive day, so it remained in a trend run down. The low of the day was 11,189, so it was still above the 42-day moving average. This was not the day to buy. It appeared to have further down to go.

On Tuesday, November 16, the DJIA finally broke below the 42-day moving average, so the minimum criterion was now being met for a primary cycle trough. The low of the day was 10,979, and the close was 11,023, which was below daily and weekly support and the daily TIP. The close was bearish and the trend run down continued. The daily stochastics were falling, but still not to the oversold 20% mark. Still no buy signal.

The next day was the three-star critical reversal date, November 17. The market traded between daily support and resistance, which is neutral. The close was below the daily TIP for the 7th consecutive day, so still no convincing buy signal. Yet we are well aware of the fact that the minimum price criterion has been met and this is a critical reversal zone, and the low so far has been 10,979 on Tuesday, November 16.

On Thursday, November 18, the market closed above daily resistance, which was the first sign that the bottom may have been in. Resistance was beginning to break. The close was also above the daily tip, so it was upgraded from trend run down to neutral. The close was also back above the 42-day moving average. It was also back above the weekly support zone, setting up the possibility of a weekly bullish trigger. A position trader could now go long with a stop-loss based on a close below the low of the move so far, which was 10,979, or even 10,500 if he wanted more room in case the market still had another sell-off ahead. If one did not buy on the bullish close, he could also look to buy on a pullback to the pivot point for the next day (11,130), for there was a two-thirds probability prices would cross the pivot point on any given day.

The next day was Friday, November 19, the end of the week. Sure enough, the market dropped back below the daily pivot point (11,130), where one could buy with a stop-loss on a close below the low of Tuesday at 10,979. The low of the day was 11,119, which was above daily support. The high of the day was 11,206, which was below daily resistance, so the close was neutral. But the close was above the daily TIP for the second consecutive day, which is neutral, while at the same time it was above weekly support, which means the weekly close was a bullish trigger. Yet the weekly close was below the weekly TIP for the first time in 12 weeks, which meant it was downgraded to neutral. The daily stochastics started to turn up from below 20%, with K crossing back above D. They ended the week with K at 32.15% and above D at 23.27%. This was encouraging, but no confirmation that the primary bottom had been completed. It would have been better (for the bullish case) if they had formed a bullish looping pattern or a bullish oscillator divergence. It would have been more bullish if there had been intermarket bullish divergence to one of the other indices at the previous week's low. But there wasn't. Each made new lows on November 16 following their primary cycle crests of two weeks earlier. What was needed to support the bullish case was two consecutive daily closes back above the 14-day moving average. It was still below that level, which started the week at 11,249. In fact, it was in between the 14- and 42-day average. It needed to close above both to resume the bullish trend and confirm the primary cycle trough was in.

The DJIA entered the week starting November 22, the 21st week of the primary cycle and the last week in which a "normal" primary cycle would be due. Both position and short-term traders would be long given our trading plan: in the case of position traders, with a stop-loss below 10,500 or 10,979 on a closing basis (depending on one's risk allowance), but in the case of short-term traders, only below 10,979. Each would know that a primary cycle low could have occurred November 16, just one day before the November 17 critical reversal date, or that it was still unfolding. There was no confirmation yet that the primary bottom had been completed.

On Monday, November 22, the market fell below daily support but closed back above it, which was a bullish trigger. It closed above the daily TIP for the third consecutive day, but it was a down day, so it was not a confirmed trend run up. It remained neutral (N*). But it would be interesting to note that the low of the day was 11,054, which was into weekly support. In other words, weekly support held, which was a positive sign.

The next day, November 23, the DJIA dropped back below 11,000, to a low of 10,992, a re-test of the prior week's low at 10,979. That was also into daily support, which held, and was thus a neutral close but with a bullish bias. But there were new concerns now. The close was below weekly support, and it was below the 42-day moving average. The close was below the daily TIP for the first time in 4 days, which meant it remained neutral. The daily stochastics however were falling again, and K went below D, the start of a bullish looping formation. What did this suggest? It suggested that prices could make a new low. And this time there would be a case of a bullish looping pattern in stochastics, and maybe even intermarket bullish divergence to another index, or a case of bullish oscillator divergence (new low in price, but not a new low in the stochastics).

Wednesday, November 24, witnessed prices closing above daily resistance, which was bullish. The close was back above the daily TIP after being below it the prior day, so it remained neutral. After Thursday's holiday, the market resumed trading on Friday, November 26. This was not such a good day for the DJIA, as it closed in daily support, which was mostly bearish. It was back below the daily TIP, which meant it was stalled in neutral. However the close was above weekly support and the low of the week was below that support zone, which meant the weekly closed on a bullish trigger. There was still hope for those long positions established on November 18 or 19, with a stop-loss on a close below 10,979 or 10,500. Entering the new week, our position would still be long (both position and short-term traders), with a stop-loss below 10,500 or on a close under the low of the move so far (10,979), or on a weekly close below next week's support (10,985-10,987), depending on your risk allowance. For the short-term trader, it would be on a close below 10,979 or weekly support.

On Monday, November 29, the DJIA dropped to a new low, 10,929, taking out the prior low of 10,979 and both daily and weekly support of 11,033-11,045 and 10.985-10,987 respectively. Yet it did not close below that prior low or daily support. It closed at 11,052 for a bullish trigger. In addition, neither the NASDAQ nor S&P futures made a new low, and all closed in the upper third of the day's range, for an intermarket bullish divergence signal. Since they made their primary bottoms on November 16, one day before the geocosmic three-star critical reversal date, and the DJIA made a lower low two weeks later, this was an excellent buy signal. Both position and short-term traders could remain long (or get long, if not already long), but it would be wise to lower the stop-loss on a close below the new low (10,929) or at a point when the S&P and NASDAQ futures also made a new cycle low and thereby negated the bullish intermarket divergence signal.

The next day, November 30, the DJIA once again fell below daily support (but not the 10,929 low of Monday), for another bullish trigger. But the close was below the daily TIP point for the third consecutive day, and it was a down day, which meant its status was downgraded to a trend run down. We now had mixed signals.

The next day, December 1, would resolve the dilemma. The market soared higher, up 250 points to close at 11,256, well above daily and weekly resistance, which was bullish and well above both the weekly and daily TIP. The daily TIP was thus upgraded right back to neutral. There were many other bullish signals that emerged that day. The stochastics turned back up after forming a bullish double looping and bullish oscillator pattern, with K rising back above D, both above 25% and K widening its distance above D. The close was above both the 14- and 42-day moving averages, confirming the probability of an expanded 22-week primary cycle now completed. The 14-day average never moved enough below the 42-day moving average to suggest the trend run up via moving averages was ever really over. That meant we could expect new highs, and traders could resume a pyramiding buying strategy very early in the new primary cycle. That is, every time the market made a new cycle high (above the 11,452 high of November 5), one could add onto long positions, especially after a two-day or greater decline. A very bizarre and distorted primary cycle had come to an end. The "Asset Inflation Express" was now back on track and would remain in effect until May 2011. Despite the difficulties encountered in labeling this primary cycle correctly from July through early September 2010, it eventually gave its bullish signal and settled into a fabulous bull market in which traders could make substantial gains following the trading plans outlined in this chapter. They are based upon the market timing and technical studies presented in these five volumes. This primary cycle ended, and the new one began, in a classical formation of buy signals generated November 18 through December 1. Both position and short-term traders would have been long from the close of November 18 (11,181) or the pivot point of November 19 (11,130) and were never stopped out via the stop-loss points that would have been enacted according to the trading plan outlined in this chapter. This is how it should be and how it usually is, when primary cycle troughs form in the stock market. It is as good as it gets.

Short-Term Aggressive Trading

The one area yet to be covered in detail is that of aggressive short-term trading. By that, I am referring to trades that are entered into with the idea of exiting within 1-5 days afterwards. Often they turn out to be day trades (in and out the same day).

Like position and short-term traders, the aggressive trader will use many of the tools provided up until this point. The major difference will be the importance placed upon solar-lunar reversal dates and intraday oscillators like stochastics and various chart patterns that might form during any particular day - especially a solar-lunar reversal day.

In terms of timing, short-term aggressive traders will look for a particular setup to unfold when entering a geocosmic critical reversal zone or solar-lunar reversal date. To be a valid setup, the market must form an isolated low or high during these time bands. An aggressive trader has to anticipate that this will happen the day before the setup is fully completed. If he waits until the day the setup is completed, he will have missed the greater part of the trade and hence lost out on potential profits.

So let us back up a moment and review the setup as explained in Volumes 3 and 4 of this Stock Market Timing series. Once a critical reversal date has been determined, we look for an isolated high or low to occur within 7 trading days, i.e. from a time band that starts three trading days before the critical reversal date through three trading days afterwards. In the case of solar-lunar reversal dates, the time band is narrowed to only 1-3 days (usually two days). That is because each solar-lunar reversal combination only lasts about 60 hours (2-½ days). That is how long it takes for the Moon to travel through each zodiac sign. When it changes signs, so does the solar-lunar combination.

An isolated high is formed when the market takes out the high of the previous day, and then that high is not taken out the next day. It is the highest price between two days of lower highs. It is a day whose high is higher than the day before and the day after. All cycle crests are isolated highs, but not all isolated highs are cycle crests - at least not of the type that we have defined as trading, major, half-primary, and primary cycle crests. They may be crests of much smaller cycles that are measured in terms of hours instead of days.

An isolated low is just the opposite. It is a lower price than the low of the day before and the day after. The low of the day before is higher than the low of this day, and the low of the day after is also higher, so it stands out as an "isolated low" day. All cycles troughs are isolated lows, but not all isolated lows are cycle troughs - at least not of the type that we have defined as trading, major, half-primary, and primary cycle troughs. They may be troughs of much smaller cycles that are measured in terms of intraday moves instead of days.

Figure 73 (on the next page) identifies examples of isolated lows and highs in the German DAX index for June 2011. Isolated high and low days are not that uncommon. They are not all that important, except when they happen during a time band for a cycle reversal, geocosmic critical reversal zone, or solar-lunar reversal period.

As one can see from the graph in Figure 73, there were 10 instances of isolated highs and lows in the 20 trading days between June 2 and June 29. They occur rather often. But they are important as a trading setup when a solar-lunar reversal date is in effect, especially if they represent the end of 2.5% or greater move (ideally 4% or more) from a recent low or high. For that matter, they are important when a geocosmic critical reversal zone is in effect too.

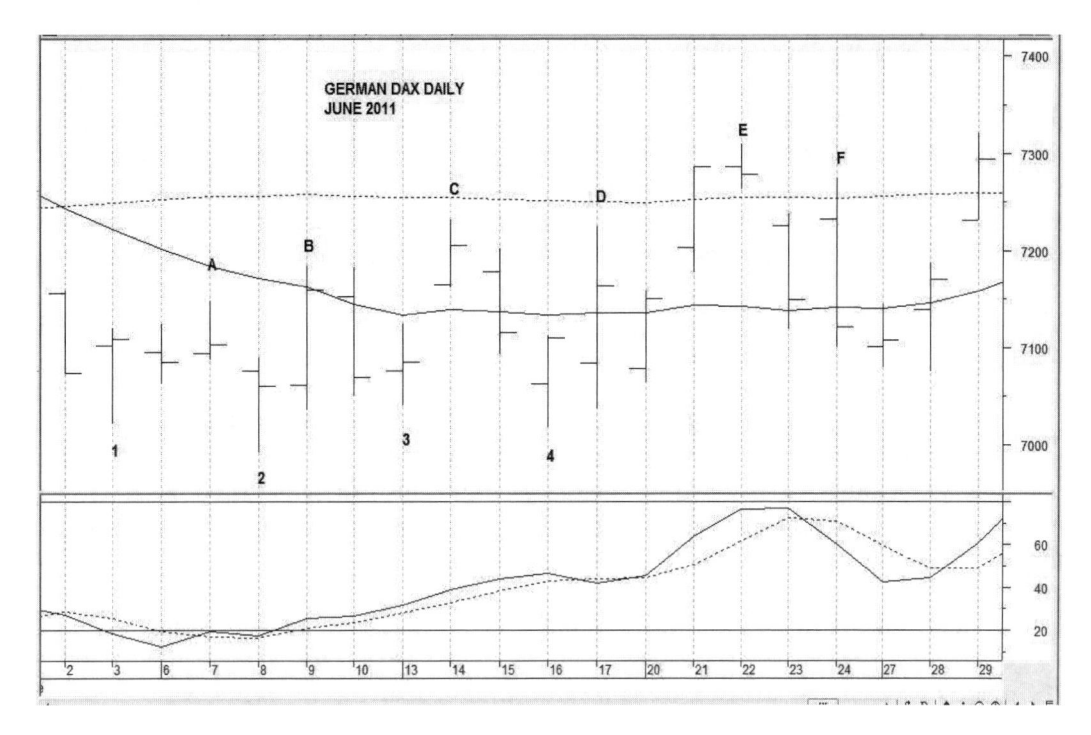

Figure 73: Daily Chart of German DAX Index for June 2011, depicting instances of isolated lows (1-4) and isolated highs (A-F).

The trading plan for the aggressive short-term trader during a solar-lunar reversal period of 1-3 days is simple. As soon as the market enters the solar-lunar reversal day(s), one looks for prices to exceed the previous day's high or low. If it takes out the low first, then the aggressive trader prepares to implement a trading plan to buy. If it takes out the high of the prior day, then he prepares to implement a selling (shorting) trading plan. It can do this on the first or second day of the solar-lunar reversal period, even the third day if there is a third day in which the Moon remains in that reversal sign. If the market takes out the low of a prior day during this solar-reversal zone, it is best if the lows that are unfolding are at least 2.5% below the most recent trading cycle crest (which may also be the major, half-primary, or primary cycle crest). If it takes out the high of the prior day first during this solar-lunar reversal zone, then it is best if this high is at least 2.5% above the most recent trading cycle trough (which may also be the major, half-primary, or primary cycle trough). This is the start of the setup. The trading plan cannot be activated until this first step to an isolated high or low has developed - it has to take out the prior day's low or high in the reversal zone.

The next step is to identify daily or weekly support points in the case of a potential isolated low, or daily/weekly resistance points in the case of a potential isolated high. You may also calculate potential price objectives for intraday swings based on the formulas given in this book, such as MCP price targets, but applied to smaller swings than those that would be used to calculate a major or greater cycle trough or crest.

The third step is to examine the 60-, 30-, and 5-minute charts, and note if they are overbought or oversold on the 15-bar slow stochastics, just as we did with the daily and weekly charts. In fact, we prefer to see these overbought and oversold levels to be even more extreme, depending on the lowest time band used. That is, the hourly and 30-minute chart may be overbought when above 80%, but it is better if they are over 90%. The 5-minute chart, however, is more revealing when it is closer to 100%. The same is true in the case of being oversold. A 20% or lower reading is required for the 60- and 30-minute stochastics, but a 10% or lower reading is even better. On a 5-minute chart, the closer the stochastics are to 0% the better. Additionally, the aggressive trader will also look for any bullish looping patterns or cases of bullish oscillator divergence on any of these intraday charts, as the market drops to a new intraday low in price. In the case of new intraday highs, he will look for bearish looping patterns or bearish oscillator divergence on the 60-, 30-, or even 5-minute chart when readying to execute the trading plan.

The fourth step is to then set the stop-loss at a favorable risk-reward point. That is, if we are looking for a 250 point or greater move in the DJIA, the stop-loss should be set approximately 100 points away from the entry point. This can be adjusted based on the market falling or closing below daily support or above resistance, depending on whether the entry position was a long or short.

So let us summarize these steps for a short-term aggressive trader's trading plan.

If Going Long:

1. Once the market enters the solar-lunar reversal zone (or even a geocosmic critical reversal zone), look for the market to fall below the prior day's low.
2. Identify daily or weekly support zones and intraday downside price targets based on the intraday pattern. It is best if these support zones are at least 2.5% below the high of the most recent trading cycle crest. However, that is not always going to be the case - it is just best when it is.
3. Once the market enters one of these downside support zones, look to see if the 60-minute chart shows a 15-bar slow stochastic reading that is oversold or at least back to the neutral 42-58% if it has been above 90%. Also, observe if there is a bullish looping pattern or a bullish oscillator divergence on the 60-minute bar chart, as prices are dropping into this support zone. If you use other oscillators that measure oversold or neutral readings, you may use them in place of stochastics. If you use other technical tools, like a sudden spike in volume for the hourly bar, you may use that as a signal to act as well.
4. Next, check the 30-minute bars for the same signals. It needs to indicate the market is oversold, and even better, if it is forming bullish oscillator patterns (i.e. bullish divergence or a bullish looping pattern).
5. Next, use the 5-minute chart to observe the same oscillator signals. Here, it may even be better to wait until the stochastics come very close to 0%, then rally, and then come down again a second time, just to be sure support is holding on the first re-test. You will often see the kind of bullish patterns we like to see at the bottom that forms on the re-test of the first low.
6. You may even use a one-minute chart, or tick chart, to help guide you into the entry point. If doing so, then that stochastic reading needs to be at - or very close to - 0% as the low is forming.
7. Set your stop-loss either 100 points below your entry (if trading the DJIA), or below one of the daily or intraday support zones that held on the move down.

You can move that stop-loss up to just below the low of the move once the 30- and/or 60-minute bars confirm the low of the move is in for this solar-lunar reversal zone (or geocosmic critical reversal date time band).
8. Your trading plan should include a point at which to take your profit. It should initially be at least 2.5% up from the low of the move, and/or based on the trading plan rules for selling short (next section). Usually this will be achieved within the next 1-5 trading days.

If Going Short:

1. Once the market enters a solar-lunar reversal zone, look for the market to rally above the prior day's high.
2. Identify daily or weekly resistance zones and intraday upside price targets based on the intraday pattern. It is best if these resistance zones are at least 2.5% above the high of the most recent trading cycle trough. However, that is not always going to be the case - it is just best when it is.
3. Once the market enters one of these resistance zones, look to see if the 60-minute chart shows a 15-bar slow stochastic reading that is overbought or at least back to the neutral 42-58% if it had recently been below 10%. Also observe if there is any case of a bearish looping pattern or bearish oscillator divergence on the 60-minute bars as the price falls into this support zone. If you use other oscillators that measure overbought or neutral readings, you may use them in place of stochastics. If you use other technical tools, like a sudden spike in volume for the hourly bar, you may use that as a signal to take action.
4. Next, check the 30-minute bar chart for the same signals. It needs to indicate the market is overbought, and even better, forming bearish oscillator patterns (i.e. bearish divergence or a bearish looping pattern).
5. Next, use the 5-minute chart to observe the same oscillator signals. Here, it may even be better to wait until the stochastics come very close to 100%, then decline, and then rally to a secondary high, just to be sure resistance is holding on the first re-test. You will often see the kind of bearish technical patterns we like to see as the secondary crest is forming.
6. You may even use a one-minute chart, or tick chart, to help guide you into the entry point. If doing so, then that stochastic reading needs to be at or very close to 100% as the high is forming.
7. Set your stop-loss either 100 points above your entry for the short sale (if trading the DJIA) or above one of the daily resistance zones that held on the move up. You can move that stop-loss down to just above the high of the move once the 30- and/or 60-minute bar chart confirms the high of the move is in for this solar-lunar reversal zone (or geocosmic critical reversal date time band).
8. Your trading plan should include a point at which to take your profit. It should be at least 2.5% down from the high of the move and/or based on the trading plan rules for going long (the previous section). Usually this will be achieved within the next 1-5 trading days.

Now let us show an example of how these rules would have worked in a real case. On June 23-24, 2011, the Sun was in Cancer and the Moon was in Aries. This has a weighted value of 144.6, which is thus a strong solar-lunar reversal signature. The DJIA had bottomed the week before, June 15, at 11,862.50. Weekly support was 11,871-11,876. Daily support was 12,058-12,074. The low of the previous day (June 22) was 12,105. The high was 12,208. Whichever broke would set up the trade for the aggressive short-term trader. Figure 74 shows what the DJIA looked like as of the close June 22.

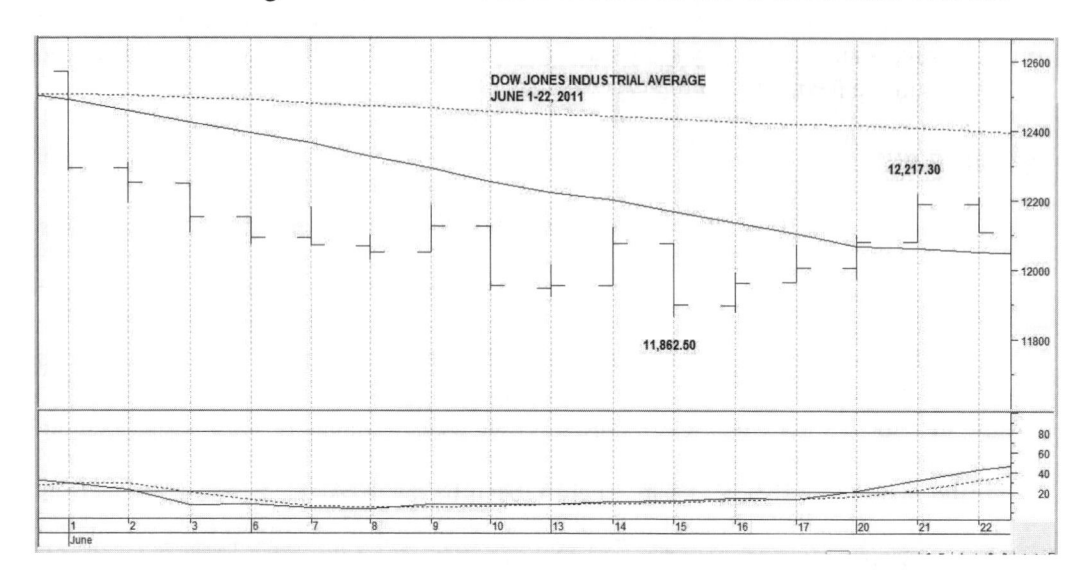

Figure 74: Daily chart of DJIA going into the solar-lunar reversal date of June 23-24, 2011.

Note that the most recent high was 12,217 on June 21. A 2.5% decline would take the market down to 11,912. If the market took out the low of the prior day at 12,105, we would like to see it continue to fall to at least 11,912 for a more optimal buying set up.

Now let us show what happened via the 60-minute, 30-minute, and 5-minute bar charts that day. The charts on the following page are intraday charts from the Charles Schwab "Street Smart Edge" Trading platform.[1] In the first hour of trading on June 23, the DJIA fell below the low of the prior day. We also note that the 60-minute stochastics fell below 20% that first hour, which was in oversold territory. K was at 7.27% and well below D at 35.24%. As you can see from the chart in Figure 75, the actual low of 10,874.90 was made in the second hour. Note that this was right into weekly support. It held. The confirmation that this was the low would not come until two days later when prices closed above the 15-hour moving average.

Now let us examine the 30-minute chart (Figure 76, next page) for that period and see if there were further signs that would help determine when and where to get long on June 23. Late the day before, the 15-bar stochastics showed the K line bottoming at 5.76% and below the D line at 20.00%. But the actual low of 10,874.90 was not realized until the third 30-minute bar of the next day, June 23, when the solar-lunar reversal signal was in effect. At the low, K was at 6.44% - higher than it was in the last 30-minute bar of the day before. D had fallen back to 7.90%, but it is K that we are most interested in for signs of bullish oscillator divergence. We got it here.

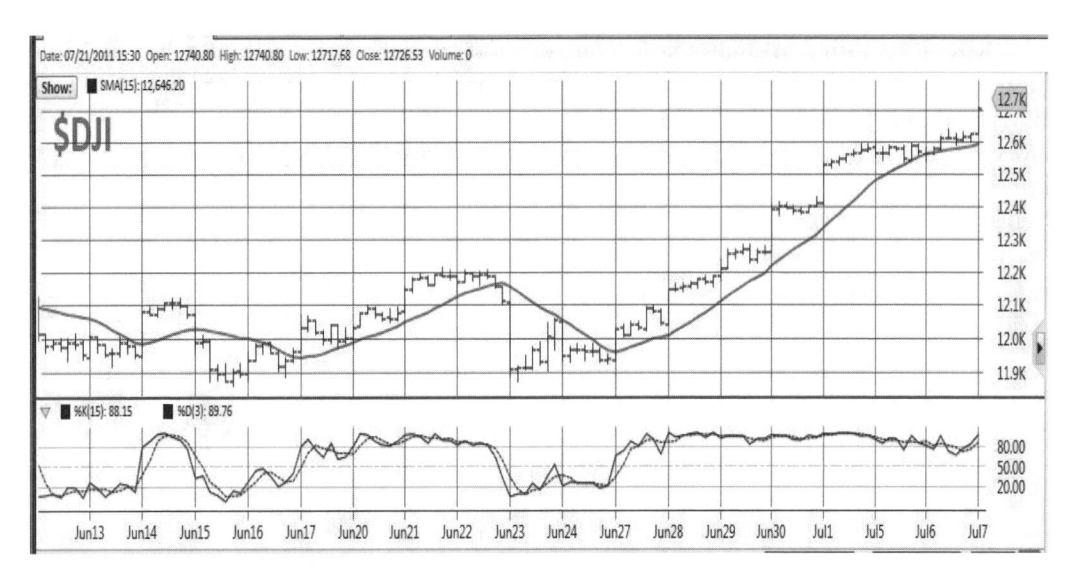

Figure 75: An hourly chart of the DJIA from June 13 through July 7, 2011. Shown here are a 15-bar moving average and a 15-bar slow stochastics. Note the double bottom lows of June 15 and June 23.

Thus as we entered the first 90 minutes of June 23, we knew several things were occurring that would lead us to buy. First, prices were below the low of the former day, so the setup was beginning. Second, the hourly stochastics were in oversold territory, which is a criterion for preparing to buy. Third, the 30-minute stochastics were exhibiting signs of bullish oscillator divergence (a new low in prices, but at a rising stochastic level). And third, prices were falling into weekly support and holding. This support level was a double bottom to the low of the prior week, which also represented support.

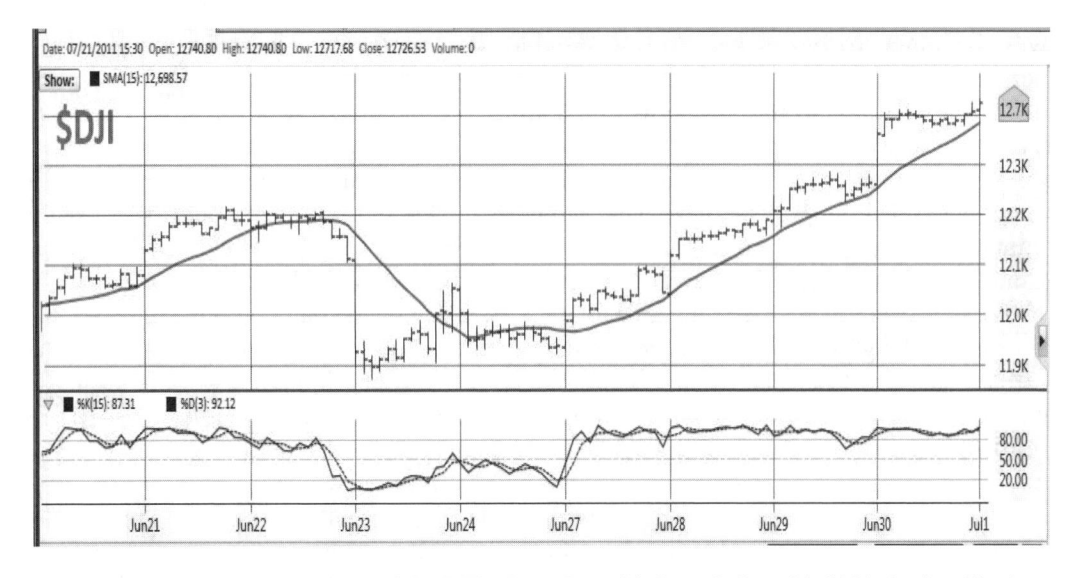

Figure 76: A 30-minute bar chart of the DJIA from June 21 through June 30, 2011. Again, this chart displays a 15-bar moving average and a 15-bar slow stochastic. Note that the low of June 23 occurs in the third 30-minute bar of that day.

Now it was time to study the 5-minute chart for further guidance on when and if to buy. Aggressive traders would use this, and perhaps even the 1-minute chart, to establish an entry point from the long side, with a 100-point stop-loss or a stop-loss based on a close below weekly support (11,871). The 5-minute chart of this period is shown below in Figure 77.

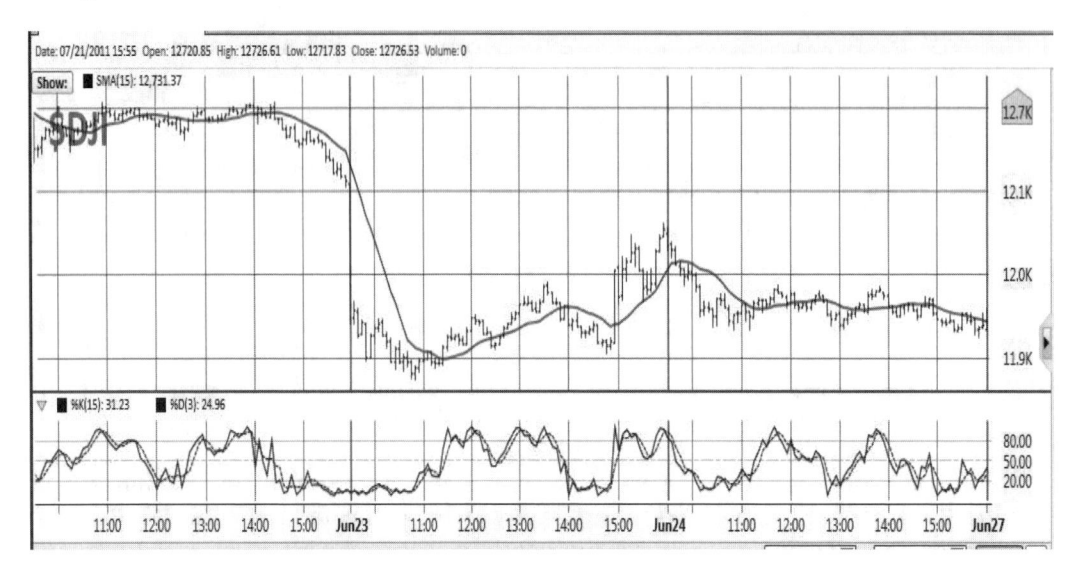

Figure 77: A 5-minute bar chart of the DJIA from June 22 through June 24, depicting the low at 10:50 AM at 10,874.90 on June 23.

Notice that the stochastics bottomed at 10:20 AM as K fell to nearly zero. It was at 0.34% and below D at 6.76%. Five minutes later the price fell lower, but the stochastics were beginning to rise. K was at 9.74% and above D at 6.25%. One could have bought here - the low was 11,887 - with a stop-loss 100 points lower, as the 60-, 30-, and 5-minute charts were all flashing signs of a bottom forming on the solar-lunar reversal date and close to weekly support. Or, as suggested in our trading plan, the aggressive short term trader could wait for a secondary low to form (it usually does) and buy that if it continues to exhibit bullish signs. That would have worked out even better, because 25 minutes later the DJIA did make a new low at 10,874.90 - right in the weekly support zone. As this secondary but lower low unfolded, the 5-minute stochastics were already rising. K was up to 16.14% and above D at 8.87%. We now had a good buy signal via the "bottom picking" strategies that these studies are designed to capture. At 2:45 PM, the DJIA tested this low again, falling back to 11,906. But then it started to rally strongly, closing the day at 12,050, up 175 points from the low of the day at 10:55 AM. In retrospect, the DJIA never looked back at that low over the next month.

Let us do one more example and then close this section on aggressive trading plans. Those lows of June 16 and 23 turned out to be a double bottom primary cycle trough. In addition to June 23 being a solar-lunar reversal zone, it was also just two trading days before June 27, which was a three-star geocosmic critical reversal date. Thus the DJIA was also in the time band for a primary bottom and within a geocosmic critical reversal date period.

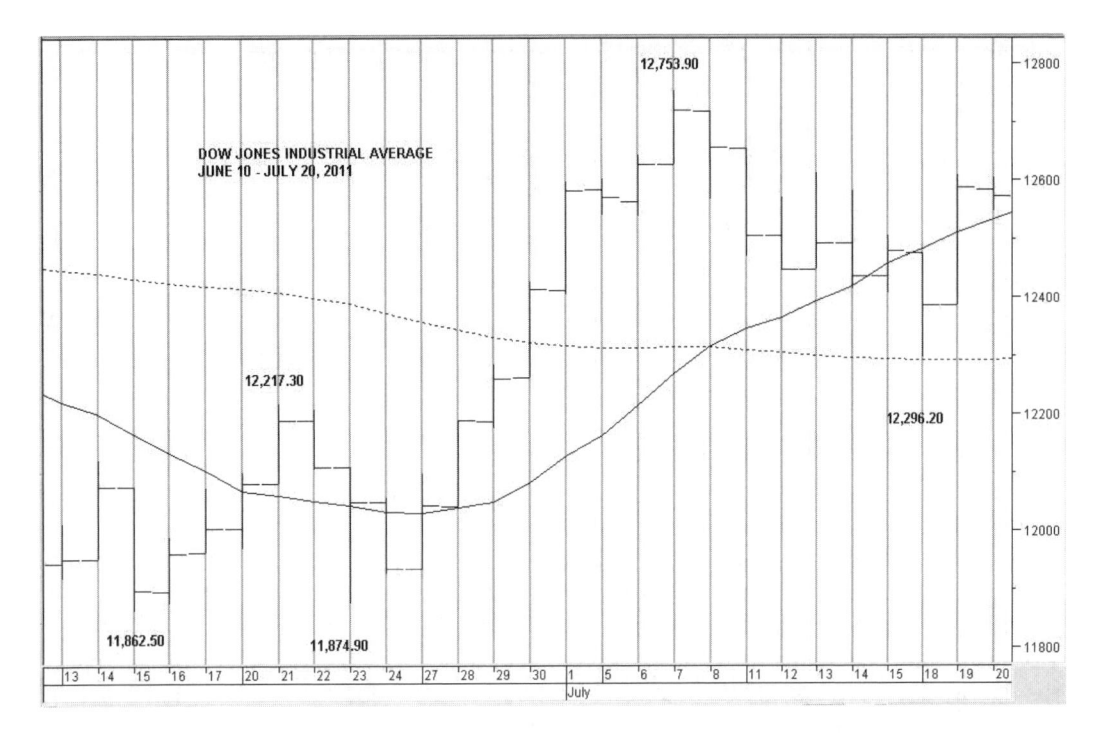

Figure 78: Daily chart of the Dow Jones Industrial Average, June 10 - July 20, depicting the double bottom primary cycle trough of June 15 and June 23, the major cycle crest of July 7, and the major cycle trough of July 18.

As one can see from the chart in Figure 78, the DJIA soared from the lows of June 16 and 23, at 11,862 and 11,874 respectively, to a high of 12,753 three weeks later on July 7. The DJIA then declined to a 5-week major cycle trough on July 18 at 12,296. That also happened to be another solar-lunar reversal date. The Sun was in Cancer and the Moon was in Pisces, which had a weighted value of 120.6 according to the studies reported in Volume 4. Any value above 120 (or in actual practice, above 114) has a higher than average expectancy for a reversal. Thus the market was falling into July 18-19 as the solar-lunar reversal signature was readying. The high of the prior day (Friday, July 15) was 12,504, the low was 12,406, and the close was 12,479. Which would break first, the high or the low, as we entered this lunar reversal zone? Whichever broke would dictate the trading plan for the aggressive trader.

The low broke first. Therefore the trading plan would be to buy. Now the task would be to determine at what price to buy. For this we can apply a couple of price objective calculations to determine support zones and possible points to buy with a 100-point stop loss. The first calculation can be a simple 50% correction of the swing up from the double bottom lows of June 15 (11,862.50) and June 23 (11,874.90), to the major cycle crest of 12,753.90 of July 7. That would yield a price target of 12,308.20 +/- 105.18 or 12,314.40 +/- 103.72. The overlap of these two price ranges would be 12,210.68-12,413.38. This is the most important price range to consider. The hourly chart in Figure 79 would show a move down from the high of 12,753.90 on July 7 to a low of 12,446 late in the day on July 12. The next day it rallied to a secondary high of 12,611. An MCP downside price target on the hourly chart would give a price target for the decline down to 12,303.10 +/- 53.20. This range would be 12,249.90-12,356.30, which overlapped with

287

the other two price ranges. Therefore this becomes our preferred price range to buy on the solar-lunar reversal dates of July 18-19, assuming the DJIA falls into there.

Second, we can simply look at the level of the 25-week and 42-day moving averages as support. For the week starting July 18, the 25-week moving average was at 12,297. The 42-day moving average was at 12,292 on July 18.

Next, we look at weekly and daily support zones or TIP points that are below 12,406, the low of the prior day. That would include weekly support at 12,354-12,372 and daily support at 12,422-12,430. There was also a former bullish crossover zone still in effect at 12,305-12,332 from June 29-30.

The trading plan would therefore be to buy in the area 12,249.90-12,356.30, if offered, with a stop-loss below 11,862.50 (the start of the primary cycle), or on a close below 12,210 (price target zone of the most important correction areas), or a close below the bullish crossover zone at 12,305, or a weekly close below 12,354 (weekly support). It all depends upon the trader's personal risk tolerance level, for any of these can be justified as a technical stop-loss point to start with. But you may prefer a "dollar-risk" stop-loss point. To adjust for that, we would want to see the 60-, 30-, and 5-minute charts display a case of oversold oscillators, or better yet, oversold and with a looping pattern and/or exhibiting a bullish oscillator divergence. Once we see the "optimal" point to enter, we may elect to set a stop-loss 100 points below the entry point, or the low of the move just prior to the actual entry point.

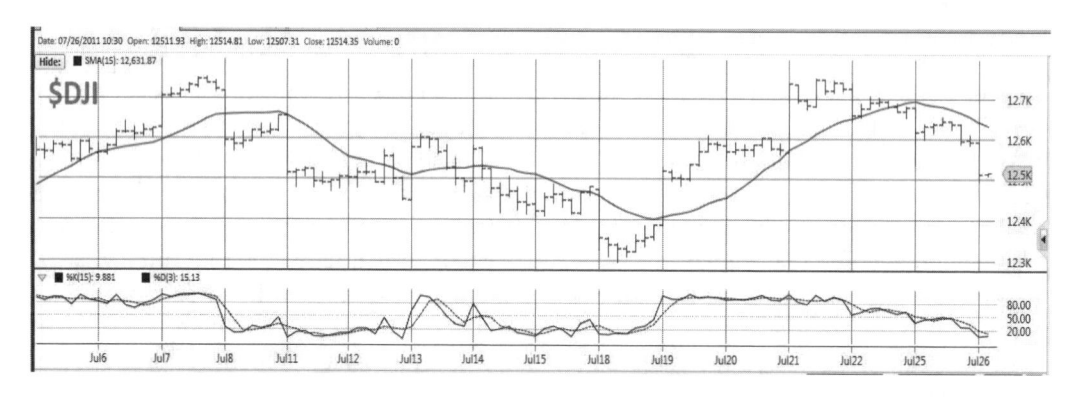

Figure 79: An hourly bar chart, with a 15-bar slow stochastics and a 15-hour moving average, showing the major cycle trough of July 18.

The 60-minute chart in Figure 79 shows each of these bullish stochastic conditions present at the low of 12,296 that formed in the third hour of July 18. Not only was there a bullish looping pattern at the low, but the stochastics were rising (bullish oscillator divergence). The low was 12,296.20, which was within the ideal price target zone.

The half-hourly chart (Figure 80, shown on the next page) displayed a similar pattern at the low of July 18 at 11:30 - noon. That is, the stochastics were oversold with K = 2.48% and below D at 9.82%. The low that formed then was the second loop of a double looping formation below 20%, and even below 10%, which is more ideal for a low.

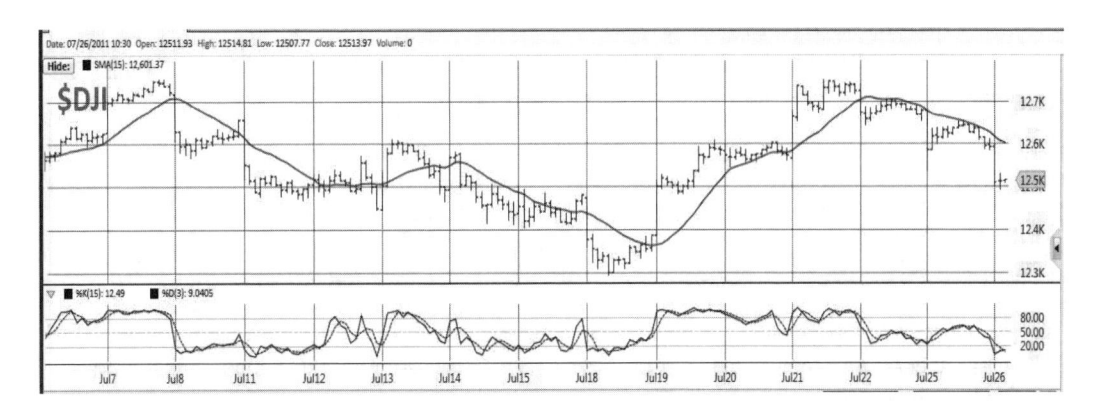

Figure 80: A chart of 30-minute bars, with a 15-bar slow stochastics and a 15-hour moving average, showing the major cycle trough of July 18.

The five-minute chart in Figure 81 (next page) shows that the low occurred at the 11:50 AM mark on July 18. The low prior to this occurred at 10:50 AM, an hour earlier, at 12,309. The K line of the stochastics at that time was at 0% and below D, which was at 8.09%. Previously we explained how we like to see the 5-minute stochastics close to 0% as a low forms, or a bullish looping formation where the second low is lower in price, but higher in its stochastic level. That happened here. At the actual low of 12,296 at 11:55 AM, the 5-minute stochastics were higher, with K up to 8.14% and still below D at 11.09%, but qualifying as a case of bullish oscillator divergence. Since both the 30- and 60-minute charts were flashing buy signals, and since the market was into the ideal price support zone for a major cycle trough, and since this was a solar-lunar reversal zone, one could now buy with a stop-loss of about 100 points below the low of the actual move (12,296) or your entry point, depending on your risk tolerance level. Or, if you have a wider risk tolerance level, you could set the stop-loss below any one of the other stop-loss points given before, but no lower than 11,862. Once the low is confirmed by a move up above a daily resistance zone, or say the 15-bar moving average on the 30-minute chart, you could move your stop-loss up to just below the low of the move. Once it appreciates at least 2.5% from that low, the aggressive short-term trader will start looking to take profits. That means the minimum price objective initially for taking profits would be 12,603. Ideally this would happen in the next 1-4 trading days. But even so, it is best to see a technical selling situation in effect in order to maximize profits from the position.

As one can see, this trade worked out very well, as the set up suggested it would. The very next day the DJIA had rallied to 12,607, already above the minimum price target of 12,603. The rally topped out at 12,751.40 on Thursday, July 21, which was already into the next solar-lunar reversal zone, as the Sun was still in Cancer and the Moon had advanced into Aries. This combination had a weighted value of 144.6 for a market reversal. That was well above the 120-weighted value necessary for a formal solar-lunar reversal possibility, and it turns out that Thursday was an isolated high. One could take profits and short the market then. That short would have worked out just fine too, as the market then declined sharply into the following week, as shown in Figure 82 on the next page.

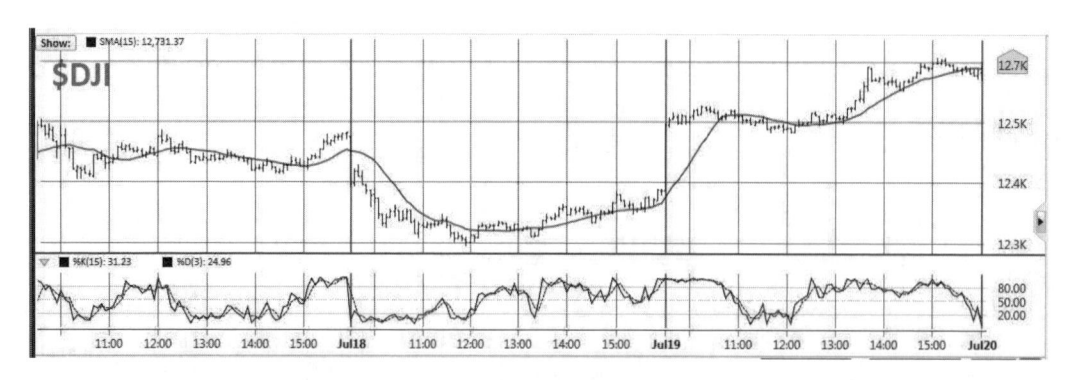

Figure 81: A chart of 5-minute bars, with a 15-bar slow stochastics and a 15-hour moving average, showing the major cycle trough of July 18.

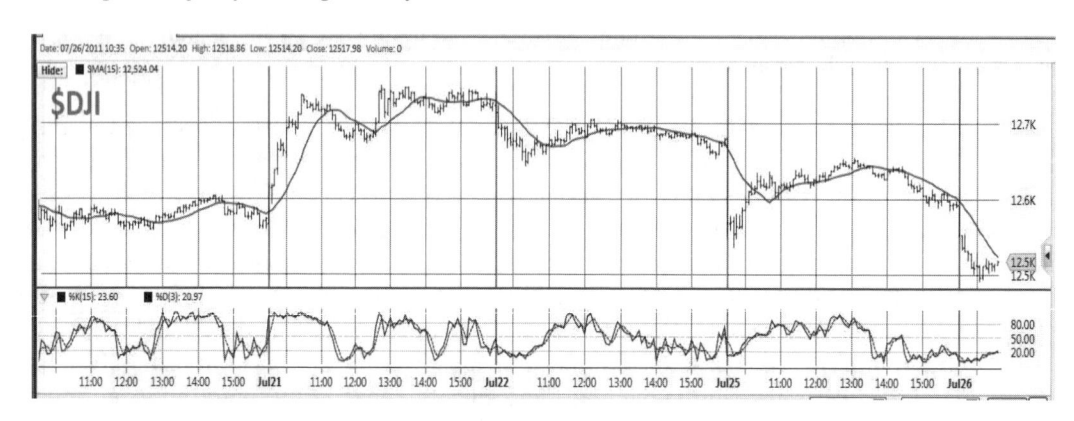

Figure 82: A five-minute chart of the DJIA showing the high that formed on July 21.

You have now seen how these formulas are designed to work and in a surprising number of cases, this is how they actually do unfold in real time. For short-term aggressive traders, this is as good as it gets.

An Additional Note Regarding Stop-Losses

For aggressive traders, it is advisable to move your stop-loss up to at least break-even once the 15-bar moving average is exceeded on the 30- or 60-minute charts. The reason for doing this is because aggressive traders will be more prone to experience sudden reversals that take away all their profits - and more - than position traders will be. Many analysts feel that position traders should also move their stop-losses up to break even once the position is in profit, but in so doing, you will experience an abundance of times when you are taken out of a position for a break-even that later would turn out to be profitable. My suggestion is to wait at least until a pre-defined resistance level is taken out before you move your stop-loss up to break even. Otherwise your stop-loss will be a "guaranteed loss", and no gain, which for a position trader is very frustrating.

References:

1. "Street Smart Edge," Charles Schwab & Co., www.schwab.com, San Francisco, CA, USA.

CHAPTER TWENTY-ONE

FINIS

After 15 years of writing, researching, and reporting the results of scores of studies on the correlation of stock markets to cycles, geocosmic signatures, chart patterns, trend analysis, and technical analysis studies, we have finally arrived at the final chapter of the fifth and final volume of this series titled "The Ultimate Book on Stock Market Timing." It has been an unbelievable journey that has been undertaken with the intention of being able to identify historical correlations of high rates of frequency that will stand the test of time. I confess one motive for creating these volumes was to serve as reference books for my own needs as a trader and investor because it was time-consuming to keep looking up what happened the last time this or that cycle was due, or this or that geocosmic signature was present. It was time consuming to keep looking up what happened the previous times in which certain chart patterns occurred under certain technical conditions and how far the resulting price moves took the market. By writing this series of books, many answers to the above-mentioned concerns would be quickly available to any student on stock market timing. And I still consider myself such a student. The learning never ends because the questions never cease and the quest is always alive.

And now we come to the final pages of this effort, which seems more like an epic because - by choice - it passionately consumed so much of my life. It is these final strokes in these last chapters that have tied it all together so that traders, investors, students, and market analysts alike will have at their disposal a truly unified system for approaching financial markets. So to bring this effort to a satisfying closure, let us demonstrate how these basic principles have continued to work in the primary cycles of the DJIA that have unfolded between November 29, 2010 and the time this last chapter has been written in late July 2011. It is a perfect way to end the book, because the primary cycles that unfolded since the distorted one of July 2 - November 29, 2010 have been almost picture perfect in terms of cycles, geocosmic studies, price objective studies, and technical studies.

The Rest of the Story that Never Ends

For this final exercise, we will focus only on the key elements of the position trader. That is, we will examine the periods surrounding the primary cycle troughs and crests that unfolded between November 29, 2010 and the time this book has been written, with an eye on both the longer-term cycles that contain these primary cycles and the subcycles (or phases) within the primary cycle. This is the manner in which multiple time bands of cycles are tied together in the effort to identify the most likely trend of the primary cycle.

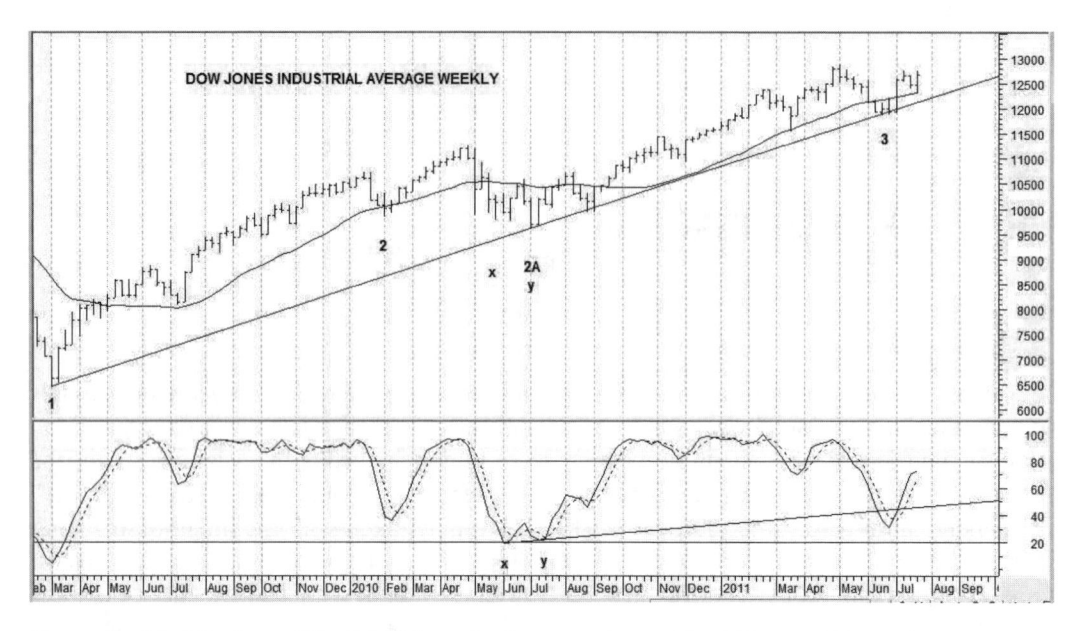

Figure 83: Weekly chart of the DJIA from the 4-year cycle trough of March 2009 through July 2011, depicting the 50-week cycle troughs so far (2A and 3) and the first phase of the 4-year cycle (2A). Note that 2 would have been a normal 50-week cycle trough, but it expanded to coincide with the first 15.5-month cycle phase of the 4-year cycle at 2A. Note the bullish oscillator divergence that occurred at 2A.

To begin this final analysis, we will commence by examining the weekly chart of the DJIA starting from the 4-year cycle trough of March 6, 2009, shown in Figure 83.

In the earlier chapters of this book, it was determined that the first phase of the 4-year cycle bottomed on July 2, 2010. It was also determined that July 2, 2010 was a distorted (expanded) 50-week cycle that actually lasted 69 weeks. Distortions like that have a less than 10% historical frequency. Therefore, connecting the 4-year cycle low of March 6, 2009 with the trough of the first phase of the four-year cycle, i.e., 15.5-month cycle of July 2, 2010, creates a bullish trendline that defines the bullish trend for the 4-year cycle. This is known as the 15.5-month cycle trendline. Once this trendline is broken, it will suggest that the crest of the next highest cycle on this trendline is probably over. That would be the 4-year cycle crest. A *confirmation* of this labeling would occur when the 15.5-month cycle low of July 2 (9614) is broken. The break of the trendline would be a strong bearish signal that this could be happening. In fact, it would be a very strong indication that this bull market has ended because it has become a 4-point trendline as shown on the chart in Figure 83. That trendline was tested - and held - at the lows of August 27, 2010 and at the primary cycle trough that occurred in June 2011, shortly before this is being written in July 2011.

The next thing to observe about this weekly chart is the 25-week moving average. From the low of July 2, 2010, the next 50-week cycle would be due 34-67 weeks later. Prices would likely break below this 25-week moving average as the 50-week cycle formed. You can see that this moving average was broken as the DJIA formed an important low on June 15, 2011. That happened to be exactly 50 weeks from July 2, 2010. Now we will wait to see if it will also turn into another expanded 50-week cycle to coincide with a 15.5-month cycle (2nd phase of the 4-year cycle), similar to what occurred at 2 and 2A in 2010 (in Figure 83). A break below the 25-week moving average would suggest that this will be the case. A close below the 4-point trendline would be an even stronger case. In fact, a break of the trendline would suggest the 4-year cycle may have topped out and the market has turned bearish. The U.S. stock market could then turn into a bear market lasting into the next 4-year cycle trough, which would "normally" be due January 2013, +/- 10 months (36-56 months after March 6, 2009). But as you will see shortly, the low at 3 (in Figure 83) fits well for a 50-week cycle trough as it was the third primary cycle phase within the greater 50-week cycle that started at 2A.

Now, let us analyze the primary cycles that unfolded since November 29, 2010, which was the first primary cycle phase of that 50-week cycle that started July 2, 2010.

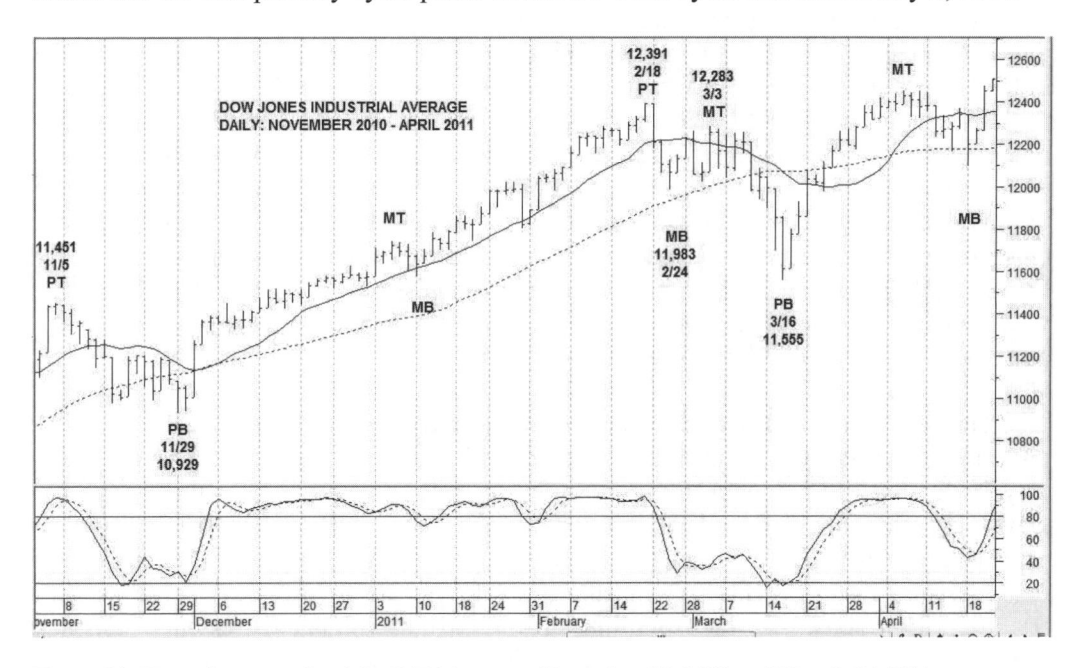

Figure 84: The primary cycle of the DJIA between November 29, 2010 and March 15, 2011.

In Figure 84, one can see that the second primary cycle phase of the 50-week cycle lasted from November 29, 2010 through March 16, 2011. The "normal" time band for the primary cycle is 13-21 weeks, and this one lasted 15 weeks, which means it was a normal primary cycle periodicity. It was also a classical three-phase pattern, consisting of three major cycles, but the last one contracted and only lasted three weeks.

As expected, this was a bullish primary cycle. Why was that expected? Because 1) it was still early in the 15.5-month cycle, and 2) the 14-day moving average remained above the 42-day moving average as the primary cycle began, which meant it was still in a trend run up. In the very first week of the primary cycle, prices were above both the 14- and 42-day averages, which simply confirmed that the market was bullish. In all likelihood, it would not top out until after Tuesday of the 9th week (the "bullish 8-week rule") and well into the second or third phase of this primary cycle. In fact, that is exactly what happened as this primary cycle topped out at 12,391 on February 18th, the 11th week of the primary cycle, and the 5th week of the second major cycle phase.

293

Was there a geocosmic critical reversal date or an important Level 1 geocosmic signature nearby to this primary cycle crest? The answer is, "Yes." Below is a list of geocosmic signatures that were present around that time.

Date	Signature	Aspect Degree	Value	Level
Feb 17	☉☌♆		9.40	1
Feb 18	♀□♄	90°	9.43	1
Feb 20	♂☌♆		8.91	2
Feb 25	♃□♇	90°	8.90	2

As one can see, there was indeed a geocosmic cluster in effect from February 17 through February 25. The midpoint was February 21, which was a Monday and a holiday in the USA. The critical reversal zone would thus be February 18-22, +/- 3 trading days. The last day of trading before February 21 was February 18, which was of course within the allowable time frame for a geocosmic critical reversal date. Additionally there were two level 1 signatures in effect during that cluster, on February 17 and 18 respectively. So time-wise via geocosmic studies, February 18 fit almost perfectly for a primary cycle crest. As a point of interest, European and Asian stock markets were open on Monday, February 21, and many of them made their cycle highs exactly on that day. Thus there were cases of intermarket bearish divergence when some indices made highs one week, and others made new cycle highs the following week.

The next step would be to calculate price objectives for this primary cycle crest. This process would start by looking at the weekly chart in Figure 83. Note that from the low of July 2, 2010 at 9614 through the primary cycle crest of November 5, there were two waves up. This would include the major cycle crest of August 9 at 10,720 and the primary cycle crest of 11,451 on November 5. If we take the difference between the high of the second swing up (11,451) and the start of the 50-week cycle at 9614, we get a result of 1837 points. Now let us multiply that by .618 to estimate the extent of this next move up. 1837 x .618 = 1135. If we add this to the primary cycle low of 10,929 on November 29, we get one of the price targets for the crest of the new primary cycle. This would be 10,929 + 1135 = 12,064. The allowable orb for this price target would be (12,064 - 9614) x .118 = 289. The range for the crest of this primary cycle, via this calculation, would be 11,775-12,353.

Next we would calculate the MCP (Mid-Cycle Pause) price objective from the previous two primary cycle lows. That is, we would add the 11,451 primary cycle crest of November 5 to the 10,929 primary cycle trough of November 29, and from that total we would subtract the 9614 primary cycle low of July 2. It would look like this: (11,451 + 10,929) – 9614 = 12,766. The orb of allowance would then be (12,766 – 9614) x .118 = 372. The range for the MCP price objective for the primary cycle crest would thus be 12,393-13,138. There was no overlap to the first price target of 11,775-12,353. What is interesting, however, is the space between these two targets: 12,353-12,393.

Next, we could calculate an MCP for the crest of the second major cycle. The crest of the first major cycle occurred on January 5 at 11,743. The major cycle trough was just a couple of days later at 11,574 on January 10. Adding these two together (11,743 +

11,574 = 23,317), and then subtracting the primary cycle trough of November 29 at 10,929 from it (23,317 – 10,929) will yield the MCP of the next crest at 12,388. Applying our .118 rule of the difference between this upside price target and the low from which the cycle began (12,388 – 10.929) for the orb gives us a price target of 12,388 +/- 172, or a range of 12,216 – 12,560. This overlapped with the prior price target at 12,393-12,560. But as one can see from the chart, the actual crest was 12,391, which was very close to the exact later MCP price target of 12,388 +/- 172. Perhaps if February 21 had not been a holiday, the DJIA would have made it up to this overlapping price range just two points higher. Thus in our final analysis, the time factors worked extremely well, and one of our price target zones was fulfilled almost exactly.

At the high, one can see that the 15-day slow stochastics were overbought. The K line was at 98.23% and above D at 95.38%. They had formed a bearish double loop. However it was not until the next trading day on February 22 that they started to curl back down. That day the market also closed below the 14-day moving average, a sign that at least a major cycle crest had been completed.

Two days later, the first leg down was completed at 11,983 on February 24. This would turn out to be a major cycle trough. The rally that followed did not make a new cycle high. The crest of the third major cycle topped out on March 3 at 12,283. We note that the daily stochastics never reached oversold levels on the major cycle trough of February 24. Consequently it was no surprise that on the rally to the major cycle crest of March 3, the stochastics did not rise beyond the neutral level of 42-58%. The market then reversed back down, on its way to the primary cycle trough, where 1) stochastics would be expected to fall below 20%, and 2) the DJIA would likely at least touch the 42-day moving average, and better yet, fall below there. They did that on March 10.

The next step would be to determine the time band for the primary cycle trough. The expectation is that it would occur 13-21 weeks after November 29, 2010, or February 28 - April 29. We would also expect it to occur 2-5 weeks after the primary cycle crest of February 18, or February 28 - March 25. The overlap would be this later time band, or February 28 - March 25. Ideally it would also overlap with the next 5-7 week major cycle, following the second major cycle trough of February 24. This would come out to March 28 - April 15, but this did not overlap the previously determined ideal time frame. As it turned out, the primary cycle low was completed on March 16, which was in the original overlap zone.

This was a case where the geocosmic signatures did not coincide with the primary cycle trough. That happens about 18% of the time, according to studies conducted in Volume 3. Between February 28 and March 25, there were no significant planetary signatures present until March 21, when the Sun formed a conjunction to Uranus. This was a very powerful geocosmic signature with a C/S value of 9.70 and an 83% correspondence to primary or greater cycles, which is very high. The low of March 16 was only three trading days prior to this aspect, so it fulfilled the minimum criteria for a reversal, although it was not the kind of precise correspondence we like to see for a primary cycle trough, which is a midpoint of a geocosmic cluster, +/- 3 trading days. The reason it didn't happen "on time" via this study may have been due to the enormity of the UFO (Unexpected Fundamental Occurrence) event that took place the weekend before.

On Friday, March 11, as Uranus entered Aries and after the U.S. markets had closed, a huge earthquake struck northern Japan, followed by a devastating tsunami and wreckage of a nuclear power plant that led to deadly radiation leaks. Stock markets around the world reeled as trading began the next week. In the study of astrology, Uranus rules earthquakes and these types of disasters. Uranus changing signs (a 7-year event) and the Sun conjunct Uranus on the spring equinox (it was also a full moon) certainly fit these events which transpired, but it was not a perfect correlation for the primary cycle trough of March 16. It would have been a better geocosmic correlation if the bottom had occurred the following week.

Like the cycle studies, however, the price objective calculations fared very well at that low. A "normal" corrective decline of the primary swing up from the 10,929 low that started the primary cycle on November 29 to the 12,391 primary cycle crest of February 18 would yield a price target of 11,660 +/- 173 for the primary cycle trough. There was a second downside price target that could be calculated by multiplying 1.618 of the first leg down from the crest at 12,391 to the major cycle low of 11,983 on February 24. Then we subtract that amount from the major cycle crest of 12,283 on March 3, to get a price target of 11,623 +/- 91. The range was thus 11,531-11,713, which overlapped the first price target range for this low given above. The final low was 11,555 on March 16, which was indeed in the ideal price range just calculated and yet another excellent call for these price target studies as presented in this book.

The stochastics also performed in a classical manner at the primary cycle trough. That is, they fell below 20%, and they formed a bullish looping formation with the second loop slightly higher than the first as the price made the new low. It was a classic case of bullish oscillator divergence and a bullish looping pattern. By March 18 the K line was back above 25% and widening its distance above D, a "confirming signal" that the bottom was in. By the next trading day, Monday March 21, the DJIA closed above the 14-day moving average, a stronger signal that at least a major cycle low was completed. Two days later, March 23, the DJIA closed above the 42-day average, a powerful signal that the primary cycle trough was over, and a new primary cycle was underway. Now we start the process all over again for this new primary cycle.

March 16 thus began the third primary cycle of the 50-week cycle that commenced on July 2, 2010. What do we know about third and probably last phases of cycles that hitherto have been bullish? We know that one of three patterns tend to happen, but regardless of which one it is, the decline from the crest to the trough will likely last longer and be steeper than the declines to the lows of the prior two phases. That absolutely happened here.

But let us start by identifying when this new primary cycle would be due to bottom. First, we know that a 50-week cycle trough would be due 34-67 weeks after July 2, 2010, or February 21 - October 14, 2011. The 50th week would correspond to the week ending June 17, 2011, so the closer to that the better. Second, we know that a "normal" 13-21 week primary cycle (following the low of March 16) would be due June 13 - August 12, 2011. This overlapped the ideal time for the 50-week cycle too. However we also know that the last phase of a cycle may distort more often than the other phases, so a cycle low as short as 12 weeks or as long as 26 weeks was possible.

Given that this would be the third and possibly final primary cycle phase of the greater 50-week cycle, we could not be sure where and when the crest would occur. However, we had a general idea based on the historical studies of Jupiter transiting through the signs of the zodiac, as reported in the Forecast 2010[1] and Forecast 2011[2] books. These studies showed that the DJIA had a high frequency of forming bull market tops when Jupiter was positioned between 23 degrees of Aries and 7 degrees of Taurus, in studies going back to the 1870's. Jupiter would be there May 2 through July 22, 2010 and again October 7, 2011 through March 7, 2012. In the latter case, Jupiter would not cover that whole ground. The retrograde would only take it back to 0° of Taurus. It would then transit 0 - 7 degrees of Taurus. The midpoint of this first Jupiter crossing would be June 4, 2011, and so one's sights would be set on the period nearby to June 4 as a possible period for the primary cycle crest, or at least May 2 through July 22.

From a purely cyclical viewpoint, we would expect the crest to unfold at the 2-5 week interval of this new primary cycle in the event it was to become a bearish pattern. More than likely the crest would be closer to the center of the primary cycle time band, or around the 8th week, which was the week beginning May 9. This was more likely to be the case than seeing a top unfold at the 2-5 week interval because Jupiter would not be in the 23° Aries to 7° Taurus zodiac range until May 2. If this was to be an extremely bullish primary cycle - always a possibility in third phases of bullish cycles where "blow-offs" can unfold - then the crest would not be due until late in the primary cycle, probably after the 13th week. When such extreme bullish markets take place in third phases, the sell-off that follows is also usually extreme. Thus we would watch for any signs of a crest forming after the second week. We would watch for those signs of a crest forming once prices tested the crest of the prior primary cycle, i.e., double top formation within 2% of the prior primary cycle crest of 12,391. We would also watch for any signs of a crest once prices entered any price objective zone for a crest, especially if nearby to a geocosmic critical reversal date. Our greatest attention would be on rallies that took place in the second major cycle phase of this new primary cycle, for we would anticipate the DJIA to at least test the crest of the first phase then. And that time frame would follow May 2, our earliest date for a projected primary cycle crest based on the transit of Jupiter.

The first major cycle phase was bullish, as expected. That is, the DJIA rallied to a new multi-year high of 12,451 on April 6. This was three trading days after the midpoint of a rather large geocosmic cluster extending from March 21 - April 11. The midpoint was Good Friday, April 1. This high occurred on the following Wednesday, and three weeks into the new primary cycle. The DJIA then declined the normal 38.2-61.8% of the swing up to form its first major cycle trough on April 18 at 12,094. A "normal" corrective decline for this major cycle trough would have been (12,451 + 11,555) ÷ 2, or 12,003 +/- 106. That low fell within the next geocosmic cluster zone of April 18-30, albeit 4 trading days before the midpoint.

Our attention would now be on heightened alert for a possible primary and 50-week cycle crest as we entered the second major cycle phase of this primary cycle. This was reinforced by the fact that Jupiter would soon enter its time frame that historically correlates with an important crest after May 2. So now it is time to calculate upside price targets for this crest. For this we can make three calculations, as follows:

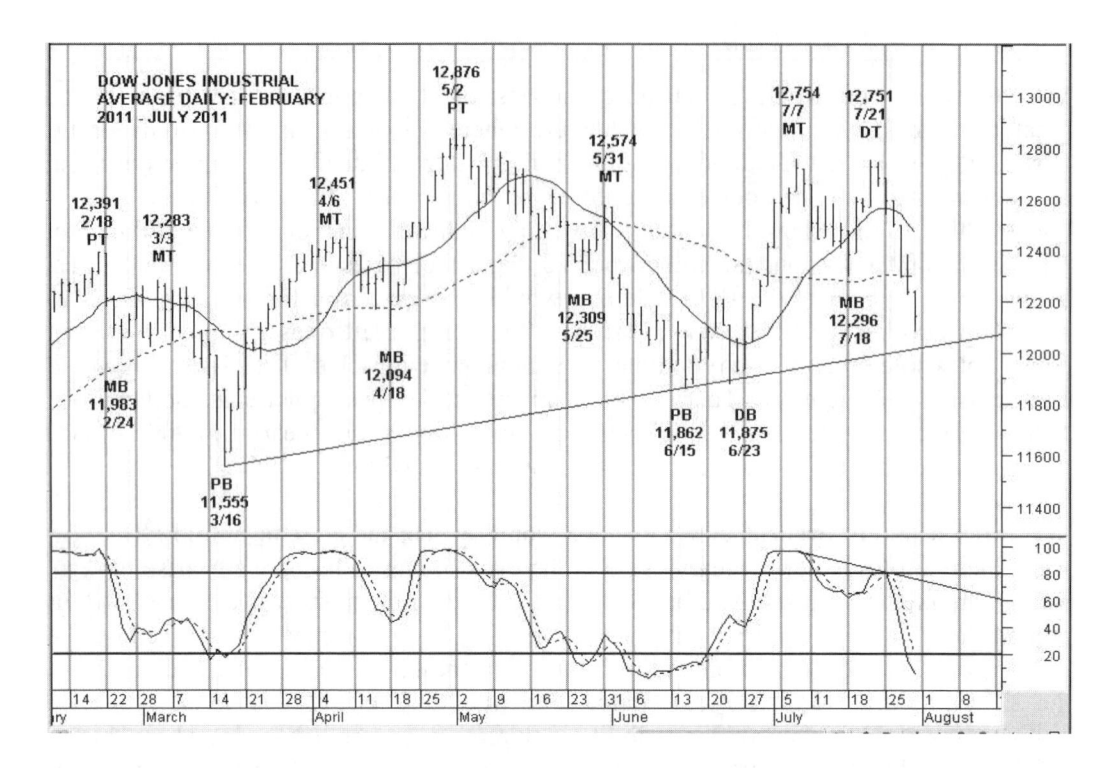

Figure 85: Daily chart of the DJIA illustrating the primary cycle of March 16 through June 23, 2011 and the first major cycle phase that followed.

1. Take the difference between the last primary cycle crest (12,391 on February 18, 2011) and the start of the 50-week cycle, which was 9614 on July 2, 2010. Multiply that by .618 and add it to the second primary cycle trough of 11,555 of March 16. It looks like this:

   (12,391 – 9614) x .618 = 2777
   2777 = .618 = 1716
   11,555 + 1716 = 13,271
   The orb of allowance is (13,271 – 9614) x .118 = 431
   The range for this price objective for a crest is 12,840 – 13,702.

2. Calculate a primary MCP based on the last two primary cycle lows (10,929 of November 29, 2010 and 11,555 of March 16, 2011) and the prior primary cycle crest of 12,391 on February 18, 2011. It looks like this:

   (12,391 + 11,555) – 10,929 = 13,017
   The orb of allowance is (13,017 - 10,929) x .118 = 246
   The range for this price objective for a crest is 12,770 - 13,263.

3. Calculate a major cycle MCP crest based on the last primary cycle low (11,555 of March 16, 2011), the last major cycle trough (12,094 of April 18, 2011), and the prior primary major crest of 12,451 on April 6, 2011. It looks like this:

   (12,451 + 12,094) – 11,555 = 12,990

The orb of allowance is (12,990 – 11,555) x .118 = 169
The range for this price objective for a crest is 12,820 - 13.189.
The overlap of these three price objective ranges is **12,840 - 13,159**.

As one can see from the chart in Figure 85, the high was right there, at 12,876 on May 2. This was the first day of the time band for the Jupiter transit that historically correlates with an important crest. It was the 7th week of the primary cycle. It was within four trading days (actually only one day) of a Level 1 and Level 2 signature that each took place on Saturday, April 30 (Venus in opposition to Saturn and Mars conjunct Jupiter). It was also a new moon period (May 3). But it wasn't within the ideal three-trading days of a critical reversal date, which would have been April 22-25. It was 5 trading days afterwards.

At that high of May 2, the daily stochastics were overbought and starting to fall. They would not issue a stronger sell signal until one week later, on the re-test of the May 2 high that took place May 10 as the DJIA rallied back to 12,781. After that, they fell below 71%, suggesting a primary cycle crest may have been achieved, and a major cycle crest had indeed been completed.

The DJIA then continued this first leg down to a major cycle trough at 12,309 on May 25. The concern here was that this low was more than a normal 38.2-61.8% corrective decline of the major cycle swing up between April 18 and May 2, which would have been 12,485 +/- 92. The decline was also below the 42-day moving average, another sign that the primary cycle had topped out. Our strategy would now switch to selling the next corrective rally to the next major cycle crest.

How high would this rally go? When would it end? If the primary and 50-week cycle had topped out as the price objective studies and technical studies and chart pattern studies suggested, then this rally to the third major cycle crest might only be corrective and might only last 3-8 trading days. So we would be vigilant for that crest if prices rallied back to 38.2-61.8% of their decline from the 12,876 high of May 2 to the 12,308 low of May 25. The price target would be (12,876 + 12,308) ÷ 2 = 12,592.50. Applying the range of 38.2-61.8% would give a price target zone of 12,525.50-12,659.50. As it was to be a major cycle crest, the DJIA should at least touch the 14-day moving average. Time-wise, 3-8 trading days after May 25 would give a time frame of May 30 -June 6 for this crest (one day later actually since May 30 was a holiday in the USA).

Geocosmics would now be helpful in determining the reversal date. There was a critical reversal date on June 1-2, as a Level 1 signature was present each day. On June 1, the Sun formed a 240° trine to Saturn, which has a 69% historical correlation to primary or greater cycles. On June 2, Neptune turned retrograde, which has an 86% historical correlation to primary or greater cycles. The midpoint of June 1-2 has an orb of three trading days. As you can see from the chart shown in Figure 85, the crest occurred May 31 at 12,574. That was within our price objective range for this crest, and it was slightly above both the 14- and 42-day moving averages, which confirmed May 25 as the major cycle trough. By the end of the next day, June 1, the DJIA was back below each of these moving averages on its way down to the primary and possibly 50-week cycle troughs of June 15 and their double bottom low of June 23.

The activity and trading plans for aggressive traders surrounding the lows of June 15 and June 23 were covered at the end of the previous chapter. But as we conclude the position trader's analysis of this chapter and this book, we can see once again that many of the signals for a primary cycle trough as outlined in this book and the previous four books were fulfilled. The second low at 11,875 on June 23, 2011 was especially significant from the standpoint of geocosmic studies and solar-lunar reversal dates, as described in the last chapter. Both lows fit very well according to the stochastic studies, as bullish oscillator divergence was in effect after falling below the oversold 20% level. Now we wait and see if the rally to the crest of the new primary cycle will make a new high for this 4-year cycle, a double top, and/or if it will break below the 4-point trendline and send the DJIA lower to its final 15.5-month cycle trough and eventually its 4-year cycle trough. (Note: the DJIA made a double top on July 21 and then sold off sharply into early August, breaking the 4-point trendline, as this is being edited).

Conclusion and Finis

And here dear reader is where we end this chapter, this book, and this journey that has lasted 14 years. With the 5 volumes of this series, I trust you will now view financial markets and trading from a completely different perspective than when you started. It is my sincere wish that with these manuals, all financial markets will now look familiar, with order and meaning, and you will know where you are at any time within any market, unlike ever before. But mostly I would like to wish each one of you great success in trading and analysis as a result of these studies and trading plans that have been introduced and an equal measure of joy and fascination for the cyclical nature of life that subtly underlies all human activity.

For me, nothing has brought me closer to God than the undertaking of these studies. I started out with the idea that I wanted to be in touch with the "soul of the stock market." But in the final leg of this journey, I realized that the soul I got most in touch with was my own and the understanding of my relationship to the cosmos. Every one of us makes up the soul of the stock market and the soul of the collective. But the mystery for me was in the understanding of the relationship between the cosmos, the collective, and the stock market. An excitement of discovery came from this realization - that it works and continues to work every day, every week, every month. It doesn't always work exactly as I expect, but that only illuminates the limits to my own understanding, which has increased tremendously as a result of this work. It is not the result of limitations or the non-existence of such macro-micro relationships. To the contrary, it is because of those relationships that I will always be a student and a humble admirer of the mystery of life and the creation of this universe in which we all exist.

Finis. For now.

References:

1. Merriman, Raymond A., "Forecast 2010," Seek-It Publications, 2009, W. Bloomfield, MI, USA.
2. Merriman, Raymond A., "Forecast 2011," Seek-It Publications, 2010. W. Bloomfield, MI, USA.

RAVE REVIEWS FOR VOLUME 3

THE ULTIMATE BOOK ON STOCK MARKET TIMING: GEOCOSMIC CORRELATION TO TRADING CYCLES

"Raymond Merriman has done it again. With his usual style and finesse, this master trader and market analyst has put together a massive piece of research that is at once deliciously arcane and eminently practical, incredibly comprehensive and wonderfully accessible, broad in its vision and absolutely rigorous in its reasoning. What's especially nice about this book is the way Merriman combines meticulous research with pragmatic recommendations. In dealing with the various planetary combinations that can impact market dynamics, for example, he not only explains the underlying energies at work—he also cites historical examples of the geocosmic interactions, lists the dates when those interactions will occur again, and offers a quick paragraph of capsule advice for the trader who wants to consider the planets in an operative trading plan. This is definitely a book that warrants a prominent place on the shelf nearest your trading station. But that doesn't mean that it's a volume that deserves to gather dust. Put Geocosmic Correlations to Trading Cycles to work as an active part of your trading analysis and this book will quickly pay for itself many times over."

- Tim Bost, Editor, Financial Cycles newsletter Sarasota, Florida

"Ray Merriman is to be congratulated. His research is excellent, his explanations very clear, and his examples that demonstrate how to use multiple indicators to identify trend reversals well articulated. Traders lacking an astrological background should easily understand and benefit from them. This is not a book for day traders (Volume IV of this series promises to do that) but for those who want to catch the +/-10% changes in the financial market indices this provides powerful, effective tools. The empirical evidence provided in this and in the previous volume clearly demonstrates that astrology works, that specific planetary combinations can be significantly associated with the changes in mass psychology, with increased optimism or depression, and these in turn are associated with ups and downs, the bull and bear markets, on Wall Street and the world's financial markets."

– Ken Gillman, Editor, Considerations Journal Mt. Kisco, NY

"I got Volume 3 last week, and find it to be what I call a "dangerous book," i.e. it is so interesting you don't want to do anything else but read/devour."

– G.W., investor and trader. Calgary, Alberta - Canada

"Merriman's work is extraordinary. He does a fine job of making this extremely tedious and complicated material readable and even fascinating. He deserves high honors for even undertaking such a task. This result of his dedication and patience deserves accolades from everyone interested in stock market forecasting. I eagerly look forward to the next two volumes in the series."

– Mary Plumb, reviewer for The Mountain Astrologer Cedar Ridge, California

"To say that Merriman is a prolific writer is an understatement. His latest exhaustive book (Volume 3) is a mere 439 pages in its 8.5" x 11" paperback format. In this work, Merriman has analyzed 3,000 geocosmic signatures that he correlated with varying cycles in the DJIA and S&P 500 futures prices. In summary, this book is a significant contribution in the area of timing the market using astrological signs and cycles in combination. For those readers with a solid understanding of these subject areas, the usefulness of this book is self-evident."

– Les Masonson, reviewer for Amazon.com Monroe, NY

"Merriman presents his findings on 148 astrological signatures on how well each one corresponds to price reversals in the Dow Jones Industrial Averages of four percent or greater. The signatures are derived from planetary stations and in aspect to each other. How much money could a trader make if he knew that within eight days of the exact trine between Jupiter and Uranus there would be a 91% chance of a major price reversal? This is just one of the stunning bits of information found in Volume 3. Wouldn't it be great to know that a rounded top is shaping up and starting to reverse because Neptune is turning retrograde? Much of the data can be helpful to even shorter-term traders than the primary cycle. For example, there's an 86% chance that within four days of when the Sun squares Uranus the market will reverse. The last few chapters summarize the data and show how to build a timetable for investing opportunities. The nature of the financial markets is undeniably cyclical, and this is where astrologers have the upper hand. Merriman's groundbreaking work is breathtaking in its scope and practical application."

– Chris Lorenz, Horoscope Magazine New York, NY

RAVE REVIEWS FOR VOLUME 4

THE ULTIMATE BOOK ON STOCK MARKET TIMING: SOLAR-LUNAR CORRELATIONS TO SHORT-TERM TRADIMG REVERSALS

"Very few researchers and market analysts have the stamina, knowledge, time, and skill to write one groundbreaking book on the markets. Merriman has accomplished that feat four times over, and he is not done yet, with a fifth volume underway.

Merriman's reviews 60 years of DJIA price data coupled with all the Sun-Moon combinations. He also reviews similar combinations with almost two decades of data for the Nasdaq composite and the Japanese Nikkei index. He focuses on determining the important reversal dates (one or three day time bands a few times a year) - 4% or more changes in value — for specific Sun-Moon combinations. Traders can get ready to act on these reversal points with minimal risk. Traders who use the QQQs, SPYs, and DIAs, as well as futures and options can benefit from Merriman's identification of these time frames.

Merriman found that certain lunar cycles and certain Sun-Moon signs correlate consistently with tradable highs and lows in the financial markets, and identifies them. At the end of the book, Merriman has a chapter devoted to a short-term trading methodology that clearly spells out the 16 steps required to take advantage of the key reversal dates... this book is another significant contribution in the area of timing the market - with specific emphasis on using solar/lunar correlations to identify high probability key reversal dates. Merriman continues to add significant value to short-term trader's ability to profit from identifiable and profitable market situations. Those who take the time to study his work will find a new tool to use."

-Les Masonsen, Trader and Reviewer, Amazon.com

"Ray Merriman has done a remarkable job of isolating high probability time periods to trade. His newest book, titled 'The Ultimate Book on Stock Market Timing, Volume 4: Solar-Lunar Correlations to Short-Term Trading Reversals,' focuses on the timing of trades through the quantification and isolation of specific high probability short-term reversals, based on Sun-Moon combinations that are likely to have a high percentage move of 4% or more – and also those time periods that are NOT likely to have much of a move. It is an excellent addition to a trader's technical toolbox for short-term entries and intraday trading, and also for identifying ideal entry time periods for longer-term moves and cycles."

-Walter Bressert, World-renowned cycles' analyst, and President of Walter Bressert Asset Management Company

"Ray has added another jewel to the collection of books he has written on Financial Astrology for traders. Ray did a brilliant, well thought out and well documented study."

"The year has been divided into the 12 Sun Signs, and the highest probability and lowest probability for a reversal of 4% or more is listed for Moon, Mercury and Venus pairings with each Sun Sign. For quick reference, and added clarity, there is a section at the end of each section called. "Traders' Advisory." The reversal dates are taken a step further, with sections for each Sun Sign on "Crest Correlations" and "Trough Correlations." The 12 chapters on each Sun sign are followed by chapters devoted to further analysis of Mercury and Venus, respectively.

"Whether you are a trader in search of an added edge, or an astrologer with an interest in research, this book is a valuable addition to your library."

-Frances E. Rackow, CSH, CPA, Atlanta, Georgia

"With his 4th book in the "Stock Market Timing Series" the author has made another valuable contribution to the development of financial astrology. While intermediate - and long-term geocosmic stock market patterns have already been researched quite well, very little has been done to cover short-term swings. That's why many contradictory and false theories are circulating. This book fills the gap and offers a good starting point for traders and researchers alike."

-Manfred Zimmel, editor of Amanita Market Forecasting, Vienna, Austria, www.amanita.at